human
ecosystems

human
ecosystems

W.B. Clapham, Jr.

Clapham Associates, Cleveland, Ohio

MACMILLAN PUBLISHING CO., INC.

New York

COLLIER MACMILLAN PUBLISHERS

London

Macmillan Publishing Co., Inc.
866 Third Avenue, New York, New York 10022

Collier Macmillan Canada, Ltd.

Library of Congress Cataloging in Publication Data

Clapham, Wentworth B.   (date)
  Human ecosystems.

  Includes bibliographies and index.
  1. Human ecology, I. Title.
GF41.C527 1981   304.2   80-16692
ISBN 0-02-322510-6

Printing: 1 2 3 4 5 6 7 8   Year: 1 2 3 4 5 6 7 8

preface

This book is about the ecosystems dominated by people. Humans, just as any other species, interact with other animals, as well as with plants and their nonliving environment. Whether or not we recognize it, we are part of the ecosystems in which we participate and have been since the dawn of our lineage. We have been able to mold the shape of ecosystems and maintain them in useful states for at least 10,000 years. Our ability to mold and maintain new ecosystems oriented toward specific goals has increased steadily since then. Today our world is changing faster than ever before. It is becoming more complex, and it is increasingly harder to keep the factors that control this complexity in perspective. Factors that appear at first to be unrelated to ecological phenomena bring major environmental change. Events in seemingly remote areas can affect countries around the world.

Society and the environment have become so interconnected that it is often difficult to separate them. Nevertheless, we often try. We are used to thinking of ecosystems as natural phenomena in which organisms interact with their nonliving environment according to certain rules. These rules may be ecological, physical, or chemical, but they are intrinsic to the ecosystem and cannot be altered by people. Human ecosystems, on the other hand, reflect the values and goals of a society, and some of the most important forces in the system are explicitly social. Even so, the ecological, physical, and chemical laws of the natural ecosystem remain valid, and the overall behavior of the system depends on the joint interaction of all of its elements, including organisms and their nonliving environment. It is nonsense to think that the behavior of human ecosystems can be understood without considering these laws in some way. But it is equally nonsense to believe that they can be understood without understanding the perceptions, values, needs, and attitudes of the controlling society.

It has become clear that the issues of environmental protection go far deeper than preserving as much of nature as possible or cleaning up polluted air and water. The environment is the foundation upon which modern industrial civilization is built. It includes the air we breathe, the water we drink, the materials we use in industrial processes, the energy that heats our homes and runs our factories, the geobiological milieu that we call agriculture, and the biological responses of our own bodies to the world around them. The environment is a set of interactions that governs the way the biosphere responds to human manipulation. Environmental protection may mean preserving the natural, but it also means creating a stable foundation for society that can endure changing economic and social conditions.

The purpose of this book is to present an introduction to human ecosystems that allows the college student to visualize the interplay of the factors and forces that shape them. Some of these are overtly ecological. Others are economic, demographic, political, and normative. An introductory text with a scope this broad cannot be complete or comprehensive, but it should be sufficient to build a base for further understanding. Examples are chosen from many parts of the world, although most are from North America. This has been done both the emphasize that environmental problems are not the exclusive province of any nation or kind of nation and to provide a sense of familiarity to readers in various parts of the world.

This book is designed to be used in conjunction with a text in ecology, such as my *Natural Ecosystems.* I have not attempted to develop all of the ecology needed to deal with the material in the book, even though it is intended for an introductory audience. Frankly, I believe that a grounding in natural ecosystems is so important to understanding human ecosystems that the amount of ecology included in most introductions to the ecology of man is insufficient. A responsible approach required either that this book is designed as a companion to *Natural Ecosystems* or that the two books be combined into a single work. Both have advantages; the choice made allows greater flexibility in the way material is presented to the student.

This book, like *Natural Ecosystems,* is primarily descriptive. Chapter 1 introduces some systems notions, oriented to human ecosystems. Chapters 2 and 3 look at human society, first with regard to its evolution and second with respect to the dynamics of its growth and change. Chapters 4 and 5 examine ecosystems that are managed in a natural or quasinatural form, while chapter 6 looks at a set of ecosystems that is managed intensively. Chapter 7 considers the role of energy in the metabolism of a modern society. Chapters 8 to 10 discuss pollution, its origin, effects, and control. Chapter 11 returns to a systems view of human ecosystems.

I would like to thank many people for their assistance in this project. The book has been read, completely or in part, by Alan Haney, Peter Frank, Ellen Knox, Peter Hammond, David Pilbeam, Howard Roepke, William Rowland, and Arthur Borror. The suggestions made by these reviewers were often maddening, but the book has been greatly improved because of them. I am also grateful for the able assistance of Charles

Stewart, Woodrow Chapman, and David Garrison of the Macmillan Publishing Co., as well as the staff of the Production Department. The manuscript was typed, at various stages, by Shelly Baum, Carolyne Raine, Carolyn LesCook, Donna Sockel, and Sandra Delroy. Finally, I want to express my gratitude to my friends and family for having put up with me at times when that was not a particularly easy thing to do.

W. B. C., Jr.

contents

1/environment and society

Ecosystems are complex self-sustaining systems that consist of organisms and the physical and chemical phenomena associated with them. Most importantly, they include interactions binding the living and nonliving components into stable systems. These interactions include those between organisms, the relationships among organisms and their nonliving (abiotic) environment, and the various phases of the abiotic environment that mold its own change.

The term *ecosystem* generally brings nature to mind. Most studies of ecosystems are of natural ecosystems. But the principles of ecology govern more than nature. Humans too are animals, and are as much a part of the ecosystems in which they participate as other animals. We can describe these as *human ecosystems*. They have a special significance to us, and they are unlike natural ecosystems in some important ways.

Human activity makes human ecosystems what they are. In ecological terms, humans are the dominant species. But there is a significant difference between the dominance of people in, for example, a cornfield, and that of elephants in the African savanna (or that of any other dominant species in any other locale). Human activity is rooted in social systems, and it is oriented toward goals whose bases are social, not biological. We cannot view a cornfield, a cow pasture, a clear-cut forest, or a polluted stream and comprehend what we see without understanding what people do. We cannot make sense of what people do without understanding their goals in the context of the society to which they belong.

Only humans, of all living species, are capable of cognitive reasoning, and they have devised many ways of interacting with their environment. A human society can alter an ecosystem, sometimes at will. It can maintain the system in a structure very different from that which would exist in nature. People's ability to reason cognitively and to act as a part of an integrated society enables changes to be made and then maintained.

However, although society can maintain ecosystems in forms that meet some of its perceived needs, it cannot alter the laws under which they operate. The laws of ecology govern the interactions among entities. The overall behavior of any ecosystem depends on its nature at a particular time: its species makeup, the details of its abiotic environment, and its history. Some of these factors can be controlled directly by people, others indirectly. Some, such as the gross climate or genetic details of most populations, are beyond the reach of society. Others get lost in the tremendous complexity of ecosystems and are simply not known.

MULTIPLE DIMENSIONS OF HUMAN ECOSYSTEMS

In order to view things as complicated as human ecosystems without being overwhelmed by complexity, it is often useful to divide them into meaningful pieces. For our purposes, it is easiest to visualize them in terms of *domains,* or interacting parts. Specifically, let us identify three of these domains: the *environmental,* the *individual-management,* and the *policy-making.* As a shorthand, we can refer to the first as "the environment" and the other two collectively as "society." The scope of these domains, as well as their most important characteristics, is summarized in Table 1.1. The environmental domain comprises those system components that react according to the laws of natural ecosystems. Here are the geobiological phenomena of plant and animal growth, population and community dynamics, and the flow of nutrients and energy throughout the food web. The individual-management domain comprises the behavior of those people and institutions who interact directly with the environment and manipulate it deliberately or unintentionally. The policy-making domain comprises the mechanisms by which society generates economic and policy signals in an attempt to channel the development of the various sectors of society in particular directions.

This division points out the different kinds of actors that have a role in molding the human environment. The people or phenomena in Table 1.1 have very different roles in molding the human environment, and they are all critical. Dividing the system into different domains also points out the different disciplinary views that are brought to bear on different aspects of the system. Each domain is characterized by one or more relatively well-defined sets of phenomena, as well as a set of disciplinary approaches, and these views can be integrated into some sort of meaningful overview.

The environment is often understood to mean something separate from society. It might mean virgin wilderness, bucolic or rustic landscapes, cities, or polluted air and water, but it is usually not understood as basic to the way people live. In fact, this view is unreasonably restrictive. The point of human ecosystems is that there is a mutual interaction between society and the environment which enables society to

Table 1.1   Domains of Human Ecosystems.

	Environmental	Individual-Management	Policy-Making
Representative Actors, Phenomena	Animals Plants Soil Water	Farmers Fishermen Industries Nature organizations	Government International organizations
Characteristics	Phenomena obey laws of natural ecosystems.	Decisions directed internally, to affect own actions.	Decisions directed externally, to affect actions of others.
Representative Actions	Individual growth Interactions among populations Soil formation Atmospheric, water chemistry	Land use decisions Capital formation Marketing decisions Management of animal and plant populations	Taxation and subsidies Coordination of different sectors of society Regulations Education, policy
Disciplines; Background of Practitioners	Ecology Applied physics and chemistry Engineering	Microeconomics Engineering Business	Macroeconomics Business Law Policy sciences

exist. The environment comprises the resource base of many of society's most basic activities, and people manipulate and mold it in an effort to meet their needs.

It is not enough to say that a managed ecosystem is shaped by the society managing it. There is a mutual interaction with feedback from the environment to society. The behavior of the environment affects the behavior of the manager, and vice versa. Policies influence management, and vice versa. Indeed, environmental problems can lead to change in policies, and government can ultimately influence environmental health and stability. The domains are so intimately linked that we cannot separate them completely. They constitute a system whose parts can usefully be looked at separately, but which is not meaningful until they are viewed together.

Orientation of Domains

The human ecosystem can be portrayed as an ordered series of processes connected by a network of flowing information (Figure 1.1). Individual managers have certain ways of managing various facets of the environment, and they monitor particular geobiological phenomena in return. They respond not only to these phenomena but also to the economic and policy signals generated through governments. Policy makers, in turn,

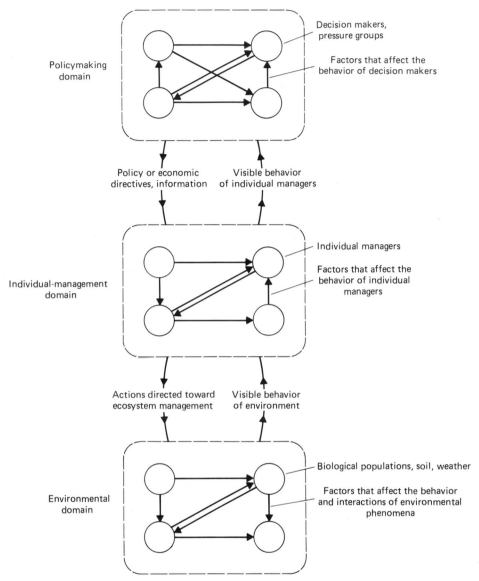

Decision makers, pressure groups

Factors that affect the behavior of decision makers

Policymaking domain

Policy or economic directives, information

Visible behavior of individual managers

Individual managers

Factors that affect the behavior of individual managers

Individual-management domain

Actions directed toward ecosystem management

Visible behavior of environment

Biological populations, soil, weather

Factors that affect the behavior and interactions of environmental phenomena

Environmental domain

Figure 1.1 Generalized schema for a human ecosystem expressed in three interacting domains. Circles in each domain represent different actors or phenomena. Arrows represent interactions that affect the behavior of actors or phenomena.

monitor the behavior of the individual managers, and design policies or attempt to guide the economy in a direction they believe most appropriate for society. Figure 1.2 gives some representative examples of the information flow.

A farm is a representative human ecosystem (Figure 1.2a). Farmers are individual managers, and the environment of concern consists of their fields, including crops, pests, weeds, soil, and the interactions among them. The interactions between farmers and their environment are very close. Most of the farmers' activities are directed to-

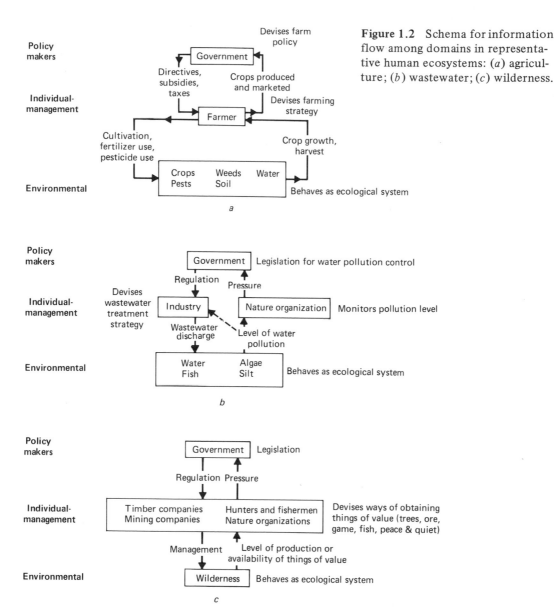

Figure 1.2 Schema for information flow among domains in representative human ecosystems: (*a*) agriculture; (*b*) wastewater; (*c*) wilderness.

ward creating conditions under which their crops will prosper. They monitor crop growth, pest activities, and soil conditions, because these provide the information they need in order to adjust their cultivating activities and chemical applications, and to judge their ultimate harvest plans. As these conditions change, they can revise their activities to make them more effective. In the same way, they respond to policies set by government. These may limit the amount of land they can plant in a given crop, set the price they have to pay for particular inputs or the price they will receive for their crops, or provide them with certain services in operating their farms. The government devises these policies because it desires to influence or control farm production, and it monitors the behavior of farmers to assure that its policies have the desired results. There is thus a tight feedback between the farmers and the environment, as well as between farmers and policy makers. The behavior of any one of them affects the behavior of one or both of the others.

Compare this system with that of the wastewater-receiving ecosystem shown in Figure 1.2b. The managers here are the industries and municipalities discharging wastes into the river, as well as one or more actors who monitor the state of the receiving streams. These may be industry personnel, downstream water users (e.g., intakes for potable water plants), nature organizations, or government observers. The receiving waterway may be considered a free repository for the wastes produced by society. It is not perceived to yield products of direct benefit to the industries or municipalities in question. Their decision-making on how much treatment to give their wastewater is not directly concerned with the potential resources of the receiving waterway which might exist in the absence of water pollution, but rather with minimizing government regulation and adverse public opinion.

There is no direct feedback between the environment and the managerial domain. The state of the receiving stream must first be communicated to government policy makers by stream monitors and result in legislation, regulation, or lawsuits. These measures are oriented toward managers, not the receiving stream. How the environment is actually managed depends on the behavior of the managers. They can blunt the effectiveness of public opinion or of the regulatory and legislative efforts of society. For this reason, environmental control is infinitely easier to justify and implement if it affects management directly rather than indirectly. The feedbacks linking the domains are much looser and more cumbersome than in agriculture. But the domains are nevertheless linked, and the behavior of any of the components of the system is felt throughout it.

The third example, in Figure 1.2c, is the management of undeveloped land. The environment here consists of the land itself. The managers comprise the various interest groups, such as timber companies, mining interests, hunters, fishermen, and nature organizations. The policy domain consists of those agencies of government that must balance the interests of these groups and allocate use of the land among them according to an assessment of what constitutes the greatest benefit to society as a whole. In the meantime, policy makers are importuned by all of the interest groups with regard to what constitutes the most appropriate use of the area. Once allocations or rights to use are granted, actor-managers then carry out whatever management is appropriate to their use, and they monitor its response to a greater or lesser degree. Some of the manager-environment interactions are quite close, and the feedback between them is very strong, as with hunters and fishermen. For others, as with mining interests, the behavior of the environmental domain may be all but irrelevant.

HUMAN ECOSYSTEMS AS SYSTEMS

The multidimensional view of human ecosystems presented here is a very simple distillation of some important ideas from systems theory (Clapham, 1980; Clapham and Pestel, 1978). There is an order to the domains. The environment is local and specific, whereas the policy making domain has a much broader scope (commonly national or within specific subunits of countries, such as states or provinces) and is much more general. Management is intermediate between these two. There are other characteristics as well, but the critical factor is that the domains have a specific order within the overall human ecosystem.

It can be shown (Mesarovič et al., 1970) that subsystems within a given domain— or even a whole domain—can be viewed as simple entities in an analysis centered on an adjacent domain. For instance, it is possible to ignore all or part of the environment in assessing a manager's behavior so long as its responses are fully predictable. People have actively manipulated ecosystems for at least 10,000 years (see Chapter 2). Our experience is often sufficient to predict the behavior of ecosystems under various kinds of management without needing to understand them in great detail.

The behavior of any subsystem is a function of that of the other subsystems with which it interacts. We can anticipate its responses only so long as the other subsystems themselves behave predictably. The environment reacts directly or indirectly to signals generated within many parts of society. As the social system changes, or as any of the linkages between the social and environmental domains change, we may lose whatever ability we had to predict the behavior of the environment. Furthermore, the individual changes may be minor, leading to incremental responses by managers. But as the structure of the overall system evolves, the loss of predictability can easily become total.

Never before in human history have the linkages between the environmental and social domains been less constant. Automation, new chemicals, population growth, and a kaleidoscope of technological innovations bring change at a rate faster than ever before. Responsible decision makers need some kind of model for the ecosystem so that they can judge the reciprocal interactions between the environment and their own efforts at control. The models most commonly used have been empirical rules of thumb that are simple and that generally work without the need for extensive data gathering. They are based on familiarity and experience rather than understanding. It may be that the environment's responses to certain kinds of change are familiar enough that these rules of thumb provide all the information we need. But the system has changed so much in so many ways that many of our current models are insufficient for long-term coordination of the ecosystem. We really do not know when our knowledge is sufficient and when it is not. There is already abundant evidence that the changes in the linkages between society and the environment have caused—as well as solved— problems. We do not know how these problems will affect the overall society in the long run. This uncertainty underlies the current "environmental crisis."

Most of what we know about ecology stems from studies on ecosystems that have minimal contact with people. Ecologists have commonly tried to study undisturbed areas and to understand the ways in which natural ecosystems function. The context of the natural ecosystem comprises those features that change but little except over geological time, including topography, basic geology, and climate. Within these confines, the responses of portions of the ecosystem to slight perturbations can be studied and predicted.

Because the human ecosystem includes the social system as well as the environment, the responses of the environment to any perturbation, natural or artificial, can be molded by society's activities. But society does not have complete control. Most particularly, it cannot assure that every configuration of the system can be sustained. It is possible, in principle, to maintain a much wider range of stable configurations of human ecosystems than would be possible in nature. But it is also possible to generate configurations that are useful to society for a few years but that decay or collapse after a while.

It is impossible to acquire, much less interpret, all of the available information about all aspects of the environment. Indeed, most natural ecosystems are so complicated that we cannot even describe completely those we have monitored for a very long time and are not even trying to alter. In addition, not all elements of the environment can be influenced directly by society. Some factors are much easier to manipulate than others. For example, it is generally much easier to add something than to subtract it. The fertility of soil in a cornfield can be increased by adding fertilizer, but we cannot simply remove a population, such as corn borers. We can reduce their number substantially by using insecticides, but this means adding a chemical to which the borer population responds by dying in large numbers.

More concretely, let us consider a specific type of human ecosystem, such as the farm model in Figure 1.2a. If we see it only as a piece of land bounded by a fence, it represents a unique ecological phenomenon in which the actions of the manager may make little direct sense. They do not reflect an ecological logic. Only when we see the field as the environmental domain of a larger human ecosystem can we interpret the logic by which the social strata act to mold the appearance of the field.

Let us be more specific. Consider an area in, say, northern France. Several thousand years ago it was covered with deciduous forests, and the people who lived there were hunter-gatherers who depended upon it as their source of food. The first farming was slash-and-burn agriculture. Trees were felled, the vegetation burned to ash, and a plot farmed for a few years, after which the land lay fallow as the forest regrew. As the resources of the society increased, slash-and-burn was replaced by crop rotations in which fields alternated with pasture for domestic livestock. This was followed by our mechanized agriculture of the present day. Through all of this, the basic features of the land have changed relatively little. Society, especially with developing agricultural technology, increasing population density, rising urbanization, and accompanying economic changes, forced the shift from subsistence to commercial farming.

In areas of Western Europe and North America with similar physical settings, the organization of farms—even highly mechanized ones—differs somewhat, reflecting the perspectives of the societies, the economic conditions under which they operate, and the resources available to the individual farmer. The differences are even more pronounced when one compares areas whose natural resource complements are similar but whose inhabitants show strong cultural differences. As an extreme example, the terraced hillsides of the Andes near Machu Picchu (Figure 1.3) were developed as productive agricultural lands many hundreds of years ago by the Inca empire because there were no other lands suitable for feeding the growing population. Similar slopes in North America would not be considered too steep to log, much less farm. The terraced farmlands of China and Java, some of which are among the world's most productive agricultural areas and have been in production for several thousand years, would not be considered even potentially farmable according to the U.S. Department of Agriculture land capability classification (Klingebiel and Montgomery, 1961).

The Incas, Chinese, and Javanese were forced by population pressure to develop

Figure 1.3 Terraced hillsides high in the Andes near Machu Picchu, the ancient capital of the Incas. These hillsides are far steeper than any that would be farmed in North America, but some have been in continuous cultivation for over 750 years. [Photograph courtesy of Dr. A. K. Stoll.]

certain kinds of food-producing ecosystems and to maintain them as stable systems over very long intervals. Other cultures depend on trade to provide the equivalent food supply. Few, if any, countries have the resources within their borders to provide their people with what we commonly think of as a high standard of living. All parts of the world are linked into a highly interdependent system. All countries depend on others for markets, raw materials, and manufactured goods. Modern communications make both rich and poor countries increasingly aware of one another's conditions. Economics, ethics, and expectations have become intertwined to a point where what goes on in almost any country on the globe can affect almost all others.

The problems of poor countries take on a special significance as their strategic importance increases. How can we enable the poor to attain a higher standard of living? Is this possible? Indeed, can countries that now have high living standards maintain them? Modern life is characterized by very high levels of consumption of materials that are in limited quantity in nature. For example, if all of the world's population consumed petroleum at the per capita rate now current in the United States, proven reserves would be used up in five years and estimated total resources in fifteen. Shifting to burning coal at the same rate would eventually release so much carbon dioxide into the atmosphere that the global energy balance would be disrupted, with severe climatic consequences. The earth's farmers now produce enough food to feed the entire world population, but it is inequitably distributed. So much goes to feed livestock in rich countries that poor countries often experience food shortages. The resources do not now exist to produce sufficient food for the world at a North American or European standard of consumption.

The oil price rises by the Organization of Petroleum Exporting Countries (OPEC) since 1973 showed the world how relatively poor countries could make their needs felt. The future will bring other changes, and many will affect human ecosystems in one way or another. We do not know what kind of changes to expect or what their implications will be. But we must recognize that further change is inevitable, and we must be able to accomodate it when it comes.

The study of human ecosystems is designed to explicate the options available to us, the constraints that limit our interactions with the environment, and the changes in our lifestyles to which we will have to adapt.

References

Clapham, W. B., Jr., 1980. Environmental problems, development, and agricultural production systems. *Envir. Conserv.,* **7**: 145–152.

Clapham, W. B., Jr. and Pestel, R. F., 1978. A common framework for integrating the economic and ecologic dimensions of human ecosystems. I: General considerations; II: Processes and problem chains within the natural stratum; III: Policy, uncertainty, and analysis. Laxenburg, Austria: International Institute for Applied Systems Analysis, *Research Memoranda* **RM-78-29; RM-78-30; RM-78-31.**

Klingebiel, A. A. and Montgomery, P. H., 1961. Land capability classification. U.S. Dept. of Agriculture *Agricultural Handbook* **210.**

Mesarovič, M. D., Macko, D., and Takahara, Y., 1970. *Theory of Multilevel Hierarchical Systems.* New York: Academic Press.

2/influence in human ecosystems

Perhaps the diagnostic characteristics of human ecosystems are the patterns of information flow among domains and the fact that the social system can consciously influence or shape the environment. It is useful to chart the development of these patterns in time and space in order to understand both where they came from and the alternatives that have existed throughout human history.

INTERACTIONS AS A FUNCTION OF TIME

We could, if we wanted to, trace our ancestry back at least 400 million years to those fishes that began the initial tentative venture onto dry land and developed first into the predatory scourges of contemporary ponds and later into amphibians. But we do not need to. Up until humans emerged some three million years ago, their interactions with their environment were basically those of any other animal that is not capable of cognitive reasoning. With the origin of thought comes at least a rudimentary ability to control: one manipulates portions of the environment not simply because one can, but rather because one chooses to in order to meet some predetermined goal. Throughout most of the last three million years our ancestors' ability to control has been limited, both because only a few factors in the environment were amenable to control and because their society was limited in the kinds of control it could exert. At first these limitations were due mainly to physical structure and capabilities. As the lineage became more and more like anatomically modern humans, the limitations ceased to be predominantly structural and became increasingly cultural. Humans were structurally able to do certain things, but they did not do them until they had learned how and had chosen to do them.

Humans as Animals

Humans belong to the animal kingdom. Like all animals, they have certain biological requirements, and they have a certain "role" in the ecosystems of which they are a part. They have sets of interrelationships with other species, requirements for nutrients or other abiotic resources from the environment, and a position in regulating or affecting the flow of these resources. This "role" is termed the species' *ecological niche*. The ecological niche of most species is relatively constant in evolutionary time. Even rapidly evolving lineages tend to change their fundamental niches very slowly. As an example, it was not until 100 million years after the first amphibians became well established on land that plant-eating vertebrates evolved. The fossil record before that shows no vertebrates that were not animal eaters even during the periods of the coal swamps, which featured some of the most luxuriant vegetation in the history of the earth. The human ecological niche has undergone a revolution in the last three million years, and especially in the last ten thousand years. The ascendancy of modern humans is the end result of one of the most interesting evolutionary sequences known.

Early History of the Human Lineage. Most dominant mammals became specialized fairly early in their histories, so that evolution progressed by increasing the viability of the lineage within a fundamental niche. Our early ancestors were relatively unimportant generalized forms existing in small numbers in a hostile environment surrounded by much more highly specialized animals. It is remarkable that enough survived to give rise to the next link in the evolutionary chain. Because of the tenuousness of their existence, their habitat, and their small numbers, fossils of our early ancestors are very uncommon, and much of our understanding of human origins is based on inference. But our knowledge is sufficient to give us a feeling for the underlying reasons why humans are the kind of animal they are and why ecosystems dominated by them have the characteristics and problems they do. We shall briefly sketch the origin of humans as a species.

Humans are members of the *primate* order of placental (unpouched) mammals. This is one of the oldest and most primitive of mammalian orders. It extends back into the Cretaceous (Figure 2.1), and its rise was part of the first adaptive radiation of mammals. It includes lemurs, tarsiers, monkeys, the great apes, and humans. The maximum number of primate species was reached some fifty million years ago. As more advanced mammals became widespread during the late Eocene and Oligocene, the primates were generally unable to compete with them. Those that survived did so by adopting an arboreal habitat. The arboreal habitat to which the early primates were driven is an important factor in the development of the critical adaptations of humans.

Arboreal animals must be able to grasp effectively in order to move through the trees. The most common tree-grasping adaptations are claws that can dig into the bark and provide a foothold, as with rodents, cats, and birds. Primates and the opossum, alone among living animals, have an opposable digit (thumb and big toe), which allows

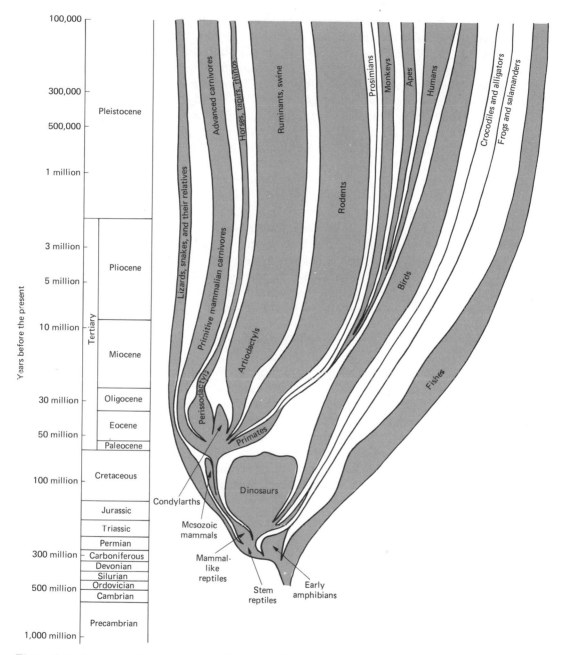

Figure 2.1 Phylogenetic and geologic history of the vertebrates.

the animal to grip the branch. The thumb was a prerequisite to our way of making and using tools.

Other primate adaptations for arboreal life that proved essential for the origin of humans included visual acuity, stereoscopic vision, quick reflexes, and good balance. A wide diversity of food is available to an arboreal animal, including insects, leaves, young birds, and fruits. Primates have had a tendency to omnivorousness throughout their history, and very few show much specialization in their diet.

The balance, good reflexes, and muscular coordination required in an active arboreal animal conferred a strong selective pressure for an increase in the flexibility and complexity of the locomotor areas of the brain. The excellent visual acuity and color vision of the primates (Harrison and Montagna, 1969) made it possible for them to gather a great deal of information about their environments. An animal with a well-developed motor nervous system and an opposable thumb can pick up objects, feel them, and look at them, as well as clamber through trees. This too enables him to gather information from his environment.

Of course, the mere potential for acquiring information is not equivalent to its assimilation. The latter depends on intelligence. Few things are more useful for an animal's survival than the ability to assimilate information about its surroundings. Hence a strong selective pressure for increasing intelligence accompanied the improvement in senses and locomotion. Increasing capacity to assimilate information built a strong selective pressure to increase the ability to acquire information. Thus there was a self-reinforcing (positive feedback) evolutionary tendency in the higher primates to improve the proficiency of the organism to gain and handle information. This led to a continual improvement in the nervous system as a whole, but especially in the brain. In almost all other respects, primates remained quite primitive and unspecialized.

During the Oligocene epoch (Figure 2.1) forests covered most of the earth. Many niches were available for arboreal primates. In east Africa, where humans originated, two major primate lifestyles began to diverge. Most species moved through the trees on all fours; these are the old world monkeys. The other group tended to be slightly larger and showed greater functional differentiation between forelimbs and hindlimbs. By the Miocene, many descendants of this second group moved through the trees by *brachiation,* swinging hand-over-hand while suspended from the branches; this lineage is that of the apes and humans. Brachiation was an important step in the development of humans for two reasons. The functions of the hands and feet are clearly differentiated, and the body is oriented in a vertical plane. A number of skeletal and visceral characteristics are prerequisites for erect bipedal locomotion. Most of these are related to the vertical orientation of the body and would have been selected for in a brachiating animal (Romer, 1966).

While these evolutionary changes were taking place, the climate was deteriorating steadily all over the earth (e.g., Axelrod, 1958). Forested areas had remained common through the Oligocene, but a dry season became well established in the plains of east Africa during the Miocene, and savanna vegetation was widespread. Forest sizes dwindled steadily, and trees were more likely to be found in groves or clumps than in large tracts. As the forests decreased in area, the habitat open to arboreal primates was squeezed so that only the forms that were most powerful and specialized to the arboreal habitat could maintain their position in the trees. The remainder were pushed out onto the grasslands. Some of the latter were lucky. They were able to survive in groves too small to serve as a habitat for fully arboreal primates but large enough for those who could take refuge in them. Their primate habitat remained in the forests, but they could move through the grass to forage for food and still escape from predators that surprised them in the grasslands. These animals derived primarily from the populations that moved by arm swinging and evolved into the African Great Apes. The modern chimpanzee is primarily a ground dweller that lives in forested areas but may venture into nearby grasslands to forage (Tuttle, 1969).

There were some populations that could not maintain territories even in the small groves. They were forced out onto the open savanna; humans are derived from them. An open grassland is not a benign place for an animal that is structurally better adapted to an arboreal hbaitat. Savanna-dwelling primates had to compete with larger, faster, more powerful, and more specialized species for their food. They had to contend with predators that were the most fleet-footed and (except for the primates themselves) the most intelligent animals alive. Most populations of savanna-dwelling primates of the Miocene must have passed quickly into extinction. In the beginning the savanna-dwelling primates had only two characteristics that allowed them to maintain any niche at all in the community: their wits, and the fact that they were not specialized in their food preferences. The former enabled them to circumvent some of their weaknesses and defenselessness; the latter allowed them to eat whatever they could safely procure, including nuts, insects, small birds, frogs, salamanders, and abandoned carrion.

But intelligence and the ability to survive on castoffs of other species are not sufficient to assure the continuity of a lineage. The structural changes in the pelvis (hipbone) and spine that had begun with the brachiators of the Miocene continued, to yield an animal that could support itself upright. The foot typical of the apes, which has an opposable big toe and can be used for grasping, became modified to produce a foot designed for support alone. We do not know when these structural modifications came about, because fossil limbs of our immediate ancestors are almost nonexistent. We can be fairly sure, however, that they were well along by the end of the Miocene (Simons, 1977; Washburn, 1978).

The defenselessness of the Miocene savanna dwellers had other implications. Only two mechanisms of defense from predators were open to them: group defense based on bands of individuals, and tool-using. The tools consisted primarily of rocks and sticks that could be thrown at enemies. Our early ancestors could use these implements both because of their well-developed hands and because the differentiation of function between hands and feet allowed them to stand and throw at the same time. It is possible that this use of tools was a factor in the rapid development of a fully upright posture and the complete separation of function of hands and feet. It is also quite likely that the Miocene savanna dwellers were gregarious (Isaac, 1978). Many animals, including many primates, are gregarious. And primates found both in forests and on the savanna, such as chimpanzees, may assume a much tighter social structure when they venture out onto the grasslands than they do in the forests (Suzuki, 1969; Izawa, 1970).

There are other reasons to believe that our early ancestors had a well-developed social structure. In order for increasing intelligence to be possible, the size and complexity of the brain must increase. Up to a point, this is not a particularly difficult problem. However, the time comes when the head of the infant becomes too large to fit through the birth canal. At this point, either the evolutionary increase in brain size must stop, or birth must take place at an earlier and more immature stage when the head is smaller. An animal born at a very immature stage must be tended for a time before it can fend for itself, and the mobility of nursing mothers is substantially reduced for long periods. Thus, a corollary of the steady increase in intelligence within the human lineage is the presence of organized groups, probably organized around families. This level of organization had probably been reached by the end of the Miocene. About this time, the fossil record discloses remains of a species known as *Ramapithecus,* which seems to have been intermediate in structure between the stage of evolution represented by the apes of the Oligocene and earlier Miocene, and humans (Simons, 1977).

Origin of Man.   Unfortunately, the fossil record of our ancestors through the Pliocene is sparse. We assume that the main evolutionary thrusts of their evolution were improvements in tool use, increased differentiation of hands and feet, greater uprightness of individual stature, and increasing degree of social development. At any rate, a critical juncture was reached during the Pliocene. Individuals belonging to the genus *Australopithecus* not only used easily available sticks and rocks as tools; they also chipped rocks and other hard objects to make implements that were more useful than the objects in their original form. With this accomplishment the number of things that the groups could do increased vastly. For instance, a sharpened stone can be used as a tool to cut through the skin of an animal. The size of the niche of *Australopithecus* was enlarged from that of its forebears, as was its geographic range.

Once toolmaking developed, there was a continual evolutionary pressure for an increase in the sophistication and standardization of tools and a differentiation of tool types, since effective tool use was a most powerful aid to survival. Change was continuous and self-sustaining, as the primitive cultures could pass on the knowledge of toolmaking from one generation to the next, including improvements as they developed. Survival of a population was no longer a function simply of its innate physical structure and intelligence, but also of the level of its cultural development. In the sense of Marshall McLuhan (1964), tools were an extension of the physical structure of the animal that could overcome many of the deficiencies of that structure.

During much of the Pleistocene cultural and physical evolution proceeded in parallel, with physical evolution gradually slowing and cultural evolution increasing in importance. Early in the Pleistocene the genus *Homo* evolved from *Australopithecus* or from a common ancestor. The two groups of hominids lived together for a considerable length of time, but competition between them drove *Australopithecus* into extinction by the beginning of the middle Pleistocene period. *Homo* itself has undergone some evolution over the last half million years, but it has been minor compared to the difference between *Australopithecus* and *Homo.* The appearance of *Homo sapiens sapiens* (Cro-Magnon Man) about 35,000 years ago signaled the conclusion of our present structural evolution. All human populations during and after the ebb of the final glacial period have belonged to a single species, *Homo sapiens.*

Cultural evolution has advanced rapidly during this time, allowing people to overcome—at least in the short term—virtually all obstacles to their existence. Slowly at first, but then with increasing speed, barriers were identified and tools and methods invented to overcome them. As environmental obstacles were overcome, the human ecological niche increased in scope and population groups expanded their geographic range. At the present time people inhabit virtually all land areas of the earth, and the human niche is so broad that we cannot even determine the earth's carrying capacity.

Humans as Cultural Animals

Humans are cultural animals. They are characterized by institutions, patterns of inter-actions among individuals, and patterns of individual behavior. These include the organization of society, systems of kinship, associations, and social stratification. They include the political structure through which decisions are made, the sets of tools available to the society and the knowledge of how, when, and why to use them, and the sets of economic rules that determine the activities of the population.

Technology. Technology is the strongest cultural determinant of the impact a society can make on the environment. It refers to the way people magnify their innate physical capacity by using things in a reasoned way to perform activities. These things include tools (in their broadest sense), fire, clothing, shelter, transport, and learned techniques and skills of various sorts. Technology implies more than the simple use of tools. It implies their *conscious* manufacture and the ability to teach others about their use. Several nonhuman species today use tools routinely. Chimpanzees, for example, use sticks to break open termite mounds to get at the termites for food, and our hominid ancestors used sticks, stones, and other available implements to meet specific needs. Technology requires a clearly thought-out protocol for how, when, and why tools should be used. The specific use to which a tool will be put is known and planned prior to its manufacture. It is the function of the tool that is important, not the simple fact that it has been used.

Technology allows people to alter their ecological niche. Be it by the use of fire, stone axes, shovels, or computers, technology extends the physical structure of the human organism and allows it to transcend the limits imposed by that structure. Some of our best records of prehistory are from caves in Europe during the height of the continental glaciation. Such a habitat would have been utterly impossible for people who had not used clothing, known the use of fire, and been able to hunt large game cooperatively.

Technology has enabled people to perform tasks that would otherwise have been impossible, and to carry out accustomed tasks more effectively, efficiently, or consistently. It has allowed repeated overcoming of barriers. It has also allowed an increase in population size and enhanced the potential for development of still newer technologies to overcome the new barriers that had replaced the old.

This process has spanned the last three million years. Development was very slow at first, with the basic materials limited to stone, bone, and wood. Only in the last 10,000 years has the list of materials grown much beyond these simple beginnings. The design of tools and the complexity and degree of refinement of tool manufacture changed rather little for the first 99.8% of human history, but has blossomed at an ever increasing rate through the last 10,000 years.

The oldest standardized manufactured tools consisted of pebbles with a few flakes knocked off one end to provide a jagged cutting edge. Simple as they were, these pebble tools represented a great advance over the random tools used by prehominids. A run-of-the-mill rock may be adequate for killing small game, but it is useless for removing the skin or fur to get at the meat. Even the simplest pebble tools made this task much easier. In addition, a pebble tool can serve as a substitute claw, a formidable weapon of defense or offense.

Pebble tool technology enlarged the hominid niche, but our ancestors were not yet dominant animals. The majority of the food they ate consisted of very small animals such as rodents, insectivores, lizards, turtles, fish, birds, and young ungulates (Butzer, 1971). They sometimes consumed large animals as well, such as elephants, but these were driven singly into swamps or bogs and then stoned or clubbed to death. The portion of the animal remaining above water was then used as food. In short, our ancestors at this stage were generalized carnivores or omnivores, making relatively little impact on the natural communities around them.

By some 700,000 years ago the continental ice sheets were spreading over the northern hemisphere for the second of their four advances (Figure 2.2). Pebble tools had given away to hand axes, which could be used for skinning animals effectively or even cutting down trees. Anthropologists speak of this as the *Paleolithic* or the Old Stone Age. About the same time humans gained the use of fire, enabling them to inhabit cold climates and to develop wooden spears with fire-hardened points. Their food supply changed, but only moderately. Small animals became relatively less impor-

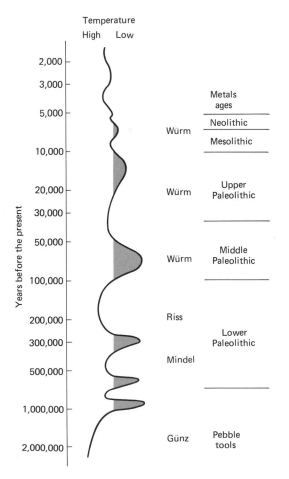

Figure 2.2 Temperatures and archaeological ages through the Pleistocene. Glacial advances are shaded.

tant, and large animals relatively more. Humans set fires in the forests, followed by re-growth of grasses and weeds. These fires may have been accidental, or they may have been set consciously as a means of encouraging rapidly growing plants that could serve as a source of food or provide a habitat for favored game (Stewart, 1956). The impact on the environment had grown significantly, but people were not yet a dominant species.

By the onset of the last major continental glaciation some 100,000 years ago, the diversity and efficiency of tools had advanced considerably beyond the hand ax. Europe, Asia, and Africa were inhabited by Neanderthals (*Homo sapiens neander-thalensis*). The record suggests that social structures were well developed and that religion was practiced. Even very large animals such as the woolly mammoth and rhinoceros were fair game for Neanderthal hunters. Even so, humans were far from being a dominant species anywhere in the world. Their populations were still small, and their overall impact on other animals was not much greater than that of other organisms of their size and population density.

Anatomically modern humans appear in the fossil record about 35,000 years ago. About the same time general purpose tools disappeared and the specialization and craftsmanship of stone, wood, and bone tools improved markedly. Tools were used not only for hunting but also for fighting and making other tools.

Shelter construction was varied, including houses of skin and wood in addition to caves. There is some evidence that family groups would winter in caves and summer in a more open structure. Great skill was shown in many activities, not only in manufacturing hand implements but also in creating ornaments of various types and in cave painting in southern France and Spain.

Humans had become dominant in the ecosystems of the late Paleolithic. The great cave paintings show scenes of group hunting which suggest that all animal species were fair game, and that people could hunt whichever they chose. We know that people had the ability to hunt herds of animals, often with extensive kills. The use of fire to remove woody vegetation favored the development of open habitats that were also the primary habitats of certain species of prey.

Toward the end of the Paleolithic the fossil record shows massive extinctions of large numbers of species of animals in both the eastern and western hemispheres. People had inhabited the eastern hemisphere for a long time, and they have been implicated in these mass extinctions. Although we are not entirely sure when people arrived in the western hemisphere, there is some evidence (Martin, 1973) that they may also have been involved in extinctions in the New World. We do not really know this (Van Valen, 1970; Martin and Wright, 1967), but it is clear that people were directly involved with the increases in many favored species (Krantz, 1970). The problem in assigning the role of humans in the faunal changes is that major climatic changes accompanied the retreat of the continental ice sheets. But if it is difficult to assess the relative importance of humans and nature in this regard, it is still clear that people's ability to manipulate the environment had increased markedly during the period of continental glaciation. The largest increases were still to come.

With the withdrawal of the glaciers, the way of life that characterized the late Paleolithic moved northward in the northern hemisphere, along with the herding animals such as mammoths and reindeer that had served as people's prime food source. Solitary animals such as deer, wild cattle, and boar took their places in the lower latitudes of Europe and the Near East. These animals could not be hunted as effectively by the group practices that had served in the late Paleolithic. The main problem for people in most of the earth was no longer survival from the cold; rather, it was assuring an adequate food supply. A markedly different strategy of hunting and food provision was necessary. What developed independently in a number of different parts of the world was a very efficient means of solitary hunting, supplemented by dependable non-game foods such as fish and plants. This is the *Mesolithic* level of technology, or the Middle Stone Age. It is transitional in many important respects between the hunting culture of the Paleolithic and the agricultural and horticultural societies of the succeeding *Neolithic,* or New Stone Age.

Human society in the Mesolithic was perhaps more vulnerable and less secure than it had been in the Paleolithic. But because of the readjustments that were necessary and could be made, the beginnings of agricultural technologies that would propel humans into a truly dominant position in their ecosystem were clearly present.

The development of agriculture in Mesopotamia, Egypt, India, China, and Mesoamerica and the Andes heralded the Neolithic level of technology. Whereas fire had given Paleolithic people the ability to expand their range into areas that would otherwise have been too cold, agriculture and horticulture gave Neolithic people the ability and incentive to expand the scope of their interactions with their environments almost to current levels. People had previously been hunters and gatherers. They had depended on wild animals and wild plants for their needs. Their use of tools had not been directed primarily toward manipulating the abiotic environment, but rather toward making hunting and gathering more efficient. The only important exception was fire, which could be used to create a habitat suitable for plant populations favored by people as food.

The most notable of these plants were the grains, but they also included most of the species that have been domesticated as crops. Mesolithic people may have aided certain species by expanding their habitat, but they did not consciously plant or husband crops. Although they may have allowed certain wild animals such as sheep, pigs, and dogs to enter their families as pets, they did not deliberately raise them either as sources of food or as beasts of burden.

With the Neolithic, cultivated plants and domesticated animals become important features of the human ecosystem. Humans created a system that was qualitatively different from that of any other animal. Domestication represented a special case of mutualism (symbiosis) in which the human species gained absolute dominance over crops and livestock. It also represented a process of intense genetic selection in which the dominant species consciously selected characteristics of greatest value. These included productivity, rapidity of growth, and gentleness. Within a short time the plants and animals that served as the basic stock of domestication had changed so much from their original state that they would not have been able to survive in the wild.

As in all cases of mutualism, the evolutionary relationship was bidirectional. Just as humans exerted selective pressure on the domesticated species, the domesticated species had a considerable evolutionary impact on people. But human evolution was not structural. As far as we can tell, people have not changed structurally in some 35,000 years. The changes were cultural. People were forced to evolve a set of behaviors and tools that would allow them to maximize the productivity of their domesticated populations.

But what a change this represented! For three million years, our ancestors had had the ability to take pieces of their environment (e.g., sticks, stones, and bones) and transform them into usable tools. But horticulture and agriculture required them to have and maintain control over essentially the total environment. If the area to be planted was forested, the trees must be cut down and the ground prepared. Certain species of plants (i.e., weeds) and animals (i.e., pests) must be consciously removed or controlled so that crop growth is favored throughout its entire development. With domestic livestock, people also had the choice of using their own labor or substituting animal draft labor for it.

For the first time in the history of the earth, a single species could mold an ecosystem into a form that it could visualize *a priori*, plan, and maintain. Neolithic people had become, for the first time in history, the overwhelmingly dominant species of their ecosystems. This is not to say that people's ability was unlimited, or even that their prowess was very far developed by modern standards. But no other species has ever had the degree of conscious control over both the abiotic and the biotic environment that is required to produce even the simplest agricultural crop.

Neolithic technology was much more specialized than those of previous societies, and it was much more productive. Each person no longer made his or her own tools (Bordaz, 1970). Some made tools and others used them. This specialization and the surpluses made possible through agriculture allowed and perhaps even encouraged the growth of large population groups. As long as people had to meet their food requirements from hunting, fishing, and gathering, it had been impossible for a population to build up a food surplus (Orans, 1966). There might be times when hunting was good, but these were matched by times when hunting was bad. Agriculture meant sufficient control over the food supply to insure that the population would generally have enough food. It was now possible for some people in a population to produce more food than they consumed. This freed others to engage in other activities such as pottery making, mining, trade, government, religion, and the development of new technologies (Mumford, 1961).

Neolithic life also brought cities. These represented nodal points for the functions of society that were not directly associated with food production. The development of cities and agriculture were closely linked. It was once thought that cities became possible because of surpluses produced by early agriculture (Smith, 1776; Lensky, 1970). It appears likely that the origin of cities as trade centers predates well-developed agriculture, and that cities provided a primary stimulus for further developments in agricultural technology (Orans, 1966; Keyfitz, 1965; Cox, 1964; Jacobs 1969). In any case, urban life could not be widespread without the surplus-producing potential of agriculture.

The growth of early cities represented a primary force in population increase. As a population grows, even very slowly, its food requirements rise. Either these requirements are met or famine and death will result. Demands placed on the food production system by growing populations were a major factor in the origin of agriculture. Once cultivation became a reality, farmers could assure sufficient food supplies to allow increasing growth in both city and countryside. This, in turn, put renewed demands upon the food production system (Boserup, 1965). Within limits, these demands could be met by increasing the amount of land under cultivation and by increasing the input of labor per unit of land.

Unlike hunting and gathering, agriculture is a sedentary lifestyle. Once a crop has been planted, it must be tended until the harvest. Farmers are bound to the land for the entire growing season, and perhaps for generations if the land is good enough. But the combination of a potential division of labor between agriculture and nonagriculture and the pressure of a group in a given place for a long time creates both a demand and a supply for nonagricultural products. These were met in the light manufacturing functions of early cities.

All activities of a society, agricultural or not, require certain basic raw materials, many of which do not exist locally and must be obtained through trade. The earliest cities were nodes on overland trade routes and coordinated the trade in essential raw materials. Their population densities were higher, and the fabric of their society was more complex than those of an agriculture area. Keeping a complex society together requires governance and organization. That means that certain people carry out governmental functions, defend the city or make war for it, practice religion, or create works of science and art. These people, in turn, represent a demand for food that must be met by surrounding agricultural areas, and they also represent a resource that is available to the agricultural population. Once the ability to produce an assured food supply larger than the subsistence needs of the individual farmer had become possible, then the positive feedback interaction between the food-producing sector of the society and the nonagricultural sector brought about increasing production of food and increasing complexity of the urban sector, and this process has continued to the present day.

Neolithic culture began at different times in different places. It probably originated in the Near East about 8,000 years ago, but it soon arose independently in China, the Indus Valley, Mesoamerica and the Andes, and west Africa. From these centers it spread first through Europe and Asia and then to the rest of the world. Even today there are isolated populations that have not attained the Neolithic level.

The end of the Neolithic, with the adoption of metals as material for toolmaking, is even more variable. In some areas metalworking grew out of Neolithic culture; in others it was imposed on groups through conquest by metal-using societies. For most of the world the first metal to come into widespread use was copper. This metal is often found in its native, or uncombined, state. Beaten copper trinkets are known from several Neolithic societies. At first copper was probably considered as a kind of rare rock that could be beaten into shape without needing to be chipped or ground. At some stage people discovered that copper could be melted in a hot fire and easily cast into shape by using a mold. They also discovered that certain kinds of minerals would break down to release copper when heated with charcoal. By some 5,500 years ago mining these copper ore minerals and smelting them to copper metal were important activities in the Near East. Soon after the use of copper had become fairly common, it was discovered that the addition of tin to copper in a ratio of 1 to 9 formed the alloy bronze, which was superior to pure copper in many ways.

Bronze use brought almost as much of social change as the domestication of plants and animals. Copper and tin ores were not found everywhere. The deposits that provided copper ore to early Bronze Age cultures of the eastern Mediterranean were located in Sinai, Cyprus, Armenia, Austria, Germany, France, Spain, Greece, the Tyrol, and Great Britain. Great Britain was visited by the Phoenicians over 2,000 years ago because of its tin deposits (U.S. Bureau of Mines, 1965). Tuscany, Bohemia, Spain, southern France, Brittany, and the Caucasus Mountains were also sources of tin. Metal ores must be mined, refined, smelted, transported, alloyed, and smithed before they have any practical value. Smelting and casting require abundant supplies of fuels. Mining requires tools of its own that are sufficiently hard to be able to work hardrock ores. Thus, before a metal-based society could maintain itself, the technologies of governmental organization and transportation had to be as well developed as those related directly to mining and smelting, and they had to extend over large areas of the world. All of these technologies needed to be supported by a stable food supply.

The Bronze Age set the tone for the direct interaction of man and his ecosystems up to the nineteenth century. Metals became cheaper, and so were used more commonly for more things by more people. And population growth brought more people. But the basic consequences of mining, refining, smelting, transporting, alloying, and smithing remained much the same as they had been at the outset of metallurgy. However, the great strength and hardness of modern materials such as iron and steel have spawned a series of technological changes that permit a greater degree of manipulation of man's ecosystems than the previous materials had allowed.

One major avenue for this manipulation resulted from the feedback from mining and metallurgical development to the other primary technology, agriculture. For instance, the development of the steel plow allowed previously nonarable lands to be cultivated. A steel plow can plow more deeply than a wooden plow, it can be handled more efficiently, it is stronger and less prone to breaking, and it is capable of plowing soils that other plows are simply not capable of plowing. Without the steel plow, it would not have been possible to develop large agricultural systems in the prairie regions of North America, South America, and Eurasia, the most inherently productive agricultural regions of those continents.

THE PLACE OF DIFFERENT SOCIETIES IN HUMAN ECOSYSTEMS

The interaction between any species and other elements of its ecosystems are related to the species' structural and instinctive adaptations, the size and dynamics of the population, and the complexity of its social organization. Every natural population is characterized by an ecological niche. People too have a niche in human ecosystems. Their niche includes the patterns by which people interact with other populations (e.g., crops, livestock, weeds, pests, pets, and so on) and by which they control the flow of materials through the ecosystem. In other species, the niche stems from the genetic makeup of the population and the structure, instincts, and behaviors determined by that genetic constitution. The human niche is determined much more by culture than by genetics. People do things differently in different places, and one cannot make universally valid generalizations. But we can make useful qualitative statements about the nature of the human niche and different broad types of culture.

The simplest way to describe the human niche is to consider the discrete resources that pass from various parts of the ecosystem into the society and back. We can represent these patterns as a qualitative flow network, showing the various sorts of actions, materials, and energy flowing between a society and the other elements of the ecosystem. We can call this network the society's *environmental economy*. Any indirect effects within the ecosystem resulting from these flows must also be included in the

---

Table 2.1 Classes of Human Social Organization

---

1. Hunting and gathering societies.
2. Agricultural societies.
   a. Subsistence level village farmers.
   b. Agriculture-based urban communities.
3. Industrial societies.
   a. Industrial urban communities.
   b. Advanced industrial societies.

---

environmental economy. In some cases, the economy is simple and does not involve many types of materials or extensive storage within the society; this is especially true of simple societies. In other cases, the environmental economy may involve many different materials, a very complex pattern of flow, and extensive storage; this is the case in advanced industrial societies.

A suitable classification of cultures is difficult at best, as there is (or has been at some time in history) a continuum from the simplest to the most complex. Also, most real societies show aspects of more than one class in any classification that might be proposed. The one adopted here points out basic patterns within the continuum that relate to the development of human social organization, and it provides a useful general frame of reference for visualizing human ecosystems. It is based on Braidwood (1960) and Lenski (1970) and is summarized in Table 2.1.

Hunting and Gathering Societies

The simplest pattern of human social organization, and the one whose flow network most closely resembles that of other animals, is that of the hunter-gatherer. This category includes most of human prehistory from the origin of man to the Neolithic. The economy of the hunter-gatherer society is basically a normal food chain (Figure 2.3). Unlike the animals that characterize the textbook food-chain model, however, people are omnivores and occupy several trophic levels. The food supply consists largely or entirely of wild animals obtained through hunting or scavenging and wild plants that can be gathered near the settlement or campsite. Primitive hunting and gathering societies do not deliberately raise much of their own food, although they may indirectly favor the growth of certain species through the use of fire.

In addition to food, food gatherers may use wood as a source of fuel, and stones are used as tools. The level of technological development limits the amount of food that can be gathered and the consistency with which that amount can be obtained. Human wastes include feces and the food or fuel materials gathered but not consumed. Those feed directly into the detritus food chain just as those of any other animal.

Hunter-gatherers may be either nomadic or semipermanent. Nomads leave little trace of their presence in most cases. Their population densities are low, individual groups are quite small, and the trampling and fertilizing that accompany human habitation get spread out over the landscape by their movements (Deevey, 1960; Murdock, 1967). Semipermanent hunter-gatherers, on the other hand, may leave a definite mark

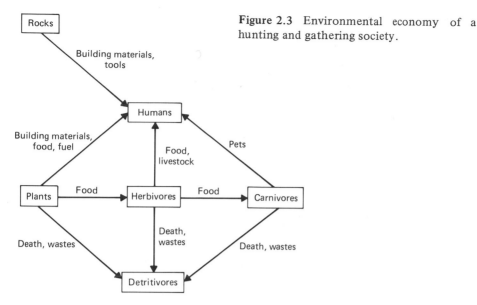

Figure 2.3 Environmental economy of a hunting and gathering society.

on their habitat. They can be semipermanent because their food-gathering technology is more efficient, and they may inhabit a more productive area than the nomads. Population densities tend to be higher, and societies tend to show some division of labor, with some people spending relatively more time with the actual practices of hunting and gathering than others.

An area that serves as a human settlement for a period of time is altered markedly by the settlement, even if it is not otherwise used as a source of food. Some degree of clearing is inevitable, whether through trampling of the underbrush, fire, or deliberate cutting of trees and shrubs, perhaps for use as building materials. The plants that repopulate such disturbed habitats are a wide range of pioneer species, including the progenitors of most of our major crop plants. Likewise, the animals that inhabit such areas are either those that are most at home in pioneer communities or those that are attracted to human settlements. These too comprise a broad group, including the progenitors of our major livestock species. Key individuals in a semipermanent community, such as headmen or priests, can experiment with the organisms found around the settlement, selecting those variants most suitable for food or other purposes (Sauer, 1969; Isaac, 1970). Most semipermanent hunter-gatherer communities use these locally encouraged species as a source of food and carry out experiments to encourage their growth—a key activity leading to the development of agriculture.

Agricultural Societies

Agricultural societies gain most of their food from crops that have been deliberately planted and cultivated, although they may supplement crops with milk, blood, eggs, meat, and game. The scope of the agricultural society is extraordinarily broad, varying from the subsistence farming hamlet to the preindustrial city. Early agricultural societies were outgrowths of relatively rich and well-organized hunting and gathering societies, where seeds collected for food were stored or lost in the vicinity of the settlement. People recognized that sprouts from these seeds were the young of edible plants, and they realized that a small amount of seed planted would yield a large amount of food at the end of the next season. This discovery in itself did not immediately raise the amount of food available to the population. Nor did it necessarily increase the efficiency or complexity of social organization (see the excellent discussion of these points by Orans, 1966). However, this discovery made it a lot easier for a population to fulfill its food needs and laid the foundation for future expansion in the size and complexity of societies.

Agricultural technology has a strong influence on the ecosystem. Farming requires major alterations in both the physical environment and the biological community. Tilling the soil changes its structure, its patterns of mineral leaching, its erodability, and virtually every other factor of importance. A relatively small number of species is planted and maintained in the field. The specific number is variable, but it may range from 40 to 50 crops, as in certain primitive tribes of tropical rain forests (Conklin, 1954), to a single crop, as in high-intensity monocultures. Even considering weeds, the diversity of field communities is drastically lower than in nature. Even the simplest pioneer community that begins ecological succession is more complex than most agricultural communities. As ecological succession acts to bring the community back into a more natural configuration, it introduces plants and animals that are not those that have been deliberately planted and maintained. These are competitors either with the crop or directly with humans. Pests and weeds are thus a feature of the orderly reconstruction of the natural steady-state community.

A field is a very different sort of ecosystem from a native forest or grassland, geochemically as well as biologically. Soils in areas at high rainfall may lose so much of their nutrients to leaching, for instance, that a field may have to be abandoned for several years so that natural succession can restore the available nutrients to useful levels. The only alternative is for farmers to take an even more active role in the geochemical part of the ecosystem and either reconfigure it structurally so that the problem is reduced (e.g., by terracing or careful selection of crops) or replace the nutrients that are leached out. The methods used depend on the resources available to the farmers and the demands made upon them.

Agriculture did more to shape man's role in the ecosystem than increase the intensity of his impact on it. It also changed the human position in the food chain. Plants may have contributed more than half of the calories to the diet of preagricultural man, but never an overwhelming majority, and the plants in the diet were generally a rather broad spectrum. Agriculture made it possible for people to increase their dependence on plants as a source of food. Some societies became almost entirely herbivorous, but all vastly reduced the number of species providing substantially to the diet.

Subsistence-Level Village Farming. Primitive agricultural communities are not very different from semipermanent hunting and gathering communities, except that relatively more of the food is derived from crops and domesticated livestock, and relatively less is obtained through hunting. The classical type of subsistence-level village farming communities are those of the Neolithic, although the peasant farmers of Europe through the last century and many present-day farmers in South America, Africa, and Asia still show the pattern.

The most important innovations in the environmental economy of a typical subsistence-level village farm, when compared with a hunter-gatherer society, are the crops grown in fields as a source of food, alterations in the balance of nutrients, water, and soil in the fields themselves, and the presence of some domesticated or semi-domesticated animals. In very primitive areas, fields tend to be small and incompletely cleared; stumps or even small living trees are left standing. Cultivation is by primitive horticulture: Implements tend to be very simple wooden digging sticks or hoes used to scratch the surface of the soil and provide a soft seed bed. Cultivation can be carried out for only a short time before weeds take over, the soil becomes permanently depleted in nutrients, or erosion begins to render the soil useless for agricultural purposes.

More advanced subsistence-level village farming may use a more effective agricultural technology based on the plow. The original plows were wooden and pulled by people, but they were quickly replaced by plows that could be pulled by domesticated animals, particularly cattle and asses. The potential for food production from a plowed field is substantially higher than that possible from a field planted with a digging stick or hoe.

Preindustrial Urban Societies. Cities have existed for at least 8,000 years, and for at least 90% of their history they have not been characterized by modern heavy industry. Their economic base has been built on trade, light manufacturing, government, and other services. Their food base is agriculture of a relatively primitive sort without the benefit of chemical fertilizers, pesticides, or tractors. The environmental economy of a preindustrial urban culture may be sharply different from that of a subsistence level village farming society. New interactions between society and the environment are implicit in an urban society and become significant for the first time.

Little food is grown in cities, and the survival of a city depends on the ability of the surrounding agricultural *hinterland* to provide a dependable supply. At the same time, cities can provide things to farmers that the latter cannot supply for themselves. These include the efficient development of new technologies of food production, markets for farm products, sources of useful materials or goods imported from other areas, the seat of government, and protection from invasion by neighbors. Once cities become part of a society's culture, they and the countrysides are linked together in a relationship like that shown in Figure 2.4, so that the size and complexity of the city and the level of agricultural production are mutually reinforcing. Both grow until a steady state is reached, at which the city can no longer exact an increase in agricultural productivity either through providing technologies or by imposing higher taxes, or the agricultural area can no longer raise its exportable surplus to sustain further growth by the city, or one of the two reaches an environmental limit to its expansion. This steady state can be maintained as long as the resources needed for both city and countryside are available and the society is politically stable (Sjoberg, 1963).

The earliest cities were market centers that controlled the trade of obsidian and flint for toolmaking. They also served as centers for manufacturing goods such as tools and cloth. The initial domestication and husbandry of certain animals, such as cattle, sheep, and goats, seem to have been related to religious ritual (Isaac, 1962, 1970), and early cities were the religious centers. Figure 2.5 diagrams the basic environmental economy of a typical metal-using preindustrial urban society. Mining and mine-related activities such as refining and smelting are as critical to the maintenance of the struc-

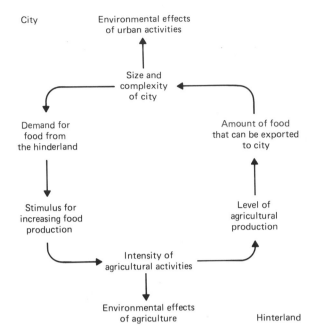

City

Environmental effects
of urban activities

Size and
complexity
of city

Demand for
food from
the hinderland

Amount of food
that can be exported
to city

Stimulus for
increasing food
production

Level of
agricultural
production

Intensity of
agricultural activities

Environmental effects
of agriculture

Hinterland

Figure 2.4 Feedback linking agricultural and urban growth in an agriculture-based urban community. Urban and agricultural sectors of the society both grow in response to the growth of the other, limited only by the availability of agricultural technology to increase the intensity of agricultural activity in the presence of a suitable stimulus and by the ability of the transportation network to transport food produced in outlying areas into the city.

ture of the society as the food supply is to the maintenance of the population. Trade between the city and its agricultural hinterland is vigorous, if for no other reason than that metal farm equipment such as plows are products of the city that make possible high and increasing productivity and stability of agricultural production.

Coincident with a burgeoning metals technology was an increased activity in forestry. Wood and wood charcoal were the primary fuels for smelters and smithies, as well as for domestic heating. Lumber was needed for construction. Exploitable forests tend to be in the hills, as the lowlands have long since been turned over to fields. In hilly areas forestry and related operations may be a significant source of environmental degradation, leading to pollution of nearby waterways and destruction of the soil to the extent that forests cannot be reestablished. Forests known to have been present before the growth of cities, such as the cedars of Lebanon and several other upland forests of the Near East, were logged heavily by preindustrial urban societies and all but destroyed by the twentieth century (Rowton, 1967).

The existence of cities implies that materials produced in one place (i.e., on farms, in forests, or from mines) are removed to a central location. The transport of biological materials harvested from farm and forest is more than the simple movement of food or wood. It is a net loss of all of the nutrients chemically bound in the harvested materials. Once in the city, the portion of the materials that is not used, or is eaten and excreted, or is used and then discarded, becomes a waste problem. In some preindustrial civilizations such as the ancient Greek city-states, the city dweller also worked the land and may have been able to cycle some wastes from the city back to the countryside, but it is unclear how widespread this practice was. Certainly, the residents of large preindustrial cities like ancient Rome or medieval London were not farmers, and most urban wastes were not recycled to the countryside. They had to be disposed of in the city.

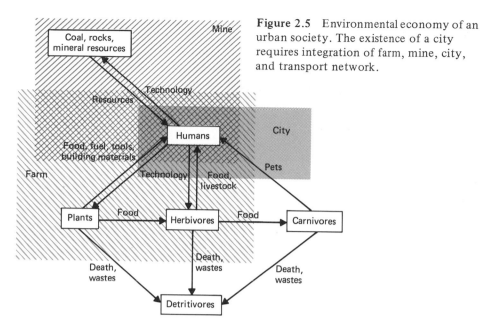

Figure 2.5 Environmental economy of an urban society. The existence of a city requires integration of farm, mine, city, and transport network.

Cities represent very different ecological systems from farms or forests. The existence of a major garbage problem is only one aspect of the difference. Cities have a much higher population density than the countryside. They may contain many thousands of inhabitats packed into relatively small space. Imperial Rome at the height of its power may have contained as many as one million. The cities of the Yoruba of western Nigeria have population densities equivalent to those of modern Chicago or New York (Bascom, 1963; Hauser, 1965). Land uses are commonly restricted to those perceived to relate to the functions of the city, such as residence, marketing, manufacturing, and transportation. Little or no thought is given to optimizing the cycling of nutrient materials or to other functions of natural ecosystems. When such provision is made it is frequently because of esthetic considerations (see, for instance, McHarg, 1969).

The abiotic environment of a city is likely to be much more rigorous than that of the open countryside, and few organisms are adapted to live there. The only truly successful urban organisms are people themselves, the animals they have intentionally domesticated such as the horse, dog, and cat, animals that have become unwanted comrades such as mice, pigeons, rats, and roaches, and very hardy species such as squirrels and some birds. The biological community within the city is simpler than in a natural ecosystem, and simple communities tend to be ecologically unstable. In a natural ecosystem, unstable communities are characterized by populations showing marked boom-and-bust rises and falls. It is not uncommon to find local or temporary extinction of a population occurring at the end of one decline, to be replaced by some other population that goes through an increase followed by an equally precipitate decline, which may be replaced by a third population, and so forth. In preindustrial cities this instability was often reflected in major epidemics and high mortality (see Chapter 3).

Despite the vulnerability of some urban populations, cities have resources that natural ecosystems of similar low diversity do not. The urban hinterlands are also part of the total urban ecosystem, as are the city's social and technological resources. As a general rule, the potential instability of a city can be counteracted, but only by paying the cost of a high level of consumption of resources from outside. A corollary to this conclusion is that the stability of the city is related to the stability of its support system in the rural hinterland.

Industrial Societies

The Industrial Revolution was a great stimulus to the development of cities and to the increase in social complexity. Its origins are rooted in the political, religious, technological, and social conditions of the sixteenth to the eighteenth century in northwestern Europe (see Lenski, 1970). The way the Industrial Revolution changed the focus of society to the cities and made possible their tremendous growth has had profound environmental repercussions. The most important developments of the Industrial Revolution for our purposes were widespread adoption of machines to perform many functions formerly carried out by human labor or draft animals, the broad-scale conversion to mechanical power sources such as hydropower and the steam engine to run these machines, the increase in the efficiency of transportation, and the growth in industrial technology.

Few of these developments were altogether new. Machines of various sorts date to antiquity; mills run by waterwheels and windmills have been around for thousands of years; vehicles and roads for moving goods and products from one place to another date from the earliest village and are essential to the supply of all cities. Technology is as old as man. What was new in the Industrial Revolution was the increase in the scale of change and the fact that the city's hegemony over the countryside became clear and undeniable. The main center of human population growth had formerly been in the countryside. It shifted to the cities during the Industrial Revolution, and migration from the countryside into the cities became the norm.

Urban Industrial Societies. From a qualitative standpoint, the basic patterns of interactions between city and countryside are the same for preindustrial and industrial urban societies. The survival of cities still depends on food from farms and on metals and fuels from mines. The requirements of farms and mines for technology and machinery are still supplied from cities. However, the quantitative patterns of the interaction are quite different. While the preindustrial city had used fuels for smelting, cooking, and similar activities, the industrial city used fuels—mainly coal—to power machines. This required a marked increase in the rate of mining and coal production over and above those required for heating and smelting (Figure 2.6), as well as an improved transportation network to get the coal to the city. The environmental effects of mines—especially coal mines—on human ecosystems can be substantial (see Chapter 7). As the demand for metal to build machines and manufactured goods increases, mining for ore and the associated smelting activities must increase apace.

As population shifts from farms to cities, agricultural production must increase sufficiently to feed it. In the preindustrial city this had been accomplished by increasing the level of agricultural technology in the area immediately surrounding the city

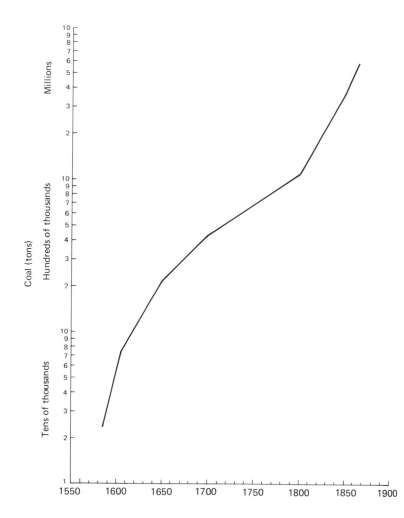

Figure 2.6 The use of coal in London, in tons. The rise in coal consumption in the 16th and 17th centuries is due to the substitution of coal for wood, which was seriously depleted in Great Britain by that time. The rise in usage after 1800 is due to the increased demand for coal resulting from the Industrial Revolution.

and providing a stimulus (money, increased technology, or coercion) to farmers to produce a surplus over their own basic needs. The growth of agricultural technology lagged roughly a hundred years behind industrial technology during the Industrial Revolution, however, and the main mechanisms of increasing agricultural production during the early stages of industrialization were those of enlarging the area supplying the city and of reducing the amount of farmland whose economy was only at a subsistence level. This could be done by improving the transportation network so that produce from outlying farms could be brought to market more easily, and products of urban industry expedited to outlying areas.

The environmental impact of the transportation network itself is considerable in an industrial society. Concentrated harbors and shipping canals represent environments quite different from natural aquatic ecosystems. The latter may connect bodies of water containing different faunas, sometimes to the detriment of the aquatic life (see Chapter 4). Railroads are the key overland transportation link in an industrial civilization. Once built, their direct effect on the environment is relatively small, outside of minor air pollution and grass fires set by primitive locomotives, but the construction of railroads is marked by types of environmental degradation such as stream siltation and the slaughter of the bison on the western range of the United States. Roads in a typical industrial society function as a link between farm and market or farm and railhead, and as distributory arteries within cities.

The indirect effect of the transportation network may be greater than the direct effect. People's economic lives are very closely linked to transportation. The distribution of population is determined to a great degree by people's ability to move. Nodes in the transportation network also tend to be points of concentration of population or industry. The kind of transport system can also affect settlement patterns. Center-to-center transport as exemplified by railroads tends to promote highly centralized cities. Automobiles and airports, on the other hand, which are not directed toward central cities, have the effect of promoting urban sprawl throughout the world.

The direct environmental impact of an industrial city is much greater than that of a preindustrial city. The biggest component of the environmental economy within an industrial city is absent or unimportant in the preindustrial city; that is, industry itself. The Industrial Revolution brought with it air, water, and solid waste pollution of a sort and on a scale that had not existed previously. Before the Industrial Revolution most waste products were of biological origin. Industrial wastes tend to be different from human biological wastes, and their impact on the environment may be pronounced. As manufacturing increased it became increasingly sophisticated, producing larger proportions of materials not found in nature. Wastes themselves became recognized as a major problem by the end of the nineteenth century. In addition to industrial pollution, virtually all of the problems of the preindustrial city are present in the industrial city as well. The major exception is that with the introduction of automobiles and trucks in the twentieth century, beasts of burden were phased out as prime mechanisms for intraurban distribution of goods and people. While this represented a reduction of some types of urban waste (e.g., horse manure), it spawned many problems in their stead.

Advanced Industrial Urban Societies.   There has clearly been a major change in the organization of major industrial societies within the last thirty years (Galbraith, 1967). The basic functions of a city in any urban society can be broken down into four areas (Bogue, 1949): retail trade, wholesale trade, manufacturing, and services. Trade was the primary function of the preindustrial city; manufacturing filled this role in the industrial city. The per capita intake of food, fuel, and minerals is greater than in earlier societies. People are better fed with higher quality foods. There is a higher per capita consumption of metals, chemicals, and other basic commodities. The flow of raw materials from areas of production to the city increases greatly.

But the increase in the flow from city to countryside is even more remarkable. New technologies of obtaining fuel have been developed, from five-story-high electric power shovels for strip-mining coal to nuclear fracturing of rock in order to release natural gas. Farming has become highly mechanized, and farm chemicals (fertilizer, pesticides, herbicides, and so on) have revolutionized agriculture. While the balance sheet shows a high yield of food being delivered from farm to city, it also shows an even higher flow of energy and materials from the city to the farm. These are in the form of heavy machinery, fuel, and chemicals that the farm cannot produce but that have attained a prominent role in the operation of modern farms. The city is linked with the countryside in a technological union, to a degree that did not exist even a few years ago. A result of this union is that a problem previously characteristic only of the city, waste disposal, has become characteristic of the countryside as well. The specific wastes are different. They include materials such as pesticides, fertilizers, and feedlot manures. But the local ecosystem on the farm cannot assimilate them any more than the city can assimilate raw garbage and industrial wastes.

Transportation patterns have shown some important changes with the onset of advanced industrial society. The automobile is the key to the system, just as the railroad was the key to industrial urban society. Highway construction has at least as great an environmental impact as railroad construction, and exhaust fumes associated with the routine operation of automobiles comprise the largest single source of air pollution.

The advanced industrial city can be regarded in general as an enlargement of the industrial city, with a higher population and a substantially greater per capita consumption of energy, especially electricity. This higher consumption has several origins. The balance of industry in the advanced industrial city is slanted toward relatively more energy-intensive industries (Commoner, 1971). New materials such as plastics, sophisticated metals, and highly refined organic chemicals all have a higher energy cost than the commodities that were the raw materials for the industrial city. Residents of the advanced industrial society are, for the most part, more affluent and have more leisure time to devote to energy intensive activities.

An offshoot of the leisure time characteristic of advanced industrial urban civilization is the great increase in the previously negligible exploitation of wilderness areas for recreational purposes. In many cases, areas of relatively low ecosystem resilience that had been almost untouched by man because of their inaccessibility have been subjected to intense pressure from tourists. The consequences of this pressure are likely to be severe. It is probable that if present trends continue, the wilderness values that people seek will be destroyed by their seeking them.

HUMAN ECOSYSTEMS IN SPACE

There is an important functional distinction between city and hinterland. Activities such as farming and mining are *dispersed* through the countryside. Their influence on their surroundings is generally diffused, except for certain types of problems such as pollution from cattle feedlots or mine-mouth drainage, in which part of the production has been concentrated in a relatively small area. Functions such as residence, commerce, manufacturing, and services are *centralized* in towns and cities. The area of direct contact between them and the wider ecosystem is much smaller and is limited to the urbanized region, although the implications of this contact may spill over into wider areas. Thus, it makes sense to recognize two separate classes of environmental problems, those that are dispersed and are related to primary production, and those that are located in cities and are related to manufacturing and consumption.

Different places are characterized by different functions for various reasons. In some cases it may be because of a feature of the natural environment. It is not feasible to develop a coal mine in an area that does not contain coal. Nor is it feasible to attempt to farm intensively in an area that is too cold or too dry. But the question is not which activities are not carried out, but rather which ones are. Simply because an activity *can* be carried out does not mean that it *will* be carried out. Ore resources for which we have the technological capability of extracting metal, or areas suited to intensive agriculture, may be left unused. The choice to carry out certain activities in certain places is related to economic and political forces within a society. The distribution patterns of man–environment interactions are determined by decisions that seldom consider details of the natural ecosystems of the area in question. They are much more likely to be concerned with factors like profit or prestige.

Dispersed functions tend to involve the primary economic sectors in which commodity production is a direct result of the management of the ecosystem. Agriculture, forestry, fisheries, and mining are representative examples. The management of centralized functions tends to ignore environmental considerations unless they are forced upon it for economic or political reasons.

There is no such thing as a typical city. All cities produce a certain minimal amount of waste equal to the biological waste of their human inhabitants plus the normal waste associated with commerce. Beyond this, an industrial city produces forms of waste that are very different from those of a service-oriented city. Small cities do not, as a rule, show qualitatively the same environmental problems as large cities.

In North America and western Europe heavy industry is one of the most specialized activities of society, and it has the most pronounced impact on the environment. Industry must be located in a place where all of its requirements for raw materials, labor, communications, and markets can be met; that is, in the larger cities. Because cities contain not only the heaviest industries, but also all other urban functions as well as the highest population densities in their regions, large cities are a major factor within the human ecosystem and are commonly centers of environmental pollution.

We cannot reduce human impact on the environment by decentralizing society into suburban rings around the central business and industrial districts of our cities. To be sure, such decentralization would reduce the impact from sources related to population density. However, this reduction would be much more than equaled by an increase in negative consequences of decentralization such as air pollution from the increased automotive traffic needed to get around a decentralized area. Decentralization cannot reduce industry-related environmental problems. It can only change them a bit. It is impossible to sweep industry—or any other function of society, for that matter—under the rug. Urban areas are dependent on their rural hinterlands for food and raw materials, and rural areas and small cities are dependent on large cities for refined materials, manufactured goods, and services. Each of these settlements has certain inherent ecological characteristics, and all have a significant role in modern society.

If the present demands of human society on its ecosystems result in soil erosion and other deterioration of farmlands or destruction of waterways from acid mine drainage, the responsibility for understanding and meeting these problems falls upon all of us, because we are all part of a culture reaping the benefits and problems of an advanced industrial society. Likewise, pollution and ecosystem deterioration both in central cities and in countrysides is a direct result of the demands made by society, and responsibility for it does not escape us because we do not live in a particular area.

References

Axelrod, D. I., 1958. Evolution of the Madro-Tertiary geoflora. *Bot. Rev.* **24**: 433–509.

Bascom, W., 1963. The urban African and his world. *Cahiers d'Etudes Africaines* **4 (14)**: 163–185.

Bogue, D. J., 1949. *The Structure of the Metropolitan Community: A Study of Dominance and Subdominance.* Ann Arbor: Horace R. Rackham School of Grad. Studies, Univ. of Michigan.

Bordaz, J., 1970. *Tools of the Old and New Stone Age.* New York: Natural History Press.

Boserup, E., 1965. *The Conditions of Agricultural Growth: The Economics of Agrarian Change under Population Pressure.* Chicago: Aldine Pub. Co.

Boughey, A. S., 1971. *Man and the Environment: An Introduction to Human Ecology and Evolution.* New York: Macmillan Pub. Co.

Braidwood, R. J., 1960. Levels of prehistory: a model for the consideration of the evidence. In Tax, S., ed., *Evolution after Darwin*, Vol. II, *The Evolution of Man: Man, Culture, and Society.* Chicago: Univ. of Chicago Press, 143–151.

Butzer, K. W., 1971. *Environment and Archeology: An Ecological Approach to Prehistory*, 2nd ed. Chicago: Aldine-Atherton.

Commoner, B., 1971. *The Closing Circle: Nature, Man, and Technology.* New York: Alfred A. Knopf.

Conklin, H. C., 1954. An ethnoecological approach to shifting agriculture. *Trans. N.Y. Acad. Sci.* **17, 2nd series**: 133–142.

Cox, O. C., 1964. The preindustrial city reconsidered. *Sociol. Quart.* **5**: 133–144.

Deevey, E. S., 1960. The human population. *Sci. Am.* **203 (3)**: 195–204.

Galbraith, J. K., 1967. *The New Industrial State.* Boston: Houghton Mifflin Co.

Harrison, R. J. and Montagna, W., 1969. *Man.* New York: Appleton-Century-Crofts.

Hauser, P. M., 1965. Urbanization: an overview. In Hauser, P. M. and Schnore, L. F., eds., *The Story of Urbanization.* New York: John Wiley & Sons, 1–47.

Hockett, C. F. and Ascher, R., 1964. The human revolution. *Current Anthrop.* **5**: 135–168.

Howells, W. W., 1967. *Mankind in the Making*, rev. ed. Garden City: Doubleday & Co., Inc.

Isaac, E., 1962. On the domestication of cattle. *Science* **137**: 195–204.

Isaac, E., 1970. *Geography of Domestication.* Englewood Cliffs, N.J.: Prentice-Hall.

Isaac, G., 1978. The food-sharing behavior of protohuman hominids. *Sci. A.* **238 (4)**: 90–108.

Izawa, K., 1970. Unit groups of chimpanzees and their nomadism in the savanna woodland. *Primates* **11**: 1–46.

Jacobs, J., 1969. *The Economy of Cities.* New York: Random House.

Keyfitz, N., 1965. Political-economic aspects of urbanization in south and southeast Asia. In Hauser, P. M., and Schnore, L. F., eds., *The Study of Urbanization.* New York: John Wiley & Sons, 265–309.

Krantz, G. S., 1970. Human activities and megafossil extinctions. *Am. Sci.* **58**: 164–170.

Lenski, G., 1970. *Human Societies: A Macrolevel Introduction to Sociology.* New York: McGraw-Hill Book Company.

Martin, P. S., 1973. The discovery of America. *Science* **179**: 969–974.

Martin, P. S. and Wright, H. E., Jr., eds., 1967. *Pleistocene Extinctions: The Search for a Cause.* New Haven: Yale Univ. Press.

McHarg, I. L., 1969. *Design With Nature.* Garden City: Natural History Press.

McLuhan, M. H., 1964. *Understanding Media: The Extensions of Man.* New York: McGraw-Hill Book Company.

Mumford, L., 1961. *The City in History: Its Origins, its Transformations, and its Prospects.* New York: Harcourt, Brace, and World.

Murdock, G. P., 1967. Ethnographic atlas, a summary. *Ethnology* **6**: 109–236. This has also been published separately, and the atlas is updated in succeeding issues of *Ethnology,* compiled by the editors.

Nef, J. U., 1932. *The Rise of the British Coal Industry,* Vol. I. London: Frank Cross & Co., Ltd.

Orans, M., 1966. Surplus. *Human Organization* **25**: 24–32.

Romer, A. S., 1966. *Vertebrate Paleontology,* 3rd ed. Chicago: Univ. of Chicago Press.

Rowton, M. B., 1967. The woodlands of ancient western Asia. *Jour. Near Eastern Studies* **26**: 261–277.

Sauer, C. O., 1969. *Agricultural Origins and Dispersals: The Domestication of Animals and Foodstuffs.* Cambridge: MIT Press.

Simons, E. L., 1977. *Ramapithecus. Sci. Am.* **236 (5)**: 28–35.

Sjoberg, G., 1963. The rise and fall of cities: a theoretical perspective. *Int. Jour. Comp. Sociol.* **4**: 107–130.

Smith, A., 1776. *An Inquiry into the Nature and Causes of the Wealth of Nations.* London: W. Strahan and T. Codell.

Stewart, O. C., 1956. Fire as the first great force employed by man. In Thomas, W. L., ed., *Man's Role in Changing the Face of the Earth.* Chicago: Univ. of Chicago Press, 115–133.

Suzuki, A., 1969. An ecological study of chimpanzees in a savanna woodland. *Primates* **10**: 103–148.

Tatersall, I., 1970. *Man's Ancestors: An Introduction to Primate and Human Evolution.* London: John Murray, Ltd.

Tuttle, R. H., 1969. Knuckle-walking and the problem of human origins. *Science* **166**: 953–961.

U.S. Bureau of Mines, 1965. *Mineral Facts and Problems,* 1965 ed. Bureau of Mines Publication **630**.

Van Valen, L., 1970. Evolution of communities and late Pleistocene extinctions. *Proc. North American Paleont. Conv., Sept. 1969,* part E: 469–485.

Washburn, S. L., 1978. The evolution of man. *Sci. Am.* **239 (3)**: 194–208.

3/growth and regulation of human populations

The human population has been growing steadily throughout the last three million years. On the average, each generation has left a population slightly larger than itself. During the Early and Middle Stone Ages, for example, growth averaged less than 1/10 of 1% per century. With the development of agriculture the growth rate increased markedly for a while, and then declined essentially to zero until the Industrial Revolution, when it rose again. In the last few decades the rate of increase in the growth rate has itself been increasing. This is a matter of concern for two reasons. First, the effect on the environment of most human activities is a function of population density: the more people, the greater the effect. Second, no population can grow indefinitely. All systems are limited. The question is, by what, and how, is the limitation imposed?

For instance a linear relationship such as line 2 of Figure 3.1 means that per capita impact on the environment is constant, regardless of population size or density. Some effects are exponential, as shown in line 1 of Figure 3.1. Here, per capita environmental degradation increases with rising population density. Still others show an effect analogous to benefits of scale, in which the rate of environmental degradation rises more slowly than the population and per capita impact falls with increasing population, as in line 3 of Figure 1.3. Examples of all three are suggested by different aspects of wastewater collection and pollution. Low-density settlements may be able to use septic tanks effectively to control human wastes. But the probability of leakage or ground saturation increases exponentially with increasing density, so that water pollution from septic tanks in densely populated areas may be significant. If on the other hand, household wastes are fed into a sewer, the per capita

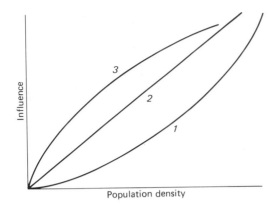

Figure 3.1 Schematic representation of the impact of a population on the environment as a function of population size: curve *1*: influence increases exponentially with population density; curve *2*: influence increases at a constant rate with population density; curve *3*: influence increases at a decreasing rate with population density.

contribution of wastes to the sewage load is approximately constant regardless of population density. Treatment plant efficiency often improves with increasing plant size as sewer districts can afford to maintain larger and better trained staffs to monitor and run the plant.

Most of the important environmental phenomena do not show the simple relationships to population illustrated in Figure 3.1. They are a collage of several factors (such as per capita waste production and treatment plant efficiency) that show different associations with population. Thus the most significant relationships tend to be quite complex.

The forces that stimulate or limit population growth are equally complex. Some are physical (e.g., temperature, water, energy, nutrients, food), while others are biological (e.g., predation, parasitism, crowding). The interactions between populations and most of the factors that control them are of a feedback kind: changes in population density lead to further changes. If the result is self-sustaining growth or decline, the feedback is said to be *positive;* if it is toward regulation around some steady-state level, the feedback is said to be *negative.*

The most important interactions limiting the growth of populations in general are of the negative-feedback sort. Some are internal, where the population adjusts its reproductive rate according to its density. More common are responses to other populations or to the abiotic environment. It is quite usual, for example, for a prey species to be limited by a predator. If its numbers get higher than some equilibrium level, predation is easier and the predator can take a higher percentage of the prey, driving the prey population back toward its equilibrium level. The reverse is true if the prey population drops below its equilibrium. Similar instances exist in nature for abiotic factors as well.

In a sense, it does not make much difference which of the three mechanisms is in effect. All can work efficiently to limit population growth and indeed many, if not most, populations are controlled by all three working together. Outside observers would be hard pressed to tell the difference if they could perceive only the population size or density statistics. Some natural populations are regulated quite precisely by negative feedback, and fluctuation about the mean is minimal (Figure 3.2, curve 1). In still others the feedback mechanism is more gross, and fluctuation may be much wider, as shown in curves 2 and 3 of Figure 3.2. But all populations are regulated. No single

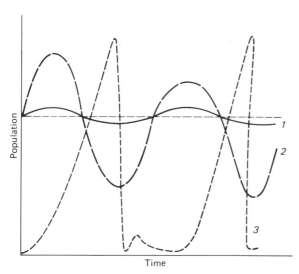

Figure 3.2 Types of fluctuation in a hypothetical population: curve *1*: very tightly controlled around a mean carrying capacity; curve *2*: very loosely controlled around a mean carrying capacity; curve *3*: not controlled at all with regard to mean carrying capacity; population expands rapidly during favorable conditions and crashes during unfavorable conditions.

population can grow to infinite numbers; the earth does not have a sufficient resource base to support an infinite population of any species.

In the case of humans the situation is not as simple as it is with most animals and plants. Controls on the human population were quite obvious at earlier stages in history. Stone Age people were limited by their food supply, by climate, and by their hunting methods. The development of agriculture removed many of these limitations. New limitations were related to motive energy, which was soon overcome by the invention of the harness for domestic livestock. This, in time, was superseded by people's ability to manipulate agricultural ecosystems. Limitations since then have been steadily chipped away by the development of fertilizers, pesticides, new crop varieties, and so on through the arsenal of the Green Revolution. In a sense, we do not know what factors constitute the limits to the present proliferation of people around the earth. There is no question that there is a limit. The question is, what determines it? By what means, and how strongly, will the limit be imposed? Can we learn enough about the cultural forces that determine the growth and regulation of human populations to bring them to a sustainable steady-state level with a minimum of social disruption? The alternative is to condemn society to a statistical roller coaster for an indeterminate period into the future.

The "population problem" stems ultimately from the fundamental regulatory structure of the human ecosystem. The environment limits the effectiveness of given technologies, but cultural development has historically been quite effective in getting around the old limitations and making new resources available. Whatever evidence we have suggests that technological growth will continue to circumvent at least some of the resource limitations acting on human populations. This does not change the basic premise that human populations cannot continue to grow indefinitely. It does make it impossible to specify the precise mechanism by which they will ultimately be limited.

One of the most frustrating aspects of the population problem is that its influences are often subtle, and their connection with population is often not even noticed. In a trenchant editorial in *Science,* Garrett Hardin (1971) recounts having been in Calcutta in 1970 when a cyclone struck in Bangladesh (then East Pakistan): "Early dispatches spoke of 15,000 dead, but the estimates rapidly escalated to 2,000,000 and then dropped back to 500,000. A nice round number: it will do as well as any, for we will never know. The nameless ones who died, 'unimportant' people far beyond the fringes of the social power structure, left no trace of their existence. Pakistani parents repaired the population loss in just 40 days, and the world turned its attention to other matters." The population density of the Ganges Delta of Bangladesh is among the highest in the world, whereas its natural endowments and standard of living are among the world's lowest. If it is possible to say that any area in the world is overpopulated, it is the Ganges Delta. And yet what brings death is a cyclone, not a too-high population density.

Several facets of population growth can be controlled. Mortality can be reduced through medical technology and health care delivery systems. It is almost a technical matter. Fertility can also be controlled, but this depends on conscious decisions and actions by the entire reproductive population. Because fertility control needs mass acceptance, it is much harder than mortality control. It may be perfectly obvious in an intellectual fashion that fertility control and consequent limitation of births is absolutely essential to the long-term survival of modern society. But this realization does no good unless it is incorporated into the attitudes of each community.

DYNAMICS OF POPULATION INCREASE

Populations grow when there are more births than deaths over a period of time. This statement is deceptively simple, and the crude measures that follow from it conceal much of the dynamism of demographic change. In order to get a feeling for the dynamics and momentum of population growth we must consider not only the size of the population, but also its age distribution and the probability of individuals of various ages to give birth or to die. Even these factors ignore migration, which is significant in many countries and is a major reason that nobody ever worried about a population explosion before the close of the frontier in the New World.

Crude Rates of Population Change

In order to assess population change it is necessary to determine the population's *vital rates;* that is, the rates of births, deaths, and growth. The simplest vital rates are the *crude rates of change.* These take into account the size of the population, the number of births, and the number of deaths, but they do not consider effects of the age distribution or the age-dependence of birth and death. The crude rates are the simplest means of denoting population growth, and they are also the most common. In some ways this is unfortunate, as it allows people to ignore the most critical factors influencing the momentum of population growth. But the crude rates are useful for making rough comparisons of population growth in different areas, and they are a direct measure of the change in a population's demand on its ecosystem at any given time.

The crude birth and death rates represent the number of individuals being born to, or dying from, 1,000 typical individuals in the population under consideration over a period of one year. By convention the population is considered at its midyear level. The crude birth rate (CBR) is obtained by dividing the number of births in the year by the midyear population and multiplying by 1,000. The crude death rate (CDR) is obtained by dividing the total number of deaths in the year by the total population and multiplying by 1,000.

$$CBR = (\text{total births/midyear population}) \times 1,000$$

$$CDR = (\text{total deaths/midyear population}) \times 1,000$$

The crude growth rate (CGR) is the difference between the crude birth rate and the crude death rate.

$$CGR = CBR - CDR$$

Doubling Period

Seemingly small differences in the growth rate of a population are magnified greatly by the fact that growth is compounded. Persons added to a population can reproduce, and the breeding population is not limited to the number originally present. To see how great this effect really is, compare the doubling periods of populations growing continuously at a constant annual rate. The doubling period is the length of time it takes for the population to double in size. Figure 3.3 shows the relationship between the different growth rates and the doubling period. The population of the world as a whole has a doubling period of about 38 years. For some countries, like Libya and Kuwait, the doubling period is less than 20 years. Other countries, like the United States, Italy, and most of northern Europe, have a doubling period over 100 years (PRB, 1979).

AGE-DEPENDENT RELATIONSHIPS

Although the crude vital rates are often used to predict population growth, they are not really appropriate for this purpose. For example, the notion of doubling time assumes that the growth rate is constant over the period in question. This is never true. Birth rates and death rates both change to reflect social factors, and both show a relationship to age that confers a powerful momentum to population growth. In order to deal adequately with population dynamics it is necessary to consider these age dependencies. Unfortunately, they complicate matters greatly, and a complete discussion requires a mathematical treatment beyond the scope of this book (see, for instance, Keyfitz, 1968, Coale, 1972). Population statistics must be much more complete and accurate than those that suffice for crude measurements. For this reason the population dynamics of many areas cannot be analyzed in adequate detail, as their census data are insufficient. This is especially true in developing countries (United Nations, 1970).

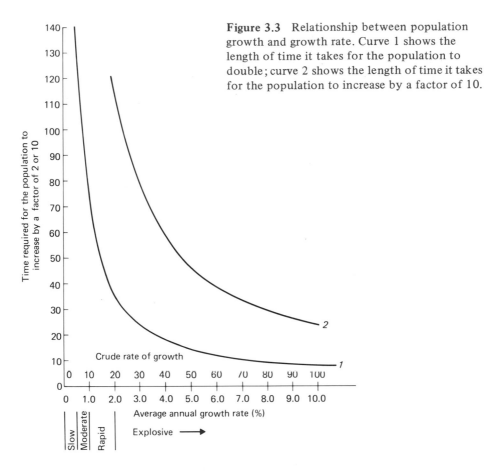

Figure 3.3 Relationship between population growth and growth rate. Curve 1 shows the length of time it takes for the population to double; curve 2 shows the length of time it takes for the population to increase by a factor of 10.

Age Distributions

Different populations have different age distributions. These distributions are commonly portrayed as age pyramids, as shown in Figure 3.4. The shapes of these pyramids provide a rapid graphic insight into a population's growth dynamics. Those whose growth rate is increasing have an expanded base similar to that of Costa Rica in 1963; those whose growth rate is stable have an age pyramid similar to that of Belgium in 1967.

Age-specific Fertility. Fertility is defined as the number of live births per woman. In all human populations fertility is far less than the physiological maximum number of conceptions possible, but it varies strongly with respect to age and culture (Figure 3.5). Fertility begins with *menarche,* the age at which ovulation begins, reaches a maximum in a woman's early twenties, and falls slowly to zero at *menopause,* the age at which ovulation ends. The age-specific fertility rate is an accurate measure of fertility in a population.

The female population of reproductive age (generally considered at 15 to 50) is considered in intervals, commonly five years in length. The total number of babies

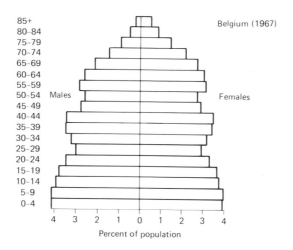

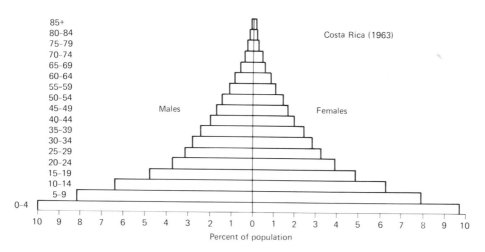

Figure 3.4 Age pyramids for Belgium, a country with a stable population, and Costa Rica, a country with an expanding population. Males and females are shown separately. [Data from United Nations, 1970.]

born to all women in a given age interval (B_i) is divided by the total number of women in that age interval at midyear (N_i), and multiplied by 1,000 to give the fertility rate for that interval (r_i).

$$r_i = 1,000 \; B_i/N_i$$

The age-specific fertility is the distribution of all r_i's for the population (see Table 3.1). Its magnitude is strongly dependent on culture. The basic shape of the age-fertility relationship is the same for most populations (Figure 3.5), although there are slight differences. Table 3.1 shows the age-specific fertility for Belgium and Costa Rica. In addition to the age-specific fertility, two parameters can be calculated from this table. The *general fertility rate* of the population is the number of babies born to all

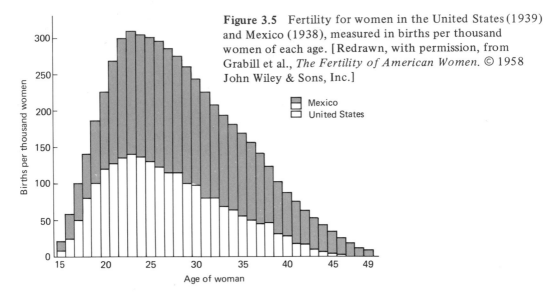

Figure 3.5 Fertility for women in the United States (1939) and Mexico (1938), measured in births per thousand women of each age. [Redrawn, with permission, from Grabill et al., *The Fertility of American Women.* © 1958 John Wiley & Sons, Inc.]

women of reproductive age in the population; the crude birth rate can also be determined if the size of the total population is known.

The fertility of a population is the chief determinant of the birth rate, but it is not the only one. Compare the number of births that would result if the age-specific fertility rates of the two nations shown in Table 3.1 were found in a society whose population had a hybrid distribution intermediate between two (Table 3.2). The crude birth rates are close to those found in the two populations whose fertility data were used, but they are not identical. The differences are due to the differences in the age distri-

Table 3.1 Age-specific Fertility and Births for Belgium (1967) and Costa Rica (1963).

Age Range	Belgium			Costa Rica		
	No. Women	*Fertility*	*Births*	*No. Women*	*Fertility*	*Births*
45–49	275,603	1.0	276	23,321	16.7	389
40–44	332,015	11.2	3,719	27,590	100.2	2,765
35–39	328,915	41.7	13,716	34,126	225.8	7,706
30–34	302,795	85.6	25,919	39,169	295.5	11,574
25–29	278,783	151.4	42,208	44,675	361.9	16,168
20–24	316,130	156.4	49,443	53,782	338.3	18,194
15–19	349,686	15.3	5,350	66,986	52.9	3,544
Totals	2,183,927		140,631	289,649		60,340
General fertility rate		64.4			208.3	
Total population	9,580,990			1,378,705		
Crude birth rate		14.7			43.8	

Data from United Nations, 1970.

Table 3.2   Age-specific Fertility Data for Belgium and Costa Rica Applied to an Artificial Population with an Intermediate Age Distribution.

Age Range	No. Women	Belgium		Costa Rica	
		Fertility	*Births*	*Fertility*	*Births*
45–49	1,043	1.0	1.0	16.7	17.4
40–44	1,249	11.2	14.0	100.2	125.1
35–39	1,349	41.7	56.3	225.8	304.6
30–34	1,369	85.6	117.2	295.5	404.5
25–29	1,404	151.4	212.6	361.9	508.1
20–24	1,643	156.4	257.0	338.3	555.8
15–19	1,943	15.3	29.7	52.9	102.8
Totals	10,000		687.8		2,018.3
General fertility rate		68.8		201.8	
Population	45,650				
Crude birth rate		15.1		44.2	

This population was calculated by adding the age distributions of Belgium and Costa Rica and extracting 10,000 females of reproductive ages.
Data from United Nations, 1970.

butions, and they are readily explainable. The Belgian fertility data give a higher birth rate in the hybrid population than in the actual Belgian population primarily because more of the women in the hybrid population are younger and in their reproductive prime. The Costa Rican fertility data also give a higher birth rate in the hybrid population, because more of the women are older and of reproductive age. The differences between the performances of the actual and hybrid populations are small and would probably be negligible in practice. This does not mean that the effects of age distribution are negligible. To see the critical importance of age distributions, let us turn to age-specific mortality.

Age-specific Mortality.   Death, like birth, bears a strong relationship to age, and tables and graphs derived from mortality data are among our most useful tools in population dynamics. By knowing the age distribution of a population at any given time and the number of people in each age group who will die during a calendar year, several useful parameters can be calculated and tabulated in the *life table* (Table 3.3).

The life table consists of seven columns. It can be used to determine several things, including the infant mortality rate, the probability of an individual of any age dying within the year, the average number of years an individual of any age can expect to live, and the probability of surviving for any given number of years (Bogue, 1969). We can compare populations on several grounds, such as life expectancy, age-specific death rate, infant mortality rate, and shape of the *survivorship curves.* The last are an especially useful graphic means of comparing the mortality of populations (Figure 3.6). A highly convex-upward curve, such as that of Belgium in 1967 (Figure 3.6a) is typical

Table 3.3   Life Table for the United States of America, 1977.

Age	nq_x	l_x	nd_x	nL_x	T_x	$\overset{o}{e}_x$
0–1	.0142	100,000	1,421	98,751	7,316,270	73.2
1–5	.0027	98,579	268	393,693	7,217,519	73.2
5–10	.0017	98,311	167	491,106	6,823,826	69.4
10–15	.0018	98,144	173	490,355	6,332,720	64.5
15–20	.0051	97,971	499	488,723	5,842,365	59.6
20–25	.0067	97,472	650	485,756	5,353,642	54.9
25–30	.0066	96,822	637	482,517	4,867,886	50.3
30–35	.0070	96,185	677	479,306	4,385,369	45.6
35–40	.0097	95,508	928	475,369	3,906,063	40.9
40–45	.0151	94,580	1,428	469,565	3,430,694	36.3
45–50	.0239	93,152	2,222	460,552	2,961,129	31.8
50–55	.0372	90,930	3,379	446,727	2,500,577	27.5
55–60	.0555	87,551	4,861	426,258	2,053,850	23.5
60–65	.0858	82,690	7,095	396,531	1,627,592	19.7
65–70	.1173	75,595	8,868	356,669	1,231,061	16.3
70–75	.1764	66,727	11,768	305,147	874,392	13.1
75–80	.2647	54,959	14,550	238,929	569,245	10.4
80–85	.3612	40,409	14,596	164,964	330,316	8.2
85+	1.0000	25,813	25,813	165,352	165,352	6.4

This table includes the entire population of the U.S.A., male and female, white and nonwhite. Columns are defined as follows:

Age   Period of life between two exact ages, stated in years.

nq_x Proportion of persons alive at begining of age interval dying during interval.

l_x Number living at beginning of age interval, out of a hypothetical population of 100,000 at age 0.

nd_x Number of individuals in the population (l_x) dying during the age interval.

nL_x Number of individuals in a stationary population, aged each interval.

T_x Number of individuals in a stationary population, aged each interval or older.

$\overset{o}{e}_x$ Average number of years of life remaining at beginning of age interval.

From National Center for Health Statistics, 1980.

of industrial societies with fairly low mortality; a curve such as that of Costa Rica in 1963 (Figure 3.6b) is typical of preindustrial societies with greater mortality.

In order to get a better grasp of the implications of some of the more common measures of death rate, let us compare the age-specific death rates for Belgium and Costa Rica, just as we did for birth statistics. Age-specific mortality rates are graphed in Figure 3.6. Note that mortality in all populations is concentrated in the very young and the very old, and that the age-specific mortality is quite different for the two countries. Table 3.4 shows the number of individuals in all age groups in both populations, as well as the number of deaths in each age group. When the deaths are totaled and divided by the population size, we obtain the crude death rate. The crude death

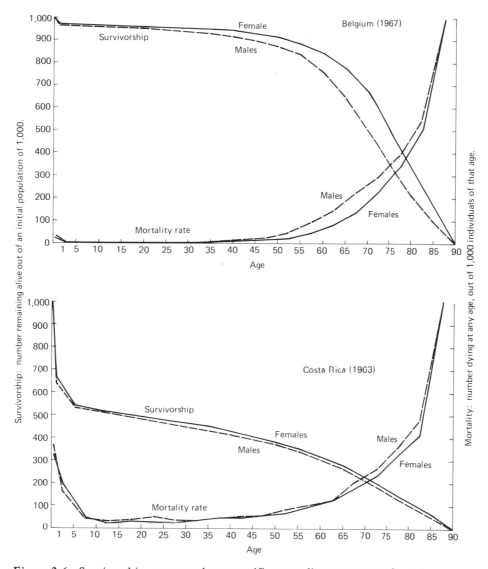

Figure 3.6 Survivorship curves and age-specific mortality rate curves for Belgium and Costa Rica. Males and females are shown separately; data are presented at five-year intervals except for infants (0–1 yr.) and ages 1–4, which are shown separately. [Data from United Nations, 1970.]

rate for Belgium is roughly 1.5 times that for Costa Rica. But Table 3.5 shows the number of deaths in the same hybrid population that was used to construct Table 3.2, using the age-specific mortality rates for Belgium and Costa Rica. The obvious conclusions drawn from the crude death rates are greatly understated. Correcting for differences in the age structure shows clearly that mortality in Belgium is not 1.5 times that of Costa Rica as indicated by the crude death rate, but rather is only 0.75 as great.

Table 3.4 Age-specific Mortality and Deaths for Belgium (1967) and Costa Rica (1963).

Age Range	Belgium			Costa Rica		
	Population	*Mortality*	*Deaths*	*Population*	*Mortality*	*Deaths*
85+	70,672	215.9	15,259	3,309	203.6	674
80–84	130,258	127.4	16,603	4,537	122.1	554
75–79	228,706	77.9	17,818	7,582	83.8	636
70–74	347,365	49.0	17,031	11,479	53.8	618
65–69	468,031	31.0	14,544	16,964	33.7	573
60–64	545,754	19.7	10,754	23,366	19.0	444
55–59	574,624	12.2	7,049	30,091	13.7	413
50–54	512,589	7.5	3,869	39,686	8.0	319
45–49	544,982	4.4	2,420	46,959	5.4	257
40–44	662,669	2.7	1,826	55,149	4.2	232
35–39	661,661	1.6	1,110	67,954	3.3	231
30–34	614,275	1.2	718	78,023	2.2	174
25–29	570,558	1.0	586	87,846	1.8	159
20–24	648,192	1.0	643	105,157	1.5	162
15–19	713,189	0.7	503	132,966	1.3	181
10–14	738,338	0.4	258	173,819	0.8	149
5–9	777,927	0.4	332	221,463	1.2	270
1–4	624,218	0.9	534	213,670	6.0	1,286
0–1	147,057	22.8	3,355	58,685	66.1	3,882
Totals	9,580,990		115,212	1,378,705		11,214
Crude death rate		12.03			8.13	

Data from United Nations, 1970.

Effects on Age Distribution of Alternations in Vital Rates

If age distributions were constant, we would not have to worry about their effects on birth or death rates. The effects would be present, to be sure, but they could be considered characteristics of the population in question. But they are not constant. Fertility and mortality both vary, and they may sometimes change rapidly. When this happens, the age distribution changes in response.

Consider what happens when a population whose age distribution shows the aggregate mortality and fertility patterns of Latin America, which experiences an across-the-board 30% reduction in mortality (Figure 3.7). We expect a general reduction in mortality to lead to increased survival of older individuals, and this happens. But a far more important result is the expansion of the base of the age pyramid, reflecting the survival of many infants who would otherwise have died (note in Table 3.4 that infant mortality accounted for about 1/3 of the total deaths in Costa Rica in 1963). A reduction of mortality has precisely the same effect on age distribution as an increase in fertility.

Table 3.5 Age-specific Mortality Data for Belgium and Costa Rica Applied to an Artifical Population with an Intermediate Age Distribution.

Age Range	Population	Belgium		Costa Rica	
		Mortality	*Deaths*	*Mortality*	*Deaths*
85+	488	215.9	105.4	203.6	99.4
80–84	845	127.4	107.7	122.1	103.2
75–79	1,469	77.9	114.4	83.8	123.1
70–74	2,229	49.0	109.2	53.8	119.9
65–69	3,058	31.0	94.8	33.7	103.1
60–64	3,695	19.7	72.8	19.0	70.2
55–59	4,089	12.2	49.9	13.7	56.0
50–54	4,114	7.5	30.9	8.0	32.9
45–49	4,548	4.4	20.0	5.4	24.6
40–44	5,458	2.7	14.7	4.2	22.9
35–39	5,918	1.6	9.5	3.3	19.5
30–34	6,035	1.2	7.2	2.2	13.3
25–29	6,163	1.0	6.2	1.8	11.1
20–24	7,197	1.0	7.2	1.5	10.8
15–19	8,544	0.7	6.0	1.3	11.1
10–14	10,157	0.4	4.1	0.8	8.1
5–9	12,091	0.4	4.8	1.2	14.5
0–4	13,902	0.9	69.5	6.0	262.7
Totals	100,000		834.3		1,106.4
Crude death rate		8.34		11.06	

This population is the same as that used in Table 3.2, adjusted to a total of 100,000.
Data from United Nations, 1970.

The number of births is slightly higher at first, as the breeding population reflects the addition of the relatively small number of children that lived because of the mortality reduction. It rises sharply after a generation, when the individuals that were infants at the time of the change enter the breeding population. The crude birth rate is slightly lower than it was before the mortality decline, as the population is larger than previously, and most of the increase is among youths who have not yet reached reproductive age. As the first cohort of individuals surviving infancy reaches sexual maturity, the crude birth rate climbs back to a point slightly higher than its former level, where it remains.

The crude death rate is never as high as it was before the decline in mortality, but it is not constant. From its original low point, it rises slightly as older people die, but the marked increase in reproduction from reduced infant mortality has not yet become a factor. With increasing reproduction, the age distribution becomes increasingly youthful and less prone to death, and the crude death rate declines to a level where it remains. After the entire population has been subjected to the same birth and death rates the age distribution will begin to assume a configuration that will not change as

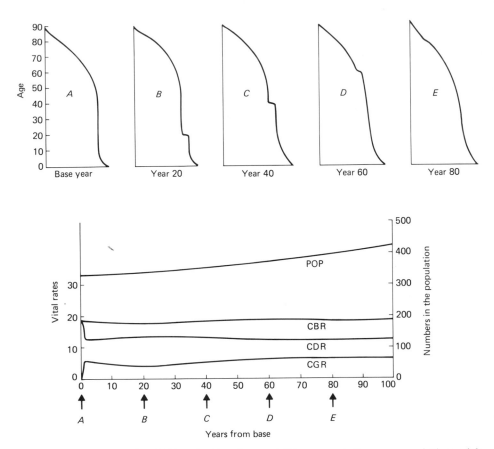

Figure 3.7 Effects of a 30% reduction in mortality on a stationary population with the mortality schedule of Latin America. The relative fertility of different age groups is also that of Latin America, multiplied across-the-board by a deflator coefficient so that the population does not grow. The age pyramids show age distributions at 20-year intervals. Lower graph shows population growth and the effects of changing age distributions on crude birth rate (CBR), crude death rate (CDR), and crude growth rates (CGR).

long as the age-specific vital rates do not change. This configuration is know as the *stable age distribution.*

If, instead of a general mortality decline, the age-specific fertility were to increase by 25%, the population would show the progression indicated in Figure 3.8. From the initial age distribution, the increased production of infants gives a strongly expanded base to the pyramid. As these individuals reach sexual maturity, the birth rate rises sharply, followed by a secondary rise as their offspring reach sexual maturity themselves. This second pulse is not as sharp as the first, however, because of the relatively long period of fertility of each individual in the population. Eventually, the birth rate evens out to its stable level.

Throughout this evolution of the age structure of the population, the pyramid gets steadily more youthful and broad-based. Because the age-specific mortality of people aged 5–50 is much lower than that of the very young or the aged, the crude death rate

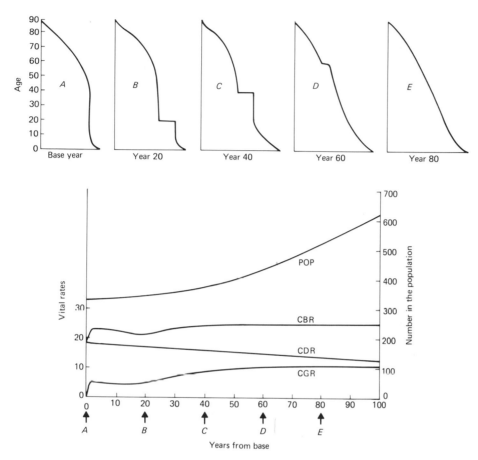

Figure 3.8 Effects of a 25% increase in fertility on the same stationary population as in Figure 3.7. Age pyramids show age distributions at 20-year intervals. Lower graph shows population and the effects of changing age distributions on crude vital rates as shown in Figure 3.7.

drops consistently as the pyramid broadens. Its decline continues even after the crude birth rate stabilizes. But it too eventually reaches a steady-state value as the age distribution approaches a stable age distribution. It should be noted that the 21% drop in the crude death rate is entirely a function of the age distribution. The age-specific mortality has not changed at all.

The effects of the age distribution can obscure the apparent simplicity of the concepts of fertility and mortality. They cannot be ignored in any meaningful discussion of population dynamics. Too much of the course of population growth is due directly to age distribution. To further underline this fact, consider what would have to be done in order to reach certain vital-rate goals. As an example, if the birth rate in the United States fell immediately to a *replacement level,* the rate at which each family produces, on the average, exactly enough children to replace itself (about 2.11 children per family, according to the U.S. Bureau of the Census, 1970), the population would continue to rise until about 2040, to a total 50% larger than the present (Frejka, 1968).

The lag effect would be even greater for a country with a very youthful age distribution, such as Costa Rica and other developing countries.

The effects of age distribution on population growth is demonstrated even more powerfully by Frejka's (1968) study on the progression of birth rates that would be necessary to establish and maintain a constant (unchanging) population size at the 1965 level (Figure 3.9). The number of children per family would have to be kept just

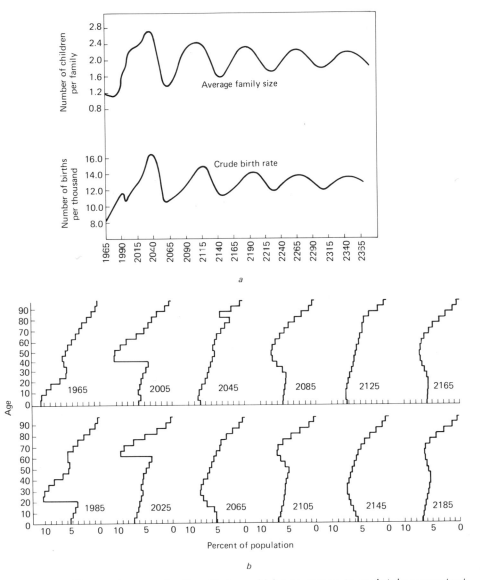

a

b

Figure 3.9 Changes in reproduction that would be necessary to maintain a constant population size in the United States at a 1965 level: (*a*) fluctuation in the family size and crude birth rate; (*b*) change in age distribution at 20-year intervals. [Modified, with permission, from Frejka, 1968. Reflections on the demographic conditions needed to establish a U.S. stationary population growth. *Population Studies* **22**: 379–397.]

over 1 as the post-World War II baby boom passes through its reproductive period. Family size would then have to climb to about 2.8 children as individuals conceived during the late 1900s reached sexual maturity and the population was weighted heavily toward older individuals. It would then drop back to about 1.4 children per family about 2065, and oscillate in this fashion for several centuries. The only way to establish a constant population immediately from an expanding one is to manipulate the age distribution by altering the birth rate over a wide range for many generations.

None of the crude vital rates can predict population change accurately over a period of time in which the age distribution varies. But there is a set of measures for population birth, death, and growth, that does consider the age distribution, the *intrinsic* rates. These are the birth and death rates that a population would have if it were characterized not only by its current schedules of fertility and mortality, but also by a stable age distribution based on these schedules. Because the stable age distribution can be calculated from any fertility and mortality schedule, even if the age distribution is changing rapidly, it is possible to determine the degree to which current patterns of fertility and mortality will affect future population growth. The intrinsic rates of birth, death, and growth may be quite different from the crude rates of birth, death, and growth, as shown in Table 3.6. As a rule they are more useful but much harder to compute.

Even the intrinsic rates of change do not spell out the length of time before the stable population can be expected, and many countries whose long-range prognosis is for population decline (i.e., a negative intrinsic growth rate) are still actually growing (i.e., a positive crude growth rate), since the age distribution has not yet caught up to the fertility and mortality schedules. This means that even when a country has been successful in controlling its fertility the population will continue to grow because of the momentum conferred by its age distribution.

There are only two ways by which population growth can be controlled: by lowering fertility or by raising mortality. Of the two, the former is preferable on many grounds. But growth responses based on birth rate changes always have a substantial built-in time lag during which the population will continue to grow, and the social and environmental problems occasioned by too-rapid population growth will continue to be felt. Death rate changes work much more rapidly.

Table 3.6 Comparison Between Crude and Intrinsic Rates of Birth (b), Death (d), and Growth (g) for Several Countries.

Crude Rates				Intrinsic Rates		
b	d	g		b	d	g
20.8	8.2	12.6	U.S.A., 1963	24.6	7.5	17.1
13.1	9.1	4.0	Hungary, 1961	11.7	16.8	−5.1
16.6	6.4	12.2	Japan, 1963	12.3	15.3	−3.0
17.5	8.3	9.2	Finland, 1960	18.7	10.6	8.1
23.4	7.9	15.5	New Zealand, 1964	27.5	6.3	21.2

HISTORY, CULTURE, AND POPULATION GROWTH

How have human populations grown? What dynamic forces and interactions have underlain their astonishing growth over the last hundred, thousand, or million years? The historical record does not lend simple answers to these questions. Indeed, it does little more than underscore their importance. For one thing, accurate demographic records, or records showing the statistics of the size, makeup, and changes of human populations, are needed. These records do not extend back very far under the best of circumstances, and accurate records do not exist for some countries even at the present time. We can gauge the relationship between changes in social organization and population growth only in the most relative fashion, and records of the geography of demographic patterns are all but nonexistent for most of human history.

This lack is unfortunate in that it forces us to base virtually our entire conception of the role of human populations in human ecosystems on recorded features of the last 60 years, even though people have had a major hand in molding them for at least 10,000 years. To be sure, many modern environmental changes are different from those of previous years. Neolithic technology did not produce automotive air pollution or industrial water pollution. But we have no datum other than the present to apply to environmental problems, and the present is a period of such flux that it is difficult to sort out the effects of population, population density, level of technology, type of social organization, and all of the other myriad variables that affect human ecosystems.

Keeping in mind the lack of sufficient data, let us surmise what we can about the long-term growth of the human population. Several estimates have been made of the population density of societies at various technological levels (e.g. Table 3.7), based on observations of the densities of modern primitive societies and inferences from archaeological research. A very rough estimate of the total world population can be obtained by multiplying the estimate of average density by the total inhabited land area. Other

Table 3.7 Estimated Human Population Density at Different Stages.

Years Ago	Cultural Stage	Density: Persons per 100km^2
Present	Industrial and farming	1,700
70	Farming and industrial	1,100
170	Farming and industrial	620
220	Farming and industrial	490
320	Farming and industrial	370
2,000	Agriculture-based urban; subsistance village	100
6,000	Subsistance village; early urban	75
10,000	Mesolithic	4
25,000	Upper Paleolithic	4
300,000	Middle Paleolithic	1.2
1,000,000	Lower Paleolithic	0.4

Adapted, with permission, from Deevey, 1960.

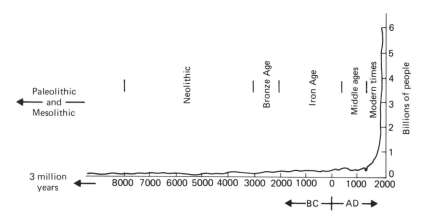

Figure 3-10 Growth of the human population. The Paleolithic is not to scale. If it were, the base line would extend over 30 m. to the left. [Modified, with permission, from Jean van der Tak, Carl Haub, and Elaine Murphy, "Our Population Predicament: a New Look." *Population Bulletin,* Vol. 34, No. 5, (Population Reference Bureau, Inc., Washington, D.C., 1979).]

estimates can be based on what census data exist (such as, in part, Population Reference Bureau, 1962) or on projections backward based on a constant intrinsic rate of natural increase (Keyfitz, 1966). None of these estimates is particularly precise, but all show the general form of Figure 3.10. If the population of the world was about 250 million persons some 2,000 years ago, it had taken well over a million years to reach that level. The population then doubled by about 1650 and doubled again (to 1 billion) by about 1825. In just over 100 years (1928) it doubled again. The world population had doubled again to 4 billion by 1976.

The rate of increase has not been constant, nor has it been the same in all parts of the world. Figure 3.11 shows an estimate of the average annual rate of increase from 1650 to the present time in industrialized countries and in the Third World. While population has always grown, really rapid growth did not begin in the industrialized countries until the onset of industrialization in the eighteenth century. It reached a peak and then dropped, only to rise again after World War II. The growth rate of the Third World countries remained fairly constant as long as these areas were backward agrarian societies. However, at the beginning of the twentieth century, their rate of growth began to rise sharply.

SOCIETAL ATTITUDES

One of the most impenetrable aspects of the man-environment relationship is the way culture feeds back upon itself. The forces that mold society are always unclear, often arcane, and at best difficult to express. But people's outlooks on population growth have changed, and it is clear that they will have to change more in the future. The only data we have about the evolution of a society's attitudes come from its past. The

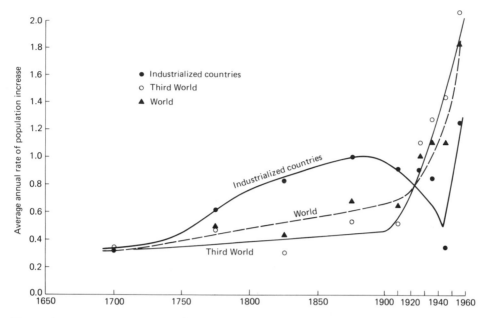

Figure 3.11 Estimated rates of population growth from 1650 to the present time. [Data from Bogue, 1969.]

changes that must come in the future have their roots in history, but they will not be like those of the past. Nevertheless, it is instructive to look at the development of the forces molding population dynamics through human history.

Development of Agriculture

The development of Neolithic agriculture apparently had several different effects on contemporary populations. By assuring a more constant supply of food than can be provided by hunting, it lowered the death rate, especially during years of poor hunting. Deevey (1960) estimates that the average life span was increased by about 6 years (from 32 to 38). This effectively lengthened the human reproductive period by a factor of 1/3, which in turn made possible a substantial increase in the birth rate. Finally, the greater availability of food had the effect of raising the carrying capacity of the land. The archaeological record indicates that there was a substantial increase—by a factor of about 25—in the human population during the Neolithic.

Population growth continued throughout the preindustrial era, although at a much slower rate than had been the case during the explosive growth occasioned by the development of agriculture. The birth rate was controlled by methods such as abortion, infanticide, coitus interruptus, douching, use of condoms, encouragement of homosexuality, and abstinence (Ehrlich, Ehrlich, and Holdren, 1977). Studies on the cultural ecology of current Neolithic peoples suggest that few, if any, societies show better developed cultural restraints than do primitive agriculturalists (e.g., Rappaport, 1967). In these cases the human population may be held to a remarkably delicate balance with the environment. The mechanism through which population control operates is often a set of taboos that have no obvious connection with the environment but clearly act to hold the population to a level with the carrying capacity of the land.

Primitive societies have always been characterized by high death rates determined ultimately by disease and food supply. As agrarian societies developed in the more progressive portions of the world, however, they made tremendous advances in their capabilities for controlling the options available to them. One direct effect of these technological and economic developments was a continual increase in the carrying capacity of human ecosystems.

More people could be supported, and there were more people. The growth of population was slow throughout the agrarian world, but the taboos and rituals which had operated to keep population under control waned in their importance as societies became increasingly sophisticated.

Urbanization

Urbanization is a potent force in the development of attitudes toward reproduction. It is also a very complex one, operating in several directions at once. Until the nineteenth century sanitary conditions in cities were poor, leading to a very high urban mortality rate and lowering the mean longevity. For instance, Deevey (1960) estimates that classical Greece and Rome showed mean longevities of 35 and 32 years, respectively; both were significant decreases from the 38-year span of Neolithic or Bronze Age subsistence farmers. In the sixteenth to the eighteenth century the mean life expectancies in European cities were significantly less than those for the surrounding countryside.

Cities had high mortality rates before the nineteenth and twentieth centuries because their high population density encouraged the spread of disease. Epidemics of smallpox, cholera, influenza, dyphtheria, typhoid, and especially bubonic plague were commonplace in preindustrial cities. For most of their history, urban populations remained fairly constant through the balancing of a moderate growth rate for several years, followed by a severe epidemic that cancelled the gain. This pattern lasted in Europe until the mid eighteenth century, when the great plague epidemics ceased. The decline in mortality that accompanied the Industrial Revolution in Europe is probably due more to concurrent improvements in contageous disease control than to a real lowering of the year-by-year mortality rates (Helleiner, 1957).

A decrease in the average lifespan cuts out a substantial part of the reproductive period, and hence must lower the birth rate unless some counteracting force raises it. But there is such a force. For a number of reasons, urbanized communities tend to be much less bound by rituals, taboos, and similar restraints than are rural communities. For example, in many agrarian societies a couple will not marry until they have a farmstead; generally this is the one that belongs to the husband's father, and it does not pass into his hands until the father's death. Such strictures do not exist in cities, and couples tend to marry earlier. Also, the economic return on capital is typically much higher in cities than it is in the countryside, so that economic well-being is enhanced by urban life. This is reflected in the standard of living, and in the ability to purchase food and amenities. Where mortality is high the birth rate tends to be positively correlated with the standard of living, so that one of the impacts of the economic success of preindustrial cities was a tendency for the birth rate to rise. But it is difficult to be certain, since a very large portion of their growth was due to migration into the city rather than reproduction within the city (Figure 3.12).

Industrialization

The rise of industry began in England in the mid eighteenth century and spread to all of Europe and North America by the end of the nineteenth. It is still spreading into the rest of the world. Industrialization has had as profound an effect on world demographic patterns as the development of agriculture eight to ten millenia earlier. But it has been much less straightforward. While the agricultural revolution affected the food supply directly, and urbanization created an environment that expedited the spread of disease, the Industrial Revolution created new kinds of societies. In every industrializing country the population growth rate increased with the onset of the

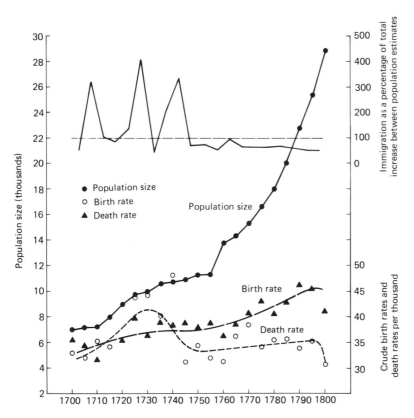

Figure 3.12 Growth of the population in Nottingham, England, a typical preindustrial city, from 1700 to 1800. During the period shown, Nottingham was a weaving center. Machines were introduced into the weaving industry during the last third of the eighteenth century as the Industrial Revolution arrived. The drop in the death rate in 1800 is due to vaccination for smallpox. Immigration percentage over 100% indicates that population grew, but that deaths outnumbered births of the city's residents. [Data from Chambers, 1960.]

Industrial Revolution. Just why this should be the case is not clear, and it has been the subject of intense debate for some fifty years (see the review by Eversley, 1965). An increase in growth rate can occur only if the birth rate increases or the death rate decreases, or both. In the presently industrialized countries during the nineteenth century and the Third World during the twentieth, both factors seem to have been present. Their relative importance, however, has not been the same in both cases, and the identifiable factors stimulating changes in the vital rates of industrialized countries were quite different from those influencing the Third World.

Industrialization in Developed Countries. Perhaps the most direct effect of industrialization on the population of presently industrialized nations was the increase in the birth rate (Habakkuk, 1953), as a response to economic factors. Industrialization brought a great increase in both supply and demand for manufactured goods, which led to a high demand for labor to staff industrial machines. This brought about a rise in the price of labor, creating increased migration from the countryside to urban centers and also an increase in the urban standard of living. Higher standards of living allowed larger families to be supported. This may have resulted from increased birth rates, but it was due also to improved dietary standards and, therefore, to decreased mortality from malnutrition (Figure 3.13).

At the same time rising demand for manufactured goods was translated into an increasing profit from their production. This allowed increasing investment and capital formation, which in turn generated ever-increasing production and ever-increasing demand. As with all positive feedback loops, this one was limited by a negative feedback loop that set the carrying capacity of the ecosystem. In the case of Europe during the Industrial Revolution, the limit was set by disease and the food supply. Agricultural technology had not caught up with industrial technology, and there was no simple way of increasing the food supply. Some increases in efficiency were possible, and legislation in a number of countries changed land tenancy practices to increase agricultural production. But the capability of the mechanisms available at that time were not sufficient to produce very large increases.

At the same time a medical breakthrough made possible a significant drop in the mortality rate. Smallpox vaccine was developed in 1796, and its use spread rapidly. It was followed by a growing awareness of the significance and importance of public health practices—those measures that would assure greater health to society as a whole. As these measures were instituted, the crude death rate began to fall, and it has fallen steadily ever since (Figure 3.14).

The tools for controlling disease and lowering the death rate have gradually and continuously improved since 1800. The relatively slow rate of change allowed society to adjust its birth rate as the death rate fell. Industrialized countries show a historical drop in the birth rate that parallels the drop in mortality. This parallel change in vital rates is commonly termed the *demographic transition.* It is a change from a high-birth-rate, high-death-rate population with a youthful age distribution and a low growth rate, through a state of rapid growth with a high birth rate and a low death rate, to a final stage when the population is once again characterized by slow growth, but with low birth rates and death rates and an older age distribution. The demographic transition has been a characteristic of all industrial societies and will be discussed more fully in this chapter.

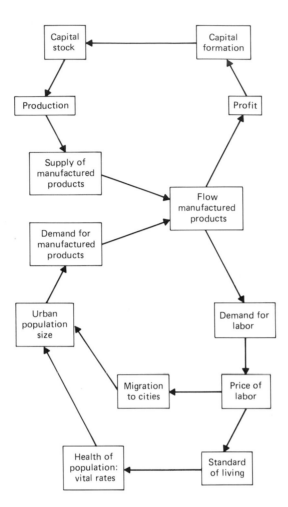

Figure 3.13 Simplified diagram showing positive feedbacks linking urban population size to the economic factors of the early industrialization process.

Industrialization in the Third World. The biggest difference between industrialization in the developed and in the developing countries is that is was an evolutionary process in the former, increasing gradually and growing out of domestic society, while it has been revolutionary in the latter, being imposed or imported from an outside source, often at a very rapid rate. The demographic consequences of this industrialization are much better known than those in the developed countries, but the problems and their environmental consequences are very different, so that one cannot equate the two. Before the 1900s industrialization in most of the Third World was almost nil, and public health measures had not permeated much beyond the large cities that served as government or depot centers for the colonial powers.

In some Third World countries, especially in Latin America and East Asia, industrialization began early in the twentieth century, with the consequent drop in mortality. In more backward countries the drop in mortality did not begin until the 1930s and 1940s, with the importation of effective public health measures.

Arriaga and Davis (1969) have compared the mortality rates (measured as expectation of life at birth, thus correcting for age distribution) of the countries of Latin

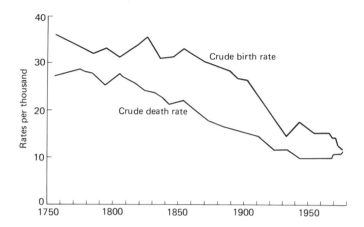

Figure 3.14 Vital rates for an industrialized country through the Industrial Revolution and extending to the present: Sweden, 1750–1979. [Modified, with permission, from Jean van der Tak, Carl Haub, and Elaine Murphy. "Our Population Predicament: a New Look." *Population Bulletin*, Vol. 34, No. 5 (Population Reference Bureau, Inc., Washington, D.C., 1979).]

America, and the highly developed countries of England and Wales, Sweden, and the United States. They note two classes of countries in Latin America. In the first group were those whose economies were well enough developed to allow a reduction in mortality and an increase in mean longevity early in the twentieth century. In the second group were the very backward countries that showed essentially no change in mean life expectancy until 1930. Beginning in 1930 the increase in life expectancy is dramatic in all countries of Latin America, regardless of their economic conditions, due to improvement in public health (Figure 3.15a). The percentage increase per decade is shown in Figure 3.15b. The rate of increase for Latin America rises throughout the entire century, while that of the industrialized countries has fluctuated about a constant rate for almost 100 years.

The very rapid decrease in mortality in the Third World is a phenomenon of the last 50 years, while the much slower decrease in mortality during the nineteenth century in Europe and North America has been with us almost 200 years. But timing and spread are not the only differences between the mortality decreases in industrialized and developing countries, nor are they even the most important. Preindustrial cities had been places of disease and relatively high mortality. Immigration from countryside to city stemmed from the economic advantages of the city, and it occurred even when urban mortality rates were high. By mid twentieth century the cities of the Third World offered not only economic advantages but also lower mortality rates than the countrysides (Arriaga, 1967). Health care has become an urban function in all societies. As a result, cities can no longer absorb the surplus of rural immigrants as easily as they once could. Indeed, the urban surplus is now larger than the rural.

Because modern health measures were thrust upon the Third World so fast, their societies have not yet had a chance to respond to the new realities of the demographic statistics. It is not difficult to berate them for not controlling their population, but it is sobering to remember that death rates have been declining in most Third World countries for only about 40–50 years; by comparison, 40 years after the death rates had started to decline in the United States the railroad had not yet reached from the eastern seaboard to Chicago.

A corollary of a rapid drop in mortality with a constant birth rate is not only a drastic increase in the population growth rate, but also a population with a much younger age distribution. As a result, it is virtually impossible to halt population

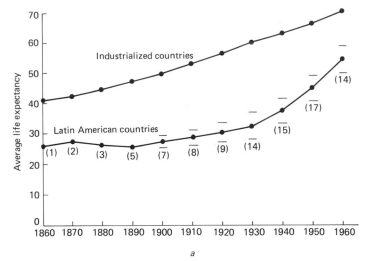

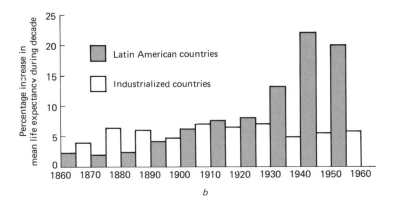

Figure 3.15 Changes in life expectancy for Latin American countries compared to that of three developed countries (England and Wales, Sweden, U.S.A.), 1860–1960: (*a*) graph of mean life expectancy; number in parentheses represents the number of countries supplying data. Ticks indicate one standard deviation; (*b*) comparison of the percentage change in life expectancy during each decade. [Data from Arriaga and Davis, 1969.]

growth quickly, and it is difficult even to slow it down. The infants who were saved from malaria (or who were born because their parents were saved) by mosquito control begun in many tropical areas during the late 1940s and 1950s have just recently reached adulthood. If the time lag for stabilizing population growth in a country with the age distribution of a developed country is measured in decades, it would take a major effort spread over an even longer time to halt population growth in the Third World.

There is some evidence that birth rates in the Third World are beginning to fall. And they are falling for much the same reason as in the industrialized countries, namely the demographic transition based primarily on economic factors—plus an effective advertising campaign for birth control devices. The long-term result is unclear. The growth rate in the Third World is the highest that human society has ever experienced, and there is no longer a frontier in the New World to provide an immigration "safety valve" as there was when Europe's population was expanding. In addition, young people in the Third World are entering the job market at a rate up to five times as fast as jobs are created (Thiesenhusen, 1971). This creates sociopolitical problems that cannot be overlooked. Creating jobs in the industrial sector requires capital. The amount varies among industries and countries, but $500 per job is a good estimate of the order of magnitude for the Third World. For a country like Mexico or Nigeria, it would require an investment of $500 million to $1,000 million per year simply to create jobs for the people entering the labor market for the first time. This is a large sum for a developing country, but it is typical of circumstances throughout the Third World.

THE DEMOGRAPHIC TRANSITION

The demographic transition is a widely recognized phenomenon in which a stable population with high birth and death rates passes through a stage of rapid growth, in which death rates drop but birth rates remain high. An intermediate stage follows in which the birth rate is substantially higher than the death rate, and growth is maximum. In the final stage, the birth rate drops to the level of the death rate, and the population once again stabilizes with low and essentially equal birth and death rates. This process has been correlative with industrialization and has been seen in Europe, North America, and parts of Asia and Oceania.

Figure 3.16 is a generalized diagram of the vital rates and population growth across

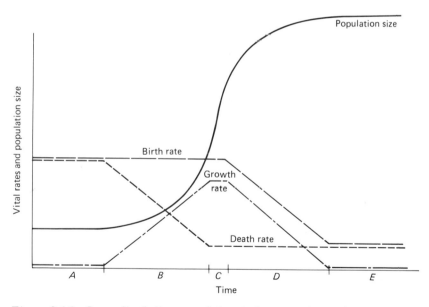

Figure 3.16 Generalized diagram of the vital rates and population size changes across the demographic transition. Characteristics of the population at various stages of the transition can be described as follows: *Pretransitional* (*A*): population size constant; birth and death rates high; growth rate zero. *Transitional* (*B*): population size increasing as death rate drops, growth rate steadily increasing; birth rate constant and high. (*C*): population size increasing at its maximum rate; death rate low, birth rate high. (*D*): population size continuing to increase, but at a declining rate as growth rate drops in response to a declining birth rate. *Post-transitional* (*E*): population size constant; birth and death rates low, growth rate zero.

the demographic transition. Several factors affect the course of population growth. The most important are the differences between the pre-transition and post-transition death and birth rates, the rates at which the death and birth rates decrease, (these rates of decrease can also be regarded as the length of time it takes for the vital rates to go from pre-transitional to post-transitional levels), and the length of time lag between the onset of the drop in the death rate to the onset of the drop in the birth rate. The most important growth indicators are the percentage increase in the size of the population across the transition and the rate of population growth.

In the most general case (Casetti, 1968), the actual increase in the size of the population across the demographic transition is a function of the absolute drop in the death rate, the time lag between the beginning of the transition and the beginning of the drop in the birth rate, and the rate at which the birth rate drops relative to the rate at which the death rate drops. It is not related to the rate of population growth. The latter is a function of the difference in birth and death rates at any specific time. Thus, it is not surprising that the present rate of growth in the Third World is the highest in human history. Mortality rates dropped much faster there than they did in the industrialized countries, so that the absolute difference between birth and death rates is the highest that man has ever known. A very high growth rate does not necessarily mean that post-transitional populations in the Third World will be relatively larger than those of the industrialized world when compared to their pre-transitional population levels. However, they will arrive there faster than the industrialized countries did. If the time lag between the initial drop in mortality rates and the initial drop in the birth rate can be kept short, and if the rate of decline in the birth rate is faster than that in the death rate, the size of the equilibrium post-transitional population can be controlled.

In some industrialized countries (Figure 3.14) the mortality rate began to fall about 1800, the birth rate about 1850; the birth rate dropped slightly faster than the death rate. In the Third World the time lag has been considerably shorter, although it is too early to judge how fast the birth rate will fall relative to the death rate. The little evidence we have suggests that the end results of population growth in the Third World will be similar to those in the industrialized world: a stable post-transitional population several times larger than its pre-transitional level. But the rate of growth will be very different, as will the cultural forces operating in the society and the precise mechanisms by which the birth rates decline.

Many families desire at least one son who will outlive his father, care for his parents in their old age, and carry on the family name. In areas of high mortality this may require the birth of several sons as well as several daughters. In a rural economy it may also be to a farmer's advantage to have several children to help with the work. In many societies a man's virility is measured by the number of his children. Many national leaders, especially in the Third World, look upon a large number of children as a symbol of hope for the future. Lowering birth rates in countries with high mortality means convincing parents that they can meet their family goals and that the family's continuity is assured with fewer children. Then and only then is it reasonable to expect people to look favorably upon birth control.

It is not a trivial matter to convince people that the expectations built up over generations of high mortality have been negated by modern medicine. Decline in the birth rate does not follow automatically once the mortality rate has begun to fall. It is necessary to insure that mortality continues to fall so that improvements are noticeable. It is also necessary to convince people at all levels of society that the future does not lie either in an individual's virility or in a nation's having a superabundance of young. This also is difficult, and a development plan that seeks to retain its credibility must be directed, at least in part, toward people's attitudes regarding family security. It is necessary to convince families that it is to their economic disadvantage to have large families and that their standards of living will rise much faster if they have fewer children.

The essence of the demographic transition is that societies contain a complex set of feedbacks linking fertility and standards of living (Figure 3.17). Technological and socioeconomic development brings an increased standard of living, which in turn makes the realization of family goals more secure. This provides families with an economic and social incentive for family planning to replace the incentives for high reproduction that characterize high mortality areas. This has certainly been the pattern in industrialized countries. It appears also to be applicable to the Third World as well, although it

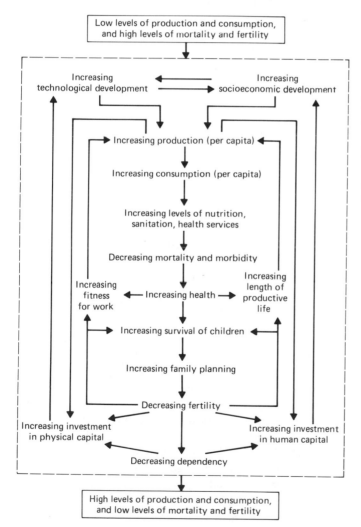

Figure 3.17   Schematic representation of social factors leading from high levels of births and deaths with low production through demographic transition to low levels of births and deaths with high production. [Redrawn, with permission, from Frederiksen, "Feedbacks in Economic and Demographic Transition." *Science* 166: 837–847. © 1969 American Association for the Advancement of Science.]

is not clear to what extent, due to cultural differences and the fact that the historical record of responses of Third World societies to mortality decline is not very long.

The demographic transition model raises questions that demand answers. In it the responsibility for lowering the birth rate lies with the individual, and the most effective focus for national birth control efforts lies not in birth control technology, but rather in reducing the number of children *desired* by the individual. If the people want large families, on the average, mortality decline by itself will not lead to a drop in the birth rate; it may even rise. The notion that the ultimate responsibility rests in the individual is deceptively simple (Colinvaux, 1976). The point of the demographic transition is not in the focus of the responsibility for carrying it out (because in fact it does not get "carried out"). Rather, the demographic transition represents nothing less than a change in the basic value structure of a society to a point where fertility reduction can be effected on an individual level.

There are many ways in which a state or quasi-governmental authority can influence the norms of the society in question. The most obvious example is the People's Republic of China, where fertility control has become a matter of patriotic principle. Another example is Singapore, where the tax structure encourages first children but becomes confiscatory when family size becomes much higher. But ultimately, the decision of whether or not to have a child rests with the individual in every society. Changes in individual norms are much more likely to come about through incentives and persuasion than through attempts to impose new values from outside.

The desired family size is a complicated issue. It is subject to change just as any other values of society. To encourage change is the major goal of the policies in China and Singapore just referred to. Many studies have been done to try to measure the desired family size in different societies (e.g., Figure 3.18 and Blake, 1969). Most show that the number of children considered ideal is more than the replacement rate. If the average family had the ideal number of children, the population would continue to climb, although perhaps at a slower rate than is now the case.

But the notion of the ideal family size is a value judgment that differs both from the actual family size and the family size that would be chosen by actual individuals if they had complete choice. The distinction between the ideal, which is a society-wide notion, and personal choice is a significant one. For example, a group of American women aged 35–44 in 1965 reported that they considered an average of 3–4 children as the ideal family size. But the average number of children that they themselves would have, given adequate access to contraception, was 2.5 (Bumpass and Westoff, 1970). This is close to the replacement level. Even under the most propitious circumstances there is no necessary connection between theoretical considerations and public policy (Harkavy, Jaffe, and Wishik, 1969). In the Third World the most progressive public policy is often frustrated simply by a lack of suitable medical personnel.

Perhaps the most important question that can be asked of the demographic transition as a model is whether or not it can possibly provide a reasonable projection of the pattern of population change. It provides a useful description of changes in the developed world. But is it also appropriate for the Third World, where data are few and contradictory? It is undeniably true that many countries show a rise, rather than a fall, in birth rates as industrialization has become a factor in the economy (Figure 3.19). This may be because a secure family is more likely to reach its goal than an insecure family.

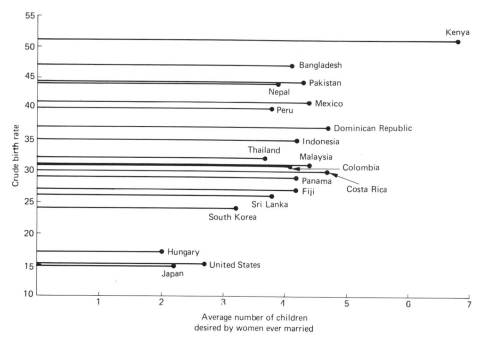

Figure 3.18 Average desired family size for several selected countries. [Data from van der Tak et al., 1979, and PRB, 1979.]

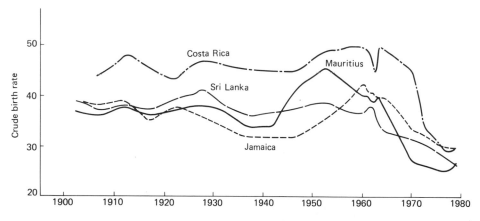

Figure 3.19 Trends in crude birth rate in representative Third World countries over the last 70 years. Note that the birth rate rises in response to the introduction of public health measures following World War II in Costa Rica, Mauritius, and Jamaica, but that there is no change in Sri Lanka. The current trend in birth rates in all of the countries is strongly down. [Data from Gille, 1967, and PRB, 1971, 1974, 1977, and 1979.]

This supports the neo-Malthusian argument that fertility and development are linked in a relatively simple way, as shown in Figure 3.20. However, the crux of the demographic transition model is that the indirect effects of development, such as increasing levels of education, a higher standard of living, and greater cosmopolitanism, are more significant in determining fertility patterns than the direct economic effects. Heer (1966; see also Frederikson, 1969; and Blake, 1969) shows that these complex indirect effects are real and are, in fact, brought to bear on the fertility of the population soon after its initial and very transitory rise.

Another major question about the usefulness of the demographic transition model is that it postulates that economic development is the engine of change in vital rates. Traditional man-environment interactions with a relatively simple and rural base evolve to urban-industrial patterns that are both more complex and more likely to increase the severity of environmental dysfunction. If the demographic transition describes the

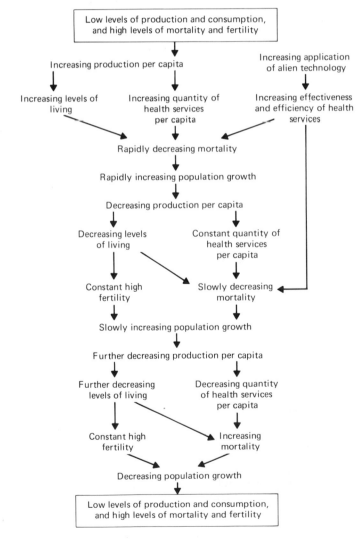

Figure 3.20 Schematic representation of the neo-Malthusian model of population growth, showing the failure of the demographic transition. [Redrawn, with permission, from Frederiksen, "Feedbacks in Economic and Demographic Transition." *Science* 166: 837–847. © 1969 American Association for the Advancement of Science.]

mechanism for bringing a society's birth rate into line with its death rate, then population regulation is accomplished at considerable environmental cost. This cost can be borne only if the structures of the ecosystems upon which the society depends for its needs are not undermined by the new patterns of man-environment interactions.

This notion suggests that either the maximum population density or the maximum level of economic development that can be sustained over an extended period is limited. But the connection between carrying capacity, or maximum sustainable population density, and level of development is not at all clear. It is clear that the carrying capacity of an ecosystem for humans is a function of the level of economic development, and that the number of people that can be sustained in an area is related to the level of their technology. It is low in primitive societies, and it is equally low in areas where over-exploitation has undermined the ability of the ecosystem to support human society. Its maximum is somewhere in between. But what determines the carrying capacity of an ecosystem for people? What role does the environment have in setting these limits, or is society so powerful that it can ignore the natural limits?

CARRYING CAPACITY OF THE EARTH

The number of people who can live together on earth represents the resolution of all of the cultural and environmental forces found in human ecosystems. It is an extraordinarily difficult concept to deal with, both because of the dynamism of the interactions involved, and because it requires that we put aside the disciplinary blinders that Western culture has cultivated assiduously for several hundred years. The carrying capacity can be established only in the context of the overall system.

Because technology allows man to change his ecological niche, it does not make sense to argue that the capacity of the ecosystem for supporting populations is determined solely by environmental factors. This is obviously not the case, and a school of thought that attempted to trace most of the basic characteristics of civilization to environmental factors (the environmental determinists as exemplified by Ellsworth Huntington, 1945) has been thoroughly discredited.

But it makes no more sense to ascribe to society the power to overcome all limits. Whenever society has pushed back the limits imposed by the environment, it has been either through substitution of one resource for another (e.g., fossil fuels for wood, animal power for human power, machine power for animal power, textured vegetable protein for meat), or understanding a specific part of the system sufficiently well that it could use it more effectively (e.g., using the existing genetic reservoir within crop plants to develop high-yield varieties through a scientific breeding program). Never has society replaced a basic human biological requirement, and never has it succeeded in overcoming the fundamental ecological principles that govern the behavior of a population in a complex community.

During the early stages of human evolution population density was limited directly by the food supply. The more food that could consistently be collected, the larger the mean population that could be supported. Increasing efficiency of hunting technology allowed the carrying capacity to rise only so long as the level of exploitation of prey species was less than the optimum for the species. (In this case, optimum refers to the level of exploitation that will provide the maximum yield of prey that can be sustained indefinitely; it is not a value judgment. See Chapter 4 for further discussion.) However, once exploitation is at or above the optimum level, further increases in the level of hunting pressure can only overexploit the species and lower the long-term yield, undermining the carrying capacity of the ecosystem.

Overexploitive technology can, of course, provide short-term yields with which people can stave off famine for a while. But these yields cannot be maintained. When the populations being exploited can no longer sustain the exploitation, their decline is a biological certainty. Whether this is followed by a collapse of the human population is determined mainly by people's ability to switch to auxiliary food sources. If switching is not possible, then collapse of the human population follows collapse of its food source. This pattern of the collapse of a prey population followed by the collapse of a predator is quite common in nature. There is no reason to view humans as somehow exempt from it.

Agrarian populations are also regulated by their food supplies. But the regulatory mechanisms are slightly different from those of hunting and gathering societies. Food is obtained through manipulation of ecosystem resources in both cases, and overexploitation results in decreased food yields. But farmers do not manipulate prey populations; they manipulate the soil. The soil, like a population, can be overstressed. In some areas, such as the wet tropics, the soil is extremely sensitive to even moderate disruption. Heavy rainfall leaches nutrient materials out of the soil so fast that irreversible deterioration can set in rapidly. A typical field becomes unproductive after a season or two, at which time it must be allowed to revert to forest for as long as ten to fifteen years before it can be cleared again (Conklin, 1954). Other areas such as the prairies of North America are much less sensitive. These ecosystems are so inherently resilient that as long as animals were used to pull the plows, enough manure was cycled through the soil that measurable fertility remained constant. When animals were replaced by tractors, even these areas began to deteriorate (Dasmann, 1972).

The relationship of technology to agricultural yield is not a simple one. In some cases technology can smooth out normal environmental fluctuations. As an example, irrigation can replace rain as a source of water in dry seasons with relatively little negative effect on the ecosystem. Yields during lean years can be brought up to the levels of good years without increasing the intensity of soil cultivation. If technologies of this sort lead to soil degradation, it is through side effects, such as the salt left behind as irrigation water evaporates, rather than a direct result of ecosystem manipulation. Because of their relative simplicity and benign nature, technologies designed to even out variations in the environment have been used successfully and continuously in some areas for over 5,000 years.

A second type of technology is that which allows increased intensity of manipulation of the land. These improvements may raise the efficiency of farming, as with the development of the steel plow or the tractor, or they may retard the degradation of the soil (everything else being equal), as with fertilizers and soil conservation engineering.

Increasing the food supply in preindustrial urban societies was done by increasing yield, paying relatively little attention to reversing environmental degradation. This limited the geographic extent of early urban societies to locations where soils are replenished fairly often as in the alluvial soils of Egypt and Mesopotamia, areas which had relatively resilient soils such as Western Europe and North America, or places that were major regional market centers such as many of the great cities of the Near East and West Africa. Industrialization, which requires even larger agricultural surpluses to supply a larger, more specialized urban population, could originate only in areas of highly resilient soils such as those of Western Europe and North America.

As the sophistication of ecosystem management has improved, it has become possible to farm intensively on virtually all kinds of land, not only those that are characterized by alluvial or resilient soils. But the cost of this capability has been high. We have come to depend largely on high-intensity mechanized monocultures grown continuously year after year. From an economic viewpoint it has been efficient to increase the intensity of agriculture, since machines and chemicals can be substituted for a great deal of expensive human labor. But economic criteria are often not the most meaningful ways to gauge the impact of activities on total ecosystems. It is often more useful to look at the implications of modern methods of production in terms of net energy costs (Odum, 1967, 1971; Slesser, 1978). The ecological simplicity of a modern crop monoculture is so unstable that it requires large inputs of chemicals to maintain the crop. In developed regions such as North America, Western Europe, or Japan, every calorie of food we eat may represent 2-10 calories of fossil fuel energy in the form of tractor fuel, chemicals, and so on—all in addition to the solar energy contained in the fixed carbon. Furthermore, we are just now becoming aware of the effects of modern agriculture on ecosystems beyond the farm. Agriculture is already the source of the largest fraction by weight of water pollution, and some agricultural pollutants are as toxic as anything put out by urban industry.

One of the biggest factors determining the carrying capacity of the earth for man concerns the length of time it takes for a system to adjust to change. Such adjustment can be quite simple in simple systems. For example, if you push the call button, an elevator arrives at your floor after a short time. But most interactions between people and the environment are not as simple as calling an elevator. The response of the elevator system is completely predictable (unless the elevator is broken). It will arrive at our floor after we push the button. How long it takes to do so is equally predictable, although it depends on where the elevator is when you push the button, what direction it is going in, and how many other people have pushed the call button on other floors. In principle, if you knew all of these things, you could predict the precise arrival of the elevator at your floor.

Man-environment interactions may show several responses to a single stimulus. Some are rapid while others are quite slow. As an example, a farmer might add a pesticide to a field to get rid of some unwanted pest. It might perform that function satisfactorily and quickly. But using the pesticide will also result in the buildup in genetic resistance to the pesticide over several years. This slow, long-range effect is no less significant than the rapid one. It is not unusual for management to consider only the responses that occur quickly and unambiguously. It may ignore, overlook, forget about, or underestimate the slow or delayed responses.

For many purposes the slow responses may be more significant than the rapid ones. By the time the environment finally responds to the stimulus, management must compensate with some further action. This does not further the goals of the ecosystem; it is a reaction to past management. That systems behave in ways we do not anticipate is not necessarily good or bad, and one need not place a value judgment on it. It is a phenomenon inherent in the operation of human ecosystems, and it becomes progressively more significant as the system becomes more complex. There have been instances in which society has had to make significant adjustments for the delayed or slow environmental changes induced by management—such as with genetic resistance to pesticides or the carcinogenic effects of asbestos. The fact that human ecosystems show different kinds of responses means that special attention should be given to them. Failure to do so leads to what one might call the Alice in Wonderland effect, in which one must, to quote the Red Queen, run faster and faster and faster simply to stay in the same place. There comes a time when we can no longer run faster.

So—what is the carrying capacity of human ecosystems for people? Very simply, we do not know. It is clear that society has become so sophisticated that the carrying capacity is considerably more than it was in hunter-gatherer days. It is not even clear, however, that the current population of the earth can be maintained over a long period of time, and there are people who believe that many countries have badly overshot their carrying capacity (e.g., Hardin, 1974). On the other hand, there are those who believe that the earth can support many times its current population (Revelle, 1971).

In the long run the sustainable population of an advanced industrial society (or for any society for that matter) will reflect the weakest part of the ecosystem upon which it is based. We know a great deal about the environment, about management, and about setting goals and strategies for society, but we know very little about how they operate together and about the mechanisms by which each limits the others. Perhaps we can be optimistic. Society's track record so far is not unblemished, but it is not so bad. Modern society appears to be thriving and the system seems to work. But nobody really knows why.

References

Arriaga, E. E., 1967. Rural-urban mortality in developing countries: an index for detecting rural underrepresentation. *Demography* **4**: 98–107.

Arriaga, E. E. and Davis, K., 1969. The pattern of mortality change in Latin America. *Demography* **6**: 223–242.

Blake, J., 1969. Population policy for Americans: is the government being misled? *Science* **164**: 522–529.

Bogue, D. J., 1969. *Principles of Demography*. New York: John Wiley & Sons.

Bumpass, L. and Westoff, C. F., 1970. The 'perfect contraceptive' population. *Science* **169**: 1177–1182.

Casetti, E., 1968. A formalization of the demographic transition theory. *Papers, Regional Science Assn.* **21**: 159–164.

Chambers, J. D., 1960. Population change in a provincial town: Nottingham 1700–1800. In Presnell, L. S., ed., *Studies in the Industrial Revolution: Essays Presented to T. S. Ashton*. London: Univ. of London Press, 97–124.

Coale, A. J., 1972. *The Growth and Structure of Human Populations*. Princeton: Princeton Univ. Press.

Colinvaux, P., 1976. Review of *Human Ecology*, ed. by Frederick Sargent, II. *Human Ecology* **4**: 263–266.

Conklin, H. C., 1954. An ethnoecological approach to shifting agriculture. *Trans N.Y. Acad. Sci.* **17, 2nd series:** 133–142.

Dasmann, R. F., 1972. *Environmental Conservation,* 3rd ed. New York: John Wiley & Sons.

Deevey, E. S., 1960. The human population. *Sci. Am.* **203 (9):** 195–204.

Ehrlich, P. R., Ehrlich, A. H., and Holdren, J. P., 1977. *Ecoscience: Population, Resources, and Environment.* San Francisco: W. H. Freeman and Co.

Eversley, D. E. C., 1965. Population, economy, and society. In Glass, D. V. and Eversley, D. E. C., eds., *Population in History: Essays in Historical Demography.* Chicago: Aldine Publishing Co., 23–69.

Frederiksen, H., 1969. Feedbacks in economic and demographic transition. *Science* **166:** 837–847.

Frejka, T., 1968. Reflections on the demographic conditions needed to establish a U.S. stationary population growth. *Population Studies* **22:** 379–397.

Grabill, W. H., Kiser, C. V., and Whelpton, P. K., 1958. *The Fertility of American Women.* New York: John Wiley & Sons.

Habakkuk, H. J., 1953. English population in the eighteenth century. *Econ. Hist. Rev.* **6, 2nd series,** 117–133.

Hardin, G., 1971. Nobody ever dies of overpopulation. *Science* **171:** 527.

Hardin, G., 1974. Living on a lifeboat. *Bioscience* **24:** 561–568.

Harkavy, O., Jaffe, F. S., and Wishik, S. M., 1969. Family planning and public policy: who is misleading whom? *Science* **165:** 367–373.

Heer, D. M., 1966. Economic development and fertility. *Demography* **3:** 423–444.

Helleiner, K. F., 1957. The vital revolution reconsidered. *Canad. Jour. Econ. Pol. Sci.* **23:** 1–19.

Huntington, E., 1945. *Mainsprings of Civilization.* New York: John Wiley & Sons.

Keyfitz, N., 1966. How many people have lived on the earth? *Demography* **3:** 581–582.

Keyfitz, N., 1968. *Introduction to the Mathematics of Population.* Reading, Mass., Addison-Wesley Pub. Co.

National Center for Health Statistics, 1980. *Vital Statistics of the United States,* Vol. II, Section 5: Life Tables. Hyattsville, Md. U.S. Public Health Service.

Odum, H. T., 1967. Energetics of world food production. In President's Scientific Advisory Committee, *The World Food Problem,* vol. III: 55–94.

Odum, H. T., 1971. *Environment, Power, and Society.* New York: John Wiley & Sons.

Population Reference Bureau, 1962. How many people have ever lived on earth? *Pop. Bull.* **18 (1):** 1–19.

Population Reference Bureau, 1971. Man's population predicament. *Pop. Bull.* **27 (2):** 1–39.

Population Reference Bureau, 1979. World Population Data Sheet, 1979.

Rappaport, R. A., 1967. Ritual regulation of environmental relations among a New Guinea people. *Ethnology* **6:** 17–30.

Revelle, R., 1971. Will the earth's land and water resources be sufficient for future populations? Speech presented at the U.N. Conference on the Environment, Stockholm.

Slesser, M., 1978. Energy Analysis: its utility and limits. Laxenburg, Austria: Int. Inst. Applied Syst. Anal. *Research Memorandum* **RM-78-46.**

Thiesenhusen, W. C., 1971. Latin America's employment problem. *Science* **171:** 868–874.

United Nations, 1970. *Demographic Yearbook,* 21st ed., 1969. New York: Statistical Office of the U.N.; Dept. of Economic and Social Affairs.

U.S. Bureau of the Census, 1970. Projections of the population of the United States, by age and sex (interim revisions): 1970–2020. *Current Population Reports,* series P–25, No. 448.

Van der Tak, J., Haub, C., and Murphy, E., 1979. Our population predicament: a new look. *Pop. Bull.* **34 (5)**: 1–48.

4/fisheries

A fishery is an ecosystem whose managerial domain is oriented to catching aquatic life, including true fish, shellfish and other mollusks, and whales. Its products constitute an important source of high quality meat, oil, fertilizers, animal feed, and protein-rich flour. Fish products account for a very high proportion of the total animal protein intake of many societies (Borgstrom, 1961). Even in the most impoverished protein-poor countries, symptoms of severe protein deficiency and the disease *kwashiorkor* tend to be rare in areas close to rivers or the sea, within which areas fish can easily be transported. Most fisheries concentrate on a few species of special economic value. The remainder of the community is essentially ignored.

The detailed study of fisheries is a combination of three historically different approaches. The first is fisheries population biology, in which the characteristics of the fish population are analyzed. The population biology of many fishes is well known, and fisheries serve as a model for other areas of applied ecology. The second field, fisheries ecosystem ecology, is much less well developed. Very few species of economically important organisms are so well known that their interactions with other populations and with the important abiotic factors of the environment can be used by managers. But the insights available from those instances in which we can deal with fisheries as ecosystems may be extremely powerful. Finally, fisheries economics looks at the rules governing the behavior of society with respect to fish populations and ecosystems.

Fish catches are very unevenly distributed over the earth's surface (Figure 4.1). Most come from an extraordinarily small zone, and most of the ocean is

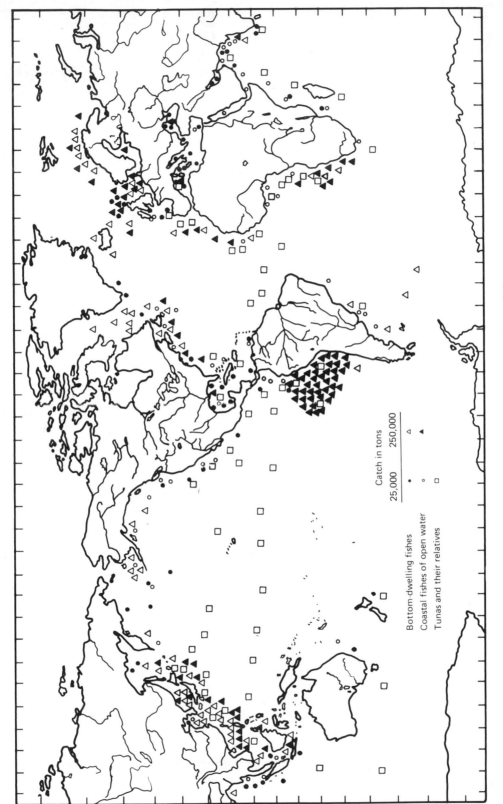

Figure 4.1 Fish catch of the world's oceans. [After Food and Agriculture Organization of the United Nations, 1972. *Atlas of Living Resources of the Sea.*]

Catch in tons

	25,000	250,000
Bottom-dwelling fishes	•	◾
Coastal fishes of open water	○	◁
Tunas and their relatives	□	◼

essentially barren. About 85% of world fisheries are marine. Of the total world fish catch, 50% comes from zones of upwelling covering some 0.1% of the ocean's total surface. The remainder of the marine catch (35% of the total) comes from fertile areas of the continental shelf and a few productive places in the high seas, especially in the Arctic and Antarctic convergence zones. The final 15% is from freshwater continental regions and fertilized fish ponds. Very little can be done to change these proportions, as they are determined mainly by the distribution of ocean fertility. Very few fertile places in the world ocean are not now exploited at-least to some degree. Altering the zonation of the marine fish catch, even in principle, would require changing the basic geographic patterns of physical and chemical dynamics of the world ocean. The most effective way of increasing fish catches very much over their current level is with highly managed fish ponds or bays.

FISHERIES AS POPULATIONS

A commercial fishing expedition is generally directed toward one population. The boat's equipment is designed for this purpose, and although a given boat may go out after more than one species over a season, it is likely to fish for only one species on a particular trip. Because the fisherman's activities are directed toward one population, the questions that appear most relevant are population questions. How many fish can be caught for a given input of labor or capital? What is the most appropriate level of fishing intensity, and what is the maximum yield corresponding to this level of pressure? What conditions are beneficial to growth or reproduction of the species, and to what degree are the factors that control its population density a function of the population density itself?

Life Cycle of Fish

A typical fish begins its life as an egg laid either in the moving water mass or in or on the bottom sediments (Figure 4.2). The egg consists of the embryo, a yolk sac, and a gelatinous covering. The embryo develops within the egg at first, hatching into a larva when the yolk sac is exhausted. The larval stage may last only a few weeks in some species, or as long as several years in others. Most larval fish are plankton-eating filter-feeders. They may be capable of swimming, but they are so small that they are at the mercy of the currents. At maturity the larvae undergo metamorphosis into fish with adult features and lifestyle. They are still quite small, and the major part of their growth is still to come.

An adolescent fish (i.e., one that has metamorphosed but is not yet sexually mature) is too small to be caught by most commercial fishing nets. Nets are generally designed so that they will take only fish that have begun to reproduce. After some time, which may be several months to several years, depending on the species, the individual fish is said to be *recruited* into the population. This is the point where it is large enough to be vulnerable to capture by normal fishing techniques.

The fertility of a sexually mature fish tends to increase as the fish ages. In general

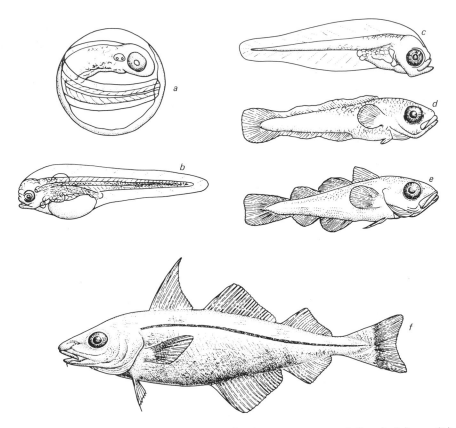

Figure 4.2   Life cycle of the haddock (*Melanogrammus aeglefinus*): (*a*) egg; (*b*) larva, just hatched, retaining yolk sac; (*c*) larva, 4.2 mm., shortly after losing yolk sac; (*d*) larva, 15 mm., shortly before metamorphosis; (*e*) young fry, 25 mm.; (*f*) adult. [After various authors. From Bigelow and Schroeder, 1953.]

it is related to size, and size is a function of age (Figure 4.3). This suggests that the reproductive potential of a fish increases steadily as it grows older, but this assumption is somewhat misleading. Figure 4.4 plots the increase in fertility per unit increase in biomass as a function of age. The rate of increase in biomass is one measure of growth rate and reflects the efficiency of energy conversion by the fish. While older, larger fish are more productive in terms of eggs produced per individual or per kilogram, they

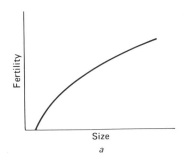

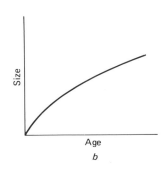

Figure 4.3   Schematic inter-relationships between fertility, size, and age in a typical fish population: (*a*) fertility as a function of size; (*b*) size as a function of age.

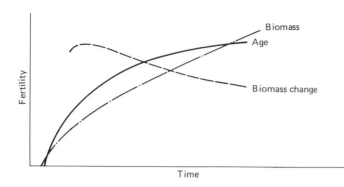

Figure 4.4 Fertility in a typical fish species as a function of several age-related factors.

are not necessarily as efficient in terms of eggs produced per unit of food assimilated by the population.

Life Forms of Fishes

Different species of fishes have vastly different lifestyles. Freshwater fishes comprise a broad range of species. Some, such as the carp and some of its relatives, inhabit slowly moving water low in oxygen and are very important food fishes. Others, such as the salmon and trout, can only be found in oxygen-rich water and are as significant for sport as for food.

Some fishes spend part of their life cycle in fresh water and the rest in the ocean. Of these, the *anadromous* fishes such as the salmon are born in fresh water but spend their adulthood in the ocean, migrating back to fresh water to reproduce. The *catadromous* fishes such as eels are just the reverse; they are born in the ocean but spend their adulthood in fresh water. These fishes are capable of extraordinarily long migrations, often thousands of miles in length and several years in duration. As an example, the eels of both North America and Western Europe reproduce in the Sargasso Sea but swim back to their respective continents as the "elvers" mature. They reach adulthood in freshwater streams (Figure 4.5). The homing mechanisms of these fishes are remarkable. For example, salmon that have spent many years in the high seas will return to reproduce in the stream where they are born.

Anadromous and catadromous species are among the most vulnerable to water pollution. They are beset not only with all the problems of living in the high seas but also all of the pollution-related problems of freshwater fishes. It is not enough to maintain the breeding grounds clean and unobstructed, as might be sufficient for a freshwater fishery. The entire river system from the spawning pool to the sea must be passable. Nevertheless, we cannot write them off as desirable but impractical to maintain. They include some of the most valuable of commercial fish species, and the salmon has been accorded a nobility of place equaled by no other fish species (Netboy, 1968). Per kilogram, it is the most valuable food fish in the world.

Ocean fishes include bottom-dwelling forms as well as those that swim in the open sea. The bottom-dwelling forms include numerous, widely sought-after species from fertile regions of the continental shelf, including herring, cod, mackerel, plaice, flounder, and sole. They typically hatch in estuaries or nearshore areas of the sea.

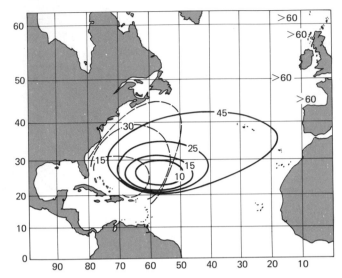

Figure 4.5 Distribution of larval eels, by size in millimeters, in the North Atlantic. Solid contours are sizes of *Anguilla anguilla,* the European eel. Dashed lines are those of *A. rostrata,* the American eel. Smallest larvae are found in the Sargasso Sea, the spawning ground for both species. [After Schmidt; redrawn, with permission, from D. H. Cushing, *Fisheries Biology,* 2nd ed. (Madison; The University of Wisconsin Press; © 1980 by the Board of Regents of the University of Wisconsin System).]

After metamorphosis they swim or are carried by currents to nursery zones, which tend also to be shallow nearshore locations, where they grow to adulthood. The adults may range over wide areas. As an example, a single adult Arctic cod may swim over 650 kilometers in a single year (Figure 4.6; Cushing, 1980).

The fishes of the high seas spend their lives in the open ocean and are not associated in any way with the bottom. Population densities in terms of numbers of fish per unit area are always very low, and adults move even more widely than the bottom-dwelling forms. Some like the tuna may move throughout most of the ocean, and some whales may migrate thousands of miles from the Arctic to the Antarctic within a given year.

Marine fisheries represent a "commons" (Hardin, 1968). Like the New England town common, the sea belongs to everybody and therefore to nobody. Fishing fleets are built up by many independent agents to maximize their economic return from fish sales. The agents may be individual fishermen operating out of a single port, or they may be highly organized and capitalized national fishing fleets operating all over the world. The fishermen using particular fishing grounds tend not to coordinate their activities, so that the fishery is not a closely managed ecosystem.

Natural populations have limited capacities for exploitation. Some can withstand a high intensity of fishing, but it is distressingly common for a multinational fishing fleet to be built up to a point where its extraction capability is significantly larger than the sustainable yield of the fish population. The reasons for this are both economic and biological. The biological reasons stem mainly from the fact that fish, like many natural populations, show a lag response to exploitation, especially if fishing pressure builds very quickly. It is not always possible to judge whether or not a population is being overfished. The economic reasons are more complex.

It is never biologically reasonable to overexploit a desirable population. Only by the preservation of its integrity does the population remain a useful resource. But human ecosystems are not simply biological systems. There are times when it may

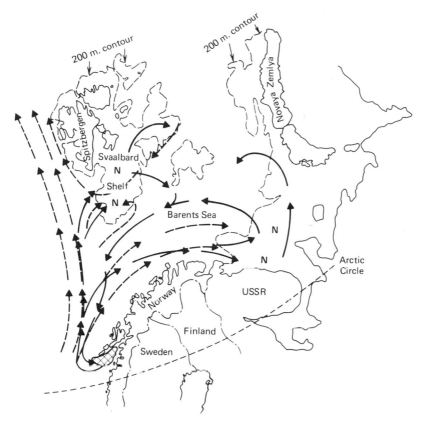

Figure 4.6 Migration patterns of arcto-Norwegian cod. The spawning grounds are in the crosshatched area off northern Norway. Larvae are carried by northward-flowing currents to the Svaalbard Shelf and the shallow shelf areas of the southeastern Barents Sea. Nursery grounds are designated "N" on the map. As the cod grow older, they migrate into the Barents Sea and swim against the northward-flowing currents to return to the spawning grounds to spawn. [After D. H. Cushing. *Fisheries Biology,* 2nd ed. (Madison; The University of Wisconsin Press; © 1980 by the Board of Regents of The University of Wisconsin System).]

appear economically justifiable to overexploit a population, even to a point where it is destroyed. Economic activities compete with each other for capital, and they must consider the time value of money, commonly expressed in the *discount rate.* This is the rate at which an investment loses its value. Clark (1973) shows that if the discount rate is sufficiently high, and if "economic sense" is defined as maximizing profit, then economic sense may best be realized by taking as many fish as possible as fast as possible for a relatively short period of time and not worrying about the long-term consequences. The basic fish resource itself is not "owned," either in the legal sense that characterizes capitalist societies, the organized community sense that characterizes socialist societies, or the abstract community sense that characterizes many primitive and animist societies. It may not seem as economically important as the costs of building boats and processing plants or carrying out the fishing operations. In this respect fisheries are very different from those sorts of exploitation in which the basic resource such as the livestock herd or the land is treated as owned capital.

Sustainable Yield

One of the most important questions about any fishery (or any other human ecosystem) is whether or not its current yield can be sustained indefinitely. Many fisheries have shown remarkable stability for as long as there have been records. Others show trends reflecting major changes in the structure of the biological community. Still others simply collapse if they are sufficiently overstressed. The decline or collapse of a fishery from overfishing represents a biological tragedy; it may also represent a human tragedy. Large amounts of capital may have been invested in the fishery along the way, mainly in the form of money for ships, canning plants, and so on. There may be times when one can justify overfishing from a profit-maximization view. But capital also includes human capital, the building of skills by people whose lives depend on fishing. When the decline comes, this investment is lost. This loss is wasteful and debilitating both to the fishery and to the human community.

If the current level of catch can be sustained, then a second question is in order. How much larger a catch might be gotten if the intensity of fishing were stepped up, and what level of fishing intensity is most likely to provide the maximum yield that can be sustained? The notion of maximum sustained yield is a simple and intuitively meaningful concept (Figure 4.7). There is no yield at all if there is no fishing intensity. All mortality in the population is due to natural causes. There is also a level at which the mortality from exploitation is so high that the population cannot withstand it, and the sustainable yield approaches zero. Between these two extremes there is a positive yield that can be sustained over time. The shape of the relationship, however, is not at all obvious, and analysts generally assume a very simple curve such as the one shown in Figure 4.7.

It is not always possible to translate an abstraction such as a simple curve into a concrete management policy for a real-world population. For example, mathematical

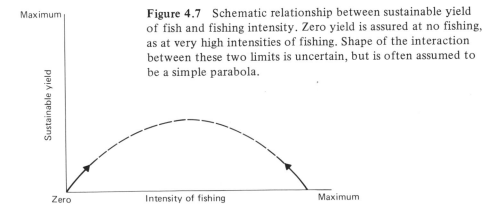

Figure 4.7   Schematic relationship between sustainable yield of fish and fishing intensity. Zero yield is assured at no fishing, as at very high intensities of fishing. Shape of the interaction between these two limits is uncertain, but is often assumed to be a simple parabola.

analyses based on the simple parabola (Shaefer, 1957) suggest that the maximum sustained yield from fish population is attained when the population is equal to 1/2 of the carrying capacity. What does this half consist of? What controls additions to the population? Most analyses consider only those individuals who have been recruited into the population, since well over 99% of the eggs and larvae are lost before recruitment in most fish species. But there is no assurance that half of the recruited population is maximally sexually reproductive, or that somewhat more than this number would not be more efficient in reproducing. The idea that the maximum catch can be sustained if the recruited population equals half of the carrying capacity is not intuitively reasonable and must be justified on the basis of the biology of the species in question.

This would be an academic question if mathematical models of fish populations were not used as the basis of fishery management. But they are, and the simple models make implicit assumptions that cannot be justified biologically. They might be useful if fish populations were regulated by negative feedback forces applied to recruited individuals. However, population regulation in fishes tends to be directed not at the adult stages but rather at the juveniles. It appears to be quite rare for adult fish to be the focus of negative-feedback mechanisms that are successful in regulating population densities.

In addition, fish reproduction like that of humans is a function of the age distribution of the population. If we wanted to assume some kind of equilibrium distribution, then a simple model that described population regulation in the juvenile stages would be an entirely reasonable way to proceed. But the age dependence of natural mortality (such as from cannibalism related to the density of the population) is different from that due to exploitation pressure. The overall age distribution of the population as a whole can change quickly as these two factors vary.

Let us examine some of the more important factors involved in the notion of maximum sustainable yield in a real-world context. This analysis is based on a very simple mathematical model that considers the roles of weather, the intensity of exploitation, and the age-specific patterns of reproduction and exploitation strategy.

The first scenario is one in which the weather is uniform and the age-specific patterns of fertility and mortality do not change from one year to the next. The intensity of catch can be designated as "low," "medium," or "high." Figure 4.8 demonstrates the responses of the population to these levels of exploitation. Let us now compare these results with similar situations in which fertility and mortality vary to reflect fluctuations in the weather. In Figure 4.9 the amount of weather-induced variation is moderate; in Figure 4.10 it is severe. The meanings of low, medium, and high exploitation pressure remain the same as in the previous examples. These figures show that population becomes increasingly vulnerable to overexploitation as the fluctuations in the natural environment increase, and that intermediate levels of exploitation are more consistently successful than intense levels.

Overexploitation is a complex phenomenon that has meaning only in the context of a specific population in a specific environment. It involves the progression of reproduction and mortality through time, but its practical manifestation is a decline or collapse of the exploited population. Any number of strategies may lead to overexploitation, depending on the circumstances. Overfishing is not a simple act carried out by unwitting or uncoordinated fishermen, but rather a whole class of strategies that

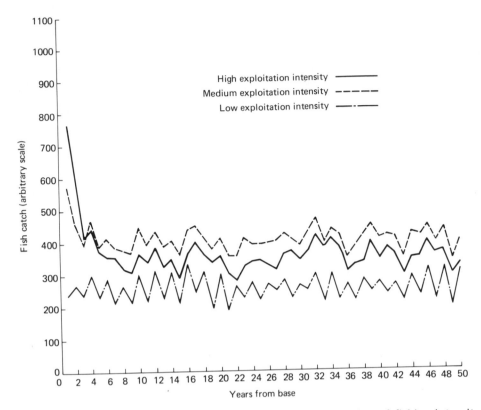

Figure 4.8   Catch of a hypothetical fish population as a function of fishing intensity in an ecosystem of low variability. The unexploited population starts at base year with an equilibrium age distribution. Fertility and mortality characteristics are those of North Pacific sardines (Murphy, 1966). The responses of fertility and mortality to variation are simulated in a simple computer model. The same relative variation sequence is used for all simulations in Figures 4.8, 4.9, and 4.10.

for one reason or another are not balanced with the fish population. These include too-intensive exploitation of adult fish, exploitation of the wrong age groups, and fishing at the wrong times.

The concept of maximum sustainable yield is therefore equally complex. Natural deaths may decline in a population that is exploited in an optimal fashion; that is, when fishermen remove individuals that are more likely to die, and exploitation reduces competition between members of the population without decimating the reproductive ability of the population. This latter effect can be quite important, and it has also been noted in a number of experimental populations to test the effects of exploitation (Watt, 1968).

Weather fluctuation affects both fertility and mortality at all ages. An adequate exploitation strategy for a real-world fish population should allow a suitable "cushion" for bad seasons. It is always possible, of course, that a given year will be characterized by excellent conditions for reproduction and that subsequent years will show favorable conditions for the survival of larval and adolescent fish. (Note that reproduction

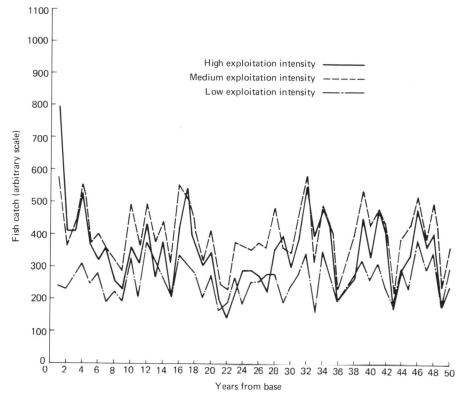

Figure 4.9 Catch of the hypothetical fish population as a function of fishing intensity in a moderately variable ecosystem. (See Figure 4.8 for details.)

and survival are two different things, and there is no particular reason why conditions suitable to one need also be suitable for the other.) Under such conditions the population could grow to rather high levels. It is also possible that conditions may be very bad for reproduction or survival of juveniles.

Except in environments which are inherently very stable, it is likely that conditions will alternate randomly between good and bad, if not for reproduction then for survival of juveniles. A cushion in the form of a guaranteed minimum unexploited breeding population is essential for survival of the fishery resource. Its minimum size is a function of the population's response to the instabilities in its physical environment. The responses of a population to environmental instability are closely correlated to the degree of environmental instability. Let us discuss some case studies of fisheries from stable and unstable habitats.

Plaice in the North Sea.   The North Sea fishery is one of the oldest and most stable fisheries of the Western world. Fish have been caught there for as long as there has been recorded history of fishing. The annual fluctuation of the catch is small (Figure 4.11), indicating exceptional stability of population density even in the context of changing exploitation intensity. The North Sea is inherently a very stable environment. Most of it is less than 100 fathoms in depth, and the Gulf Stream moderates summer

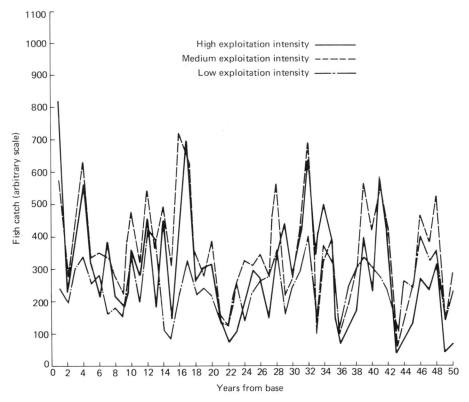

Figure 4.10 Catch of the hypothetical fish population as a function of fishing intensity in a highly variable ecosystem. (See Figure 4.8 for details.)

surface temperatures between 15.5 and 17.5°C, and winter temperatures between 4 and 5°C. There is a very rich plankton supply and many areas are suitable both as spawning grounds and as nursery grounds for commercial species of fish.

The North Sea is a stable environment but it is not static. Different species respond differently to its fluctuations. For example, haddock has shown a number of wide leaps in its catch. While this may be due in part to patterns of fishing, it is more likely that some real factor in the biology of the organism causes large differences in annual reproduction in the species.

Plaice, on the other hand, is very stable (Figure 4.11). Figure 4.12 graphs an index of survival to recruitment in plaice plotted against biomass in the parent population. The extremely small scatter indicates a very strong relationship between the number of recruits of the year and the number of fish already in the parent population. This suggests a powerful negative-feedback mechanism regulating recruitment.

Beverton (1962) points out that the plaice is a very fertile fish. Out of every million eggs spawned, only an average of 10 can live to recruitment if the population is to remain stable. The total observed range of variation has been from 5 to 30, and the average range of survivors is from 7 to 15. This is a very narrow range. In comparison, recruitment to haddock and sole populations in the same area over the last 30 years has varied over an extreme range of 500-fold.

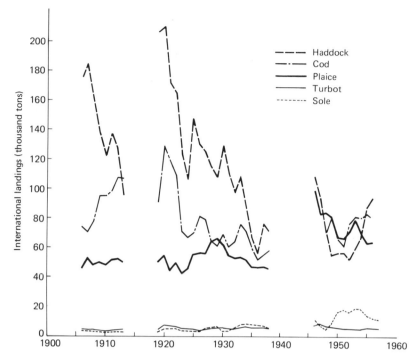

Figure 4.11 Total international landings of important fish species in the North Sea, 1906–1957. [Redrawn, with permission, from Beverton, 1962.]

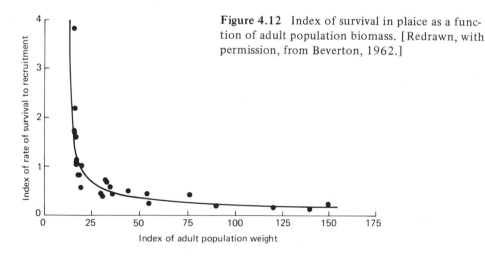

Figure 4.12 Index of survival in plaice as a function of adult population biomass. [Redrawn, with permission, from Beverton, 1962.]

Figure 4.13 shows the distribution of plaice eggs at the peak of spawning in the southern North Sea spawning grounds for two years of very different spawning density. In 1937 relatively few eggs were deposited. Spawning was very heavy in 1947, since fish populations had rebuilt themselves during World War II, when fishing had not been very heavy. Several intra-population factors known in other species might be suggested to account for the differences observed. These include behavior, the effect of

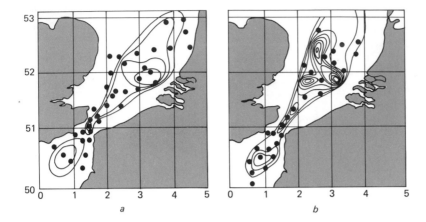

Figure 4.13 Distribution of plaice eggs at peak spawning time in the southern North Sea in two years of very different overall egg production: (*a*) January, 1937, a low reproduction year; (*b*) January, 1947, a high reproduction year. [Redrawn, with permission, from Beverton, 1962.]

overcrowding on hatching efficiency, and the ability of females to produce healthy and viable eggs. Beverton (1962) suggests that they are not significant for plaice. Eggs are produced in numbers roughly proportional to the number of adult fish in the population, but they are spawned only in restricted spawning grounds with little spillover beyond these areas.

There is some evidence that the rate of predation from other species increases as the density of hatchling plaice increases, and plaice eggs have been reported in the guts of herring. But the main control mechanism for the remarkable stability of plaice appears to be associated with the food supply of the larvae. They subsist almost entirely on the copepod genus *Oikopleura*. Shelbourne (1957) has shown that the viability of plaice hatchlings is directly related to the abundance of *Oikopleura*. A small *Oikopleura* population may bring about outright starvation of the young plaice. It may also lead to a deterioration of the condition of the larvae so that other factors not normally density-dependent become so. Malnourished larvae may be more vulnerable to predation or to changes in the physical environment. Food shortage may also delay metamorphosis, so that the larval stage lasts relatively longer. This would increase the length of time for factors that operate against larvae to act on the young fish.

In short, the biology of the plaice population is characterized by two primary factors that create a highly efficient negative-feedback regulating mechanism. The first is an extreme circumscription of the spawning zones, so that the density of eggs tends to be proportional to the density of adult fish in the population. Second, there is the overwhelming dependence of the hatchling plaice on *Oikopleura* as a food source, so that too high larval density cannot be sustained by the copepod population (Figure 4.14). A relatively small adult population lays relatively few eggs in the spawning grounds, so that the predation on *Oikopleura* is relatively mild. Under this level of feeding, the *Oikopleura* flourish, insuring a solid food supply for the developing hatchling fish. This is reflected in high proportions of recruitment.

These patterns can be contrasted with those of other fishes in the North Sea that

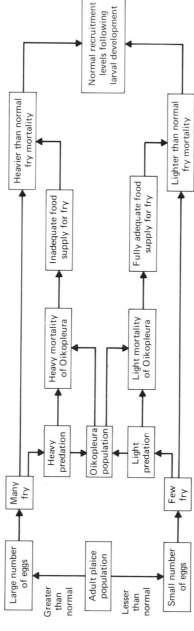

Figure 4.14 Interaction between plaice population, especially larvae, and the copepod *Oikopleura*, which is the main regulatory factor for recruitment levels.

inhabit the identical environment but are not characterized either by the restricted spawning grounds or by the narrow feeding preferences of the young fish. Even in the relatively stable environment they show greater fluctuations in both recruitment and catch (Figure 4.11).

A strong caveat must be thrown in at this point. Whatever has been said about the effectiveness of controls on fish populations in stable environments is valid only so long as the environment remains stable. So long as the nursery grounds remain inviolate, and so long as the *Oikopleura* population remains stable itself, plaice populations will not fluctuate greatly. However, plaice are much more dependent on these factors than are other North Sea fishes on the factors that control them. If pollution or some change in the spawning and nursery grounds removed them from habitability by plaice, or if some catastrophe befell the *Oikopleura* population, the impact on the plaice population would be much greater than the impact of similar kinds of changes on a sister population. One must recognize that the populations of all of the commercial fish species in the North Sea are remarkably stable for populations of wild animals.

Sardines of the Eastern Pacific Ocean.   The eastern Pacific Ocean is inherently a much less stable environment than the North Sea. Nevertheless, its sardine fisheries have comprised some of the world's most important fisheries. There are two main centers. The first is in the North Pacific, running from Baja California to British Columbia; the second is in the South Pacific, around Peru. The former is the older, although it has fallen on hard times as of late, and in many ways the latter is the more interesting. Both shed considerable light on the problems of exploiting a population in an unstable environment. Figure 4.15 shows the location of these two fisheries. Both are characterized by cold currents that bring nutrient-laden waters to the surface. Both of these currents vary in the strength of their flow and in their location, conferring a substantial instability on the physical environment. The California fishery shows an intense interspecific competition between sardines and anchovies, which are closely related and have somewhat similar requirements (Murphy, 1966a, 1967). The California sardine population was partially replaced by anchovies following its collapse.

Figure 4.16 shows the rise and fall of the North Pacific sardine fishery. Between 1935 and 1945 it was the largest fishery in North America in tons of fish harvested. Only tuna and salmon outweighed it in dollar value. During the late 1930s and early 1940s the total catch of North Pacific sardines was relatively constant. Additional fishing boats were constantly entering the sardine fleet, and pressure on the population was continually increasing.

Even if sardines were regulated by as profoundly effective a negative-feedback regulatory mechanism as the North Sea plaice, it would not have been surprising to see the population collapse simply as the result of overfishing. But regulation in sardines is not strong, and the California current is a much more variable habitat than the North Sea. Spawning was essentially nil in both 1949 and 1950. Coupled with the very intense fishing pressure, the northern race of the California sardine collapsed in 1950 and spelled the end of the sardine fisheries in British Columbia, Oregon, and Washington. The major drop in California occurred in 1952.

The pacific coast sardine population comprised at least two races, of which the larger and more important prior to 1950 was the northern race (Murphy, 1966b). They overlapped considerably in area, although they did so at different times of the year.

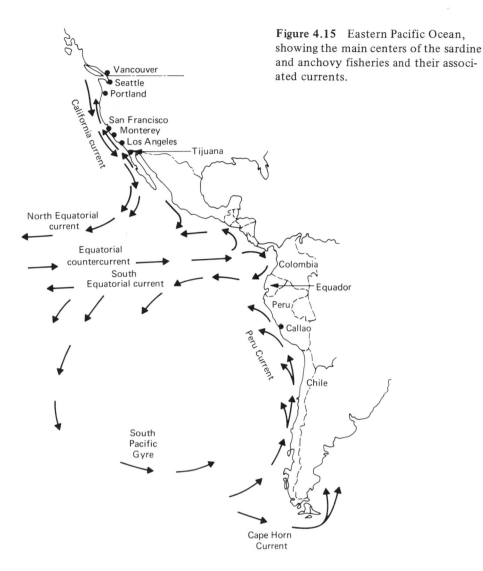

Figure 4.15 Eastern Pacific Ocean, showing the main centers of the sardine and anchovy fisheries and their associated currents.

The most important difference between them is that the northern race was characterized by a considerably lower natural mortality than the southern race. Fishing activities in the northern Pacific waters were so intense that virtually all of the older individuals were stripped from the population. During good years or even average years this would not make a great deal of difference, since the sardine is a very prolific reproducer and relatively young recruits can provide enough eggs to keep the population at a reasonable level. When reproduction failed almost entirely in two successive years, the fishing pressure wiped out any chance that the northern race could bounce back. Its population was so reduced that interbreeding between the races resulted in its genetic incorporation into the southern race. The resulting sardine population was characterized by the higher natural mortality and consequently slower population growth which had characterized the southern race.

Why did reproduction in the California sardine fail in 1949 and 1950? It is difficult

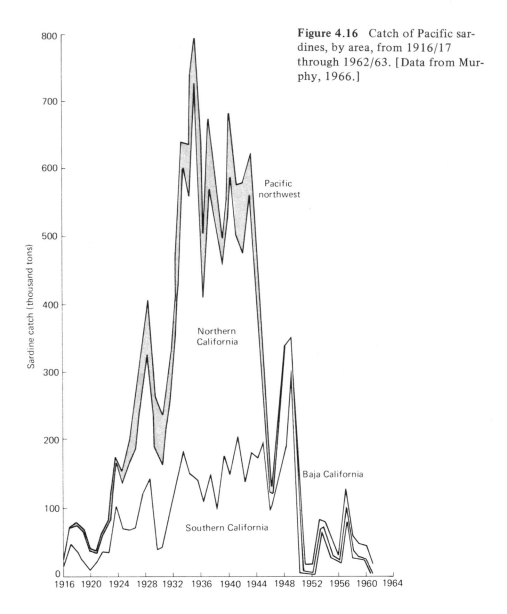

Figure 4.16 Catch of Pacific sardines, by area, from 1916/17 through 1962/63. [Data from Murphy, 1966.]

to be certain, but the most logical explanation appears to be the temperature of the spawning grounds. The season of 1949 was one of the coldest off the coast of California (Figure 4.17). While 1950 was not as cold as 1949, it was still colder than normal. The temperature optimum for sardine spawning is relatively high. Therefore, one would expect that the lower-than-normal temperature would be accompanied by a lower-than-normal reproductive success.

But there is more to it than this. Even highly impaired spawning should not spell the complete failure of reproduction that seems to have occurred in 1949. The California current itself may play a prominent role in sardine reproductive success. Sardines spawn in offshore waters but their nursery grounds are near the coast, where they are transported by the current. If it is strong and unsteady as it moves down the coastline,

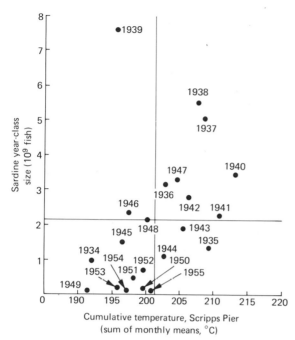

Figure 4.17 Relationship between sardine year-class sizes and the temperature of the water off southern California. Year-classes are estimated fish populations, and temperature index is the sum of the monthly mean temperatures at Scripps Pier from April to March. [Redrawn from *Ecology and Natural Resource Management* by K. E. F. Watt. © 1968 McGraw-Hill Book Co. Used with permission of McGraw-Hill Book Company.]

the young sardines are carried southward and then out into the Pacific ocean. Because very few of them arrive at the nursery grounds, the survival of larval fish is very low and recruitment is correspondingly poor. If the current is relatively weak, it carries the hatchling fish into the nursery grounds and survival and recruitment are much higher (Sette, 1960).

The strength of the California current is strongly correlated with low temperature in the spawning grounds. Not only is spawning likely to be depressed during very cold years, but the hatchling fish are more likely to be carried away from the nursery grounds. This, coupled with an exploitation policy that selected very strongly against older fish and altered the age distribution so that reproduction was carried out almost exclusively by new recruits, could in fact spell the decimation of the population.

The North Pacific sardine fishery had another important operative factor. Many of the requirements of the California anchovy are quite similar to those of the sardine. It is also shorter lived and more prolific, so that its reproductive characteristics have evolved in a way that does not depend on reproduction spread over a number of years. The decline of the sardine allowed a vast expansion of the anchovy, so that the current biomass of the anchovy population is roughly equivalent to the biomass of the sardines at their height. Because of the very high degree of niche overlap between the two species, it will take a very long time for the sardine to regain its former abundance—and it may no longer even be possible.

The Peruvian Anchovy. The anchovy fishery of the southern Pacific Ocean off the coast of Peru is similar to the North Pacific sardine fishery in many ways. Development of the fishery began during World War II, and construction of the first fishmeal plant on the Peruvian coast began around 1950 (Paulik, 1971). The fishery expanded at an incredible rate, so that Peru had become the world's leading fishing nation, measured by live weight of catch, by 1963. This record was based almost entirely on the stocks of the Peruvian anchovy that inhabit the rich upwelling zones of the Peru current.

It has been estimated (Cushing, 1969) that the Peru current is one of the two largest zones of upwelling in the world's oceans, about 2–3 times as important with respect to potential fish production as the California current. The Peru current is the northward flowing expression of the giant South Pacific gyre (Figure 4.15). Nutrient-rich waters are forced to the surface very close to shore by the contours of the sea bottom. These nutrients make possible a tremendous amount and diversity of phytoplankton, which in turn support great quantities of zooplankton. Zooplankton provide food for the juvenile and larval anchovies, while zooplankton and phytoplankton together provide the food supply for the adult anchovies.

The main natural predator of the anchovies are the millions of cormorants, gannets, and pelicans that nest on islands offshore from Peru and feed on great quantities of the fish. These are the guano birds, whose fecal material accumulates to great thicknesses on the rainless guano islands off the coast of Peru. Guano has been a major fertilizer resource for many years. Even the Inca were aware of the great value of this material. Until the development of the anchovy fishery, the birds had been the main (and most efficient) means for converting a resource that had no direct benefit (i.e., the fish) into a material with immense economic value. Unreachable fish were converted without human effort into useful fertilizer. But in the 1950s the fish became reachable in their own right, so that the birds became competitors for this resource. Because fishmeal carries a considerably higher price than guano, the importance of the birds as competitors began to outweigh their value as a conversion agent.

The Peru current is as variable an environment as the California current. It normally shifts offshore to some degree every year, generally during the winter months. The degree of shift, however, varies considerably from year to year, and every few years it shifts further offshore than usual. The shift is known as El Niño, the Spanish word for child, because it comes approximately at Christmas time. As the current shifts from shore a wedge of warmer water covers the colder water. Sometimes El Niño is so mild that it can scarcely be noticed by the fishermen; at other times (generally occurring about every seven years) El Niño is pronounced and is accompanied by heavy rains and a strong north-south surface flow of relatively low-salinity, low-fertility warm water. During such times the anchovies, which normally feed fairly near the surface, are forced down into the cold waters underlying the surface flow. This makes it impossible for all but the strongest birds to reach the fish, so that a strong El Niño is accompanied by mass starvation of birds. Normally, after it has passed the birds regain their former numbers. However, following a severe El Niño in 1965 the bird population fell from 17 million to 4.3 million, and it has not recovered. Many plankton living between the current and the shore may not have an adequate nutrient supply during El Niño. These also die, so that El Niño is the source of mass mortality of all kinds of organisms at all stages of the food chain.

The natural fluctuations of the Peru current and its associated biota are entirely normal, but the growth of the Peruvian fish industry changed the qualitative balance among the actors. What once was a wide-ranging dynamic equilibrium between fish and guano birds has become a race between man and birds much akin to the gold rush days in the North American west (Paulik, 1971). The fishing industry has grown so fast, and its catching capacity is already so much greater than the sustainable yield of the anchovy population, that one might doubt seriously whether an equilibrium among fish, birds, and man is likely or even possible.

What then determines the sustainable yield of the Peruvian anchovy? As it happens, the anchovy population is inherently more stable than that of the California sardine. Anchovies are much smaller, shorter-lived fish. They are recruited to the fishery at about five months of age, and they become sexually mature about 1 year old. Most adults are less than 3 years old. Such a short-lived organism cannot afford reproductive failure, especially in an unstable environment like the Peru current. Reproduction must be successful every year.

In fact, recruitment to the population in the Peru current has been remarkably successful and consistent. It has typically been within a factor of 2-3 of the historical mean. The reason is that the fish has evolved a reproductive strategy that insures the survival population. Spawning is continuous throughout the year. Anchovies are filter-feeders and are easily capable of ingesting their own eggs. Thus the proportion of eggs lost to cannibalism is directly proportional to the population density of the adult population. At the same time the carrying capacity of the environment for juvenile fish is closely regulated by the food supply. An anchovy egg has virtually no energy supply. When the egg hatches, the anchovy larva must eat promptly or it will have exhausted its entire stored energy supply. These two factors plus predation by birds and other fishes were sufficient to stabilize the population levels of the anchovy until recently.

Stability for the anchovy, then, is high natural mortality balanced by high fertility, moderated to a degree by negative feedback. If this leads to a balance in nature, it leads to problems when exploitation becomes excessive. Since the natural population only includes 2 or 3 age classes on the average, excess capacity can easily strip off all but the newly recruited individuals. Failure of reproduction is always conceivable in an unstable environment. While the normal population structure of the anchovy provided an adequate cushion for reproductive failure, the heavily exploited population had none whatsoever. A reproductive strategy that is dramatically successful under natural conditions can lead to devastation under conditions of heavy fishing pressure.

Paulik (1971) suggested a scenario for annihilation of the Peruvian anchovy population. The fish catch has removed almost all fish greater than one year old. (This has been roughly the case for the last few years.) Upwelling currents are weak from January to March, causing a near failure of reproduction. The catch falls and the price of fishmeal climbs in response, tending to increase exploitation pressure on the population. The weakness of the upwelling currents concentrates the remaining population into a relatively narrow band along the coast. If catching capacity were sufficient, it would be possible at this point to decimate the entire reproductive population of the fishery.

It would also be possible to call a moratorium on fishing, given the extraordinary vulnerability of the population at this time. But this is very unlikely in practice. Most of the fishermen and fishmeal factory workers would become unemployed *barriados* in the slums of Lima. It is very unlikely that a poor country would have the option of acting in a way that would appear most responsible under the relatively narrow considerations of conservation or economics.

The rising price of fishmeal would be an extraordinarily effective stimulus for increasing rather than decreasing fishing intensity. The fishing industry of Peru is financed largely on short-term loans that must be paid off. If the only way to pay off these loans would be to decimate the fishery in the process, then this is probably what would happen. It did happen, in 1973.

FISHERIES IN COMMUNITIES

A fishery in the real world is not limited to a single population. Any aquatic ecosystem is characterized by a great number of fish species; these species compete with each other for at least some of the same resources such as spawning grounds, nursery space, and zooplankton. Some species may be predators on others, and it is conceivable that both the predator and the prey are economically significant. In addition, most ecosystems include both valuable fish and the coarse fishes that bring a very low price. A realistic study of a fishery must concern itself not only with the obvious questions of the requirements of the population of interest, but also with the requirements and realities of populations that are not of direct interest. At the very least, it must consider the community in enough detail to understand how exploitation of valuable species affects the other populations in ways that feed back on the valuable species. Examples already touched on include the way in which *Oikopleura* serves as a "safety valve" for plaice in the North Sea, and the complex patterns of competition between the guano birds and fishermen over the Peruvian anchovy.

There are many other categories of competitors. Large predacious vertebrates include sharks, seals, toothed whales, and marine birds, as well as other fish. Myriad parasites attack fish of economic importance, including bacteria, molds, protozoa, trematodes (flukes), tapeworms, and crustacea. As an example, cod has over a dozen species of trematode parasites.

Numerous toxins can affect fisheries. Some of these are natural. For example, the red tide dinoflagellate is a small unicellular alga that undergoes major "blooms" every so often. Its waste products are highly toxic not only to other marine organisms but even to animals as large as people. Other toxins are completely artificial. These include oil spills, pesticides, and the whole range of industrial pollutants. Large quantities of oil globules are no longer uncommon. At several points along the journey of Thor Hyerdahl's reed boat, the *Ra,* the crew disdained to brush their teeth in seawater because it was so polluted with oil. Plastic and other debris accumulate to a noticeable degree in some of the formerly cleanest parts of the ocean such as the Sargasso Sea (Carpenter and Smith, 1972).

Great Lakes of North America

One of the most interesting and best studied examples of a fishery at the community level is that of the Great Lakes in North America. The Great Lakes have always been a major fishing ground for the United States and Canada. Many different species have been commercially important over the past 200 years, and different species have been favored at different times. The species distribution of the catch was roughly stable during the first half of the twentieth century in most of the Great Lakes, although it was significantly different before about 1890 and after about 1950. This stability reflected the dynamic equilibrium between the natural community and human exploitation that existed between 1890 and 1950.

The problems of the lower lakes (Erie and Ontario) are somewhat different from those of the upper (Superior, Michigan, and Huron) (Figure 4.18). The fishery in Lake Ontario suffered during the 1800s with the buildup of large cities such as Buffalo, Rochester, Syracuse, and Toronto. Unlike the other Great Lakes, Lake Ontario is also accessible directly from the ocean via the St. Lawrence River. The other Great Lakes were protected from marine invasions by Niagara Falls, which lies between Lakes Erie and Ontario. Not until the early nineteenth century were Lake Erie and the upper Great Lakes linked to the sea through the extensive canal systems that were then under construction. The most important of these were the Erie Canal linking the Niagara River at Buffalo with the Hudson River at Albany, the Welland Canal running from Lake Ontario at St. Catherines to the eastern basin of Lake Erie, and the various canals through Ohio linking Lake Erie with the Ohio River. Even with the canals in place, however, it took almost 100 years for the most destructive of the marine influences, the sea lamprey, to swim up the Welland Canal into Lake Erie, where it proceeded to decimate the most important fish populations in the upper Great Lakes.

Lake Erie has always had the largest and most important of the Great Lakes fisheries. It is the shallowest of the Great Lakes and it has always been the best nourished. Its western basin has a mean depth of about 7.4m., and light can penetrate to the bottom. Many shoals and rocky reefs in the western basin have long served as valuable spawning and nursery grounds. Even today, despite the presence of Detroit and Toledo together with innumerable smaller cities, the western basin of Lake Erie is still the most important spawning ground for fish in the entire Great Lakes system. By con-

Figure 4.18   Map of the Great Lakes of North America, showing the Welland (W) and Erie (E) canals.

trast, the eastern and central basins are deeper and are stratified in the summer. The target species in the early nineteenth century were the valuable lake trout, lake herring, and lake whitefish. Fishing was carried out on a relatively small scale before 1850. The hooks, seines, and small stationary gear that were used did not make a great impact on the community as a whole, although they did allow for substantial yields (Figure 4.19).

A major change in fishing technology about 1850 brought about the demise of the first of a string of species in Lake Erie. Large gill nets and pound nets were much more effective in catching the salmonids that formed the basis of the fishery, and they were widely adopted. Unfortunately, they could be severely damaged or even destroyed if a lake sturgeon got caught in one of them. Sturgeon is a relatively large fish (sometimes over 80kg) that grows very slowly and matures very late and has few natural enemies. It had been completely outside the fishery up to that point, but it quickly became regarded as a pest of major proportions. As a result, sturgeons were fished very heavily in a conscious effort to reduce the population to insignificance. This was not difficult since the sturgeon is so slow in growing and so late in maturing sexually.

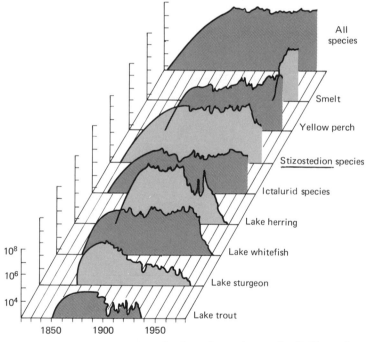

Figure 4.19 Annual catches of selected species, and of all species combined, in the Lake Erie commercial fishery since 1820. Continuous lines represent data reported annually by commercial fishermen; dashed lines represent data requiring interpolation; dotted lines are based on semiquantitative estimates. *Stizostedion* species include walleye, blue pike, and saugers; Ictalurid species include channel catfish and bullhead. [Redrawn, with permission, from Regier and Hartman; "Lake Erie's Fish Community: 150 Years of Cultural Stress." *Science* 180: 1248–1255. © 1973 American Association for the Advancement of Science.]

The slaughter of the sturgeon was reminiscent in many ways of the contemporary slaughter of the buffalo in the western plains. The fish were often caught, killed, and dumped back into the lake. On some occasions they were even piled in stacks on the shore, doused with oil, and burned (Regier and Hartman, 1973). Since the species does not become sexually mature until it is 15–25 years old, it did not take long to reduce the sturgeon to commercial insignificance. Not until 1860 did American fishermen learn how to smoke and render the sturgeon, make caviar from its eggs, and manufacture isinglass from its air bladder. By 1870 the fish had become a species of considerable commercial value, and it was also much less common. By the 1920s sturgeons were so rare in the upper Great Lakes that they were protected in the U.S. waters of those lakes. For the last 50 years only incidental catches have been permitted (Smith, 1968). At this point sturgeons seem to be holding their own in the upper Great Lakes, although they have declined seriously in Lake Erie since 1950. This is probably a result of pollution, however, rather than fishing pressure.

With the exception of the sturgeon, the commercial fishery of Lake Erie held fairly constant until 1925. In 1925 the lake herring population collapsed. The lake herring had traditionally been the most important species of the Great Lakes, and Lake Erie herring were particularly abundant and large. It was not unusual for annual production from Lake Erie to range over 20 million pounds, and the annual catch ranged up to 2 1/2 times that average. As with so many similar instances, the herring was treated as an infinite resource. If catches were so high as to glut the market with fish, they were often simply discarded and left to rot (Van Oosten, 1930). After the initial collapse the herring population produced only one strong year class, that of 1944. Substantial spawning stocks were present until the mid 1950s, but they are now very scarce.

The original collapse of the lake herring seems due mainly to overfishing. Because of its great value pressure on it was quite heavy, especially in the early 1920s. The year 1924 saw an unusual concentration in the eastern basin of the lake. The catching capacity of the fishery had been building up for some time, and by 1924 it was probably well above maximum sustainable yield of the population. In any case, fishermen converged on the concentration in the eastern basin and decimated the population to a point where it could not recover for another 20 years. Niche overlap between the lake herring and other salmonids such as the lake whitefish slowed whatever comeback might have been possible for the herring. Its final demise in the 1950s was most likely due to increasing chemical pollution. Lake Erie had always produced the largest and fastest growing Great Lakes herring. Fish collected after 1955 show a growth rate much slower than previous records either from Lake Erie or from the other Great Lakes.

The decline of the lake herring stemmed from a complex interaction of excess fishing capacity, behavioral irregularities of the fish population itself, interaction with other fish species, and water pollution. The second commercially important population to collapse was clearly due to overfishing. The lake whitefish was second only to the lake herring in importance in the Great Lakes. A large gill net, intended for the lake whitefish, came into widespread use in United States waters in the late 1920s. It was an efficient net capable of taking large numbers of immature whitefish. Although it was never permitted in Canadian waters, it was so effective that whitefish stocks were depleted far below those needed to maintain the population on a sustained basis.

It was outlawed by most jurisdictions between 1929 and the mid 1930s, but the damage had already been done. Whitefish catches fluctuated at a relatively high level in Lake Erie, but they had dropped by 1942 in the upper Great Lakes to roughly 1/10 of the catch in 1935 and 1/20 of the record of 1931 (Smith, 1968). There have been some very successful year classes subsequently but these have been the exception rather than the rule.

While excess fishing has been a factor for all of the fish populations that have collapsed in the Great Lakes, it is by no means the only important one and for some species it is not even the most important. The most valuable fish species was the lake trout. The most important factor in its demise in the upper Great Lakes was the invasion of the sea lamprey. The sea lamprey is native to Lake Ontario and other species of lampreys have been known in Lake Erie for many years (Van Meter and Trautman, 1970), but they were balanced with the other species in the community and hence caused no problem.

The sea lamprey was first reported in Lake Erie in 1921. It had evidently entered Lake Erie via the Welland Canal from Lake Ontario. It could spawn in a few of the rivers entering the two lower Great Lakes, but they were too warm to allow effective reproduction. The sea lamprey thus never reached very high populations in Lake Erie or Lake Ontario. However, once in Lake Erie it could spread rapidly through the upper Great Lakes. Their watersheds had clear cold streams that were ideal spawning grounds for it. The sea lamprey is a far more vicious predator than its naturally occurring relatives, and it preyed especially on the three largest populations inhabiting the lakes, namely the lake trout, the lake herring, and the lake whitefish. It was well established throughout the upper Great Lakes by the mid 1940s. After 1944 the lake trout population was so heavily infested with sea lamprey that it collapsed and neared extinction by the mid 1950s, with an almost complete failure of natural reproduction after 1948.

The sea lamprey provided the *coup de grace* for all of the large salmonid fishes. But these were more than commercially important species. They were also the keys to controlling the populations of the smaller fishes of the Great Lakes. These smaller fishes expanded as the larger fishes declined. The fish catch of the 1950s began to be dominated by fish such as catfish, perch, smelt, and small chubs, notably the species of chub known as the bloater. All are much smaller than the large salmonids, and their value per pound is much less.

Almost unnoticed, the alewife entered the upper Great Lakes in the 1930s. This is a small brackish-water fish quite common in coastal areas of North America. It is considered a valuable food fish in these areas and alewiving is a popular a sport on the Maine coast as smelting is in the Great Lakes. The alewife was first discovered in Lake Erie in 1931, but it never became common there because the shallowness of the lake means that the water in winter is relatively cold. Alewives do much better in deep lakes whose bottom waters have a constant temperature throughout the year. If Lake Erie was not a favorable habitat for the alewife, the upper Great Lakes were. This is especially true for Lake Michigan, whose waters are deep enough to offer the alewife refuge and are not as cold as those of Lake Superior. Even so, the alewife was held in check in the upper Great Lakes during the 1940s by the large salmonid carnivores. The decimation of the salmonid carnivores in Lakes Huron and Michigan have freed the alewife from interspecific population control, and they have expanded to nuisance proportions. The situation is somewhat different in Lake Superior because it is the coldest of the Great Lakes and because there are still large populations of predators.

In many ways the alewife represented as important a change in the food webs of the Great Lakes as the sea lamprey. It is an effective filter-feeder that competes directly with other fish low on the food chain. It is very gregarious and forms large schools that move throughout a lake and are remarkably efficient in removing plankton from the water.

The very high population density and wide-ranging movements of the alewife have had a pronounced effect on a large number of species. It seeks the warmest deep waters of the lake during the coldest part of the winter. This is the area that had been occupied by the small chub, *Leucichthys kiyi*. This chub was fairly abundant during the mid 1950s, but it had been reduced so much through competition with the alewife that it was practically extinct by 1965 (Smith, 1968). Great schools of alewives moved toward shore during the early spring and late fall through the areas occupied by the bloater. During the early 1960s the bloater had constituted the major chub in the commercial fish catch, but it declined rapidly to insignificance as the alewives increased.

The alewives move into very shallow waters during the late spring and summer, where they spawn during June and July (Wells, 1968). This had been the area occupied by the lake herring and certain other species of fishes. These two showed marked declines that were correlated with the alewife expansion. Even the rugged yellow perch, which originally showed a positive response to the increase in the alewife population, was forced into deeper water as the dense schools of alewives began to crowd the shore. It is possible that alewives provided an abundant food source for adult perch, but they also invaded the spawning grounds, causing a substantial disruption of perch reproduction. The result was a markedly increased perch catch during the early 1960s followed by a sharp decline by 1966 (Figure 4.20). Along with the perch, the American smelt declined sharply as the alewife expanded. It is likely that the smelt will not be damaged as much as the other species displaced by the alewife. It is still abundant

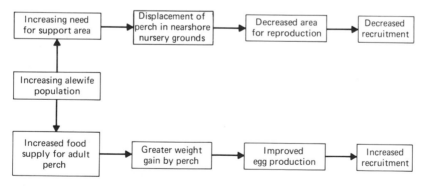

Figure 4.20 Interaction between alewives and perch in Lake Michigan during the early 1960s. Both pathways were operative throughout the period, but at different intensities. As long as alewife density was low, the lower pathway dominated, so that perch density increased and the population thrived. As the alewife population increased, however, the upper pathway became increasingly important and took a serious toll of the perch population.

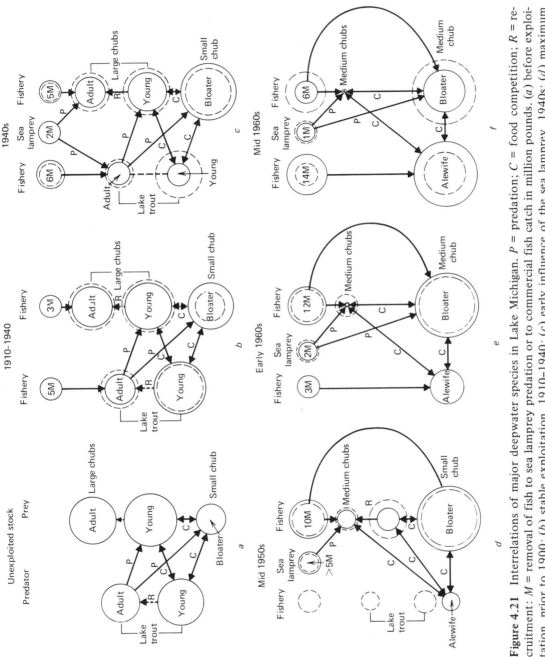

Figure 4.21 Interrelations of major deepwater species in Lake Michigan. *P* = predation; *C* = food competition; *R* = recruitment; *M* = removal of fish to sea lamprey predation or to commercial fish catch in million pounds. (*a*) before exploitation, prior to 1900; (*b*) stable exploitation, 1910–1940; (*c*) early influence of the sea lamprey, 1940s; (*d*) maximum abundance of the sea lamprey, 1950s; (*e*) maximum abundance of bloaters, early 1960s; (*f*) maximum abundance of the alewife, after mid-1960s. [Redrawn, with permission, from Smith, 1968, "Species Succession and Fishing Exploitation in the Great Lakes." *Journal of the Fisheries Research Board of Canada 25*: 667–693.]

in Lake Ontario, where the alewife has long been common, even though the other fishes displaced by the alewife are quite rare.

The fisheries of the Great Lakes have shown some remarkable changes over the last 50 years (Figure 4.21). This has been due to a combination of many factors including overfishing, pollution, and especially the invasion of several exotic species that changed the structure of interspecific interactions within the fish community. By 1960 the dominant species in the community had shifted from large predators such as the large salmonids to the parasitic sea lamprey and the planktivorous alewife.

It would be necessary to re-establish a large predator in order to control the alewife, but this had not been possible so long as the sea lamprey held its position within the community. However, it is now possible to control the sea lamprey. It spawns in certain streams and then swims into the open lake water. As the spawning streams became known, mechanical and electric weirs were used experimentally, followed by chemicals toxic to larval lampreys. The lamprey populations have declined. By the late 1960s it made sense to begin to attempt to re-establish salmonid predators in the Great Lakes (Lawrie, 1970). Several species have been introduced, notably the Coho and Chinook salmon, as well as the lake trout. There is some hope (Smith, 1968) that a combination of large salmonids, judicious management of the alewife, and careful management of those populations that yet inhabit the Great Lakes, can led to a re-establishment of a stable equilibrium that can be exploited in a useful way by people.

SOCIETY AND FISHERIES MANAGEMENT

This chapter has presented several case studies of fisheries in different parts of the world. All share certain characteristics. All are ecosystems exploited by humans without the intention of altering their basic characteristics. It is difficult to manipulate the oceans and large lakes, and what we do to them as ecosystems is almost never intentionally directed to improving the fishery. But society does affect fisheries, often dramatically, and almost always unintentionally. Sometimes these impacts are related to fishing, as with overfishing or the deliberate slaughter of the Lake Erie sturgeon. Often they are by-products of practices oriented toward other societal goals, as with the role of the Welland Canal in allowing the sea lamprey and the alewife to reach the upper Great Lakes or with water pollution in general.

A fishery represents an extreme type of human ecosystem in that there is so little direct intentional manipulation of the environment. Fish are totally wild animals, and virtually the only habitat modification that can be carried out is the creation of spawning beds by dumping old cars or other debris near shore, or deliberate fertilization of closely managed fishponds. Because fish live in water they are difficult to see, to measure, or to understand. They are not like a forest, where we can go out into the field and see immediately what is going on. Virtually the only information we have about a fishery comes from the commercial catch. This is a highly biased and unrepresentative source.

Planning in fishery management is difficult, especially when fishing grounds are in international waters. It is not always even clear what the objective of planning should be. Decisions on where and when to fish are made on the boat. Indeed, the decisions on the type of gear and what kinds of fish to fish for are made on the boat in most countries; the most notable exceptions are the highly centralized fleets of Japan and the Eastern European countries. Few other human ecosystems concentrate so much of the basic decision making in the hands of the individual manager, as opposed to society as a whole.

The societal domain in fisheries is very small. Institutions tend to be oriented much more toward fisheries research than policy formulation, and regulation of fishing operations has been very weak up until recently. International regulatory agencies exist for a few key fisheries such as whales and tuna, but these are the exceptions rather than the rule. They are also oriented toward single-species fisheries and have grown in response to problems of overfishing. Because these bodies are intergovernmental policy-making organizations, they act exceedingly slowly, and their decision-making authority is limited. The best example is the International Whaling Commission (IWC), which debated many years over the fate of the great whales, could not agree on what data were correct, and did not ban the capture of the most endangered species until 1979. A response to their ban has been the outfitting of a number of "pirate" whaling boats registered in countries that are not members of the IWC. The net result of the ban may be nil or even an increase in overall whale capture.

One of the most effective devices for fishery conservation is the recent adoption of 200-mile-wide economic zones or territorial limits by coastal nations. This allows countries to regulate fishing activities within those limits. While the contentions that have arisen over extended territorial limits are entirely of a "national self-interest" nature, they have often led to extreme measures. Numerous American tuna clippers have been taken into custody by the Equadorian and Peruvian Navies, and Iceland's enforcement of its territorial limit against British fishermen has resulted in frequent clashes between the Icelandic Coast Guard and the Royal Navy in what has been dubbed the "cod war." Nevertheless, these regulations have resulted in the assumption of real responsibility for fisheries management by one party and a reduction in the intensity of fishing.

The governmental and intergovernmental agencies that regulate fisheries have done little or nothing to control the intensity of fishing on an ecosystem level. Even the research being done tends to be oriented more toward populations than toward communities and ecosystems. Fishing is becoming increasingly intensive, with high-powered factory ships and world-ranging fishing expeditions that may last for a year or more. Our experiences with terrestrial ecosystems demonstrates that intensification of effort increases the impact of that effort and requires increasing amounts of information about all aspects of the system. This is doubly hard with fisheries, where we cannot even see the populations we are most interested in.

The management of fisheries will ultimately require social institutions attuned to the realities of fish populations and ecosystems as well as to managers who must make significant decisions outside the direct control of any high authority. Such institutions must be oriented to fishing areas such as the Georges Bank, the North Sea, or the upwelling zones of the east Pacific, and they must have a long-term view of the needs of the commercial fish, the fishermen, the markets, the financing of fishing expeditions, and all the biological and geophysical components in the fishery ecosystem. Thus far no such institutions exist. Effective, sustainable, intensive fishing is not likely until they are widespread.

References

Beverton, R. J. H., 1962. Long-term dynamics of certain North Sea fish populations. In LeCren, E. D., and Holdgate, M. W., eds., *The Exploitation of Natural Populations.* Oxford: Blackwell Scientific Pub., Ltd., 242–259.

Bigelow, H. B. and Schroeder, W. C., 1953. Fishes of the Gulf of Maine. *U.S. Fish Wildlife Serv. Fish. Bull.* **74.**

Borgstrom, G., 1961. New Methods of appraising the role of fisheries in world nutrition. *Fishing News International Magazine* (October, 1961): 33–38.

Carpenter, E. J. and Smith, K. L., 1972. Plastics on the Sargasso Sea surface. *Science* **175:** 1240–1241.

Clark, C. W., 1973. The economics of overexploitation. *Science* **181:** 630–634.

Cushing, D. H., 1969. Upwelling and fish production. *FAO Fish. Tech. Paper* **84:** 1–38.

Cushing, D. H., 1980. *Fisheries Biology: A Study in Population Dynamics.* 2nd ed. Madison: Univ. of Wisconsin Press.

Food and Agricultural Organization, 1972. *Atlas of the Living Resources of the Sea.* Rome: F.A.O.

Hardin, G., 1968. The tragedy of the commons. *Science* **162:** 1243–1248.

Lawrie, A. H., 1970. The sea lamprey in the Great Lakes. *Trans. Am. Fish. Soc.* **99:** 766–775.

Murphy, G. I., 1966a. Population biology of the Pacific sardine (*Sardinops caerulea*). *Proc. Calif. Acad. Sci.,* 4th ser., **34 (1):** 1–84.

Murphy, G. I., 1968b. Population dynamics and population estimation. In Calhoun, A., ed., *Inland Fisheries Management.* Sacramento: Calif. Dept. of Fish and Game.

Murphy, G. I., 1967. Vital statistics of the Pacific sardine (*Sardinops caerulea*) and the population consequences. *Ecology* **48:** 731–736.

Netboy, A., 1968. *The Atlantic Salmon: A Vanishing Species?* Boston: Houghton Mifflin Co.

Paulik, G. J., 1971. Anchovies, birds, and fishermen in the Peru current. In Murdoch, W. W., ed., *Environment.* Sunderland, Mass.: Sinauer Assoc., 156–185.

Regier, H. A. and Hartman, W. C., 1973. Lake Erie's fish community: 150 years of stress. *Science* **180:** 1248–1255.

Schaefer, M. B., 1957. A study of the dynamics of the fishery for yellowfin tuna in the eastern tropical Pacific Ocean. *Inter-American Trop. Tuna Comm. Bull.* **2 (6).**

Sette, O. E., 1960. The long-term historical record of meteorological, oceanographic, and biological data. *Calif. Coop. Oceanic Fish. Invest. Rept.* **VII:** 11–194.

Shelbourne, J. E., 1957. The feeding and condition of plaice larvae in good and bad plankton patches. *J. Mar. Biol. Ass. U.K.* **36:** 539–552.

Smith, S. H., 1968. Species succession and fishery exploitation in the Great Lakes. *J. Fish. Res. Bd. Canada* **25:** 667–693.

Van Meter, H. D. and Trautman, M. B., 1970. An annotated list of the fishes of Lake Erie and its tributary waters exclusive of the Detroit River. *Ohio Jour. Sci.* **70:** 65–78.

Van Oosten, J., 1930. The disappearance of the Lake Erie cisco—a preliminary report. *Trans. Am. Fish. Soc.* **60**: 204–214.

Watt, K. E. F., 1968. *Ecology and Natural Resource Management.* New York: McGraw-Hill Book Company.

Wells, L., 1968. Seasonal depth distribution of fish in southeastern Lake Michigan. *U.S. Fish Wildlife Serv. Fish. Bull.* **67**: 1–15.

5/wilderness, wildlife, and forestry

Human ecosystems span a continuum from those on which people make virtually no impact to those that are completely controlled for human use. This chapter looks at the lower end of the spectrum. Human impact on the landscape is relatively small; little or no attempt is made to change it to a more "useful" configuration. Organized intervention in the environment ranges over a relatively small spectrum from simple use to deliberate management of existing resources.

WILDERNESS AND RESERVE AREAS

The least touched ecosystems are those of wilderness. It is probably inaccurate to say that these are untouched, because there are virtually no places on earth where no person has ever walked, and there are certainly no places that have not been exposed to anthropogenic air pollutants or pesticides carried by the wind. But there are many places that are almost as they were before people reached them, and many societies are trying hard to maintain at least some of this land as wilderness.

The essence of wilderness is purity and naturalness. This is commonly taken to mean that the land is as it was before the arrival of high technology human society. There are no roads, and what footpaths exist make a minimal imprint on the landscape. Such ecosystems either show a steady state or their communities change in a continuous cycle. Both situations reflect a natural balance among the dynamic forces represented by the community and the abiotic components of the ecosystem.

There is a conceptual difference between wilderness and a natural ecosystem. The former is a cultural notion implying a lack of manipulation by people; the latter is an ecological notion referring to a particular structure of ecosystem. It is true that wilderness is a natural ecosystem, just as it is true that all ecosystems could be described as wilderness before about the Mesolithic. But certain areas may be subject to intense management for a while and then abandoned. After a period of time they return to a natural state through the well-known phenomenon of ecological succession. One can walk through many a lovely old second-growth forest in New England and suddenly stumble upon a stone wall built during a time when the land had been cleared and farmed. Many areas have been logged and have grown back to their natural state. Whether such areas are wilderness or not is perhaps a moot point. Most parts of the world have been places of human habitation for so long that the only natural ecosystems left are those that have been abandoned and returned to their nature state via succession. Many countries have special legislation allowing them to preserve wilderness areas. The argument that wilderness must be pure has been used as the basis of refusing preservation to secondarily natural areas for wilderness uses.

Wilderness is not a type of ecosystem. It is an expression of a type of land use. As such, it represents society's commitment to preserve certain areas in their natural state even if conflicting uses are possible. This implies that society considers wilderness as "the highest and best use" for at least some land. What does this mean? Numerous value judgments are tied up with land use, and one must be careful to separate those value judgments from things that represent hard reality. The judgments include matters like the "highest and best use for a piece of land." The hard reality includes the nature of the ecosystem in a given location, or its resource complement.

The most common basis for choosing a given land use is the profit generated by that use. There are some cultural differences about how profit is measured, but the principle is recognized in capitalist, socialist, and mixed economies. The direct costs of different forms of land use are relatively easy to measure, although some of the external costs are not so easy. The direct benefits of economic land uses are measurable. But numerous land uses also have external benefits whose measurement tends to be even more difficult than their external costs. There is no direct economic benefit to wilderness; all of its benefits are indirect. Placing a monetary value on it is virtually impossible, and if wilderness is to be preserved it must be because society wants to preserve it.

We often hear of bringing new lands into "productive use." Most parts of the world have the majority of their land neither under the plow nor urbanized (Table 5.1). The undeniable truth is that the lands that are developed first are those most economically suited to early development. The lands that are not developed are marginal. Any discussion of ecosystems that are not intensively exploited by man must necessarily include some discussion of land use. Being suited in this context implies that whatever use is proposed can be sustained over a long period of time. This is nothing more than the extension of the sustainable yield principle to land. If the use cannot be sustained, then it is probably not economically sound, much less ecologically sound.

It is often difficult to judge whether or not a proposed land use can be sustained. An unequivocal answer is feasible, at least in principle. When the use can be sustained, we then run into the murkier question of whether the proposed use *should* be sustained in the area. Several alternatives are almost always available. If one of the alter-

Table 5.1   Patterns of Land Use in Selected Countries.

	Land Use (thousands of hectares)					
	T	A	P	M	F	O
Africa						
Algeria (1970)	238,174	6,240	552	37,416	2,424	191,542
Egypt (1972)	100,145	2,723	129	–	2	97,291
Ivory Coast (1971)	31,800	7,807	1,080	8,000	12,000	3,359
South Africa (1960)	122,104	11,578	480	90,390	4,105	15,551
North America						
Canada (1971)	922,107	–43,767–		24,896	443,094	485,857
Mexico (1970)	197,255	25,776	1,693	69,789	18,478	86,470
United States (1969)	912,689	189,283	1,770	244,277	212,457	208,525
South America						
Argentina (1968)	277,689	23,851	2,177	144,947	62,700	44,014
Brazil (1970)	845,651	26,047	8,035	107,274	517,936	191,905
Colombia (1970)	103,870	3,596	1,458	17,084	51,251	40,502
Asia						
Bangladesh (1968)	14,227	– 9,069–		600	2,242	2,366
China (1971)	959,696	–127,000–		200,000	118,000	514,696
India (1971)	328,048	161,340	4,340	13,000	65,930	40,660
Turkey (1971)	77,076	24,978	2,636	26,135	18,273	6,036
Europe						
France (1970)	54,703	17,417	1,684	13,934	14,013	7,655
Poland (1972)	30,468	14,844	303	4,224	8,553	3,344
Sweden (1972)	41,148	–3,031–		703	22,713	18,528
USSR (1972)	2,240,220	227,500	4,931	375,300	910,009	722,480
Oceania						
Australia (1971)	768,685	44,605	166	454,768	37,938	231,208
Papua-New Guinea (1970)	46,169	102	329	89	37,000	8,649

T   Total land area.
A   All land used for temporary crops.
P   Land in permanent crops including perennials crops that do not need to be replanted for some time after initial planting.
M   Permanent meadows and pastures.
F   Forested land.
O   Other land, including urban land, wasteland, parks, roads.
Data from FAO, 1974.

natives involves very low-intensity development or no development at all, a decision maker must be able to weigh monetary and nonmonetary values in his assessment.

The demands a society makes on its resources change as its population grows and moves and as its values change. Most land uses can be altered fairly rapidly. Wilderness cannot. Its value is its pristine state, and this is lost forever once the wilderness is converted to some other use. Even to recreate a natural ecosystem through ecological succession requires waiting between 50 and 200 years following the abandonment of economic land use. It is impossible to alter the wilderness characteristics of an area but retain its basic wilderness value without having to wait for ecological succession to take place. This requires a planning horizon about ten times as long as is normal in land use planning. When wilderness is abundant it may not matter much if people make basic land use decisions quickly. But when it is rare, the most efficient decision-making processes in the world cannot overcome the fact that the response time of the environment is set unalterably by natural succession, or that the end product of that succession is a secondary climax and not virgin wilderness.

Wilderness preservation in a developed country thus requires a commitment to the future and an explicit analysis of the tradeoffs between land uses of various levels of intensity in and around the proposed wilderness preservation area. This level of planning is not common in most countries.

Values of Wilderness and Reserved Areas

The values of wilderness that would normally be included in the planning process are many. Some are quantifiable in some form or other, and some can even be expressed in monetary terms. Wilderness areas serve as sources of new organisms or strains of organisms that may have human application. Sometimes such new strains turn out to be very useful. The most dramatic example of an organism that had never been consciously cultivated and was even regarded as somewhat of a pest, but turned out to be of tremendous importance to human health, is the bread mold *Penicillium,* the source of the drug penicillin. Obscure strains of fish have been found to be useful agents for controlling mosquitoes in the seasonal lakes and drainage ditches of the deserts of New Mexico (Miller, 1968). Some wild animals may be much more efficient at converting forage into meat than domestic livestock. Game ranchers in southern Africa can produce more meat per hectare with a balanced mixture of native animals, with less damage to the overall environment, and at a lower cost than other ranchers in the same area growing cattle and other species of domesticated livestock (Dasmann, 1964a; Pollock, 1969). Bison on the western ranges of North America, once hunted almost into extinction, seem also to be able to produce more meat per hectare than domestic cattle (Nelson, 1965). The raw materials for numerous drugs and pharmaceuticals are found only in tropical forests (Myers, 1979).

Wilderness is a vital resource for scientific research. It comprises the only set of large undisturbed ecosystems left in the world today. Many basic scientific studies, notably in ecology, require undisturbed areas. This has been a major consideration in land use management in a number of countries. For example, parts of national parks in Canada have not been developed even to the point of providing trails for hikers, and hikers are specifically discouraged from entering these areas at all. A portion of the lakes district of western Ontario has been set aside as a limnological study area. There is a large number of lakes of rather different characteristics in this area, and it is possible to perform both observational and experimental ecology in this setting. Natural areas provide benchmarks (Moir, 1972) for what the landscape was like before intensive human intervention began.

Perhaps the most obvious justification for the preservation of wilderness is recreation. It is undeniably true that modern human society operates in a highly tense environment, and a quiet place for contemplation is useful and necessary for large numbers of people. Henry David Thoreau proclaimed that "in wilderness is the preservation of the world." Many people depend on sojourns into the wilderness to recoup a sense of who they are and where they are going. Even for those who do not actually enter natural areas, simply being aware that they exist can contribute to a sense of personal value. The most eloquent exponent of the relationship between wilderness and personal well-being was the late Aldo Leopold. His "A Land Ethic" (Leopold, 1949) is a classic and beautiful statement of it.

Wilderness areas are often remarkably practical. Cities often rely on wild tracts to insure the stability of some part of the overall urban system, especially its water supply. Many cities in the world are built in areas that depend on superficial groundwater to sustain the demand for water. This is notably true in well-watered areas where natural lakes are rare and the bedrock is impervious to groundwater motion. Examples include Hawaii, the Caribbean, and volcanic islands in general. In order to maintain the groundwater supply these areas have set aside broad areas of land (Figure 5.1). This is not because they are beautiful (although they generally are), nor is it because they are wild. It is because their soils provide the only water storage capacity in the area. Development of the reserved areas would mean reduction, contamination, or even failure of the city water supply. Even low-intensity development would result in increased runoff, compaction of soil, and increased erosion. Urbanization would bring construction of roads, lawns, and other relatively impervious surfaces. Water that would normally have seeped into the ground would now run off into the nearest stream or sewer, where it would be carried to the sea. Even if intensive development of recreation areas did not increase the runoff rate, the sheer increase in the number of visitors would tend to increase the probability of fire. Few things have a more pronounced short-term effect on soil capacity, permeability, and erosion potential than deforestation from severe fire.

Reserved areas may also be important for maintenance of water supplies in regions that depend on reservoirs rather than groundwater for their water storage. Runoff rates tend to be relatively high in arid regions. If all else were equal this would be good, because runoff is a major source of supply for rivers, and hence for reservoirs. But all else is not equal. As water runs off it also erodes the soil over which it runs, so that sediment as well as water is carried to the reservoir. As a general rule there is a strong negative correlation between the amount of vegetation in an area and the erosion rate. The more vegetation, the less soil erosion for a given amount of runoff, and vice versa.

The surest way to encourage maximum vegetation density, especially in arid areas, is to limit human contact. This limits soil compaction and reduces fire, both of which are inimical to vegetation growth. Water supply management in arid areas must do everything possible to reduce soil erosion. This can be a very significant problem, and a reservoir may fill rapidly with sediment washed into it during heavy rains. This problem may be compounded by fire, especially considering that many arid areas are popu-

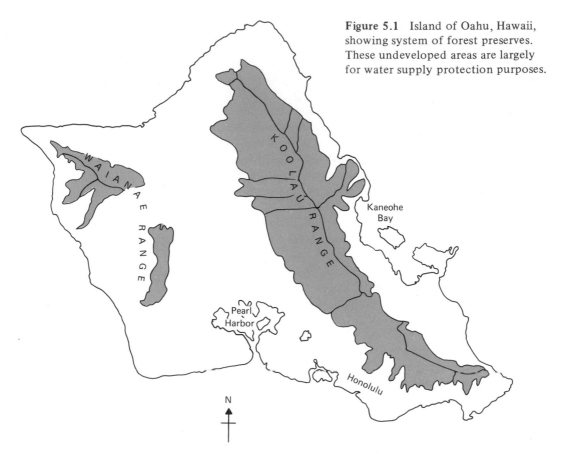

Figure 5.1 Island of Oahu, Hawaii, showing system of forest preserves. These undeveloped areas are largely for water supply protection purposes.

lated by a number of fire prone species (Mutch, 1970). Fire removes whatever erosion protection a soil may have had.

Figure 5.2 shows Mono Reservoir in California. This artificial lake was built to provide protection from siltation for Gibraltar Reservoir, the main water supply reservoir for the city of Santa Barbara. Gibraltar Reservoir, completed in 1920, had been filling with silt for several years, and it had become obvious by the early 1930s that its capacity would be lost by the end of the decade. It took only 2 years for Mono Reservoir to silt up completely. This formerly protective reservoir became open woodland within 10 years. In the meantime it had become necessary to build Gibraltar Dam higher than it had been, and even this did not stop water shortages through the 1940s. The much larger Cachuma Dam and Reservoir downstream from Gibraltar Dam was begun in 1948 to meet the water needs of Santa Barbara.

To be sure, Santa Barbara is in a very unfortunate position for water supply. The chaparral vegetation characteristic of this part of southern California is extraordinarily fire prone, so that deforestation and high rates of runoff, erosion, and siltation are very common. The situation was more serious here than in other parts of the world because the reservoirs involved were small and the demand for water was high. But all reservoirs in dry areas, be they big or small, and regardless of what country they happen to be located in, are subject to the same general kinds of problems as the reservoirs of Santa Barbara. The easiest and cheapest way to minimize erosion in the watershed is

Figure 5.2 Mono Reservoir in California: (*a*) 1938, when the reservoir was silted in; (*b*) 1949, after succession to open woodland. [Photographs courtesy U.S. Forest Service.]

a

b

to preserve it in natural vegetation. When this is possible, and it may be very difficult in fire prone areas, it can act as an efficient filter for runoff water and an effective sedimentation trap.

WILDLIFE MANAGEMENT

The considerations noted above all constitute valid reasons for maintaining reserve areas. But they are not the main reasons that wilderness is preserved in most parts of the world. The most common rationale is for fish and game purposes. Even people who are neither fishermen nor hunters can respond to fish and game as being of demonstrable usefulness.

Wildlife management shares some characteristics with fishery management. Like fish, game animal populations are not intensively and deliberately manipulated by human's but the sustainable yield depends on hunters' or game managers' awareness of the biological requirements of the populations and their responses to exploitation.

The biggest difference is that habitat plays a more central role in wildlife management than in fisheries. There are very few ways in which a manager can intervene directly to manipulate an aquatic habitat. The important habitat variables for fisheries relate to patterns of pollution, oxygenation, thermal stratification, and so on. The terrestrial environment is much more complex. Individual populations, especially of large woody plants, have a role in molding it in ways for which there is no analogue in streams, lakes, or the ocean. Terrestrial environments in most countries are subject to property law, so that land uses may change over relatively small areas because different people own the land.

Habitat is the key to wildlife conservation. Even if the intensity of hunting and the age distribution of exploitation are attuned to the needs of a game population, that population cannot survive unless its habitat needs are met. The physical and biological structure of the environment must permit or encourage the existence of the desired wildlife species, and the designated range must be large enough to support it. Even if an area has all of the characteristics required by a wildlife species, the population cannot survive if the area is not big enough to support the normal ecological unit, be it a herd or a dispersed population of minimal size. If the summer feeding grounds are ideal but the winter feeding grounds are inadequate, the population will be limited by the winter feeding grounds. Some species may be able to survive in a relatively small area. The large game that tend to be valued most highly such as moose, caribou, and mountain goat need quite large basic ranges. Predators such as wolf, grizzly bear, or mountain lion require larger areas yet.

There is often a basic conflict between the environmental geography of wildlife populations and the geographic thinking of society. The ecological needs of the wildlife represent the end result of several million years of evolution, and they are not very likely to change. All populations show minimum ranges that need not correspond to political boundaries. These ranges tend to increase in size both as the animal gets larger and as it gets higher in the food chain. For example, extensive studies have been carried out on the wolf–deer interaction in Algonquin Provincial Park, Ontario. In both places the density of wolves is roughly one wolf per 25 sq. km. Isle Royale is an island in Lake Superior where moose are the only large ungulate prey population for the world. Moose density is roughly 1.15 moose per sq. km. (Mech, 1966). In Algonquin Park deer are the overwhelming abundant ungulate, although some moose are present. Deer density is roughly 5 per sq. km. (Pimlott et al. 1969).

This does not mean that preservation of a square kilometer or two of otherwise suitable habitat is sufficient for survival of moose or deer. What must be maintained is not a few individuals, but rather the minimum breeding population. In principle, we could estimate the size of a minimum breeding population and multiply it by the area requirement per individual in the population to calculate a minimum species range.

This is probably adequate for solitary animals. But for gregarious animals like the wolf, the important factor is the average range per pack and the degree of overlap between the territories of different groupings.

Figure 5.3 shows the distribution of territories maintained by wolf packs on Isle Royale. These included several small packs of 2-3 individuals, the "big pack" of about 10-15 individuals, and several lone wolves. Some lone wolves maintained territories separate from that of the big pack, while others followed the big pack and fed on the remainder of its kills (Mech, 1966). Studies on wolves in other parts of North America make it clear that the pack habit is the norm and that the average pack size varies between 6 and 10 individuals (Pimlott et al, 1969). This implies that to maintain a single pack of wolves requires the maintenance of a continuous wolf habitat on the order of 150 to 300 sq. km. A stable population of wolves can exist only if the pack can survive as a unit. The same holds for all other animals that exist in assemblages.

In principle, the problem is less complicated for populations that are dispersed throughout the environment. Clearly, each animal must have a continuous range large enough for its survival, but it may not be necessary for the range of the entire population to be continuous, at least all of the time. How uniform an environment must be depends, obviously, on the biology of the species. If its behavioral adaptations are based on continuous range, then it does not matter that the animal is not a herding animal. A continuous range of adequate size must exist.

Ecological Succession and Types of Wildlife

The question of wildlife is often clouded by the number of qualitatively different types of animals that may exist in any one place. For example, muskrats live in New York's East River. There are more deer just north of New York City in suburban Westchester County today than there were when Europeans arrived. On the other hand, many species of large game, such as the caribou or the bighorn sheep, are in danger of becoming extinct even in habitats far from population centers. We cannot make sweeping statements about wildlife in general. We must speak rather in terms of specific types.

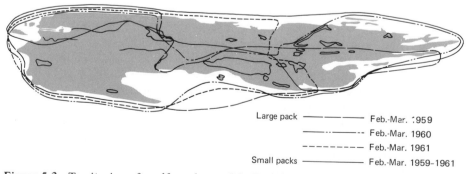

Large pack	———————	Feb.-Mar. 1959
	———··——··	Feb.-Mar. 1960
	- - - - - - -	Feb.-Mar. 1961
Small packs	———————	Feb.-Mar. 1959–1961

Figure 5.3 Territories of wolf packs on Isle Royale National Park, Michigan. [After Mech, 1966.]

Perhaps the most useful organizing concept for wildlife at this point is the concept of ecological succession. Some species are climax species and depend on a climax habitat for their survival, while other species require disturbed conditions. Climax ecosystems were once widespread, but development has been eating away at them for many years. As the habitat is changed, the basis for the maintenance of the climax species disappears as well. At the same time, as climax areas are destroyed they are replaced by preclimax environments that may be maintained in a preclimax state by human activity. Some of the animals adapted to preclimax environments, such as deer and several game birds, are quite valuable and they adapt well to a certain amount of manipulation of the environment. Indeed, they show a pronounced benefit both from society's maintenance of an early succession ecosystem and from its tendency to reduce the population density of predators.

Figure 5.4 shows the development of a herd of Columbian black-tailed deer inhabiting the chaparral region of Lake County, California, during the four years following a wildfire burn (Taber and Dasmann, 1957). The normal level of deer for the area was about 4.5 per sq. km., or about 3,000 for the 675 sq. km. study area. Following the burn there was a dense sprouting from living root crowns, as well as a rapid germination of seeds in the ashy soil. The young tender browse was ideal food for deer. Deer whose normal home range was outside the burn entered the burned area, in addition to the herd already present. This was reflected in a marked population increase for the area. Because of the high quality of the diet in the burned area, reproduction was better than in unburned areas, further accentuating the high population density. The beneficial effects of the burn are shown for about two years, after which the herd declined to its normal level.

In the chaparral discussed by Taber and Dasmann (1957) the cycle following a burn is about four years. The same pattern is shown in forested areas (Dasmann, 1964b), but the period of the cycle is longer because ecological succession is slower. The underlying force is the same: removal of older vegetation stimulates high-quality browse, which in turn stimulates the growth of deer. Burning is the most common underlying factor for the pattern in nature, but any factor that establishes open places and stimulates sun-loving early-successional plants may show the same pattern. Many kinds of land use may have this effect, including fire, logging, recreational development, and even minor suburbanization.

Let us contrast the behavior of deer populations with the behavior of a climax population in a changing environment. Wells Gray Provincial Park is a wilderness park in the Cariboo Mountains of the Canadian Rockies of British Columbia. Before 1926 it was a complex tapestry of glaciated mountains, mature cedar-hemlock forest in the lower elevations, and subalpine spruce-fir forest and alpine meadows at higher elevations. In 1926 a fire began south of the park and burned over 500 sq. km. of the mature lowland forest. The burn was a very severe one, destroying humus as well as vegetation. Recolonization was by fast-growing deciduous vegetation such as aspen, willow, and birch. The climax cedar-hemlock forest had not reestablished itself after 3 decades.

Woodland caribou had been the chief large ungulate in the park before the fire. Mule deer inhabited the more open forests in the drier portions of the park but avoided the mature forest except to travel through it. Cougar and coyotes were found along with deer, and the coyotes often ventured to the alpine meadows where mice were

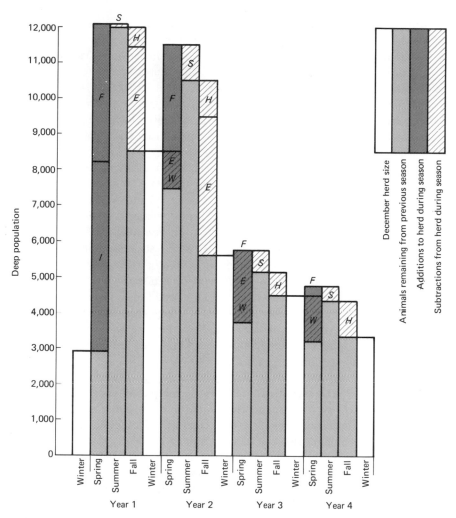

Figure 5.4 Schematic diagram of the dynamics of a deer herd in the chaparral region of California following a burn which killed all above-ground plants. The herd is followed for four years after the burn, after which time the habitat has essentially reestablished itself. The best single index of changes in the population size is the December herd size (white bars). E = emigration from the burned area; F = fawn drop; H = hunting, crippling, and miscellaneous fall losses; I = influx to burned area from surrounding areas; S = summer mortality; W = winter mortality.

easy prey. Wolverines, marten, beavers, and small numbers of black and grizzly bears were found in the forests. Moose were unknown and wolves were rare.

For a few years after the fire only mice and deer could be found browsing in the burned areas. As the early-successional aspen, willow, and birch became established, deer and mice underwent a spectacular increase followed by cougar and coyotes. Beavers and black bears also found new food and flourished. The first moose were wanderers that entered the park in the early 1930s. They increased quickly to very high densities by 1945; wolves increased apace. This new type of community remained for at least the next decade.

The fires that had allowed these increases in deer, moose, and their fellows had destroyed 60% to 70% of the winter range of the caribou, which required mature forest for the lichens and browse that were their winter staples. Another 450 sq. km. of lowland forests burned in a series of fires during the 1930s, so that only three restricted areas of mature forest were available for winter caribou range by 1940. The herd had declined noticably as a result, and its survival requires habitat maintenance as a major component of any management scheme.

The simple correlation between habitat destruction and decline of the caribou herd does not demonstrate that a straightforward relationship exists between them, much less indicate why the relationship exists. Indirect effects are also present and they may be more significant than the direct relationships. As pointed out by Bergerud (1974), lichens may constitute their favored food supply, but caribou can lose weight when provided with only lichens and can survive without them. Habitat destruction limits the favored food supply and this limitation may be an important factor in the decline of the population, but it is neither a necessary nor a sufficient condition for this decline. In Wells Gray Provincial Park the change in habitat led indirectly to an increase in the wolf population. The wolves preyed mainly on moose, but they were fully capable of taking caribou that happened to be in the area. This seems to have been more important to the maintenance of Wells Gray caribou at reduced levels than the simpler changes in vegetation occasioned by the fire.

Many populations occupy several habitats. Some may be relatively easy to preserve; others may represent weak links in the overall chain. The best examples of these involve migratory waterfowl, which may fly many thousands of miles along well-developed flyways (Figure 5.5). The nesting grounds at each end of the flyway may be fairly well defined and easy to maintain. However, the birds must be able to rest in order to make the trip. They need ponds or lakes at strategic intervals along the way. But such wetlands may not be considered desirable commodities by the average farmer or real estate developer. Vast numbers of swamps and small ponds have been filled in for conversion to agricultural fields or subdivisions. As the area of shallow wetlands has declined, the entire migrating population has become concentrated in the remaining wetlands, until these have become key limiting factors for the waterfowl populations. The crowding that accompanies conversion of wetlands can be detrimental to migratory species both by increasing the pressure on the wetland ecosystem and by increasing the vulnerability of the crowded population to hunting pressure.

In principle, it is possible to maintain wildlife refuges along the flyways to insure an adequate number of resting stations for migrating birds. In practice, it is difficult to obtain adequate wetland within the public sector. Even if this is possible, it is difficult to provide adequate protection for the migrating birds. Not only must there be adequate resting grounds; there must also be enough of a buffer zone around the pond that the birds who use it are not sitting ducks, as it were, to hunters. It is not uncommon during hunting season for hunters to gather by the thousands around certain refuges and kill great numbers of birds as they rise off the ponds to continue their flight. In many cases the birds fall inside the refuge, where they cannot be retrieved, and thus are wasted (Sherwood, 1970).

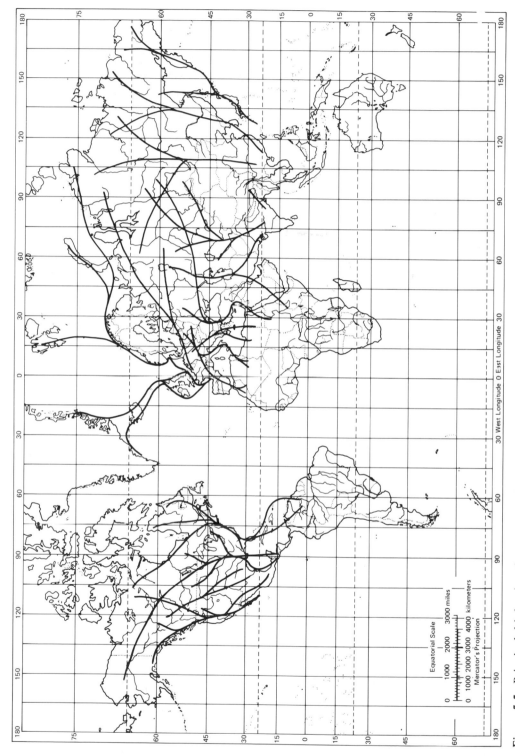

Figure 5.5 Principal bird migration routes of the Northern Hemisphere. [After J. Dorst, *The Migration of Birds*. Copyright © 1961 by Houghton Mifflin Co., and William Heinemann Ltd. Map Copyright © 1939 by the University of Chicago Press.

Wildlife, Parks, and Ecological Units

A wildlife management planning program should deal with entire communities and the resource base upon which they depend. The planner should consider the behavior of each species, especially in terms of feeding and migration patterns. Territories of different individuals of different species commonly overlap each other, and the ranges of different species tend not to coincide. The maintenance of the community therefore requires the maintenance of a continuous range sufficiently large to include the minimum required ranges of all populations in the community. This is a difficult requirement, and there are few areas in the world where it can be met. Even the great national parks of North America and Africa are smaller than the minimum area necessary for an ecological unit, and their boundaries represent political compromises rather than ecological understanding.

The special problems of maintaining ecological units in a natural state are probably best exemplified by the great national parks in the savanna zone of East Africa. These form a chain of natural areas running from Kenya to South Africa, as shown in Figure 5.6. Some of these parks are very large. Yellowstone, the largest park in the United States, has an area of 23,000 sq. km. Kenya's Tsavo and Zambia's Kafue are both greater than 55,000 sq. km. Kruger National Park in South Africa is 48,000 sq. km., and Serengeti has an area of 40,000 sq. km. As with all political entities, the boundaries of the parks were not based on a thorough study of the populations that inhabited them, but are rather a reflection of the political considerations that were needed in order to set up the parks in the first place.

The animals in these parks are savanna animals. They evolved in response to an open environment and they are adapted to ranging over large areas. The savanna is an extremely variable environment, with pronounced wet and dry seasons. Many species have well-developed migration patterns extending over hundreds of kilometers. Many parks have shown profound changes in their faunal makeup since they were established, when, among other things, the presence of a fence or agricultural zone around the perimeter blocked traditional migration routes of animals that had "always" lived there (Myers, 1972a,b). Lake Manyara in Tanzania had been characterized by large herds of wildebeest and zebra, as well as large stands of acacia trees, before it was established as a reserve in the early 1960s. The zebras and the wildebeests are now rare, since their natural migration routes are blocked. Elephant populations have skyrocketed throughout Tsavo and other parks of savanna Africa, where they are destroying great quantities of acacia trees. Myers (1972b) points to dramatic differences in vegetation inside and outside the national parks that are due to destruction of trees inside the parks by the many elephants. The parks, where elephants are protected, is open savanna; outside, where they are not, is thick brush. It is very difficult to say which has been more modified by human decisions and activities.

If the most meaningful geographic basis for a population is its range, then the most useful geographic basis for the community is the *ecological unit*. This is the minimum area that is still large enough to provide an adequate basis for all of the populations making up the community. It includes all seasons' ranges for those species in the community with seasonal ranges, and it is large enough to provide a minimim sized habitat for all of the species in the area. It is unlikely that the area will be homogeneous, as very few populations in a community inhabit precisely the same habitat, and different populations show considerable overlap in range.

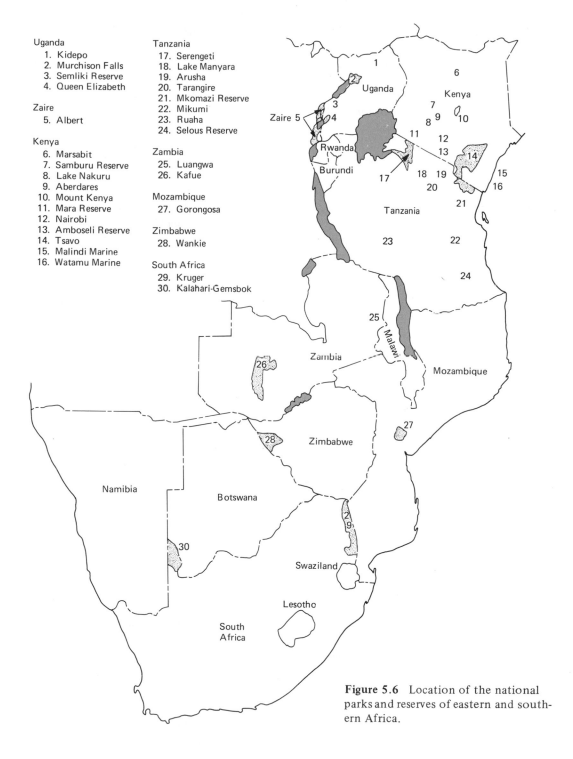

Uganda
1. Kidepo
2. Murchison Falls
3. Semliki Reserve
4. Queen Elizabeth

Zaire
5. Albert

Kenya
6. Marsabit
7. Samburu Reserve
8. Lake Nakuru
9. Aberdares
10. Mount Kenya
11. Mara Reserve
12. Nairobi
13. Amboseli Reserve
14. Tsavo
15. Malindi Marine
16. Watamu Marine

Tanzania
17. Serengeti
18. Lake Manyara
19. Arusha
20. Tarangire
21. Mkomazi Reserve
22. Mikumi
23. Ruaha
24. Selous Reserve

Zambia
25. Luangwa
26. Kafue

Mozambique
27. Gorongosa

Zimbabwe
28. Wankie

South Africa
29. Kruger
30. Kalahari-Gemsbok

Figure 5.6 Location of the national parks and reserves of eastern and southern Africa.

In a sense, the concept of the ecological unit is self-evident. An ecosystem responds to the signals imposed on it by society, and it is not possible for a society to do nothing. Even as innocent an action as drawing a line on a map is a powerful signal if the line is the boundary of a park; it can exclude species that used to be common, as with the wildebeest and zebra of Manyara, and it can bring total discontinuities of vegetation such as those caused by the elephants of Tsavo. Wildlife communities are extraordinarily dynamic, and preservation requires that management recognize the forces that link organisms and their environment. Where the conservation area approximates an ecological unit the problem is small. Management can be of a hands off sort, and nature will take care of itself. But where the ecological unit is larger than the political unit a laissez faire attitude is not sufficient, and definite steps must be taken to counter the problems generated within the community and retain the pre-existing balance.

This is not to say that a laissez faire attitude will not lead to some balance; it simply will not and cannot be the natural one. It may sound paradoxical to maintain that a hands off attitude can lead to an ecosystem structure less natural than an intensive management approach, but it is not. Wildlife management, like that of any human ecosystem, depends on numerous decisions. Once a set of management goals is chosen, and the area is chosen for the goals to be applied, the die is cast. The goals may be to maintain the pre-existing natural order, but they need not be. The only constraint is that the goals be sustainable under feasible management practices. The dynamics of the interaction among populations need to be understood sufficiently well that management strategies can be worked out. This means recognizing when the usual controls on population growth no longer apply—or are too effective—and designing remedial measures of thinning or enhancing. It means recognizing when migration routes are blocked and designing artificial relocation schemes. It may be necessary to manipulate populations of competitors or predators of a particular species, or it may be necessary to alter physical aspects of the habitat.

Intervention on this level may strike many people as being inappropriate and somehow "unecological." Such an argument would carry a lot of force if the management goals were for something other than a natural ecosystem. But the experience of the great national parks of East Africa shows clearly that wildlife cannot coexist in a natural state with man unless people take the responsibility to counteract the side effects of their presence.

It does not matter whether the critical decision is the deliberate imposition of specific management goals or practices, or whether it is the seemingly benign act of drawing a line on a map. Both have their impact. The issue is nothing less than the basic point of the study of human ecosystems. Policies made by society, and the management acts of individuals, result in changes to the environment. The dynamic interactions among domains are often difficult to predict. The sustainability of a given ecosystem depends on the behavior balance among the various domains, and requires that society have sufficient feeling for the realities of the natural environment that it designs policies and management activities to preserve the dynamic balance.

FORESTRY

Perhaps the most intensive use of otherwise unmanaged land is forestry. Forest management practices span a range from maintaining almost natural conditions to practices that cause complete devastation of the landscape. Timber and pulpwood constitute the largest economic justification for keeping land in a relatively undeveloped state. The largest areas of forests in the private sector are owned by lumber and paper companies. Even within the public sector, many lands are held in a quasi-natural state mainly so that trees can be harvested, with royalties reverting to the public treasury.

Most types of ecosystem exploitation are characterized by a narrow range of land-use practices in a given area. Fishermen, for example, fish a given body of water in roughly the same way. Farmers tend to use similar methods to produce a particular crop within a given area. But this is not true of forestry. Widely different practices may be carried out by different operators, ranging from very intense to low-key. The entire gradient may represent economically and ecologically sound forestry ventures, depending on details of the operation. Some types of forestry operations encourage other uses that can mesh with forestry activities. The reason for the diversity is that a typical forest takes many years to develop, and this is followed by a rapid harvesting phase.

The income from the forest itself is shown schematically in Figure 5.7. It is zero during the growth period of the trees, and it reaches a sharp maximum when the trees are cut. During much of this cycle, however, the forest can be used for many other things such as game reserves or recreational areas. These alternative uses can contribute to income from the forest during the growth phase, but committing land to multiple use may also increase the costs of the growth phase or delay the beginning of harvesting. A tradeoff is thus implicit in multiple use, and it may be evaluated differently by public and private managers. Private landowners are more likely to consider it in strictly economic terms, so that they favor minimizing the cost of alternative uses and minimizing deferral of harvest. Public officials, on the other hand, are more likely to weigh the tradeoffs in political terms. It is worth emphasizing the alternative uses, which tend to be low-income high-mass-appeal activities, and planning tree harvests on grounds that consider factors in addition to their value as economic resources. This may mean delaying or proscribing tree harvesting, or cutting at a rate much higher than the ecologically sustainable rate in order to control consumer prices for wood.

In either case, the major income is by the sale of lumber and pulpwood. Income

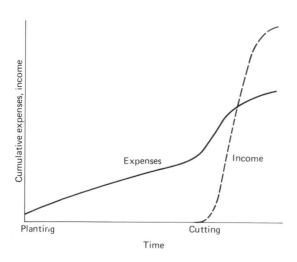

Figure 5.7 Schematic representation of cumulative expenses and income over a forestry cycle from planting to cutting. The expenses stem from minimal maintenance costs, taxes, and debt service. Expenses rise sharply with cutting and its associated overhead, but income rises much more sharply.

from other uses of the land as the forest is developing, such as permits for hunting, fishing or camping, count on the positive side of the ledger, but they are less important. Regardless of the forest management technique used, taxes must be paid on private land, and buildings and equipment on the land must be maintained. All other costs are variable costs. They include all efforts made to increase the productivity of the forest, such as thinning, fertilization, pest management, or species manipulation. If multiple use management is carried out, then the costs of allowing the alternative uses must be paid.

There are other considerations as well. For example, it is easier and cheaper to harvest a lot of trees from a small area than it is to harvest the same number of trees spread out over a much wider area. But intensive logging tends to expose the soil surface to vastly increased rates of erosion and nutrient leaching, which can render it much less productive in the long run. "Cut-and-run" forestry is not appropriate to existing conditions in most parts of the world. Two different questions should be addressed in a discussion of forest management. First, how do we go about increasing the forest resource, in terms both of trees and of the characteristics of the forest ecosystem? Second, what are the implications of harvesting these resources, either by cutting trees or by multiple use of forest land?

Trees, like all plants, exhibit very strong intraspecific competition for root space, sunlight, water, nutrients, and so forth. The growth of individual trees can be stimulated by reducing intraspecific competition for these resources. Thinning the stand allows only established trees at controlled distances to compete for nutrients (Figure 5.8). The manager can also alter competitive interactions between layers of the forest (Weetman and Alger, 1974). The faster the harvestable trees grow, the shorter the period between harvests. By favoring rapidly growing species over slowly growing varieties, one can also reduce the interval between harvests. As an example, one common practice is to harvest the hardwoods in a forest and replace them with faster growing softwoods. Of course there is a tradeoff between rapidity of growth and value of the ultimate lumber. As a general rule, hardwood lumber is more valuable than softwood lumber, so that it sometimes makes some sense to allow a longer interval between cuttings and to increase the value of the lumber realized at harvest.

A corollary of this substitution is the establishment of a forest comprising very few species of trees, of which only one or two are reseeded. This is typical of many other types of human ecosystems, in which management reduces ecosystem diversity. Of course, even the most intensive forests are much more diverse communities than agricultural fields. Understory plants are present, even if the canopy trees belong to a single species, and a relatively large diversity of animals may be supported. But such communities are more simple than natural ones, and they are special prey to a number of pests.

Reducing the interval between cuttings is generally carried out by physical or chemical methods of stimulating individual trees to grow faster. The physical method most widely used is scientific thinning based on the resource needs of individual trees and the resources available to the forest. Trash lumber is removed, and the trees to be harvested at some later period are left at controlled intervals. Chemical methods include fertilization, chemical pest control, and irrigation.

Forest fertilization has been carried out for some time on a fairly extensive basis in Europe and on a more experimental basis in North America. It will probably increase

Figure 5.8 Intensively managed and thinned Scots pine forest at Jädraås, Sweden.

in the future in most parts of the world. Most observations suggest that trees respond very well to fertilization, although the results are not as clear as they are with field crops, perhaps because individual trees are able to garner nutrient resources from large volumes of the soil through their extensive root systems (Morrison and Foster. n.d.; Weetman and Alger, 1974).

What happens to the nutrient materials introduced as fertilizer? Forest ecosystems are ideally suited to cycling nutrients through natural channels. Nutrient influx and outflux are roughly the same and both are quite small. The number of pathways for nutrient cycling in a fertilized forest appears to be sufficiently high that relatively little nutrient material need be lost through washing into nearby watercourses or volatilization into the air, although there is a correlation between the intensity of forest management and the surface-water pollution from fertilizer runoff. A series of experiments on nutrient cycling in forest soils (Overrein, 1968, 1969, 1971a,b, 1972a,b) has

demonstrated that losses of fertilizers into the ground water system or into the atmosphere vary considerably depending on the type of fertilizer used (Figure 5.9). Losses
may be substantial, and they may cause substantial pollution of surface waters, but
they need not.

Phytophagous Insects

Perhaps the most controversial aspect of intensive forestry is its responses to insect
pests. Many hectares of forests have been damaged, in some cases quite severely, by
phytophagous insect pests. As a general rule defoliation of trees is not complete, but a
partially defoliated tree is more subject to disease than a healthy tree. The most devastating insect pests for North America have been the spruce budworm, which has
attacked great areas of spruce trees in Canada and the northern United States; tent
caterpillars, which attack a number of species of temperate zone trees; and bark
beetles, which are prominent in the mountain regions. Such insects have been credited
with losses of timber in the millions of dollars.

Phytophagous (plant-eating) insects have been around much longer than humans
have. They are a normal part of all forest ecosystems and they often comprise a major

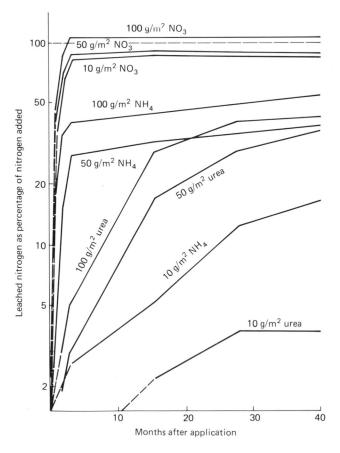

Figure 5.9 Leaching of nitrogen fertilizer from podzol forest soil as a
function of type and amount of fertilizer and time. The three forms in
which nitrogen was added were urea,
ammonium (NH_4^+) and nitrate (NO_3^-).
The three rates shown in this figure
are 10 g. N per m.^{2}, 50 g. N per m.^{2},
and 100 g. N per m.^{2}. [After Overrein, 1971b.]

link in the nutrient cycling mechanism. It is naive and misleading to view phytophagous insects simply as defoliators of useful timber trees. They are that, but their impact on the total ecosystem goes far beyond simple defoliation. Not all of the impacts are negative. Indeed, the defoliation of forest trees by insects may have benefits that outweigh the damage they do (Mattson and Addy, 1975). Because of the issues involved, it is not a trivial thing to assess whether or not defoliation is beneficial, or the degree of defoliation that constitutes economic damage. It depends to a degree on the level of abstraction at which people are willing to make decisions and on the importance they ascribe to normal ecological processes.

As a general rule, phytophages consume somewhat less than 10% of the total net primary production of forest ecosystems (Golley, 1972, Wiegert and Owen, 1971, Reichle et al., 1973, Gosz et al., 1972, Whittaker and Woodwell, 1968). Most temperate zone forests are characterized by roughly half this level of foliage removal. But there are extremes. Defoliation in some forests can reach up to 100%. This represents the total foliage production for the year in question in a deciduous forest. In an evergreen forest it represents the loss of several years' foliage production. Very light defoliation generally causes no problem. It can even stimulate plant production, and plants can compensate for defoliations of less than 40% to 50% (Rafes, 1970).

Mattson and Addy (1975) compare two different hypothetical situations. In the first type, aspen is defoliated by the forest tent caterpillar. A typical forest tent caterpillar infestation begins slowly, reaches a peak where it remains for about 3-4 years, and then subsides. Figure 5.10 graphs stemwood and foliage production in an infested and a noninfested forest. During the years of severe defoliation stemwood production in the affected forest is minimal, whereas foliage production is much higher, as the forest must compensate for insect defoliation. Within roughly 10 years after the defoliation episode, the biomass production in the two forests is virtually identical. This is not to say that the tent caterpillars have had no effect; they obviously have. The effect has indeed been severe in the short run, but it has not been a major factor in the long run.

In the second hypothetical situation, balsam fir is defoliated by the spruce budworm. The spruce budworm is one of the primary economic pests infesting forests in North America. More effort has been made to control it than any forest insect other than the gypsy moth. It attacks numerous species of evergreen trees, including the balsam fir. Defoliation by it can bring widespread death to mature trees in infected forests. A spruce budworm infestation may kill most of the mature overstory trees. This is shown in Figure 5.11, where forests of 55 to 60 years of age experience an extensive spruce budworm episode. But the focus of the spruce budworm attack is mature overstory trees. It does not attack younger trees in anywhere near as great intensity. The understory trees in forests attacked by the spruce budworm are commonly saplings and other juveniles of the mature trees making up the forest. A result of forest infestation by the spruce budworm is often, if not always, the resurgence of the forest from the saplings of the same species of tree.

The episode itself destroys most trees. For the next 10 years wood production in the affected forest is much less than that of an unaffected forest. However, production in the defoliated forest is even higher than that of the undefoliated forest by 15 years after the episode. This is because the undefoliated forest is characterized by large mature trees that have passed their most rapid growth stage. The defoliated forest is in-

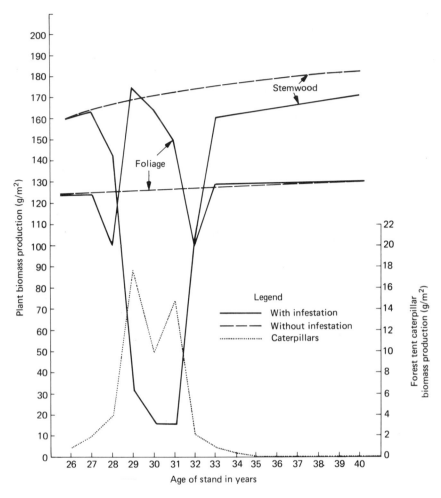

Figure 5.10 Annual biomass production in two hypothetical stands of aspen with and without forest tent caterpillar infestations. [Simulation data from Mattson and Addy, 1975.]

habited by younger, more vigorous trees. Thus the case of the spruce budworm is not at all a simple one. In the short run, it is a very serious pest that is capable of killing large proportions of the forest and leaving it more susceptible to fire. In the long run, it allows the forest to be more productive of stemwood than it would otherwise be.

This is not to say that the spruce budworm is a friend of the forester and that it should be protected. But the case points out once again the very significant differences between the short-run and the long-run considerations. On one hand, the system is healthier and more productive in the long run if the spruce budworm is allowed to defoliate. On the other hand, the harvest of large, economically valuable trees is aided by budworm control. One study has even suggested (Clark, 1979; Holling, 1978), that an effective method of budworm control would be to harvest those trees in the epi-center of budworm outbreaks. They would be killed anyhow, and depriving the bud-

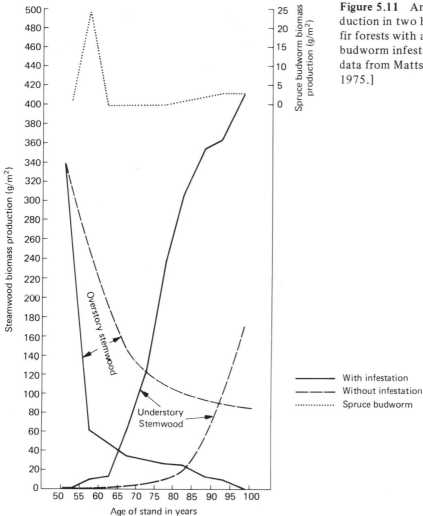

Figure 5.11 Annual biomass production in two hypothetical spruce-fir forests with and without spruce budworm infestations. [Simulation data from Mattson and Addy, 1975.]

worm of its food supply would reduce its numbers and therefore lower defoliation levels in adjacent areas. If people harvested trees just before the budworm got them, the trees would develop just as long as they would be likely to in any case, economic loses to the budworm would be minimized, and forest production would be maximized.

The case is not this simple, though, since it makes certain assumptions about what a commercial forest should be. A commercial forest is, among other things, a quasi-agricultural situation whose primary product is trees. If tree production is not encouraged, then the forest cannot meet the goals that the manager has set for it. On the other hand, a commercial forest is a managed community with considerable diversity of animals and plants. Because of the slow growth of the forest ecosystem, it is not necessarily feasible to exercise the same degree of control in a forest that would be possible in an agricultural field. The natural dynamics of the ecosystem are more prominent, since any given influence has a much longer period of time to make its impact on specific individuals in the system. Phytophagous insects have a pronounced role in maintaining the interspecific and intraspecific diversity of the forest. They are important as decomposers in regulating nutrient cycling throughout the system. They represent a part of the forest ecosystem that has evolved after roughly 400 million years of interaction between plants and insects. They affect many other populations either directly or indirectly through the mechanisms of energy flow and nutrient cycling.

Forest Fire

Fire is another important factor in forest management. It is as capable of destroying trees as a defoliating insect. Fires consume great quantities of forests every year. They are faster, more devastating, and more effective in their destruction than the most virulent of the phytophagous insects. Yet the place of fire in a natural ecosystem is not unlike that of the phytophagous insects, and a comparison between the two is appropriate. Forest management once emphasized the destructive power of fire to the exclusion of everything else, so that fire suppression was the watchword. A tree that did not burn was assumed to be available for harvest, and the forest's recreation value preserved. But forest fires were not invented by human society. They have existed as long as there have been forests. Most forests, at least in the temperate zones, have developed in concert with natural fires, so that fire has a specific place in the growth cycle of the forest. Indeed, many species, including some valuable ones, depend on forest fires for their existence or propagation, and fire has had a key role in molding ecosystem structure since time immemorial (Wright, 1974, Stone and Vasey, 1968).

There are two primary ways in which forest fire suppression affects the development of a forest ecosystem. Certain branches of any tree are more shaded than others. They die, as do entire trees that are too shaded, diseased, defoliated, or weak. Dead wood accumulates on the forest floor. In a tropical rain forest dead wood can be broken down relatively quickly by the detritus food chain. In virtually no other ecosystem is this possible; the lignin that comprises most of the tree's biomass is simply too tough and too difficult to break down during the season available to detritus organisms. Under normal circumstances periodic fires remove the dead wood but do not kill the healthy trees (Figure 5.12). If a forest is not burned, there is no diminution in the rate in which fuel accumulates. Under an extreme regimen of forest fire suppression, so much fuel accumulates that if a fire ever does get started there will be so much fuel that control will be impossible, and trees that would not normally be damaged by the fire are killed by it (Figure 5.13, Dodge, 1972).

Of course, fire does a great deal more than consume fuel. It has a pronounced effect upon the physical soil. For one thing, woody debris on the forest floor contains considerable amounts of nutrient minerals that would be released for recycling only very slowly through decomposition without fire. Fire releases them to the environment virtually immediately. Nitrogenous materials may be released either into the soil or into the atmosphere, depending on the intensity of the fire. Other nutrients are concentrated in the ashes on the forest floor.

The rich ashy residue is an excellent seed bed for many species of trees. Some

a

b

Figure 5.12 Photographs (*a*) before and (*b*) after prescribed burning at Redwood Mountain Grove, King's Canyon National Park, California. Initially the forest had a great deal of combustible material and white fir saplings. The trash was consumed in the burn and the white fir saplings were killed, restoring the forest normal for the region. [Photographs courtesy Bruce M. Kilgore, U.S. National Park Service.]

Figure 5.13 Photograph of a 65-year Douglas fir stand in the Gifford Pinchot National Forest, Washington. Limbs are dead to a height of 25 m., and self-pruning has led to the accumulation of a great deal of fuel on the forest floor. Should a fire become started, it would be very destructive and difficult to control. (Compare with figure 5.12*a*.) [Photograph courtesy U.S. Forest Service.]

species depend on it and their reproduction is vastly decreased without it. One example is the "big tree" (*Sequoiadendron giganteum*) of the Sierra Nevada. Table 5.2 shows the number of seedling sequoias in three different burned areas of the Sierra Nevada for the three years following a rescribed burning on Redwood Mountain in Kings Canyon National Park. The first year after the burning, the average seedling sequoia population was over 54,000 per hectare. Not a single seedling sequoia could be found in an unburned control plot in the same general area. Sequoia as a population depends on fire to release nutrients and to prepare a seed bed for the population.

Natural forest fires do not damage soil excessively. Some humus may be burned, but the humus layer is not terribly flammable and it is augmented by the ash from the burned debris. A very hot fire, on the other hand, destroys the humus layer as well as the dead wood. This often brings a pronounced drop in the soil's fertility and it may be very difficult for a forest to become restarted (Figure 5.14), Wagle and Kitchen, 1972).

Many natural communities are maintained by fire. Natural fires set by lightning have been characteristic of redwood forests of the Sierra Nevada from time immemorial, with the average period between fires on the order of about 9 years (Kilgore and Taylor, 1979). Trees such as the white fir would normally be killed while very young,

Table 5.2   Sequoia Seedling Responses to Prescribed Burning in 1969 on Redwood Mountain, King's Canyon National Park, California.

	Size (ha)	Mature Sequoia, (No. per ha)	Seedling Sequoia (No. per ha)		
			1970	1971	1972
Burn 1	1.52	7.2	32,560	5,382	1,211
Burn 2	2.47	11.3	31,350	3,230	941
Burn 3	2.53	22.9	99,161	10,764	1,077
Total	6.52				
Mean		14.9	54,357	6,459	1,077
Control	2.14	14.5	0	0	0

After Kilgore, 1973.

since they are not nearly as fire resistant as the giant sequoia and sugar pine that make up the mixed sequoia-pine forests of the high Sierra. Young fir trees are not significant competition for the sequoia or the sugar pine, but adult trees can be if they become established. Fire suppression in the mountain areas inhabited by the giant sequoia have caused a marked proliferation of white fir in these forests, to the detriment of the natural environment of the sequoia forest and also to the sequoia itself (Figure 5.15; Kilgore, 1972, 1973). Similar phenomena can be seen in other forests throughout the world.

Harvesting Trees

People manage fire, phytophagous insects, the spacing of trees, and the varieties of trees in commercial forests, but their most powerful impact on the forest ecosystem is in harvesting. This involves cutting and removal, and both have several variants. Which ones are used depends on esthetics, the regeneration potential of the forest trees to be favored, topography, erosion potential and fire hazard of the general environment, proximity to markets, requirements for wildlife maintenance, and cost of operation.

The least intensive method of cutting is the *selection* system (Figure 5.26a). Selected trees are identified, marked, and cut. In one sense, selective cutting represents a thinning of the trees that are not harvested. Those that remain mature more rapidly since they no longer compete with the mature harvested trees, and they can be cut relatively quickly. Selective cutting is the closest thing there is to a continuous management type of forestry. Regeneration in the areas opened up by tree removal takes place from saplings already in the area. This minimizes changes in the overall structure of the forest. Selective cutting works well only when the young trees of the desired species are tolerant of shade and can exist in the shade of harvestable trees. This is true for many of our most important timber species. They include Pacific coast redwood, white fir and incense cedar in California, ponderosa pine on the eastern slope of the Sierra Nevada and Cascade Mountains, Englemann spruce and alpine fir in the western

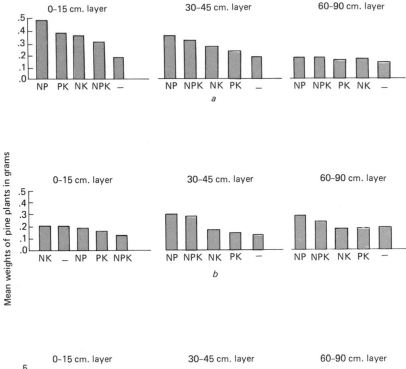

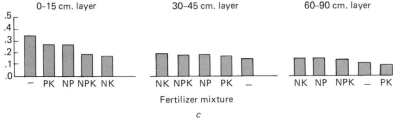

Figure 5.14 Bioassay showing loss of fertility from wildfire in ponderosa pine forests. Samples were taken from 3 levels of soil (0–15 cm., 30–45 cm., 60–90 cm.) and used as growth medium for ponderosa pine seedlings. Three different areas were used as the soil source. One (*a*) had no history of wildfire; the second (*b*) had been burned by wildfire 14 years before the study; the third (*c*) had been badly burned 3 years before the study. Mixtures of nitrogen (N), phosphorus (P), and potassium (K) were added to some of the soils; others were not fortified (–). [After Wagle and Kitchen, "Influence of Fire on Soil Nutrients in a Ponderosa Pine Type." *Ecology* 53: 118–125. © 1972, Ecological Society of America.]

portion of the Rocky Mountains, sugar maple and beech among the northern hardwoods, and most white and red oaks in central North America.

Some species require a certain amount of shade to reproduce. These include especially heavy-seeded species such as most oaks, yellow poplar, basswood, hickory, and white ash. In order to harvest these species, selection as such is often not used. Instead, all of the mature trees in a stand are harvested, but not at once. They are removed in a series of harvests so that there is always an overstory to shelter the site and to provide

a

b

Figure 5.15   Two photographs of the Confederate Grove in Mariposa Grove, Yosemite National Park, California, showing changes in forest composition following fire suppression in the forest: (*a*) 1890, before any fire supression policy; (*b*) 1970, after almost 50 years of conscious fire suppression. [The 1890 photo by J. J. Reichel, courtesy of Mrs. Dorothy Whitener; historical documentation by Bill and Mary Hood; 1970 photo by Dan Taylor. Both photos courtesy of U.S. National Park Service.]

a

b

c

d

Figure 5.16 Different kinds of tree harvesting operations: (*a*) selective cutting operation on lands of the Weyerhauser Timber Company west of Klamath Falls, Oregon; trees are individually marked and removed; (*b*) shelterwood harvest in a 148-year-old red pine forest in Minnesota; all mature trees are removed, but enough shade is left to encourage reproduction of the desired tree type; (*c*) seed trees left after cutting a stand of longleaf pine in Florida. All trees in the area are removed except for about 10 seed trees per hectare, which will be allowed to reseed the area; (*d*) clear-cutting operation in the St. Joe National Forest in Idaho; all trees in the area are removed, and the area is reseeded. [Photographs courtesy of U.S. Forest Service.]

shade for the young growing trees. This *shelterwood* method of cropping retains many of the esthetic advantages of selection harvesting, but all of the commercially important mature trees in the area are removed by the end of a few years' cutting cycle (Figure 5.16b).

A more extreme method of cutting is the *seed tree* method (Figure 5.16c). Almost all of the trees are removed at once from the area of the cut, leaving a small number of mature trees to provide seed for the stand. This method is very well adapted to trees such as the southern pines, which have very light seeds that can be born efficiently by the wind. After the forest is reseeded, even the seed trees may be harvested. The resulting forest is therefore even-aged and fairly uniform in its composition.

The most extreme of all methods of cutting is the *clear-cut* method (Figure 5.16d). All trees in the logged area are cut whether they are merchantable or not. There are two purposes to clear-cutting. The first is to harvest the trees. The second is to establish a new stand that is even-aged and of uniform composition. After the area is cut it is seeded or planted with valuable fast-growing species that do not reproduce satisfactorily under competition from other species. Clear-cutting may be carried out in patches, strips, or whole watersheds.

Once trees are cut, the logs must be carried to a yarding area where they are transferred to trucks, water, railroad, or some other medium for transportation to market. This is usually the most environmentally damaging phase of the harvesting operation. Normally the logs are simply dragged from one place to another by tractor. Tractors can be used effectively with any kind of logging system and in virtually any topography. However, since the log is dragged over the ground the soil surface is disturbed, and soil erosion generally increases greatly as a result.

There are other ways of transporting logs from the stand to the yarding area. We can touch briefly on a few to point out the relationship between different parts of the harvesting phase of timber management and the ultimate impact of forestry on the total environment. The *high lead,* for example (Figure 5.17a), is basically a line that runs from a mobile spar to the place of the logging operation. One end of the log is hoisted up by the line, and the other is dragged over the ground toward the loading yard. The fact that the front end of the log is off the ground makes it possible to clear obstacles relatively easily without building more complicated roads, and a skilled operator can "fly" even a large log over short distances such as streams or other unstable areas.

A variant of this is the *skyline cable* (Figure 5.17b). There are two spars, one at the yarding area and the other at the logging site. The entire log is carried above the ground, so that minimum damage is done to the soil. The skyline cable requires only about 1/10 of the road construction needed for tractor or high lead logging systems. The skyline cable may consist of a single span, or there may be multiple spans going over hills or very long distances. An important feature is that the yarding area may be either at the top or the bottom of the watershed.

Perhaps the least intensive method of transporting logs is balloon logging (Figure 5.17c). It is adapted to steep slopes and very fragile soils, because the yarding areas can be further apart than in any other transportation scheme (almost 1,000 m.). However, the yarding areas must be downhill, and therefore relatively close to streams.

The ultimate method of transporting logs is by helicopter. This does not require any ground-fastened equipment at all, but the helicopter is such a voracious user of

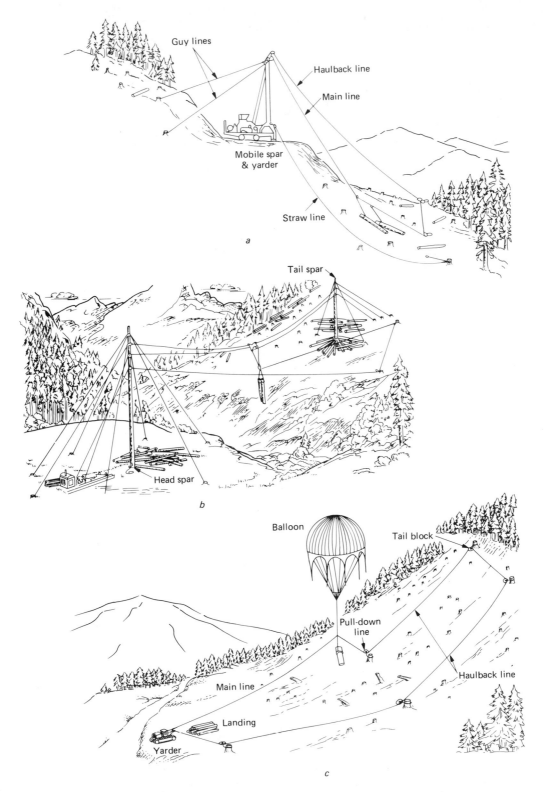

Figure 5.17 Different ways of transporting trees from cutting area to staging area: (*a*) high-lead; (*b*) skyline cable; (*c*) balloon logging; [Redrawn from EPA, 1973.]

gasoline that this is neither a very common nor an ecologically responsible way of transporting logs.

The assessment of any system of forest harvesting must include both cutting and transporting. It must consider the tradeoff between intensity of cutting and intensity of transportation. There is a gradient from selective cutting through shelterwood through seed tree to clear-cutting. But there is also a gradient from tractor transportation through high-lead to skyline cable and balloon. As one goes up the gradient from less intensive to more intensive cutting techniques, the costs per log decrease somewhat, but environmental disruption increases greatly. As one goes up the gradient from tractor transport through high-lead to skyline cable and balloon, there is a clear transition not only from greater to lesser disturbance of the soil, but also from a relatively low to a very high capital requirement per hectare. In addition, a tractor can go anywhere. It would be feasible to drag one large log per half hectare of cut by tractor, but it would not be feasible to run a skyline cable for the same cut. In other words, as one goes to the increasingly less damaging method of transporting logs, one must also go to increasingly more intensive patterns of cutting in order to make it feasible.

The basic impacts of logging operations are qualitatively similar for all kinds of cutting and transportation; the differences are in degree. In all cases the area loses much of its vegetative covering. If the slash and other logging debris are not burned, they litter the ground and constitute a major fire hazard. If they are burned, then the burned-over area may be deprived of whatever other plants were there that might have helped stabilize the soil, although the ash bed resulting from careful burning may provide a useful seed bed for the establishment of new vegetation. The disturbances inherent in logging operations may cause landslides that leave exposed, unstable, unsightly, and very erodable surfaces. The probability of landslides is related to the degree of disturbance resulting from the logging operation.

Skid trails from logs pulled by tractors or high leads compact the ground. This may dramatically increase the erodability of a fragile soil. The soils in the yarding and staging areas are even more compacted, having received many tons of logs. The exposed, compacted mineral soil has little ability to absorb water, and it is therefore a major source of runoff that may initiate erosion in less disturbed areas. But the principle sources of sediments are the roads that have been built to facilitate the logging operation. Not only are the soils more compacted there than anywhere else in the area, therefore being the most prone to increased runoff rates, but the roads also serve as conduits for running water.

As if to underscore the relative importance of the transport system in determining the levels of sediment losses, Fredriksen (1970) compares three experimental logging systems from deep unstable soils in western Oregon (Table 5.3, Fig. 5.18). The slopes were high, up to 110%, and sediment yields were monitored for nine years following the logging operation. In addition to an unlogged control forest watershed, one watershed was harvested by clear-cutting, with the logs transported by a skyline cable. This method of transport was feasible for the completely clear-cut watershed. Another watershed was clear-cut in patches, so that only 25% of the total area was harvested. The transport system was the high lead, which would be considered the most appropriate kind of transport for a harvesting system of this type. The clear-cut forest showed a sediment loss 3.3 times that of the control watershed. But the watershed that was clear-cut in patches showed a sediment 26 times that of the clear-cut forest.

Table 5.3 Sediment Losses Resulting from Logging and Transport Systems.

Logging System	Transport System	Roads (km)	% Area Harvested	9-Year Sediment Losses (m.t. per km.^{2} per yr)
None (control)	None	0	0	32.57
Clear-cutting	Skyline	0	100	107.50
Patch clear-cut	High-lead	265	25	2,795.00

Data from Frederiksen, 1970.

If clear-cutting in itself were the major problem, one would have expected these numbers to be the other way around. The major affront to the forest ecosystem was due more to the way logs were transported than to the way they were cut. If, in fact, clear-cutting makes it possible to have a less damaging transport system, then it would appear to be preferable to a more localized logging scheme, at least with reference to the delivery of sediment to streams.

Such a conclusion is oversimplified. Standard logging practices are not the only choices. Feasible engineering developments can negate some of the disadvantages of the more intensive methods of log transport. Figures 5.19a and 5.19b, for example, show two kinds of logging roads in one of the experimental watersheds of the Coweeta National Forest in North Carolina. The first shows a traditional logging road. Coupled with the poor logging methods typical of small operations in Appalachia, the watershed produced turbidities in the streamwater as great as 5,700 parts per million (ppm) during storms with average rainfall. A nearby watershed was logged in a way that attempted to minimize the impact on the soil. Roads were constructed on engineered grades, 2/3 of the area was clear-cut, and 1/3 was merely thinned. The road was planted in grass immediately following cessation of the logging operation. The maximum recorded turbidity from this watershed was 400 ppm from a very heavy rainstorm. Figure 5.19c shows the confluence of the streams draining the two watersheds. The clean-flowing stream on the left drains the watershed that had been logged using advanced methods. The dirty stream coming in from the right drains the area that had been logged using traditional methods.

Although the main insult to forest ecosystems from timber operations is the sediment delivered to nearby streams, other effects must also be considered. Especially in public land, hiking and recreation are significant uses. A clear-cut forest is not an attractive place, at least for the first few years after cutting. Widespread clear-cutting can create large landscapes whose esthetic value is very low. Less intensive cutting methods are not so displeasing, at least from a distance.

Streams flowing through forests are commonly shaded by trees and do not receive the full impact of the sun. Removing vegetation can allow the stream to receive full or at least greater summer sunshine, so that its temperature may be raised several degrees. This can be a significant change, and its impact on fish life is not very different from heat pollution from an electric power plant.

Figure 5.20 shows the temperature effect by comparing seven different watersheds in the Coweeta experimental forest of North Carolina. One of these, an unlogged

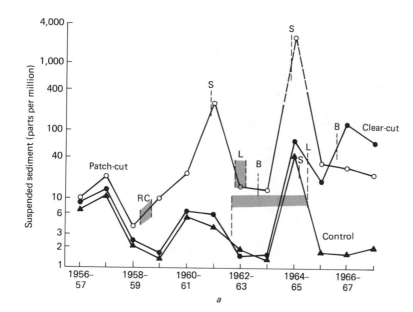

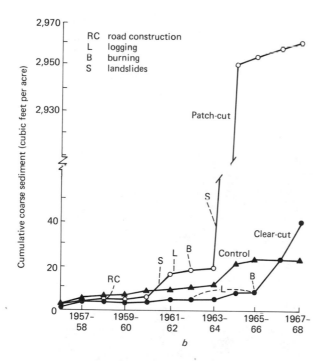

Figure 5.18 Sediment erosion from clear-cut, patch-cut, and control watersheds in Oregon: (*a*) suspended sediment in streams; (*b*) accumulated volumes of coarse sediment delivered to streams. [Redrawn, with permission, from Frederiksen, 1970.]

control, is shown in the illustration as "the line of no effect." The other six experimental watersheds are shown relative to the temperature of the control.

The most extreme temperature deviation occurred in a watershed from which the forest had been permanently removed. This was a demonstration mountain farm showing good agricultural practice in this part of the Appalachians. Even good agricultural

a

b

c   142

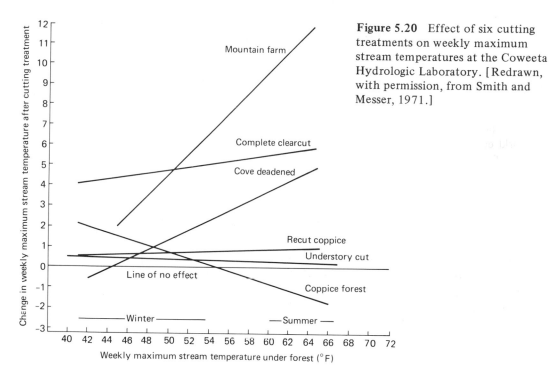

Figure 5.20 Effect of six cutting treatments on weekly maximum stream temperatures at the Coweeta Hydrologic Laboratory. [Redrawn, with permission, from Smith and Messer, 1971.]

practice brought a substantial increase in stream temperature, especially during the summer. The second watershed was clear-cut in its entirety. This watershed recorded the highest temperatures in the winter, but it was lower than the mountain farm in the summer. The cove forest typical of the area was killed by the use of herbicides in the third watershed, but the forest itself was left standing. All understory trees and plants with green leaves were cut to the ground. The next two watersheds showed almost the same temperatures as the control forest. The fourth watershed (recut coppice) comprised the brush forest that grew after clear-cutting 6 years earlier. The dense growth was cut both in January and in late July, but the total vegetation was not killed. In the fifth watershed (understory cut), all evergreen understory trees in the forest were cut, but the deciduous trees of the canopy were not. This accounted for roughly 22% of the basal area of the forest. The final experimental watershed was the coppice forest that followed clear-cutting some eight years earlier. While the stream draining the coppice forest was warmer than the control in the winter, it was actually cooler than the control in the summer.

Of course, the simple act of logging a watershed does not imply extreme tempera-

Figure 5.19 Two watersheds in Coweeta National Forest, North Carolina, showing the effects of different kinds of logging roads: (*a*) traditional unimproved road abandoned following logging; (*b*) road engineered to specific grade through forest, planted to grass following abandonment; (*c*) confluence of streams draining the watershed shown above; traditional practices were followed in the watershed to the right: improved practices were followed in the watershed to the left. [Photographs courtesy of James E. Douglass, U.S. Forest Service.]

ture rises in the streams draining it. One solution to the problem is simply to leave a forested belt along the streams. This particular choice has advantages. Leaving a border of natural environment between logging roads and dragways and a stream provides a buffer zone wherein much of the sediment eroded from the disturbed area can be deposited before it reaches the stream.

EPILOGUE

The spectrum of ecosystem types considered in this chapter demonstrates the way even the smallest management efforts ramify throughout the system. One cannot even draw a line on the map, so to speak, without risking substantial changes on the ground. One cannot try to minimize the effects of human actions, even the sincere attempt to suppress forest fires, without risking far worse problems in a few years. Modern society is so widespread that there are virtually no areas on earth that are not affected in key ways by people. Society is responsible, whether it recognizes it or not, for the status of world ecosystems. This is obvious for intensively managed systems such as agriculture, or for urban areas, or for polluted streams. But it is no less true for most natural ecosystems.

Any form of ecosystem management begins with a goal. This goal may be set explicitly as a matter of policy, or it may be set by default. Unless there is some way of insuring that there is no contact whatever between human society and nature over an entire ecological unit, the effects of people will be felt on the ecosystem. If society's goals are to be met, then it is necessary to understand both the behavior of the environment and the kinds of interactions that exist between society and the environment, so that management activities can be designed to complement the natural behavior of the communities in question and also the unavoidable effects of people. Whether we are talking about wilderness preservation, which ought to be the lowest intensity of management possible, or lumber operations, the key words are responsibility and stewardship. Society has the responsibility for maintaining ecosystems. The level of stewardship that is actually practiced depends on society's understanding both of the environment in question and of its own role in the human ecosystem.

References

Bergerud, A. T., 1974. Decline of caribou in North America following settlement. *Jour. Wildl. Manage.* **38**: 757–770.

Clark, W. C., 1979. Talk given at the International Institute for Applied Systems Analysis, Laxenburg, Austria, based on work done at the Institute for Animal Resource Ecology at the University of British Columbia discussed in Holling (1978).

Dasmann, R. F., 1964a. *African Game Ranching.* Oxford: Pergamon Press.

Dasmann, R. F. 1964b. *Wildlife Biology.* New York: John Wiley & Sons.

Dodge, M., 1972. Forest fuel accumulation—a growing problem. *Science* **177**: 139–142.

Dorst, J. P., 1962. *The Migration of Birds*. Boston: Houghton Mifflin Co.

Environmental Protection Agency, 1973. Processes, procedures, and methods to control pollution resulting from silvicultural activities. Washington: U.S. EPA report EPA 430/9-73-010.

Food and Agricultural Organization, 1974. *Production Yearbook 23: 1973*. Rome: F.A.O.

Fredriksen, R. L., 1970. Erosion and sedimentation following road construction and timber harvest on unstable soils in three small western Oregon watersheds. *U.S.D.A. Forest Service Research Paper* **PNW-104**: 1-15.

Golley, F. B., 1972. Energy flux in ecosystems. In Wiens, J. A., ed., *Ecosystem Structure and Function*. Corvallis: Oregon State Univ. Press, 69-90.

Gosz, J. R., Likens, G. E., and Bormann, F. H., 1972. Nutrient content of litter fall on the Hubbard Brook Experimental Forest, New Hampshire. *Ecology* **53**: 769-784.

Holling, C. S., 1978, ed. *Adaptive Environmental Assessment and Management*. Chichester: John Wiley & Sons.

Kilgore, B. M., 1972. Fire's role in a sequoia forest. *Naturalist* **23**: 26-37.

Kilgore, B. M., 1973. The ecological role of fire in sierra conifer forests: its application to national park management. *Jour. Quat. Research* **3**: 496-513.

Kilgore, B. M. and Taylor, D., 1979. Fire history of a sequoia-mixed conifer forest. *Ecology* **60**: 129-142.

Leopold, A., 1949. *A Sand County Almanac*. New York: Oxford Univ. Press.

Mattson, H. J. and Addy, N. D., 1975. Phytophagous insects as regulators of forest primary production. *Science* **190**: 515-522.

Mech, L. D., 1966. *The Wolves of Isle Royale* U.S. National Park Serv. *Fauna Ser.* **7**.

Miller, H. T., 1968. *The Naturalistic Control of Mosquitoes in Dona Ana County, New Mexico*. Santa Fe: N.M. Dept. of Public Health.

Moir, W. H., 1972. Natural Areas. *Science* **177**: 396-400.

Morrison, I. K. and Foster, N. W., n.d. Ecological aspects of forest fertilization. From *Proceedings of a workshop on forest fertilization in Canada*. Great Lakes Forest Research Center: Forestry Tech. Rept. **5**: 47-53.

Mutch, R. W., 1970. Wildland fires and ecosystems—a hypothesis. *Ecology* **51**: 1046-1051.

Myers, N., 1972a. National parks in savannah Africa. *Science* **178**: 1255-1263.

Myers, N., 1972b. *The Long African Day*. New York: Macmillan Publishing Co.

Myers, N., 1979. *The Sinking Ark: A New Look at the Problem of Disappearing Species*. New York: Pergamon Press.

Nelson, K. L., 1965. Status and habits of the American buffalo (*Bison bison*) in the Henry Mountain area of Utah. *Utah State Dept. Fish and Game Pub.* **65-2**.

Overrein, L. N., 1968. Lysimeter studies on tracer nitrogen in forest soil, 1. Nitrogen losses by leaching and volatilization after addition of urea-N^{15}. *Soil Sci.* **106**: 280-290.

Overrein, L. N., 1969. Lysimeter studies of tracer nitrogen in forest soil, 2. Comparative losses of nitrogen through leaching and volatilization after the addition of urea-, ammonium-, and nitrate-N^{15}. *Soil Sci.* **107**: 149-159.

Overrein, L. N., 1971a. Isotope studies on the leaching of different forms of nitrogen in forest soil. *Med. Norske Skogforsøksvesen* **28**: 333-351.

Overrein, L. N., 1971b. Isotope studies on nitrogen in forest soil, 1. Relative losses of nitrogen through leaching during a period of forty months. *Med. Norske Skogforsøksvesen* **29**: 263-280.

Overrein, L. N., 1972a. Tracer studies on the internal nitrogen cycle in forest soil. *Med. Norske Skogforsøksvesen* **29**: 443-466.

Overrein, L. N., 1972b. Isotope studies on nitrogen in forest soil, 2. Distribution and recovery of ^{15}N-enriched fertilizer nitrogen in a 40-month lysimeter investigation. *Med. Norske Skogforsøksvesen* **30**: 308–324.

Pimlott, D. H., Shannon, J. A., and Kolenosky, G. B., 1969. The ecology of the timber wolf in Algonquin Provincial Park. Ontario Dept. Lands and Forests: Research Branch *Research Rept. (Wildlife)* **87**.

Pollock, N. C., 1969. Some observations on game ranching in Southern Africa. *Biol. Conservation* **2**: 18–24.

Rafes, P. M., 1970. Estimation of the effects of phytophagous insects on forest production. In Reichle, D. E., ed., *Analysis of Temperate Forest Ecosystems.* New York: Springer-Verlag, 100–106.

Reichle, D. E., Goldstein, R. A., Van Hook, R. I., and Dudson, G. J., 1973. Analysis of insect consumption in a forest canopy. *Ecology* **54**: 1076–1084.

Sherwood, G., 1970. Carnage at Sand Lake. *Audubon* **72(6)**: 66–73.

Smith, L. W., Jr., and Messer, J. B., 1971. Forest cuttings raise temperatures of small streams in the southern Appalachians. *Jour. Soil Water Conservation* **26**: 111–116.

Stone, E. C. and Vasey, R. B., 1968. Preservation of coast redwoods on alluvial flats. *Science* **159**: 157–161.

Taber, R. D. and Dasmann, R. F., 1957. The dynamics of three natural populations of the deer *Odocoileus hemionus columbianus. Ecology* **38**: 233–246.

Wagle, R. F. and Kitchen, J. H., Jr., 1972. Influence of fire on soil nutrients in a ponderosa pine type. *Ecology* **53**: 118–125.

Weetman, G. F. and Alger, D., 1974. Jack pine fertilization and nutrition studies: three-year results. *Can. Jour. Forest Research* **4**: 381–398.

Whittaker, R. H. and Woodwell, G. M., 1968. Dimension and production relations of trees and shrubs in the Brookhaven forest, New York. *J. Ecol.* **56**: 1–25.

Wiegert, R. G. and Owen, D. F., 1971. Trophic structure, available resources, and population density in terrestrial vs. aquatic ecosystems. *J. Theor. Biol.* **30**: 69–81.

Wright, H. E., Jr., 1974. Landscape development, forest fires, and wilderness management. *Science* **186**: 487–495.

6/agriculture: the growing of crops

No class of man-environment relationships is more critical to human survival than managing the food supply. Crops comprise a restricted set of plants that have the special characreristics of rapid growth, high yields of specific organs used as food or fiber, and good taste, nutritive quality, or fiber strength. A few dozen species out of the entire plant kingdom constitute the overwhelming majority of cultivated crops. In any one area, the number of cultivated species may vary from as few as one in a high-technology monoculture to about 50 or so in a primitive slash-and-burn agriculture. (For an interesting view of gardening in which some four dozen crop varieties may be planted together in a single field, see Conklin, 1954).

An agricultural ecosystem includes five classes of organisms. These are the crop itself, animal pests, weeds, helpful species that are not used for food either by man or by domesticated livestock, and benign species that do not seem to have either a helpful or harmful role in expediting crop production. Management signals include choices of the crops grown, cultivation, irrigation, and the use of agricultural chemicals. The policy making domain in agricultural systems typically is very well developed. Farmers are numerous enough in most countries that policy makers respond to them, and ministries of agriculture are typically large and powerful.

CROP SPECIES

Considering the enormous diversity of the plant kingdom, the number of domesticated species is small indeed. Most major crops come from fewer than ten families of plants (Table 6.1). Most crop varieties are derived from early-successional species. Such plants are characterized by rapid growth and high yield, and they are the plants most likely to have grown up in the disturbed areas surrounding early human settlements. Thus, they are the natural candidates for having been noticed, planted, and cultivated by Mesolithic and Neolithic gatherer-cultivators.

The relationship between people and their crops is a symbiotic one. The crop population provides food for people, and people provide the kind of environment in which crops can succeed and even thrive. Indeed, most crop varieties are so unlike their ancestors that they would either quickly become extinct or revert to their wild ancestral form, were it not for people. Many weeds, in fact, are crop varieties that have escaped from human cultivation and care and have reverted to their ancestral weedy nature.

Table 6.1 Botanical Classification of Some Common Annual and Bush Crops.

Family Gramineae:
  Triticum (wheat)
  Oryza (rice)
  Hordeum (barley)
  Zea (corn)
  Secale (rye)
  Avena (oats)
  Setaria (millet)
  Sorghum (sorghum)
  Saccharum (sugar cane)

Family Cucurbitaceae:
  Cucurbita (pumpkin, squash)
  Cucumis (cucumber)
  Citrullus (watermelon)
  Melons, various genera

Family Liliaceae:
  Allium (onions, garlic)
  Asparagus (asparagus)

Family Solanaceae:
  Solanum (potatoes, eggplant)
  Lycopersicon (tomatoes)
  Nicotiana (tobacco)

Family Cruciferaceae:
  Brassica (mustard, cabbage, cauliflower, broccoli, rapeseed)

Family Euphorbiaceae:
  Manihot (cassava)
  Ricinus (castor beans)

Family Leguminoseae:
  Phaseolus (beans)
  Pisum (peas)
  Vicia (broad beans)
  Vicia (vetches)
  Cicer (chickpeas)
  Vigna (cowpeas)
  Cajanus (pigeon peas)
  Lens (lentils)
  Lupinus (lupins)
  Glycine (soybeans)

Family Asteraceae:
  Carthamus (safflower)
  Cynara (artichokes)
  Helianthus (sunflower)

Family Rosaceae:
  Rubis (raspberries)
  Fragaria (strawberries)

Various families:
  Ipomoea: Convolvulaceae (sweet potatoes)
  Calocasia: Araceae (toro)
  Dioscorea: Dioscoreaceae (yams)
  Papaver: Papaveraceae (poppy)
  Gossypium: Malvaceae (cotton)
  Piper: Piperaceae (peppers)
  Daucus: Apiaceae (carrots)
  Vitis: Vitaceae (grapes)
  Beta: Chenopodiaceae (beets)
  Cannabis: Cannabaceae (hemp)

CHARACTERISTICS AND CONTROLLABILITY OF AGROECOSYSTEMS

Many different kinds of agroecosystems exist even in an area characterized by one type of natural ecosystem. The reasons for their differences are the resources available to the farming society, the history and traditions of that society, and the specific goals of the farmer concerned. Precisely how these factors are translated into farming type is not at all a simple matter.

Agroecosystems, like all human ecosystems, are not fully controllable. No controller (in this case the farmer or farming community) can maintain the structure of the system in any arbitrary configuration. It makes a lot of sense to view agroecosystems as comprising two kinds of phenomena, which we can call factors and interactions. A factor is something that can be seen or measured, like a plant, a soil particle, or the concentration of some nutrient. Interactions describe connections among factors, such as the growth of a plant under a particular soil nutrient regime or the predation of a particular insect pest on a particular crop. Factors are physical entities; interactions are abstractions.

As a general rule, the factors are the things that can be manipulated by farmers, although many are beyond their grasp. The interactions are the keys to the dynamic behavior of agroecosystems, and very few, if any, are accessible to human manipulation. The farmer cannot wave a magic wand and get a plant to absorb phosphorous faster from a given soil; he can only add chemicals that alter the pH of the soil in order to make phosphate ions more mobile. He cannot remove pests from the ecosystem (except under the most labor intensive conditions, where laborers pick pests off crops one by one); he can only add chemicals or perform activities that kill a certain percentage of pests or disrupt their reproduction.

In the very early stages of agriculture, about the only thing cultivators could do was to fell and burn trees and to plant their seeds in the resulting ash-enriched seedbed. They could not turn over the soil, determine which populations were more beneficial to the soil, or do much to reduce the number of pests beyond handpicking them and pulling weeds. Nor could they affect the fertility of the soil other than by burning the vegetation that had previously been there or by implanting fish along with the crop.

Later, when domesticated animals became available they could plow the soil and create a medium in which crop growth was more controllable than in the unplowed soil. Likewise, cultivation could be used as a way of killing weeds. Soil fertility had to be maintained through crop rotations of various sorts. These typically included a pasture phase in which nitrifying plants such as clover and legumes enriched the soil in nitrogen, and droppings from domesticated animals provided other essential soil nutrients. Later on these resource requirements could be met at least in part by inorganic means. Indeed, for societies whose agricultural systems have essentially unlimited resources (or which are at least perceived not to be resource-limited), the resource requirements of the crops for nutrient materials can be met so well by inorganic means that demanding crops such as grains and certain fibers can be grown continuously year after year without being rotated with soil-building plants.

Until several hundred years ago the only means of pest control were picking them off the crop by hand and cultural methods of intercropping, timing of planting, and so on. Then chemicals such as arsenic-based poisons and botanical insecticides became available. These allowed a certain measure of control for certain kinds of pests. Only following World War II did farmers become aware of the tremendous power of chemical insecticides for controlling pest populations. Many pests that had never had any regulation could be attacked with the new insecticides.

Chemical pesticides represent an indirect control mechanism. They do not remove pests directly from the environment like the method of picking them one by one. Rather, they alter the abiotic environment with which the pest, as well as the other species in the community, must interact. The pest population is reduced because of the new toxicity of the environment. But the current generations of pesticides are not very selective, and they kill non-target species as well. The result can be a major change in the insect community. While pesticides have had some unquestionable successes, their effects have permeated the entire agricultural ecosystem to a point where in many cases the system is less rather than more stable.

Agriculture represents the establishment and maintenance of an artificial and unstable ecosystem, buttressed by the full resources of modern society. Fortunately, these resources have so far been sufficient to support agriculture despite all of the problems inherent in it. The survival of modern society depends on this continuing to be the case. The question—and there is a question—is to what degree of instability can modern agroecosystems be maintained. The trend has been to a simpler, more productive, but increasingly unstable community, maintained through increasing levels of technological inputs. There is obviously a limit to this trend, but it is not at all clear where it is.

Composition and Nutrient Balance of Soil

Any agricultural activity is carried out with the expressed goal of producing crops. To this end, the soil serves the critical functions of supporting plants physically and providing them with nutrients. Soil fertility is controlled by several factors. Some, such as the innate number of nutrient ions present in the soil, are fairly obvious. Others, such as texture, ion exchange capacity, or organic content are less obvious but no less important.

Texture and Structure.   Texture refers to the size distribution of mineral fragments within the soil. It is important for soil fertility, the ease with which it can be worked, and the physical support it provides to the plant. Soils comprise particles of many different sizes. They can be classified into various catagories, as shown in Table 6.2. The most important particle sizes in the mineral soil are sand, silt, and clay. Any soil can be analyzed to determine its percentage composition of the three components. It can then be classified as a loam, as a sandy, silty, or clayey soil, or as an intermediate, using a chart like Figure 6.1.

The physical properties of different textured soils are quite different. Clay-rich soils tend to be very coherent and plastic. They are often referred to as heavy because they are more dense and difficult to plow or to dig, and they may become quite hard if they dry out. Sandy soils, on the other hand, tend to be quite loose and are easy to plow and dig, but they tend to be relatively infertile. In general, the loams are the most desirable groups of soils, but there are plants that are well adapted to living in each of the major soil textural types.

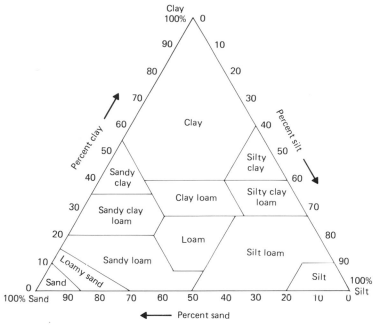

Figure 6.1 Diagram showing the designations of soil textures as a function of percentages of sand, silt, and clay. The percentage of each of these three components in the soil is determined by mechanical analysis, and the corresponding position of the soil on the ternary graph is found. Every point on the graph represents percentages of the three constituents, adding up to 100%. Thus a point at the three apices represents 100% of the constituent at that apex, whereas a point somewhere in the middle represents a mixture of the three constituents at the percentages indicated. [Redrawn, with permission, from N.C. Brady, *The Nature and Properties of Soils,* 8th edition. Copyright © 1974 by Macmillan Publishing Co., Inc.]

Table 6.2   Size Ranges of Soil Particles.

Soil	Range
Gravel	Greater than 2.0 mm.
Sand	0.02–2.0 mm.
coarse	0.2–2.0 mm.
fine	0.02–0.2 mm.
Silt	0.002–0.02 mm.
Clay	less than 0.002 mm.

Classification of the International Society of Soil Science.
There are other classifications, which vary slightly.

There is much more to a soil than its mineral constituents. Air and water are major components of soils, occupying the interstices between particle grains. Water is an important factor in determining soil properties in several ways. It surrounds every particle in a typical soil. The intensity with which it is held depends on the thickness of the water film, and it may vary over several orders of magnitude. When a soil is waterlogged, water in the pore spaces is held very weakly and can flow under the force of gravity. When the soil is very dry, there is still considerable water left but it is so tightly bonded to the soil particle that it must be heated in order to be driven off, and it shows few properties of liquid water. The thinner the film of water surrounding a soil particle, the greater the tension at which it is held (Figure 6.2). Plants are unable to utilize water held at tensions tighter than a level known as the *wilting coefficient*.

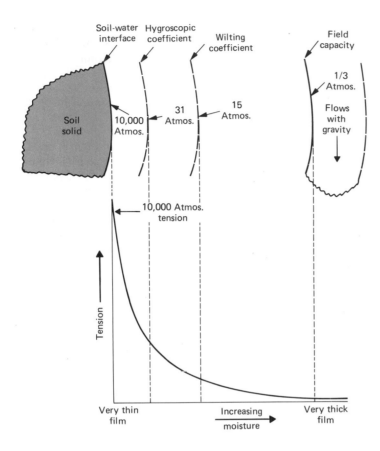

Figure 6.2 Relationship between thickness of water films and the tension at which water is held at the liquid-air interface. Above: diagrammatic representation of the thickness of the water film held at several levels of tension; below: graph of tension vs. thickness of water film. Tension is expressed in atmospheres. [After N. C. Brady, *The Nature and Properties of Soils,* 8th edition. Copyright © 1974 by Macmillan Publishing Co., Inc.]

Clay soils are made up of small particles. Pores are thus very small, and water can be held efficiently by molecular attraction. Such soils are poorly aerated, and water tends not to flow by gravity once it has entered the soil, even to unsaturated soils immediately beneath. Percolation through clay soils is very slow. Rain impinging on the surface tends to run off rather than infiltrate, because the available pore spaces near the surface get filled quite rapidly. Most of the particles in a sandy soil, on the other hand, are large. Pores are correspondingly large, and they cannot hold a lot of water through capillary attraction. Water percolates through these soils rapidly, making them well drained and well aerated, but with little water in the root zone.

Neither of these conditions is very useful for agriculture. Excess runoff represents a waste of available water, and too-rapid infiltration removes water from the root zones. Intermediate-textured soils, such as loams, contain both large and small pores because of the different sizes of soil particles. Infiltration of water is intermediate, as is water retention throughout the soil profile. Some of the pore spaces are filled with water, and the soil is moderately well aerated.

Another important characteristic of soils is structure. This refers to the organization of soil aggregates in the field. We can identify different structures based on the appearance of a soil when it is broken into clods. There are several important classes (Figure 6.3). The structure of a soil stems from its parent material, the climatic condi-

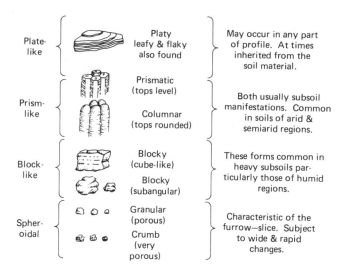

Plate-like	Platy leafy & flaky also found	May occur in any part of profile. At times inherited from the soil material.
Prism-like	Prismatic (tops level)	Both usually subsoil manifestations. Common in soils of arid & semiarid regions.
	Columnar (tops rounded)	
Block-like	Blocky (cube-like)	These forms common in heavy subsoils particularly those of humid regions.
	Blocky (subangular)	
Spheroidal	Granular (porous)	Characteristic of the furrow—slice. Subject to wide & rapid changes.
	Crumb (very porous)	

Figure 6.3 Various types of soil structure, showing their location in the soil profile. [After N. C. Brady, *The Nature and Properties of Soils*, 8th edition. Copyright © 1974 by Macmillan Publishing Co., Inc.]

tions under which it was formed, the organisms living in it, and hydrogen bonds among soil particles.

The most ordered structures are typical of virgin soils and are found in agricultural soils only beneath the furrow slice. Granular and crumb structures are characteristic of the furrow slice and are derived from other structures that have been shattered by plowing and cultivation. If the aggregates have been completely broken down by cultivation, the structure is considered amorphous.

The genesis of soil structure is a complex mechanism including the dynamics of wetting and drying, freezing and thawing, the physical activities of roots and soil animals, the progress of decaying materials such as roots and other large plant or animal residues through the detritus food chain, the chemical interactions between the soil solution and soil colloids, and tillage practices (if the soil in question is plowed and cultivated). Many of these factors lead to aggregation of soil particles; others can create lines of weaknesses or shift particles to force contact that otherwise would not occur. For a detailed view of the aggregation process, see Brady (1974) or Harris et al (1966).

In general, structural organization promotes water infiltration, and the more organized soil structures are more erosion-resistant than the less organized forms. It is very rare for arable land to have a highly organized structure in the furrow slice. The simple act of cultivation precludes this. Judicious plowing can improve the granular structure, but cultivation generally degrades it, and even plowing may have a deleterious effect unless it is timed properly. Overplowing or plowing when clays are too wet or too dry can lead to subsurface hardpans that are impermeable to root growth. Overaeration of the plow layer through excessive plowing or cultivation may lead to excessively high rates of breakdown of organic molecules. This is a very serious problem, as the organic fraction of the soil is the most efficient contributor to the aggregation process and hence to satisfactory structure.

Organic Fraction of Soils. In addition to their mineral components, soils also have a small but critically important organic fraction. Organic material is incorporated into the soil by the death of plants and animals (or parts of plants and animals) and their gradual breakdown by detritus-feeding organisms. Depending on the rate of detritus breakdown, the organic fraction may consist of relatively small organic molecules that otherwise might be suitable food for detritus-feeders, or it may include only the most refractory organic particles. In swamps and arctic tundras, for example, the soil is so waterlogged that detritus breakdown is very slow even though production may be relatively high. The soil's organic fraction is correspondingly large, and it includes molecules that would have been broken down in more aerobic environments. In tropical rainforests, on the other hand, detritus production is extraordinarily high, but its decomposition is so rapid that very little detritus remains in the soil, and it comprises only the most refractory molecules.

The organic materials in the soil are collectively termed *humus*. This is a very mixed bag chemically, but most humus particles have certain critical characteristics in common. These are very small size—even smaller than a typical clay—a colloidal nature, and a high surface chemical reactivity, so that ions can become adsorbed readily onto the surface of the organic molecule.

Humus contributes to soil fertility in much the same way as clay minerals. (This will be discussed directly below.) Unlike the clays, humus shows a dynamic balance between formation and destruction. Moreover, both of these factors are affected by farmers through what they grow and what tillage practices they use. Once an area has been turned over to arable cropping, the only source for humus is the debris remaining from the crops, unless the field is fallowed, a "green manure" crop planted, or mulches from other sources are used. The more the field is plowed and cultivated, the greater the oxidation of humus materials.

It is difficult to overstate either the importance or the vulnerability of the organic fraction of an agricultural soil. It is the chief "glue" that holds soil aggregates together, and its ability to bind ions to its surface makes it a critical component of soil fertility. Increasing levels of organic matter can mean better organized soil structure, increased infiltration of water and erosion resistance, and higher crop production. Plowing and cultivation expose the soil to excess oxidation, which increases the rate of humus destruction. To a degree, as content is reduced through continuous cropping, the losses in inherent fertility can be overcome by liming and fertilization, which change the ion balance of the soil. But these only increase the amount of nutrient in the soil. They do not increase the soil's ability to store ions and make them available to plants. In all, humus is the most important binder of the soil, and gram for gram it is the most significant contributor both to tilth and to soil fertility.

Composition of Mineral Soil.   Any number of minerals can be found in the typical soil. The most important are quartz, which is the mineral of common sand, and a large group of minerals called the clays. It may be somewhat confusing that the word *clay* can refer either to a type of mineral or to a size fraction, but there is little confusion in actual practice, because most mineral particles of the clay size belong to the clay group.

Clays as a group are characterized by very small flat particles. Largely because of their small size, the clay particles in soils are colloidal in nature. Because of their chemical structure, they are very surface-reactive. This means that the surface of the clay crystal is electrically charged, so that ions in the soil solution can be bound to it.

Different materials show different degrees of surface reactivity. One type of clay might be able to absorb a large number of ions onto its surface, whereas another might only be able to adsorb a very few. A measure of the adsorptive ability is the *ion exchange capacity*. This identifies the number of spaces available for ion adsorption per clay particle, or *micelle*. A high ion exchange capacity indicates that the clay can adsorb a large number of nutrient ions, while a low exchange capacity indicates lower ability to adsorb ions.

The exchange capacity of a soil is one of the best indicators of its potential fertility. This is because the soil represents the reservoir for almost all of the nutrients needed by plants. The soil solution does not act as a nutrient source analogous to, say, the water of a lake. The overwhelming majority of the nutrients in a soil are adsorbed onto surface-reactive clay and organic particles. They are released when other ions replace them on the micelle surface. Extensive substitution is possible, and in essence any ion can be freely exchanged for any other of the same charge. Nutrient ions that have been released into the interstitial waters are directly available to plants, but they are also easily leached from the root zone if a net downward movement of water carries the nutrients along with it.

One of the most critical factors in the ion balance of the soil is pH. As the pH decreases more hydrogen ions become available, and hydrogen ions tend to replace other ions (such as plant nutrients) on the micelles. The nutrients are easily leached from the root zone. As the pH goes up, hydrogen ions are released from the micelles and are replaced by other ions in the soil solution. Figure 6.4 shows the relative avail- ability of the most important nutrients as a function of pH.

Soil Fertility

Soil fertility is not a simple thing. It has no single and unique measure. It implies standard of yield: A fertile soil is productive; an infertile soil is not. We do not even commonly distinguish production of what. This has caused a great deal of confusion and sometimes tragedy, especially with regard to tropical soils. The humid tropics, including the tropical rainforests and monsoon forests, are among the most lush and productive forests anywhere in the world. But the soils are very infertile. High produc- tivity is maintained by very rapid turnover of what nutrients exist rather than by high storage capacity. When these soils are planted to crops that normally do well in the temperate zone, the resulting yields tend to be very poor. The crop ecosystem cannot cycle nutrients efficiently enough to overcome the tendency of percolating rainwater to leach them out of the soil profile.

Soil fertility has several obvious connotations. The most obvious are the presence of nutrient ions in the soil and the ion exchange capacity. The first parameter refers to the absolute soil fertility, but it includes no measure of where the nutrients are, how available they are, or where they are going. In a natural soil we might be able to ignore these factors, since natural soils are characterized by a dynamic equilibrium or quasi-equilibrium that can be described and understood. Indeed the empirical observa- tion of this equilibrium is sometimes a more useful estimate of gross fertility than a knowledge of precisely how many nutrient ions are actually present in the soil.

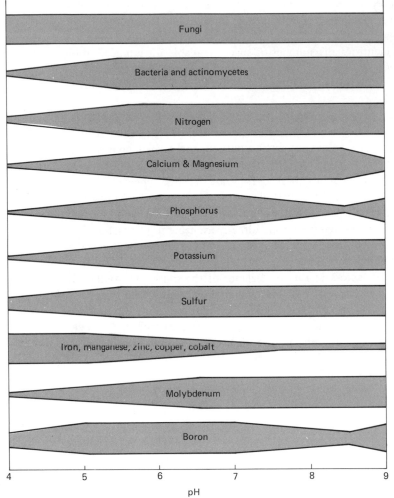

Figure 6.4 Relative activity of microorganisms and availability of plant nutrients as a function of pH. The optimum zone for most purposes is a pH between 6 and 7. [Redrawn, with permission, from N. C. Brady, *The Nature and Properties of Soils,* 8th edition. Copyright © 1974 by Macmillan Publishing Co., Inc.]

The condition of an agricultural soil is influenced greatly by farmers. They may do things that improve soil fertility or that degrade it in some way. If they use chemical fertilizer, it is to add nutrients to the soil in a form available to the crop. But what happens to these nutrients once they are added to the soil? Are they, in fact, available to plants, are they bound somehow in the soil, or are they leached out of the root zone? All of these things happen. The balance among them depends on the ion exchange patterns and is the key to a soil's ability to hold nutrients so that they are available to plants. Nutrients can react chemically with particles in the soil in such a way that they become bound permanently and are unavailable to plants. If the ion exchange capacity is not high enough, there may be no adsorption sites on the soil to hold nutrients, so that they are flushed out of the soil by moving water. Water moving through soils may also leach colloidal materials out of the root zone and into the subsoil. These are the clay minerals and organic materials that contain adsorbed nutrients.

To be sure, the leaching of colloids is slower than the leaching of materials dissolved in the soil solution, but it is characteristic of some soils.

Nutrient ions can be replaced by non-nutrient ions and then be leached out of the soil. The probability that one ion will replace another (or be replaced) on the surface of a colloidal micelle is roughly proportional to its frequency in the soil. If a very large number of non-nutrient ions is present in the soil solution, then these ions will tend to replace the nutrient ions. This is typical of high-rainfall areas, where hydrogen ions are abundant in the percolating rainwater. This effect is magnified in rain downwind from industrial or urban areas, where the pH of the rain is very low because of acids derived from gaseous emissions (see Chapter 9). When irrigation is carried out with saline water, large quantities of sodium are present in the soil solution. Ions that are much more useful than sodium may be removed, replaced, and leached out of the soil profile.

Structural breakdown may also affect soil fertility indirectly. The water-holding capacity of cultivated soils tends to be lower than soils occupied by a natural community. The percolation and erosion characteristics of agricultural soils are markedly different from those of natural soils. As a result, the patterns of percolation and leaching are also markedly different. As structure deteriorates, relatively more of the water passes through the soil or runs off the surface than remains within the profile.

If soil fertility is related to available nutrients, and if it is reflected in the production of crops, then one of the most important questions confronting both the farmer and the larger society is how to maintain or improve soil fertility. The specter of world hunger makes this even more imperative, as the only way that people can be fed in many parts of the world is by increases in yield per hectare. The logical strategy would appear to be one in which the structure of the soil is maintained at its optimal level, ion exchange capacity is maximized, the abundance of nutrient ions in the soil is improved, and water retention capacities of the soil is maximized. Unfortunately, there is no simple rapid way of doing all of these things.

The simplest way of improving the gross amount of nutrient in the soil is by fertilization. This is a valid and legitimate practice. It does not by itself exclude any other activity that might affect soil fertility. Fertilizers have been a keystone in the Green Revolution, by which modern genetic crop lines and cropping practices replaced traditional varieties in developing areas. But fertilizers are not a panacea. It often happens that more fertilizer is applied than can be taken up immediately by the plant. Most nutrient ions are adsorbed onto soil particles at least to some degree; most of the important nutrients can be fairly well stored in the soil. An exception is nitrogen, which is added most commonly as ammonia (NH_3 or NH_4^+) or as nitrate (NO_3^-). The ammonium ion can undergo ion exchange, but it tends not to be held in the soil by adsorption as simply as many other ions. Rather it is oxidized to nitrate, which is one of the most soluble of ions (Kurtz, 1970). It can then be leached easily from the soil profile. There is evidence that so much fertilizer nitrate has leached from corn fields in Illinois as to cause a human health problem (Kohl, Shearer, and Commoner, 1971).

Fertilizer production requires prodigious amounts of fossil fuel energy. More energy is required to manufacture the fertilizer used on many crops in the United States and Western Europe than is realized in harvest of the crop. The major feedstock for nitrogen fertilizer is natural gas or petroleum naphtha (Pratt, 1965). Nitrogen fertilizer alone accounts for over half of the total energy used in growing corn in the United States corn belt.

World patterns of fertilizer use developed under a regime of cheap fertilizers based on underpriced fossil fuels. The rise in oil prices in the 1970s has led to a corresponding rise in fertilizer prices and a reduction in the growth rate of fertilizer demand. Farmers in developed countries have had to adjust their practices in line with economic reality. Farmers in the Third World have often had to forgo fertilizers, even though they were commited to a crop variety that did not produce well without them.

Some new methods of producing food maintain the fertility of the soil in a different way. Minimum-till or no-till methods, for example, place special emphasis on maintenance of soil structure and protecton of the soil from erosion. Mechanical cultivation is held to an absolute minimum. The soil may be broken with a chisel plow to provide a seedbed, but it is not turned over as in standard plowing. Mechanical cultivation is not done; herbicides are used instead. Crop yields are generally at least as good as for conventional tillage, and they are sometimes much better (Bennett et al, 1973, 1975). Water retention is better, to be expected with improved structure (Blevins et al, 1971), as is nitrogen retention (Bennett et al, 1975). Erosion is reduced, and the energy requirements of the method are shifted from tractor fuel to herbicide manufacture, for a slight decline. In all, the move to minimum tillage and no-till cropping appears to be a beneficial one. The biggest problem is the vastly increased dependence on chemical herbicides. This has public health as well as pollution aspects, but it is not yet clear how serious it is.

One of the most effective ways of controlling soil fertility is also one of the simplest. Adding organic material provides exchange capacity and supports improved soil structure. Humus can be added in the form of mulch or a cover crop that is plowed under at maturity (i.e., a green manure crop). Vigorous growth of the cash crop leaves extensive below-ground materials that can also decompose into humus if soil erosion is suppressed. Crop rotations that allow the land to remain fallow for a time or that involve soil-building forage crops also add organic material to the soil. Some of the plants, such as the legumes, have symbiotic nitrogen-fixing bacteria that improve absolute soil fertility as well as structure and organic material content.

There are many alternative ways of improving the soil. Some require removing land from the cash crop, or at least alternating the highest-value crop with others that produce less income; others do not. Some involve purchased inputs; others do not. The farmer must assess the tradeoff between different kinds of costs, as well as between present and future values. This is not a strictly economic assessment; it has a strong ethical component. There used to be a wide variation in people's attitudes toward their land, from those who viewed the land as a trust to be passed along to their children, to those who would brag that they had "farmed out" several farms in their lifetime. For the first, farming meant stewardship and care of the soil to improve it; for the second it meant using it up and moving on. Today land is increasingly viewed as a commodity, as suburban areas sprawl and as corporate farms increase. This brings still a different dimension to the way farmers evaluate their responsibilities toward the land.

The primitive methods of soil building that sufficed for hundreds of years require rotations that imply large amounts of land per unit of main crop production. It is likely that current knowledge and technological capacity will permit patterns of land use that are more efficient and that will allow maintenance of soil fertility for the future. But it is not clear what the overall costs of these methods will be or precisely what mix of government policy and farmers' attitudes will be required to meet the goals.

CROP HYBRIDIZATION

Crop hybridization has become one of the most important tools in modern food production. It is a technique by which plant breeders manipulate the genetic character of crop varieties to tailor them to farmers' requirements. These include resistance to certain diseases or insect pests, characteristics which affect the ease of harvesting or salability of the crop, length of growing season, and so forth.

The key to crop hybridization is to identify desirable genes and combine them into a variety whose seeds can be sold to farmers. The actual selection process is nothing new. It has been going on for at least 10,000 years, and all of our present day crops have come into being as a result of selection of certain genes held advantageous by farmers. What is new is the way genes are identified and combined into seed stocks.

Like most populations, a typical field crop is genetically quite diverse. The rapid identification of specific genes requires crop lineages that are highly *inbred*. Pollen is used to fertilize the ova of closely related plants (or even the same individual), until the genetic contribution from both parents is identical. The quickest way to do this is by self-pollination, in which a single plant serves as both parents to all of the seeds produced.

After several generations of enforced self-fertilization, series of inbred lines are produced consisting of individuals with random combinations of the genes that existed in the original parent lineages. The genetic variability of the crop population as a whole has not necessarily been lost or even reduced. It has simply been channelled into a different form so that the expression of each gene can, at least in principle, be perceived. Selection takes place at this point. Plants showing desirable characteristics can be mated with plants showing other desirable characteristics until a lineage is created that includes all of the desirable characteristics that have been identified in the various inbred lineages.

Actually it is not quite this simple, as most inbred populations are stunted, lacking in vigor, and generally with few obvious redeeming characteristics. They must be back-crossed with open-pollinated varieties before their genetic advantages become clear. Also, most crop plants are normally open-pollinated, and a rigorous inbreeding program requires special procedures to minimize cross-fertilization. Once inbred lines with the desired genes are identified, they can be planted next to each other and pollen from one allowed to fertilize the other. This too is not a trivial task. At one time it meant hiring large numbers of people to remove the pollen-producing parts of the flower by hand. This is still the case for many crops. In others cases genetic or cytoplasmic factors have been discovered that render a lineage male-sterile. If one of the two lines to be crossed has this factor bred into it, it can be regarded as "pure female," as it were, so that all of the seeds produced represent pollen from the adjacent row. Once two inbred lineages have been crossed, the resulting progeny contain a larger number of desirable characteristics than either of the original lines, and they can be further inbred to localize these characteristics in a single inbred lineage. The cycles of identification and evaluation of desirable characteristics can be continued until the requisite number of desirable characteristics has been localized in two lineages. At this point, the marketed hybrid is created.

The new hybrid seeds have sparked an unquestionable improvement in crop production worldwide. Figure 6.5 shows the yields of several crops in production per hectare in the United States. The growth in yield reflects several changes in farm technology, but most are either directly associated with the use of hybrid seeds or are indirectly associated through cultural or fertilization practices that become feasible when hybrid seeds are used. Hybrid seeds have also spread throughout many parts of the Third World and have promised to multiply yields severalfold, assuming the other necessary inputs such as fertilizers are present.

Benefits and Costs of Hybridization

The benefits of crop hybridization have been so dramatic as to have entered the mythology of agricultural science. Hybrids have increased yields, allowed crops to be tailored to specific farmers' needs, and conferred resistance to insect pests and crop

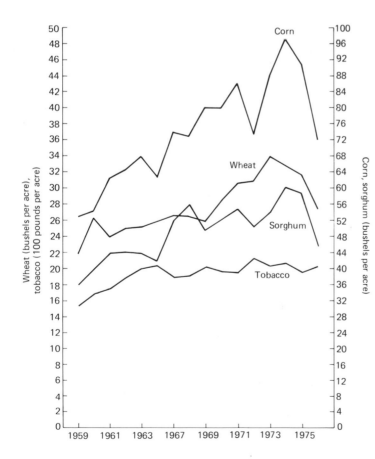

Figure 6.5 Yields for four crops in the U.S. [Data from USDA.]

disease. Hybridization is also relatively cheap. A study of hybrid corn suggests that the return on investment has been at least 7 to 1 (Griliches, 1958).

There is, however, a fly in the ointment for which no pesticide has yet been developed. The very essence of the hybrid crop is the inbreeding followed by the choice of lineages with desirable characteristics. Only lineages that have been identified as desirable are selected. Because of space limitations on the breeding farm, the remainder may be allowed to die out. This leads to an erosion of the genetic base of the species. As an example, 70% of the American corn crop is derived from 6 parent lines (Vietmeyer, 1979). This would not be a problem if the genes that were not used for further hybridization had no value. But who is to say that some characteristic that has not been identified as being desirable at one point in time will not turn out to be desirable at some future date? Today's problems may not be the most significant ones tomorrow. A new race of insect pest or disease may arise, so that the genes that confer resistance to the current strain are no longer effective. This has happened several times in several crops, often with severe consequences (Horsfall et al., 1972). Or genetic characteristics that are not particularly needed in one area may prove extremely beneficial in another. The problem of the erosion of the gene pool has long been recognized, and numerous gene banks exist for most major crops. However, these banks tend to be notoriously underfunded, and most of them are not very effective (Miller, 1973; Nabham, 1979). We do not really know how serious the overall erosion of the gene pool has been, and it is the kind of thing that has dimensions that may not be apparent until a catastrophe occurs.

Alternatively, weedy relatives of cultivated crops may exist unrecognized, even though they could contribute valuable genes to the crop line. But because their growth form is weedy, they are vulnerable to agricultural activity, especially if they are rare. A particularly good example is the corn relative, perennial teosinte (*Zea diploperennis*). This is the closest perennial relative to domestic maize. If current cross-breeding efforts are successful in conferring perennial genes on corn, which is an annual, the discovery of perennial teosinte would be worth billions of dollars. Yet its range is limited to slightly more than 1 ha. in the Sierra de Manantlán in Mexico, and the entire species would have been lost if a single Mexican farmer had decided to plant hybrids instead (Vietmeyer, 1979).

A related problem is that the hybrid plants in the field are genetically identical. While their genetic makeup may confer resistance to certain problems, it cannot confer resistance to everything. If a disease comes along to which the variety is susceptible, crop mortality is likely to be much higher than in a genetically diverse population. This is bad enough when it happens on a farm level, but it can be extremely serious when it happens on a national scale.

An example is the North American corn blight of 1970. By the late 1960s most of the hybrid corn growing in North America had a cytoplasmic factor known as Texas-T. As early as 1962, two Philippine workers discovered that Texas-T corn was more highly affected by a virulent strain of the fungus *Helminthosporium maydis,* or corn blight, than was normal corn (Horsfall et al., 1972). It was clear by 1965 that *H. maydis,* like most diseases, had several races, some of which were more harmful than others, and that new, even more virulent races, could be expected. Unfortunately, these two findings were not tied together. By 1970 thousands of miles of corn in North America, ranging from Florida into Canada, were all hybrids based upon

Texas-T. The weather conditions in 1970 were unusually wet, favoring the spread of *H. maydis*. It hit with a vengeance in Florida, destroying up to 50% of the corn crop, and moved north into Canada. All in all, about 15% of the North American corn crop was destroyed. One of the major reasons was its tremendous uniformity.

Genetic uniformity as a major factor in crop failure is well known. A "miracle" variety of oats called Victoria, discovered in 1942, was resistant to the crown rust fungus. By 1946 almost all of the oats in the midwestern portion of the United States contained the Victoria gene for crown rust resistance. A new disease called Victoria blight (*Helminthosporium victoriae*) arose in wild grasses in 1946 and spread throughout the North American oat crop, destroying a major portion. The Irish potato crop in 1840 was based on the genetically uniform "lumper" variety of potato. When the potato blight hit in the 1840s, not a single potato in Ireland was resistant to it.

There is another negative side to hybridization as well. Like many new technological developments, it has an overhead that is not always obvious. The need for germ plasm banks is only one part of it. Almost all hybridization programs select for increased yield per hectare. This almost always means improved response to fertilization. Hybrid seeds require more fertilizer, and they respond well to it. But if fertilizers are not used, or if they are used in an incorrect way, the yields may not be significantly better than those of traditional varieties, and they may even be less (Figure 6.6). When farmers in a region adopt hybrid seeds they also commit themselves to major programs of fertilization and mechanization. Even hybridization programs directed to shifting cultivators, the most primitive farmers in the world (Greenland, 1975), assume that they will use manufactured inputs and that they will be incorporated into a cash economy. Hybrid grains were once thought of as the cornerstone for solving the hunger problem in the Third World (Brown, 1970). Their adaptability and higher yields held out the promise of great increases in the ability of Third World farmers to produce their own food. This was to be a Green Revolution in people's ability to feed themselves. The 1970 Nobel Peace Prize was given to Norman Borlaug, a major developer of hybrid corn and wheat for tropical areas, for his contributions to eradicating world hunger.

It had become abundantly clear by the mid 1970s, however, that the overhead costs associated with the Green Revolution were strongly favorable to the rich farmers

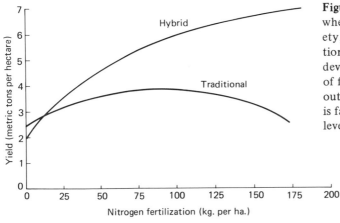

Figure 6.6 Yield of a typical hybrid wheat compared to a traditional variety, as a function of nitrogen fertilization under controlled conditions in a developing country. At very low levels of fertilization, the traditional variety outperforms the hybrid, but the hybrid is far superior at moderate to high levels.

of the Third World. Those who were already in the commercial economy could afford the fertilizer and the more expensive seeds. Those who were not could not, and they were even worse off than they had been. While the Green Revolution has raised the Third World's food production, it has also brought some undesirable social disruptions.

All in all, then, crop hybridization has been one of the most significant steps in modern agriculture. Its successes have been unquestionable, and it will always have a major role in agricultural production. However, the intensive levels of fertilization and pesticide use associated with hybrids lead to water and soil pollution, and the genetic uniformity of hybrid crops brings a strong potential for destabilizing the system, and this must be taken very seriously.

NONCROP POPULATIONS

In a typical modern agricultural cropping scheme, only one crop species is planted or cared for in a given field. That field is an ecosystem, and all of the forces that act upon any ecosystem act in the field. In addition to the abiotic factors of soil, weather, and water, there are noncrop species that are predators on the crop (pests), competitors with it (weeds), or predators on other noncrop species. We cannot wish these populations away, and dealing with them is one of the key jobs of agricultural science.

Weeds use resources in the ecosystem that would otherwise be available to the crop. Pests consume the crop in competition with man. Both are classical ecological interactions and are to be expected whenever there is a food supply for a potential predator. Because pests and weeds tend to be neither edible nor marketable, the crop losses they bring represent an absolute loss to the farmer's cash income or food supply. Some attempt to control or minimize the impact of the weeds and pests is clearly appropriate.

Until the seventeenth century pest control was not very sophisticated, and consisted of little more than erecting scarecrows or picking off bugs as they were encountered in the field. To be sure, Homer reported the use of sulfur as a pesticide around 1000 B.C., and Cato records fumigation of grape arbors with boiling asphalt around 200 B.C. Arsenicals were in use in China by A.D. 900, and they were used as ant poisons in the Western world by the late seventeenth century. Marco Polo is reputed to have brought back the use of pyrethrum, an insecticide derived from chrysanthemums, from his journey to the Far East. Ground tobacco was used as an insecticide before the French Revolution. Sabadilla mixtures have been used by South American natives against lice for centuries. Rotenone-containing plant preparations have been used since the mid nineteenth century. Arsenic based insecticides such as Paris green have been used since the 1860s, and fumigation with hydrogen cyanide was introduced in 1886.

The use of plant extracts and inorganic compounds as insecticides created a major new role for the farmer, although it is entirely analogous to a common ecological phenomenon. Farmers' use of chemicals to protect plants from the ravages of their natural predators is not very different from the natural secretions of many plants to reduce competition or predators in nature. The only difference is that it is the human symbiont that uses the chemical, rather than the plant. Also, the chemicals can be developed and put to use quickly; they do not need to arise through evolution.

Chemical biocides numbered in the dozens before 1940. Most were extremely toxic heavy-metal or arsenical inorganic poisons. The rest were petroleum-based oils and natural toxins extracted from plants. Some use of synthetic organic pesticides had been made as early as the 1840s, but very few had spread beyond the chemist's laboratory into field use. The breakthrough came in Switzerland in 1939, when the Swiss chemist Paul Müller recognized the remarkably effective insecticidal power of DDT. He pointed out the potential of such a chemical to food production and disease control. As a result he won the 1948 Nobel prize for medicine. The similar properties of benzene hexachloride (BHC) were identified in France and England in 1940.

DDT especially represented a compound that was very effective in killing large numbers of insects over a rather broad spectrum, and it was very cheap, unlike most of the earlier pesticides. It entered the world's consciousness in a particularly dramatic way, and it has occupied a central position in that consciousness ever since. As the United States Army entered Naples in 1943, the disorganization left by the war put the populace in extreme danger of an epidemic of louse-carried typhoid. DDT was used to eliminate the vector, saving many thousands of lives. For the next few years DDT was looked upon as a savior of mankind. It would eliminate major insect-carried diseases, and it would reduce crop losses materially. Not until the publication of Rachael Carson's *Silent Spring* (Carson, 1962) did opposition to the use of the new generation of chemical pesticides become organized.

Even since *Silent Spring* biocides have been increasing in their use, and they have become as much a staple in the arsenal of modern agriculture and disease control as fertilizers and hybrid crops. They number on the order of 1,000 active chemicals formulated into over 60,000 different preparations (Mrak et al., 1969). A military analogy is apropos. One can look upon biocides as a weapon in a genuine war between humankind and pestkind. The dramatic rises in food production per hectare all over the world and the by-and-large successful control of insect-borne diseases in many parts of the world attests to the tremendous successes of chemical biocides in meeting the challenge posed by the insect pests. Conservation tillage depends on the use of chemical herbicides as a substitute for plowing.

The victory has been real; it has also been Pyrrhic. The costs of biocide use have been high. Pesticides do not solve pest problems in any lasting way. They are more like a drug that offers symptomatic relief with the surety that the same problem will crop up soon and need additional treatment.

Types of Chemical Biocides

In order to take an intelligent look at biocides, we need to understand what kinds of things they are. They are oriented toward many target groups. Herbicides, fungicides, and pesticides, respectively, are directed toward weeds, plant disease, and animals, respectively. The pesticides include insecticides, rodenticides, molluscicides, and nematicides, directed against insects, rodents, molluscs, and nematodes, respectively. The modes of action of different biocides covers a broad range. Insecticides alone include at least three basic types. The stomach poisons are eaten by the insect and kill as they are absorbed through the gut; these are used mainly to control chewing insects. Contact insecticides are absorbed through the body wall and need simply come into contact with the insect in order to kill; they are most effective against sucking insects. Fumigants enter the insect's respiratory system as a gas; these are most effective against insects living in some kind of an enclosure.

Biocides comprise several broad chemical classes. It is convenient to view pesticides as existing in three generations: pre-1945, or first-generation biocide; second-generation organic chemicals, which came into widespread use about 1945 with DDT; and third-generation biocides, which have been developed mainly in response to some of the problems inherent in the second-generation biocides.

The first generation pesticides are largely insecticides. They comprise the botanicals, the oils, and inorganic pesticides. The botanicals are extracts of chemicals produced naturally by plants to protect them from their enemies. They break down into harmless compounds relatively soon after their application. Their mammalian toxicity is fairly low, so they are relatively safe to handle. They are most effective against soft-bodied insects such as aphids, certain young caterpillars, and so forth. Their use goes back hundreds of years.

Oil may be spread over water to act as a larvacide for mosquitoes, and several oils are widely used to control insects in fruit trees and ornamental trees. The dormant oils are relatively nontoxic. They are sprayed on fruit trees during their dormant season to smother overwintering eggs of mites and aphids and also to control scale insects. More highly refined oils even less toxic to plants may be used to control aphids, mites, and scale insects during the summer when foliage has appeared. Using oils as insecticides goes back to the eighteenth century.

The inorganic insecticides comprise a large number of very toxic chemicals, including several heavy-metal compounds, hydrogen cyanide (HCN), and elemental sulfur. Most of these chemicals are extraordinarily toxic, and will kill practically anything from man to the smallest of pests. Their toxicity spectrum is the broadest, and their persistence is the longest of all pesticide groups.

Biocide *spectrum* refers to the diversity of organisms affected by the chemical. A broad-spectrum biocide affects most organisms in the community, while a narrow-spectrum biocide kills only a small number of species. *Persistence* refers to how long it takes for the chemical to decompose into harmless residues in the field. Some biocides break down within a few days; others never do. For example, mercury is always mercury no matter what it is combined with, and most mercury compounds are quite toxic. There are fields on which inorganic insecticides have not been used for many years but which still contain enough insecticide that it can be recovered in the agricultural product.

The second-generation insecticides are organic chemicals not normally found in nature. They are manufactured as poisons, and their main function is to kill. They are cheaper than the first-generation biocides, more restricted in their toxicity, and easier to use. This group includes three major chemical groups of insecticides, as well as several minor herbicides, fungicides, and pesticides. It would not be difficult to get lost in the chemical details of the biocidal chemicals that have entered agricultural practice in the last 35 years. We shall take a brief look at some representative groups and leave the bulk to more detailed treatments (e.g., Mrak, 1969; ACS, 1978; Bent, 1979).

The best-known group of second-generation insecticides is the chlorinated hydrocarbon group, which includes DDT. These are likely to be persistent, lasting for months or even years. They are essentially insoluble in water and they tend not to be absorbed into the plant. They kill certain insect groups effectively but are rather ineffective in killing other major groups. They work both by contact and by stomach action. Most of the chlorinated hydrocarbons are relatively safe to use.

The organophosphate insecticides, on the other hand, are very broad-spectrum insecticides, acting mainly through contact or fumigant action. They are derivatives of nerve gases developed during World War II. Most are very hazardous to people, with the exception of Malathion, which can be broken down by a healthy human liver. They tend to be very short-lived in the environment and are broken down into non-toxic residues rather quickly by bacterial action.

Fungicides are toxic to plant diseases, most of which are caused by fungi or bacteria. They work both by preventing disease from getting started and by arresting disease that is already present. A satisfactory fungicide must be able to penetrate the cell membrane of the fungus and disrupt its metabolism without becoming established in the crop cell. It must also be sufficiently stable to be used effectively. Many of the formulations in longest use are compounds of mercury, copper, and zinc. Newer organic formulations are also in widespread use. Fungicides are used in many ways, including treatment of bulbs and seeds to prevent fungal attack during the crops' dormant stages, or treatment of foliage or soil to control diseases of actively growing plants. The effect of treatment of actively growing plants may be either local to the area of application, or systemic throughout the plant.

Herbicides include about one hundred different chemicals that kill higher plants. Some kill directly on contact with the foliage and act in such a way that the plant dies very quickly after contact. Others are absorbed by the foliage or by the roots and are translocated throughout the entire plant, killing it slowly. Still others sterilize the soil and prevent plant growth for periods of time ranging from a couple of days to several years. Herbicides are used in a number of ways, including field clearing, selective control of undesirable plants, and maintenance of waterways and the right-of-ways for highways and railroads. They have also had military applications, most notably the defoliation of much of Indochina by the U.S. Air Force during the Vietnam War. As with other agricultural chemicals, the oldest are the heavy-metal compounds. Numerous organic chemicals have become common in the last 30 years.

Biogeochemical Cycles

The biogeochemical cycles of essential mineral nutrients such as nitrogen, phosphorus, and potassium are well known and well understood. But every material in an ecosystem moves from organism to organism and back and forth between living tissue and the abiotic environment. Thus every material has a biogeochemical cycle of some sort. This notion is particularly useful for following and understanding the movement of agricultural chemicals through the ecosystem.

The biogeochemical cycle of a pesticide (or any other agricultural chemical, for that matter) can be viewed in the context of Figure 6.7. This is a highly schematic view, since most agricultural chemicals are complex molecules whose breakdown is an important aspect of their cycles. Agricultural chemicals in general are chemical compounds subject to the metabolism of the full range of bacteria, plants, insects, soil

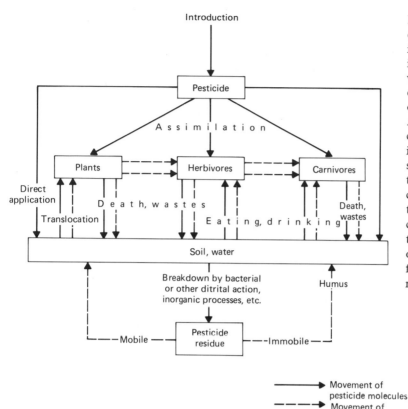

Figure 6.7 Biogeochemical cycle of a typical pesticide. It is introduced into the environment, where it cycles much as any other mobile substance. At the same time it decomposes (or is altered) into other chemical substances, which also enter the cycle. This process continues until the pesticide has decomposed completely into residues that are either insoluble or indistinguishable from naturally occurring substances.

organisms, and so forth. Whether they are naturally occurring or synthetic, broad-spectrum or narrow, persistent or not, affects only the type and rate of the metabolism. As long as they retain their structural integrity they retain their biological activity. They lose their biocidal properties as they are metabolized by the organisms in the community and decompose. What residues remain merge with the refractory organic molecules in the soil humus.

The evidence thus far is that the process of biocide detoxification by the metabolism of organisms is final and irreversible. However, surprisingly little research has been done on the precise nature of the ultimate residues, so that one cannot be sure that the residues have lost all of their biocidal properties (see Katan et al., 1976). Once a certain amount of breakdown has occurred, it is virtually impossible to trace the residues back to the parent chemical unless the experiment is very carefully controlled and each chemical substance is carefully labeled radioactively.

Adsorption of Pesticides. Most biocides tend to carry an electric charge that enables them to be adsorbed onto soil particles in much the same way as inorganic ions. The sorption behavior is a function of pH. The degree of ionization of a typical herbicide, for example, is greater under moderately acid than under basic or neutral conditions, so that the molecule competes better for acid sites on micelles in an acid soil.

This is significant because the phytotoxicity of herbicides is strongly affected by the degree of adsorption. Figure 6.8 shows the responses of cucumber to different levels of 2, 4-D in four different soil mixtures. Curve 4 shows the response of cucumber grown in quartz sand, which has no adsorptive capacity. Curve 3 shows the same curve for a mixture of sand and kaolinite, a clay with little adsorptive capacity for 2, 4-D. Curve 2 is for a mixture of sand and 2.0g organic soil, which has numerous acid sites, and Curve 1 reflects a mixture of quartz sand and 4.0g organic soil. The vertical axis in all cases records growth of the herbicide treated cucumbers as a percentage of that of cucumbers grown in the same medium without herbicide treatment. At high levels of herbicide treatment, the percentage growth of plants in the adsorptive medium was roughly 6–7 times that of those in the sand (Scott and Weber, 1967). Similar effects can be shown for other herbicides.

Pesticides behave in similar ways, and we know somewhat more about their decomposition mechanisms. As with herbicides, they are much more strongly adsorbed onto soils with a high exchange capacity, and the degree of adsorption is dependent on pH. The *rate* of adsorption (and, conversely, of movement through the soil) differs from pesticide to pesticide (Figure 6.9), but all behave in the same basic way (Huang and Liao, 1970).

Biocide Degradation.   In addition to soil adsorption, biocides undergo major structural changes that completely alter their toxic properties. Some of these changes are primarily biochemical; others are photochemical. Still others are inorganic chemical reactions with water or other inorganic substances in the soil. Biochemical decomposition represents the quasi-normal activities of the detritus food chain. Biocides serve as a source of energy for bacteria and are broken down by them. This breakdown commonly detoxifies the chemical, but it may reduce or alter its toxicity spectra. In

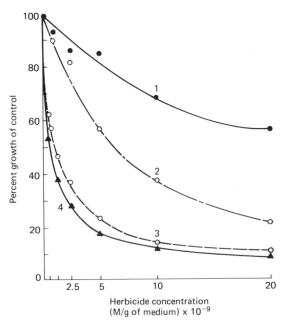

Figure 6.8 Responses of cucumbers to various concentrations of 2,4-D in artificial soils containing various quantities of organic material and kaolinite clay. Growth is expressed as a percentage of the growth of untreated plants in the same soil medium. Soil types: 1: 2.5% organic soil, 0% kaolinite, 97.5% sand; 2: 1.25% organic soil, 0% kaolinite, 98.75% sand; 3: 0% organic soil, 2.5% kaolinite, 97.5% sand; 4: 100% sand. [After Scott and Weber, "Herbicide Phytotoxicity as Influenced by Adsorption." *Soil Science* 104: 151–158. © 1967 The Williams & Wilkins Co., Baltimore.]

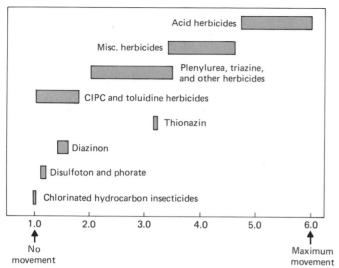

Figure 6.9 Relative mobility of several biocides in an irrigated soil column. [Reprinted, with permission, from C. I. Harris, "Movement of Pesticides in Soils." *Jour. Agricultural and Food Chemistry* 17: 80–82. Copyright © 1972 American Chemical Society.]

some cases it may even amplify them. Photochemical breakdown has similar results. The basic difference is that the chemical reaction is carried out through the adsorption of solar energy rather than by bacterial metabolism. Inorganic decomposition is commonly by hydrolysis or reaction with acids or bases in the interstitial waters.

Of the various decomposition routes, biochemical breakdown is by far the most important. Six conditions must be met before it can take place (Alexander, 1966).

1. The enzyme systems for biodegradation must be present. Considering the incredible array of molecules that can be broken down by microbes, it is easy to forget that there is a limit. But there are molecules that either cannot be broken down by the normal soil flora or for which special strains of microbes must be developed.

2. The chemical must be able to enter the detritus food chain. Microbes cannot ingest everything. They are limited to chemicals that resemble metabolites. If a chemical is to be biodegraded (or is to be biologically active for that matter) it must be capable of being ingested.

3. The biodegradation process must not damage the organisms doing the degradation. If the biodegradation of organic molecules leads either to the death or inhibition of the degrading organisms, then degradation will cease.

4. The chemical to be degraded must be accessible to the decomposer. It is entirely possible, for example, that a degradable pesticide may be readily attacked when it is in the soil solution, but that it is inaccessible when adsorbed onto a clay or other colloid or somehow protected through encrustation with a relatively impregnable coating.

5. As compounds are broken down, they may be readily attacked at first but modified to a point beyond which bacteria can no longer attack it. Thus biodegradation cannot always go to the level of ultimate decomposition. Each stage of the breakdown must be appropriate for further decomposition to take place.

6. If some other materials (O_2, iron catalysts, and so on) are necessary for enzyme action, they must be present or the enzyme system responsible for bacterial degradation cannot operate.

These rules might seem very restrictive. But virtually all organic biocides that have come on the market are capable of being degraded, at least slowly and under some condition by some enzyme system that exists in the soil. Some can be degraded remarkably rapidly.

The significance of biocide degradation within the biogeochemical cycle is twofold. First, insofar as the biocide is detoxified it is removed from the biocide's biogeochemical cycle. Second, if its toxicity is changed in some way, a second biogeochemical cycle parallel to the first must now also be considered. A good example of the second phenomenon is that of DDT. In its most common form, DDT is quite toxic to many varieties of insects and relatively nontoxic to birds. It is metabolized by numerous organisms, mainly detritivores, along two pathways (Figure 6.10). Under anaerobic conditions, dechlorination and reduction to TDE (also called DDD) and subsequent dechlorination to DDNS is the main route (Matsumura, Patil, and Boush, 1971).

Under oxidizing conditions, DDE is the most common metabolite; it is very common in DDT-treated soils and in vertebrates fed or dosed on DDT. DDD and DDE are both toxic, and the fact that DDT has been altered in no way means that biocidal activity has been removed from the environment. But the biocidal activity of the metabolites is different from that of the DDT. DDE is relatively nontoxic to insects, but it has a pronounced effect on birds, especially female birds. It disrupts their calcium metabolism so that calcium-requiring functions are slowed. Most notably, the eggs laid by affected birds may have substantially thinner shells (Ratcliffe, 1970; Cade et al., 1971; Peakall, 1974). The effect of DDT on calcium metabolism of birds

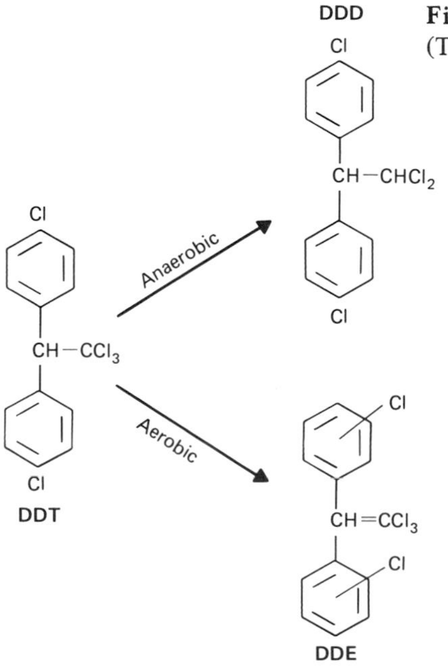

Figure 6.10 Breakdown paths of DDT into DDD (TDE) and DDE.

was the subject of some dispute for a long time (Gunn, 1972), but it has now been demonstrated beyond reasonable doubt. Figure 6.11 shows the historical trend of eggshell thickness for two species of birds of prey in Britain, and Figure 6.12 shows the empirical relation between eggshell thickness and DDT concentration.

The birds most pronouncedly affected by DDT poisoning are the raptors, or large agile carnivorous birds (e.g., eagles, hawks, owls). They are particularly vulnerable to pesticide poisoning, since they are the end of the food chain. Biocides show the phenomenon of *food chain magnification,* by which species at the end of the food chain ingest far more of the chemical than those at the beginning. We shall have more to say about this phenomenon shortly. Their numbers began to decline precipitously following the introduction of second-generation pesticides after World War II. Controlled experiments were carried out in which some birds were fed DDE and others

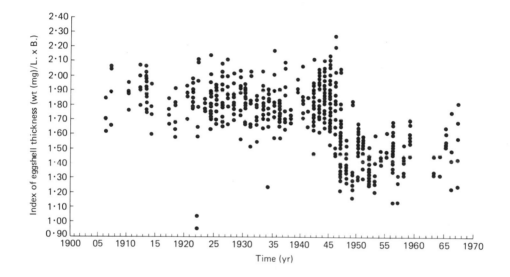

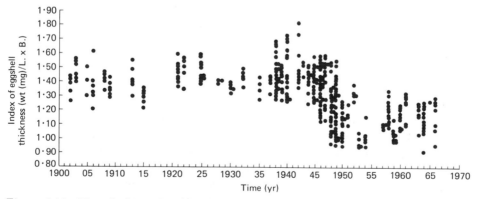

Figure 6.11 Historical trends of eggshell thickness for British birds: (top) peregrine falcon; and (below) sparrow hawk. [Redrawn, with permission, from D. A. Ratcliffe, "Decrease in Eggshell Weight in Certain Birds of Prey." *Nature* 215: 208–210. Copyright © 1967 Macmillan Journals, Ltd.]

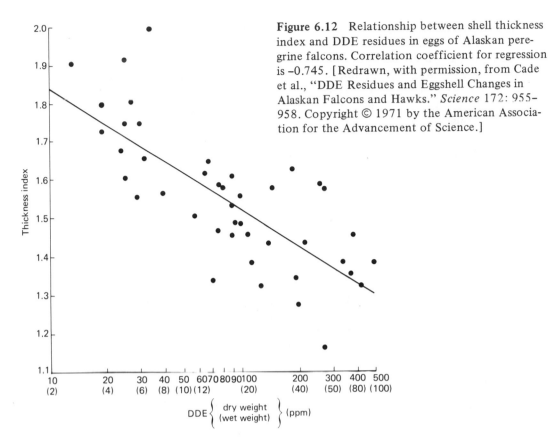

Figure 6.12 Relationship between shell thickness index and DDE residues in eggs of Alaskan peregrine falcons. Correlation coefficient for regression is –0.745. [Redrawn, with permission, from Cade et al., "DDE Residues and Eggshell Changes in Alaskan Falcons and Hawks." *Science* 172: 955–958. Copyright © 1971 by the American Association for the Advancement of Science.]

were not. These demonstrated that the observed correlation between the DDE content of the birds' bodies and the thinness of their eggshells represented cause and effect and that it was not due to correlation with some third factor such as degree of urbanization (Heath, Spann, and Kreitzer, 1969; Porter and Wiemeyer, 1969).

Other chlorinated hydrocarbon insecticides show similar patterns of biodegradation. Aldrin is transformed bacterially into its epoxide, dieldrin, a potent pesticide in its own right which is even more toxic than the parent molecule. In addition, both aldrin and dieldrin can change photochemically to still other highly toxic chemical substances.

Many studies have examined the deterioration of pesticides in the soil (e.g., Lichtenstein et al., 1971). The breakdown rate (generally measured by the half-life) is strongly affected by edaphic conditions such as temperature, soil moisture, soil texture, and cultivation levels. A single pesticide may show decomposition rates that vary over an order of magnitude for different conditions. The metabolism of pesticides in the field is a complex and difficult subtopic of applied chemistry. Each chemical compound has its own distinctive behavior. Every variable in the system, whether human or natural, can influence the degradation pattern. Even birds and mammals may have a role in pesticide breakdown; their influence may approach that of the detritus food chain in the rapidly biodegradable organophosphates and carbamates (Dorough, 1970; Kuhr, 1970). As in the more stable chlorinated hydrocarbon insecticides, biodegradaton by higher animals produces metabolites that are more toxic than the original pesticide (Menzer and Dauterman, 1970). The metabolic pathways for any given biocide may be different for different types of organisms (Menzer and Dauterman, 1970; Kapoor et al., 1970). It is this feature that enables a pesticide to be highly toxic to insects and much less so to mammals—or vice versa. Different pesticides—even close relatives—may be metabolized completely differently by different animals (Kapoor et al., 1970).

Cycling of Biocides. The dynamics of biocides in the soil show similarities and differences from those of nutrients. Once they have been introduced they pass along the grazing food chain and through the detritus food chain, as well as back and forth between the two. They are adsorbed onto and desorbed from soil particles and passed to and from the soil by microorganisms. This is the essence of a biogeochemical cycle. Unlike a nutrient cycle, where the nutrient has a structural integrity regardless of what specific form it happens to be in, the chemical nature of the biocide changes as it passes from one actor to another within the cycle. Ultimately it loses its identity as a biocide, broken down into materials indistinguishable from humic colloids already present in the soil.

Impact of Pesticides on Nontarget Populations

Biocides are introduced into the environment at large, where they commonly adhere to foliage or soil particles. Their targets are economic pests, but they can be ingested and assimilated by any organism capable of consuming the foliage, the soil, or another organism that has somehow become contaminated. Once the biocide has been ingested it may be metabolized by the organism. It may be detoxified or changed, it may kill it, or it may remain in the organism's body.

The range of nontarget organisms affected by biocides includes desirable animals and plants as well as species that are neither. Most significant economic pests are insects. But the number of beneficial or neutral insect species is many times larger than that of the economic pests. The effects of pesticides on nontarget organisms may be physiological or behavioral, direct or indirect; it is almost always detrimental.

Physiological Effects. The simplest biocide effects on nontarget organisms are physiological. Death, sterility, or some other measurable dysfunction occurs. Biocides most commonly act on nontarget populations just as on a target population, with high mortality due to the toxicity of the chemical. This is especially significant (and not at all uncommon) when the nontarget population is a beneficial insect such as a pollinator or the natural enemy of an economic pest.

In the former case, the transfer of pollen from male floral parts to female is slowed or stopped, with a corresponding decline in fruit set. Many crops are totally dependent on insect pollinators for fruit production, and disruption of pollinating species may be very harmful to crop production. As an example, the most common pollinator for many fruit crops is the honeybee. Unfortunately, the bee is very susceptible to chlorinated hydrocarbons, and it can easily be exterminated locally through their use.

Predators and parasites on economic pests are often more susceptible to insecticides than the pests themselves. When this is true, using a pesticide may cause some pest mortality, but relatively higher mortality of the natural enemy. This can release the pest from predator control so that the abundance of the pest actually increases. DeBach (1974) documents several predator-prey pairs in the citrus areas of California alone where pests can be raised from rarity to economic importance simply by using chemical pesticides. As an example, Figure 6.13 shows the effect of DDT in inhibiting normal biological control of the olive parlatoria scale *Parlatoria oleae* (Huffaker, 1970). When pesticides are not used two parasitic wasps, *Aphytis maculicornia* and *Coccophagiodes utilis* are so effective that 1,000 to 15,000 leaves must be examined to find a single individual of the scale. The wasps are so efficient that 70% to 95% of the female hosts that are found are commonly parasitized. However, as soon as pesticides enter the system, the parasites are so much more susceptible than the scale that their use results in a tremendous increase in the scale population.

It is not always obvious how a biocide will affect a given population. In some biocide-related problems it is difficult to demonstrate that the biocide is the source of the problem. As an example, Burdick et al. (1964) recount the effects of pesticide treatment in the watershed of Lake George, New York, on the lake trout population in the lake. A large decline in the lake trout population was noted following several years of treatment with DDT. It seemed clear that some DDT was getting into the lake, but since DDT is very insoluble in water, the amount was not thought to be very great. High concentrations of DDT residues could be found in adult lake trout (up to 835 ppm) as well as in lake trout eggs (3 to 355 ppm). Mature lake trout seemed unaffected and the eggs hatched normally. No clear-cut relationship between the DDT and the decline in the trout population could be noted until it was discovered that the young fry were highly sensitive to DDT at certain key points in their life cycle. They developed normally in the egg until the time of hatching even with high concentrations of DDT in the egg. But with hatching, the yolk is finally absorbed and the young are ready to feed. With the last absorption of the yolk, all of the remaining DDT is taken into the body of the fry. The fry are especially vulnerable at this time and the flux of DDT into the body is most rapid. Burdick et al found that as long as the DDT concentration in the egg was on the order of 3 ppm or less, some fry could survive. Above 5 ppm, mortality of the young fry approached 100%.

In a well-known case, Clear Lake, north of San Francisco and Sacramento, California, was the home of a large flock of western grebes. It was also characterized by a high population of gnats. DDD was applied to the lake in large amounts in an effort to control the gnats. An ancillary result was the death of several hundred grebes (Hunt and Bischoff, 1960). Each spraying of DDD for midge control was followed, after some delay, by the death of more grebes. As it happens, the grebes are fish-eaters, and

Figure 6.13 (Opposite) Control of diaspine scale, *Parlatoria oleae* by biological means and the effect of pesticides on the control mechanism: (*a*) trees on the right have not been sprayed; they are clean and vigorous, with scale under control by parasites; trees on left have been treated with DDT; they are heavily infested with scale and are dying back; (*b*) Typical infestation of scale on DDT-treated trees; (*c*) Typical healthy fruit, stems, foliage on untreated trees. [Photographs by F. E. Skinner, furnished by C. B. Huffaker, California Agricultural Experiment Station.]

a

b

c

the fish they consumed had accumulated large concentrations of DDD. The DDD concentration in a composite fat sample of Clear Lake grebes during the year following spraying was up to 1.6 gm/l. Even five years after spraying had ceased, DDD concentrations in body fat of grebes was almost 2/3 gm/l.

Many pesticides affect the reproduction of higher animals in addition to the raptorial birds already discussed (see numerous reviews in Pimentel, 1971). The fawns of white-tailed deer treated with 25 ppm of dieldrin have higher mortality than those of untreated does, and chlorinated hydrocarbon insecticides have disrupted reproduction in many species of birds. The herbicides 2,4-D and 2,4,5-T at relatively high dosages lower reproduction in chickens, while chickens exposed to thiram produce soft-shelled eggs of abnormal shape. Mosquito fish abort their young after surviving sublethal dosages of DDT, TDE, methoxychlor, aldrin, endrin, toxaphene, heptachlor, and lindane. Ovulation time of finches increases by a factor of two as a result of DDT in the diet, and embryo mortality during egg incubation increases up to 50% in mallard ducks whose diet includes 40 ppm of DDE. Biocides may increase reproduction as well as decrease it. As an example, when bean plants are exposed to 2,4-D, aphid reproduction increases during a 10-day period from 139 to 764 per aphid female.

Biocides can change the growth rate of numerous organisms. As an example, dieldrin is known to decrease the growth rate of female white-tailed deer. The herbicide 2,4-D slows down the growth and development of predaceous coccinellid beetle larvae by up to 60% (Adams, 1960). These ladybird beetles are often important biological control agents deliberately introduced to control aphids and similar insect pests. When the larvae grow more slowly, they are much less effective as control agents. Thus, 2,4-D both stimulates reproduction in the pest and suppresses the growth rate of the control agent. It has also been known to stimulate the growth of the rice stem borer. Borer larvae are up to 45% larger on treated plants than on untreated rice plants (Ishii and Hirano, 1963). DDT has been known to stimulate the growth of corn, so that soil treated with 100 ppm of DDT produces corn weighing nearly 40% more than corn produced in untreated soil. On the other hand, beans weigh almost 30% less if grown in DDT-treated soil.

Several insecticides cause significant changes in the essential element concentration in food plants. In beans treated with 100 ppm of heptachlor, for example, zinc was 50% higher than the controls, and nitrogen was 50% less. Wheat exposed to 2,4-D had an increased protein content, while beans grown on 2,4-D treated soil showed reduced protein content. It caused a level of potassium nitrate in sugar beets that would be highly toxic to cattle. It also causes ragwort to produce an unusually high level of sugar. This is significant because ragwort is a weed that is naturally toxic to many animals including cattle (Willard, 1950). High sugar content makes it much more attractive to domestic livestock, and therefore a much more serious poisonous plant. The herbicide 2,4,5-T has increased the hydrocyanic acid content of Sudan grass to a level at which it too is toxic to many animals.

The community effects of pesticide usage are also noteworthy. It has long been known (Wurster, 1968) that DDT at unusually high concentrations causes significant decreases in the photosynthetic rate of several algal populations. How significant this phenomenon is has not been clear, and the use of very high dosages of DDT in the initial experiment has led some to assert its meaninglessness (e.g., Singer, 1970). But the pesticide concentration of the oceans is increasing (Cox, 1970), and some algal species are, in fact, sensitive to certain pesticides at concentrations that could exist under reasonable conditions (Menzel, Anderson, and Randke, 1970, Mosser et al, 1972). The mechanism for the decrease in photosynthesis is now known to be a reduction in the reproductive rate of the sensitive algae (Fisher, 1975). Despite the fact that the phenomenon has been demonstrated and a mechanism shown, it would be only of minor interest were there not a parallel mechanism for spreading the effect through the oceans (Mosser et al., 1972). Because some phytoplankton are much more strongly inhibited than others, the influx of pesticides into the seas may cause disruptions within algal populations that can ripple through the algal community.

Algae do not occur alone in any aquatic ecosystem. When Hurlbert, Mulla and Willson (1972) established a controlled set of model freshwater ecosystems and treated them with feasible levels of an organophosphate insecticide, they found that the effects of the insecticide on the insects in the system were sufficient to release certain algal populations from herbivore control. As a result, the use of the insecticide was capable of generating an algal bloom. Algal blooms in the ocean are not inconceivable, especially in nearshore waters that are especially contaminated. Already there has been an increase in blooms of the highly toxic red tide organism, a marine dinoflagellate. It would seem that these have some connection with human pollution activity, but nobody has yet documented a mechanism.

Behavioral Changes. It is much more difficult to document behavioral changes than physiological changes, because one must observe larger numbers of organisms for longer periods of time. But some serious effects of pesticides on animals have been noticed. As an example, sublethal dosages of dieldrin increase the number of trials required by sheep to relearn a visual discrimination test (Van Gelder et al, 1969). Likewise, sublethal doses of DDT cause trout to forget most of their learned avoidance responses. Salmon exposed to a sublethal dose of DDT become increasingly sensitive to cold water, and might even be led to lay their eggs in abnormally warm water (Ogilvie and Anderson, 1965). Indeed, salmon fry cannot survive in water of the temperature preferred by salmon exposed to relatively high levels of DDT. Mosquitofish exposed to relatively low concentrations of DDT (0.1 to 20 parts per billion) tend to prefer waters that are more saline than usual for the species. All of these behavioral changes might have quite serious impacts on the populations of desirable species.

Biological Concentration

It is commonly observed that the biocide concentration in the bodies of many animals and plants is considerably higher than that of the surrounding medium of the soil or water. There are two mechanisms for this, both of which can be subsumed under the rubric of *biological concentration*. The first is that in which the individual organism concentrates the biocide directly from the medium. This involves an expenditure of energy to translocate a chemical or an essential nutrient across the cell membrane. This kind of concentration is especially characteristic of the chlorinated hydrocarbon insecticides, and it is well known in aquatic organisms. As an example, oysters can concentrate DDT by some 70,000 times in their bodies from water containing DDT at 1 ppb (Butler, 1964). Water fleas can concentrate DDT 100,000 times even if the DDT concentration in the water is only 0.5 ppb. Certain organisms can concentrate many materials far above ambient levels. Oysters, for example are also able to concentrate radioactive zinc by a factor of tens of thousands (Salo and Leet, 1969; Chipman, Rice, and Price, 1958).

The other kind of concentration is *food-chain magnification*. Most organisms do not have mechanisms for excreting many man-made chemicals such as chlorinated hydrocarbon insecticides, since there was no selective pressure to develop them until some 35 years ago. Since the insecticides are not excreted, they accumulate at a rate roughly proportional to the ingestion of food and also the concentration of insecticides in the food. Insecticides commonly enter the food chain at the base, where organisms ingest treated plants, soil, or water directly. Each animal at each step in the food chain must ingest roughly 10 calories of energy for every one that is incorporated into its biomass, since the other 9 are, on the average, lost to respiration. Thus, the biocide content of an organism one step above the base tends to be about 10 times that of the organism at the base, which served as its food source. Other animals that consume this species must likewise take in roughly 10 calories for every one they assimilate, so that they retain roughly 10 times the biocide content of the lower organisms or 100 times that of the base. In short, we can expect that as we go up the food chain each trophic level will be represented by an increase in insecticide concentration by a factor of roughly 10.

This has been observed in numerous empirical observations. The killing of the Clear Lake grebes discussed above in this chapter is an example of the phenomenon. It is not uncommon that populations relatively high on the food chain show pesticide poisoning even though those lower down do not. This is one reason why predators and parasites are often much more susceptible to pesticides than are the herbivorous insects against which they are intended. Table 6.3 shows the tremendous increases in pesticide content possible from food chain magnification of DDT. Those organisms with low concentrations tend to be at the bottom of the food chain, while those with high concentrations are at the top.

Public Health Considerations

It is extraordinarily difficult to document the public health aspects of biocides. They have been criticized for being toxic, carcinogenic (cancer causing), teratogenic (causing birth defects), and mutagenic (causing genetic mutations). Thousands of formulations are in widespread use, most of which can be applied in several different ways. There are *synergistic* interactions among biocides, by which the combined effect is greater than the sum of the separate effects. Their ambient levels in the environment are so low that in studies of their toxicity single substances must be examined under controlled conditions in order to detect the significant health effects. The number of different combinations possible under field conditions is so high, though, that experimental work can give only partial insight into the overall public health problems posed by biocides. It is clear that most pesticides are toxic, although they vary from very low toxicity to virulent poisons. Some are clearly carcinogenic, teratogenic, or mutagenic; some do not in themselves show these properties, but impurities commonly found in them do. The verdict is not in for a great many. For a detailed look at the

Table 6.3   DDT Residues in Various Organisms from Carmans River, Long Island, N.Y.

Organism	Residue (ppm)
Larus delawarensis (ring-billed gull)	75.5
Phalacrocorax auritus (double-crested cormorant)	26.4
Mergus serrator (red-breasted merganser)	22.8
Larus argentatus (herring gull)	3.5–18.5
Pandion haliaetus (osprey egg)	13.8
Sterna hirundo (common tern, egg)	3.1–7.1
Sterna albifrons (least tern)	4.7–6.4
Butorides virescens (green heron)	3.5–3.6
Spartina patens (marsh grass roots)	2.80
Strongylura marina (Atlantic needlefish)	2.07
Esox niger (chain pickerel)	1.33
Paralichthys dentatus (summer flounder)	1.28
Fundulus heteroclitus (mummichog)	1.24
Anas rubripes (black duck)	1.07
Cyprinodon variegatus (sheepshead minnow)	0.94
Mercenaria mercenaria (hard clam)	0.42
Spartina patens (marsh grass shoots)	0.33
Diptera (flies and other flying insects)	0.30
Anguilla rostrata (American eel)	0.28
Gasterosteus aculeatus (threespine stickleback)	0.26
Nassarius obsoletus (mud snail)	0.26
Crickets	0.23
Menidia menidia (Atlantic silverside)	0.23
Opsanus tau (oyster toadfish)	0.17
Shrimp	0.16
Cladophora gracilis (colonial alga)	0.083
Plankton, mostly zooplankton	0.040
Water	0.00005

After G. M. Woodwell, C. F. Wurster, Jr., and P. J. Isaacson. DDT residues in an east coast estuary: a case of biological concentration of a persistent insecticide. *Science* 156: 821–824. Copyright © 1967 by the American Association for the Advancement of Science.

public health aspects of the most important pesticides, the reader should consult major reviews such as Mrak et al, 1969. This book can treat only the highlights.

The first distinction that needs to be made is between *chronic* and *acute* effects. The former are the relatively low-level effects that debilitate people for some period but do not kill them outright. The latter refer to severe and rapid debilitation or death. Acute effects are easier to measure, and they are generally considered more important.

Table 6.4 summarizes various epidemics of pesticide poisoning from different parts of the world. Several things should be noted. The pesticides concerned were, for the most part, organophosphate pesticides, especially parathion, or the very potent organo-

Table 6.4 Representative Epidemics of Pesticide Poisonings.

Pesticide	Material Contaminated	Numbers of Cases	Deaths	Locations
Spillage During Transport or Storage				
Endrin	Flour	1,033	26	Wales, Qatar, Saudia Arabia
Diazinon	Doughnut mix	20	0	U.S.A.
Parathion	Wheat	398	111	India, Malaysia
Parathion	Flour, sugar	500	25	Egypt, Mexico
Parathion	Bed sheets	3	0	Canada
Mevinphos	Trousers	6	0	U.S.A.
Eating Formulation				
Hexachlorobenzene	Seed grain	3,000+	3–11%*	Turkey
Organic Mercury	Seed grain	400	59	Pakistan, Iraq, Guatemala
Warfarin	Bait	14	2	Korea
Improper Application				
Toxaphene	Greens	7	0	U.S.A.
Nicotine	Mustard	11	0	U.S.A.
Parathion	Louse control	17+	15	Iran
Miscellaneous				
Parathion	Crops	400+	0	U.S.A.
Pentachlorophenol	Nursery linens	20	2	U.S.A.

Data from Mrak et al., 1969.

*Annual mortality. Percentage different in different years.

chloride pesticides, endrin and dieldrin. They were not DDT. Second, pesticide poisonings can take place in many different ways, and they can enter the human body by many different paths. Food contamination is the most common, but contamination of clothes and linens is also known. Third, the number of deaths is generally considerably smaller than the total number of affected people, and pesticide epidemics are worldwide.

Figure 6.14 shows the toxicity of some representative organophosphate and chlorinated hydrocarbon insecticides. The differences, both within and between groups, is impressive. Toxicity is measured in 50% lethal dose, or LD_{50}. This is defined as the dosage of pesticide that, if given in one increment, would kill 50% of the total population in question. Its units are milligrams of pesticide per kilogram of body weight. These figures are drawn from laboratory animals, most commonly rats.

Figure 6.15 summarizes the results of a detailed study of acute pesticide poisoning in Dade County (Miami), Florida, from 1963 to 1968. Different pesticides have strikingly different incidences of poisoning within the population as a whole. These are significant socioeconomic and occupational differences. People in contact with pesticides, such as farmers or farm workers, are much more likely to be poisoned by them than

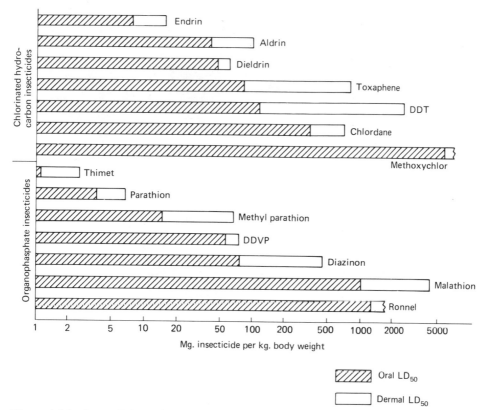

Figure 6.14 Acute LD_{50} of several chlorinated hydrocarbon and organophosphate insecticides, in mg. pesticide per kg. body weight. [Data from Bureau of Occupational Health, California Department of Public Health, as quoted in Mrak et al., 1969.]

the general population. In the Dade County area these people tend to be nonwhite, conferring a much greater load of pesticide burden on this particular part of the population than would be expected if all other factors were equal.

The chronic human effects of biocides are much less obvious and much more widely spread throughout the population, although they also seem to indicate the same socioeconomic differences, with higher exposure of nonwhite Americans than of white Americans. Pesticides enter the body by a number of routes: through the intestines after the pesticide has been ingested, through the lungs after inhalation of pesticide-laden dusts, vapors, or aerosols, by penetration through intact skin, and by absorption directly into the bloodstream through broken skin. The first is probably the most important. Inhalation is also an important factor, however, especially in poorer households where bug bombs are used to control cockroaches and other pests. Pericutaneous absorption is significant for agricultural workers, but is not terribly important for the general population except where very toxic pesticides such as parathion are made available for home garden usage.

The chlorinated hydrocarbon insecticides remain in the body, and they are stored preferentially in certain organs, especially in adipose (fat) tissue. Table 6.5 shows the

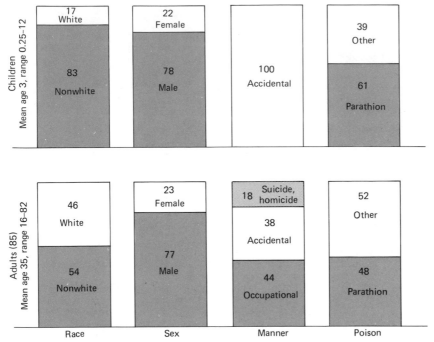

Figure 6.15 Epidemiology of pesticide poisonings in Dade County, Florida, 1968. [After Davies et al., 1969.]

distribution of DDT in chickens dosed with 10 mg. DDT per kilogram of body weight for 90 days. Table 6.6 shows the distribution of DDT (and metabolites) and dieldrin in the general human population. Empirical evidence has demonstrated a rather simple correlation between DDT or dieldrin in the diet, and storage of the pesticide or its breakdown products in adipose tissue, liver, blood, brain, and other tissues (Figure 6.16). For a given rate of intake of DDT there is a saturation level of DDT storage in the organs of the body, and the insecticide is gradually excreted if intake ceases. Different people respond to pesticides in different ways. Most are not affected adversely even by high chronic doses of the chlorinated hydrocarbons (Hayes et al., 1956; Stein and Hayes, 1964), while some people are extraordinarily sensitive and may be completely incapacitated by very low dosages.

Less is clear about the chronic effects of other biocide groups. Perhaps this is because some of them, such as the organophosphates and the carbamates, are so highly toxic in their own right that chronic effects are unlikely. These pesticides also happen to be detoxified by the body (especially the liver) relatively quickly, so that they are either rendered harmless or excreted if their rate of ingestion is so low that they do not first do serious damage. This is especially true for malathion, which has a reputation of being the "safe" member of the organophosphate insecticide group. It is readily detoxified by an enzyme widely found in mammals, especially in the liver (Menzer and Dauterman, 1970). It thus does not reach acutely toxic levels unless exposure is very intense. For this reason it is widely used as a home insecticide. Unfortunately, certain people do not possess the detoxification enzyme and are unable to detoxify

Table 6.5   Average DDT Residues in Adult Chickens.

Tissue	Females	Males
Brain	4.3	25.1
Abdominal fat	1,558.2	4,252.5
Subcutaneous fat	1,531.2	3,190.0
Gizzard	7.9	13.1
Heart	25.6	150.8
Kidney	18.8	29.5
Liver	24.3	39.1
Breast muscle	5.0	8.2
Thigh muscle	55.4	55.6
Gonad	42.0	24.8
Preen gland	271.9	1,179.7

All data are in ppm DDT and its primary breakdown products based on adult chickens dosed with 10 mg. DDT per kg. body weight per day over a period of 90 days.

Reprinted with permission from F. C. Wright, J. C. Riner, and R. L. Younger. Residues in chickens given DDT. *Jour. Ag. Food Chemistry* 20: 17-19. Copyright © 1972 American Chemical Society.

Table 6.6   Pesticide Levels in Tissues of Human Population.

Tissue	DDT + DDE	Dieldrin
Adipose	10.56 ±0.88	0.215±0.023
Liver	0.889±0.106	0.035±0.007
Kidney	0.141±0.024	0.013±0.002
Brain	0.123±0.017	0.035±0.005
Gonads	0.059±0.011	0.035±0.007

Data are in ppm. Figures are mean ± standard deviation.
After Fiserova-Bergerova et al., 1967.

malathion. For them it may be as toxic as other organophosphate insecticides that would be far more toxic than malathion to the general populace. This is especially the case if people are unaware of their sensitivity, and use it thinking that it is, in fact, safe.

Biocides as a group are hazardous chemicals with a significant role in modern agriculture. Many have public health consequences that go beyond acute toxicity, and their consequences are sufficiently serious that regulation of some sort is necessary. Legislation requiring stringent measures to protect society from the most negative consequences of pesticide use requires experiments and data collection which may run 10-15 years before the full public health consequences of the chemical are understood.

It has never been clear how best to regulate pesticide use so as to minimize their public health problems. Most countries have an office within their Ministry of Agricul-

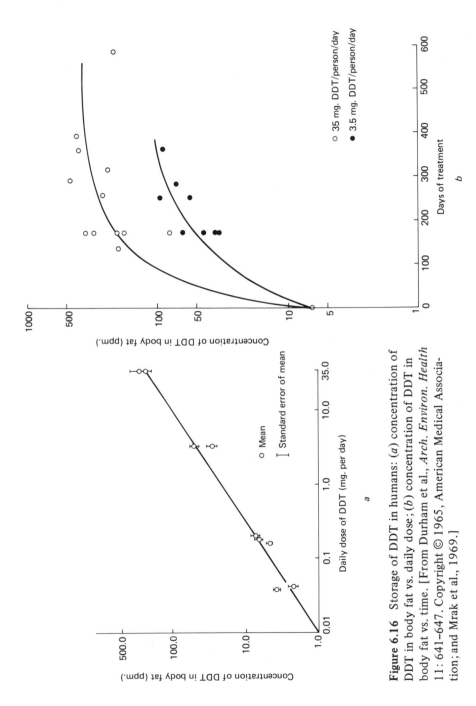

Figure 6.16 Storage of DDT in humans: (*a*) concentration of DDT in body fat vs. daily dose; (*b*) concentration of DDT in body fat vs. time. [From Durham et al., *Arch. Environ. Health* 11: 641–647. Copyright © 1965, American Medical Association; and Mrak et al, 1969.]

ture or Environment to regulate pesticide use. In the United States it is the Office of Pesticide Programs of the Environmental Protection Agency. In addition, the Food and Agriculture Organization and World Health Organization of the United Nations have assembled a set of international tolerance levels for pesticide residues that recognize the different needs of different nations. Because countries may set limits for pesticide residues in imported foods, the actions of one country may affect agricultural practices in another. Both the national and international standards have been criticized as being too restrictive by some and as too weak by others. All standard-setting groups and agencies are dealing with the same basic problem. Standards must be set on the basis of difficult experiments that cannot give a complete picture. It is very unlikely that the fundamental data problem will ever change. Society's needs require that pesticide regulation be carried out using the best and most appropriate mechanisms available. These estimates will be controversial and subject to error for the foreseeable future. It will be virtually impossible to assess the tradeoffs between the risks and benefits inherent in agricultural chemicals by objective means, so procedures become extra important. For some insight on the experiences of the United States, see NRC, 1977.

Genetic Resistance

The phenomenon of genetic resistance is a decrease in effectiveness of any chemical, such as a biocide, due to a change in the genetic composition of the target population. Resistant individuals are no longer as strongly affected by the chemical as they were previously. This is a widespread phenomenon, and virtually every target species can develop at least some degree of genetic resistance to every artificial pesticide used against it, given sufficient time. By 1967 second-generation insecticides had been in use for some 20 years. Resistance had built up throughout the insect group by that time and it has gotten worse since then (Figure 6.17).

The mechanism for genetic resistance is simple. All populations contain a certain amount of natural variation in numerous characteristics, including susceptibility to specific chemicals. When an insecticide is used it tends to kill individuals who are susceptible to the poison more effectively than those who are resistant. The generation following the application of the insecticide is characterized by a different genetic composition from that of its forebears. Specifically, it comprises the progeny of those individuals left following the use of the insecticide. Because the individuals carrying genes that conferred sensitivity to the chemical have been selectively killed, those that were left were less sensitive to the insecticide (Figure 6.18). The following generation will accordingly have a greater frequency of resistant genes. Continued use of the same chemical acts as a strong selective agent to remove sensitive genes from the population and thereby to increase the frequency of resistant genes in the population. After some time, the population is so resistant that either dosage must be increased substantially or the pesticide is no longer effective at all. Only if the population does not contain the gene for resistance (and this is not common, although it does occur) is resistance to a chemical not assured by its continued use.

How does one minimize genetic resistance in target populations? This is equivalent to asking how to minimize the selection of resistant genes at the expense of susceptible genes. If chemicals could eradicate a pest population we would not need to worry

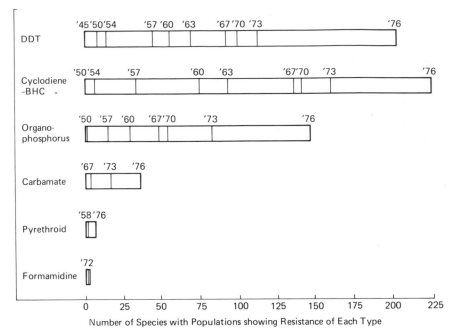

Figure 6.17 Numbers of arthropod species in which populations have developed resistance to insecticides of the six principal types available. [Reprinted with permission from Brown: *Ecology of Pesticides,* © 1978 by John Wiley & Sons, New York.]

about resistance, but this is seldom possible and almost never feasible. A 95% control of a species is very good in most cases, but even 95% is a far cry from 100%. If the pest control scheme removed individuals of all genetic constitutions at random, there would be no selection for resistant genes. But as long as pest control schemes favor resistant genes, then resistance is conferred on the population. In this regard the presence of the pesticide in the environment is precisely equivalent to any other environmental factor that exerts selective pressure on a population. One of the key tasks in designing a chemically based pest control scheme is to judge the rate at which genetic resistance builds up in the target population at different levels of use, so that the tradeoffs between killing efficiency, public health side effects, nontarget influences, and genetic resistance can be assessed.

Economic Threshold

As a general rule, we do not need to be concerned with phytophagous pests simply because they eat desirable crop plants. Many such insects have been around for thousands of years in association with the crop, doing little or no damage. The only pests we need to become really concerned about are those that cause economic damage directly to the farmer and indirectly to the consumer. Most pests are not economically important below certain levels of activity, so that we do not even need to try to exterminate them. Simply reducing them below a certain threshold level is sufficient to keep them from destroying too much crop. (Figure 6.19).

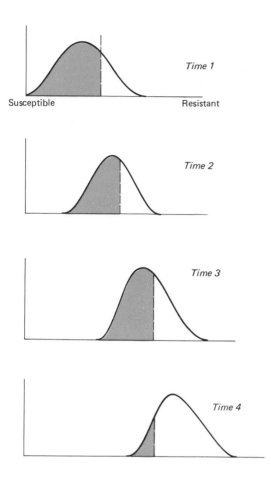

Susceptible · Resistant

Time 1
Time 2
Time 3
Time 4

Figure 6.18 Schematic representation of the development of genetic resistance in a target population. At *Time 1*, the frequency distribution of pesticide resistance is normal. Pesticide is applied at a concentration that kills the shaded portion of the distribution, leaving the unshaded portion to reproduce and serve as the parents of the population at *Time 2*. A higher application of pesticide is made at this point, with similar results, so that the unshaded portion of the distribution represents the parents of the population at *Time 3*. The process continues, with resistant genes becoming very common in the population by *Time 4*.

Three population densities are significant in pest control. The *general equilibrium density* is the average density for the area. The *economic injury level* is the density at which economic damage is done and for which control is called for. The *economic threshold* is a warning density. Economic damage has not yet occurred, but it is likely unless control measures are taken. The fluctuations of many pests around the general equilibrium never carry it above the economic injury level (Figure 6.18a). These need never to be controlled. For others (Figure 6.18b), the population maximum occasionally carries it above the economic threshold. Control is needed only on these occasions. In still others (Figure 6.18c) the general equilibrium is below the economic injury level, but the peak populations are above. Such pests need considerable control effort, with the explicit intent of depressing population. Finally, there are those populations whose general equilibrium level is above the economic injury level (Figure 6.18d). Not only must the equilibrium level be reduced, but frequent measures must also be applied in order to retain control over the population (Stern et al, 1959).

Controlling pests in relation to the economic injury level will minimize, at least for the short run, the amount of insecticide entering the environment. But the fewer the number of individuals killed by the poison, the more are left to produce the next generation. This may affect the rate at which genetic resistance builds in the population. In many cases, a "responsible" program of chemical pest control designed to reduce

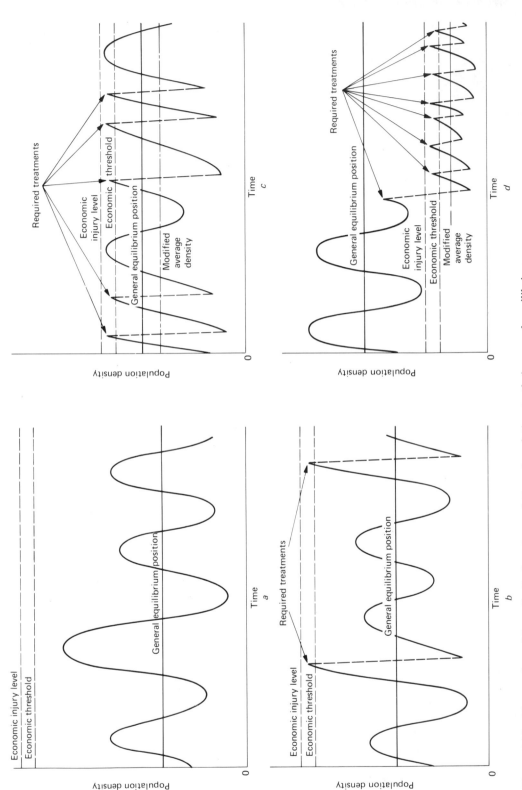

Figure 6.19 Fluctuation of hypothetical pest populations in relation to their general equilibrium levels, economic injury levels, and economic thresholds: (a) noneconomic pest; (b) occasional pest; (c) perennial, but relatively minor pest; (d) perennial severe pest. [Redrawn, with permission, from Stern et al., 1959.]

the population below the economic threshold will maximize the buildup of genetic resistance. Unfortunately, the laws of genetics will not allow us to have it both ways, and the question of genetic resistance is the one which more than anything else casts doubt on the ultimate utility of the chemical strategy as the dominant means of pest control.

Alternative to Biocides for Pest Control

One might get the idea from some sources that the goal of pest control is to use chemicals wisely, whatever that means. For others, chemicals represent a pariah that should be prohibited from entering the environment. Agriculture is an artificial ecosystem designed to maximize the growth of a crop. This requires that pest growth be minimized or at least held below the economic threshold. It does not really matter how either of these goals is attained so long as society's needs are met over the long run. Biocides are now the most widely used methods of pest control. But several alternative methods are under development, and some are in widespread use.

Food Chain Control. In some ways, the most straightforward of these methods is also the oldest, *food chain control.* Control over the pest is vested in an organism higher up in the food chain than the pest itself, so that the natural food chain processes confer adequate control for the pest. Familiar examples of this kind of control involve the vedalia beetle and the cottony cushion scale in the California orange groves, or the cactus eating moth, *Cactoblastis cactorum,* and the alien prickly pear cactus in Australia. DeBach (1974) presents case studies of numerous others from all over the world.

In food chain control the natural enemies of a pest are either allowed to exist or are encouraged by several means. Parasites can be raised in insectories or collected in nature and sold to farmers for introduction into the fields. Examples are the praying mantises and ladybird beetles that can be bought for home gardens at most garden stores.* Nesting sites can be prepared, especially for birds, and one can always choose not to remove the critical habitat of a species with a key role in the control scheme.

A variant on food chain control is the development of pest diseases that can be spread through the environment and cause increased mortality of the pest population. Several of these have already been marketed. One, milky spore virus, affects certain species of beetles, including the Japanese beetle. At one time the Japanese beetle was a very serious pest on roses and other ornamental shrubs, and people with rose gardens during the 1950s could expect to pick thousands off their rose bushes during the summer. Today, milky spore virus has spread through most of North America to a degree that the Japanese beetle population is held down to an acceptable level most of the time.

A species of bacterium known as *Bacillus thuringiensis* has proven to be quite toxic

---

*De Bach (1974, p. 236) points out an important caveat that should be borne in mind with regard to the widespread use of certain common beneficial insects such as the ladybird beetle. The behavior of these animals depends on their state of development and position within their life cycle. Most ladybird beetles sold are in a state of ovarian diapause and are not ready either to feed heavily or to reproduce. Only preconditioned beetles are capable of providing effective control of insect pests. Fortunately these are available from some sources.

to soft-bodied insects such as the caterpillar stages of many obnoxious moths. This bacterium has recently been released for commercial use against certain insects, and tests of this and other bacteria indicate that bacteria will be a very potent weapon for controlling these insects in the future (Table 6.7). More highly pathogenic bacteria and viruses, quite specific to given pest groups, are also under development (CEQ, 1972).

Pheromones. Chemicals can be used in alternative ways to control pest populations. For example, many flying insects locate each other at mating time by secreting volatile substances termed *pheromones*. If these can be collected or synthesized in sufficient quantity, they can be used to jam the olfactory apparatus of the flying insects, so that males and females cannot locate each other (Marx, 1973). Release of these

Table 6.7   Representative Pathogens Intended for Use Against Agricultural and Forest Pests in the United States.

Pathogens	Pests Controlled
Under Commercial Production	
Bacillus popilliae	Japanese beetle.
Bacillus thuringiensis	Larvae of various moths and butterflies.
Nuclear polyhedrosis virus	Cotton bollworm; Corn earworm.
Under Serious Development	
Viruses	Cabbage looper; diamond back moth; beet armyworm; tobacco budworm; pink bollworm; cotton leaf perforator; alfalfa looper; fall armyworm; saltmarsh caterpillar; Douglas fir tussock moth; gypsy moth; codling moth; red banded leaf roller; European pine sawfly; pine sawfly; spruce budworm; soybean looper; citrus red mite; mosquitoes.
Fungae	Citrus rust mite; pecan weevil; corn borer; leafhoppers; sugarbeet curcuilio; cutworm froghopper; rhinoceros beetle; wheat cockchafer; corn rootworm; white fringed beetle; Colorado potato beetle.
Protozoa	Grasshoppers.
Not Under Serious Development	
Nuclear polyhedrosis virus	Yellow striped armyworm; almond moth; indian meal moth; cotton leafworm; alfalfa looper; Great Basin tent caterpillar; western tent caterpillar; eastern tent caterpillar; hemlock looper.

After Council on Environmental Quality, 1972.

nontoxic chemicals into the environment in large enough quantities (many times smaller than normal insecticide usage levels) can destroy the normal pheromone gradient that would lead the male to the female. As an example, fertile female gypsy moths are so loaded down with eggs that they cannot fly. They must somehow lure the flying males to them. One sex attractant known as Disparlure has been tested experimentally in the northeastern United States and has been moderately effective in controlling the gypsy moth (Beroza and Knipling, 1972).

Conversely, pheromones can be used in conjunction with a relatively small amount of toxic insecticide in an enclosed box. The pheromone issues from the trap as though it were a female (indeed, trapped females may be used as the pheromone source), so that males are attracted to the trap thinking that it is the female of the species.

The chemistry of pheromones is not simple. They are typically mixtures of complex molecules. The substances comprising a given pheromone are often closely related and may be isomers with the same basic formula. Figure 6.20 shows the different responses of two very closely related species of peach stem borer to different mixtures of two isomers of a single chemical (Tumlinson et al., 1974). Similar phenomena are reported for the European corn borer and red-banded leaf roller by Klun et al., (1973). The pheromone of the oak leaf roller was found to consist of a mixture of up to ten related compounds (Hendry, et al, 1975).

Pheromones do not kill the target species. They are used in very much lower concentrations than insecticides, and they are highly species-specific. Unfortunately, they cannot be used with all insects, and isolation and synthesis of a pheromone complex requires years of expensive research. But once the pheromone has been tested and proven effective, the monetary costs of applications are much less than those of standard chemical pesticides, and the external costs are infinitesimal. In many ways they represent the ideal chemical control method.

Other Third-Generation Chemicals.   Other third-generation chemicals are the *juvenile hormones* or *molting hormones*. These are extremely powerful hormones nor-

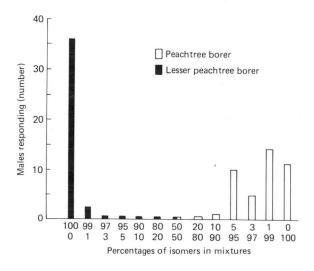

Figure 6.20 Relative responses of male peach stem borers of two closely related species to mixtures of two isomers of a synthetic pheromone in the proportions shown; 120 nanograms of pheromone mixture is equivalent to 1 peachtree borer or 30 lesser peachtree borers in attractive ability. [Redrawn, with permission, from Tumlinson et al., "Sex Pheromones and Reproductive Isolation of the Lesser Peachtree Borer and the Peachtree Borer." *Science* 172: 955–958. Copyright © 1974 by the American Association for the Advancement of Science.]

mally present in the body of the larval pest. Their presence must be timed very closely if the insect is to develop normally. If they can be introduced into the environment in such a way as to be absorbed by the pest at the critical time, the larvae do not metamorphose into adulthood, but rather into an intermediate but basically larval insect that does not survive long. The specificity of the juvenile hormones is much higher than most chemical pesticides, but lower than that of the pheromones. One such hormone, altoside SR-10, has been approved for use on floodwater mosquitoes, but other applications can be devised. A serious drawback to their use is that they are effective only at the final larval instar stage. That is after many pests have done their worst damage. But these have great promise for relatively light infestations of insects whose most detrimental stage is the adult (Marx, 1973).

Another hormone that may prove to have some use is the *anti-juvenile hormone* (Bowers et al, 1976). This has been recovered from a common plant, and its effect is to cause a larva to molt into a precocious adult. The adult is sterile and often dies quickly. Anti-juvenile hormones represent compounds of very high specificity and low toxicity that have many of the advantages and few of the disadvantages of chemical insecticides.

Physical Methods of Control. Numerous mechanisms can be lumped together as physical methods of pest control. One of them is as old as agriculture, the simple mechanical cultivation of crops. This removes weeds and may affect a number of insects as well. The physical removal of insects from a crop is often possible, especially for large insect pests. Scarecrows have been used to frighten birds, as have noisemakers of various sorts. One of the more interesting variants of the noisemaker is the underwater loudspeaker to keep fish out of water intakes to electric power plants. Loud radio programs frighten the fish away. (It has been observed in empirical tests that rock music is the most effective at driving fish away.) Electric lights shining in fields may either attract or repel insects, depending on what kind of light is used. Attracting in-

Figure 6.21 Standing rows of young wheat are resistant to the Hessian fly; other rows are susceptible. [Photograph courtesy of U.S. Department of Agriculture.]

sects to grates on which they are electrocuted, and shining ultraviolet light that repels the insects, are equally effective (Osmun, 1972).

A very important variant on the physical control method is cultural control, by which cultural practices are so synchronized with those of the pest that planting, harvesting, and other activities are adjusted to minimize the problem. The best example of this is the Hessian fly, a serious pest of wheat. At one time the Hessian fly took large percentages of the North American wheat crop and represented potential economic disaster (Figure 6.21). At this point it is possible to control the Hessian fly largely by using resistant varieties of wheat and delaying planting until after the hatching of Hessian fly eggs. If their primary food supply is not present, the population never grows large enough to do much damage. The wheat can still be planted early enough to allow a sufficient crop. Figure 6.22 shows the approximate dates after which wheat can be safely planted to avoid Hessian fly damage.

Sterile Male Technique.   The sterile male technique of pest control is one that has been used rather effectively for a very small group of insects, but that shows some promise of being modifiable to a much larger and more significant group. Large numbers of pest males are sterilized through irradiation or chemical sterilization in the laboratory and released into the environment, where they mate with wild females. The sterile male technique depends on the laboratory's ability to irradiate just enough to disrupt the genetic information in the nucleus but not so much as to prevent the sperm from fertilizing the egg. As a result, viable young do not result from the mating. This is a most effective way of pest control where it can be used, since it is absolutely nontoxic to the environment. It does not involve the relase of any chemicals, and it is dif-

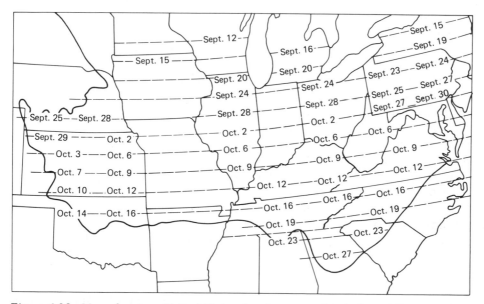

Figure 6.22 Map of eastern United States showing approximate dates following which wheat can safely be planted to minimize damage from Hessian fly. [Redrawn, with permission, from Gallun, 1965.]

ficult for insects to develop genetic resistance to a method based on simple sexual reproduction.

It was first tried on a broad scale with an important livestock pest, the screwworm, a species of fly that lays its eggs on open sores (Knipling, 1972, Bushland, 1974). The maggots feed on the wound, enlarging it so that even more eggs are likely to be laid there. The screwworm is seldom fatal but is the source of great pain and weight loss to the animals. The screwworm had a characteristic that made it ideal for a first test of this method. The female screwworm mates once and then does not remate. For this reason a female screwworm that mates with a sterile male will never produce viable young. Furthermore, the screwworm is an animal that can be raised under insectary conditions and sterilized quite efficiently.

The technique of sterilizing the male screwworm was demonstrated on a laboratory basis by the U.S. Department of Agriculture in the early 1950s. It was necessary to demonstrate it in the field before it could be put to any practical use. For obvious reasons, few stock farmers in the United States were enthusiastic about having large numbers of screwworms released into their areas, even when they were assured that the operation would not cause increases in the screwworm population. In addition, since the screwworm is an important economic pest, ranchers were taking precautions of various sorts against it, and it would not have been possible to get a sufficiently controlled large-scale experiment in the continental United States.

A demonstration was made on the island of Curacao. This island of 448 sq. km. has a large livestock industry, and the livestock growers are quite poor. The screwworm is an endemic and important pest. Large numbers of irradiated screwworm males were spread across the island by airplane. By 1954 the screwworm had been essentially irradicated and was no longer an economic pest on the island. The success with the screwworm program in Curaçao convinced the U.S. Department of Agriculture to try to expand the program to the mainland United States. Starting in Florida in 1958, the screwworm program worked its way north and west until it had covered all the screwworm-infected areas in the continental United States. A buffer zone was established at the southern end of the Mexican desert, with billions of irradiated male screwworms released every year. This aids the Mexican livestock industry and limits the recolonization of the pest.

It has been estimated that the amount of money saved through the screwworm program approaches $120 million per year, at an annual cost of $6 million. This represents a significant cost-benefit ratio for effective control of an important pest. The sterile male technique has also been used with some success on several species of oriental fruit flies, and local control of the cotton boll weevil has been obtained. For other insects, including the codling moth, the method has proven an expensive failure. According to E. F. Knipling (1972), the "father" of the sterile male technique, the approach is unlikely to have a wide application to large numbers of species. But for some species, and as part of an integrated control program, it may be spectacularly successful.

Integrated Pest Management

There are often reasons why biological control based on one or two predators or parasites cannot be used to control a given pest. The enemy may not exist in the area or may have been killed off by excessive use of pesticides. The sterile male technique is not useful when the pest is so common that it is not possible to infuse the area with enough sterile males to disrupt reproduction. The insect may not respond effectively to light or other physical devices.

In such instances, which comprise the majority of cases, a combination of methods is needed, so that the pest population is manipulated by whichever method is most effective at the current pest density. This is *integrated pest management.* A typical scenario would be to use chemical pesticides to reduce the pest population in a brute force fashion, to a point where biological controls could be brought to bear effectively. One or more biological methods can be used, together or *seriatim,* whichever is most effective. As an example, a highly toxic organophospate pesticide might be used to knock the pest population down to a threshold level. As soon as it has been degraded, parasites could be introduced *en masse.* When these have lowered the population even more, the pest can be largely eradicated by means of the sterile male technique. There are many variants on the same basic theme of "the most appropriate control method given the conditions of the population at the time."

The integrated management strategy has had several marked successes in several places (CEQ, 1972). In the Cañete valley of Peru, where cotton yields responded quickly to the initial uses of chlorinated hydrocarbons but quickly declined to a point of economic and ecological disaster, integrated pest control has allowed a doubling of yield over the pre-DDT levels. In Los Baños, California, 600 acres of tomatoes formerly required spraying four to five times each season, at a cost of $20 to $50 per acre, without adequate control of the fruit worm. Integrated pest management was able to reduce the cost of pest management to $8 to $10 per acre with adequate control. Spraying is often not needed at all, but it may be used for very local outbreaks. Integrated pest management is now the accepted means of cotton pest control in the southwestern United States.

The key to a successful integrated pest management scheme is information. If farmers have no information, they may feel compelled to use prophylactic spraying as an insurance measure. In cotton lands in Arizona, tobacco acreage in North and South Carolina, and in the apple-growing Annapolis valley of Nova Scotia, there are well-developed networks of field scouts who monitor fields to report insect densities. Only when levels are above the warning level need pesticides be used. The important thing is that the farmer can be convinced that he is not endangering his livelihood by not spraying. Considering the added costs to the farmer of the scouts, but the reduced expenditures on pesticides, farmers in such programs typically save considerable money on pest control alone, and it is generally coupled with higher yields. The Council on Environmental Quality (1972) estimates that one scout per 2,000 acres and one professional crop protection specialist to 15 scouts would allow the adoption of integrated control on field crops throughout the country. This is a total manpower requirement of roughly 180,000 persons.

THE WORLD FOOD SUPPLY

Agriculture, as all sectors of modern society, is in a state of flux in all countries, rich and poor. How it changes in the present will determine its direction for the future. The problems of agriculture discussed so far are common to most countries. But their impact on society is very different in different places. Few countries are self-sufficient in food. Even in countries like Egypt and India, whose agricultural exports account for significant percentages of the country's export earnings, the exports are of cash crops. Food production is inadequate, and the country must import much of its food. Other countries such as those of Europe can grow enough food to feed themselves, but they use substantial amounts of grains as livestock feed rather than as human food and so must also import a great deal of food.

The food that passes from country to country in international trade can be regarded as coming from two major producing areas, North America and Australasia, and spreading throughout the world. It makes little difference to the producing area whether the grain is shipped to a rich country or a poor country, but it makes a great deal of difference to the people in the country of destination, and hence to world foodstuff demand. We hear a lot about the world food problem, but it is a multifaceted phenomenon with social, economic, and environmental dimensions. Many people are not eating enough. The Food and Agricultural Organization of the U.N. has estimated that some 10 million people die annually of starvation (or of diseases that would not have killed them had they been having enough to eat), and that the long-term trend in this figure is increased. At the same time, enough food is now produced to provide a good diet to all of the world's people. Indeed, Revelle (1972) has estimated that the earth could easily feed some ten times the likely maximum world population to an acceptable level of nutrition if all potentially arable land were cultivated. People are starving in the midst of what ought to be plenty.

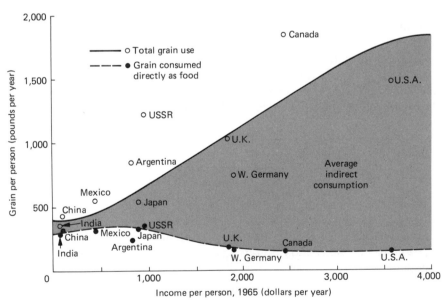

Figure 6.23 Grain use as a function of income in different countries of the world. Shaded area shows how indirect consumption increases with income per person. [Redrawn, with permission, from L. R. Brown. Population and affluence: growing pressures on world food resources. *Pop. Bull.* **29**(2): 1–32. Copyright © 1973 Population Reference Bureau.]

Table 6.8   Percentage Consumption of Selected Foodstuffs in Various Parts of the World.

	North America	Latin America	Western Europe	Africa	South Asia
Wheat	59/13	64/2	49/16	71/0	79/1
Corn	1/94	33/47	3/87	77/5	75/4
Rice	53/13	59/0	54/1	64/0	59/1
Starchy roots	70/9	43/17	50/29	67/0	67/8
Vegetables	90/0	81/7	84/1	91/0	90/0
Pulses	87/1	90/0	45/37	84/0	78/8

Numbers refer to percentage of foodstuff used as human food/livestock feed. They do not sum to 100%, as use in manufacturing and waste are not noted. Data are an average of 1964–68.
Data from FAO, 1971.

Enough food is produced, but it is not produced in the places that need it most. And the poor countries that need it most cannot afford to pay as much for it as the rich countries that feed imported grain to their livestock. As income rises, the proportion of grain diverted through livestock increases markedly, necessitating a much greater production of grain per unit of food than would have been the case had it been fed to humans directly. If all of the world's grains were consumed directly by humans instead of being fed to livestock, many more people could be fed than is now the case (Figure 6.23, Table 6.8).

In many developing countries where the land is good enough to support sharply higher production using modern methods, farmers are too poor to be able to buy the requisites of modern agriculture; modernization of the agricultural sector is impossible because the land tenure system does not provide sufficient incentives to modernize; and the other sectors of the economy cannot absorb the people who would be displaced by a rapid modernization. In many cases, the efforts of farmers to realize maximum production brings soil erosion or erosion of the genetic basis of the crop. Either can lead to disaster.

The world food problem is typical of agricultural phenomena in that its social and environmental domains are so closely intertwined with each other. Ultimately, people in poor countries cannot be fed unless they can increase their own production. This requires increasing the arable land base as well as the intensity of cropping in order to meet the demands of a growing population. They must be able to do this in a way that is economically feasible and sustainable over the long term. This cannot be done without social readjustments that are highly unlikely without improved productivity. This is the classic "Catch 22" that confronts agricultural development and assistance efforts designed to aid development.

Traditional Development Patterns: Evolution vs. Involution

Those of us who live in agriculturally progressive areas of North America, Europe, Australia, New Zealand, and elsewhere may view agricultural development as a process of constant improvement. Technological innovations allow crop yields to rise at a relatively small price, with fewer and fewer farmers being able to feed more and more of the total population. Technological innovations allow increased productivity per unit of land and per farmer, as well as increased capital returns on investment. These lead to still more technological innovations. This process has allowed 5% of the North American population to feed the other 95% and to maintain relatively large amounts of food as exportable surpluses. This agricultural *evolution* is based on the replacement of human energy with energy from other sources: first draft animals, and later fossil-fuel-powered machines. As nonhuman power became available in the fields, labor was released from agriculture to go to the city and produce more energy, more machines, and more technology to increase the efficiency of the labor left in the field. There is a positive feedback between labor productivity in the fields and productivity of the urban-based economy.

Most poor countries have no market for the labor released by agricultural evolution. The number of people who remain on the farm rises, and the system becomes increasingly labor intensive. Productivity per unit area rises, as with the evolutionary pattern. But instead of increasing labor productivity per farmer, this pattern of *involution* leads to decreasing labor productivity, as increasing labor per hectare shows diminishing marginal return (Figure 6.24). Ultimately the limits of the system are reached in which each person can produce just enough to feed himself, and further infusions of labor into the field cannot produce enough to feed the additional hands.

Both evolutionary and involutionary agricultural development show diminishing returns of production as a function of energy input. Involution is ultimately limited by the nutritional efficiency of the food supply system. Modern agriculture is limited either by the availability of energy or material inputs or by the pollution effects of using high technology products and methods. For those of us who live in the developed world, involution is an unsatisfactory solution because it perpetuates the life pattern of past ages when life was "nasty, brutish, and short." It does not possess the amenities that we take for granted and value highly. But the resources of an involutionary agriculture are home-grown, so that it is always a possible option for any society. A highly capitalized technology-based agriculture is possible only when the technological and energy resources are present.

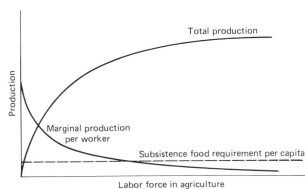

Figure 6.24 Total and marginal production as a function of labor force given a fixed land base and technological level. [After Mellor, 1966.]

Solving the World Food Crisis

The fuel crisis of the mid 1970s has clearly demonstrated the vulnerability of an agricultural system that requires continuous input of fossil-fuel-based products. In their own way, evolution and involution are both traps for the Third World. Evolution as the developed countries have known it is too expensive, both in monetary and sociocultural terms. Involution perpetuates poverty and may not be able to withstand the challenges posed by relentless population growth (Boserup, 1965). The world food problem means more than people going hungry. It is a collapse of people's ability to manage the most basic of their needs, and it may mean the collapse of societies as well. This happened in the African Sahel in the mid 1970s and in Cambodia in the late 1970s. Empires such as the Maya of Central America and several cultures of the ancient Near East have collapsed because their agricultural systems could not cope with the stresses imposed jointly with the environment and population growth (Turner, 1974; Culbert, 1973).

It is not a trivial matter to design and build nontraditional agricultural technologies in poor countries. It is bad enough to incorporate nontraditional methods of, say, pest control in developed countries where a farmer can afford to take a loss. But a loss for a subsistence farmer in the Third World spells personal starvation. Farmers must be shown that new methods will work, assured that they can afford them, and convinced that adopting them does not risk disaster for their family. Methods that work well in developed countries may not be appropriate for developing countries. Different areas of the world are differently endowed, and some places are inherently capable of much higher production than others. The world's temperate zones, which include the breadbaskets of all of the continents, are intrinsically more capable of producing field crops than are the tropics, the arctic regions, or the world's deserts. Here are the developed countries. The problems and needs of the tropics, where most developing countries are located, are very different.

To "solve" the world food problem requires a new outlook that focuses on the village and treats the social, cultural, and environmental dimensions of agriculture as a total system. The problem is not so much to generate new knowledge and new technologies or to mold new goals for public policy, as it is to take what we know about agriculture as an ecological activity and mesh it with known technologies that are adapted to the cultural realities of the people concerned, so that they can meet their own needs from their own resources. This is a slow process. The first few decades of foreign assistance following World War II have not been outstanding or shining successes. But developments in the villages of the Third World are going on, and recent information suggests that there is hope (Critchfield, 1979).

References

Adams, J. B., 1960. Effective spraying of 2,4-D amine on coccinellid larvae. *Can. J. Zool.* 38: 285–288.

Alexander, M., 1966. Biodegradation of pesticides. In S.S.S.A., *Pesticides and their effects on soil and water*. Am. Soc. Agron. Special Publ. 8: 78–84.

American Chemical Society, 1978. Pesticides in the environment. Ch. 7 in *Cleaning Our Environment: A Chemical Perspective.* Washington: Am. Chem. Soc., 320–377.

Bennett, O. L., Mathias, E. L., and Lundberg, P. E., 1973. Crop responses to no-till management practices on hilly terrain. *Agron. Jour.* **65**: 488–491.

Bennett, O. L., Stanford, G., Mathias, E. L., and Lundberg, P. E., 1975. Nitrogen conservation under corn planted in quackgrass sod. *Jour. Environ. Qual.* **4**: 107–110.

Bent, K. J., 1979. Fungicides in perspective: 1979. *Endeavour* **3**: 7–14.

Beroza, M. and Knipling, E. F., 1972. Gypsy moth control with the sex attractant pheromone. *Science* **177**: 19–27.

Blevins, R. L., Cook, D., Phillips, S. H., and Phillips, R. E., 1971. Influence of no-tillage on soil moisture. *Agron. Jour.* **63**: 593–596.

Boserup, E., 1965. *The Conditions of Agricultural Growth: The Economics of Agrarian Change under Population Pressure.* Chicago: Aldine Pub. Co., Inc.

Bowers, W. S., Ohta, T., Cleere, J. S., and Marsella, P. A., 1976. Discovery of insect anti-juvenile hormones in plants. *Science* **193**: 542–547.

Brady, N. C., 1974. *The Nature and Property of Soils,* 8th ed. New York: Macmillan Pub. Co.

Brown, A. W. A., 1978. *Ecology of Pesticides,* New York: John Wiley & Sons.

Brown, L. R., 1970. *Seeds of Change: The Green Revolution and Development in the 1970's.* New York: Praeger Publishers.

Brown, L. R., 1973. Population and affluence: growing pressures on world food resources. *Pop. Bull.* **29**(2): 1–32.

Burdick, G. E., Harris, E. J., Dean, H. J., Walker, T. M., Skea, J., and Colby, D., 1964. The accumulation of DDT in lake trout and the effect on reproduction. *Trans. Am. Fish. Soc.* **93**: 127–136.

Bushland, R. C., 1974. Screwworm eradication program. *Science* **184**: 1010–1011.

Butler, P. A., 1964. Commercial fisheries investigations in pesticide-wildlife studies. *U.S. Fish and Wildlife Serv. Circular* **199**: 5–28.

Cade, T. J., Lincer, J. L., White, C. M., Roseneau, D. G., and Swartz, L. G., 1971. DDE residues and eggshell changes in Alaskan falcons and hawks. *Science* **172**: 955–957.

Carson, R. L., 1962. *Silent Spring.* Boston: Houghton-Mifflin Co.

Chipman, W. A., Rice, T. R., and Price, T. J., 1958. Uptake and accumulation of radioactive zinc by marine plankton, fish, and shellfish. *U.S. Fish and Wildlife Serv. Fish. Bull.* **50 (135)**: 279–292.

Conklin, H. C., 1954. An ethnoecological approach to shifting agriculture. *Trans. N.Y. Acad. Sci.* **17, 2nd ser.**: 133–142.

Council on Environmental Quality, 1972. *Integrated Pest Management.* Washington: U.S. Govt. Printing Office.

Cox, J. L., 1970. DDT residues in marine phytoplankton: increase from 1955 to 1969. *Science* **170**: 71–72.

Critchfield, R., 1979. The world's villages—a fresh look. *Humanist* **39 (6)**: 4–11.

Culbert, T. P., ed., 1973. *The Classic Maya Collapse.* Albuquerque: Univ. New Mexico Press.

Davies, J. E., Jewett, J. S., Welke, J. O., Barquet, A., and Freal, J. J., 1969. Epidemiology and chemical diagnosis of organophosphate poisoning. In Deichman, W. B., Radomski, J. L., and Penalever, *Pesticides Symposia.* Miami: Halos and Assoc., 183–191.

DeBach, P., 1974. *Biological Control by Natural Enemies.* New York: Cambridge Univ. Press.

Dorough, H. W., 1970. Metabolism of insecticidal methylcarbamates in animals. *Jour. Ag. Food Chem.* **18**: 1015-1022.

Fiserova-Bergerova, V., Rodomski, J. L., Davies, J. E., and Davis, J. H., 1967. Levels of chlorinated hydrocarbon pesticides in human tissues. *Indust. Med. and Surg.* (Jan., 1967): 65-70.

Fisher, N. S., 1975. Chlorinated hydrocarbon pollutants and photosynthesis of marine phytoplankton: a reassessment. *Science* **189**: 463-464.

Food and Agricultural Organization, 1971. *Food Balance Sheets, 1964-1966.* Rome: F.A.O.

Gallun, R. L., 1965. The hessian fly: how to control it. U.S. Dept. Agric. Leaflet 533.

Greenland, D. J., 1975. Bringing the green revolution to the shifting cultivator. *Science* **190**: 841-844.

Griliches, Z., 1958. Research costs and social return: hybrid corn and related innovations. *Jour. Pol. Econ.* **66**: 419-431.

Gunn, D. L., 1972. Dilemmas in conservation for applied biologists. *Ann. Appl. Biol.* **72**: 105-127.

Harris, C. I., 1969. Movement of pesticides in soil. *Jour. Ag. Food Chem.* **17**: 80-82.

Harris, R. F. et. al., 1966. Dynamics of soil aggregation. *Adv. Agron.* **18**: 107-169.

Hayes, W. J., Jr., Durham, W. F., and Cueto, C., Jr., 1956. Effects of known repeated oral doses of chlorophenothane (DDT) in man. *J.A.M.A.* **162**: 890-897.

Heath, R. G., Spann, J. W., and Kreitzer, J. F., 1969. Marked DDE impairment of mallard reproduction in controlled studies. *Nature* **224**: 97-98.

Hendry, L. B., Anderson, M. E., Jugovich, J., Mumma, R. O., Robacker, D., and Kosarych, Z., 1975. Sex pheromone of the oak leaf roller: A complex chemical messenger system identified by mass fragmentography. *Science* **187**: 355-357.

Horsfall, J. G. et al., 1972. *Genetic Vulnerability of Major Crops.* Washington: National Academy of Sciences.

Huang, J.-C. and Liao, C.-S., 1970. Adsorption of pesticides by clay minerals. *J. San. Eng. Div., Proc. Am. Soc. Civil Eng.* **96 (SA5)**: 1057-1078.

Huffaker, C. B., 1970. Life against life—nature's pest control scheme. *Envir. Research* **3**: 162-175.

Hunt, E. G., and Bischoff, A. I., 1960. Inimical effects on wildlife of periodic DDD applications to Clear Lake. *Calif. Fish and Game* **46**: 91-106.

Hurlbert, S. H., Mulla, M. S., and Willson, H. R., 1972. Effects of an organophosphorus insecticide on the phytoplankton, zooplankton, and insect populations of freshwater ponds. *Ecol. Monog.* **42**: 269-299.

Ishii, S. and Hirano, C., 1963. Growth responses of larvae of the rice-stem borer to rice plants treated with 2,4-D. *Entomol. Exp. Appl.* **6**: 257-262.

Kapoor, I. P., Metcalf, R. L., Nystrom, R. F., and Sangha, G. K., 1970. Comparative metabolism of methoxychlor, methiochlor, and DDT in mouse, insects, and in a model ecosystem. *Jour. Ag. Food Chem.* **18**: 1145-1152.

Katan, J., Fuhremann, T. W., and Lichtenstein, E. P., 1976. Binding of [^{14}C]Parathion in soil: A reassessment of pesticide persistence. *Science* **193**: 891-894.

Klun, J. A., Chapman, O. L., Mattes, K. C., Wojtkowski, P. W., Beroza, M., and Sonnet, P. E., 1973. Insect pheromones: Minor amount of opposite geometrical isomer critical to attraction. *Science* **181**: 661-663.

Knipling, E. F., 1972. Use of organisms to control insect pests. *Jour. Env. Qual.* **1**: 34-40.

Kohl, D. H., Shearer, G. B., and Commoner, B., 1971. Fertilizer nitrogen: contribution to nitrate in surface water in a corn belt watershed. *Science* **174**: 1331-1334.

Kuhr, R. J., 1970. Metabolism of carbamate insecticide chemicals in plants and insects. *Jour. Ag. Food Chem.* **18**: 1023-1030.

Kurtz, L. T., 1970. The fate of applied nutrients in soils. *Jour. Ag. Food Chem.* **18**: 773-780.

Lichtenstein, E. P., Fuhremann, T. W., and Schultz, K. R., 1971. Persistence and vertical distribution of DDT, Lindane, and Aldrin residues, 10 and 15 years after a single soil application. *Jour. Ag. Food Chem.* **19**: 718-721.

Marx, J. L., 1973. Insect control (I): Use of Pheromones; (II): Hormones and viruses. *Science* **181**: 736-737, 833-835.

Matsumura, F., Patil, K. C., and Boush, G. M., 1971. DDT metabolism by organisms from Lake Michigan. *Nature* **230**: 325-326.

Mellor, J. W., 1966. *The Economics of Agricultural Development.* Ithaca, N.Y.: Cornell Univ. Press.

Menzel, D. W., Anderson, J., and Randke, A., 1970. Marine phytoplankton vary in their response to chlorinated hydrocarbons. *Science* **167**: 1724-1726.

Menzer, R. E. and Dauterman, W. C., 1970. Metabolism of some organophosphorus insecticides. *Jour. Ag. Food Chem.* **18**: 1031-1037.

Miller, J., 1973. Genetic erosion: crop plants threatened by government neglect. *Science* **182**: 1231-1233.

Mosser, J. L., Fisher, N. S., and Wurster, C. F., Jr., 1972. Polychlorinated biphenyls and DDT alter species composition in mixed cultures of algae. *Science* **176**: 533-535.

Mrak, E. M. et al., 1969. *Report of the Secretary's Commission on Pesticides and their Relationship to Environmental Health.* Washington: U.S. Govt. Printing Office.

Nabham, G. P., 1979. Who is saving the seeds to save us? *Mazingira* **9**: 54-59.

National Research Council, 1977. *Pesticide Decision Making.* Washington: National Academy of Sciences.

Ogilvie, D. M. and Anderson, J. M., 1965. Effect of DDT on temperature selection by young Atlantic salmon, *Salmo salar. J. Fish. Res. Bd. Canada* **22**: 503-512.

Osmun, J. V., 1972. Physical methods of pest control. *Jour. Env. Qual.* **1**: 40-45.

Peakall, D. B., 1974. DDE: its presence in peregrine eggs in 1948. *Science* **183**: 673-674.

Pimentel, D., 1971. *Ecological Effects of Pesticides on Non-Target Species.* Washington: U.S. Govt. Printing Off.

Porter, R. D. and Wiemeyer, S. N., 1969. Dieldrin and DDT: Effects on sparrowhawk eggshells and reproduction. *Science* **165**: 199-200.

Pratt, C. J., 1965. Chemical fertilizers. *Sci. Am.* **212 (6)**: 62-72.

Ratcliffe, D. A., 1967. Decrease in eggshell weight in certain birds of prey. *Nature* **215**: 208-210.

Ratcliffe, D. A., 1970. Changes attributable to pesticides in egg breakage frequency and eggshell thickness in some British birds. *J. Appl. Ecol.* **7**: 67-115.

Revelle, R., 1972. Will the earth's land and water resources be sufficient for future populations? Paper presented to the U.N. Conference on the Environment, Stockholm.

Salo, E. O. and Leet, W. L., 1969. The concentration of ^{65}Zn by oysters maintained in the discharge canal of a nuclear power plant. *Symposium on Radioecology: Proc. of the Second National Symposium, Ann Arbor Mich., May 15-17, 1967.* Springfield, Va.: Clearinghouse for Fed. Sci. and Tech. Inf., 363-371.

Scott, D. C. and Weber, J. B., 1967. Herbicide phytotoxicity as inferred by adsorption. *Soil Sci.* **104**: 151-158.

Singer, S. F., 1970. Will the world come to a horrible end? *Science* **170**: 125.

Stein, W. J. and Hayes, W. J., Jr., 1964. Health survey of pest control operators. *Indust. Med. and Surg.* **33**: 549–555.

Stern, V. M., Smith, R. F., van den Bosch, R., and Hagen, K. S., 1959. The integrated control concept. *Hilgardia* **29**: 81–101.

Tumlinson, J. H., Yonce, C. E., Doolittle, R. T., Heath, R. R., Gentry, C. R., and Mitchell, E. R., 1974. Sex pheromones and reproductive isolation of the lesser peachtree borer and the peachtree borer. *Science* **185**: 614–616.

Turner, B. L., II, 1974. Prehistoric intensive agriculture in the Mayan lowlands. *Science* **185**: 118–124.

Van Gelder, G. A., Buck, W. B., Sandler, R., Maland, J., Karas, G., and Elsberry, D., 1969. The effects of dieldrin and ruelene exposure on experimental behavior and encephalogram. In Gillett, J. W., ed., *The Biological Impact of Pesticides on the Environment.* Env. Health Ser. 1, Oregon State Univ.: 125–130.

Vietmeyer, N. D., 1979. A wild relative may give corn perennial genes. *Smithsonian* **10** (9): 68–76.

Willard, C. J., 1950. Indirect effects of herbicides. *N. Central Weed Control Conf. Proc.* **7**: 110–112.

Woodwell, G. M., Wurster, C. F., Jr., and Isaacson, P. J., 1967. DDT residues in an east coast estuary: a case of biological concentration of a persistent insecticide. *Science* **156**: 821–824.

Wright, F. C., Riner, J. C., and Younger, R. L., 1972. Residues in chickens given DDT. *Jour. Ag. Food Chem.* **20**: 17–19.

Wurster, C. F., Jr., 1968. DDT reduces photosynthesis by marine phytoplankton. *Science* **159**: 1474–1475.

7/ energy, materials, and the metabolism of a modern society

The metabolism of an organism is the process by which it procures materials and energy and converts them into its tissues or consumes them to keep itself alive and operating. In the same way, the metabolism of a modern society is the process by which society procures and uses resources to keep itself in operation. Some of these resources consist of food to satisfy the biological needs of the population, but a functioning society requires much more than food. It needs energy in numerous forms, as well as inorganic resources. Some forms of energy resources are renewable. They are constantly being replenished by the sun. Others, as well as most nonenergy resources, are nonrenewable. The earth contains a finite amount of them.

Energy is the capacity to do work. An energy resource is a material that contains within it the capacity to do work of some sort. It may be potential energy attributable to the chemical nature of the material, as in the fossil fuels. It may be a physical characteristic of the material in question, as in the nuclear fission potential of heavy atoms and the heat from geothermal springs that can be harnessed to heat houses or run electric turbines. Finally, it may be a function of the material's environment, as with hydroelectric energy that can be obtained by harnessing moving water or wind power that can be harnessed using a windmill.

Energy is unique in that it is subject to transformations that are governed by the laws of thermodynamics. Potential energy can be changed to electricity, kinetic energy to potential, or electricity to heat. Doing work requires energy transformation. But whenever energy is changed from one form to another to do useful work, the energy transfer process is never perfectly efficient. Some of the energy is always wasted. The energy that is not used is still energy, but it is no longer available to do work; this unavailable energy is called *entropy*.

Materials, on the other hand, are those things that are useful to society because of their physical and/or chemical properties. They obey the laws of conservation of matter, so that using them does not render them unavailable. They simply change their form. This is a significant difference, although it might not seem so at this point. For example, iron after it has been mined and cast into a bridge is still iron. After it has passed its usefulness and is scrapped, it is still iron and can, in principle, be refabricated to use for anything that iron can be used for. On the other hand, once the energy in gasoline has been transformed into mechanical energy to move a car, it is gone. When the gas tank is empty and the car has coasted to a stop, the energy cannot be retrieved.

Many materials are present in large quantities in the earth's crust. But the resources from which we can obtain useful forms of particular materials may be relatively expensive or rare. A resource is a substance that can serve as an economically feasible source of a material or fuel. Thus, granite and the mineral sylvite (KCl) both contain potassium. Granite is quite common and it contains many times more potassium than the rare mineral sylvite. But granite is difficult to break down, and potassium is a minor constituent, so that granite does not constitute a resource for potassium. Potassium can be obtained cheaply from sylvite through electrolysis, even though this mineral is rare.

At one time the iron ore resources of North America consisted mainly of the hematite deposits of northern Michigan and Minnesota. Many other iron-containing deposits existed, but none was as rich as these, so that none was considered a resource for this element. But the hematite deposits were largely played out by the end of World War II, and other sources for iron had to be located. Stockpiles of hematite were retained for national security purposes, but the technology for using taconite was developed. Taconite is a processed, pelletized ore derived from low-grade mine tailings. As the price of the iron ore (and also that of the iron) rose, taconite became the chief ore for iron in steel mills of the north central United States. Indeed, the technology of taconite-based iron smelting is so highly developed now that the reserves of the formerly valuable hematite are no longer as useful as the formerly useless taconite.

RESOURCE CLASSIFICATION

In order to get a feeling for resources, it is useful to discuss them by using the economist's terms *supply* and *demand*. The economist's meaning is quite specific. The terms represent a relationship between quantities supplied or demanded and an associated price (Figure 7.1a). The quantity of a commodity that is purchased is a function of the price at which it is offered. Less is purchased as the price goes up; more is purchased as the price goes down. Demand is the relationship between quantity and price (and not the quantity itself). Supply is the relationship between price and the quantity that can be provided at that price. At very low prices only commodities easiest to obtain (i.e., at least cost) can be supplied to the market; as the price rises, more of the commodity can be supplied from more marginal or recalcitrant sources.

The notion of price implies a market (Figure 7.1b). Suppliers and demanders (sel-

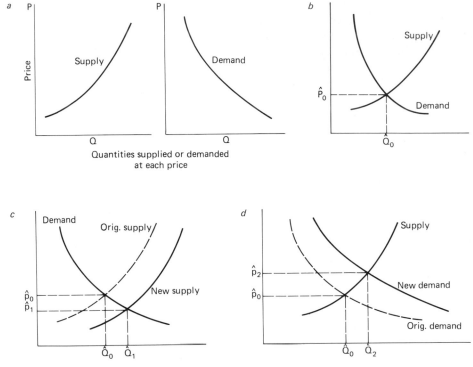

Figure 7.1 Economic notions of supply and demand: (*a*) supply and demand are both quantities transacted as a function of price; (*b*) a market reaches equilibrium where the supply and demand curves for each commodity cross; $\hat{P}$ and $\hat{Q}$ represent equilibrium levels of P and Q, respectively; (*c*) equilibrium can shift with shifts in supply; the new equilibria are $\hat{P}_1$ and $\hat{Q}_1$ rather than $\hat{P}_0$ and $\hat{Q}_0$ as in part *b*; (*d*) equilibrium can also shift with shifts in demand; the new equilibria are at $\hat{P}_2$ and $\hat{Q}_2$.

lers and buyers) both enter the market. Each is characterized by a relationship between quantity and price. There is one price, however, at which the quantity demanded and the quantity supplied are equal. This is the *equilibrium price*. The market price tends to move to this level so that the equilibrium quantity of the commodity moves from seller to buyer.

No market is static. Technological developments may lower the production cost of a commodity. This allows the supply curve to *shift* to the right (Figure 7.1c). Instead of the original supply curve (the dashed line), a greater quantity can be supplied at each price (the solid line). If consumer demand does not shift, the equilibrium market shows greater commodity transfer at lower prices. Demand can also shift (Figure 7.1d) in response to numerous factors. This does not mean that a greater quantity is desired; it means that people are willing to pay more for a given quantity or that they will purchase more at the same price. If supply does not shift, the equilibrium market shows greater commodity transfer at higher prices.

Of course this is a highly idealized version of supply, demand, and equilibrium markets; the interest reader is referred to an economics text such as Samuelson (1980) for greater detail. The important factors for our purposes are the gross causes and effects of shifts in demand and supply. Supply shifts generally occur when the costs of producing a commodity change. The supply curve can shift to the right with discovery of new supplies, lower labor costs, technological innovation, and so on. It tends to shift to the left as a result of supply exhaustion, increases in taxes or labor costs, or removal of low-cost sources through political trade restrictions.

Demand shifts are more subtle. They may involve public taste, but they are more likely to involve the interactions among different commodities. For example, consider the response of demand for a commodity such as the iron drainpipe to the introduction of plastic drainpipe. The latter is cheaper, easier to install, and lower in its maintenance cost. With its introduction and acceptance, the demand curve for the iron pipe shifted greatly to the left. The same thing happened to coal as a home-heating fuel in the United States when the construction of large transcontinental gas pipelines allowed natural gas to become a feasible alternative. The hematite stockpiles in the Mesabi range do not lie unused because their iron content is low; it is still higher than that of the taconite. Rather they are unused because the technology of taconite handling is sufficiently well developed that its costs are lower than those of hematite handling. The demand curve for hematite has been shifted because of substitution by taconite.

Supply and demand can also be influenced by advertising and by policies such as taxation or subsidies. Price itself may be influenced by nonmarket factors. The whole notion of market behavior for commodities subject to substitution, price manipulation on the supply side, and so forth, is a complex one. Nowhere are the complexities better shown than in energy resources, where supply can be controlled to a high degree by policy decisions in both producer and consumer countries, and demand is determined by people's expectations, tempered by propaganda, advertising, and politically motivated statements of all sorts.

Resource Classification and Supply

One of the most basic questions regarding nonrenewable resource supply is, how much of it is there? For various reasons, we do not know how much of any of our basic mineral and fuel resources may exist in the ground at any time. The best estimates are quite crude. A simple classification for resources has been devised by McKelvey (1972). It has been adopted by the U.S. Geological Survey and the U.S. Bureau of Mines and is shown in Figure 7.2. It recognizes that two dimensions of ignorance preclude our understanding the resource situation completely and concisely. The first of these, represented by the horizontal axis of the diagram, is geological; the second is economic or technological, represented by the vertical.

Geologically, a resource may be identified or it may be undiscovered (Schanz, 1976). That is, we may have geological evidence that a mineral or fuel exists in a specific place, or we may believe that unspecified bodies of mineral-bearing material exist in a broad area based on accumulated geologic knowledge and theory. Identified resources may be demonstrated (measured within accepted limits of error from well-known samples or indicated on the basis of fewer samples and reasonable geologic projections) or merely inferred. The undiscovered resources may be hypothetical (i.e., undiscovered minerals reasonably expected to exist in a known district under known

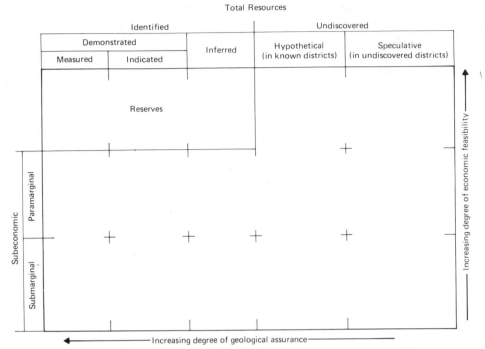

Figure 7.2   Graphic classification of resources and reserves of nonrenewable resources. [Redrawn, with permission, from Schanz, 1976.]

geological conditions) or speculative (i.e., undiscovered minerals occurring in known types of deposits in undiscovered districts or in unknown or unrecognized types of deposits).

Along the technoeconomic gradient, a resource may be economic or subeconomic, and subeconomic resources can be further classified into paramarginal and submarginal. An economic resource is one whose concentration and geologic environment allow its extraction at a cost (economic and social) sufficiently low that it can be brought to market economically and legally. All resource production is from demonstrated economic deposits. The sum of all identified economic resources is termed the reserves. The proportion of the subeconomic resources that cannot be produced economically or for political reasons, or that borders on being economically producible, is termed the paramarginal. The submarginal resources are those that would require a substantially higher price (and no increase in costs) or a major cost-reducing advance in technology for production to become feasible.

Other resource classifications (see Schanz, 1976 for a review of American classifications) recognize these two gradients of ignorance. The boundaries of classes are by no means static. A given deposit may change from paramarginal to economic by an improvement of extraction technology. Conversely it may go from economic to paramarginal by a drop in price or a change in legal status. A deposit may go from hypothetical or inferred to demonstrated by being discovered and measured. As examples, the minimum grade of copper ore that can be profitably worked has declined steadily from 3% copper content in 1880 to 2% about 1910 to 1% about 1940 to 0.5% by

1970. The discovery of oil in Prudhoe Bay, Alaska, and the Gulf of Mexico off Mexico added major new fields to the world's proven oil reserves. What had been speculative deposits in untested districts quickly became measured.

In trying to assess the state of nonrenewable resources at any point in time, we are constrained by experience and current practices. We do not know and cannot often predict the developments in technology, exploration, or hazards that will move the boundaries shown in Figure 7.2. These movements are the source of uncertainty in detailed estimates of mineral resources.

Resource Substitution and Demand

A large literature within resource economics charts the consumption patterns of various resources as functions of both time and price. It suggests that market forces are sufficiently powerful to assure that shortages of basic resources will never develop. An accessible statement of this viewpoint is that of Barnett and Morse (1963). The viewpoint depends on two premises, both of which are generally acceptable. First, price rises will tend to stimulate supply responses in the form of new technology, which increases the availability of resources. Paramarginal supplies become economic, and the supply curve shifts to the right. There may be a limit to this response, but we have not yet reached it. Second, the consumer can substitute among materials (e.g., aluminum for copper, Buick for Mercedes, Oakland for San Francisco, gas for oil), based on his personal preferences and on price. Consumers seldom care about the precise commodity they are buying; its function is the important consideration. As relative prices change, substitutions alter demand patterns, and commodities whose supply responses are easiest are favored. This buffering process extends to the entire system and minimizes the role of shortages in any given commodity. Continued economic growth requires substitution among different resources and further technological growth.

We can probably assume continuing technological growth for some time. Probably there are limits, but we do not yet know what forms these limits will take. Some limits to substitution are already clear. For example, while petroleum (in the form of plastics) can be substituted for many metals for numerous purposes, metals cannot be substituted for petroleum as a fuel. Energy materials have a unique role in the economy of society. While they may be substituted for each other to a degree, they have no easy substitute.

MATERIAL RESOURCES

The material resources of a society include a remarkable assortment of everything under the sun. There are metals, nonmetallic elements, and common aggregate materials such as sand and gravel. They are used as building materials, chemical resources and intermediates, vessels, elements in the transportation link, and as the material basis for every other function of society. Depending on the value of the material, it may be obtained purely locally as in the case of sand and gravel, or it may be an element in worldwide trade networks such as chromium or tin for metal alloys. No modern society is self-sufficient in all the mineral resources of which it makes use. Some industrial nations such as Japan are dependent on outside sources for virtually all their requirements, while other countries may be self-sufficient in a few (see, for example, Table 7.1). But no region of the world could survive as a modern society if it were not part of the worldwide trade networks of the major mineral resources.

Mineral resources are nonrenewable. There is a finite number of atoms of every

Table 7.1 Proportions of Key Materials Imported into the United States, 1974.

Mineral	Percent Imported	Major Source Countries
Strontium	100	Mexico, United Kingdom, Spain.
Columbium	100	Brazil, Malysia, Zaire.
Mica (sheet)	99	India, Brazil, Malagasy Republic.
Cobalt	98	Zaire, Belgium, Luxembourg, Finland, Norway, Canada.
Manganese	98	Brazil, Gabon, South Africa, Zaire.
Titanium	97	Australia, India.
Chromium	91	USSR, South Africa, Turkey, Philippines.
Aluminum	88	Jamaica, Australia, Surinam, Canada.
Asbestos	87	Canada, South Africa.
Platinum group	86	United Kingdom, USSR, South Africa.
Tin	85	Malaysia, Thailand, Bolivia.
Fluorine	86	Mexico, Spain, Italy.
Mercury	82	Canada, Algeria, Mexico, Spain.
Bismuth	81	Peru, Mexico, Japan, United Kingdom.
Nickel	73	Canada, Norway.
Gold	69	Canada, Switzerland, USSR.
Silver	68	Canada, Mexico, Peru, Honduras.
Selenium	63	Canada, Japan, Mexico.
Zinc	61	Canada, Mexico, Peru, Australia, Japan.
Tungsten	60	Canada, Bolivia, Peru, Thailand.
Potassium	58	Canada.
Cadmium	53	Mexico, Canada, Australia, Japan.
Antimony	46	South Africa, Mexico, China, Bolivia.
Tellurium	41	Peru, Canada.
Barium	40	Ireland, Peru, Mexico.
Vanadium	40	South Africa, Chile, USSR.
Gypsum	37	Canada, Mexico, Jamaica.
Petroleum	35	Canada, Venezuela, Nigeria, Netherlands Antilles, Iran.
Iron	23	Canada, Venezuela, Japan, European Common Market.
Lead	21	Canada, Peru, Australia, Mexico.
Copper	18	Canada, Peru, Chile, South Africa.
Salt	7	Canada, Mexico, Bahamas, Chile.
Natural Gas	4	Canada.

After Kirby and Prokopovitsh, 1976.

element and this number does not change regardless of the rate at which minerals are mined, smelted, fabricated, used, or thrown away. There is every bit as much silver or mercury in the world today, when they are in short supply, as there was 10,000 years ago when both elements could be found pure in nature. The significance of mineral resources does not lie in themselves but rather in their relationship to specific functions. There really are very few products whose specifications are so rigid that different materials could not be used under certain circumstances. Substitution of one material for another is almost always possible and should be regarded as standard practice when there is a reason for the substitution. However, all materials are limited, and uses compete with one another for the same materials. If any factor limits the degree of development for resources in general, then it may also limit the substitutability of one resource for another. There is such a limit; it is energy.

ENERGY

Energy is a critical requisite of any society, and it is also one of the most complex. It includes the fuels, which are materials found in the earth's crust and that enter the human consumption stream much as any other material resource. It includes all of the conversion processes between fuel and the form of final use. Some of these conversions are very simple; others represent complex phenomena not found in nature. Some forms of energy have finite resources; others will last as long as the sun. Some forms are more directly useful than others. Unfortunately, the more limited sorts of energy tend also to be the most useful and efficiently converted, while the unlimited forms tend to be dispersed and less easily used.

In a global sense, there are only three ultimate sources of energy: the sun, gravity, and the atomic nucleus. Some forms comprise the normal and continuing processes that occur routinely in ecosystems due to the energy constantly being intercepted by the sun. This is the natural energy source for ecosystems in general. It has been an integral part of living systems for over four billion years. In a sense, this is analogous to income and it is available to people whether or not it is tapped. It is commonly stored only in the tissues of living organisms. But these tissues can accumulate slowly under peculiar geological conditions to form energy "capital" such as petroleum and coal. These are, in essence, stored sunlight. While they are being formed currently and continually, their rate of formation is slower by several orders of magnitude than the rate at which they are being used. Table 7.2 summarizes the different types of energy sources.

Sun-derived Energy Sources

Of all the energy sources that might conceivably become available to society, the sun is unquestionably the most powerful. Häfele (1975) has estimated that insolation (solar energy reaching the earth's surface) in the Federal Republic of Germany, a northern industrial country, is almost 90 times the country's total fossil-fuel consumption in 1970. Solar energy harnessed at even a low conversion efficiency could make a substantial contribution in a modern industrial society. In more primitive societies the sun is

Table 7.2 Classification of Energy Sources.

Solar-derived Natural Energy Types
  Very short time-scale (hours to days):
    Wind.
    Water power.
    Direct solar radiation.
  Medium time-scale (months to years):
    Biomass (photosynthesis).
    Ocean thermal gradient.
  Long time-scale (centuries to millions of years):
    Peat, lignite, and coal.
    Petroleum, tar.
    Natural gas.
Gravity-derived Energy Types
  Water power.
  Tidal power.
Nuclear Energy Types
  Fission by fissile isotopes.
  Fusion of small nuclei.
  Radioactive decay of radioactive isotopes.
Derived Energy Types (derivable from any of above)
  Energy forms essentially similar to natural sources:
    Synthetic petroleum liquids.
    Synthetic natural gas, power gas, etc.
  Energy as heat collected from primary energy source conversion:
    Heat engine: turbine, engine, power plant, etc.
    Heat usable directly as heat.
  Electricity.
  Electromagnetic radiation (e.g., microwaves).

still the primary energy source. Firewood and other combustible photosynthetically derived materials represent controllable forms of solar energy stored in chemical form. Firewood is still the major energy source for most of the world's population (Eckholm, 1975).

Almost as old as their use by people are windpower and waterpower. These too are forms of solar energy. Wind is a phenomenon caused by the uneven heating of different air masses in different places and their consequent moving to regain physical equilibrium. Waterpower is the result of the interaction of gravity and the hydrologic cycle. The sun evaporates the water; rainfall deposits it at higher elevations, where gravity carries it back downhill.

A less obvious sort of solar energy is the ocean's thermal gradient. Just as the uneven heating of air masses gives rise to wind current, ocean currents result from uneven heating of the ocean's waters. These currents may extend many thousands of kilometers across the sea. Water in an ocean current moving over water of different temperature establishes a high thermal gradient. These gradients have not been tapped as commercial energy sources. But the energy is there, and mechanisms for using it are under development. The final type of solar energy source is, of course, the direct insolation from the sun.

Biomass Energy.   The average insolation at ground level in the temperate zone is about 0.26 langleys (cal./sq. cm./min.), or 182 watts/sq. m. (von Hippel and Williams, 1974).* The chemical reactions involved in photosynthesis have a theoretical maximum efficiency of 5% to 7%. Things are never this good in the real world, however. Even in tropical bogs photosynthesis is only about 4% efficient, and typical values for plants in the temperate zone are between 0.25% and 1%. These efficiencies are lower than the theoretical maximum because a real plant must maintain other vital functions. Much of the energy fixed through photosynthesis is lost in respiration. Also, a plant is part of a larger community and it cannot put all its resources into primary production. There is a balance between photosynthetic efficiency and all the other functions necessary for the survival of the plant in its total context.

Photosynthesis is perhaps the cheapest conversion process for solar energy into a directly usable form. Firewood has been used as a fuel for many thousands of years. It is familiar to a broad range of potential users, and the installed capacity of wood stoves and fireplaces far outstrips the combined total of all other solar-energy-based sources. Wood and woody crop residues have an energy content similar to lignite (2.3 kwh/kg) and even bituminous coal (8.1 kwh/kg). Furthermore, their sulfur and ash contents are low, and they can be burned or gasified as easily as coal (Hammond, 1977). In addition, they can be fermented to alcohol or digested anaerobically to methane. The obstacles to their greater use are mainly handling difficulties and land-use constraints.

Several industries obtain a considerable proportion of their energy needs from biomass. In the United States the forest products industries get some 40% from this source, and in Sweden the proportion is nearer 60%. A walnut factory near Stockton, California, expects to halve the cost of its gas supply by building a gasifier that can produce gas at a rate of 41,400 kw. from walnut shells. It has been estimated that forest product wastes already collected in California alone could produce 31.8 billion kwh. of gas annually using similar gasifiers.

It is not certain how much energy could be obtained from sources outside of the forest-product industries, however. It has been estimated that about 6% of the total energy consumption of the United States could be produced by short-rotation forestry on about 10% of the country's now idle land. Sycamore trees planted in rows and harvested after five years yield between 22 and 36 metric tons of harvestable biomass per hectare per year. This is equivalent to 120,000 to 200,000 kwh per year. The Swedish Secretariat for Future Studies has estimated that energy plantations, largely of fast-

---

*For the rest of this discussion we shall speak of energy in kilowatt-hours (kwh) and power (i.e., energy per unit time) in watts (w). The basic unit of energy in the metric system is the joule; this is the energy needed to move a 1-kilogram object one meter. It takes 4.2 joules to equal 1 gram-calorie, or 4,200 to equal 1 kilogram-calorie, so the joule represents a very small amount of energy and is not very useful for our purposes. A watt is the amount of power generated by a machine producing one joule per second. A kilowatt is 1,000 watts. A kilowatt-hour is the amount of energy supplied by one kilowatt of power for one hour. It is equal to $3.6 \times 10,000,000$ joules.

growing hardwoods in Swedish bogs, could produce almost 50% of the nation's total energy needs by 2015 (Johansson and Steen, 1978).

Aquatic plants have been proposed as energy sources. From blue-green algae growing on sewage wastes to water hyacinths that clog numerous inland waterways around the world, yields of 20 to 80 tons per hectare of dry biomass can be produced and digested anaerobically to produce methane. Wilcox (1975) proposes a series of marine "farms" covering an area over 40,000 sq. km and costing over $2 billion. Nutrient-rich bottom water would be pumped up to the surface. Large seaweeds (kelp) would be harvested periodically and used as a source of energy, food, fertilizer, and industrial feedstock.

Regardless of the potential of biomass, however, most estimates suggest that the contributions of biomass fuels to energy consumption in an industrial country such as the United States is limited to about 10%. In Sweden, which is a leader in biomass energy and which has a large forest products industry, the contribution is now about 7%. The only fields likely to be dedicated to biomass fuel production are marginal lands, since standard field crops return more to the farmer on prime agricultural land than do fuel crops (von Hippel and Williams, 1975).

Certain field crops lend themselves to multiple-use agricultural systems producing food, fiber, and energy simultaneously. Corn, for example, is an excellent source of ethanol (grain alcohol). This can be burned as a fuel or mixed with gasoline to make gasohol. Corn husks and stalks can be used as fiber for paper production as well as fuel. The stillage (mash) remaining after ethanol fermentation can be used as a protein-rich animal feed. The markets for corn are such that it is unlikely that energy will ever be its primary use. But alcohol production would strengthen the market for corn and would support prices during bumper years when supplies were high.

The cellulose residue from sugarcane, or *bagasse,* has a yield of about 9 metric tons per hectare. This has an energy content equivalent to almost 6 tons of coal. Given appropriate collection and processing facilities, sugarcane could be visualized as a fuel crop as well as a source of a valuable edible commodity. The sugar can also be fermented to make ethanol. Brazil is already looking into producing enough ethanol from sugarcane to run the country's automobiles on alcohol (Goldemberg, 1978).

Short-rotation silviculture can be carried out as part of a larger term soil conservation program, as harvesting small trees for energy is much less damaging than harvesting large trees for timber or pulpwood, and the unharvested root system would remain behind to help stabilize and add organic matter to the soil.

Ironically, a drawback to the expansion of biomass energy is precisely that its biggest advantage is its ability to be part of a larger system. As pointed out by Hammond (1977), bureaucracies that might expedite or regulate new technologies such as biomass energy are not oriented toward integrated systems with several radically different goals. Few ministries of energy have experience with integrated developments of which energy production is a part. The field stations capable of tailoring multiple-use biomass production systems to local environmental, economic, and sociological conditions exist within ministries of agriculture, but few ministries of agriculture have a charter in the energy field. Nevertheless, photosynthesis can provide a share of the energy requirements of any country that wants to make the commitment to do it. The technology required is, for the most part, of a relatively simple sort, and it generally exists.

Wind Power. The windmill is one of the oldest and best known converters of solar power. It is also one of the most flexible. The biggest disadvantage of wind power is that it is available only when the wind is blowing, and the wind does not always blow. Efficient use of wind power requires either an effective way of storing energy or a power grid connecting windmills (and other energy converters) so that power is always being produced somewhere on the grid and is feeding power into the total system.

Wind tends to be more concentrated than normal incoming solar radiation. For example, it is not at all unusual for an area to be characterized by winds averaging over 30 kilometers per hour (kph). This is equivalent to an energy flux of roughly 485 w/sq. m., or 3 times the average insolation. Furthermore, the wind blows at night when the sun does not shine. It represents high-grade mechanical energy that can readily be converted to electric power or used as is (e.g., to pump water). An ideal windmill can extract about 59% of the energy incident on the area swept out by the propeller. Real windmills are not so efficient; the best are 30% to 40% efficient as electrical power generators (Sørenson, 1975). The extractable power increases as the cube of the wind velocity, so that power generated from wind blowing at 40 kph is over twice that available at 30 kph. For this reason, the average power output of a windmill may be considerably higher than the power that would be produced by wind of the average speed at the location, even though it does not produce power continuously.

The technology of windmills is an old one. They have been around for thousands of years, and in some places they are still the main source of power. Electricity generation from windmills has been both a commercial venture and a staple for farms for many years. Before rural electrification came to the United States in the 1930s, the main source of electricity in most rural areas was a windmill that ran a direct current generator hooked to a series of 28-volt storage batteries. At the opposite extreme, and for rather different reasons, an apartment house in New York City has recently constructed a windmill-powered alternating current generator to run the common services of the building (e.g., stairway and basement lights). When the wind is not blowing the building receives backup power from the local electric utility.

Commercial electric power from windmills has also been demonstrated. The first such large electric plant was a 1.25-megawatt installation built by the Vermont Power Company at Grandpa's Knob, Vermont, in 1941. It functioned during World War II before it broke down in 1945 because of metal fatigue. It was not replaced at that time because the economics of constructing and operating fossil-fueled power plants were better than those for wind-powered plants. An experimental plant in Gedser, Denmark, provided electricity to the Danish public electric power network from 1958 to 1967. It is being used as the model for other wind electric generators, both in Denmark (Sørenson, 1975, 1976a,b) and in the United States (Metz, 1977b). Pilot project wind-powered electric generators are being erected in many countries (Inglis, 1975, 1978).

Few industrialized countries will ever be able to use wind power to provide the bulk of their energy needs. Metz (1977b) estimates that wind could contribute 1% to 2% of the total United States electric generating capacity by 2000, and Sørenson (1975) suggests that it would be feasible for a combination of wind and direct solar converters to provide most or even all of Denmark's energy needs. Gustavson (1979) suggests that the upper limit of wind energy utilization for the United States is about

75% of the current level of energy consumption. The capital costs per kilowatt of small and moderate-sized windmills are on the order of those for nuclear power plants. But the physical size per unit output of electricity is quite large.

Because windmills must be located in places where wind velocities are relatively high, they would be quite prominent features of a landscape. It has been estimated (von Hipple and Williams, 1975) that it would take roughly one million large windmills to equal the fossil-fuel electric generating capacity of the United States. This is on the same order as the number of transmission towers for high-tension lines in the country. If the size of the individual towers was very large, subtending a circle with a diameter of 1/3 km, the total area covered with windmills would come to about 1% of the total land area.

This might be considered a reasonable use of land, especially if deployment of windmills on this scale would essentially obviate the problem of air pollution from electric generating plants while providing shorter distances between the generator and many dispersed electricity users. But such a system would interfere with television reception, and there might be a measurable impact on the climate. We do not yet have the data to be sure.

The most important factors in the practical harnessing of wind power are the way the wind generator is interfaced with the rest of the system and the way in which energy is stored, if at all. A wind generator contributes nothing when the air is calm. Conversely, it may contribute a great deal of power to a grid when the wind is blowing very strongly. Figure 7.3 compares the power duration curve (solid line) for a wind energy generator and a nuclear power plant. Both produce electricity for about 70% of the time. The nuclear plant produces between 70% and 80% of its rated capacity for over 60% of the time it is operating. It is relatively consistent. But the wind plant varies almost continuously from very low output to output over three times the average.

If wind generation were a relatively small portion of the total power grid capacity, it could simply be let run at full power and other plants could be used to take up the slack. If wind power were developed near hydropower dams, the hydroelectric capacity could be used to even out the low points in wind electricity generation. Alternatively, the windmill could be used as a mechanical water pump for pumped storage (see below in this chapter, Structural Conservation) rather than for generating electricity directly. When there are no complementing energy sources of this sort, it is useful to store energy so that the plant can operate on a more consistent basis near the average level (the broken line in Figure 7.3). In addition to pumped storage, energy can be stored by air compression, batteries, flywheels, and hydrogen produced through electrolysis of water. All of these have been used on at least a pilot basis, and it is not clear what types of storage or complementing power sources will be used as wind power regains commercial acceptance. It would appear that to some degree at least, wind power will become an increasingly important source of power throughout the world.

Ocean Thermal Gradient.   The sea absorbs more solar energy than all of the earth's lands. Surface waters in the tropical areas are almost continuously at a temperature of 25°C. The deep waters of the oceans are at or below 5°C even in the tropics. Ocean currents circulate worldwide; only in the Arctic and Antarctic do cold surface waters sink to the bottom, and only in restricted zones of upwelling do cold bottom waters rise to the surface. Over the rest of the ocean, mixing of surface and bottom waters is

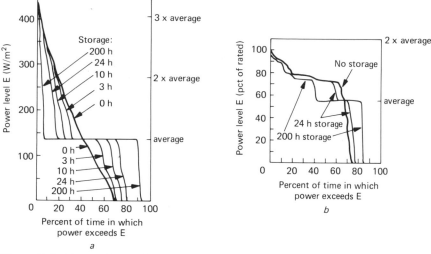

Figure 7.3 Comparison of power duration curves for: (*a*) a wind electric generator (Risφ, Denmark, 1961); (*b*) a nuclear power plant (Vermont Yankee, 1974). The vertical axis records level of power generation both as absolute power (left side) and as multiple of average power generation. The horizontal axis is the percentage of time in which the level of power generation exceeds the level of power generation shown on the vertical axis. Thin lines show the power duration that would obtain with storage of energy sufficient to assure average production for between 3 and 200 hours. [Redrawn, with permission, from B. Sφrenson, "Dependability and Energy Generation with Short-term Energy Storage." *Science* 194: 935–937. Copyright © 1976 by the American Association for the Advancement of Science.]

inhibited by density differences due both to vertical temperatures and vertical salinity changes.

As pointed out by Othmer and Roels (1973), the Gulf Stream alone carries some 2,200 cu. km. of water per day along the east coast of the United States. It is heated by the sun in the Caribbean and the Gulf of Mexico at a rate almost 1,000 times the total rate of energy use in the United States. If the energy in the Gulf Stream alone could be tapped at an efficiency of 2% to 3%, the energy that could theoretically be realized would be 20 to 30 times the total power consumption of the United States. This efficiency seems feasible for Ocean Thermal Energy Conversion (OTEC) plants. Ocean thermal gradients are there whether or not we use them. They do not come and go like the winds. If the energy in the warm surface waters could be extracted and transmitted to markets, there would be no need for storage as in a wind or direct solar conversion plant.

Figure 7.4 shows a diagrammatic representation of the power generation cycle in a thermal power plant. A heat-rich (i.e., hot) medium adjacent to a heat-poor (cold) medium is separated by a power generator. As an example, the heat-rich medium in a typical electric power plant is boiler steam; the heat-poor medium is water cooled by the condenser, and the power generator is a steam turbine. The temperature difference is high, so that energy conversion is fairly efficient (30% to 40%). The working fluid in an OTEC generator is ammonia (or a fluid with similar physical characteristics). It is

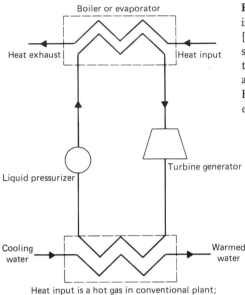

Figure 7.4 Basic power generation cycle in OTEC or conventional power plants. [Reprinted from Zener, 1976, by permission of the Bulletin of the Atomic Scientists, a magazine of science and public affairs. Copyright © 1976, Jan., by the Educational Foundation for Nuclear Science, Chicago, Illinois.]

heated by the warm surface waters and sent to the turbine generator, where electricity is generated. The temperature drop across the turbine is accomplished by the condenser cooled by deep ocean water that has been pumped to the surface. The cooled working fluid is then compressed and reheated, and the cycle starts over. The thermal efficiency of such a plant is very much lower than in a conventional plant, as the thermal gradient is much smaller, but the "fuel" (i.e., the solar-heated surface water) is free, continuously supplied, and very abundant. How this generalized cycle would be implemented in an OTEC plant is indicated in the cutaway diagram, Figure 7.5.

Electric power would not be the only result of OTEC power generation. The nutrient-rich bottom waters released at the surface would have two effects. First, they would create artificial zones of upwelling that would allow a great expansion in biomass production. A demonstration plant in St. Croix, U.S. Virgin Islands, has shown great potential for artificial upwellings of this sort as tools in mariculture of valuable shellfish (Othmer and Roels, 1973). Such plants can also be used to produce hydrogen to send ashore in addition to or instead of electricity.

The bottom waters are not only rich in nutrients, they are also very rich in dissolved carbon. As they are raised to the surface, the carbon can escape as CO_2. It has been estimated that the CO_2 released by an OTEC plant would be roughly equivalent to a third that of a fossil-fueled plant of equivalent capacity. The buildup of CO_2 in the atmosphere from the proliferation of fossil-fueled powered electric generating plants has been suggested as a significant factor in bringing about climatic change. Adding to this might be an unfortunate development in the use of "income" energy.

A possible undesirable result of an OTEC plant is that the temperature of the surface water declines as the surface waters are cooled and released and as the deep waters are released at the surface. Depending on the degree of temperature reduction, this might be serious. However, there is some evidence that the cooling effect would be

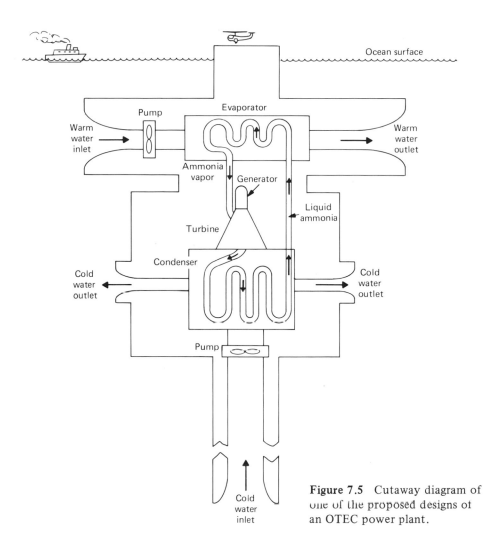

Figure 7.5 Cutaway diagram of one of the proposed designs of an OTEC power plant.

counteracted by an increase in the thermal absorption of the ocean's surface layer, so that increased solar absorption would more than make up for the heat extracted by the plant.

Just as the Gulf Stream is the most obvious candidate for OTEC plant development, it is also the major moderator of the climate of western Europe. OTEC generation from the Gulf stream sufficient to meet the current U.S. electricity consumption would cause a temperature drop of as much as .25°C, assuming expected plant efficiency and no counteracting increase in surface absorptivity (von Hippel and Williams, 1975). We do not know what this would do to the climate of western Europe. It might be negligible, or it might be catastrophic. Computer modeling efforts such as those of Murphy et al, (1976) might give some insight into this matter, but they have not yet been carried out.

OTEC can be regarded as a dark horse in the stable of potential income energy production processes for the time being. Unlike wind and biomass approaches, the technology is very new and no functioning demonstration plants exist. But the capital costs can probably be brought down to the same level as nuclear power plants (Zener, 1976), and the basic technology is both simple and appropriate to mass production. Thus, if the first very expensive demonstration plants are successful, volume production at much lower costs should follow shortly after. OTEC represents an option whose potential risks and benefits are both high. The tradeoffs are quite clear, and a detailed assessment should be possible in the near future.

Direct Conversion of Solar Energy. It was once standard practice in many areas for hot water to be heated by rooftop solar heaters. There were tens of thousands in the southern United States in the 1920s, but they were largely abandoned as fossil fuels fell in price. The current price rise for fossil fuels has reawakened interest in direct solar conversion not only for hot-water heating, but also for space heating and electric generators. More efficient solar hot-water and space heaters are being developed and many companies are manufacturing and marketing these products. They are widely used in Australia, Japan, Israel, and the U.S.S.R.

Small-scale technology exists to convert the sun's energy directly into electricity by means of solar cells similar to those of a photographic exposure meter. But these cells are very expensive, and most experts feel that direct solar production of electricity will be limited to special purposes for some time. Solar thermal energy production, on the other hand, in which solar radiation heats a working fluid (e.g., water or a water-ethylene glycol mixture) that generates electricity using a familiar turbine, is well within the realm of possibility.

The capital costs of most methods of direct utilization of solar energy are now too high to be competitive with fossil fuels. But space and hot-water heating are both fairly well developed and are already economically competitive in some areas. Figure 7.6

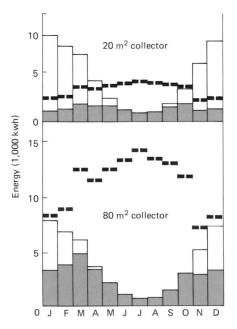

Figure 7.6 Month-by-month performance of heating systems of two different collector areas on a Wisconsin home with a floor area of 180 m.[2]. Insolation on the collector is shown by the heavy lines; total heating and hot water load is shown by the height of the bars. The shaded portion represents the part supplied by the solar system, the unshaded portion the part supplied by the backup system. [Redrawn, with permission, from Duffie and Beckman, "Solar Heating and Cooling." *Science* 191: 143–149. Copyright © 1976 by the American Association for the Advancement of Science.]

compares the contribution of two solar heating systems of different sizes to meeting the total hot-water and space heating load of a typical home in Wisconsin. It also shows the total energy intercepted by each collector and the amount of heat that must be supplied by the auxiliary heating system. Even in the dead of winter, more solar energy impinges on a 300 sq. m. south-facing roof than is burned by the same house in fossil fuels. Thus a solar collector would not have to be 100% efficient in order to provide all the needs of the house for space heating and hot-water heating. Even if the collector were only 30% to 40% efficient, it would still be able to provide between 50% to 70% of the heat required.

A typical home solar heating unit consists of several parts (Figure 7.7). The collector is typically a flat plate mounted on the south-facing roof with a slope approximately equal to the latitude. Metal tubes containing the working fluid are bonded to a black metal sheet and mounted in an insulated pan or trough covered with glass. Solar energy is absorbed by the black sheet, and the infrared reradiation from the metal backing is captured by the glass cover. This greenhouse effect allows maximum energy retention at minimum cost. The working fluid is pumped through the collector and the absorbed heat is stored. Heat for hot-water or space heating can be obtained directly from the storage tank via a heat exchanger. The energy stored in the tank can also be used for air conditioning.

Solar collectors designed for home use vary in their efficiency. The biggest variable in solar heating systems is the way the tradeoff between storage capacity and backup reserves is handled. Heating needs are greatest when the sun is not shining. In order to provide reasonable stand-alone performance, a solar heating system would have to be able to store sufficient heat to allow the system to function even when the sun is overcast for several days. For typical North American conditions this would require a well-insulated water tank of about 30 cu. m. capacity (30 tons) for a solar heating system,

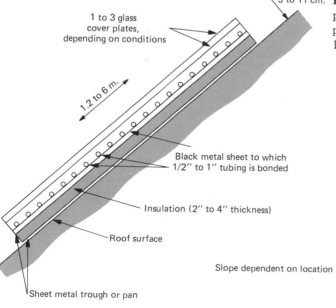

Figure 7.7 Design of a typical flat-plate solar collector. [Redrawn, with permission, from Donovan et al., 1972.]

or several tons of lead-acid storage batteries for a solar electric home system. Because of the costs involved, a generally preferred strategy is to provide a much lower heat storage capacity of about two days. A backup system provides heat when the storage is depleted.

Even so, solar thermal home heating with fossil-fuel backup is close to competitive with traditional heating methods at the present time. In the northern United States a 40% efficient solar collector can save the equivalent of 30.5 liters of heating oil or 215 kwh of electric resistance heat for each square meter of solar collector over the six-month heating season. This is roughly equivalent to $8.00 worth of heating oil or $11.00 for electricity in 1979. If a typical mortgage is for 20 years at 10% interest, then these savings would justify the expenditure of $80 per square meter as a replacement for oil heat or $110 per square meter as a replacement for electric resistance heat. Few solar collectors are currently this inexpensive, and those that are tend to be the least efficient. Nevertheless, solar buildings are being erected as demonstration projects, and experience with other new technologies suggests that solar collectors will come down in price as the technology matures and demand increases. There is little question that home solar heating will become commonplace within the next 25 years.

Solar energy systems in which a collector heats a working fluid are often termed *active* systems. In *passive* solar heating, the area being heated serves as its own collector. An example is a south-facing window that, if used with properly insulated draperies or shutters, can capture much of the energy needed by a typical house for space heating.

Solar electricity generation is considerably less advanced than solar heating. It is very difficult to project how the field will develop over the next 10 to 50 years. Home photoelectric cells may become feasible if electricity doubles in price over the next couple of decades. Solid-state technologies in general are advancing rapidly, and photoelectric cells are no exception. Research and development can be justified on the basis of applications for the military and for communications satellites. Myriad civilian uses will become possible as costs decline. The largest scheme for photoelectric power conversion so far suggested is a giant solar power satellite placed in a synchronous orbit with the earth (i.e., always located over a single point). Electricity could be produced there with radiation intensity at the full solar constant and beamed down to a receiving station on the surface by microwave (O'Neill, 1975). This scheme is currently being investigated in some detail.

A different approach to direct solar conversion is that of large solar-thermal electricity generation plants located in sun-rich areas such as the southwestern United States or the Middle East. These would concentrate solar radiation to very high temperatures and reject the waste heat directly into the air. The most common conception of a large solar-thermal generation facility is a field of *heliostats,* or efficient mirrors mounted so that they can track the sun over the sky. These heliostats would focus solar energy on a single absorber atop a tower (sometimes called the *power tower,* Figure 7.8). Electricity would be generated in the towers using well-known steam or gas turbine technology (Wolf, 1974; Hildebrant and Vant-Hull, 1977; Metz, 1977a; Weingart, 1977).

A 100 megawatt (electric) power plant would require roughly 15,000 to 20,000 heliostats over a 40 sq. m. area with a tower 200 to 250 m. tall. The total area of the station would be about 1.5 sq. km. This is a rather large area for a plant that is small

Figure 7.8 Photograph of a power tower. Heliostats in foreground track the sun and focus its radiation on the collector at the top of the tower in the background. [Photograph courtesy of Sandia Laboratories, Albuquerque, NM.]

in comparison to modern fossil-fueled or nuclear-fueled steam power plants. But the conventional plants have significant indirect land requirements that are often over-looked. Roughly 40 sq. km. must be strip-mined to provide the coal required over the 30-year lifetime of a 1,000 megawatt power plant in the southwestern United States. Solar thermal electric power plants are also less polluting than either fossil or nuclear power plants, although their capital costs are much higher. Even here, the situation is likely to improve as the technology matures.

Fossil Fuels

The fossil fuels are the residues of carbohydrates fixed through photosynthesis over the last several hundred million years. These were refined *in situ* into coal, petroleum, natural gas, and so forth. All are formed in essentially the same way. Detritus accumulates in various depositional environments. It is incorporated into the sediments and carried through the rock-forming process or *diagenesis*. The diagenetic and post-diagenetic environment is one of tremendous pressures and temperatures that are capable of altering organic materials physically or chemically, or both. In some cases, as with coal, only the very most refractory solids are left behind, broken down largely to pure carbon. In other cases the materials that remain are fluid hydrocarbons that flow under pressure and work their way through the rocks until they are trapped by an impermeable barrier. Natural gas comprises the gaseous hydrocarbons, largely methane; petroleum comprises the liquid hydrocarbons and related materials.

Petroleum.   Petroleum is the most important fuel in the world today. It has supplanted coal from first place, just as coal supplanted hydropower and wood. It is relatively easy to handle, since it is a liquid. It will flow through pipelines, it can be stored in tanks either on-site or off-site, and it can be carried easily in a self-contained vehicle such as an oil tanker or a truck. It burns quite cleanly producing less particulate and sulfur-oxide pollution than coal and much less ash to be discarded by the furnace operator. It has also been historically quite cheap to produce.

It is not without problems. All phases of petroleum extraction and use affect the environment directly, as well as indirectly as petroleum use patterns govern the way people do things. A few examples may illustrate this adequately. Exploration is often carried out by a seismographic crew consisting of at least three heavy trucks and associated smaller vehicles operating on poorly engineered temporary roads that last only as long as the crew is in the area. The soil erosion from such roads approaches that from lumbering roads.

The drilling operation has hazards for wildlife. Every oil well needs a mud pond to store water and excess drilling mud. This mud lubricates the drill bit during drilling, and its weight resists blowouts and explosions if the bit encounters a pocket of gas or oil under pressure. These ponds are commonly left in place after completion of the drilling operation, where they attract migrating waterfowl. Unfortunately, they remain highly polluted with mud, oil, and all the other effluvia of the drilling operation. Birds have often landed in a drilling pond, got their feathers soaked with oil, and died of exposure.

A different hazard from petroleum production is land subsidence. Whenever great quantities of materials are removed from the earth, a certain amount of equilibration is to be expected. When oil is pumped out of the earth, it is not unreasonable to expect the surface to settle as a result. In Long Beach, California, withdrawal from the Wilmington Oil Field has caused up to 30 feet of slumping in the 40 years following 1928. The maximum subsidence is on Terminal Island at the Long Beach Naval Yard, which is practically under water (Figure 7.9).

Oil refineries are among the dirtiest of heavy industries, and they are also one of the most difficult to clean up. Oil pipelines can break, and they are especially vulnerable to seismic activity. Petroleum-carrying trucks, barges, and railroad trains are also

Figure 7.9 Aerial photograph of Long Beach, California, showing subsidence due to pumping of oil. Gradations in feet. [Photograph courtesy of D. R. Allen, City of Long Beach Dept. of Oil Properties.]

known to spill their contents on occasion. The most vulnerable link in the transportation chain is the oil tanker. Petroleum is relative easy to handle in bulk, and oil handling and transport show great benefits of scale. The larger the tanker, the cheaper it is to operate per ton of oil. Thus the size of oil tankers has grown steadily (Figure 7.10). It is sobering to note that the *Torrey Canyon,* which ran aground and broke up off the coast of France in 1967, was considered in its day to be a large tanker at 127,000 tons. It is much smaller than the generation of tankers now entering the service of all of the world's major oil companies.

At the same time, the world is becoming increasingly dependent on the Middle East for its oil supply. Even the United States, which until recently produced most of its own oil, must now import almost half of its consumption from the Middle East. Most other developed countries must import practically all of their petroleum.

As international ocean transport becomes increasingly important and as tankers increase in size, they also become increasingly fragile. A modern oil tanker is about 350 m. long and 52 m. wide; it is basically a single-walled storage tank with an engine, bridge, and various navigation aids. It is subject to considerable torsion in heavy seas.

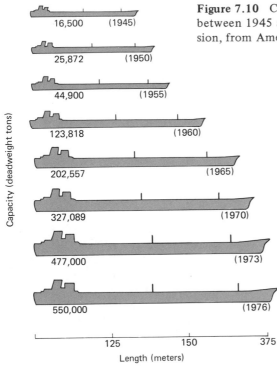

Figure 7.10 Comparative sizes of oil tankers built between 1945 and 1976. [Redrawn, with permission, from American Petroleum Institute, n.d.]

The greatest danger posed by tankers is collision. It has become fairly common for tankers to run aground or to collide with each other, with other ships, with bridge abutments, and so on. A supertanker under full steam travels at 30 kph and takes over 10 km to stop. Even the best navigation aids cannot preclude a supertanker from getting into trouble, especially if the collision is somebody else's fault.

Tankers are made to travel loaded. The trip from the Middle East to, say, Rotterdam, is made with a full load of oil. The tanker must take on ballast after it has discharged its oil if it is to ride correctly and controllably back to the Middle East. The ballast is obviously sea water. Upon arrival in the Middle East it pumps out the sea water in order to take on a new load of oil. If only sea water were in the ship's hold this would cause no problem, but it is not possible to pump all of the oil out of any tanker. A fraction clings to the walls and bottoms, and the heavier fraction of the petroleum may settle out and solidify on the bottom. So when the sea water ballast is pumped out it contains a certain amount of residual oil.

At one point the problem of oil discharge from ballast pumping was more serious than it is now. Tanker companies make an effort to pump out only the water and not the oil. They may have water treatment facilities on shore to reclaim the oil from the ballast water. Taking care in these ways makes good economic sense, since the oil contained in the ballast of a modern supertanker may be worth over $500,000. Relatively little oil is lost during bilge and ballast pumping operations on a given ship, but the tanker trade is so large that the gross result is quite substantial. It is significant that the tremendous oil spills such as the *Torrey Canyon* or the *Amoco Cadiz,* or blowouts such as those in the Santa Barbara Channel, the Ekofisk field in the North Sea or off Mexico in the Gulf of Mexico, contribute less to the total marine oil pollution problem volume for volume than the routine discharges that are a basic part of tanker operations.

Resource Supplies. The short-run problems of petroleum pollution are obvious, but as the world becomes increasingly dependent on oil the long-run problems become even more important. Petroleum is a finite resource. How much is there? Can we estimate when the resource will be used up, and what impact this will have on the pulse of modern life? What substitutions are possible, and what new sources will become available in the future?

Petroleum is found underground. We do not know for sure how much there is until we find it. Certain areas, such as the continental United States, are very well known, and we can be fairly sure that we will find no more large oil fields. We know much less about the situation offshore or in new provinces, especially in the Third World. New fields such as those of northern Alaska and the western Gulf of Mexico have recently added to world reserves, but we do not know how many more such fields remain to be discovered. Also, it is possible to recover only a fraction of the oil in a given field. This fraction, known as the *recovery rate,* is on the order of 30% to 40%. It can be increased, but this increases production costs and it can never reach 100%. Petroleum production in the continental United States peaked in about 1970 and is now in decline (Hubbert, 1974). Demand has continued to climb, however, placing economic pressures on the system that complicate the already complex matter of resource reserves.

There are numerous ways to look at resource limits, some of which are summarized in a useful volume edited by Grenon (1975). Since the uncertainty of such analyses is so high, let us summarize one of the simplest approaches, recognizing that the exact numbers may be somewhat in error. In one of the most useful studies so far, M. King Hubbert of the U.S. Geological Survey has analyzed the resource situation for petroleum, gas, and coal (Hubbert 1962, 1970, 1974, 1975). His most detailed analysis has been of petroleum.

The Hubbert approach is a very simple method of using published data to make rough estimates of total reserves. It looks at three quantities: the cumulative production (P), the proved reserves (R), and the cumulative discoveries (D). It assumes a logistic production cycle of a resource such as petroleum or gas (Figure 7.11). For United States petroleum, data for P are available since 1860. Detailed data for R are available beginning with 1937, and approximate data go back to 1900. D = P + R. Cumulative discoveries lead production by an interval (t), but they eventually reach the maximum usable reserves. Cumulative production follows and eventually uses up the original resource. Proved reserves rise from zero to a peak in the middle and then drop back to zero as production reaches its maximum. Figure 7.12 shows the equations and curves for the three variables for crude oil from the coterminous United States. In 1956 Hubbert predicted that the maximum United States petroleum reserves were on the order of 150 billion to 200 billion barrels (bbl), and that production would peak between 1966 and 1971. In 1974 he revised that estimate to 170 billion bbl of maximum reserves, with production peaking in 1968. It appears to have peaked in 1970.

Hubbert has used a different method of estimating ultimate reserves, in which the rate of discoveries per foot of drilling is plotted as a function of cumulative explora-

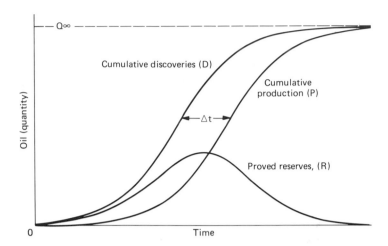

Figure 7.11 Variation with time of proved reserves (R), cumulative production (P), and cumulative proved discoveries (D), during a complete cycle of petroleum production. Q_∞ represents the total recoverable resources. [Reproduced, from *Energy Resources*, 1962, with the permission of the National Academy of Sciences, Washington, D.C.]

tory drilling (Figure 7.13). The area under the curve represents the total ultimate resource. It is 172 billion bbl, in substantial agreement with his earlier analyses.

One does not have to agree with Hubbert. The actual figures for the ultimately recoverable reserves is not really very important. What affects human ecosystems is the fact that levels and costs of production are related in several ways to ultimately recoverable resources. Expansion is possible only so long as reserves make it possible. When producers believe that they must stabilize production because of resource con-

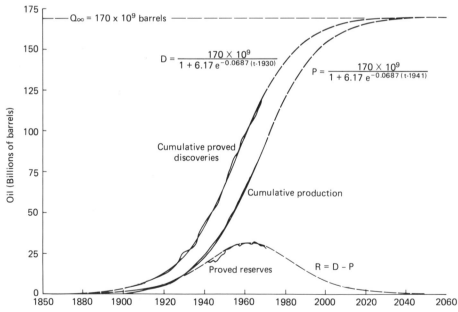

Figure 7.12 Logistic equations as in Figure 7.11, fitted to data of cumulative discoveries, production, and proved reserves in the coterminous U.S., 1900–1971. Dotted lines represent extrapolations to the probable level and date of Q_∞. [Redrawn, with permission, from Hubbert, 1974.]

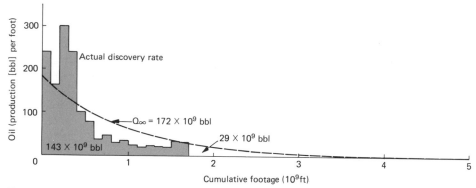

Figure 7.13 Estimates of ultimate crude oil production in the coterminous U.S. by means of curve of discoveries per foot vs. cumulative footage of exploratory drilling. [After Hubbert, 1974.]

straints, as the OPEC countries have done since about 1970, then this has an impact on price, which in turn affects people directly and indirectly. It almost does not matter whether the resource limit is real or not (although for petroleum they are). People's perception of and reaction to the limits is what shifts supply and demand.

Perceiving a resource limitation to petroleum is equivalent to changing from a stable or rightward-shifting supply function to a leftward-shifting supply curve. The vast and seemingly inexhaustible supplies of petroleum before 1973 made its use ubiquitous in today's world. There was no substitute for gasoline for cars, diesel fuel for trucks, buses, or trains, or even kerosene for cooking in the Third World. Lifestyles were built around certain patterns of consumption. The demand curve was very steep. OPEC raised petroleum prices in 1973, partially because of Western involvement in the Arab-Israeli war of that year, and partially because of a realization that their main natural resource would be gone within the foreseeable future, and that whatever modernization they could do would have to be financed by using their petroleum.

The world's response to the OPEC price increase was almost total acceptance of the higher prices (Figure 7.14a). The quantity of petroleum traded did not change very much; the price rose markedly. The usual economic wisdom in such cases is to try to flatten the supply curve by bringing in new technology. This is not very easy for liquid fuels, since the things that could replace petroleum in the foreseeable future are all much more expensive. The only way to contain price increases is to flatten the demand curve (Figure 7.14b). Prices would still rise, but not so much, and the quantities consumed would decrease. These two results would reduce the import bill faced by petroleum-importing countries, and it would also give exporting countries a reason not to treat oil prices as a political tool.

Various governments have attempted to moderate demand in different ways, such as rationing, advertising, tax credits for insulation, increased taxes on gasoline and petroleum products to raise consumer prices even more without affecting the import bill, or encouraging more efficiency through lowering maximum speed limits. It appears that the most effective ways of moderating demand are by manipulating price. It is interesting that the United States, whose oil imports cost roughly 1.5 times the country's overall trade deficit, has not tried nearly as hard as western Europe to de-

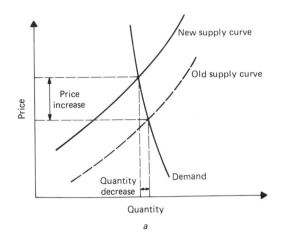

Figure 7.14 Responses of market to changes in OPEC oil prices: (*a*) response when consumers accept price increases; (*b*) response when consumers attempt to flatten demand curve.

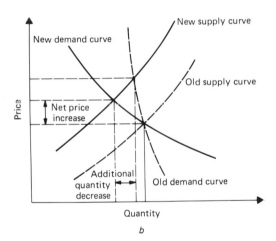

crease demand by increasing costs. People have not slackened their consumption very much, and the resulting balance of payments deficit has been one of the main factors in the tremendous erosion of the value of the dollar. European countries, on the other hand, have tended to adjust the price of gasoline to discourage wasteful use. Their import bills are very high, but they are in line in most cases with the countries' export earnings.

Natural Gas. Natural gas consists largely of methane (CH_4), although it may contain other gases as well. Because of its very simple chemical form and complete combustibility, natural gas is the easiest and cleanest of fuels to deal with. It requires minimal handling, processing, or cleaning. Of all the fossil fuels it is the one that burns most completely to carbon dioxide and water, and it leaves virtually no other pollutants.

Because of its cleanliness and its ease of working, it is ideal for home use. Its very low level of pollution caused many industries to rely upon it to reduce air pollution from their factories. The demand for natural gas in the home is much higher in winter than in summer. Gas is shipped in pipelines whose capacity is related to the expected peak capacity. Increasing industrial use reduced the unevenness in gas consumption through the year, but it did so by raising the peak. For various reasons, the demand for gas has grown so fast that construction of pipelines and storage facilities has not been able to keep pace. Likewise, gas supplies are not growing as fast as demand. The result is a periodic shortage of fuel that has made it necessary for industries, schools, and commercial buildings to shut down for long stretches of winter because they could not get gas to run their boilers, and it has even endangered the supply of gas to homes.

This periodic shortage has several reasons. Natural gas is finite, just as petroleum. Indeed, Hubbert's analysis of natural gas shows its world supply to be more precarious than that of petroleum. At the same time, it is very difficult to turn to overseas sources of gas the way most nations have done with petroleum, since the gas must be compressed under very high pressure in order to be transported by tanker or truck. A new generation of tankers specifically designed to carry liquified natural gas from gas-rich areas to other parts of the world is now coming on the scene. While they may be able to alleviate severe problems in gas-short regions, they will not be able to carry anywhere near the percentage of world gas consumption that oil tankers carry of oil.

Natural gas, like oil, has a politico-economic dimension. Gas production and shipping are quasi-monopolies that require regulation to avoid monopolistic pricing policies by the producers. In the United States the federal government has regulated the wellhead price of all gas that is shipped interstate, and left the other aspects of production and distribution in the hands of private enterprise. Retail prices have been regulated by state law to allow gas companies a fair return on investment. These policies have kept prices somewhat lower than those that would have prevailed had supply and demand been the main arbiter. By the early 1970s gas was already somewhat cheaper in dollars per kwh than coal or petroleum. The cost of gas for the kwh-equivalent of one barrel of oil in 1973 was $1.50, and the retail rate in New England was $.18 for the energy equivalent of a gallon of heating oil. The corresponding prices of petroleum were $5.25 per bbl for controlled domestic interstate petroleum and over $10.00 for imported OPEC-controlled petroleum (CED, 1974). Industries thus had an incentive to convert from these fuels to natural gas, even in the absence of air pollution control legislation. Gas is so much easier to handle than other fuels, and it burns so cleanly, that the clean air legislation of the early 1970s was met by a wholesale industrial changeover from coal to gas, and demand for natural gas skyrocketed.

This increase in demand is a rightward shift in the demand curve in Figure 7.1. The result should have been that more gas would become available, but at a higher price. The regulated prices did not rise, and there was no concomitant shift in supply that would tend to allow more gas to be available at the same price (Figure 7.15). As demand rose and price remained constant, gas became even more underpriced than it had been previously, causing an acceleration of the upward spiral. The gas industry, fearing shortages such as happened in 1976 and desiring to increase its rate of return, called for higher prices to allow gas to approach the cost of an equivalent amount of oil.

Indeed, gas should be worth substantially more than petroleum considering its greater ease of handling, but gas price affects so many people so directly that price adjustments are politically difficult and the issue is still not resolved.

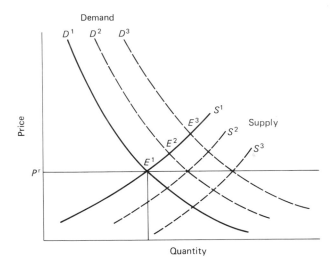

Figure 7.15 Schematic diagram of the supply-demand relationships of natural gas with regulated price, under conditions of strong increases in demand. At the beginning, the supply curve S^1 and the demand curve D^1 are characterized by an equilibrium price/quantity pair E^1. The price of gas is set by regulation at P^r, which corresponds to this equilibrium price. A major demand shift to demand curve D^2 should bring about equilibrium E^2. But the regulated price forces the market to behave as though S^2 rather than S^1 were the supply curve. This, in essence, drives down the value of gas and may exacerbate the demand shift to D^3, and so on.

Coal. Coal was the first of the fossil fuels to come into widespread use, and for many years it was the most commonly used. It is the solid residue of plants that lived many years ago, were buried in contemporary sediments, and underwent diagenetic change with the energy-rich materials remaining in it. It includes not only the energy-rich materials, but also the solid sulfides, dirt, and any other contaminants that might have been present in the original sediment.

Coal is the dirtiest of all fossil fuels to mine, to handle, and to burn. Mining is one of the most dangerous of all occupations, and miners' deaths from cave-ins, fire, explosion, and flooding are so frequent as to form dominant elements in the folklore of mining communities. In its wake coal mining leaves chronic black lung for the miners, surface lands scarred by strip mining and spoil banks, the threat of subsidence from underground mines, and acid mine drainage. Processing and burning coal leads to "black water," fly ash and acid sulfates in the air, and sludges of several sorts that must be disposed of. The use of coal creates public health and solid waste problems of great magnitude. Nevertheless, coal is the only fossil fuel with sufficient reserves to be counted on as a fuel after 50 years hence, and it is the only completely proven energy technology capable of serving as the basis for an industrial society into the next century.

The image of coal mining conjures up different things to different people; some think of deep mines in Pennsylvania or Wales; others think of strip mines in Illinois or Wyoming. Still others think of peat bogs in Minnesota or Ireland. In fact, coal comprises a wide range of deposits with different geologic properties and problems.

The most important properties of coal are its heating value, ash and volatiles content, and thickness of overlying strata. We can integrate these concepts by viewing the formation of a coal deposit as a dynamic function of time (Figure 7.16). Photosynthetic energy is fixed by green plants, which die and are incorporated into the accumulating sediments of the swamps in which they grew. Limited breakdown, pressure, and temperature produce peat. As peat deposits are covered by other sediments, the pressures and temperatures increase, driving off water, nitrogen, and other plant elements. The peat is transformed by the process of *coalification* to lignate and then to higher

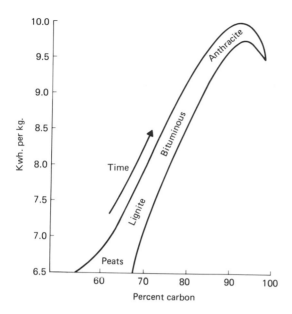

Figure 7.16   Schematic representation of the formation of a coal deposit. [Brian J. Skinner, *Earth Resources* © 1969. p. 111. Adapted by permission of Prentice-Hall, Inc., Englewood Cliffs, New Jersey.]

ranks of coal such as bituminous and anthracite. In general, the higher-rank coals have much higher heating values and lower volatiles content, and they are much older. Low-rank coals generally lie fairly close to the surface. High-rank coals are typically deeply buried and can be mined economically only if several million years' accumulation of rock are removed by erosion to bring them close to the surface again.

Strip Mining.   Strip mining has deservedly been cited as one of the most voracious land users in an industrial society. Land in timber, pastures, or crop (Figure 7.17a) is leased by the coal company, and the coal is exposed (Figure 7.17b–d). Following extraction of the coal, it is left in whatever state is required by law or the conscience of the coal company operators (Figure 7.17e).

Stripping is a feasible method of mining when the coal seams are relatively flat-lying and close to the surface. It has both advantages and disadvantages over deep mining. The recovery factor is higher (80% as opposed to 57%; CEQ, 1973), and the output per mine is also higher (34.6 tons per man-day as opposed to 11.2 tons per man-day; U.S. Bureau of Mines, 1974b), with a lower risk of injury or death. (Surface mining has an injury rate of 30.4 injuries and 0.3 work fatalities per million man-hours, as opposed to 53.0 and 0.9, respectively, for underground mining; U.S. Bureau of Mines, 1974a; Moyer and McNair, 1973.) Surface vegetation, buildings, and so on must be destroyed, at least temporarily. Conscientious reclamation can return surface-mined lands to productive use quickly. Knabe (1964a) documents the return of these lands to agriculture in Germany, with grain crop yields of 3 to 4.5 metric tons per hectare the first year after reclamation is complete. Reclamation by the British National Coal Board often results in better drained and superior farmland than had previously existed. But reclamation is not always conscientious. Surface mines are not always planned to minimize the adverse effects of environmental processes found in all coal mines.

A typical mining cycle is shown in Figure 7.18. The coal seam is located and its

Figure 7.17   Before, during, and after photograph of a strip mined area in Belmont County, Ohio. [Photographs courtesy of Dr. T. Voneida.]

geological extent is estimated. The water table is adjusted, if necessary, so that it lies below the coal seam, and the pit is opened. Ideally, the topsoil is separated from the underlying overburden and the remaining overburden is piled into an initial spoil heap. The coal is removed. Overburden is removed from the adjacent part of the mine and is placed in the part from which the coal has been removed. The newly exposed coal is removed, and the procedure continues until the final cut is made. The last coal is removed, and the contour of the spoil heap and the high wall (the face formed by the final cut) are adjusted. The surface is prepared, the water table is allowed to return to its normal level, and the spoil heaps are planted. The processes of overburden removal, coal removal, contour adjustment, and planting are continuous, and go on at the same time with a large mine. If all of these steps are followed efficiently and conscientiously, there is no reason why the resulting man-made topography cannot be at least as useful a landscape as the original.

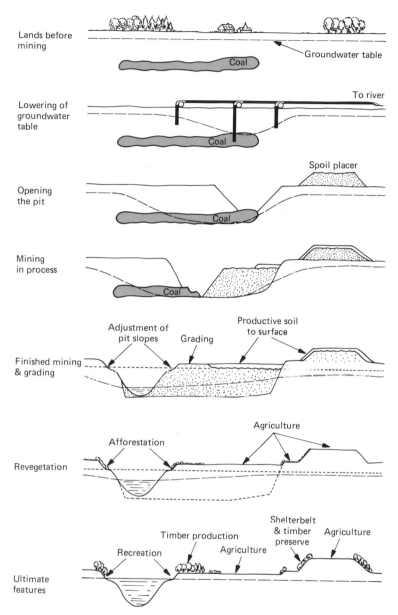

Lands before mining

Lowering of groundwater table

Opening the pit

Mining in process

Finished mining & grading

Revegetation

Ultimate features

Figure 7.18 Idealized schematic procedure of the typical coal mining cycle in the brown coal beds of Germany, from initialization of mining to completion of reclamation. [Redrawn from Knabe, 1964, by permission of *Ohio Journal of Science.*]

Coal contains many materials in addition to carbon; the most important in many ways is iron pyrite FeS_2. In a typical coal such as that found in the Appalachians of eastern North America, pyrite can be found in the coal and the assorted shales, but especially in the roof shale immediately overlying the coal. When the overburden is stripped off into the spoil heaps, the most pyrite-rich fraction is exposed to whatever elements can attack it in the spoil heap. When oxygen-rich rainwater percolates through the porous heap, pyrite reacts with oxygen and water:

$$4FeS_2 + 15O_2 + 2H_2O \rightarrow 2H_2SO_4 + 2Fe_2(SO_4)_3$$

The sulfuric acid produced by this reaction is leached out with the percolating rainwater, which becomes exceedingly acid. The water commonly emerges at the surface, either within the mine or in a nearby stream where it can do considerable damage to surface-water ecosystems. The ferric sulfate can be hydrolized under certain conditions to produce even more sulfuric acid:

$$Fe_2(SO_4)_3 + 6H_2O \rightarrow 2Fe(OH)_3 + 3H_2SO_4$$

For each ton of pyrite oxidized by normal percolation, up to 1.7 tons of sulfuric acid can be formed. This goes on as long as the pyrite or other material or organic sulfides can come in contact with air and water.

In flat-lying areas with relatively high groundwater tables, such as the German coal region studied by Knabe (1964a) and shown in Figure 7.18, acid mine drainage is important only during the active mining stage. As the pit is backfilled and reclaimed, the soil replaced on top of the spoil is sufficiently active biologically to remove the oxygen from the percolating rainwater. The pond remaining in the final cut quickly develops an organic-rich underclay bottom that removes much of the oxygen in the water and cuts down on the diffusion of the rest. Deprived of oxygen, the sulfides are not mobilized and acid drainage does not form.

Knabe (1964 a,b) presents a very useful classification for overburden that can clarify some of the practical reclamation problems encountered in surface mining. Five classes of material are recognized (Table 7.3). All of these materials may or may not be present in a region. The *A* material is almost always topsoil, and the *P* and *F* materials are typically topsoil or at least subsoil. The *T* materials are the sulfide-containing layers, and they can be found at the surface only in exceedingly arid regions where the sulfides are not leached naturally into the subsoil. It is fairly easy, in principle, to minimize acid mine drainage from strip mines by separating the nontoxic portion of the overburden from the toxic, minimizing the surface area of the toxic overburden (such as by replacing it in the mined-out sections and landscaping it to grade), and placing the nontoxic overburden over it. This is the standard European practice.

If the most agriculturally useful fraction is placed on top, the land can be returned at least to its previous use. In a large mine the final grade can be more level than the original, so that it is agriculturally superior. This is not to say that well-reclaimed land is immediately as good as virgin soil; it is not. The structure has been destroyed and the use of heavy machines has compacted it. But these factors can be corrected relatively quickly through good agricultural practices (Chapter 6).

When different classes of overburden are mixed, the reclaimed land is suitable for the use appropriate to the poorest class in the mixture (Table 7.4). Cropland is likely only if good topsoil is saved strictly for this purpose. When toxic overburden is mixed with the surface materials, it renders the surface toxic. Plant growth is extremely slow and any value it might have had for sealing out acid drainage is lost.

Underground Mining. Underground mining is the predominant method of mining in much of the world and will remain the only way for extracting deep coal deposits over about 100 m. deep. The basic operation of underground mining is simpler than that of strip mining. Only the coal seam is removed, along with whatever other rock is necessary to allow miners and their equipment to work. Both coal and refuse are

Table 7.3 Classification of Overburden with Regard to Reclamation.

Value	Class	Usefulness	Examples	Suitable Management during Mining Process
1	A	Agriculture: Cropland. Can be used for field crops soon after reclamation complete.	Topsoil, loess, glacial till, soft shales, calcareous clay.	Separate excavation and transport. Dumping on surface of bank separate from lower layers.
2	P	Agriculture: Pasture. Can be used for pasture; not sufficient for crops.	Calcareous rocky material, rocky till, hard shale.	As above.
3	F	Forestry; not useful for agriculture.	Nontoxic sands, loams, clays.	As above, if class A overburden is lacking.
4	S	Sterile or barren. Can be revegetated, but will not bear a crop.	Quartz gravel, poor sand, subsoil, other nontoxic layers.	Preferably not brought to surface unless quickly buried by A, P, or F layers.
5	T	Toxic, with ingredients that poison plants.	Layers containing pyritic or other toxic materials.	Not to be brought to surface. Must be covered as quickly as possible with A, P, or F or at least S material.

After Knabe, 1964a,b, by permission of The Ohio Journal of Science.

carried to the surface, and the refuse is piled in a spoil heap (Figure 7.19). The remainder of the overburden is allowed to remain in place over the mine.

Acid drainage is found in deep mines as well as in surface mines. Also significant in deep mines are subsidence and slumping, fire, and respiratory tract illness. An open mine is an obvious entrance for oxygen to the pyrite-containing shales that would nor-

Table 7.4 Optimal Uses of Reclaimed Overburden Containing Mixtures of Classes of Overburden.

		Class of Poorest Overburden in Mixture				
		A	*P*	*F*	*S*	*T*
	A	Crops	Pasture	Forest	Nil	Dangerous
Class of Best P			Pasture	Forest	Nil	Dangerous
Overburden in F				Forest	Nil	Dangerous
Mixture S					Nil	Dangerous
T						Dangerous

Figure 7.19 Gob pile consisting of fine coal, low-grade coal, and associated slate and clay on the outskirts of Murray City, Ohio. Mine tipple is in the background. [Photograph by L. J. Prater, courtesy of the U.S. National Forest Service.]

mally be buried far out of its reach. Liquid water is commonly found in subterranean rock and is usual in mines. Likewise, the spoil heap from a deep mine consists largely of the roof shale above the coal. It cannot be protected by nontoxic overburden as in surface mining, because no overburden is mined. At best, acid drainage can be controlled only by treatment of drainage water, by backfilling the mine, or by other positive control measures after the mine (or at least the spoil heap) has been abandoned. Acid drainage from a deep mine is inherently less amenable to control than that from a surface mine, although it may be no worse in practice if effective drainage control measures are not carried out in the surface mine.

The subsidence problem can be severe. The mine operation by its very nature undermines the rock overlying the coal seam. If the overlying strata were perfectly supported and very strong they would withstand the undermining. But many kinds of underground mining (including those with the highest recovery factors) leave behind no support for the roof, so that its eventual collapse is inevitable. Of the 3 million hectares in the United States underlain by coal mines, subsidence has occurred on about 800,000 hectares, and 60,000 hectares have been in urban areas. When an abandoned mine collapses in an urban area, the damage can be very severe. Even in rural areas, land can be made unusable for crops, and drainage patterns can change. In one instance a car was swallowed up in the middle of a Pennsylvania state highway and never seen again; its driver scrambled to safety (Flawn, 1970).

A related problem is slumping of spoil heaps and related structures. Because great quantities of material are channeled through a small number of surface entrances, the spoil heaps from a large underground mine are more likely to be concentrated than those of a large strip mine. Since spoil consists largely of the shales surrounding the coal, it is very rich in clay minerals that can become quite plastic when wet and that can lubricate the readjustment and even cause collapse of the pile. The collapse of one such heap in 1965 in Aberfan, Wales, buried much of the town, including the school, and killed a large proportion of the populace, among them over 100 children. Spoil is also used for acid-control or coal-cleaning pond dams. Collapse of one such dam on Buffalo Creek, West Virginia, in 1972 flooded 14 towns and killed 130 people, damaging or destroying some 1,000 homes and doing property damage amounting to $50 million.

Fire is a factor in underground mines. Coal, like petroleum, is associated with natural gas. Every so often miners reach a pocket of gas that may explode. Most mining disasters that make the newspapers are of this sort. Fire may also begin in abandoned mines or spoil heaps and burn uncontrollably, sometimes for many years. These fires deplete resources, destroy vegetation, release toxic gases, and lower property values. They are found in all mining districts, and they are difficult either to prevent or to stop once started (McNay, 1971). Roughly 300 spoil heap and 200 mine fires are now burning within the United States alone. Of the latter, one has been burning for over 90 years near New Straitsville, Ohio, and another has cost over $5.5 million in unsuccessful control efforts.

The most tragic legacy of underground mining is the chronic debilitating respiratory disease of coal workers' pneumoconiosis, or *black lung,* and its relatives. These are a series of respiratory diseases caused by inhaling coal dust that lead to total debilitation. They affect 150 thousand to 300 thousand American miners, and their cost is over $75 million annually, along with great intangible damage such as pain and suffering, loss of family cohesion, and serious frustration (Commoner et al., 1974).

Coal Processing. Coal should be cleaned and ground to the proper consistency before it can be sold. It is relatively easy to grind it to the specifications of a boiler; it is much more difficult to remove the sulfides and noncombustible ash particles.

The basic means of processing coal for sulfides is known as deep cleaning. The coal is ground to size and subjected to liquid flotation. The heavier pyrites settle, and the lighter coal can be floated off the top. Routine coal cleaning is oriented toward ash removal, but some sulfur is also removed. Currently, feasible technologies of coal cleaning can remove 30% to 50% of pyritic sulfur, and methods under development will be able to remove up to 90% of the pyritic sulfur, as well as some of the organic sulfides (Strauss et al., 1979). As coal replaces oil and gas as primary industrial fuel, we can expect coal cleaning technology to improve and routine cleaning to approach the 90% level.

Other types of coal processing currently in an experimental stage may become commercial in the foreseeable future. Solvent refining of coal is a chemical process that produces a heavy carbon fuel with greatly reduced sulfur and ash content. Raw coal is mixed with oil (which can be derived from either petroleum or coal) at high temperatures (450°C) and pressure (70,000 gm./sq. cm). Up to 90% of the coal is dissolved. Hydrogen is added to convert some of the organic sulfides to volatile hydrogen sulfide gas, and the solid sulfide and ash can be removed by filtration. The recovery factor of this process is about 67%, and solvent extracted coal has an energy content of about 10.4 kwh/kg, about 30% higher than that of high-grade coal. The United

States Office of Coal Research expects this process to become competitive with physically treated coal in the near future.

Synthetic Hydrocarbons.   The biggest drawback to coal as a general purpose fuel, in addition to its pollution potential, are the difficulties of transport and handling. Fluid fuels such as gas, gasoline, and oil are much more appropriate for small-scale and moving-point uses such as automobiles or home cooking and home heating. Because of the coming resource limitations and price increases in these fuels there is considerable interest in producing synthetic fluid fuels from coal.

The most obvious coal-derived gas is not synthetic at all; it is the methane that occurs naturally with the coal. Osborn (1974) reports that the recoverable methane in United States coal beds is approximately equal to the total proven resources of natural gas—about 7.4 trillion cu. m. These could be exploited directly by only minor investments in exploration and new technology. Exploitation of this gas would also make underground mining safer.

Coal can also be used as a feedstock for fluid fuel production. There are three basic alternatives: substitute natural gas, a high-energy gas with the same physical and chemical properties as natural gas and a heating value of about 10 kwh/cu. m., low-energy gas with a heating value of 1 to 5 kwh/cu. m., and synthetic oil.

Conversion to high-value synthetic gas has long been considered the ideal way to use coal. It would solve almost all of the problems associated with its use and handling, leaving only those associated with mining. Even these could be overcome to a large degree if gasification could take place in the mine. Several substitute natural gas processes are now in an experimental operation stage within the United States (Hammond, 1976a). A low-energy gas comprising hydrogen and carbon monoxide is first obtained, its composition is shifted so that the ratio of hydrogen to carbon monoxide is 3 to 1, and the gases are cleaned. The two gases are reacted with each other to form methane and water. The technologies involved are fairly complex and novel. The price tag on high-energy gas produced directly from coal would be quite high.

There is some question that pipeline-quality gas of this sort is the most appropriate focus for research in coal gasification (Hammond, 1976b). It is unlikely that much synthetic natural gas will be available before the turn of the century in any case, and the need for high-energy gas will be acute long before then. It would be much easier to release the gas now being burned in electric power generators by converting gas-burning generating plants to coal. As shown in Table 7.5, electric power generators in the United States use a tremendous amount of natural gas. Of course, a boiler built to burn natural gas cannot be retrofitted to burn coal directly, and no utility would voluntarily retire a boiler early without good cause.

One way to adapt these generators to using coal would be to have them burn low-energy gas with a heat content of 1 to 3 kwh/cu. m., which can be produced by a scaled-up gasifier whose technology is reasonably well understood and proven (Squires, 1974). This gasifier can operate on New Mexican high-ash, low-sulfur coal, and the gas can at least theoretically be used to replace natural gas in an electric power generating plant with a decrease in overall boiler efficiency from 85% to 84%. Retrofitting power plants in this way is feasible in the short run. And even if the gas is not sufficiently energy-rich for many applications, its applicability to certain very high volume indus-

Table 7.5 Annual Use of Fossil Fuels for Electric Power Generation in the United States, 1973.

Fuel	Power Generated (10^9 Mw)	Capacity (Mw)	Consumption
Coal	771	156,375	351×10^6 tons
Oil	272	53,921	432×10^6 barrels
Natural Gas	376	76,569	$3,764 \times 10^9$ std. cu. ft.

Reprinted, with permission, from E. F. Osborn. Coal and the present energy situation. *Science* 183: 477–481. Copyright © 1974 by the American Association for the Advancement of Science.

trial processes (including, but not restricted to, electric power generation) allows it to substitute for a tremendous amount of natural gas.

Producing synthetic oil is more difficult than making synthetic gas, and synthetic oil is much more expensive than naturally occurring petroleum. It is not a particularly new technology, however. Coal-derived oil was one of Germany's main fuels during World War II, and a synthetic oil plant has been operating for over 20 years in South Africa. The methods used to date are inherently inefficient two-step processes in which the coal is first gasified and then synthesized to a mixture of liquid hydrocarbons. It is likely that developments in coal liquification will lag behind those in gasification for some time.

Synthetic fuels have several things in common. They provide substitutes for fuels that are being rapidly depleted from feedstocks that are in great abundance. They have been presented as the answer to fossil fuel resource problems. They are all very expensive, both in direct costs and in their impact on the landscape around them. Wholesale dependence on synthetic fuels would entail vast increases in the level of strip mining. This could be done in traditional mining areas, but synthetic fuels have most often been associated with lands now used for agriculture and pasture on the High Plains of North America. This would disrupt people's ways of life, and it is not clear that enough water exists in these areas to allow synthetic fuel production to proceed simultaneously with coal mining and processing, adequate reclamation, and productive agriculture.

Energy Resources Based on Nuclear Energy

Nuclear energy is a more complex subject than it might seem. It includes several basic energy sources (including that of uranium, the largest nucleus occurring naturally on earth, as well as that of the smallest, hydrogen). Several types of energy transformations either are or might be developed for commercial use. Three kinds of nuclear transformations are significant: radioactive emissions, nuclear fission, and nuclear fusion.

In all three cases the principle that describes the release of energy from a nuclear event is Einstein's famous equation, $E = mc^2$, where E is energy in joules, m is mass in kilograms, and c is the speed of light (3×10^8 m/sec). Normally, physical and chemical transformations show conservation of both mass and energy. The mass of every element is the same after the reaction as before (although it may be in a new chemical compound), and there is as much energy in the system after the reaction as there was before. But nuclear rearrangement involves the conversion from mass to energy. During radioactive decay, the fission of heavy nuclei, or the fusion of light nuclei, minute amounts of mass are lost. Multiplying through Einstein's equation, we can calculate that 2.5×10^{10} kwh of energy are produced for each kilogram of mass converted.

A radioactive emission is a relatively common occurrence in nature and is characteristic of all radioactive isotopes.* An atom is unstable if the configuration of protons and neutrons in its nucleus is too large for some reason. Such a nucleus tends to lose particles or energy or both at a characteristic rate as it rearranges itself into a more stable configuration.

Three kinds of radiation are given off in such events. The alpha particle is essentially a helium nucleus. It consists of two protons and two neutrons and is, when compared to the others, a very heavy particle loaded with energy. It is emitted when the overall size of the nucleus is too large for stability and is characteristic of elements of atomic weight 200 or higher. The beta particle is an electron released when a neutron decomposes into a proton. It is much smaller and, although it has greater penetration potential because of its smaller mass, it is generally much less energetic than an alpha particle. It is emitted when there are too many neutrons in a nucleus and is characteristic of smaller elements. The gamma ray is electromagnetic radiation similar to, but more energetic than, X rays.

Radioactivity is a common phenomenon in many isotopes of common elements. Most of the radiation released by radioactive emissions comes not from the heavy elements related to uranium but rather from an isotope of potassium (^{40}K). Most of the common minerals in the earth's crust contain potassium as one of their basic elements, and roughly 1% of the potassium is ^{40}K. While ^{40}K is far too dispersed ever to be a reasonable source of nuclear fuel, it is so widespread and so common that the spontaneous breakdown of ^{40}K represents an important source of energy. This is a source of heat, so that the temperature increases as one goes deeper into the earth's crust. In areas of recent geologic activity, the combination of radioactivity-related heat and heat from earth movements provides high temperatures close to the earth's surface, where they can be tapped for useful purposes.

Fission is the process by which a large, relatively unstable nucleus is broken up into two daughter nuclei. Unlike radioactivity, this does not happen spontaneously.

---

*Slightly more than 100 chemical elements are now known. Each element is characterized by a fixed number of protons in its nucleus. Most elements have several different forms, or *isotopes,* of different atomic weight. The difference is the number of neutrons in the nucleus. Each isotope can thus be characterized by two numbers. The first, the *atomic number,* is the number of protons in the nucleus. The second, the *atomic weight,* is the sum of the protons and nuetrons. It is often convenient to include these numbers (or at least the atomic weight) in the chemical symbol of an element. For example, the common variety of uranium (chemical symbol U) has 92 protons and 146 neutrons. Thus its atomic number is 92, and its atomic weight is 238. It can be designated $^{238}_{92}$U. Other isotopes, with different nuclear properties, include $^{235}_{92}$U and $^{233}_{92}$U.

Any heavy nucleus can be made to undergo fission by being bombarded by a sufficiently energetic particle, generally a neutron. A neutron that can cause fission in a typical heavy nucleus is considered an energetic or "fast" neutron.

Not all heavy nuclei are typical. Some (notably uranium-235 and 233 and plutonium-239) have the particular ability to absorb and bind a relatively low-energy or "slow" neutron into their nuclear structures. This binding releases sufficient energy that the nucleus begins to vibrate and undergo fission spontaneously. Fission results not so much from the kinetic energy of the neutron as from the relase of binding energy when the neutron is captured. An isotope that is capable of fission when it captures a slow neutron is termed a *fissile* isotope.

Other isotopes can capture slow neutrons and not undergo fission. Two such reactions are significant. Thorium-232 and uranium-235 are each capable of accepting a slow neutron. The release of binding energy does not cause fission. Rather it produces an unstable isotope of thorium, ^{233}Th, which loses a beta particle to become protoactinium-233. This is also unstable, and loses a second beta particle. The overall reaction can be expressed:

$$^{232}_{90}\text{Th} + ^1_0\text{n} \rightarrow ^{233}_{90}\text{Th} \rightarrow ^{233}_{91}\text{Pa} \rightarrow ^{233}_{92}\text{U}$$
$$\downarrow \qquad \downarrow \qquad \downarrow$$
$$\beta \qquad \beta \qquad \beta$$

^{233}U is fissile and can undergo fission when it captures a slow neutron. In a similar way ^{238}U can capture a fast neutron to form unstable ^{239}U, which loses a beta particle to become an unstable isotope of neptunium, which loses a second beta particle to become a fissile isotope of plutonium:

$$^{238}_{92}\text{U} + ^1_0\text{n} \rightarrow ^{239}_{92}\text{U} \rightarrow ^{239}_{93}\text{Np} \rightarrow ^{239}_{94}\text{Pu}$$
$$\downarrow \qquad \downarrow \qquad \downarrow$$
$$\beta \qquad \beta \qquad \beta$$

An isotope that is not itself fissile but can be transformed into a fissile isotope through neutron capture in a reactor is termed a *fertile* isotope.

Fusion is also a rearrangement of nuclei that causes the conversion of mass to energy, but the process is very different. Instead of the splitting of a single large atom, two smaller atoms fuse to form a single larger one. This occurs naturally in very high-temperature environments such as stars. It has been harnessed thus far on earth only in the hydrogen bomb, where two heavy hydrogen nuclei fuse to form a helium nucleus. As with fission, it is somewhat easier to use fusion energy as an explosive than as a more useful form of energy.

The specific reactions involved in fusion are a varied lot, most of which involve heavy isotopes of hydrogen. The energy released by a typical fusion event is roughly 2½% that of a fission event. But a fissile atom is roughly 120 times as heavy as a heavy hydrogen nucleus, so that the energy released per unit mass from fusion is much higher than that of fission.

We do not have as much experience with nuclear processes as we do with combustion, and we do not think of them as being "natural" in the same sense as fire. But fission and fusion are both completely natural. What is unfamiliar is the lengths to which one must go in order to control and harness the processes to make them useful. The sun itself is basically a large thermonuclear (fusion) device, and it can be regarded as a continuous uncontrolled hydrogen bomb that is far enough away so that the usual unfriendly influences of hydrogen bombs do not affect us here on earth. Spontaneous nuclear fission is also known to have occurred on the earth's surface. A spontaneous chain reaction resembling that in a thermal reactor occurred some 2 billion years ago in Oklo, Gabon (Brookins, 1976; I.A.E.A., 1975; Cowan, 1976). It ran for 1 million years and averaged a power output of 11.4 kw during that time. This is about 1/10 of the 1969 thermal output of the Shippingport (Pennsylvania) Atomic Power Station, the first civilian nuclear electric power plant in the world (DRDT, 1969).

Controlled Nuclear Fission.   Nuclear fission has been used for over 30 years as a source of controlled power. The current fuel is almost always uranium, although plutonium and thorium are sometimes included in the fuel mixture. The fission process takes place in a reactor, heating water that either is used as hot process water or turns an electric generating turbine.

The nuclear power plant is similar in many ways to the familiar fossil-fueled power plant that has been in existence for decades. In the latter (Figure 7.20a) water is heated in a boiler, from which it is sent to a turbine at very high temperatures. The exit side of the turbine is cooled by a condenser, from which the water is returned as liquid to the boiler. Electricity is produced by a generator attached to the turbine, and the efficiency of the generation process is directly related to the temperature difference between the entrance and exit sides of the turbine. Only the temperatures involved are really important to the electricity generation process; it makes very little difference whether the turbine is fed by steam heated in a fossil fueled boiler or in a nuclear reactor.

Two types of reactors predominate in nuclear electric power plants around the world. These are the boiling water reactor (BWR; Figure 7.20b), and the pressurized water reactor (PWR; Figure 7.20c). Both of these were developed in the United States and are collectively called light water reactors (LWR), because the neutron flux in both is moderated by normal, or light, water. They were popularized at least in part because General Electric and Westinghouse, their most important respective manufacturers, were able to use them as "loss leaders" in the world market, and because the U.S. Atomic Energy Commission showed little interest in supporting development of alternative (and competing) designs (Rose, 1974). In both cases water is heated by fission of the nuclear fuel and sent either directly (as in the BWR) or indirectly via an intermediary heat exchanger (as in the PWR) to the turbine.

As far as the electricity generation process is concerned, the reactors are no more than a large, expensive, relatively novel design of boiler. The water serves two functions. It is the heat transfer medium (as in the fossil fuel plant), and it is also the moderator of the nuclear fission process (unlike the fossil fuel plant). Hydrogen nuclei in the water can slow neutrons and moderate their energy so that they remain slow neutrons. Boron, which can absorb neutrons and slow the neutron flux, is dissolved in the water circulating through the core, and there are boron-rich rods termed *control rods* that can be pushed into the core to regulate, slow or even stop the reaction.

The actual generation of electric power is precisely the same in nuclear and fossil-fuel power plants except that LWR's operate at slightly lower temperatures; this limits

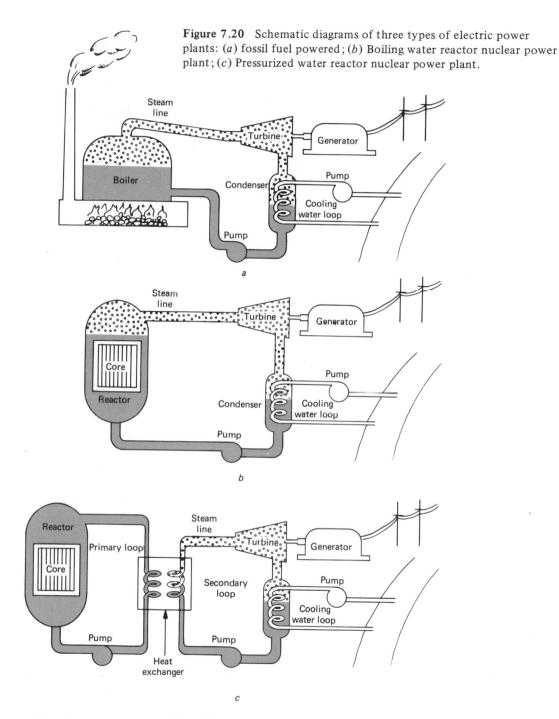

Figure 7.20   Schematic diagrams of three types of electric power plants: (*a*) fossil fuel powered; (*b*) Boiling water reactor nuclear power plant; (*c*) Pressurized water reactor nuclear power plant.

their efficiency to about 32%, while a modern fossil-fuel power plant has an efficiency of about 40%. For every unit of electricity generated in a fossil-fuel power plant, 1.5 units of heat are rejected into the environment. In a nuclear plant, each unit of electricity represents 2.1 units of waste heat. Also, about 15% of the heat rejected by a fossil-fuel plant goes up the stack, while the nuclear reactor discharges it all in the cooling water. This means that per unit of electricity a typical nuclear power plant expels about 40% more waste heat into the environment than a typical fossil fuel plant (and about 2/3 again as much heat in the cooling water). This makes a significant difference to the receiving streams, but it is a difference in degree. There are some other basic differences between fossil-fuel and nuclear power plants. With some obvious exceptions, most are surprisingly minor.

Both fossil-fueled boilers and nuclear power plants vent radioactive particles, or radionuclides, into the atmosphere and into nearby watercourses. Indeed, coal-fired plants in urban areas meeting U.S. Environmental Protection Agency standards commonly release more radiation than LWRs meeting their regulations (McBride et al., 1978). But the primary pollutants from a fossil-fuel plant are not radioactivity; they are fly ash, sulfur oxides and nitrogen oxides (see Chapter 9). These pollutants are abundant, and they are serious health hazards. A nuclear plant produces none of them. A study by Lave and Freeburg (1973) estimates that for normal power plant operations a coal-fired plant is 24 times the health hazard of a BWR and 18,000 times the health hazard of a PWR of the same size.

The degree of hazard from normal operation of an electric power plant is very low. The degree of hazard from catastrophic accident may not be. Fossil-fuel power plants are subject to breakdown and even boiler explosion, but it is extremely unlikely that injury would go beyond the plant operation. In a LWR, however, the results of a serious accident such as loss of cooling waters, leading to serious overheating and melting of the reactor core, could be catastrophic. The probability of an accident, while low, is not infinitesimal.

Once cooling water is lost from a reactor core, there is only a limited time to shut down the plant before serious damage begins. Few issues have grabbed public attention more strongly than the chance of catastrophic accident in a power plant, especially with the actual failure of the cooling system at the Three Mile Island plant in Pennsylvania in 1979. An early analysis of the consequences of a catastrophic accident from a civilian nuclear power plant (the famous WASH 740; USAEC, 1957) projected as many as 3,400 deaths and 43,000 injuries. An updated version of this report in 1965 considered the effects of the new larger generation of nuclear power plants. It projected as many as 45,000 deaths and a disaster area as large as England or the state of Pennsylvania. It did not analyze the probability of an accident of this size, however, and many people considered the numbers presented "somewhat like analyzing (say) the consequences of the New York World Trade Center falling over" (Rose, 1974).

A later and very controversial study, generally known as the Reactor Safety Study (Nuclear Regulatory Commission, 1975), has suggested that the probability of catastrophic accidents is about one per 20,000 reactor-years. Most critics are in general agreement that the absolute numbers presented in the study are far too optimistic, but there is still no consensus of how dangerous fission power plants are or even how to measure the danger (Hohenemser et al., 1977). This critical view has been supported by the accident at Three Mile Island in 1979.

There are very few data on which to base a definitive estimate of the hazards associated with nuclear electric power. We know that serious accidents can happen. Three Mile Island is only the most dramatic to date. Nuclear reactors are designed with very high safety standards, but they are not foolproof. Nuclear power plants are operated, after all, by people who are neither perfect nor perfectly trained. Civilian nuclear technology is relatively new, and we cannot always identify all of the factors that must be considered in engineering design. One of the truly disturbing things about the Three Mile Island accident is that the plant was a new one that contained safety features that many older plants did not, and its operators were above average in their training and skill.

It is not fair to expect any technology to be problem-free, and the nuclear industry and its government backers have been remiss in suggesting that nuclear power is completely safe. It is not, and we cannot expect it to be. Nevertheless, the record shows that more people have been killed building nuclear plants than in all of the recorded accidents from running them. The health effects of routine operations of coal-fired plants are far worse than those of nuclear plants. But there exists a potential for catastrophic accident with nuclear fission that does not exist with conventional electricity generation plants, and the data do not exist to assess that potential in a precise way.

The Nuclear Fuel Cycle.   More public concern has been directed to nuclear reactors than to the fuel cycle that supports them. The fuel cycle is more vulnerable in many ways than the power plants. Like other fuels, the first two steps of the fuel cycle are mining and then fuel processing and fabrication (Figure 7.21). The third is "burning" it in reactors. In a fossil-fuel plant the next and final step would be waste disposal. The nuclear fuel cycle, however, is a cycle and the waste products can be reprocessed into new fuel. When the fuel is emplaced in a light water nuclear reactor it consists of about 3.3% ^{235}U and about 96.7% ^{238}U. In the three years that a fuel charge is in the reactor, the percentage of ^{235}U drops to its natural level of 0.8%, and several new products are created.

The composition of the spent fuel removed from the reactor is determined by two processes that have been going on during the three-year period: neutron absorption and fission. Both ^{235}U and ^{238}U are beginning points of strings of neutron absorption reactions. Some of the atoms produced are exceedingly unstable, breaking down almost immediately by releasing beta particles; others are capable of absorbing still other neutrons. At least two, ^{239}Pu and ^{241}Pu, are fissile. In a typical modern LWR some 60% of the power is produced from fission of ^{235}U, but at least 35% is obtained from fission of these two isotopes of plutonium (Cohen, 1977). Roughly 1.4% of the original uranium charge is transformed into new members of the heavy actinide group of elements (Table 7.6). The actinides that are sufficiently stable to be removed from the reactor typically have half-lives measured in thousands of years. They also tend to emit very energetic alpha particles. They are very dangerous, and they must be segregated from the biosphere for several half-lives—up to hundreds of thousands of years in the case of plutonium.

Fission daughter products are also removed with spent fuel, at a rate of 1½ times that of the actinides. These elements are more familiar and much smaller. They include iodine, strontium, cesium, barium, and cobalt. Many are essential elements closely identified with particular organs (i.e., iodine and the thyroid gland), and they migrate to the organ, so that radiation damage is concentrated and therefore more severe. Other elements are chemically similar to the elements that are used in great quantities in specific tissues, as in the case of the similarity between strontium-90 and calcium, used in bone tissue. They are also capable of being concentrated in specific places in

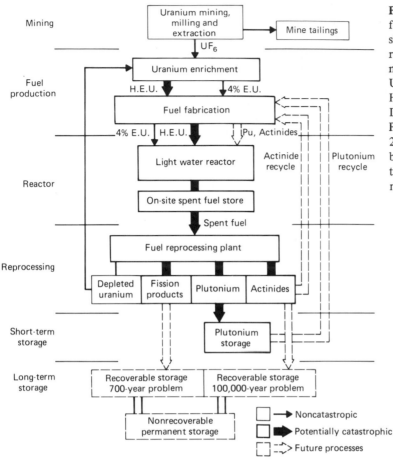

Figure 7.21 Fuel cycle for a light water reactor, showing portions currently operational and nonoperational in the United States. [After Hohenemser et al., "The Distrust of Nuclear Power." *Science* 196: 25–34. Copyright © 1977 by the American Association for the Advancement of Science.]

the body and causing significant problems. The radioactive characteristics of these elements tend to be very different from those of the actinides. They emit beta particles and gamma rays, and their half-life is relatively short. Among the longest are strontium-90 and cesium-137 with half-lives of 29 and 30 years, respectively. Some of these isotopes have great value. Cobalt-60 and iodine-131 have been useful in cancer radiation therapy. But most are dangerous. Indeed they are more dangerous than the actinides because of their high level of radioactivity and their greater rate of production.

The most intense radiation from reactor wastes as they are removed from the reactor is from the light elements. These break down relatively quickly, however, leaving the actinides as the long-term products of radiation energy. They must be stored for several half-lives to reduce them to a point where they are indistinguishable from background radiation.

The uranium fraction of the fuel can easily be reused, although it must be reenriched with fissile ^{235}U. Plutonium has a special role in nuclear science. Both fissile and fertile isotopes are removed from nuclear reactors. Depending on how it is reprocessed,

Table 7.6 Actinide Elements, with Atomic Numbers.

Atomic Number	Symbol	Element Name
89	Ac	Actinium
90	Th	Thorium
91	Pa	Protactinium
92	U	Uranium (heaviest natural element)
93	Np	Neptunium
94	Pu	Plutonium
95	Am	Americium
96	Cm	Curium
97	Bk	Berkelium
98	Cf	Californium
99	Es	Einsteinium
100	Fm	Fermium
101	Md	Mendelevium
102	No	Nobelium
103	Lw	Lawrencium

it can be used as the primary fuel for breeder reactors or made into atomic bombs. It is as toxic a substance as is known (Edsall, 1976, Bair and Thompson, 1974). The rest of the actinides tend to be neither fissile nor fertile. Their half-lives are so long that their radioactivity is low, but as alpha emitters they must be kept out of the biosphere for hundreds of thousands of years.

We have the choice of either recycling many of the actinides into new fuel or storing them for several half-lives (i.e., several hundred thousand years, or roughly 30 times the recorded human history from ancient Egypt to the present time). The composition of the uranium in spent fuel is similar to that in the original ore. It can be recycled relatively easily by the same process that was used to fabricate it in the first place. The actinides other than plutonium are not very common, and they are not fissile. They can be separated chemically from the spent fuel and (at least in principle) put into long-term storage. Plutonium presents a special problem. Spent reactor fuel is merely highly radioactive and dangerous. Recycled plutonium could be used to manufacture crude but effective bombs, and the availability of large amounts of recycled plutonium could, in the wrong hands, be used to blackmail cities or even national governments.

The best developed process for recycling spent nuclear fuels is the Purex process, developed in the United States in the early 1950s. It is designed specifically to produce weapons-grade plutonium. Spent fuel rods are chopped up, and the fuel is dissolved in nitric acid, leaving behind only the metal casing. The fuel-nitric acid solution is mixed with an organic solvent to which the uranium and plutonium migrate but the fission products do not. This solvent extraction is carried out several times to remove over 99% of the uranium and plutonium. The plutonium is then separated from the uranium by oxidizing it to insoluble plutonium nitrate. All new reprocessing plants represent some variant of this process, and the result of the commercial operation is necessarily the production of significant amounts of high-grade plutonium.

Not only is this plutonium produced during recycling, but it must be transported from the reprocessing plant back to the reactors. We may be able to assume adequate security at the reactor site and the reprocessing plant, but it is all but impossible to provide adequate security for plutonium when it is carried from one to the other. Some estimates of fuel recycling imply that there will be 50,000 annual shipments of spent fuel and waste covering a total of 80 million truck-kilometers by the year 2000 (Hohenemser et al., 1977). The black market value of plutonium is extraordinarily high, so that the incentive for theft or diversion is quite high. Indeed whole ships loaded with nuclear fuel have already been diverted from their presumed destination, and it is difficult to believe that trucks on the open roads are less vulnerable than a ship on the high seas.

There are two reasons why recycling has loomed so large in the nuclear power discussion. The first is because LWRs, which account for the vast majority of reactors in service around the world, are very wasteful of uranium, and the overall efficiency of the fuel cycle can be improved markedly by fuel recycling (Table 7.7). The second is that most breeder reactor designs require a certain amount of plutonium in their original charge, and they produce a great deal more. This plutonium cannot be used unless it can be purified and burned in a LWR or similar reactor. In other words, the fuel advantages of breeder reactors evaporate without recycling plutonium as part of the fuel cycle.

Plutonium recycling was an official policy goal in most countries until recently. The tide in the United States began to turn in 1975, when the issues of arms control and nuclear proliferation began to be joined with issues of nuclear power. Why this should be is suggested by Alvin Weinberg (1976), who describes the assumptions of

Table 7.7 Approximate Productivity of Natural Uranium for Various Reactors and Fuel Cycles.

Reactor Type	Fuel Cycle	Productivity (Kw electricity per kg. per yr.)
Light water	Enriched U, once-through.	5.1
"	Enriched U, plus uranium recycle.	6.3
"	Enriched U, plus plutonium recycle.	8.8
"	Thorium-burning (^{235}U makeup).	15.4
CANDU	Natural U, once-through.	7.7
"	Natural U, plus plutonium recycle.	16.7
"	Thorium-burning (^{235}U makeup).	50.0
High temp. gas	Highly enriched U + Th.	10.0
Fast breeder	Uranium + plutonium recycle.	500.0

After W. D. Metz, Reprocessing alternatives: the options multiply. *Science* 196: 284–287. Copyright © 1977, by the American Association for the Advancement of Science.

the original developers of the nuclear reactor. The breeder was originally thought to be the only practical design, and indeed the first two nuclear reactors to generate electricity were breeder reactors. The current generation of LWRs was originally intended only as a stepping stone from the bomb to the breeder.

These assumptions had held sway for 30 years. In 1977, the decision was made that the dangers of plutonium recycling outweighted its benefits and that commercial plutonium recycling would not be carried out, at least in the United States. Thus all high-level wastes must be stored. Regardless of the method of storage, two criteria must be met. Because of the high level of radioactivity, the heat generated must be dissipated in such a way that it does not endanger the containing vessel or the environment around it. The vessel must be constructed of materials that will not themselves be damaged by the radiation. Second, an explicit decision must be made whether to allow waste recovery at some time in the future or to seal off the waste from the environment completely and (insofar as possible) irreversibly.

Most schemes for long-term disposal of high-level wastes involve solidifying them in a ceramic matrix something like Pyrex glass. Glass has the advantage of being more resistant to most chemical alloys than metals or mineral aggregates such as concrete, but it is sensitive to both radiation and heat and can break down quickly if they get too high. The practical thermal limit for glass is about 700°C, and radiation damage is not severe if the temperature is held below this level.

The thermal release is very high when the fuel is first removed from the reactor. After an interim storage period of ten years, it drops to a level sufficient to keep the temperature of the wastes well below 700°C during subsequent storage. The standard method of interim storage for spent fuel rods is to place them under water; this is being practiced around every nuclear power plant in the world.

In theory, wastes will be congealed in glass after an interim storage of about 10 years, transported to an underground disposal site, and placed in salt deposits. The salt is highly corrosive and would quickly destroy the stainless steel cannister jacket, but the glass matrix in which the wastes were congealed would be impervious to the saline ground water. Salt is, in principle, sufficiently stable and plastic to provide a fairly good seal from groundwater. Other means of disposal have also been suggested, including granite, and "permanent" Greenland or Antarctic ice as well as the open ocean (Nielson, 1974) and outer space. Variants on ultimate disposal include solidification of wastes *in situ* without first congealing them in ceramic (Cohen et al., 1972). Other schemes have been proposed, but thus far there is no operating ultimate disposal site for high-level nuclear wastes anywhere in the world.

The ^{235}U fuel is consumed during nuclear fission, and it is quite rare. Were fission of ^{235}U to meet all of the energy requirements of the United States, the longevity of the world's ^{235}U resources would be on the order of 35 to 100 years; depending on whose estimates of reserves were used (Rose, 1974; Lieberman, 1976; Selbin, 1977; Bethe, 1977).

It has been clear for years that LWRs are very inefficient uses of uranium, and that they are at best transitions to another type of power generation source. The obvious next step is the breeder reactor, which can utilize ^{238}U and so can multiply the fuel supply by a factor of over 100 (Weinberg, 1972; Metz, 1977c). The current generation of nuclear reactors was intended to provide experience and plutonium fuel for the breeder (Inglis, 1971; Vendryes, 1977).

In no reactor is the fission of ^{235}U the only thing going on. The formation and fission of fissile ^{239}Pu, ^{241}Pu, and ^{233}U from ^{238}U and ^{232}Th happens to some degree in all. The conversion of fertile to fissile materials is a very important phenomenon. Let Q_o represent the amount of fissile material in a nuclear fuel charge when it is first emplaced and Q_c the amount of fissile material remaining in the reactor when its energy production is equal to the energy that was available through fission of the original charge of the fissile material. The ratio of the two (Q_c/Q_o) is called the *conversion ratio*. If conversion of fertile materials has been nil, then all of the fissile material will have been consumed and the conversion ratio is equal to zero. If, on the other hand, some conversion has taken place, the conversion ratio is larger than zero.

Under some circumstances the ^{238}U or ^{232}Th that may have been converted to ^{239}Pu or ^{233}U is greater than the ^{235}U consumed during the production process. In this case Q_c is higher than Q_o, so that the conversion ratio is greater than one. When the conversion ratio is greater than 1.0, fissile material is being created faster than it is being consumed. This is not to say that *uranium* is being created faster than it is being consumed, for it is not. Fertile materials are being changed into fissile materials. A typical modern LWR has a conversion ratio of about 0.4. The breeder reactor has a conversion ratio greater than 1.0. The most common design in North America is the liquid metal fast breeder reactor (LMFBR; Figure 7.22). It is like the pressurized water reactor in many ways, except that the coolant is liquid sodium and there is an extra sodium loop in the heat transmission system. Sodium is used rather than water because it has the requisite physical properties (i.e., melting point low enough, boiling point high enough) and because it does not slow down fast neutrons. Unfortunately, the sodium in contact with the core becomes intensely radioactive; hence the need for the extra loop. The secondary sodium loop does not become radioactive, and it can heat the turbine water just as the core water in a PWR.

In addition to the radioactivity of the primary sodium loop, the more intense radioactivity of the LMFBR causes the metal in the fuel rods to deteriorate much more quickly, so that fuel must be removed and reprocessed more often than in a LWR (Hammond, 1971). The breeder is also intrinsically subject to more rapid changes than lower-energy reactors. In the latter, the release of thermal neutrons is delayed to some degree. This allows adequate time for an operator to respond to a problem, whereas a nuclear excursion may begin without dalay in a LMFBR. Once a problem gets started in a LMFBR, it is potentially much more serious than in an LWR. The energy content of the core is much higher and the moderation of the reactor is much

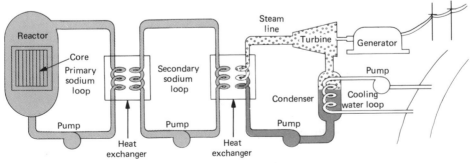

Figure 7.22 Schematic diagram of a liquid metal fast breeder reactor.

lower. The recognition that breeder reactors, with their dependence on plutonium recycling, are not only inherently more dangerous than LWRs but are also "the most proliferation-prone technology yet conceived" (Metz, 1977c), has forced a great many questions about the future of breeder reactors in civilian electricity production.

There are other nuclear alternatives in both the LWR and the LMFBR. For example, the Canadian CANDU is an efficient design that can operate on natural or enriched uranium (Robertson, 1978). Alternatively, the fuel can be enriched with thorium to give a conversion ratio well above 0.5. The moderator for the CANDU is heavy water (deuterium oxide), which allows excellent neutron economy. The efficiency of fissile uranium conversion is much higher than for a LWR (Table 7.7), but the thermal efficiency is lower.

Another alternative to the LWR is the high temperature gas cooled reactor (HTGR). The cooling medium is helium gas, which transfers its heat to water in current designs, as in a PWR, but which could in principle be fed directly to a gas turbine for greater efficiency. The moderator in the core is graphite. This design requires a highly enriched ^{235}U fuel, approaching weapons grade, but like the CANDU it can also be enriched with thorium for a similar high conversion ratio of 0.7. The thermal efficiency of the HTGR is as good as that of a coal plant, and its fuel efficiency approaches that of the CANDU.

The opportunities for near-breeders (reactors with conversion ratios between 0.7 and 1.0) are almost wide open (Weinberg, 1976; Metz, 1977c; Rickard and Dahlberg, 1978; Feiveson et al, 1979). There are many candidates and many ultimate configurations for nuclear power production systems. The decision not to emphasize plutonium recycling has caused a change in the orientation of nuclear power development, and its repercussions will probably extend throughout the world. Whereas we seemed only a few years ago to be closing options and focusing on the LMFBR, we are now taking a new look at the problems and potential of nuclear power, conscious of new options and new configurations. Nevertheless, no nuclear power program has solved the problem of dealing with high-level wastes, and the decision cannot be put off much longer.

Nuclear Fusion.   Nuclear fusion has not yet been developed to commercial levels, and there is a considerable doubt that it ever will be. Thermonuclear (hydrogen) bombs have been around for some time, but we cannot yet control thermonuclear fusion well enough to use it as a source of electric or other usable energy. The basic reactions are quite straightforward, and all involve the fusion of one or more small atomic nuclei to form larger ones. Fusion has commonly been considered a very clean and inexhaustible source of energy. Of the products only tritium (a heavy isotope of hydrogen) is radioactive, and the technology exists to hold it until radioactivity drops to acceptable levels. The main fuel is deuterium, of which an all but infinite supply exists in seawater available at economic and environmental costs far below those of coal, uranium, petroleum, or gas. But fusion is not a "clean" process, and it appears that the costs will be far higher than those of other energy sources.

A practical power plant, unlike a bomb, must be a controlled reaction. Fusion is inherently much more difficult to control than fission. The latter reaction occurs when a neutron bearing no charge collides with a positively charged nucleus. The energy of the neutron can be relatively low. In fusion two nuclei bearing positive charges must collide and fuse. Their kinetic energy must be so high that the momentum of the moving nuclei overcomes the electromagnetic repulsion between them. The fuel must exist in an extraordinarily hot (100 million to 6 billion °C) ionized gas, or plasma, so that the charged nuclei have sufficient energy to react. Confinement must be so tight that the nuclei have a high probability of colliding with one another. The very high temperatures have been reached, although the combination of factors needed to get fusion with a net positive release of energy has not. The probability that it will at some time in the future is fairly high.

It is true that fusion fuel is virtually inexhaustible. There is enough deuterium easily accessible to last for millions of years. But it is not clean. The fusion process releases very large numbers of very high-energy neutrons. The fusion reaction is contained by powerful magnetic fields that channel the highly charged plasma. Only such a medium could contain materials at temperatures as high as those required for fusion to take place. But a neutron has no charge and it is not contained by the magnetic field. Many if not most of the neutrons released by the primary fusion reaction leave the plasma and go crashing into the solid containment wall of the reactor. It has been estimated that the lifetime of the first containment wall would be 2 to 5 years. For a 1,600 megawatt (electric) reactor, some 250 tons of stainless steel would have to be replaced every two years. About 200 tons of other radioactive materials would also have to be removed, on the average, each year. The volume is something like 10 times that of the high-level wastes produced by a current-generation fission plant, and all of the removal would have to be carried out by remote control as the materials would be too radioactive to be handled directly by workmen (Metz, 1976; Parkins, 1978).

Decommission.   No plant of any sort is built to last forever. Most nuclear power plants are expected to last between 25 and 40 years. By the end of that time parts of the plant itself are highly radioactive. Most of the radioactive elements have relatively short half-lives, but not all do. Nickel-58 alloyed in the stainless steel can capture neutrons to become nickel-59 (half-life 80,000 yrs.) or nickel-63 (half-life 125 years). Carbon-14 has a half-life of 5,600 yrs. Because of their very long periods of radioactivity, it is not sufficient to weld a reactor shut to cut it off from the public. It must either be entombed in concrete like a modern pyramid or dismantled—by remote control due to high radiation levels—and added to the solid wastes. This is expensive, but it is an inherent cost of using nuclear power plants (Garret, 1976; GAO, 1977).

Geothermal Energy

The earth's geothermal gradient can be tapped as a source of energy. Some of this is derived from spontaneous radioactive decay of potassium-40. Some heat comes from friction of large rock bodies along subterranean fault zones or compression in areas of great geological pressure. One should not underestimate the amount of energy released by the earth. Between radioactive decay of granite in the crust and heat flow to the surface from the interior, the energy at the surface averages about .06 watts per square meter. Worldwide, this is greater than ten times the total energy used by society, and the geothermal energy reaching the earth's surface in one day would be sufficient to lift the Rocky Mountains over 850 kilometers.

There is a distinct geothermal gradient as one goes down into the earth. In most

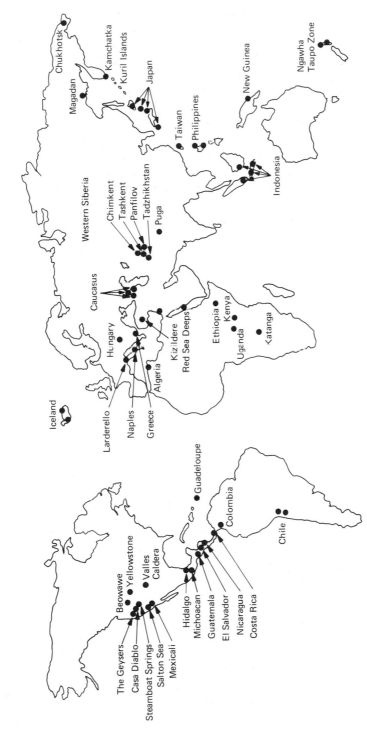

Figure 7.23 Map of major high-temperature areas of the world. Most are located in areas of current or recent volcanism or tectonic activity. [Redrawn, with permission, from Ellis, 1975.]

places the gradient is relatively low. For every 100 meters below the surface the temperature rises by 2 to 3°C in a typical geologically stable region. But many places, especially those characterized by recent geological activity (see Figure 7.23), have a higher gradient than this, with relatively high temperatures close to the surface.

The practical use of geothermal heat is very old. Its use for space heating predates both plumbing and writing. Its uses in electricity generation go back to 1904 with the development of a steam field in Larderello, Italy. There is usually some surface expression of a suitable geothermal area, such as geysers, hot springs, or fumaroles (steam vents). But there need not be. There need only be heat stored in rock with sufficient permeability that water can flow through it. There is nothing mystical about geothermal power. Naturally occurring heat is transferred to naturally occurring water; that water can be tapped and used as though it had been heated in a boiler.

Geothermal steam and water are produced in developed fields. Dry steam is preferable if available, as it can be fed directly into an electric turbine or other end-use device. But steam mixed with water or hot water alone are much more common. Of the 18 projects listed by Ellis (1975), only three produce steam without water.

Geothermal energy has many uses. The most famous (Larderello, Italy; Wairakei, New Zealand; the Geysers, California) are all used to generate electricity. Geothermal wells in and near Reykjavik, Iceland, are used to heat the city. Other uses include salt recovery, mining, animal husbandry, horticulture, and fisheries (Lindal, 1973). The precise use depends on the temperature of the water. Water under 200°C is not used for generating electricity. But water of 85°C can be very effective at space heating and cooling.

Geothermal power has several advantages. It uses no fuel whatever, and it dissipates no heat on the earth's surface that would not be dissipated anyhow in roughly the same place. Thus far, geothermal power has used naturally occurring water as a transfer medium (Figure 7.24), although other fluids have been proposed and have some clear

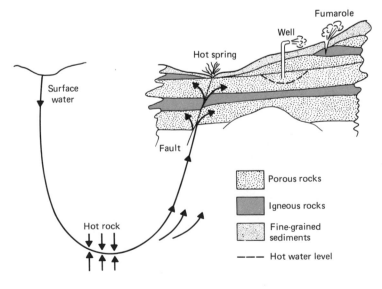

Figure 7.24 Diagram of a high-temperature geothermal system. Surface waters are heated by hot rocks, then flow through permeable zones to the surface. Porous rocks are saturated with hot fluid. Steam leaks out as fumeroles at high surface levels, and water leaks out in hot springs at low surface levels. Wells may initially tap both hot water and steam for power generation. Discharge of fluid often forces the hot water level deeper into the system, at least in the vicinity of the well. [After Ellis, 1975.]

advantages (Hammond, 1972). The system is commonly open, and little or no water is recycled back into the ground. An alternative that is being tested experimentally is to circulate water through rocks containing great geothermal heat but little or no water (so-called hot rocks; Figure 7.25; Hammond, 1973).

Superheated water is a powerful solvent. Geothermal heat tends to be concentrated in areas characterized by igneous or metamorphic rock containing minerals not common at the earth's surface and including many toxic materials. Water from a geothermal power project may contain a wide variety of toxic or corrosive substances. At Wairakei, New Zealand, the levels of arsenic, mercury, and both gaseous and dissolved H_2S, as well as several species of radionuclides, are very high. Thermal efficiency of the plant is so low (about 7.5%) that high effluents of thermal water are added to the Waikato River in relation to the amount of electricity produced (Axtmann, 1975). Nevertheless, most or all of these pollutants would be released to the river anyway even if the electricity generation plant were not present, and the development of a geothermal field may make it possible to control pollution to some extent. The high dissolved mineral content of the water leads to scaling and corrosion of equipment to an unusual degree. Maintenance expenditures may be much higher than in conventional plants. But the "fuel," as with solar power, is free, and the capital costs are much lower, so the overall cost may be considerably less than for a conventional plant.

Because so little of a geothermal field is specifically engineered (i.e., the "boiler," the "fuel" and water supply, and most of the "plumbing" are underground and only indirectly under the engineer's control), it may take some time for the field to equili-

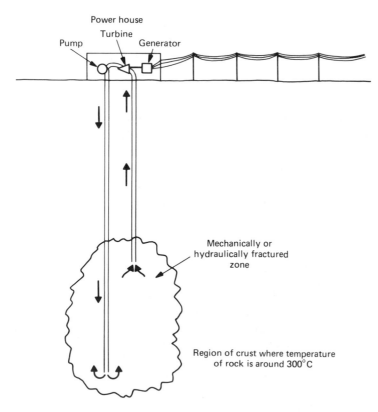

Figure 7.25 System for extracting energy from a dry geothermal reservoir. The hot rock is fractured so that water can flow through it. Cold water is pumped down from the surface, hot water released at the surface.

brate with the changes induced by exploitation. Development of a field may cause the ratio of water to steam to shift, the water level to change, a gas vent to appear or disappear as the field reaches equilibrium with its new conditions. But the basic stability of geothermal systems appears to be very long—on the order of millions of years (White, 1974). The water rather than the heat is the uncertain variable, and this can be controlled to a degree by pumping water back underground. A geothermal field may thus have a very long lifetime compared to conventional plants, further compensating for the shorter turbine life. The costs per kilowatt of installed capacity are roughly the same for extensive or limited development of a given field. This means that developing countries may find geothermal power a very attractive option if they have fields available. Power plants can be built slowly as capital is available without prejudging the course of future field development or closing options for future exploitation.

Power From Gravitational Sources

The other energy source is the gravitational attraction between bodies. Gravitation, combined with the solar energy of the hydrologic cycle, is the basis of hydropower. The pure gravitational attraction between the moon and the earth that sets the tides in motion can also be tapped for energy.

Hydropower. Hydropower has been a familiar energy source for several thousand years. A dam built on a stream serves two functions. First, the impoundment evens out variability in stream flow and makes water continuously available; second, a *hydraulic head* is created. This is the pressure of the water at the level at which work is done, and it is proportional to the height of the water above that level. Water impounded behind a dam thus represents potential energy like the chemical energy in gasoline or the nuclear energy in a ^{235}U atom. Conversion does not involve a thermal intermediate step, however.

At first waterwheels were connected directly to machines in the factory. Most medium-sized streams in most countries of the world have numerous small dams that once served to provide power directly to a grist mill, a forge, or a small factory. Very few of these mills are left, as the conversion process is not very efficient. Hydropower now almost always means hydroelectric power. Electricity is convenient, and very large hydroelectric projects show benefits of scale. The very large reservoirs that produce the hydroelectric power can be used for other things such as irrigation, recreation, and transportation.

Building a dam is commonly an extremely capital-intensive task, and the number of suitable dam sites is restricted. In some parts of the world most of the potential dam sites are already developed, including all or at least most of the best ones. In others the level of development is very small (Table 7.8). A dam site is stable over geological time. The dangers to life and property that accompany the collapse of a dam are too great to make geologically unstable sites appropriate dam sites. But reservoirs are not terribly long-lived. Because of sedimentation, an unavoidable natural process, the useful life of a dam is typically between 5 and 200 years. And a dam site, once developed, is developed. One cannot start over with a new reservoir the way one can with a power plant.

Table 7.8   World Hydroelectric Potential and Developed Capacity.

Region	Potential		Developed Capacity	
	10^3 Mw	Percent of Total	10^3 Mw	Percent of Total
North America	313	11	75	24
Central and South America	577	20	11	2
Western Europe	158	6	83	53
Africa	780	27	3	1–
Middle East	21	1	2	10
Asia	497	17	30	6
Australasia	45	2	5	11
USSR, China, Eastern Europe	466	16	35	8
Total	2,857	100	244	9

Potential data from Hubbert, 1962.
Developed capacity data from FPC, 1969.

Tidal Power.   Several estuaries in the United States and Canada, Argentina, England, France, and the Soviet Union are sufficiently large and have sufficiently high tides that it is feasible to develop tidal power systems. A dam is built to close off an estuary from the sea (Figure 7.26). As the tide comes in, the dam is closed until a substantial hydraulic head is established between the ocean and the lower water in the estuary. At that point the gates are opened, and water flows through the turbines into the estuary. As the tide goes out, the turbines are turned in the other direction as water flows back into the ocean. Most existing tidal energy schemes have a conversion efficiency on the order of 8% to 20%, although a project at la Rance, France, has an efficiency approaching 25%.

The potential for development of tidal energy is not large when compared with other energy sources. Not enough estuaries are sufficiently large and have sufficiently high tides to make it economically feasible. Where these do exist electricity can be generated with no noxious fumes, caustic water, water pollution, or radioactive wastes. Tidal generators do not flood river valleys and displace people who formerly lived there. But they do alter the estuaries in which they are built, and estuaries are unique environments for many critical functions. Paramount among these are shipping, and nursery grounds for fish. The development of tidal power may damage an estuary for these uses. The extent of damage depends on the way the project is engineered.

THE METABOLISM OF A MODERN SOCIETY

Energy includes much more than the resources, supply, and technology of energy conversion. The role of price is very important, both as relative prices of different energy sources affect the choices people make among different ways of doing things, and as

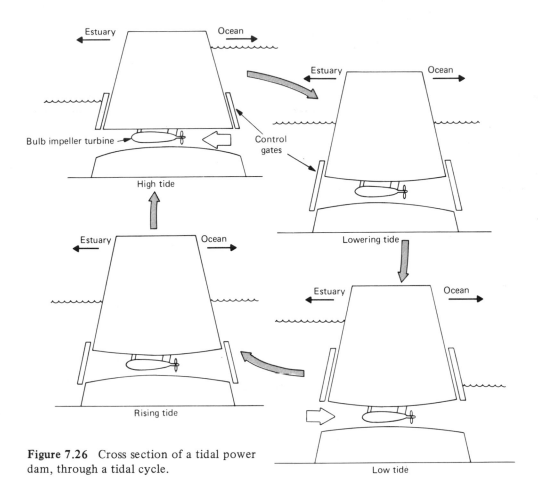

Figure 7.26 Cross section of a tidal power dam, through a tidal cycle.

the current increase in energy prices will affect the patterns of societal development on a global scale. There is no question that the oil and gas that most of the world now depends on will cease to be primary fuels during the lifetime of people now being born. We can argue about the date, but the range of probabilities is not very great.

There is no worldwide shortage of energy. Solar energy in its various guises, geothermal, fission, and perhaps fusion can provide society with all of the energy it needs for several millions of years, if it comes to that. Even coal is sufficiently abundant to bail us out for several hundred years. The issue is not what kinds of energy resources exist; it is rather what forms of energy are available for what end uses by industries and consumers and at what price.

Society has a metabolism not unlike that of a living organism. Different functions are carried out in different places; the requisite inputs must be brought in and the wastes and outputs transported away. So long as the basic functions are carried out, the society prospers. The composition of the input does not really matter so long as the process works. Changing inputs is very difficult in a living organism. If an organism wanted to alter the characteristics of a process such as photosynthesis, it would have to undergo tremendous genetic changes and it would likely become extinct. But people can respond very quickly to cultural changes in inputs. Technological innovation and substitution of materials and methods can be rapid, and a society need not risk extinction in order to develop. Basic resources are the limiting factors in natural ecosystems, but patterns of conversion limit human ecosystems. If a resource turns out to be limiting, it is because nothing else could be substituted for it in the conversion process for which it is the key.

With few exceptions, the energy that fuels the critical functions of society is not in the form in which the resource exists, but is a derivative product. As an example, cars do not run on petroleum. They run on gasoline made from petroleum (or perhaps from coal, oil shale, or municipal wastes). They can also run on diesel fuel, natural gas, electricity, hydrogen, alcohol, or even the sap of certain plants (Maugh, 1979). The function served by the car is to produce controllable mechanical power, and there are many primary energy sources that can be converted to do this. The function of the car is what is important. The primary energy sources are only precursors of final energy form.

Energy Grade and Ecosystem Metabolism

To clarify the relationship between energy type and use, it is often convenient to speak of the *grade* of energy and the specifications required for different uses. We can distinguish two meanings of energy content in a gross sense. The first is total energy content, or *enthalpy*. The second is the available thermodynamic energy. Consider, for example, two vessels filled with water, one with a volume of 1 cu. m., the other with a volume of 1 l. (1,000 cm.^{3} or .001 m.^{3}). Both are heated from absolute zero over a Bunsen burner with precisely the same amount of natural gas (Figure 7.27). Their heat contents are identical. But the temperature of the smaller vessel is considerably higher, and the energy available for performing useful work (like cooking an egg) is much higher.

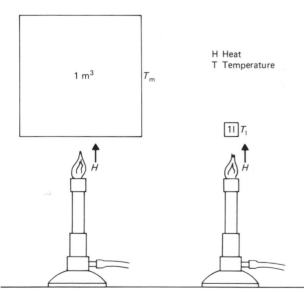

Figure 7.27 Diagram illustrating difference between heat content and available energy. Two units of water (1 m.^{3} and 1 liter) are heated from absolute zero. Precisely the same amount of heat (energy) H is transferred into them, until they reach temperatures T_m and T_1, respectively. T_m is much lower than T_1.

A useful index of the value of a type of energy is the practical question, "What can I do with a piece of it?" The more that can be done, in general, the higher its grade. Petroleum, natural gas, enriched uranium, high-temperature steam, electricity, and most types of mechanical energy are all high-grade energy types. Sunlight, low-energy synthetic gas, natural uranium, low-temperature steam, and hot water are all low-grade energy types. Most functions of society can be identified qualitatively with an energy grade. Electric motors, automobiles, computers, and communication equipment require high-grade energy, whereas space heating requires only low-grade energy.

There is no way that any modern society can maintain its current patterns of energy use over the next hundred years or so. Energy use has been expanding at a high rate in all countries of the world, sparked by petroleum and natural gas. Yet these will no longer be primary fuel sources after a few decades. The present is a transition stage to some future. If that future is to be sustainable over a long time, its energy sources must be either "income" sources or one of the finite sources with essentially infinite fuel, such as breeders or fusion. It is not clear how or when the new state will come, nor whether we shall reach it voluntarily or through coercion, or at what cost.

Indications of the possibilities for the future can be seen by comparing different societies in the present. Most European countries, Sweden in particular, are much more efficient in their use of energy than the United States (Figure 7.28) and some of them have a standard of living at least as high (Schippen and Lichtenberg, 1976). This clashes with a common belief that a high standard of living requires a high level of energy consumption. It is quite true that there is a correlation between per capita gross national product and energy usage on a national level (Figure 7.29). But the data also suggest that energy use is not closely correlated with indicators that reflect actual standards of living (Mazur and Rosa, 1974). Many changes could easily be made that would allow great energy savings in all sectors of the economy (Hirst and Moyers, 1973).

Even industry, where one would not expect to find costly waste, holds broad opportunities for improvement. Brown and Berkowitz (1974) document savings of almost 30% in the energy usage of one chemical research and development plant. Berg (1974) points out several ways in which fuel conservation can be carried out, often with substantial savings. Many of these are standard practice in Europe.

People have gotten used to thinking of energy as cheap; personal or corporate decisions do not need to consider the efficiency of energy use. A surprisingly large proportion of the population of the United States does not recognize that there is an energy problem (Abelson, 1977). Those who do not cannot be expected to respond to it, but once they do they are capable of responding relatively quickly with good results.

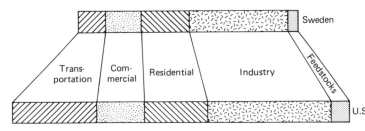

Figure 7.28 Comparison of per capita energy consumption in Sweden and the U.S. in 1971. [Data from Schipper and Lichtenberg, 1976.]

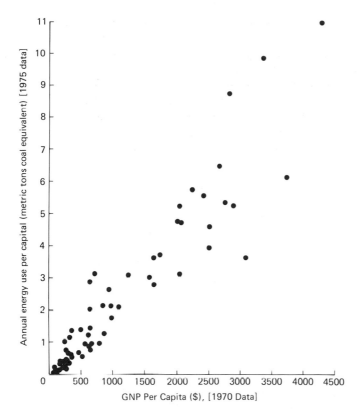

Figure 7.29 Correlation between national per capita gross national product and energy usage. [Data from U.N., 1977.]

Europe, Japan, and the Third World have always had energy shortages. For them a sensitivity to efficiency in energy use is second nature.

Structural Conservation. Conservation means reducing waste. Conservation at the point of end use is the quickest, cheapest, and most efficient way to release supply. Most conservation measures are not very dramatic. They may involve insulating houses or retrofitting furnaces with devices to retain heat in the furnace, or producing cars that get higher mileage. They may involve turning down the thermostat at night. Some of the most useful kinds of conservation do not involve increased expenses or discomfort. They involve things like closing draperies at night so that cold air does not escape, or carrying out maintenance on cars when it is due. The value of these little things was shown clearly during a recent power shortage in Los Angeles (Stobagh and Yergin, 1979). Individual efforts, most of which entailed little or no cost, were able to cut power consumption markedly with little noticeable effect on the people of the city.

Deeper changes in the structure of the energy system can also be remarkably effective in reducing waste. For example, many houses, apartments, and commercial buildings are heated by gas or oil with a thermal efficiency of 80%, when there is an electric power plant nearby operating at a thermal efficiency of 35% and rejecting its waste cooling waters into a nearby stream or lake. Even under the best of conditions the water from the power plant is discharged at a temperature higher than ambient, and it may cause a thermal pollution problem (see Chapter 8). If the plant were willing to operate at a thermal efficiency of about 29%, its waste water would be hot enough to heat the buildings around it with an overall thermal efficiency of heating of about 83%; the overall efficiency of the combined electric power and space heating system would be on the order of 75%. The overall fuel savings in the heated buildings would be about 2/3 the fuel originally used by the power plant. This is shown schematically in Figure 7.30. This is the district heating principle, widely used in Europe. It represents a highly efficient use of fuel as well as a way of reducing an important type of water pollution. Figure 7.30 shows a fossil fuel power plant. If the plant were a nuclear plant the resulting efficiency would be even higher, since all of the waste heat would go into the cooling water. District heating has never been popular in North America, but it could be successful in several American cities and it can be used successfully with power plants burning all sorts of fuels, fossil and nuclear (Karkheck et al., 1977).

The most popular end-use form of energy is currently electricity. This need not be the case, and there would be advantages in changing. Electricity is exceedingly difficult to store. Although batteries are improving they are still relatively inefficient. Figure 7.31 shows the hourly power output of a southern utility system for the peak week in

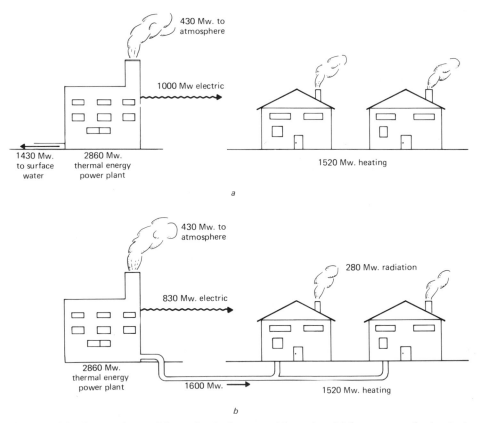

Figure 7.30 Comparison of hypothetical community *a*, in which a power plant rejects its waste heat into surface waters and buildings are heated separately, and community *b*, in which waste heat from the power plant is used to heat buildings.

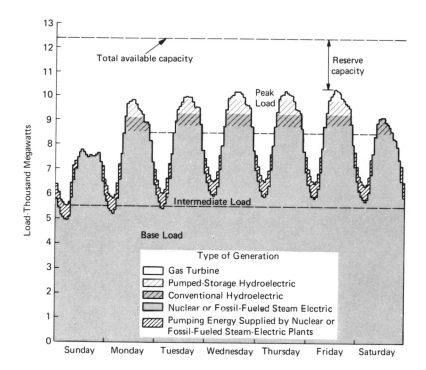

Figure 7.31 Hourly power output from a utility system in the U.S., August, 1968. [After FPC, 1970.]

August, 1968. There is a base load of about 5 megawatts demanded continuously, and fluctuating loads up to 10 megawatts at midday during the week. Different kinds of generators are used for different parts of the load. The base load is provided by the largest nuclear and fossil fuel steam generators. These are designed to run at all times, and it is both inefficient and costly to turn them on and off. Intermediate loads can be met by older, smaller, and less efficient steam plants and by hydroelectric power. These facilities can be turned on and off, as it were, much more easily and quickly. Peak loads are met with pumped-storage hydroelectric and inefficient (25% to 30% thermal efficiency) gas turbines or diesel generators that can go from off to full power in 3 to 5 minutes (FPC, 1971).

Figure 7.31 shows both supply and demand. Because electricity is virtually unstorable, generation capability must be able to meet demand fluctuations. Some elements of the supply system must thus be more costly and inefficient than might otherwise seem necessary, due to the tradeoffs that must be made between fuel efficiency, capacity, and the speed with which a plant can go from zero to spinning reserve to full load and back.

Pumped storage is so far the only way in which electricity can be stored on a large-scale commercial basis. During low periods in the daily cycle, water is pumped from a lake or river up to a relatively small reservoir above it (Figure 7.32). During peak demand this water is allowed to run back down through hydroelectric generators. The entire operation is about 67% efficient. That is, for every two units of energy produced from a pumped storage generator, three have to be expended to pump the water uphill. If this energy is generated by a 38% efficient fossil-fuel steam generator, the overall efficiency of the pumped-storage generator drops to 25%. This is about as good as

Figure 7.32 Diagram of a pumped storage hydroelectric project. [Redrawn, with permission, from FPC, 1970.]

the gas turbines and diesel generators that comprise the currently available alternatives, and the use of off-peak electricity to pump water has the great advantage of allowing utilities to increase production during off hours and raise their base load. This allows more efficient use and lower maintenance of the largest and most efficient generating plants in the system.

There are other ways of storing energy. Batteries, magnetic fields, and flywheels can all store energy efficiently as chemical or mechanical energy and regenerate it as electricity quickly on demand. The storage efficiency of some experimental batteries is about 70%, and the efficiency of magnetic-field and flywheel storage is as much as 90% to 95%. Both are higher than pumped storage, and units can be located closer to load centers, thus reducing transmission losses.

Another approach is to use electricity generated during off-peak periods to produce hydrogen gas through electrolysis of water. This can currently be done at an efficiency of 60% to 70%, but prototype electrolysis can reach 85%, and the theoretical maximum is about 120%, allowing for some heat absorption from the environment (Maugh, 1972). The hydrogen could be converted back into electricity by fuel cells at an efficiency of about 60%, or it could be used in its own right as an alternative to electricity.

Many of the chemical processes for which natural gas or petroleum is a major feedstock (e.g., manufacture of nitrogen fertilizer) require hydrocarbons mainly as a cheap source of hydrogen. If hydrogen itself were widely available as a by-product of electric power off-peak generation, a substantial amount of natural hydrocarbons might no longer be required. Hydrogen can also be used as a motor fuel (Jones, 1971), or as a home heating and cooling fuel. The costs and energy losses of distributing hydrogen are considerably lower than those of electricity, and the technology of distribution is essentially the same as that of natural gas. It has been proposed (Bockris, 1972; Winsche et al., 1973) that new power plants should produce hydrogen on-site and distribute hydrogen rather the electricity. Only small appliances really need electricity to power them. Space heating and cooling, water heating, and cooking can be done at a higher efficiency using hydrogen than using electricity. Widespread adoption of hydrogen would allow all electric plants to be designed for continuous base load operations at high thermal efficiencies, and the phasing out of the less efficient fossil-fuel plants now used for intermediate and peaking loads.

EPILOGUE

Energy poses challenges that are both frightening and exciting. It is a critical and vulnerable input to our way of life, and there is no question that the way we think about energy, as well as the price we pay for it, must change. We will probably see committed efforts to increase supplies of new (generally nuclear or synthetic) fuels. This tendency is even stronger in Europe than in North America (Häfele, 1974; Bauer et al., 1976). Sufficient new supplies can mean that the present inefficient use of energy can be sustained. This is the easier route in many ways, as societal norms would not have to change very much. But it is an unstable and expensive solution.

There is reason to believe that the supply-increase approach will not work. Even though there are great quantities of fossil fuels, uranium, oil shale, and heavy hydrogen, the new fuels of the future will tend to be of lower grade than those currently available. The development of new fuel resources will take time, money, and energy. Using lower-grade energy sources will be more expensive than using the high-grade fuels we compare them with today. It seems much better to make the changes in our thinking that will allow us to increase the efficiency of energy use, and to anticipate the impacts of future shortages or bottlenecks in energy supply or of rapid escalation of energy prices.

For example, it is well known that the cost estimates for synthetic fuels have escalated steadily over the past few years. One reason for this is that synthetic fuel technology is not a method for fuel production, but rather one of fuel conversion. It takes a lot of energy in addition to the basic coal feedstock to make this conversion, and the energy feedstocks are rising steadily in price. Of course, this price increase is passed through to the synthetic fuel.

Likewise, a nuclear power plant represents a very high investment of energy. Its core must be complete at startup, and the energy expended in the fuel mining and fabrication processes to build the core represent something like 12% to 20% of the total output of the plant over its entire life. A given power plant may produce considerably more energy than that invested in its construction and startup, but if it is part of a program in which great numbers of plants are built quickly, the nuclear power program as a whole can represent a net loss rather than a net gain in energy. It will show a net energy deficit as long as the program continues to expand (Chapman, 1974; Price, 1975).

There are outside barriers to the growth of energy consumption. The most important is the global climate. Our climate is a function of heating and cooling of different layers of the atmosphere and surface at different places and times. Energy absorption and re-radiation in the atmosphere can be affected by carbon dioxide and particulate matter emitted by power plants, as well as by the local "heat islands" (see Chapter 9) found in areas of high energy consumption. We also know that the general climate has been much cooler and much warmer in the past, and we know that it can change fairly rapidly. The net effect of increasing carbon dioxide and particulate matter from growth in energy use or shifting to synthetic fuels is not clear. It will most likely lead to a warming of the earth's global climate, which would be potentially disastrous. This is especially likely if there is a wholesale change to synthetic fuels. Because these fuels must be processed, the carbon dioxide released from synthetic fuels is 1.4, 1.7, and 2.3 times greater than that from direct combustion of coal, petroleum, and natural gas, respectively.

Few things show the dynamism and the complexity of human ecosystems more effectively than energy and materials. The things going on in the various domains shown in Figure 1.2 are exceedingly diverse and often contradictory. The forces controlling the flows of energy and materials in human ecosystems are those of technological development, political and economic tradeoffs, and public perception of an inconsistent and imperfect world with changing patterns of risk. One of the greatest challenges facing us is to understand these forces and their interactions so that the metabolism of modern society represented by the flow of energy and materials can be assured over the long term.

References

Ableson, P. H., 1977. Public opinion and energy use. *Science* **197**: 1325.

American Petroleum Institute, n.d. *Large Tankers–Our Energy Lifelines.* Washington: Am. Petrol. Inst.

Axtmann, R. C., 1975. Environmental impact of a geothermal power plant. *Science* **187**: 795–803. Comments and reply on this article in *Science* **189**: 328–330.

Bair, W. J. and Thompson, R. C., 1974. Plutonium: biomedical research. *Science* **183**: 715–722.

Barnett, H. J. and Morse, C., 1963. *Scarcity and Growth: The Economics of Natural Resources Availability.* Baltimore: Johns Hopkins Univ. Press.

Bauer, E., Puiseux, L., and Teniere-Buchot, P.-F., 1976. Nuclear energy–a fateful choice for France. *Bull. Atom. Sci.* **32** (1): 37–41.

Berg, C. A., 1974. Conservation in industry. *Science* **184**: 264–270.

Bethe, H. A., 1977. Nuclear power, a safe bet. *Bull. Atom. Sci.* **33** (7): 55.

Bockris, J. O'M., 1972. A hydrogen economy. *Science* **176**: 1323.

Brookins, D. G., 1976. Shale as a repository for radioactive waste: the evidence from Oklo. *Env. Geol.* **1**: 255–269.

Brown, A. E. and Berkowitz, E. B., 1974. Energy conservation at an industrial research center. *Science* **184**: 271–272.

Chapman, P. F., 1974. The ins and outs of nuclear power. *New Scientist* **64**: 866–869. See also comments on this article in *New Scientist* **65**: 66–67, 97, 160, 230.

Cohen, B. L., 1977. The disposal of radioactive wastes from fission reactors. *Sci. Am.* **236 (6)**: 21–31.

Cohen, J. J., Lewis, A. E., and Braun, R. L., 1972. *In situ* incorporation of nuclear waste in deep molten silicate rock. *Nuclear Technol.* **14**: 76–88.

Committee for Economic Development, 1974. *Achieving Energy Independence.* New York: Committee for Economic Development.

Council on Environmental Quality, 1973. *Energy and the Environment–Electric Power.* Washington: Council on Environmental Quality.

Cowan, G. A., 1976. A natural fission reactor. *Sci. Am.* **235 (1)**: 36–47.

Division of Reactor Development and Technology, 1969. *Operating History: U.S. Nuclear Power Reactors.* Washington: U.S. Atomic Energy Commission.

Donovan, P. et al., 1972. An assessment of solar energy as a national energy resource. Washington: National Science Foundation and National Aeronatics and Space Administration.

Duffie, J. A., and Beckman, W. A., 1976. Solar heating and cooling. *Science* **191**: 143–149.

Eckholm, E., 1975. The other energy crisis: firewood. *Worldwatch Paper* **1**. Also in Eckholm, E., 1976. *Losing Ground: Environmental Stress and World Food Prospects.* New York: W. W. Norton.

Edsall, J. T., 1976. Toxicity of plutonium and some other actinides. *Bull. Atom. Sci.* **32 (7)**: 27–37.

Ellis, A. J., 1975. Geothermal systems and power development. *Am. Sci.* **63**: 510–521.

Federal Power Commission, 1969. *World Power Data, 1967.* Washington: U.S. Govt. Printing Office.

Federal Power Commission, 1971. *The 1970 National Power Survey, Part I.* Washington: U.S. Govt. Printing Office.

Feiveson, H. A., von Hippel, F., and Williams, R. H., 1979. Fission power: an evolutionary strategy. *Science* **203**: 330–337.

Flawn, P. T., 1970. *Environmental Geology.* New York: Harper & Row.

Garret, P., ed., 1976. *An Engineering Evaluation of Nuclear Power Reactor Decommissioning Alternatives.* Washington: Atomic Industry Forum, Inc.

General Accounting Office, 1977. Cleaning up the remains of nuclear facilities—a multibillion dollar program. Report to the Congress by the Comptroller General of the United States.

Goldemberg, J., 1978. Brazil: energy options and current outlook. *Science* **200**: 158–164.

Grenon, M., ed., 1975. Energy resources. Laxenburg, Austria: International Institute for Applied Systems Analysis *Conference Proceedings* **CP-76-4**.

Gustavson, M. R., 1979. Limits to wind power utilization. *Science* **204**: 13–17.

Häfele, W., 1974. Energy choices that Europe faces: a European view of energy. *Science* **184**: 360–367.

Häfele, W., 1975. Nuclear energy and its alternatives. Laxenburg, Austria: International Institute for Applied Systems Analysis *Research Memorandum* **RM-75-73**.

Hammond, A. L., 1971. Breeder reactors: power for the future. *Science* **174**: 807–810.

Hammond, A. L., 1972. Geothermal energy: an emerging major resource. *Science* **177**: 978–980.

Hammond, A. L., 1973. Dry geothermal wells: promising experimental results. *Science* **182**: 43–44.

Hammond, A. L., 1976a. Coal research: II—gasification faces an uncertain future; III—liquifaction has far to go; IV—direct combustion key site potential. *Science* **193**: 750-753; 873-875; **194**: 172-173, 218.

Hammond, A. L., 1976b. Questioning the synthetic fuels option. *Science* **193**: 752.

Hammond, A. L., 1977. Photosynthetic solar energy: rediscovering biomass fuels. *Science* **197**: 745-746.

Hildebrant, A. F., and Vant-Hull, L. L., 1977. Power with heliostats. *Science* **197**: 1139-1146.

Hirst, E. and Moyers, J. C., 1973. Efficiency of energy use in the United States. *Science* **179**: 1299-1304.

Hohenemser, C., Kosperson, R., and Kates, R., 1977. The distrust of nuclear power. *Science* **196**: 25-34.

Hubbert, M. K., 1962. Energy resources. *N.A.S.-N.R.C. Pub. 1000-D.*

Hubbert, M. K., 1970. Energy resources. In N.A.S.-N.R.C. Commission on Resources and Man, *Resources and Man.* San Francisco: W. H. Freeman & Co., 157-242.

Hubbert, M. K., 1974. U.S. energy resources, a review as of 1972, Part I. U.S. Senate Comm. on Interior and Insular Affairs, Ser. 93-40 (92-75). Washington: U.S. Govt. Printing Office, No. 527002419.

Hubbert, M. K., 1975. Hubbert estimates from 1956 to 1974 of U.S. oil and gas. In Grenon, M., ed., *First IIASA Conference on Energy Resources.* Laxenburg, Austria: International Institute for Applied Systems Analysis Conference Proceedings *CP-76-4.*, 148-166.

Inglis, D. R., 1971. Nuclear energy and the Malthusian dilemma. *Bull. Atom. Sci.* **27** (2): 14-18.

Inglis, D. R., 1975. Wind power now! *Bull. Atom. Sci.* **31** (8): 20-26.

Inglis, D. R., 1978. *Wind Power, and Other Energy Options.* Ann Arbor: Univ. of Michigan Press.

International Atomic Energy Agency, 1975. *The Oklo Phenomenon.* Vienna: I.A.E.A. *Symposium Volume* **204**, 646pp.

Johansson, T. B. and Steen, P., 1978. *Solar Sweden: An Outline to a Renewable Energy System.* Stockholm: Secretariat for Future Studies.

Jones, L. W., 1971. Liquid hydrogen as a fuel for the future. *Science* **174**: 367-370.

Karkheck, J., Powell, J., and Beardsworth, E., 1977. Prospects for district heating in the United States. *Science* **195**: 948-955.

Kirby, R. C. and Prokopovitsch, A. S., 1976. Technical insurance against shortages in minerals and metals. *Science* **191**: 713-719.

Knabe, W., 1964a. Methods and results of strip-mine reclamation in Germany. *Ohio Jour. Sci.* **64**: 75-100.

Knabe, W., 1964b. A visiting scientist's observations and recommendations concerning strip-mine reclamation in Ohio. *Ohio Jour. Sci.* **64**: 132-154.

Kubo, A. S., and Rose, D. J., 1974. Disposal of nuclear wastes. *Science* **182**: 1205-1211.

Lave, L. B. and Freeburg, L. C., 1973. Health effects of electricity, generation from coal, oil, and nuclear fuel. *Nuclear Safety* **14**: 409-428.

Liebermann, M. A., 1976. United States uranium resources: an analysis of the historical data. *Science* **192**: 431-436.

Lindal, B., 1973. Industrial and other applications of geothermal energy. In Armstead, H. C. H., ed., *Geothermal Energy.* Paris: UNESCO Earth Science Series No. 12: 135-148.

McKelvey, V. E., 1972. Mineral resource estimates and public policy. *Am. Sci.* **60**: 32-40.

McNay, L. M., 1971. Coal refuse fires, an environmental hazard. U.S. Bureau of Mines *Information Circular* 8515.

Maugh, T. H., II., 1972. Hydrogen: synthetic fuel of the future. *Science* **178**: 849–852.

Maugh, T. H., II., 1979. Unlike money, diesel fuel grows on trees. *Science* **206**: 436.

Mazur, A. and Rosa, E., 1974. Energy and life style. *Science* **186**: 607–610.

McBride, J. P., Moore, R. E., Witherspoon, J. P., and Blanco, R. E., 1978. Radiological impact of airborne effluents of coal and nuclear plants. *Science* **202**: 1045–1050.

Metz., W. D., 1976. Fusion research. (I) What is the program buying the country; (II) Detailed reactor studies identify more problems; (III) New interest in fusion-assisted breeders. *Science* **192**: 1320–1323; **193**: 38–40, 76; **193**: 307–309.

Metz, W. D., 1977a. Solar thermal electricity: power tower dominates research. *Science* **197**: 353–356.

Metz, W. D., 1977b. Wind energy: large and small systems competing. *Science* **197**: 971–973.

Metz, W. D., 1977c. Reprocessing alternatives: the options multiply. *Science* **196**: 284–287.

Moyer, F. T., and McNair, M. B., 1973. Injury experience in coal mining, 1970. U.S. Bureau of Mines *Information Circular* **IC-8613**.

Murphy, A. H., Gilchrist, A., Häfele, W., Kroemer, G., and Williams, J., 1976. The impact of waste heat release on simulated global climate. Laxenburg, Austria: Int. Inst. Appl. Syst. Anal. *Research Memorandum* **RM-76-79**.

Nielson, S. O., 1974. Nuclear waste disposal, a response to Kubo and Rose (1974). *Science* **185**: 1183.

Nuclear Regulatory Commission, 1975. *Reactor Safety Study: An Assessment of Accident Risks in U.S. Commercial Nuclear Power Plants*. Washington: Nuclear Regulatory Commission. Report WASH-1400 (NUREG 75/014), 9 vols.

O'Neill, G. K., 1975. Spare calories and energy supply to earth. *Science* **190**: 943–947.

Osborn, E. F., 1974. Coal and the present energy situation. *Science* **183**: 477–481.

Othmer, D. F., and Roels, O. A., 1973. Power, fresh water, and food from cold, deep sea water. *Science* **182**: 121–125.

Parkins, W. E., 1978. Engineering limitations of fusion power plants. *Science* **199**: 1403–1408.

Price, J. H., 1975. Dynamic energy analysis and nuclear power. In Lovins, A. B. and Price, J. H., *Non-nuclear Futures: The Case for an Ethical Energy Strategy*. Cambridge: Ballinger Pub. Co., 105–223.

Rickard, C. L. and Dahlberg, R. C., 1978. Nuclear power: a balanced approach. *Science* **202**: 581–584.

Robertson, J. A. L., 1978. The CANDU reactor system: an appropriate technology. *Science* **199**: 657–664.

Rose, D. J., 1974. Nuclear electric power. *Science* **184**: 351–359.

Samuelson, P. A., 1980. *Economics,* 11th ed. New York: McGraw-Hill Book Co.

Schanz, J. J., Jr., 1976. Problems and opportunities in adapting U.S. Geological Survey terminology to energy resources. In Grenon, M., ed., *Energy Resources*. Laxenburg, Austria: Int. Inst. Appl. Syst. Anal. *Conference Proceedings* **CP-76-4**: 85–120.

Schipper, L. and Lichtenberg, A. J., 1976. Efficient energy use and well-being: the Swedish example. *Science* **194**: 1001–1013.

Selbin, J., 1977. Unreal thinking about energy. *Bull. Atom. Sci.* **33** (7): 54–55.

Skinner, B. J., 1969. *Earth Resources*. Englewood Cliffs, N.J.: Prentice-Hall, Inc.

Sørenson, B., 1975. Energy and resources. *Science* **189**: 255–260.

Sørenson, B., 1976a. Wind energy. *Bull. Atom. Sci.* **32** (7): 38–45.

Sørenson, B., 1976b. Dependability of wind electric generators with short-term electric storage. *Science* **194**: 935–937.

Squires, A. M., 1974. Clean fuels from coal gasification. *Science* **184**: 340–346.

Stobagh, R. and Yergin, D., eds., 1979. *Energy Future: Report of the Energy Project of the Harvard Business School.* New York: Random House.

Strauss, J., McCandless, L., Buroff, J., Hylton, B., Keith, S., Large, D., and Sessler, G., 1979. Technology assessment report for industrial boiler applications: coal cleaning and low sulfur coal. EPA Technical Report for Contract 68-02-2199, Task 12.

United Nations, 1977. *Statistical Yearbook, 1976.* New York: United Nations Statistical Office.

U.S. Atomic Energy Commission, 1957. *Theoretical Possibilities and Consequences of Major Accidents in Large Nuclear Power Plants.* Atomic Energy Commission Report WASH-740.

U.S. Bureau of Mines, 1974a. Mineral industry surveys, coal mining fatalities monthly. Coal mining fatalities in 1973. Jan., 1974.

U.S. Bureau of Mines, 1974b. Mineral industry surveys, weekly coal report No. 2950, March 29, 1974.

Vendryes, G. A., 1977. Superphenix, a full-scale breeder reactor. *Sci. Am.* **236 (3)**: 26–35.

Von Hippel, F. and Williams, R. H., 1975. Solar technologies. *Bull. Atom. Sci.* **31 (9)**: 25–31.

Weinberg, A. M., 1972. Social institutions and nuclear energy. *Science* **177**: 27–34.

Weinberg, A. M., 1976. The maturity and future of nuclear energy. *Am. Sci.* **64**: 16–21.

Weingart, J. M., 1977. Systems analysis of large-scale solar energy conversion. Laxenburg, Austria: Int. Inst. Appl. Syst. Anal. *Research Memorandum* **RM-77-23.**

White, D. E., 1974. Diverse origins of hydrothermal ore fluids. *Econ. Geol.* **69**: 954–973.

Wilcox, H. A., 1975. The ocean food and energy farm project. *Calypso Log* **3**: 1–6.

Winsche, W. E., Hoffman, K. C., and Salzano, F. J., 1973. Hydrogen: its future role in the nation's energy economy. *Science* **180**: 1325–1332.

Wolf, M., 1974. Solar energy utilization by physical methods. *Science* **184**: 382–386.

Zener, C., 1976. Solar sea power. *Bull. Atom. Sci.* **32 (1)**: 17–24.

8/the use and degradation of aquatic ecosystems

Water is one of the most common compounds on earth. Aquatic ecosystems cover over 3/4 of the world's surface and far more of the volume of the biosphere. They span the range from marine to fresh water, large to small, shallow to deep. Some flow, while others are still. With very few exceptions, we do not manage aquatic ecosystems intensively but rather are content to exploit them as natural or quasi-natural ecosystems. Nevertheless, people's activities often change them so completely that they become of minimal use. They are altered not because they are used for some specific purpose, but rather because they serve as a sink for by-products of other activities of a society.

The use of aquatic ecosystems as a sink for the effluvia of civilization is by no means new. Even in Greek mythology, one of the tasks of Hercules was to cleanse the Augean stables within a single day. These stables contained a great wealth of cattle and had never been cleaned. Hercules harnessed the River Alpheus and ran it through the stables and washed them out quickly. If only he had put a handle on it, perhaps he could have gotten a patent for the original flush toilet. Aristotle noticed white filamentous threadlike organisms in polluted water 2,400 years ago. We know these today as the sewage fungus complex. Imperial Rome in Augustine times had a population over one million people. The high population densities required some means of dealing with their domestic wastes. The *cloaca maxima* was built to drain the upper-class sections of the city. Even today, you can go into some of the old buildings near the Coliseum and walk down to what was once the street level of Imperial Rome. Below you, you can hear sewage still flowing through the *cloaca maxima,* which has been in continuous use for almost 2,000 years. The temple in Jerusalem is built over a spring that could be diverted at the appropriate time to wash away the blood from recent sacrifices.

Water carriage of household wastes was developed to a very high degree by the Romans. In consequence, it was widely used in most countries of Western Europe that had either been part of the Roman Empire or were influenced by it. In these countries the attitude grew that this was the "proper" way to handle domestic wastes. Other parts of the world where Roman technology had never spread developed different attitudes toward the domestic waste problem. In the Far East undiluted human wastes have been used as crop fertilizers for thousands of years, and a set of methods for dealing with night soil has been developed and is still used in several parts of Asia. As pointed out by Pradt (1971), night soil treatment is much cheaper than Western style sewage treatment, capital costs are about 6% of water carriage systems, and operating and maintenance costs are about 33%. There are other advantages as well, including much lower rates of water use and water pollution.

Following the demise of Imperial Rome urban population densities fell considerably, and water pollution did not become widespread again until the Industrial Revolution and the consequent rise of large cities. Isaac Walton (1653) described fishing in waters of England that today are little better than industrial sewers. Even so, Spenser (1596) described the polluting effects of mine drainage in England. Until the Industrial Revolution population densities were low enough that the traditional methods of composting, earth closets, and so on, were adequate to solve most waste disposal problems. But so much waste was being generated in industrial countries such as England by the eighteenth century that the old methods simply could not keep up with the production. Garbage and excrement accumulated in the streets, and industries that had grown up along rivers to tap readily available power sources were dumping their by-products into the same rivers. Early in the nineteenth century sewers were introduced into industrialized countries and quickly became the norm (Hynes, 1960; Tarr and McMichael, 1977). The streets were undeniably cleaner, and removing wastes from contact with the population had important health benefits.

The cost in terms of water pollution was high. In England, for example, the state of many rivers had become so bad that Parliament was forced to act. London was plagued by cholera outbreaks, and the salmon were disappearing from important salmon streams such as the Thames and the Mersey. In 1847 the first act to regulate water pollution in an English-speaking country was passed; this was the Gas-Works Clauses Act of 1847, which prohibited the discharge of gas wastes into streams. The Salmon Fisheries Acts of 1861 and 1865 prohibited the pollution of salmon waters so as to kill fish. Unfortunately, the salmon had already been driven from the important rivers of England, so these laws had little effect. The year 1898 saw the establishment of the Royal Commission on Sewage Disposal in England, which published ten reports during the first 15 years of the twentieth century. This Royal Commission represented the first in-depth look at the overall question of water pollution, and our current understanding of the nature and causes of water pollution dates in a real sense from the establishment of this Royal Commission.

We often think of water pollution as though it referred to a single kind of phenomenon. Like so many things, it is a very complex set of phenomena that stem from many different sources and have different kinds of expression in different kinds of ecosystems. Some types of pollution are more common than others, but there is no way that we can speak of a pollutant or even a type of pollution that is in any way typical. Indeed, one of the most significant problems of the Royal Commission reports is that they identified biochemical oxygen demand (BOD; we shall have a lot more to say about this shortly) as the appropriate measure of pollution and that which should be treated. They were correct in that it should be treated. But concentrating on BOD as a proxy index for all pollution to the neglect of other significant pollutants is a gross oversimplification that has led to numerous subsequent problems, many of which are serious in themselves.

OXYGEN AND EUTROPHICATION

For most purposes, the best indicator of the health of an aquatic ecosystem is its dissolved oxygen content. The cycle of oxygen in a simple aquatic ecosystem can be shown diagrammatically as in Figure 8.1. It enters the water biochemically via photosynthesis and physically by absorption across the air-water interface. The rate at which photosynthesis takes place is a function of the temperature, plant biomass, and sunlight. The rate of absorption across the air-water interface is a function of the turbulence of the water and the deviation of the dissolved oxygen concentration from saturation. Under most circumstances, the oxygen concentration of the water is less

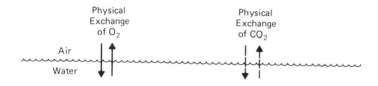

Figure 8.1 Schema for exchanges of oxygen in aquatic ecosystems. Solid arrows represent movement of oxygen; dashed arrows represent movement of CO_2 or oxygen in organic molecules.

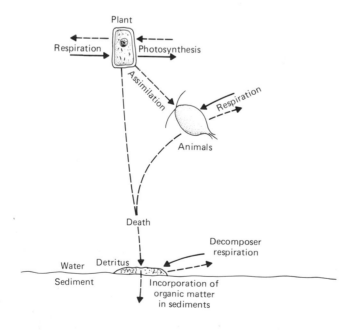

than saturation, so that oxygen tends to cross the interface into solution. Respiration converts food consumed by heterotrophs into usable energy and carbon dioxide. Oxygen is removed from solution in the process.

Lakes show a balance between the amount of oxygen crossing the air-water interface or produced through photosynthesis and the amount consumed through respiration. Most carbon fixed by plants is consumed and broken down by animals and bacteria in the same ecosystem. A little bit is incorporated into the bottom sediments and builds up as humic debris at the bottom of the lake. Photosynthesis *in situ* accounts for relatively little of the fixed carbon found in a typical stream. Most washes in from surrounding terrestrial ecosystems. However, the typical stream is often turbulent enough that adequate amounts of oxygen can also enter the system to break down the carbon contributed to the food chain.

Simple respiration is not the only way in which oxygen is withdrawn from solution. For example, other reduced chemicals such as amino or sulfhydral compounds (i.e., compounds containing $-NH_2$ or $-SH$ chemical groups) are relatively energy-rich. Their energy is released when they are oxidized. Most aquatic ecosystems include at least some bacteria capable of oxidizing these compounds. Oxidation of reduced compounds may be entirely inorganic as well.

The chemistry of the water-sediment interface is especially complex. The interstitial water within the sediment is in quasi-equilibrium with the surrounding sediments. Transfer of water between the water column and the interstitial water is only by slow diffusion. Many of the organic molecules in the sediments can serve as food for sediment-dwelling bacteria. If the interstitial waters are oxygenated, the bacterial flora is aerobic and these molecules are oxidized. If oxygen is low, some of the bacteria may be anaerobic and much of the chemical breakdown proceeds through hydrolysis. As long as aerobic bacteria are found in the sediment, they can lower the oxygen concentration of the interstitial waters until only anaerobic bacteria can survive. Because interstitial water does not mix readily into the water column, it may be anoxic even when the water column is fairly well oxygenated. Its oxygen content is controlled almost entirely by the sediment characteristics rather than by the water body itself.

Because conditions within the sediments are generally anoxic, the strictly inorganic reactions that occur there may be important. Many elements, such as iron and phosphorus, exist in several different oxidation states. If they are normally found in one such state, they may become oxidized or reduced to others under the proper conditions. As an example, sulfur is generally found as sulfate (SO_4^{--}), its oxidized state. Under highly reducing conditions, however, it can be reduced to sulfite (SO_3^{--}), sulfide (S^{--}), or elemental sulfur. One effect of these oxidization-reduction reactions is the release of a certain amount of oxygen, as shown by the equations below.

$$2SO_4^{--} \rightarrow O_2 + 2SO_3^{--} \rightarrow 3O_2 + 2S^{--}$$

$$2SO_4^{--} + 2H_2O \rightarrow 2S + 4OH^- + 3O_2$$

But changing oxidation states does not only alter the oxidation potential of the sediment. It also changes the physical properties of the material in question. For example, a relatively insoluble substance may become even more insoluble. Conversely, it may become more soluble, so that it is released into solution in the interstitial waters. As an example, iron phosphate is normally found in the water column as Ferric phosphate ($FePO_4$). The iron is in its ferric or oxidized state (Fe^{+++}). Ferric phosphate is highly insoluble. If for some reason the ferric iron becomes reduced to ferrous iron (Fe^{++}), two things happen. First of all, a certain amount of phosphate is released into solution:

$$3Fe^{+++}PO_4 \rightarrow Fe_3^{++}(PO_4)_2 + PO_4^{--}$$

| Ferric | Ferrous | Dissolved |
| Phosphate | Phosphate | Phosphate |

The ionized phosphate is dissolved in the interstitial waters. It may react with something else there, in which case it will not leave the sediment mass. But it may also diffuse across the sediment-water interface and enter the water column. In addition, ferrous phosphate itself is much less insoluble than ferric phosphate. The proportion that can dissolve in water is still very small, but it is many times that of the ferric phosphate. This may be important if iron phosphates are precipitated in lake-bottom sediments and if something brings about a reduction in the iron's oxidation state. The resulting release of phosphate under anoxia can be observed, and it may have a very profound effect on water quality.

An important fraction of nutrients such as phosphate are not precipitated as insoluble compounds, but are rather adsorbed onto organic or clay micelles. Here too, the oxidation state of the sediment affects the mobility of the ions. Phosphate is much more soluble under anaerobic conditions than under aerobic conditions (Patrick and Khalid, 1974; Li et al., 1972). Empirical observations suggest that the concentration of phosphate in bottom waters can increase by a factor of over 100 when anoxic conditions are reached (Mortimer, 1941, 1942). The regeneration rate of phosphate in Lake Erie under anoxic conditions is over 11 times that under oxic conditions (Burns and Ross, 1972).

As might be expected, the relative regeneration rates of different ions under oxic and anoxic conditions depend on the chemistry of the ions and the complexes involved. Phosphate is a good example since its behavior is representative, and it is in many ways the most significant of the mineral nutrients. It is quite possible for the bottom waters of a lake to go from oxygenated to anoxic relatively quickly, both within a year and over a span of a several years, as the lake evolves. Given this, the behavior of nutrients under anoxic conditions becomes especially important. Changes in the oxygen level of the bottom sediments may affect the nutrient content of the water.

Understanding the dynamics of oxygen in an aquatic ecosystem requires looking not only at the water column itself, but also at the air-water and water-sediment interfaces bounding it. It must consider all substances dissolved in the water or entering it across one of the interfaces, including oxygen itself, molecules that use oxygen for their breakdown, and nutrients that influence the development of oxygen demand. In addition to the physical processes of diffusion and changes in oxidation state, the mechanisms controlling oxygen dynamics include plants, animals, and bacteria, as well as any inorganic chemical reactions involving oxygen.

Oxygen-Demanding Materials and Biochemical Oxygen Demand (BOD)

Oxygen-demanding substances is an aggregate term describing organic materials in aquatic ecosystems. Most are derived from naturally occurring carbonaceous materials that may be produced within the lake or stream or washed into it from outside. All watercourses have at least some oxygen-demanding materials. They comprise a very wide range of chemical composition, come from many different sources, and exhibit a wide range of chemical properties.

Oxygen-demanding substances enter the detritus food chain, where they serve as food for bacteria or other organisms in the water. These organisms require oxygen to carry on their normal respiratory functions, and they remove dissolved oxygen from the water as they break down the carbonaceous materials. In general, the greater the amount of oxygen-demanding substances in the water, the greater the amount of oxygen that is removed from the water by its decomposition.

The most common measure of oxygen-demanding materials in aquatic ecosystems is BOD, or *biochemical oxygen demand.* Strictly speaking, it is a measure of the oxygen removed from a sample of water that is incubated under standardized conditions. As such, it aggregates the effects of all of the oxygen-demanding substances in the water and provides information on their impact on the oxygen balance in the lake or stream. It is a simple and very useful notion. For most practical purposes, it is more important to know how much oxygen is demanded by organic wastes than it is to know how much of what kinds of oxygen-demanding wastes actually occur in the water.

However, the simplicity of the BOD notion is a limited one, and its limitations must be borne in mind. Different chemicals behave differently in real watercourses, and the differences are sometimes important. For example, municipal sewage and the effluents from a beef rendering plant or a paper mill all produce wastewater with high loadings of oxygen-demanding materials. A measurement of BOD would not show much difference between them, but treatment plants to handle the wastes would face different problems and their design would have to reflect these problems. The rendering plant and the paper mill must both treat a narrow spectrum of wastes. The substances generated by the rendering plant are quite easy to break down, while those of the paper mill are quite difficult. The municipal sewage treatment plant, on the other hand, has to treat everything that comes down the sewers. Some of the organic matter may be easy to treat; some is very difficult. But the diversity and lack of control over the wastewater stream represent problems significantly different from and perhaps greater than that of the paper mill.

Even from the perspective of the lake or stream, the notion of BOD is often too aggregated. The point of a measure of biochemical oxygen demand is to indicate the amount of dissolved oxygen that will be removed from receiving watercourses. BOD as it is measured provides a rough approximation of this. It assumes that decomposition is continuous and proportional to the material remaining in solution, so that the amount of oxygen consumed during the test is asymptotic to the total amount of oxygen that will decompose in the field (Figure 8.2). Homogeneous carbohydrates behave this way, but real wastewaters do not. For example, the proteins found in most putrescible wastes contain nitrogen. The carbohydrate portion of the molecule breaks down relatively quickly, but the nitrogen-containing portions do not exert all of their

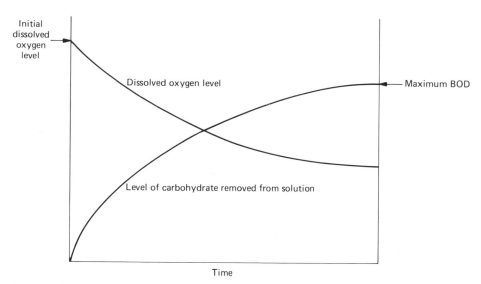

Figure 8.2 Cumulative oxygen removal curve from a solution of a simple organic molecule. The rate of decomposition is proportional to the amount of material remaining in solution.

demand for dissolved oxygen until some time later. The nitrogen accounts for a substantial portion of the oxygen demand. The standard incubation period catches the first (carbonaceous) stage, but not the second (nitrogenous) stage. Thus, the measured BOD is an underestimate of actual oxygen demand.

The notion of BOD is a very important one even though interpreting its measurements is difficult and imprecise. Organic wastes do exert oxygen demand, and the withdrawal of oxygen is their most significant practical impact on aquatic ecosystems. There are other measures of organic content that are easier to standardize, but they do not reflect the ecological fact that organic wastes are broken down by bacteria and other detritivores, as well as by some inorganic oxygen-requiring reactions.

Organic materials are normally broken down aerobically into simple compounds such as carbon dioxide and water, leaving only the refractory organic materials to collect in the bottom sediments. However, if the receiving waterway is low in dissolved oxygen or if the wastewater stream contains more oxygen-demanding substances than the receiving stream contains dissolved oxygen, the system becomes anoxic and decomposition proceeds through fermentation. In this case much less energy is released per molecule, so that decomposition takes place more slowly. If a given amount of BOD exists in the stream it will take significantly longer for all of it to decompose anaerobically, and hence the stream will be polluted for that much greater distance from the influx of BOD. Furthermore, the breakdown products tend to be more objectionable.

Anaerobic decomposition proceeds by breaking chemical bonds in organic molecules, often inserting a hydrogen atom on one side of the bond and a hydroxyl ion on the other (Figure 8.3). Rather than the chemically stable and unobjectionable carbon dioxide and water, the products are commonly unstable, smelly, and toxic. Many are volatile and escape into the atmosphere, where they are oxidized quickly. But some have such unpleasant odors that most people find them highly offensive. Examples

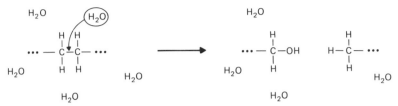

Figure 8.3 Schema for hydrolysis of an organic molecule. Note that the water molecule "attacks" the organic molecule and breaks a C–C bond. It itself is broken up in the process with H^+ being attached to one side of the broken carbon bond and HO^- being attached to the other.

include putrescine and cadaverine, both of which provide much of the pungency of rotting flesh, and butyl mercaptan, a substance produced most noticeably by the anal glands of a skunk.

Oxygen-demanding substances can remove large amounts of dissolved oxygen from rivers and lakes. This in turn can bring wholesale changes in their flora and fauna. Under extreme conditions, the discharge of large amounts of oxygen-demanding substances into a river can turn it into a foul-smelling entity largely devoid of macroscopic life. This is possible even if the substances being discharged are completely nontoxic in themselves.

Nutrients

When the Royal Commission of 1890 began publishing their reports on the nature of the water pollution and how to deal with it, they concentrated, for obvious reasons, on BOD. It was oxygen demand that caused dissolved oxygen to be lost from the water, and it was the resulting low oxygen levels that led to declines in fish populations and the objectionable smells that pervaded cities around the turn of the century. But oxygen-demanding substances are not the only pollutant discharged into waterways, and from the viewpoint of the dynamics of ecosystems they are not the most serious. Nutrients can have more far-reaching effects, as very small amounts can lead to the production of large amounts of BOD *in situ*. Their effect is also much longer-lived.

Nutrients enter aquatic ecosystems the same way as oxygen-demanding materials. Those biological materials which contain carbon also contain nutrients such as phosphorus, nitrogen, and sulfur. Raw organic debris contains these nutrients in roughly the proportion needed for rapid organic growth. The form of nutrients as they are delivered in wastewaters is as parts of large organic molecules. They are stripped off these molecules by the same decomposer organisms that bring the decline in dissolved oxygen concentration. Stripping nutrient ions, however, does not cause a further direct decrease in the dissolved oxygen concentration. The nutrient becomes available to organisms that can convert them to their own biomass. In essence, the addition of nutrient elements to an aquatic ecosystem fertilizes it. Just as in a field, when a lake or stream is fertilized production rises.

If increase in production were the only effect of fertilizing a lake or a stream, the nutrient addition would not be a problem. But there are significant secondary effects. All living things, be they autotrophs or heterotrophs, must meet certain respiratory requirements. Autotrophs can manufacture food and release oxygen only when the temperature and the light intensity are sufficiently high. At night they, as well as the heterotrophs, respire. The combined respiration may be enough to deplete the dissolved oxygen concentration. At the same time, the saturation level for dissolved oxygen is lower at the high temperatures found during the day, when plants can produce oxygen by photosynthesis, than it is at night (Figure 8.4). If conditions become unfavorable to autotrophs for any reason, their death transforms what had been oxygen-producing organisms into oxygen-demanding organic material.

Under conditions of very high productivity, aquatic ecosystems often show *algal blooms,* in which an algal population multiplies to very high densities. It is not uncommon for a lake surface to resemble green pea soup of a rather bad quality. During the bloom itself, virtually all of the available nutrients are included in the algal biomass, although some are released back to the water as the bloom ages. Ultimately a combination of effects limits further algal growth, and they begin to die. Tremendous blooms of algae are followed by equally remarkable die-offs. A dead alga (or a dead anything else, for that matter) is not an autotroph producing oxygen through photosynthesis. It is detritus demanding oxygen. Even if increasing productivity did not lead to algal blooms, the simple increase in plant production resulting from fertilization would lead to increased heterotroph activity. This also represents an increase in oxygen demand generated *in situ* by the increased nutrient level.

Two things should be noted about nutrient enrichment as compared with pollution by oxygen-demanding substances. First of all, both entail major increases in the BOD load on the ecosystem. But the timing of that influx is very different. Oxygen-demanding substances remove oxygen from solution immediately and continue to do so until they have been broken down. The expression of nutrient pollution, on the other hand, is delayed for some time. The effects of oxygen-demanding substances

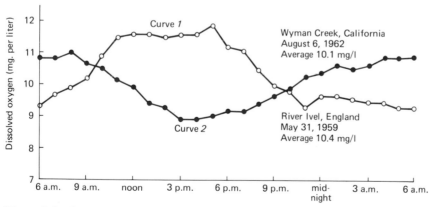

Figure 8.4 Curve showing the dissolved oxygen concentration in two small streams over a 24-hour period. Curve *1,* for the River Ivel, England, is controlled by photosynthetic oxygen production *in situ,* which reaches its maximum by noon and then declines in the late afternoon. Curve *2,* for Wyman Creek, California, does not have a large plant population. Its dissolved oxygen curve is temperature controlled: The highest levels are during the coldest part of the day, when oxygen saturation levels are at their peak. Oxygen is lost during the day, as the temperature rises and the saturation concentration declines. [Redrawn, with permission, from Slack, 1971.]

are transient, whereas those of nutrient pollution are much longer lasting. Oxygen-demanding carbonaceous materials provide detritivores with energy. When the energy of the carbonaceous materials is discharged there is no remaining oxygen demand. Nutrients, on the other hand, are not energy sources that are respired away. Once a nutrient atom has entered an ecosystem, it may remain there indefinitely, cycling constantly through normal biogeochemical cycles and continuing to allow higher production.

The fate of nutrients in enriched watercourses is a function of their biogeochemical cycles. The basic form of the biogeochemical cycle in a waterway receiving nutrient-containing wastes is shown in Figure 8.5. The nutrient material enters the food chain as they are taken up by aquatic plants. They are passed on to animals through the grazing food chain and through detritivores back to solution in the water.

The productivity of an aquatic ecosystem is controlled by the sum of the nutrients dissolved in the water within the photosynthetic zone plus those actually present in autotroph tissue. This pool constitutes the total available nutrient resources for primary production. It may be a very large proportion of the total nutrient content of the system, or it may be a rather small one. Only nutrients in solution are actually available to phytoplankton. They can also be found in particulate form, combined into molecules of partially decomposed tissues of dead animals or plants, or in insoluble

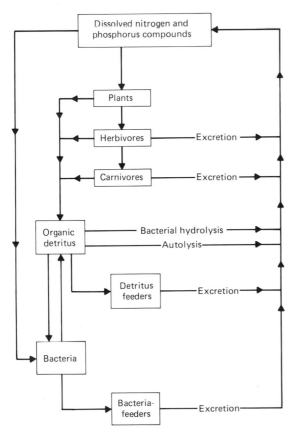

Figure 8.5 Biogeochemical cycle of nutrients in an aquatic ecosystem. [Redrawn, with permission, from Johannes, 1968, "Nutrient Regeneration in Lakes and Oceans." *Advances in Microbiology of the Sea* 1: 203–213.]

inorganic minerals. During periods of active growth, soluble nutrients cycle rapidly from solution into autotroph biomass. Whatever is excreted is picked up quickly by other plants. Nutrient-containing dead tissues are rapidly broken down, and the nutrients are regenerated into their dissolved form. The more rapid the algal growth, the faster the nutrient regeneration and uptake. Dissolved nutrients build up during periods that are not favorable for plant growth, bringing about a seemingly paradoxical inverse relationship between dissolved nutrients and ecosystem productivity.

The nutrient regeneration patterns in an aquatic ecosystem differ from those of a terrestial ecosystem. Most regeneration in the latter is by bacteria in the detritus food chain. Relatively little is excreted by organisms in soluble form. The reverse is true in the aquatic ecosystem. Most nutrients regenerated into solution are excreted by zooplankton feeding on the algae, so that the zooplankton provide nutrients under normal circumstances fast enough to supply algal growth requirements. Bacteria are very much involved with the breakdown of carbonaceous matter, but breakdown tends not to be as complete as on land, and those nutrients that are chemically bound to a refractory molecule are likely to remain so after the molecule has become permanently incorporated into the bottom sediments. Experimental data suggest that only about 50% of the particulate nitrogen and phosphorus are actually regenerated into usable form (Foree et al., 1971).

Algae can assimilate nutrients in several ways. Like other organisms, they take up the amounts actually required by cell metabolism. These nutrients become part of the algal biomass. Since they are required, a failure to take in the minimum amount inhibits growth. But most algae can assimilate much larger amounts of certain key nutrients. This so-called *luxury uptake* is a useful adaptation to rapidly changing dissolved nutrient levels. The excess nutrients are held relatively loosely, so that cell growth and division can continue when concentration of limiting nutrients dissolved in the water falls below what would normally be a critical level. In a way, luxury uptake can be regarded as evolution's unemployment insurance. Indeed, experiments have shown that certain essential nutrients (notably phosphorus) can be held so efficiently that algal populations can become established and grow in a phosphate-free medium. Luxury uptake is an evolutionary mechanism whereby algae take advantage of optimal conditions and reach very high population densities, even though the demand generated by those levels causes massive deterioration in key growth conditions (i.e., nutrient concentration). The selective advantage to the population is that it can thrive under the ensuing low-nutrient conditions, while other populations cannot. Algal blooms can start as a response to favorable conditions and continue even when the most important nutrients are all but absent from the solution at the height of the bloom.

It is significant that a very high proportion of the nutrient pool is assimilated in algal tissue during a bloom. The very high population levels thus constitute a scavenging mechanism for nutrients. With the aging of the bloom and the death of cells, a certain amount of nutrients are regenerated by excretion and cell breakdown. But the chemically bonded nutrients sink to the bottom as particulate matter, and a significant proportion is incorporated permanently into the sediments. By the end of the bloom, higher than normal proportions of the nutrients are tightly bonded, and the nutrient regeneration rate from a large algal bloom is less than for more normal algal growth conditions. In one algal bloom in Lake Sebasticook, Maine (Mackenthun et al., 1968), the algae contained over 2 tons of phosphorus and over 20 tons of nitrogen. This was about 33% of all of the phosphorus in the lake. If as much as 20% of the phosphorus were incorporated permanently into the sediments following the bloom (Golterman, 1960), the result would be that almost 1/2 ton of phosphorus, or 7% of the total phosphorus in the lake, would be scavenged from the water column.

Between the incomplete regeneration of nutrients from particulate matter and the tendency for certain materials, notably phosphorus, to become adsorbed onto sediment particles, the sediments represent a tremendous sink for nutrients. Despite the tendency for many nutrients to become mobile under anoxia, there is empirical evidence that sediments tend not to release their sorbed nutrients into the overlaying water unless the concentration in the water column is quite low (Laterell et al., 1971; Taylor and Kunishi, 1971).

Inorganic Reducing Agents

The inorganic reducing agents comprise several inorganic chemicals that can combine with and remove dissolved oxygen. Some are also nutrients, including amino nitrogen and sulfhydryl sulfur. Both of these can be oxidized by specially adapted bacteria, and these reactions are normal parts of their biogeochemical cycles.

Other reduced inorganic chemicals found in watercourses are either uncommon or unknown in natural ecosystems. Bacterial or inorganic oxidation of these materials can remove dissolved oxygen just as efficiently as respiration of carbohydrates. The best example is acid mine drainage, discussed in Chapter 7. The oxidation in each molecule of iron pyrites requires 7.5 molecules of oxygen, so that pyrites entering a watercourse during a mining operation exert a very strong demand for oxygen in addition to acidifying the water and rendering it toxic to most forms of life.

Many metals exist in several oxidation states, with the most common being the highest. When such a metal enters the environment in a lower oxidation state it tends to be oxidized, and it constitutes a potential inorganic reducing agent. The most common example is ferrous iron (Fe^{++}). This is the form in which iron is discharged from steel mills as "pickle liquor." The more common form of iron is ferric iron (Fe^{+++}). A moderately strong oxidizing agent can easily transform Fe^{++} into Fe^{+++}. Oxygen is the only strong oxidizing agent common enough to be important in typical waterways.

$$2Fe^{+++} + O_2 + H_2O \rightarrow 2Fe^{++} + 2OH^-$$

This kind of reaction is not as significant as BOD in real watercourses, but it can be locally important.

Patterns of Oxygen Dynamics in Space and Time

The phenomena discussed here so far are general and hold equally well for lakes and streams. But there are important differences between these two.

Dissolved Oxygen Depletion in Streams.   The consequences of discharging an effluent rich in BOD into a stream depend on the amount and type of material being discharged, the temperature of both the water and the effluent, and the quality and size of the receiving stream. They are a complex mixture of chemical and biological phenomena. Of the two, the chemical effects are simpler in many ways, but the flora and fauna are often more sensitive than chemists' measuring devices, so that biological examination will often show more than all but the most detailed of chemical observations.

The course of BOD breakdown in a stream is relatively straightforward (Hynes, 1960). Imagine a finite loading of BOD entering a stream at some specific place. Decomposition, and hence dissolved oxygen removal, proceed at a rate characteristic of the temperature, the oxygen concentration, and the type of materials in question. If the initial dissolved oxygen concentration was at a constant and high level in the system at the point of discharge, and if no oxygen was allowed to cross the air-water interface, the relevant variables would probably show the patterns in Figure 8.6. The rate of oxygen removal is highest at the beginning when the most digestible organic materials are being broken down. It declines gradually with the actual concentration of organic materials, as the residue becomes more refractory. Ultimately, the residue is entirely refractory and undergoes no further breakdown. The rate of dissolved oxygen depletion drops to zero.

In an actual stream, oxygen does cross the air-water interface and it is promoted by turbulent stream flow. Everything else being equal, the reaeration rate is proportional to the oxygen deficit of the stream (i.e., the difference between the actual oxygen concentration and the saturation level; Figure 8.7). Reaeration increases as the dissolved oxygen level drops, at least partially offsetting deoxygenation induced by the bacterial breakdown. The dissolved oxygen level continues to drop as long as decomposition is fast enough that respiration exceeds reaeration. When the level of organic matter drops low enough that reaeration exceeds respiration, the dissolved oxygen curve begins to rise back to saturation. Assuming no new wastes enter the stream, it reaches saturation when only refractory carbonaceous matter remains, and it stays there.

This characteristic temporary decline in dissolved oxygen levels downstream from waste discharges is termed the *oxygen sag*. Three variants on the oxygen sag curve,

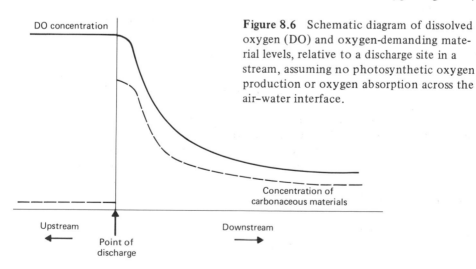

Figure 8.6 Schematic diagram of dissolved oxygen (DO) and oxygen-demanding material levels, relative to a discharge site in a stream, assuming no photosynthetic oxygen production or oxygen absorption across the air–water interface.

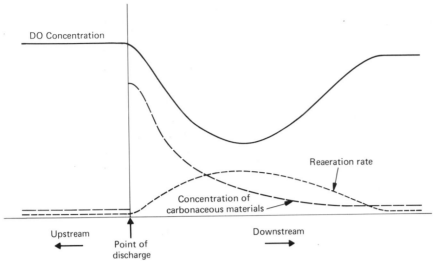

Figure 8.7 Schematic diagram of dissolved oxygen, oxygen-demanding materials, and reaeration levels, relative to a discharge site in a stream.

differing in the intensity of BOD discharge, are shown in Figure 8.8. They are representative of the conditions in actual streams. If a particular river does not show a smooth oxygen sag curve, it is because real rivers do not have constant velocity or uniform turbulence (and hence reaeration rates). For a given set of physical conditions, the depth and length of the sag is a function of the amount of BOD injected into the stream. Unless the waste load contains toxic materials, the river can be expected to return to its original purity by the end of the sag zone.

The process by which an organically polluted river shows an oxygen sag and then returns to its original level is commonly called *self-cleaning*. It occurs because the carbonaceous materials dumped into the river represent energy. Energy is dissipated in a unidirectional way, and it does not cycle. When it is gone, there is nothing left to support bacterial metabolism.

Not all pollutants are pollutants because of their energy content. Some are not dissipated like BOD, but rather remain within the ecosystem. The best examples are the nutrients, but they also include radioactivity, suspended solids, and other forms. They are often collectively termed *conservative* pollutants because they are not used up in the process of oxidative decomposition. All respond to the physical movements of water, and some are also affected by biological activity. None is inert, and none is simply carried downstream unaffected by the characteristics of the stream.

Radioactive substances remain radioactive regardless of their chemical behavior. Suspended solids, on the other hand, settle out in quiet parts of the river, but they can be re-suspended if the shear forces of the stream increase. Nutrients that are parts of insoluble molecules or particles behave in part like suspended solids, but they are active biologically and can be removed from and excreted readily into the water.

Let us follow the levels of some of the important components in wastewater following its discharge into a stream. The materials are partially dissolved and partially in particulate or colloidal form, reflecting the fact that most wastewater treatment plants

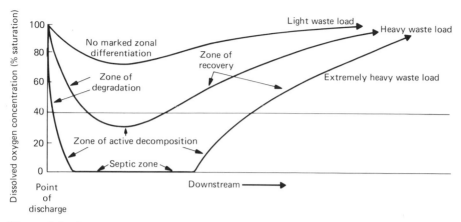

Figure 8.8 Oxygen sag curves and zonal classification for a typical river when different amounts of organic wastes are introduced.

do not retain water longer than a few hours before discharging it. The discharge almost invariably raises the dissolved nutrient concentration of the receiving stream, allowing an increase in productivity. But because of the BOD discharge and the consequent oxygen sag phenomenon, the organisms that prosper close to the outfall are bacteria, as well as low-oxygen-tolerant algae and animals (Figure 8.9). Carbonaceous materials decompose within the sag zone, and nutrients are stripped off organic molecules and released to solution. In general, the algae and zooplankton that would normally assimilate the nutrients are scarce, and the nutrient content rises as breakdown nears its peak. For nutrients such as phosphate the peak is a simple one. For nitrogen there is an ammonia peak that is reached first as amino nitrogen is hydrolyzed from organic material, then a nitrate peak as ammonia (NH_3) is oxidized to nitrate (NO_3^-).

Below the oxygen sag, production in the stream increases, reflecting increasing dissolved oxygen and high nutrient levels. Algae and other biota absorb nutrients from solution and reduce concentrations to the low levels that hold thereafter. Some nutrients are excreted and recycled quickly in soluble form, but much material is precipitated as insoluble particulates. The dissolved nutrient levels decline to steady state levels. The steady state is determined by the amount of nutrient entering the system from the atmosphere, from slow regeneration of particulate nutrients being carried along the current, and from dispersed sources surrounding the stream. These are balanced by formation of particulate nutrients from the death of living organisms, sedimentation in quiet water or during floods, and inorganic precipitation of insoluble materials. This balance is a dynamic one that may bring conditions quite similar to those before any human contact, or it may bring a somewhat higher level of production.

The biological patterns in a stream relative to large BOD outfalls are closely related to the oxygen and nutrient characteristics of the water. The organisms often provide much more insight into the health of the stream than the chemistry (Wielgolaski, 1975), as the changes in whole communities are generally more sensitive to the state of the ecosystem than the measurable concentrations of chemicals in the water at any one time. The nutrient-enriched, low-oxygen waters of a polluted river are not at all natural for most streams, and the flora and fauna reflect this. Many organisms are able

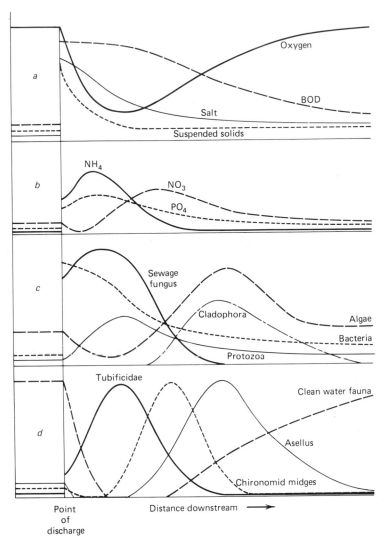

Figure 8.9 Diagram of the effects of an organic effluent in a river as one passes downstream: *a* and *b* show the physical and chemical changes; *c* shows the changes in the algae and microorganisms; *d* summarizes the changes in the larger animals. [Redrawn, with permission, from Hynes, *The Biology of Polluted Waters*. Copyright © 1960 Liverpool University Press.]

to feed directly on carbonaceous sewage. These include a complex assemblage of bacteria that reach their peak with the peak BOD concentration and fall off as the BOD declines. Some are generalized forms capable of feeding on any carbonaceous matter, while others are specialists on things like cellulose, starches, proteins and fats. Nitrogen bacteria, sulfur bacteria, and methane-producing bacteria can also be found in this bacterial assemblage.

As BOD breakdown continues downstream, and simpler organic molecules become more common, another group of organisms becomes relatively more important. This is the *sewage fungus* complex, which includes a number of colonial organisms that can be seen with the unaided eye. Relatively few organisms in the sewage fungus assemblage are true fungi. Most are colonial bacteria that congregate to form dense colonies. Still others are single-celled protozoa and multicellular animals such as rotifers. The sewage fungus assemblage is a very noticeable and unsightly aspect of polluted streams. It tends to form in dense dirty-white clumps that break off as they become large enough and float downstream. They can foul beaches, fishermen's nets, or anything else that comes in their way. The main organism in the complex is generally colonial bacterium *Sphaerotilus.* Whatever other organisms are involved in a particular sewage fungus complex, the *Sphaerotilus* mass makes up a considerable portion of the assemblage and gives it its slimy gelatinous feel. As it is washed downstream from the zone in which it is most active it begins to die, and it may cause local pockets of deoxygenated water.

Algae are quite sensitive to the state of water pollution, especially with regard to nutrients and oxygen. They may be able to live in oxygen-poor waters, as they do manufacture oxygen through photosynthesis during the day. But absolutely anoxic conditions cannot support algae, which need oxygen at night for their respiration. Where the level of pollution is low enough that some oxygen is always present, algae can be found throughout the sag zone. In this case they first decline through the sewage fungus zone and then expand rapidly. In general the clean-water algal flora is dominated by diatoms, with a few species of green algae. As pollution becomes more pronounced the diatoms decrease markedly in density. Bluegreen algae and the resistant species of green algae become much more common. Bluegreen algae sometimes even take part in the sewage fungus assemblage. Many secrete gelatinous sheaths that are slimy to the touch but may be ideal sites for mutualistic bacteria.

The most common alga found in the zone of improvement beyond the sewage fungus zone is the long green colonial alga, *Cladophora.* Its filaments are attached to rocks, submerged tree trunks, and anything else that can provide an attachment surface. It may cover an entire river bottom and resemble large green blankets. Its growth is enhanced by very high nutrient levels, as it occurs most abundantly in the zones in which nutrient regeneration is at its peak. *Cladophora* requires relatively high levels of oxygen, at least at night. It forms such dense masses that the respiration of a dense *Cladophora* mass can remove most of the oxygen from a river.

Like the sewage fungus, *Cladophora* is a nuisance growth. Under the best of circumstances it has an odd smell. It requires relatively high temperatures and is most abundant during the summer. When temperatures fall and the *Cladophora* die they are dislodged from their holdfasts and float downstream. They may pile up against bridge abutments, snag industrial water intakes, or accumulate in lakes or still portions of rivers, where their decay can deoxygenate the river. Decaying *Cladophora* has an odor somewhat akin to untreated sewage.

Beyond the *Cladophora* zone BOD breakdown is essentially complete, and nutrients fall to their normal levels. The biological community is much more diverse and competition for nutrients is much keener. The number and diversity of macroinvertebrates is considerably higher, and these tend to be herbivorous species capable of keeping the growth of algae under control.

One of the most striking things about the oxygen sag zone of a river is the progression of changes in its invertebrates. The normal invertebrate assemblage for a typical river consists of macroinvertebrates including mayflies, stoneflies, damselflies, dragonflies, and true flies. A half hour's search in a clean stream may result in the recovery of several dozen species of insects, along with snails, clams, and several species of protozoa, rotifers, and other lower animals. As the dissolved oxygen content drops following sewage discharge, there is an almost complete demise of the macroinvertebrate fauna. Two kinds of animals are relatively common in the sewage fungus zone. The first is protozoa. Some are detritivores that can feed directly on decaying material. These are often part of the sewage fungus complex. Others are carnivores or herbivores and feed on the sewage fungus and on other protozoa. These single-celled organisms fill most of the ecological niches that had been filled in clean water by macroinvertebrates.

A few macroinvertebrates, however, become quite common in the sewage fungus zone. These are tubificid worms, more commonly known as tubeworms or sludgeworms. Their blood contains hemoglobin for the most efficient collection of oxygen. Thus they can exist at very low oxygen concentrations. They are detritivores and live in tubes in the bottom mud. Under normal conditions they extend from the top of their tube and wave their bodies back and forth to gain what little oxygen they can from the water. In a grossly polluted stream there may be so many sludgeworms that they resemble nothing more than a dusky red carpet that disappears as if by magic when it is touched, as the tubeworms withdraw into their tubes. Occurring with the tubeworms are the bloodworms, or midge larvae. These also contain hemoglobin in their blood and can withstand almost as low a degree of oxygen concentration as sludgeworms. As the dissolved oxygen content rises, a third group of macroinvertebrates, the sow bug or water louse (*Asellus*), becomes quite common. Its presence in large numbers can be taken as an indication of the early stages of recovery for the stream.

The clean-water fauna makes its reappearance as the dissolved oxygen content approaches normal. First are the organisms that are tolerant of some temporary pollution, such as short periods of relatively low oxygen concentration when *Cladophora* or other algae are washed in from upstream, higher than normal nutrient levels, or a higher density than normal of certain kinds of organisms. As chemical conditions return to normal, even the very sewage-intolerant species return.

Higher plants follow a pattern very similar to that of the macroinvertebrates, but for a rather different reason. Immediately downstream from the outfall, most rooted plants are eliminated because of silt deposition, sewage fungus, or the increased turbidity of the water. The grossly polluted parts of a stream tend to be too turbid to allow any photosynthesis either by algae or by rooted plants. By the *Cladophora* zone the main factor holding down the number of higher plants is the presence of *Cladophora* itself. Some plants such as *Potamogeton natans* can survive in slowly flowing water with their leaves floating on the surface. Other species such as the moss *Fontinalis antipyretica* can live in very rapidly flowing water where the current keeps the rocks free of drifting sewage fungus. The full river-weed community does not re-establish itself until below the *Cladophora* zone.

Fishes are almost always affected by organic pollution. As a general rule they are not found at all in the sewage fungus zone, and only sparingly so in the *Cladophora* zone. The reasons for this appear to be multiple and unclear. There is some evidence that they may be limited by high levels of carbon dioxide (Allan, 1955; Allan et al., 1958). CO_2 is produced in large quantities as a by-product of BOD breakdown, and concentrations up to 50 mg./l. can be found in polluted water. The physical mechanisms by which fish take oxygen into their gills is such that this level of dissolved CO_2 can double the minimum oxygen concentration required by fish species. At the same time high levels of CO_2 can make ammonia less toxic to fishes. The very complex "chemical soup" downstream from a wastewater treatment plant outfall doubtless causes other changes in nutrient requirements, chemical toxicities, and so forth.

In addition, desirable fish tend to be relatively high on the food chain and they require certain food species in order to live. Even when the invertebrate density is quite high, as in the *Cladophora* zone, the invertebrates are the sewage-tolerant forms that are not suitable food for clean-water fish. Even if clean-water fish were not repelled or killed by low oxygen or high carbon dioxide, and even if they had adequate food, several factors would make successful reproduction unlikely. The eggs of many of these fishes can be asphyxiated if they are covered by silt and suspended solids. Sewage fungus, algae, deposition of organic materials of any sort, or short periods of anoxia may also asphyxiate the fish eggs. There is a series of less active fishes which inhabit the low-oxygen zones characterized by *Cladophora* and its ecological relatives. These include the carp, goldfish, and other cyprinids.

Dissolved Oxygen Depletion in Lakes. The patterns of oxygen depletion in lakes are different from those in streams, because lakes do not flow. Patterns in a river can be visualized in terms of space, with "downstream" being equivalent for most practical purposes to "later." In a lake the patterns of oxygen depletion develop *in situ,* so that we must see them in three dimensions rather than one. Furthermore, none of the dimensions in a lake corresponds in any way to time. In some ways, however, lakes are simpler than streams, because we generally do not have to worry about the tremendous diversity of physical environments over which a river flows.

The key to the patterns of oxygen depletion in lakes is their stratification. Lakes tend to stratify into three zones (Figure 8.10). Water in the *epilimnion,* or upper lake zone, is circulated by the wind, and heat is continually added to or taken from this zone by contact with the atmosphere. It is as deep as storms and inlet streams can mix the water, commonly 10 to 15 m., depending on the lake's size and shape. Below the epilimnion water circulation is not driven by storm winds, and little heat or water is exchanged between the upper and deep layers. During the summer the epilimnion may be considerably warmer than the *hypolimnion,* or deep lake zone. The stratification is maintained by the density differences of the epilimnion and hypolimnion. Between them typically exists the thermocline, or zone of temperature change. This *thermocline* (or *metalimnion* as it is often called) represents a physical barrier through which circulation does not take place.

Stratification typically develops during the summer and winter, and it typically

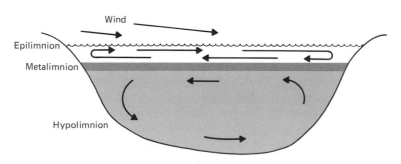

Figure 8.10 The patterns of wind-induced circulation in the hypolimnion and epilimnion of a thermally stratified lake. Circulation in the hypolimnion is much less pronounced than that in the epilimnion. [From Clapham, 1973.]

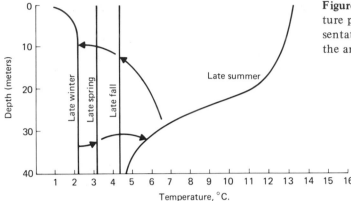

Figure 8.11 Progression of temperature profiles through a year in a representative shallow lake. Arrows indicate the annual cycle.

breaks down during the spring and fall (Figure 8.11). When the epilimnion warms or cools to the temperature of the hypolimnion, the thermocline separating them disappears, allowing vertical circulation to occur. Oxygen is incorporated into lake water from top to bottom during overturn. As summer approaches, heat is absorbed by surface water and distributed throughout all of the waters that can be mixed by the wind. The surface waters warm and become lighter than the bottom waters, until the surface water mass floats on the bottom water mass. Convection between top and bottom ceases, and the top continues to warm as it absorbs heat from the sun. As the seasons continue the epilimnion loses heat just as it absorbed it, until the epilimnion and hypolimnion are once again the same temperature and density. Following the fall overturn, the weather cools still more, and the lake loses heat to the atmosphere. Because water is most dense at 3.94°C, the surface waters become less dense as they cool below this level. Ultimately the cold light water may once again form a separate water mass floating on the more dense but now warmer hypolimnion, and the lake restratifies. With spring, the epilimnion absorbs heat from the sun and the stratification disappears.

Materials can move between the epilimnion and the hypolimnion in a stratified lake by one of three means. Gravity allows any material heavier than water to sink from the epilimnion to the bottom or anything lighter to rise from the hypolimnion to the top. Particulate matter and gases move by gravity, but the dissolved materials that control organic growth, such as oxygen and nutrients, do not. Diffusion allows molecules to move at random from one part of the ecosystem to another. It is very slow, however, and it can be neglected for most practical purposes. Finally, there is biological action, in which an organism actively moves, (e.g., swims) from one part of the environment into another.

As oxygen crosses the air-water interface it becomes dissolved in epilimnion waters and may even become saturated there. But diffusion is the only mechanism for oxygen to get down to the hypolimnion once stratification has set in. Because light reaches only into the epilimnion or the metalimnion, no oxygen is generated in the dark hypolimnion by photosynthesis. The only oxygen that enters the hypolimnion does so during the periods of overturn when the entire lake is at uniform temperature. All heterotrophic life in the hypolimnion during stratified intervals depends on this oxygen charge. The oxygen remaining in the hypolimnion at the end of a period of stratification is directly related to the amount of respiration that had gone on while the lake was stratified.

All fixed carbon in the hypolimnion enters either by gravity or by active motion, as organisms living in the epilimnion die or swim into it or as carbonaceous materials wash in from outside the lake. This fixed carbon is the energy source for hypolimnion heterotrophs. The greater the amount of fixed carbon entering the hypolimnion, the greater the respiration there and the greater the depletion of dissolved oxygen.

In most cases the overwhelming majority of the fixed carbon entering the hypolimnion is produced in the epilimnion. Thus the more productive the lake, the greater the leakage of carbonaceous materials into the hypolimnion and the greater the oxygen uptake in the bottom waters. This can be shown by comparing the oxygen profiles in lakes of different sorts (Figure 8.12). There is a typical progression of dissolved oxygen distribution curves from a lake that is almost biologically sterile to one that is exceedingly productive.

BOD, nutrients, and inorganic reducing agents affect lakes much as they do streams. Nutrients function as fertilizers, and BOD and inorganic reducing agents lead to dissolved oxygen depletion in all aquatic ecosystems, whether they be streams, lakes, or oceans. As in streams, the oxygen depletion from BOD and inorganic reducing agents is a moderate problem if it takes place in the epilimnion, as the oxygen can be made up slowly through physical uptake across the air-water interface or photosynthesis *in situ*. Oxygen-demanding materials that sink into the hypolimnion lead to substantial dissolved oxygen depletion there. And oxygen lost from the hypolimnion cannot be replaced until the next overturn. So an influx of BOD into the hypolimnion of a lake can do relatively much more damage than the same level of BOD introduced into a stream, because lakes have no self-cleaning capacity.

The organic material causing hypolimnion oxygen depletion commonly originates within the lake. Algae and their associated zooplankton in the epilimnion die and settle into the hypolimnion, where they exert oxygen demand. Nutrients in the epilimnion support algal growth and produce far more problems, gram for gram, than an equivalent amount of carbonaceous materials. More oxygen demand in the form of algae can be produced by 10kg. of phosphorus than by a ton of dry garbage.

The introduction of nutrients into a lake can initiate a cycle of oxygen depletion that continues until they have been removed from active circulation. They can be removed in several ways, but none of them is simple. For example, amino nitrogen and ammonia nitrogen can be oxidized by specialized bacteria to gaseous molecular nitrogen. But other specialized bacteria can take molecular nitrogen and fix it into amino nitrogen. Depending on conditions in the lake, the net flux of fixed nitrogen may be into or out of it.

A nutrient such as phosphorus has no volatile form that can be removed from a lake altogether. The only way it can be taken out of circulation is by accumulation in the bottom sediments. Most phosphorus compounds and complexes tend to be fairly insoluble, so this route is quite available. Even after phosphate has been incorporated into the sediments, it may still be released back into the water if the chemistry of the sediments and their interstitial waters change.

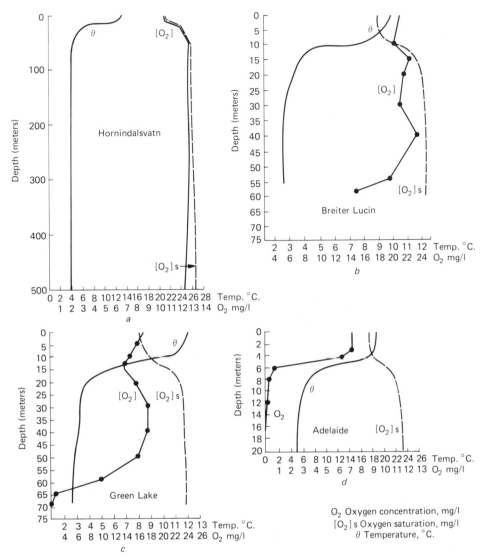

Figure 8.12 Temperature and oxygen distribution curves in several lakes: (*a*) Lake Hornindalsvatn, Norway, a biologically sterile mountain lake; (*b*) Lake Breiter Lucin, North Germany, an oligotrophic lake; (*c*) Green Lake, Wisconsin, a eutrophic lake; (*d*) Adelaide Lake, Wisconsin, a eutrophic lake with an extremely high degree of oxygen uptake. [Redrawn, with permission, from G. E. Hutchinson, *Treatise on Limnology, I: Geography, Physics and Chemistry.* Copyright © 1957. John Wiley & Sons.]

Eutrophication: Natural and Cultural

The most significant consequence of human waste disposal in waterways is the accelerated *eutrophication* of lakes. Eutrophication is a natural phenomenon whereby the productivity of a lake increases from some initial unproductive, or *oligotrophic*, stage, through a moderately productive, or *mesotrophic*, stage, to a very fertile, or *eutrophic* stage. A typical lake can be expected to age at some natural rate. The discharge of large amounts of nutrients into surface waters accelerates the eutrophication rate many times over its natural rate.

Natural Eutrophication.   The lake cycle is a well-known natural progression seen in all small lakes. Lakes are born when some quirk of history determines that a part of a river's drainage will be wider and deeper than the rest. As sediments build up in the lake, the bottom rises until the lake disappears altogether, leaving an organic soil within the river's flood plain as its only record. When a lake is geologically young, it typically has a very low concentration of dissolved nutrients. Because of this, gross production is limited and it is a typical oligotrophic lake. The animals that inhabit its lower reaches include active fishes such as lake trout, whitefish, herring, and cisco. The bottom community comprises organisms with little tolerance of low-oxygen conditions, such as burrowing mayflies, bloodless midge larvae, and mollusks. The phytoplankton are diverse, consisting mainly of diatoms and other golden-brown algae. As time progresses, nutrient materials accumulate in the lake. Most nutrients are carried by rivers either in solution or in the bed load, but some are also washed out of the atmosphere by rain (Chapin and Uttormark, 1973). For some shallow lakes the atmospheric nutrient contribution alone is sufficient to cause nutrient enrichment problems.

As the nutrient level of the lake rises, so does productivity. Eventually production reaches a maximum in the eutrophic state. The active fishes intolerant of low oxygen levels in the hypolimnion are gone, replaced by coarse fishes such as perch and carp. The only animals that can survive in the bottom sediments are those that can obtain oxygen from virtually deoxygenated water, such as tubeworms and bloodworms. Some species of bloodworm can respire normally if the oxygen concentration is as low as 1% of saturation (about 0.1 ppm). They can survive in lakes where relatives that can obtain adequate oxygen from water at 2% of saturation cannot. The phytoplankton contain a large complement of green and blue-green algae, and the lake is subject to periodic algal blooms. These blooms were characteristic of eutrophic lakes long before modern sewage-producing society came upon the scene. Lake Oneida in New York, for instance, was so prone to blooms of blue-green algae that the Indians of the area used to call it "Stinking Green" even in the eighteenth century.

The evolution of a lake from oligotrophic to eutrophic is much more complex than a simple increase in productivity. This process of eutrophication also involves drastic changes in the role of various environmental factors, and it commonly results in an ecosystem whose biota is very different from the original. Natural eutrophication has been observed many times for small lakes. Eutrophication has also been observed in large lakes, but the additional nutrients tend to be of human origin and eutrophication is cultural. In both small and large lakes, however, the basic process is similar.

The eutrophic, highly productive stage is not the end of the lake's ontogeny. It may be the longest lasting stage, but sooner or later the sediment carried into the lake builds up to a point where the lake again changes drastically. Typically, old lakes may do one of two things. They may simply fill up, or they may proceed to a *dystrophic* (from the Greek, "ill-fed") condition before filling in completely. The oxygen deficit for the dystrophic lake is very high, because detritus is so abundant as to deoxygenate the entire lake. Its anaerobic breakdown produces the highly acid "brown water" typical of bogs. Because of the very harsh conditions arising from the low oxygen concentration and low pH, the community—insofar as it exists at all—is very simple, consisting of many individuals of a few species. Production drops to a minimum.

Eventually the dystrophic lake fills with sediment or becomes covered over by a floating mat that is filled in from beneath. In either case the level of production again begins to rise, reaching a stable maximum as a terrestrial community. The changing productivity through the various stages of the ontogeny of a lake are sketched in Figure 8.13. There are variations on this basic theme, but all lakes eventually fill and become stable terrestrial communities. The time scale may be quite variable. A small lake may pass from oligotrophy through eutrophy, through dystrophy to climax forest in a few thousand years. Lake Baikal in the USSR is still oligotrophic after nearly 100 million years. There is no uniform rate of ontogeny; it depends on the total complex of factors affecting the lake and the lake communities.

The driving force of natural eutrophication is the progressive increase in total available nutrients, especially phosphorus, through time. The available phosphorus is very different from the accumulation of all of the phosphorus that has entered the lake, however. It depends on the interactions among organisms, air, water, bottom sediment, and the surrounding watershed (Figure 8.14). Some of these, such as the transfers across the air-water interface and the contribution from the watershed, do not change much in a natural ecosystem. Others, such as the dynamics of nutrient transfer across the sediment-water interface and the phosphorus balance within the community, show progressive change as the lake ages.

Productivity in the oligotrophic lake is limited by the low level of available nutrients. As the nutrient pool rises, so does production. But why should the available nutrient concentration in an oligotrophic lake rise? It is not altogether obvious that it should, since bottom sediments perform a scavenging function to remove phosphorus from biological availability. Several alternative hypotheses suggest why the nutrient content of a lake increases. For example, there may be a decrease in the sediments' scavenging ability. Phosphorus is more soluble and less easily adsorbed under the reduced-oxygen conditions that accompany eutrophication. In addition, the siltation and consequent increases in shallow water area may allow an expansion of rooted plants that are capable of pumping phosphorus out of the sediments, even when it is buried sufficiently deeply that it would otherwise be unavailable. Either mechanism would allow the flux of phosphorus through the biota to rise with the aging of a lake even if the only physical change were sedimentation to the lake bottom and even if

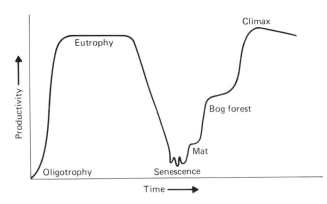

Figure 8.13 Generalized development of the productivity of a lake through the lake cycle, from oligotrophy to eutrophy to dystrophy, then eventually to a stable climax as a forest. [Redrawn, with permission, from Lindeman, 1942.]

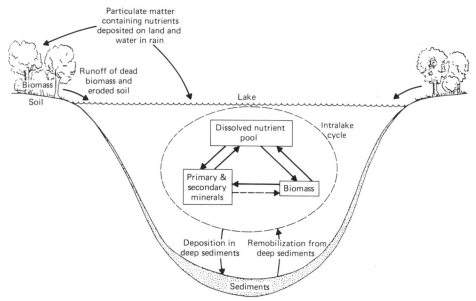

Figure 8.14 Processes determining flow of nutrients such as phosphorus into and within aquatic ecosystems.

there were no change in the net influx of phosohorus from the atmosphere or the watershed.

Other potential controlling mechanisms lie outside of the lake. The typical watershed may supply phosphorus to the lake faster than it can be removed in sediments and outflow. This kind of situation is not uncommon, and it places control of the rate of eutrophication for such a lake largely on characteristics of the watershed. In fact, paleolimnological studies have demonstrated that natural changes in nutrient delivery patterns in streams can lead to acceleration and reversals in eutrophication rate (Hutchinson, 1969).

The changes that accompany eutrophication are not completely reversible. Any changes in the input of a limiting nutrient affects production. They will also affect the composition of the biota and the scavenging behavior of the sediments. Returning a key variable such as nutrient influx from the watershed to its original level imposes a change on an altered ecosystem in response to the new conditions. There is no reason to assume that the lake would return to its original state, although it might. The behavior of nutrients, communities, and sediments in lakes are complex, and their status at any point in time is a function of their overall history.

Cultural Eutrophication. Eutrophication due to human influences is a very serious problem around the world (see the "geographic concepts" section in NAS, 1969). All sectors of the economy contribute to it in some degree. It, in turn, affects recreation, fisheries, water supply, and public health. Algal blooms reach nuisance proportions in lakes in which they were once unknown. Fish populations are excluded from lakes or even driven into extinction by the reduction of dissolved oxygen in the hypolimnion. Bacteria are most commonly present in eutrophic lakes, and some can cause public health problems.

The significance of cultural eutrophication led to an intensive search for its limiting nutrient. For some people this meant the nutrient that *causes* cultural eutrophication; for others it meant the nutrient whose control will stop or reverse it. This distinction is significant. The first definition is inappropriate to the real-world problem. Under the right experimental conditions in the laboratory, additions of phosphorus, nitrogen, carbon, chelating agents, iron, silica, trace elements, and vitamins can all lead to large expansions of algal populations. None of these experiments does much more than to suggest the factors controlling production in lakes. Nevertheless, for many years there was a consensus that phosphorus and nitrogen were the most important influences on production and that additions of these nutrients would be likely to result in eutrophication. Of the two, phosphorus was thought to be the most important in freshwaters (IJC, 1969), and nitrogen the most important in marine waters (Ryther and Dunston, 1971).

To say that something is important does not necessarily mean that it represents a lever by which the system can be manipulated or controlled. The ideal situation for any system with a severe problem is to find a single manipulable factor whose control can mitigate the problem. Phosphorus in freshwater ecosystems is such a factor. The Fresh Water Institute of the Fisheries Research Board of Canada has carried out a significant series of whole-fertilization experiments in the Experimental Lakes Area of Northwest Ontario. In one of the more significant of these, a small lake with two similar basins separated by a narrow neck was divided by means of a nylon-reinforced vinyl sea curtain (Schindler, 1974). Nitrate and sucrose were added to both basins in twenty equal weekly amounts. One basin also received phosphate along with the other inputs. The flora in the basin not receiving the phosphate was similar to that prior to fertilization, while the other basin underwent a tremendous bloom of the blue-green alga *Anabaena spiroides* (Figure 8.15).

This experiment, among others, indicated that adding phosphorus to a lake was indeed capable of bringing about cultural eutrophication. In this sense phosphorus was the limiting nutrient. But this is not the most important point. The more practical issue is whether a culturally eutrophic lake can recover when only phosphate is removed from the input. This was tested in a parallel experiment in Ontario. Phosphorus, nitrogen, and sucrose were added in quantities similar to those of the first lake in 1971 and 1972 (Table 8.1), and a pronounced algal bloom resulted each year (Figure 8.16). Addition of phosphorus was discontinued in 1973, but those of nitrogen and carbon were retained at their previous rates. Algal production dropped to its previous low level.

It would be difficult to imagine more conclusive evidence that control of any single nutrient could reduce eutrophication. But there is other evidence to support the notion that reducing the phosphorus entering a lake can arrest or reverse cultural eutrophication. In 1971 Syracuse, New York, and surrounding areas banned detergents with a phosphorus content greater than 8.7%. The result was a sharp reduction of the phosphate concentration in the water of Lake Onondaga and an absence of noxious blue-green algal blooms during the following year (Murphy, 1973). It is not as well controlled an experiment as Schindler's whole-lake experiments, but it represents a realistic experiment in a modern urban society.

More radical approaches have been aimed primarily at phosphorus reduction, but they have also resulted in reduction of other ions. Lake Washington, in the State of

Figure 8.15 Lake 226 in the Experimental Lakes Area of northwestern Ontario. The far basin has been fertilized with phosphorus, nitrogen, and carbon, while the near basin was fertilized only with nitrogen and carbon. The far basin was covered by an algal bloom within two months of the beginning of fertilization, while no increases in algal numbers or species were seen the near basin. [Photograph courtesy D. W. Schindler; Freshwater Institute, Environment Canada.]

Table 8.1 Rates of Fertilization for Whole Lake Experiments.

Lake	PO_4-P	NH_3-N	Sucrose–C
226 (SW basin)	–	3.16	6.05
226 (NE basin)	0.59	3.16	6.05
304 (1971, 1972)	0.40	5.2	5.5
304 (1973)	–	5.2	5.5

Data are in g/m.^{2} of lake surface per year. Applications were made weekly, spanning a period of 20 weeks.
Data from Schindler, 1974.

Washington (Edmondson, 1969, 1972), lies east of Seattle and served as a drinking water source for that city until 1965. Beginning in 1941 a series of sewage treatment plants was built around the shore, discharging into the lake and its tributaries. By 1960 the discharge capacity of these plants was 75,600 cu. m. per day and was equivalent to the total effluent from 120,000 people. Beginning in 1963 the discharge from these plants was diverted to Puget Sound; diversion was completed in 1968. The eutrophication of Lake Washington reached a maximum in 1964, with large blooms of the blue-green alga *Oscillatoria rubescens*. As sewage diversion continued production fell rapidly, so that its level in 1969 to 1970 was about the same as that of the mid 1950s (Figure 8.17).

One of the most interesting aspects of Lake Washington is that an oligotrophic lake had attained a very high level of eutrophication. For most of its studied history there was an excess of nitrogen over phosphorus during the height of summer algal production. But in its most eutrophic stage, in 1962 to 1964, the lake showed an excess of phosphorus over nitrogen. So much phosphate was in the lake that available nitrogen had replaced it as the production-limiting nutrient (Edmondson, 1970). The diversion of sewage was followed by a decline in dissolved phosphorus but not in dissolved nitrogen. The fact that production declined to its original low level indicates that as phosphorus was incorporated in the sediments it reassumed its role as the limiting nutrient. The Lake Washington story provides a very strong support for the idea that cultural eutrophication can be controlled if phosphate inputs are reduced. Even when it is not the most important limiting nutrient, it is still the key to eutrophication control.

Diversion of treated sewage is only one method of phosphorus reduction, and it is feasible only when there is a convenient alternate disposal place nearby. Other methods include source reduction and better sewage treatment. Source reduction is in some ways the simpler, especially with respect to detergents.

Detergents. A detergent comprises several components. The *surfactant,* a petroleum-based "synthetic soap," is responsible for the actual dirt removal. It comprises 15% to 20% of the total formulation. When detergents were first marketed they contained little else, and they were ineffective on cottons and in most wash waters. Sur-

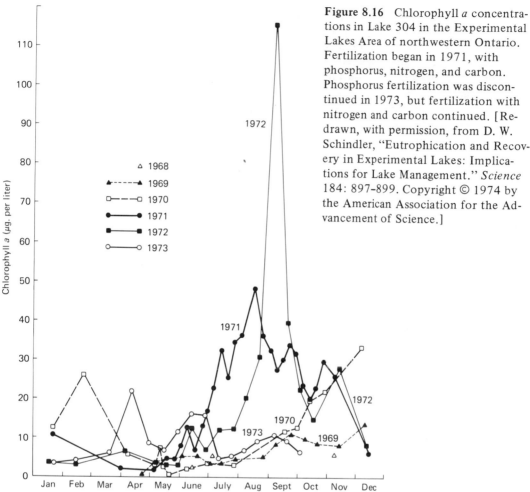

Figure 8.16 Chlorophyll *a* concentrations in Lake 304 in the Experimental Lakes Area of northwestern Ontario. Fertilization began in 1971, with phosphorus, nitrogen, and carbon. Phosphorus fertilization was discontinued in 1973, but fertilization with nitrogen and carbon continued. [Redrawn, with permission, from D. W. Schindler, "Eutrophication and Recovery in Experimental Lakes: Implications for Lake Management." *Science* 184: 897–899. Copyright © 1974 by the American Association for the Advancement of Science.]

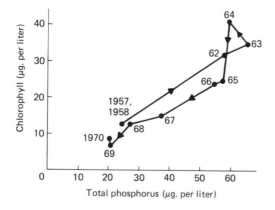

Figure 8.17 Progression of algal growth, measured as chlorophyll concentration, and total phosphorus in Lake Washington, Washington from 1957 through 1970. They are correlated very highly (the correlation coefficient is 0.933). Chlorophyll measurements were averages for July and August of each year; phosphorus measurements are means for the top 10 m. during January–March. [Redrawn, with permission, from Edmondson, 1972.]

factants work best under controlled conditions. These conditions are now provided by what are called *builders*. Surfactants and builders were not marketed together until 1947, with the production of "Tide." Since then the effective washing ability of detergents has practically driven soaps from the market in North America and Europe. The most common and effective builders are complex phosphates, although washing soda and metasilicates are also used and are somewhat cheaper. Before the early 1970s detergents typically included 35% to 55% sodium tripolyphosphate (STP). Since then typical detergent formulations have dropped to 35% STP (8.7% elemental phosphorus), replacing some of the STP with washing soda (Rukeyser, 1972). The remainder of the detergent consists of miscellaneous brighteners, enzymes, perfumes, inhibitors, and so on.

The builder is the largest single component of a typical detergent and also its most important in causing eutrophication. Why has STP proven so useful as a builder? The first function of a builder is to soften water and sequester otherwise objectional elements. Hardness due to calcium and magnesium salts can react with fats in dirt to form insoluble curds. STP ties up these ions, leaving the fats accessible to the surfactant, which can then emulsify them and wash them away. Ions such as iron, which would otherwise be deposited on clothes, can also be tied up by STP and remain in soluble form so that they can be washed away. STP can combine with dirt and grease, and its surficial charge keeps dirt suspended. It induces formation of surfactant micelles that allows the surfactant to perform its functions most effectively. Finally, STP provides and maintains the proper pH for the detergent to do its job best (Weaver, 1969).

STP is the only builder that performs all of these tasks well and is biodegradable under aerobic (as in municipal wastewater treatment plants) and anaerobic (as in septic tanks and in cesspools) conditions. It is also safe to use. The carbonate and metasilicate builders of some nonphosphate detergents work at significantly higher pH than the phosphates (10.5 to above 11, as opposed to 9 to 10), and some are dangerously caustic. Several children have been killed or severely burned when they ate nonphosphorus detergent by mistake. Polyelectrolyte builders have good washing characteristics, but they are not biodegradable. Sodium nitrilotriacetate (NTA) was once introduced into detergents in the United States and is still being used in Canada, Sweden, and other countries. It is not biodegradable under anaerobic conditions, although it breaks down quickly in aerobic treatment plants. With lack of oxygen it can chelate—and hence mobilize—dangerous heavy metals that occur commonly in many wastewaters. Some of its breakdown products can form nitrosamines, a class of organic compounds that includes many carcinogens and teratogens (Epstein, 1970). In fact, it may cause more of a eutrophication problem in coastal areas than phosphates, as nearshore marine areas represent an environment in which nitrogen is clearly limiting (Ryther and Dunstan, 1971).

The great advantage to limiting or lowering phosphorus in detergents is that it can cut the phosphorus load in raw sewage by an average of 25% to 50%, and up to 70% near metropolitan areas (Hammond, 1971), by a simple legislative action involving the emplacement of no additional sewage treatment facilities or other capital. As in the case of Onondaga Lake, this can be significant. But so many other sources of phosphorus cannot be banned so easily (e.g., human excreta and agricultural runoff), that controlling phosphorus in detergents provides only short-term relief at best. As population and urbanization continue to grow, and as domestic and agricultural wastes and urban runoff expand, the nondetergent phosphorus input will become sufficiently large to nullify the effect of detergent-phosphorus control after a few years. This does not say that the short-term relief is not useful or that it is not important to control phosphorus in detergents as part of an overall plan that includes increased control of other sources. But it is not a solution for eutrophication in itself.

OTHER WATER POLLUTANTS

The most important pollutants tend to be those involved in oxygen depletion, but many others may cause serious problems.

Poisons

A poison is a substance that causes either chronic or acute toxicity. Acute toxicity shows itself rapidly; the toxin causes disability, death, or some other noticeable effect relatively quickly after exposure. Chronic toxicity, on the other hand, may become apparent only very slowly, so that an organism may be exposed for long periods of time. Its effect is progressive debilitation rather than obvious damage. Both modes of action are serious, and neither one can be considered "better" than the other.

We often think of poisons as isolated phenomena. If a poison such as cyanide is discharged at high levels, it is easy to concentrate on its toxic effects without looking at potential interactions between the cyanide and other chemicals in the water. Some of these interactions may be quite significant and may alter the toxicity of the poison or the response patterns of the community to it. Toxicity may also depend on the physical characteristics of the water such as pH, temperature, and the ion exchange capacity of suspended sediments.

The most significant interactions affecting toxicity are the synergistic effects by which the toxicity of a mixture of chemicals is greater than the sum of the toxicities of individual poisons. Even past experience with synergists may be quite important. As an example, zinc is the most common heavy metal in most streams, and detergent surfactants are also common toxins. In an experiment by Brown et al. (1968), rainbow trout showed the same level of chronic responses to surfactants in water with and without zinc. However, the mixture of surfactant and zinc was more toxic to fish previously exposed to zinc than to those that had not been so exposed. Chronic exposures to zinc generally confer some degree of resistance to acute zinc poisoning, but surfactants nullify this resistance. The complexity of this pattern is typical of the synergistic interactions between chemicals in ecosystems.

We generally wish to know whether some chemical is poisonous and how poisonous it is. Public policy can then act appropriately to control the distribution and permissible levels of poisons in the environment. Determining toxicity levels is done through two basic types of experimental procedures. The first is the assessment of median tolerance level (TL_m). This is the amount of material that is lethal to 50% of the test population. Several replicates of fish, oysters, or other suitable test populations are grown in a standard medium in which different concentrations of the poison are maintained.

The mortality within a predetermined time interval is graphed against concentration of toxin, and the median tolerance is observed (Figure 8.18).

The experimental medium is a standard, rather than the river water in which the population actually lives. Thus it is not possible to assess potential synergistic activity between the toxin and other substances normally present in rivers. Of course, a standard medium allows the test to be readily repeatable, and it can generate a high degree of scientific credibility. But the differences between the standard and the actual conditions encountered in real streams are sometimes significant.

The other basic tool is the *bioassay*. It is run very much like the test of TL_m, except that samples of actual river water are used instead of a standard medium. This makes it possible to include synergisms with other chemicals in the river water. But the composition of river water is not constant from place to place or from day to day, so that the test medium is never standardized; hence repeatability is not always possible. It is more specific for conditions in a given river, but only in the sense that it reflects the conditions at the time of testing.

No test of toxicity can consider all of the physical and chemical factors that are found in all rivers. It would require entirely too many replicates to consider all of the permutations that would be needed. Like the BOD test, assessments of TL_m and the bioassay are useful indications of the actual behavior of organisms in real watercourses toward particular chemicals, but they cannot be regarded as precise.

Some toxins show thresholds below which they seem not to represent problems. It is appropriate to set standards for discharges of such materials with the threshold level in mind. Most micronutrients (e.g., copper) and even some macronutrients (e.g., ammonia) are quite toxic at high concentrations. But discharges of these would have little or no toxic effect if their concentrations could be maintained at a lower level. Determination of threshold toxicity levels is fraught with all of the problems of assessing toxicity in general. The only difference is that instead of trying to find the point that affects 50% of the population, the test attempts to find the level that affects none. Theoretically as well as practically, this is more difficult than trying to find TL_m. The chronic effects of toxins are also more important at low concentrations.

Death is not always the only effect of toxins in aquatic environments, and it may not even be the most important. Algal primary production can be reduced, (e.g.,

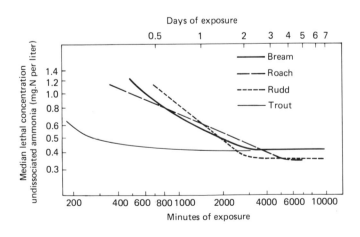

Figure 8.18 Comparison of susceptibilities of four species of freshwater fish to undissociated ammonia. [From I. R. Ball. The relative susceptibility of some fresh-water fish to poisons. *Water Research* 1:767–775, 1967. Reproduced with permission of Her Majesty's Stationery Office, London.]

Brook and Baker, 1972; Hamilton et al., 1970). Animal reproduction can be depressed or even destroyed. Behavioral changes may be noted. Growth rates can be depressed and tissues can be systematically damaged by exposure to toxins (Mitrovic et al., 1968). Swimming performances, respiratory movements, and disease resistance can all be reduced by exposure to toxins. For reviews of the effects of toxins on indicator organisms, see Doudoroff and Katz (1950, 1953) and Sprague (1969, 1970, 1971).

Pollutant concentrations may be much higher than average for rivers in certain places, such as near the outfalls of industries or wastewater treatment plants. Substances whose effects would be negligible if they were evenly distributed become locally toxic. If organisms are aware of toxins and can recognize a concentration gradient, it is not unreasonable to expect them to respond to it by moving down the gradient and away from the source. Fishes are broadly able to recognize specific chemicans at very low concentrations (Hasler et al., 1978), and their most common response is a protective avoidance reaction. This can overcome even strongly ingrained instincts such as the homing behavior of the Atlantic salmon returning to spawn. The presence of a heavy metal gradient in spawning streams can be sufficient to turn them around and drive them downstream (Sanders and Sprague, 1967). Acids and many salts have the same effect.

Some fish may be attracted by dilute solutions of poisons that would repel them in higher concentrations. Sticklebacks, for example, are repelled by high concentrations of phenol, but they are attracted by dilute solutions and may become incapacitated before they can flee. Likewise, they are repelled by strong ammonia solutions but attracted by weak ones. Dilute solutions of lead nitrate, a heavy metal poison, are repellent, but strong solutions are attractive. Interactions between pollutants influence behavioral responses to those pollutants as much as they do acute toxicity. For example, copper sulfate is normally avoided by ten-spined sticklebacks only when concentrations are relatively high. Low concentrations that normally would not be avoided destroy the fishes' sensitivity to alcohol, chloroform, formaldehyde, and mercuric chloride, all of which are highly toxic and are normally avoided.

Oxygen concentration and pH both affect toxicity. As a general rule, the toxicity of most poisons increases as dissolved oxygen concentration decreases. This may be related to most organisms' doing better in high-oxygen than low-oxygen conditions, and toxicity response is simply carried along in the process. It may also be due to a synergistic interaction between oxygen and the chemical toxin. The effect of pH is often significant, especially for ionizing chemicals. For example, ammonia is more toxic in alkaline than in acid water, because the un-ionized form (NH_3) is more toxic than the ionized form (NH_4^+). For a similar reason, cyanide is more poisonous in acid than in alkaline waters, and sulfides become much more toxic in acid waters, where they often form the highly poisonous gas, hydrogen sulfide (H_2S).

The mechanism for toxicity is quite different for different species, and a control technique that is effective for one may be totally ineffective for another. As an example, the effluent from bleached kraft paper mills is highly toxic to Atlantic salmon and lobsters. Oxidation of these wastes in a treatment plant quickly neutralizes the effect on the salmon but not on the lobster (Sprague and McLeese, 1968).

Some toxins are discharged as such in wastewater streams; others may be formed in a watercourse or as part of the waste treatment process. For example, biphenyl organic compounds are common components of certain industrial process wastes. If any of these compounds remain in the final effluent when that effluent is chlorinated to remove pathogenic bacteria, they may react with the chlorine to form polychlorinated biphenyls (PCBs), a toxic group of compounds with characteristics very much like those of DDT (Gaffney, 1977).

Many toxins exist in all aquatic ecosystems. Some are chemical forms found in nature, others are entirely man-made. The full range of toxicity responses is extraordinarily broad and difficult to generalize about. Controlling the discharge of poisons into waterways is serious, and it is often easier to design a treatment process for treating wastes than it is to design a policy, a set of standards, or a rationale for the treatment process to meet.

Suspended Solids

Suspended solids comprise the solid materials carried by water. All water contains some suspended solids. Moving water can dislodge and move solid particles from the bottom of a stream or river. Wave action along the shore of a lake is sufficient to dislodge particles, and currents can distribute them. The particles can be mineral grains, or they can be whole or partially decomposed fragments of plants and animals.

The most obvious effects of suspended solids are physical. Light entering the water is absorbed or scattered by sediment particles and thus is not available to algae below the uppermost levels of the ecosystem. In very polluted streams that are full of suspended organic solids, light may not penetrate more than a few centimeters. The solids may also clog the gills of fish or invertebrates, making it impossible for them to survive even when there is adequate oxygen and levels of toxicity are sufficiently low. Even if the suspended solids do not kill the animals themselves, they may kill their eggs by settling on spawning beds and shutting off the oxygen supply. This is notably true for species such as the salmonid fishes (salmons, trouts, and their relatives) that lay their eggs in gravel. The eggs depend on oxygen carried in water washing through the gravel. Silt from any origin settling even temporarily on top of the gravel can disrupt the flow of water.

Suspended solids are sometimes deposited rapidly on the bottom of parts of lakes or streams. The rate of deposition during such periods may be faster than the rate at which bottom-dwelling animals can burrow upward through the new silt. Those that cannot reach the surface will perish. Suspended solids also increase the viscosity and abrasiveness of moving water, so that rooted plants are more likely to be uprooted and swept away. It is very difficult for most fishes to feed under conditions of high suspended solids because they hunt by sight, and they cannot see through a dense fog of suspended matter.

A large proportion of suspended solids may consist of particulate organic material that can exert BOD or can break down to supply nutrients to solution. One of the common trends in cultural eutrophication is an increase in particulate BOD. This is suspended oxygen-demanding material with all of the chemical properties of BOD and nutrients, as well as the physical properties of suspended solids.

The particles comprising the suspended solid load of a lake or stream tend to be small. They are rich in clay minerals and organic materials, which can serve as adsorption surfaces for all sorts of materials. Many pesticides, for example, are easily adsorbed onto the surfaces of suspended solids carried by streams. One of the main sources of suspended solids is agricultural soil treated with pesticides and fertilizers. Because most pesticides are not highly soluble in water, adsorption onto soil particles is their major means of transport into streams; the same is true for phosphates and other nutrients in fertilizers.

Oils

Oils are among the most troublesome of water pollutants, and they are among the most common, especially in the ocean. They include a variety of hydrocarbons varying widely in density from some very light oils that float on the surface to heavy oils that sink immediately. Oils combine the effects of suspended solids and poisons, with a few special features of their own thrown in for good measure. The most familiar are the light varieties such as gasoline and lubricating oil, which float on the surface. They coat the surface of the water so that oxygen cannot pass readily across the air-water interface, and they can plug the breathing apparatus of surface-dwelling insects. The heavy oils that sink in water include bunker oils, residual fuel oils used in power plants, asphalt, and long-chain fluid hydrocarbons.

Oils show differing degrees of toxicity. In general the lighter oils are more toxic than the heavier oils, and the aromatic hydrocarbons are more toxic than the alkanes (see Figure 8.19 for a description of the basic hydrocarbon classes). However, the light oils are also more volatile than the heavier ones, so that they are lost from the water more quickly. The heavy oils are more effective at sealing sediments and suffocating organisms.

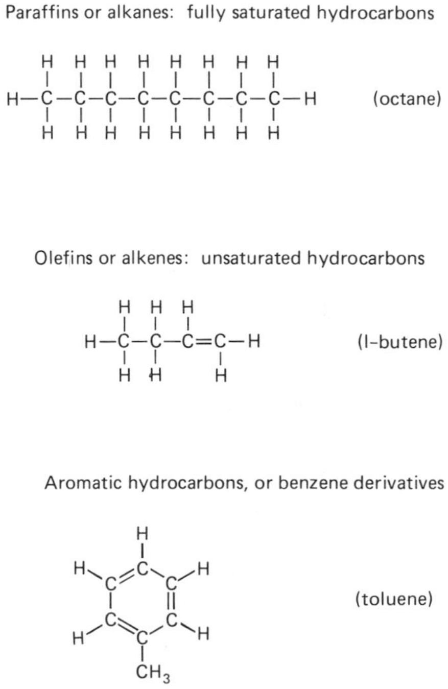

Paraffins or alkanes: fully saturated hydrocarbons

(octane)

Figure 8.19   Examples of some of the most important classes of hydrocarbons.

Olefins or alkenes: unsaturated hydrocarbons

(I–butene)

Aromatic hydrocarbons, or benzene derivatives

(toluene)

Because oils are such a diverse group, it is only natural that the fate of different components in the water should be quite different. Some components dissolve, including the acids and inorganic salts found in crude oil but normally removed in refining. Others form oil-in-water emulsions stabilized by various chemical compounds. More prominent, especially in marine oil spills, is the water-in-oil emulsion, sometimes known as chocolate mousse because of its resemblance to the fancy dessert. Its consistency ranges from thick cream to tar, and it may form broad layers, globs, or balls. Oil may also spread out on the surface of water in a layer a few microns thick.

The following things can happen to oil discharged into the water (after Pilpel, 1968):

1. Volatilization of light fractions.
2. Washing onto shore, generally followed by oxidation.
3. Remaining in sea as one of the following:
    a. Solution in water by soluble components.
        i. Dispersion and metabolism.
    b. Spreading out in thin layer over the surface.
        i. Dispersion over the surface.
        ii. Oxidation.
    c. Oil-in-water emulsion.
        i. Autooxidation.
        ii. Microbial oxidation.
        iii. Dispersion through water column.
    d. Water-in-oil emulsion.
        i. Autooxidation.
        ii. Microbial oxidation.
        iii. Sinking to bottom, ultimately as coquina, often with several cycles of floating and sinking.

The oil-in-water emulsion is miscible with water, and it is one way for oil to disperse. Bacteria in the water can attack and metabolize these emulsions relatively easily, but higher organisms can ingest them as well. Their toxic effects can be significant if the concentration is high enough.

Detergents are sometimes used to form oil-in-water emulsions from severe oil spills. This was the case, for example, with the tanker spills from the *Torrey Canyon* in 1967 and the *Amoco Cadiz* in 1978. Unfortunately, the detergents used for this type of operation may be much more toxic than the oil (McKeown and March, 1978), and the net result of detergent used for oil dispersion may do more harm than good to the biota, although beaches near an oil spill that has been treated with detergents are generally cleaner and more inviting than those that have not. A detergent-emulsified spill such as that of the *Torrey Canyon* or the *Amoco Cadiz* can spread toxic levels of oil and detergents over a much wider area than would have been subjected to the oil if detergents were not used.

Water-in-oil emulsions are a different matter. They contain about 30% water, but they are not miscible with it. They are the source of the tarballs that are becoming ubiquitous both in the world's oceans and in inland shipping or industrial waterways

(Blumer et al., 1970a). They remain on the surface until they wash out onto a beach, sink as they absorb particles of sand, silt, and organic skeletons, or are oxidized by bacteria or spontaneous inorganic reactions. Oxidation proceeds first in the lighter fractions, causing the tarballs to get heavier and ultimately to sink.

Oil may be mixed throughout a sizable portion of the water column. In a spill in Deception Bay, Hudson Strait, in the Canadian North, 10% of the oil was mixed to a depth of 20 meters in the water column (Ramseier et al., 1973), and oil droplets were found in suspension up to 80 meters below the surface in Chedabucto Bay, Nova Scotia, after the grounding of the tanker *Arrow* (Forrester, 1971).

Oil in the sea can be destroyed slowly by auto-oxidation and biochemical oxidation. The photolytic reactions require metallic catalysts, but these are readily available in the sea as dissolved salts. Most oil degradation is through microbial breakdown. This may proceed rapidly in well-oxygenated tropical waters, where the rate of oxidation may be several hundred grams per cubic meter per year. It hardly proceeds at all at temperatures below 5°C. The forms that are most prone to break down are highly dispersed oil-in-water emulsions and thin surface films. Under ideal conditions, fairly thin films of oil can be colonized by bacteria within 1-2 weeks and decomposed within 2-3 months (Pilpel, 1968). Hydrocarbons are converted into intermediate organic compounds, including aldehydes, alcohols, ketones, and acids. These tend to be more readily metabolized than the original hydrocarbons, and they break down quickly. The remainder sinks to the bottom as a mixture of polymer and smaller organic molecules. In many cases the portion that sinks can undergo further aerobic and anaerobic breakdown. Breakdown products include nitrogen, carbon dioxide, methane, and other gaseous materials. These often bring the decomposing oil back to the surface, where it undergoes another cycle of aerobic oxidation. A given oil glob may undergo several cycles of aerobic and anaerobic decomposition before it reaches equilibrium.

To say that oils can decompose in aquatic ecosystems does not mean that breakdown is quick or complete. The most favorable conditions for petroleum decomposition are in the open ocean, whereas the biggest problems are in enclosed marine bays, estuaries, rivers, and ship channels. It is very difficult to study the degradation of oil spills in these areas. In the heavily traveled ship channels, so much oil enters from so many different sources that it is virtually impossible to follow any one spill. Regions sufficiently isolated for a single spill to be followed, tend to be too distant from research centers to allow long-term study.

A fortuitous exception is a spill in West Falmouth, Massachusetts, a few miles from Woods Hole Oceanographic Institute. On September 16, 1969, the oil barge *Florida* grounded and discharged 650 to 700 cu. m. of No. 2 fuel oil. The effects of this spill have not been confounded with those of other spills, and a team of researchers from Woods Hole has been studying them for several years. The immediate results were catastrophic to the local fauna. Nearshore-dwelling fishes, worms, crustaceans, and mollusks covered the tidal pools, beaches, and banks of a nearby river (Figure 8.20). Even bottom-dwelling fishes and lobsters normally found below the tidal limit several hundred meters offshore were killed by the spill. A prodigious loss of marine life was visible on shore, and a trawl of the bottom some 300 m. offshore recorded almost complete mortality of the bottom fauna. Within a week after the spill, however, the evidence of mortality had decayed and washed to sea. Had the research center not been

Figure 8.20 Photograph of Fasset's Point Beach following the grounding of the barge, *Florida*. The beach is covered with oil globules, and massive mortality of all kinds of organisms is evident. [Photograph courtesy George M. Hampson, Woods Hole Oceanographic Institution.]

so close, the extent of the damage would never have been realized (Hampson and Sanders, 1969).

The oil carried by the *Florida* had a fairly high content of volatiles (Blumer et al., 1970a), but evaporation was slow. Wave action mixed the oil with sediments to at least 10 m. of water depth, and oil was released more slowly from the sediments than it would have been from open water. The concentration and spectrum of petroleum compounds in the sediments was essentially constant for at least 4 months after the spill (Blumer et al., 1970b), and the oil in the sediments below 2.5 m. was little changed two years later (Blumer and Sass, 1972). Even seven years after the spill (Krebs and Burns, 1977), the concentration of oil had not yet dropped very much and organisms were still inhibited from colonizing the worst affected places (Figure 8.21).

Hydrocarbons assimilated by oysters, scallops, and clams in the nearshore environment had a very different history from those attacked by bacteria. They were taken into the lipid (fat) pool and retained rather than being broken down. Even removal to

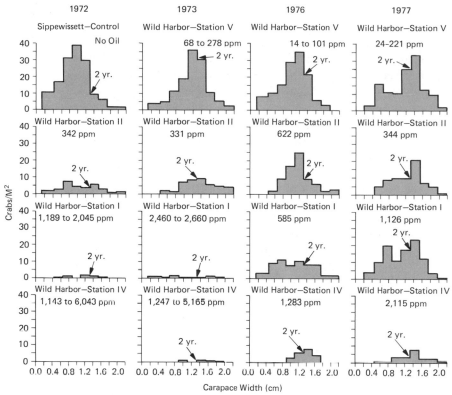

Figure 8.21 Size distribution of fiddler crabs, *Uca pugnax*, in salt marsh plots after the 1969 oil spill at West Falmouth, Mass. The concentration of petroleum hydrocarbons in surface sediments is also shown. [Figure courtesy C. T. Krebs. St. Marys College, St. Marys City, Md.]

clean water did not remove the oils from the shellfish muscles. The edible shellfish beds of western Cape Cod were more toxic in 1970 than they were shortly after the spill in 1969, as bacterial oxidation attacked the least toxic hydrocarbons preferentially, leaving the highly toxic aromatics to be absorbed by the shellfish.

Oils are solvents that have different properties from those of water. They can dissolve many substances that are insoluble in water. One of the most important examples is the chlorinated hydrocarbon insecticides. The common vehicle for these insecticides is kerosene. Various observers have noted that several chlorinated hydrocarbons could, if their concentration in the ocean were higher, cause some reduction in algal photosynthesis or a change in relative constitution of algal communities (Wurster, 1968; Menzel et al., 1970; Fisher, 1975). As oil pollution from international tanker transport becomes increasingly common, it may become substantially easier for the chlorinated hydrocarbons to become concentrated enough in the oceans to do some damage. It has also been suggested that oil pollution in certain vulnerable regions such as the Arctic may even lead to major changes in the earth's global climate (Campbell and Martin, 1973).

Pathogens

Water is a carrier for several different kinds of human diseases, and has been implicated in major and minor epidemics as well as smaller-scale problems. Typhoid and cholera are bacterial diseases, infectious hepatitis is a viral disease, and dysentery a protozoal disease. All are carried by water and all show the basic cycle shown in Figure 8.22. The disease organism is taken into the body in drinking water, where it undergoes a marked population increase and causes illness. It is passed back into the watercourse by feces or urine, when the cycle begins again. Urine and fecal material constitute a more significant public health problem than eutrophication. Their effects on human well-being are direct and very fast.

Humans are not the only hosts for organisms that can cause health problems. All warm-blooded and many cold-blooded animals can dishcarge the colon bacteria *Escherichia coli* with their feces (Geldreich, 1970). Specific races of *E. coli* are normally found in the colon and are tolerated without problem. But there are many different races, characterizing different parts of the world or different types of water supplies. When different races are ingested, as by drinking water one is not accustomed to, the result may be the well-known tourist diseases. Enteric bacteria are routinely tested for in water supplies. Total coliform (i.e., *E. coli* and related forms) as well as those races that are exclusively fecal can easily be isolated. Total and fecal *Streptococcus* (the bacterium of strep throat) and *Salmonella* (the bacterium of salmonella and typhoid) are all routinely found in water supplies (Geldreich, 1970), although they can be removed from drinking water by filtration and chlorination. Indeed, proper treatment of drinking water would have a tremendously beneficial effect on waterborne diseases worldwide, especially in developing countries where the problems are worst and the solutions are furthest from realization. For example, McCabe (1970) discusses the design for a water treatment system in Bangladesh that could have a major role in controlling cholera in that country.

Some of the world's most debilitating diseases are caused by microscopic worms whose eggs are passed in urine or feces. The best example is schistosomiasis, caused by the trematode worms *Schistosoma haemotobium, S. japonicum,* and *S. mansoni.* The larvae of these worms infect adults of a few species of snail (Figure 8.23). The worms undergo asexual reproduction in the internal organs of the snail to produce many

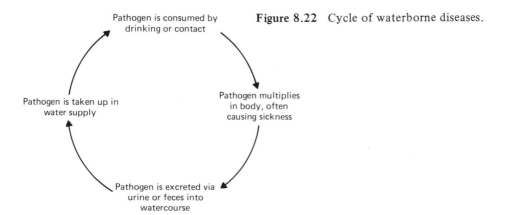

Figure 8.22   Cycle of waterborne diseases.

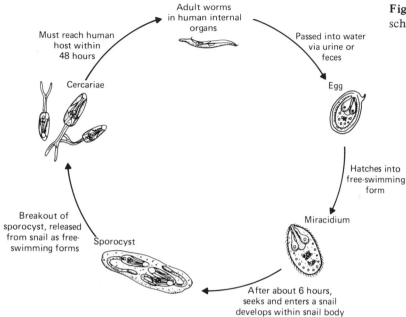

Figure 8.23 Life cycle of schistosomiasis.

thousands of larvae that are released into the water. They swim until they make contact with human skin. They bore their way into the person's body and enter the blood system. They then travel to the liver, where they grow to maturity and mate. Next they travel against the blood flow to the intestine or bladder wall, where they lay their eggs in large numbers. These are defecated or passed into the urine. Some, however, can get into the blood stream and are carried to organs such as the liver, kidney, or bladder. These organs may be seriously damaged as capillaries are blocked with eggs. At its worse, debilitation can be total (Warley, 1974).

Heat

Waste heat rejected into watercourses from electricity generation and industrial plants constitutes a substantial problem in many areas. Approximately 80% of the water used by industry, as well as virtually all water used for electric power generation, goes for cooling (Löf and Ward, 1970).

Cooling-water effluent is relatively clean. It may be chlorinated to cut down on fouling by plants, and it may contain phosphate or other chemicals added to cut boiler scale. It is low in dissolved gases such as oxygen, due to the lower solubility of gases at elevated temperatures. But the main effect of heated-water discharge comes from the heat itself. Biochemical reactions tend to speed up as temperatures rise. (A good rule of thumb is that a 10°C temperature rise causes a doubling of reaction rate.) This includes all of the reactions that deplete oxygen, including BOD, inorganic oxidation, and the metabolic rate of cold-blooded animals. The saturation level of dissolved oxygen in warm water is lower than it is in cold water. Thus increasing temperature has the effect of simultaneously decreasing supply of dissolved oxygen and increasing demand for it. Toxins also tend to become more toxic as the temperatures rise.

Different groups of organisms are favored by different temperatures. For example, the algae of typical lakes in the temperate zone tend to be dominated by diatoms with small numbers of green and bluegreen species. As temperature rises to about 32°C green and bluegreen algae become increasingly common, with the greens reaching a peak and diatoms rapidly falling off. Above about 33°C the greens also begin to decline, and the bluegreens reach their peak about 40°C (Figure 8.24).

Similar responses are shown by fishes and shellfish. The most desirable fishes that characterize oligotrophic waters high in dissolved oxygen are also characteristic of cold water. The coarse fishes, which can survive in waters of lower dissolved oxygen, are characteristic of warm waters. Thus as waste heat is discharged into a cold-water lake or fishing stream, the balance tips from desirable to coarse fishes on a thermal basis alone even if no other effects are noted.

Fish can become acclimated to a new temperature so that survival is possible at temperatures that would otherwise be too high (Figure 8.25). Fish acclimated to higher average temperatures show higher lethal temperatures and a greater capacity to withstand temperature fluctuation. But there are species limits, and fish are not infinitely adaptable to changes in temperature. Even when a population is acclimated to unusual temperatures, for example in an area heated by a power plant effluent, the rapid temperature shock that accompanies plant shutdown and operating problems can cause problems with growth and may also contribute to reproductive failure.

If survival is related to temperature, so is reproduction, and reproduction tends to be much more narrowly circumscribed than gross survival. Cold-water fishes such as salmon, trout, and grayling reproduce at temperatures of 2° to 10°C, even though they can survive at temperatures up to 20°C. It is possible to discharge hot water across a spawning bed with minimal impact on adult fish metabolism, but this may drive a population into local extinction because it prevents reproduction. Whether the effect of heat is directly on mortality or on reproduction, it often brings significant shifts in the competitive balance among species.

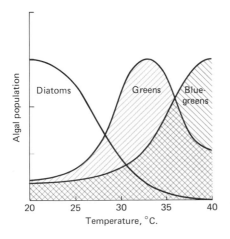

Figure 8.24 Density distribution of algal groups as a function of temperature. [Redrawn, with permission, from Cairns, 1971.]

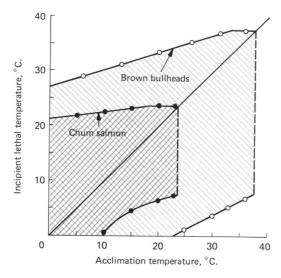

Figure 8.25 Relationship between incipient lethal temperature and acclimation temperature for chum salmon (*Onchorhynchus keta*) and brown bullheads (*Ameirus nebulosis*). The upper lines are the incipient lethal high temperatures; the lower lines are the incipient low temperatures. Zones of tolerance are shaded. Note that the zone of tolerance extends only to acclimation temperatures that are not lethal (i.e., where the incipient lethal temperature is above the 45° line). [Redrawn, with permission, from J. R. Brett, Some principles in the thermal requirements of fishes. *Quart. Rev. Biol.* 31: 75–87, 1956.]

LAND USE AND POLLUTANT GENERATION

Pollutant generation stems from people's activities on land. Understanding what goes on in the water is not very useful unless one also understands how land use is related to pollutant generation, and how to assess different alternatives such as source reduction or wastewater treatment. Figure 8.26 diagrams the system of water distribution and use in an industrialized country. There are four basic sources: groundwater, surface water, rainfall, and the oceans. Some activities such as agriculture can use rainwater directly but most need to tap continuously available water and pipe it to the point of use. These include the typically urban kinds of uses: municipal, residential, industrial, and electric power generation.

It does not make very much difference to the user whether his water comes from groundwater sources or from surface water, but it may make considerable difference to the water balance of the ecosystem. Only 2¾% of the earth's free water is usable fresh water, and the lakes and streams that are our most accessible and useful sources for water comprise only a third of that. Water cycles vary rapidly between oceans, the atmosphere, and the land surface. The average turnover time for water in the atmosphere is about 11.4 days. The average residence in lakes is generally on the order of 1 to 25 years, depending on the size of the lake and its drainage basin. Estimating a residence time for the groundwater system is extremely difficult as it is so large, but it is clearly several orders of magnitude higher. The oceans constitute an almost infinite reservoir. If the average rainfall over the earth is 81.1 cm per year (Furon, 1967), it would take over 3 million years for a volume equivalent to the oceans to pass through the hydrologic cycle.

The recharge characteristics of different groundwater reservoirs may be different. In some areas withdrawals of groundwater can be readily made up by recharge, so that the water behaves in much the same way as a surface watercourse. In others the groundwater is so-called "fossil water," and the recharge rate is very slow or even nil. All intermediates exist. Because the amount of water in surface waterways and a few

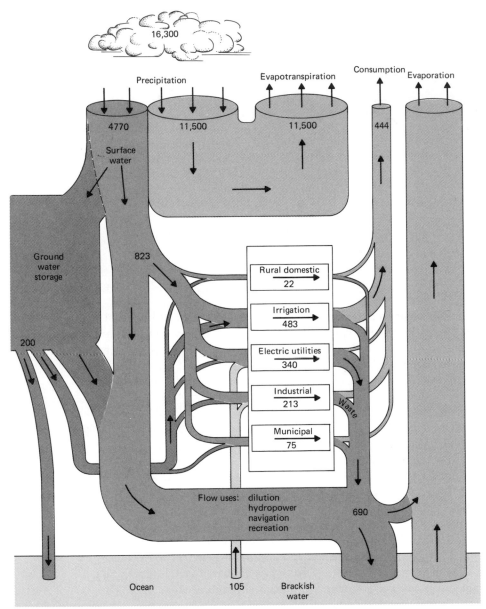

Figure 8.26 Estimated water supply and use in the coterminous U.S., 1958. The estimates are rough, but the relative magnitudes of various sources and uses are meaningful and realistic. All figures are in 10^6 m.^{3}. [After G. White, *Strategies of American Water Management*. Copyright © 1968 University of Michigan Press.]

shallow groundwater reservoirs is dependent more on cycling rates than on size, use of the water does not in itself prejudice future water availability. It may lower the downstream quality, but that is a different matter. Using groundwater that is not replenished, on the other hand, may be equivalent to a permanent reduction in the size of the resource.

Society's main concern with aquatic ecosystems is that its needs be met. The combined demands of agriculture, forestry, pastureland, and undeveloped lands account for the overwhelming majority of the flux of water through human ecosystems. These activities can use water either as it falls or as it is supplemented with water from other sources. The largest user of water over and above rainfall is unquestionably agriculture, through irrigation. Even in areas that have sufficient total annual precipitation, it is often economically useful to provide irrigation so that plants may have a sufficient supply of water during occasional droughts or periods of stress. In more arid parts of the world, irrigation is either very useful or essential for crop growing.

Of the urban users, electric power generation utilizes the most water. Electric utilities are considered separately from other industries because they use water in a different way and they produce different pollutants, both in water and in air. They use a third again the amount of water of all other industries combined. Other industries, both heavy and light, use some 3 times as much water as municipal and residential water users. The inputs to the different activities in Figure 8.26 are categorized as water, but what comes out may or may not be so simple. Something almost invariably is added, if only heat. More often a wide range of substances had been added, and the average stream flowing through an urbanized industrial area may have as much in common with the contents of a beaker in a chemistry laboratory as with the typical clear-flowing mountain brook.

It is useful to distinguish between *consumptive* and *nonconsumptive* water use. Consumptive use is that in which the water no longer has the properties of liquid water following its use. It may be water vapor, as when a boiler releases steam for running an electric turbine. It may become part of an industrial product, as when water molecules react chemically with organic chemicals to form certain plastics. The more common uses of water are nonconsumptive. These include the water used to flush wastes down toilets and drains. Almost all of the water used for electric power generation is nonconsumptive cooling water. Practically every industry uses heat in some way and therefore needs water to cool either the product or the machine that manufactures the product. Process water is part of the industrial process itself, such as the water used as a solvent or cleaning agent.

Since consumptively used water is returned to the ecosystem in some form other than liquid water, it does not contribute to water pollution in any large degree. The nonconsumptive uses lead to water pollution, as they return water to the ecosystem with whatever it contains at the time. Domestic wastes include BOD, microorganisms, and the whole gamut of pollutants from bodily elimination, food processing, normal household items, and small-scale commercial effluents. Cooling water always contains a heat load as well as some boiler scale. There may be other pollutants in cooling water, but they tend to be minor. The widest range of industrial pollutants comes with discharges of process water. This is the source of most of the industrial poisons entering surface waters, as well as large proportions of the BOD, suspended solids, and oils.

Basis for Water Quality Management

The requirements of different uses for watercourses are different and often contradictory. For example, transportation requires that a waterway be sufficiently wide and deep to accommodate any ship intended to use it. This may not be a serious problem on the open seas, but it may be the deciding factor in the kind of management policies followed for inland waterways, especially if they are man-made. It may stimulate the expenditure of many millions of dollars on operations such as dredging and harbor construction. For public water supply, on the other hand, it is not particularly important how deep or wide the source water body is. But oxygen levels must be fairly high and levels of BOD and various other nutrients must be low. Even more important, pathogenic organisms should be as rare as feasible. In water used for industrial cooling, low oxygen levels minimize corrosion of pipes in the factory. Process water must also be "clean enough" chemically. This means it must meet very high purity standards in some industrial processes; in others practically anything will do. For waters whose prime use is recreation, the requirements of aquatic life can be determined and standards be established so that the water will remain suitable for fish.

Considering the wide range of often conflicting demands society makes on a finite number of waterways, how can we best manage the aquatic ecosystems under our control? In principle we could bring all waterways up to the highest standards, so that the water would be always clean enough to drink, or at least to fish and swim in. Another approach is to zone a watercourse so that certain reaches meet very restrictive standards and other reaches meet lower standards. Some reaches, and even some entire streams, might be turned over to very intensive uses with high levels of pollution. This can be done by using both technology and the natural self-cleaning characteristics of the stream to protect other streams or other reaches of the same stream.

Both of the approaches sketched above have been suggested for most waterways in most countries, and both form the basic motivations of public policy in industrialized countries. There is a continuum between the two extremes. The first is a special case of the zoned-stream approach in which all reaches of the stream are zoned for natural watershed or contact-sport conditions. Both require a comprehensive plan with a management strategy that is consistent with the capacities of the stream and the uses desired for it. For example, it is not reasonable to use the upper reaches of a river for discharging large quantities of heavy metals or other conservative pollutants if the downstream reaches are intended for recreation or public water supply. Likewise, a salmon fishery cannot survive with its spawning beds in the upper reaches of a river if the lower reaches are so polluted that the adult fish cannot migrate through them.

It is never obvious how dirty a stream should be allowed to get. Nor is it always clear how to allocate the economic and political costs needed to clean up already polluted waterways. The ecologist cannot dictate what uses are appropriate or what the water quality at any point should be, any more than the industrial manager can dictate acceptable levels of pollution below his own outfall. Once we accept the premise that it is appropriate to use a given stream or lake for some purpose (including retention in its wild state), we accept implicitly that the responsibility for managing it is vested in people.

It is easy for the decision making process to be arbitrary and to deny the importance of either the demands being placed on the system by different sectors of society or the natural processes that occur in the stream. It is often easier to mandate a high level of cleanliness that cannot be realized even by responsible managers in an industrial society than it is to devise a strategy for the cooperation and informed regulation needed to reach a feasible solution. In the same way, it used to be considered appropriate for industrial managers to abdicate responsibility for their effluent quality without thought for the burden this placed on downstream users.

The goal of enlightened decision-making in water quality management should be to make it possible to accommodate the needs of society and the characteristics of the watercourses so that the overall ecosystem confers the greatest benefit to society. This requires a careful understanding of the environmental domain of the waterway, the mechanisms by which individual managers make decisions, and the needs and mores of the society at large.

WASTEWATER TREATMENT

Until fairly recently, wastewater treatment has meant treatment of BOD. There are numerous types of treatment, depending on the type of wastewater and the resources of the agency responsible for its treatment. The basic strategy has been to oxidize as much of the carbonaceous material as possible and to minimize the BOD load from the treated wastewaters discharged into receiving streams.

All wastewater treatment systems include collection, treatment, and discharge. Collection is generally via a sewer system, treatment is accomplished by some sort of sewage treatment plant, and discharge is typically into the nearest river or lake.

Septic Tanks

Domestic wastewater consists basically of human biological wastes. One of the simplest methods of disposal is the common septic tank. Wastes from a single house are directed through a very small sewer into a holding tank (Figure 8.27), which acts both as a detention chamber and as a vehicle for biological degradation of the waste products. Solid materials settle to the bottom of the tank, leaving liquid in suspension and a floating scum. Baffles minimize the amount of suspended materials in the upper part of the tank. Ideally anaerobic bacteria in the septic tank break down the BOD. Up to 50% of the BOD can be broken down and 73% of the suspended solids settled under ideal conditions, although the bacterial content of the effluent may be higher than that of the sewage influent. Much of the sludge is inert, and it gradually accumulates

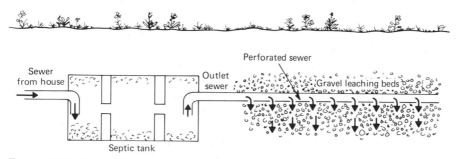

Figure 8.27 Schematic diagram of a septic tank.

on the bottom of the septic tank until it clogs the baffles and leads to system failure. Septic tanks should be cleaned on the average of once every 2 to 4 years. Their biggest advantage is their great simplicity. Maintenance costs after installation are limited to routine cleaning and repair.

The effluent from the septic tank is discharged into a broad gravel drainage field that distributes the wastes and provides an aerated environment. Bacterial breakdown continues here, so that the water becomes cleaner as it percolates down into the groundwater system. Substances remaining in the septic tank discharge can become adsorbed onto the surface of particles in the drainage bed or in the subjacent soil, or they can be carried into the water table along with the treated wastewater.

At its best the septic tank can treat small quantities of wastewater well enough to return them to the groundwater without harm to nearby wells or surface water. The soil and system design should be appropriate, the system should be adequately maintained, and other septic tanks, surface waters, and wells should be sufficiently distant. The septic tank is appropriate only in areas of low population density. As wastewater percolates out from the drainage fields, it may move some distance from the septic tank itself. It is essential that the areas into which the wastes from several septic tanks percolate do not overlap.

Standard Municipal Sewage Treatment

Where population densities are higher, standard methods of sewage treatment are practiced. Wastes are collected from each individual house by a sewer system that carries them from the house to the sewage treatment plant.

Sewer Systems. A sewer is a pipe through which wastewater flows. Small sewers connect individual buildings to larger sewers in the street. These in turn connect to larger trunk sewers that lead to the sewage treatment plant or the general outfall. The sewer system is designed to carry wastes as cheaply as possible. Among other things, this means that wastewater commonly flows under gravity from individual buildings to the treatment plant and is seldom pumped.

No sewer has unlimited capacity. Only so much wastewater can be forced into a sewer before it overflows. This limit is set by its size and the angle at which it is pitched. When more water enters a sewer than can be transported adequately by it, overflows must be available to drain the excess (Figure 8.28). The only question is where they should be placed. Basements and roadways are generally inappropriate for public health reasons, although they serve informally when the overflows are blocked or inadequate, and they would always serve this purpose if overflows were not placed in the sewer line. Overflows normally drain into nearby surface water. Well-designed sewers can easily carry the normal load of wastewater passing through them. They overflow under high flow conditions with wastewater proceeding untreated into a nearby waterway, where it does the least direct harm to people. Unfortunately, sewer system overflows may be one of the most important causes for stream degradation in an urban area. According to U.S. Environmental Protection Agency figures, they account for significant percentages of the fish kills reported in American rivers.

Why do sewer systems overflow at all? A design engineer can obviously estimate

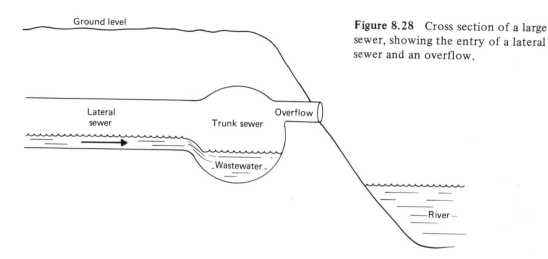

Figure 8.28 Cross section of a large sewer, showing the entry of a lateral sewer and an overflow.

the average wastewater load for the average house in a given part of a city and design a sanitary sewer system that is conservatively rated to meet the demand that will be put on it, given current housing densities and projected use changes. If the main function of the sewer system is to carry off human fecal and household wastes, there should be no reason why these cannot be estimated closely enough that one never has to worry about peaks in wastewater production exceeding the capacity of the sewer to carry the wastes.

The peaks in wastewater production are not due to household or commercial wastewater production; they are due to storms. If surface transportation networks are to work efficiently, stormwater must be channeled off the streets, subway tracks, and other transportation arteries. In a typical older city stormwaters were fed into the same sewers as sanitary wastes. When it is not raining there is no stormwater runoff, and the load in the combined sewers is domestic wastes. After a rain the stormwater inlets direct great quantities of water to the sewer. Heavy storms can easily overload a combined sewer system. When this happens large quantities of domestic wastes, including fecal material and pathogenic bacteria, are washed into local surface waters.

Several years ago many communities began to put in a different kind of sewer system, wherein sanitary wastes were directed to a sanitary sewer that was somewhat smaller than the old combined sewer but led to the sewage treatment plant without stormwater inlets. Stormwater was directed to a separate storm sewer system, which also led to the sewage plant but which could be shunted directly into the receiving waters if volumes were too high for the treatment plant to handle. Domestic wastes could always be treated with a minimum of overflows. Wastes from small storms could also be treated, with overflows being confined almost entirely to stormwater during heavy storms.

The advantages of the separate sewer system over the combined sewer system would appear to be compelling. The separation of sanitary wastes minimizes the occurrence of untreated discharges of human fecal matter and BOD. But the capital costs of separate sewer systems are considerably higher than those of combined systems. And stormwater is not pure.

As it washes over streets, lawns, alleys, railroad tracks, roofs, and the other surfaces of a city, storm runoff picks up large quantities of debris. Some are chemically and biologically inert, others are not. From a series of studies of urban runoff in several countries, it has become clear that the amount of BOD, coliform bacteria, and suspended solids in stormwater is equal to or even up to 10 times greater than that of treated sanitary wastewater, and that the shock load value may be up to 1,000 times as high (Bradford, 1977). Storm sewage is also high in nutrients, bacteria, and heavy metals (Whipple and Hunter, 1977). To be sure, the fecal wastes are not from human sources. They are from dogs, horses, rats, and similar warm-blooded members of the urban melange. But storm runoffs are not clean, and it is not desirable to discharge them directly into surface waters without treatment. Table 8.2 compares stormwaters and raw sanitary sewage and shows the ranges of variation of some significant components.

Sewer overflows from combined and separate sewers show a flushing effect, wherein pollutants reach a peak shortly after the beginning of a storm and tail off (Figure 8.29). Pollutant loadings also tend to drop from one storm to the next, if consecutive storms are close enough together and if surface materials washed off by the first have not yet reaccumulated by the time of the second (deFilippi and Shih, 1971). Even so, the intensity of pollution from stormwater runoff is potentially very high, and the only adequate way to control it is to minimize storm runoff. Mechanisms for holding water until it can be treated include surface waste stabilization ponds or underground tunnels. No method of holding and treating sewer overflows has yet been widely adopted.

Wastewater Treatment Plants.   A wastewater treatment plant is a complex in which

Table 8.2   Characteristics of Stormwater Runoff.

Constituent	Stormwater Runoff	Sanitary Sewage (raw)	Stormwater as per cent of Sanitary
1. Comparison of Stormwater Runoff and Sanitary Sewage			
Suspended solids	818.0	605.0	135
Volatile suspended solids	179.0	403.0	44
BOD	37.0	605.0	6
Phosphate	2.8	30.0	9
Nitrogen	10.0	91.0	11

2. Characteristics of Urban Stormwater			
BOD	1–700	Suspended solids	2–11,300
Organic N	0.1–16	Volatile susp. solids	12–1,600
NH_3-N	0.1–2.5	Soluble PO_4	0.1–10
Chlorides	2–25,000	Total PO_4	0.1–125
Oils	0–110	Total coliform bact.	$200–146 \times 10^6$
Fecal coliform bact.	$55–112 \times 10^6$	Fecal streptococcus	$200–1.2 \times 10^6$

Data in 1. are in kg./ha./yr., and are from Weibel et al., 1964. Chemical data in 2. are in mg./l.; bacteriological data are in bacteria per 100 ml. They are taken from EPA, 1973.

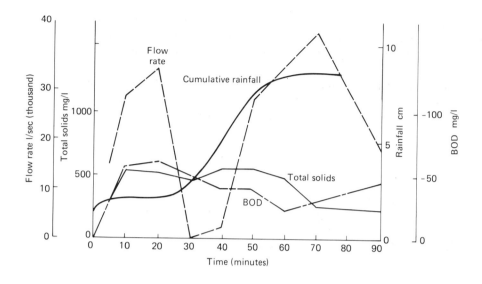

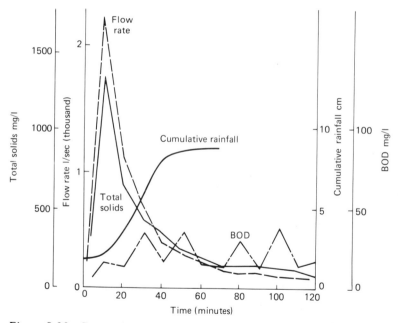

Figure 8.29 Comparison of characteristics of combined sewer runoff (above) and separate sewer runoff (below) during a long 65 to 73 minute intense (7.3 cm.) storm in Washington, D.C. [Redrawn, with permission, from DeFilippi and Shih, 1971.]

organic materials are oxidized and other chemical species are treated to minimize their impact on the environment. Most wastewater treatment is based on aerobic bacterial oxidation, although physical settling and anaerobic bacteria also have important roles. Although it might seem a very mundane kind of technology, a sewage treatment plant is one of the most efficient chemical plants in widespread operation today. Typical sewage is more than 99% pure water. BOD and other undesirable constitutents generally constitute less than 1/2 of 1% of the sewage. A well-operated treatment plant can remove roughly 90% of the BOD and large percentages of bacteria, suspended solids, and nutrients.

A wastewater treatment plant is a multiprocess operation (Figure 8.30). The largest contaminants are strained out by a large grate. These include pieces of automobile bodies, tree branches, and large animals (living or dead). The water flows into a large

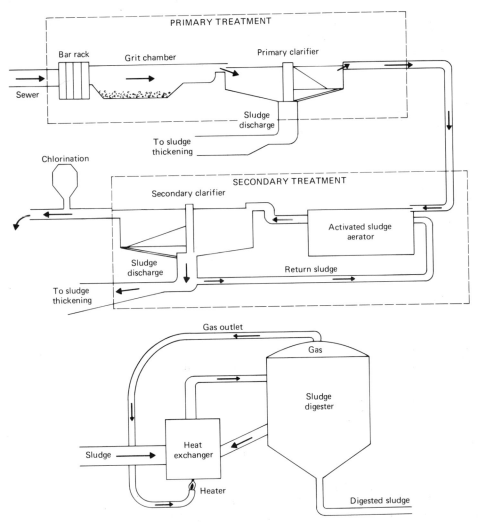

Figure 8.30 Schematic diagram of a typical municipal secondary sewage treatment plant. Primary treatment includes screening through a bar rack, with coarse material settling in a grit chamber and fines settling in a primary clarifier. Secondary treatment includes aeration with detritivorous sludge bacteria in an activated sludge aerator and particle removal in a secondary clarifier. Primary and secondary sludges are thickened in a heated sludge digester and landfilled. Effluent from secondary clarifier is chlorinated and returned to surface waters.

shallow settling basin called a degritter, where sand and gravel settle out quickly. It then enters a primary clarifier.

In *primary treatment,* a large settling cone allows fine solid particles to settle out. A typical detention time for a primary clarifier is about 1 to 4 hours. Coagulant chemicals are often added to the wastewater to allow certain materials to precipitate more rapidly. Skimmers remove floating components such as oils, and sludge scrapers at the bottom concentrate the sludge so that it can be removed at the bottom. Clarified water (i.e., wastewater without its settleable solids) flows over a weir and is sent to secondary treatment. Primary treatment removes about 30% to 35% of the BOD, along with most of the suspended solids.

There are two common types of bacterial *secondary treatment.* The simpler is by means of a trickling filter, which is actually a framework designed for aerobic organisms. The second is by activated sludge. As a general rule of thumb a trickling filter is most useful for small installations, and activated sludge is suitable for large installations.

The *trickling filter* is a large tank filled with a loose aggregation of rocks or other suitable substrate for a wide variety of organisms including bacteria, protozoa, rotifers, and fungi. Wastewater is sprayed over the top of the filter (Figure 8.31), where it trickles down across the slime-organism substrate. The surface area of the filter is so large that movement of wastewater across it is very slow. The biota inhabiting the filter slime have constant access to organic materials in the moving wastewater stream, and they are entirely aerobic. BOD is broken down through respiration and nutrients are incorporated into the slime biomass. Every so often pieces of slime wash off and are carried by the water as it exits from the bottom of the filter into a clarifier. The water that passes over the weir of this secondary clarifier is relatively clean, with a BOD content roughly 15% to 35% of the raw sewage influent.

In the *activated sludge* process the wastewater flows through a very large tank into which air is pumped at high rates (Figure 8.32). The air passing through the water mixes and oxygenates it. A community including bacteria, rotifers, protozoa, and fungi inhabit the aeration tank and break down the BOD aerobically. The detention time is typically on the order of 6 hours. BOD removal ranges from 50% to 75% to upwards of

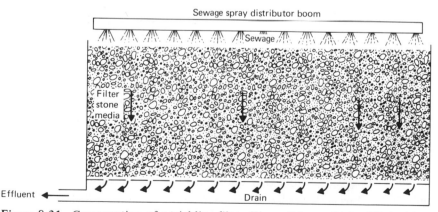

Figure 8.31 Cross section of a trickling filter. The unit is a cylinder filled with crushed rock, slag, or plastic. The "filter stone" is coated with microbial growth fed by organic materials in the wastewater. Wastewater is sprayed over the filter stone by the rotary distributor, flows over the filter stone, and drains out beneath the filter unit.

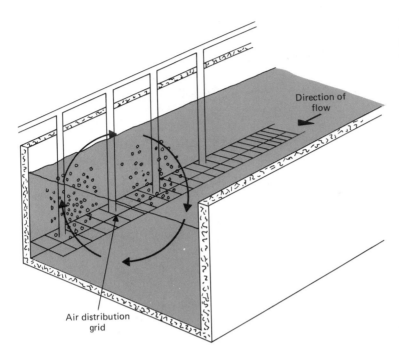

Figure 8.32 Cutaway diagram of an activated sludge aerator. Large volumes of air are forced through grids immersed in the wastewater. The airlift effect creates mass circulation to maximize aeration and mixing.

99%, depending on the design and operation of the plant. Substantial nutrient reductions are also possible, especially by judicious use of chemicals in conjunction with aeration. As with the trickling filter, the effluent from the aeration chamber flows into a secondary clarifier, where solid materials settle to the bottom, and treated wastewater flows over the top of the weir. In general, effluent water treated to this degree is returned directly to surface waters with no further treatment. The sludge, on the other hand, must be further treated before it can be disposed of. A small amount is returned to the oxidation tank to replenish the decomposer community.

Sewage sludge comprises the solid materials that settle during primary and secondary treatment. It includes everything from mineral particles and large organic molecules to members of the decomposer community. Despite its name it is still about 97% water, and disposal is not a trivial matter. It is fed into a *sludge digestor* (Figure 8.33), where it undergoes anaerobic degradation and concentration. The sludge digestor is a large vessel with a floating top. It is kept at the relatively high temperatures (35°C) required for efficient anaerobic degradation. Methane and other gases given off as part of the digestion process can provide much of the heat to maintain the digestor at its elevated temperature.

Roughly 80% to 90% of the biodegradable organic wastes can be converted to methane and carbon dioxide, and the remaining "solid" materials can be drawn off at the bottom. The solids drawn off from a sludge digestor still contain 86% to 98% water, and they must be "dewatered" before they can be disposed of. They can be physically treated until they contains only 70% to 80% moisture, at which point they may be landfilled, incinerated or used as soil conditioner. Sludge treatment is a significant component in wastewater treatment, accounting for about 25% of the total operating cost for a typical wastewater treatment plant (Jones et al., 1977).

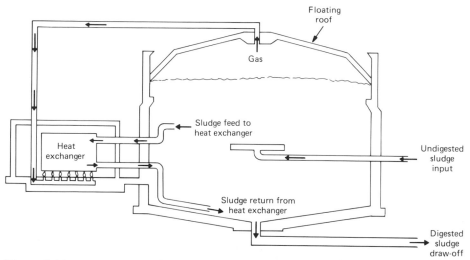

Gas

Floating
roof

Sludge feed to
heat exchanger

Heat
exchanger

Undigested
sludge
input

Sludge return from
heat exchanger

Digested
sludge
draw-off

Figure 8.33 Cross section of a sludge digestion tank and its associated heat exchanger. Sludge is recirculated through the heat exchanger, where it is heated to maintain a temperature in the main digester around 35°C. The heat exchanger is commonly gas fired, and it can run on gas produced by sludge breakdown, with backup from commercial gas systems. The top of the generator floats on the decomposing sludge, to maintain anaerobic conditions, and sludge may be withdrawn from several places within the digester.

Other Types of Wastewater Treatment

Standard wastewater treatment methods are ideal for urban types of installations where space is at a premium. There are alternatives that use more land but require less energy and maintenance. The sewage lagoon or oxidation pond is a pond into which wastewater is fed. It acts as a combined clarifier and biological treatment facility. Solids settle to the bottom and BOD is broken down by bacteria. High levels of nutrients promote luxuriant growth of algae and consequent oxygen production through algal photosynthesis. Retention times are very long. The oxidation pond is well suited to industrial applications where BOD is the main pollutant and land is relatively cheap. Examples include paper mills, feedlots, and canneries.

In *land treatment,* partially treated wastes are disposed of on land (Figure 8.34). The land may be recreational as in San Francisco's Golden Gate Park, which is fertilized by sewage sludge. It may be agricultural as in Muskegon, Michigan, where crops are irrigated and fertilized by municipal sewage. It may be grazing land as in Melbourne, Australia. It may also be wetland as in Wildwood, Florida (Boyt et al., 1977). The practice is an old one. Melbourne and Berlin have been spray-irrigating sewage since the 1890s, and *sewage farming* involving the use of treated sewage sludge has long been practiced in several European cities (Allen, 1973).

Municipal sewage and sewage sludge have some very useful qualities. They are mostly water and irrigate the receiving area. They are rich in both organic materials and nutrients, so that they condition and fertilize the soil. Soil organisms can oxidize

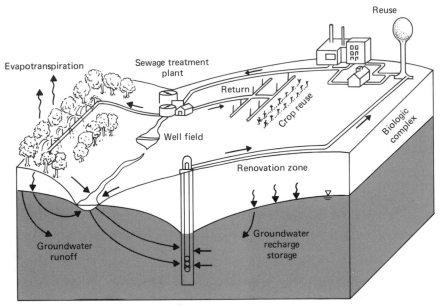

Figure 8.34 Schema for wastewater renovation and conservation based on land discharge of treated waters on crops and forests. Water that is not lost via evapotranspiration percolates to the groundwater table and is cleaned by its passage through the soil, so that it can be reused. [Redrawn, with permission, from Parizek and Myers, 1968.]

BOD, and soil micelles adsorb nutrients and even heavy metals from the wastewater or sludge.

Wastewaters and whatever dissolved or colloidal materials they contain percolate through the soil as long as it is sufficiently permeable. A first requisite of a land treatment site is, thus, that the soil be able to accept a great deal of water. The soil biota must be kept active so that the soil is constantly worked and the permeability remains high despite the deposition of solids in the pore spaces. As long as the soil community is active the pores can be kept open, and the wastewater and sludge provide both the energy and nutrients to sustain that activity. As these materials percolate through the soil, those that are not immediately assimilated by living organisms may become adsorbed onto surface-active particles such as clays or organic material.

Experiments have shown that for a suitable soil up to 100% of the nutrients in sewage treatment plant effluent are removed by land treatment (Sopper, 1968). Few pathogenic bacteria can live outside the human body, and those that can must compete for their needs with soil bacteria in a soil environment. They do not do very well, and experiments have shown that both bacteria and viruses are removed rather efficiently by land treatment. Heavy metals do not appear to accumulate to a degree that biologically active forms reach significant concentrations (Sidle et al., 1977).

Transmission of parasitic metazoans (e.g., tapeworms) to man by land treatment of untreated sewage has been documented, and transmission of parasites to animals has also been observed in land treatment of untreated and partially treated sewage (Hays, 1977). The risk of parasitism from land treatment of treated sewage appears to be very low, although complete destruction of parasite eggs is not feasible. They are destroyed satisfactorily by the soil biota if access to receiving areas is restricted to minimize contact between people or livestock and raw sewage or sludge.

Tertiary Wastewater Treatment. Tertiary wastewater treatment is a generic term for anything that follows secondary treatment. There is no standard form analogous to trickling filters or activated sludge. It is tailored to specific wastewaters, and it is called for whenever the effluent of secondary treatment is not pure enough to be discharged into surface waters. It is so new a technology that different methods are still in a shakedown phase, and we shall not discuss them in detail here.

Land treatment is often used as a tertiary treatment method. It may be designed so that the net flow of water is down into the groundwater system, or for discharge at the surface after the water has passed through a wetland. Spangler et al. (1977) documented experimental discharge cycles in marshes in which wetlands can remove considerable amounts of phosphate from wastewater effluent streams passing through them. In Wildwood, Florida, the discharges of BOD, phosphorus, and bacteria from a swamp used as a final treatment area were lower than the ambient levels of natural runoff into the receiving stream (Boyt et al., 1977).

The two most common additional methods of tertiary treatment are physical-chemical and advanced biological treatment. Physical-chemical treatment includes the addition of reagents to wastewater to precipitate various entities, as well as carbon adsorption columns, ion exchange, and reverse osmosis. It is especially suited to industrial applications such as those involving heavy metals, and to wastes with very high or very low pH. It can also be used with standard municipal waste. It is a very attractive means of wastewater treatment to municipalities or industry whose capital budget is low, because the cost of building a physical-chemical treatment plant is less than the cost of building a conventional treatment plant. However, the cost of operation is a great deal more, since it may involve the use of immense quantities of reagent chemicals. For a more complete discussion of physical-chemical treatment see ACS (1978).

In advanced biological treatment, wastewater is treated by biological communities after secondary treatment and before it is discharged into receiving waterways. For the most part these communities are algae that remove nutrient materials. In warm areas the water hyacinth, which often grows so rapidly in natural waterways that it can be a genuine hazard, may also be grown. It is capable of assimilating large quantities of nutrients, which can be removed permanently if the hyacinths are harvested. The nutrients can even be recycled by composting the harvested plants (Cornwell et al., 1977).

SYSTEM EFFICIENCY AND EVOLUTION

The amount of water on earth is finite, and it is part of the closed hydrologic cycle where it moves at all. We tend to view water resources, their extraction and use, and water treatment and pollution, as an open system. Water is a cheap (if not a free) commodity. It is sufficient to meet one's own perceived needs, and one need not worry too much about one's neighbor since water is cheap for him too.

Of course this is not so. There are so many users and so many pollutants returned to watercourses that downstream users must sometimes bear very heavy costs to meet their water needs. The model of the natural ecosystem suggests that society ought to view water as part of a closed system in which human uses are part of the hydrologic cycle. The effluent from one user would be the influent for another, and so on until it evaporates or reaches the sea. There are places where the effluent from a relatively nonpolluting user is used as the water supply by a relatively tolerant user, and there are attempts to create the kinds of cooperation that are required to use the natural self-cleaning of a river successfully. But it is more typical for downstream users never to have the benefit of water that is as clean as that available to upstream users.

There are few instances in which the cycle of water is almost closed. In Windhoek, Namibia, much of the potable water supply is treated wastewater. Many industries find it more profitable to recycle cooling water than to pay sewer user charges to discharge it. But these instances are special cases. Many legal conventions and regulations tend to make closing the cycle and reusing water difficult or even illegal (Dugan and McGaughy, 1977). Water will continue to be discharged in ways that ignore both society's legitimate needs and the characteristics of the environment. We seldom reach the ideal situation in which upstream water use does not prejudice the water supply for any downstream user (including fish), and in which the overall system is healthy.

The most common solutions suggested for deficiencies in aquatic ecosystems are those that would increase the level of treatment, but there are others that deserve consideration. In the Ruhr valley of West Germany, for example (Kneese, 1963, 1966), seven water-management cooperatives, or *Genossenschaften,* manage the small tributaries to the Rhine that serve as the foci for this intensively industrialized area. Of the five major streams of the Ruhr area east of the Rhine (which are all quite small; their combined discharge into the Rhine is less than a fourth of the low flow of record for the Delaware River at Trenton), four are relatively clean. They serve as industrial water supply and provide contact recreation such as swimming and boating. The fifth, the Emscher, has been converted into the *cloaca maxima* of the Ruhr. It is fully lined with concrete and it carries the combined wastes not only of its own watershed but also of the surrounding watersheds. An in-stream waste treatment plant treats the entire Emscher flow before it empties into the Rhine. This allows great economies of scale and efficiency of treatment. The use of a single river as a sewer also frees the other rivers for a broad and creative set of uses, so that they and the society depending on them are better off than they would be if all five were consigned to industrial uses.

Of course this is not the perfect answer. The Emscher puts a heavy load on the Rhine. But this load is probably less under the strategy being used in the Ruhr than it would be if the industries in the watersheds of the other rivers discharged directly into those rivers rather than into the Emscher.

Water resource and use systems will probably evolve under the force of two antagonistic directions at once. Demands for water, and consequent water pollution, will increase with population and material prosperity. Attempts to improve the health of watercourses will also increase with greater understanding of society's dependence on functioning ecosystems. The tension between these two directions is increasing noticeably, and we can expect it to force serious consideration of new ideas and new trade-offs. What they will be cannot be predicted at this time. Different societies will make different choices, and even a single society will choose differently at different times.

No single model or decision making process is appropriate to all situations or to all communities.

The case of the Ruhr *Genossenschaften* is an instance of a nonstandard solution to an important problem. Sometimes the problems themselves are nonstandard. For example, the discharge of tertiary effluents of drinking-water quality into Lake Tahoe, California-Nevada, would cause a substantial impairment in the quality of the lake water. The only way to maintain the quality of the water is to divert treated wastes outside the basin. Adaptation of the best available sewage treatment technology in Kaneohe Bay, Hawaii, in 1962, resulted in secondary land development in the area that led to a worsening of bay conditions. In Honolulu, on the other hand, the assimilation capacity of the adjacent Pacific Ocean is so high that the difference in water quality resulting from advanced primary treatment and much more expensive secondary treatment would be insignificant. In all three areas, the requirement of secondary treatment for municipal wastewater mandated by the U.S. Federal Water Pollution Control Act is not appropriate. The first case requires tertiary treatment with diversion of effluent and its subsequent reuse as irrigation water supplement. The second requires land use controls and either tertiary treatment or diversion of the effluent to an area of higher assimilative capacity. The third can be satisfied by a much cheaper and simpler approach to the problem.

There has been a steady evolution of strategies for managing aquatic ecosystems. None adopted so far is entirely appropriate, largely because of the difficulty of ascertaining society's true interest, assessing the capabilities of ecosystems, and translating these factors into regulations that are meaningful in the context of an ecosystem subject to multiple use and multiple users. Standards promulgated *en masse* cannot reflect the differences that exist in real ecosystems. At the same time, regulations that reflect these differences may not bring equitable treatment to people who live in different areas. It is not clear how to resolve this conflict in any given case. But its ultimate resolution is essential for the long-term survival of society and the aquatic ecosystems it depends on.

References

Allan, I. R. H., 1955. Effects of pollution on fisheries. *Verh. Int. Ver. Limnol.* **12**: 804–810.

Allan, I. R. H., Herbert, D. W. M., and Alabaster, J. S., 1958. A field and laboratory investigation of fish in a sewage effluent. *Fish. Invest. Lond.* 1,6,2.

Allen, J., 1973. Sewage farming. *Environment* **15** (3): 36–41.

American Chemical Society, Committee on Environmental Improvement, 1978. The water environment. Ch. 5 in *Cleaning Our Environment: A Chemical Perspective*. Washington: American Chemical Society, 188–274.

Baker, J. M., 1978. Marine ecology and oil pollution. *Jour. Water Poll. Control Fed.* **50**: 442–449.

Ball, I. R., 1967. The relative susceptability of some species of fresh-water fish to poisons. *Water Research* **1**: 767–775.

Blumer, M. and Sass, J., 1972. Oil pollution: persistance and degradation of spilled fuel oil. *Science* **176**: 1120–1122.

Blumer, M., Sass, J., Souza, G., Sanders, H., Grassle, F., and Hampson, G., 1970. The West Falmouth oil spill. Unpublished manuscript, Woods Hole Oceanographic Inst., Reference 70–44.

Blumer, M., Souza, G., and Sass, J., 1970. Hydrocarbon pollution of edible shellfish by an oil spill. *Marine Biol.* **5**: 195–202.

Boyt, F. L., Baylet, S. E., and Zoltek, J., Jr., 1977. Removal of nutrients from treated municipal wastewater by wetland vegetation. *Jour. Water Poll. Control Fed.* **49**: 789–799.

Bradford, W. L., 1977. Urban stormwater pollutant loadings: a statistical summary through 1972. *Jour. Water Poll. Control Fed.* **49**: 613–622.

Brett, J. R., 1956. Some principles in the thermal requirements of fishes. *Quart. Rev. Biol.* **31**: 75–87.

Brook, A. J. and Baker, A. L., 1972. Chlorination at power plants: impact on phytoplankton productivity. *Science* **176**: 1414–1415.

Brown, V. M., Mitrovic, V. V., and Stack G. T. C., 1968. Effects of chronic exposure to zinc on toxicity of a mixture of detergent and zinc. *Water Res.* **2**: 255–263.

Burns, N. M. and Ross, C., 1972. *Project Hypo: An Intensive Study of Lake Erie Central Basin Hypolimnion and Related Surface Water Phenomena.* Ottawa: Canada Centre for Inland Waters Paper **6**, and U.S.E.P.A. Tech. Report **TS-05-71-208-24**.

Cairns, J., 1971. Thermal pollution—a cause for concern. *Jour. Water Poll. Control Fed.* **43**: 55–66.

Campbell, W. J. and Martin, S., 1973. Oil and ice in the Arctic Ocean: possible large-scale interactions. *Science* **181**: 56–58. See also discussion and response in *Science* **186**: 843–846.

Chapin, J. D. and Uttormark, P. D., 1973. Atmospheric contribution of nitrogen and phosphorus. U. Wisc. Water Res. Ctr. Tech. Report **WIS-WPC-73-2**.

Clapham, W. B., Jr., 1973. *Natural Ecosystems.* New York: Macmillan Pub. Co.

Cornwell, D. A., Zoltek, J., Patrinely, C. D., Furman, T. de S., and Kim, J. I., 1977. Nutrient removal by water hyacinths. *Jour. Water Poll. Control Fed.* **49**: 57–65.

DeFilippi, J. A. and Shih, C. S., 1971. Characteristics of separated storm and combined sewer flows. *Jour. Water Poll. Control Fed.* **43**: 2033–2058.

Doudoroff, P. and Katz, M., 1950, 1953. Critical review of literature on the toxicity of industrial wastes and their components to fish. I. Alkalis, acids, and inorganics; II. The metals, as salts. *Sew. Ind. Wastes* **22**: 1432–1458; **25**: 802–839.

Dugan, G. L. and McGauhey, P. H., 1977. A second look at water reuse. *Jour. Water Poll. Control Fed.* **49**: 195–205.

Edmondson, W. T., 1969. Eutrophication in North America. In N.A.S., *Eutrophication: Causes, Consequences, Corrections.* Washington: National Academy of Sciences, 124–149.

Edmondson, W. T., 1970. Phosphorus, nitrogen, and algae in Lake Washington after diversion of sewage. *Science* **169**: 690–691.

Edmondson, W. T., 1972. Nutrients and phytoplankton in Lake Washington. In Likens, G. E. et al., *Nutrients and Eutrophication: The Limiting-Nutrient Controversy.* American Society of Limnology and Oceanography *Special Symposium* **I**: 172–188.

Environmental Protection Agency, 1973. *Characteristics of Urban Stormwater.* Environmental Protection Agency Report EPA–670/2–73–077.

Epstein, S. S., 1970. NTA. *Environment* **12**: 2–11.

Fisher, N. S., 1975. Chlorinated hydrocarbon pollutants and photosynthesis of marine phytoplankton: a reassessment. *Science* **189**: 463–464.

Foree, E. G., Jewell, W. J., and McCarty, P. L., 1971. The extent of nitrogen and phosphorus regeneration from decomposing algae. *Proc. 5th Int. Water Res. Conf.* **III-27**: 1–15.

Forrester, W. G., 1971. Distribution of suspended oil particles following the grounding of the tanker *Arrow. J. Mar. Res.* **29**: 151–170.

Furon, R., 1967. *The Problem of Water: A World Study.* New York: American Elsevier Pub. Co., Inc.

Gaffney, P. E., 1977. Chlorobiphenyls and PCBs: formation during chlorination. *Jour. Water Poll. Control Fed.* **49**: 401–404.

Geldreich, E. E., 1970. Applying bacteriological parameters to recreational water qualities. *Jour. Am. Water Works Assn.* **62**: 113–120.

Golterman, H. L., 1960. Studies on the cycle of elements in fresh water. *Acta Botanica Neerlandica* **9**.

Hamilton, D. H., Flemer, D. A., Keefe, C. W., and Mihursky, J. A., 1970. Power plants: effects of chlorination on estuarine primary production. *Science* **169**: 197–198.

Hammond, A. L., 1971. Phosphate replacements: problems with the washday miracle. *Science* **172**: 361–363.

Hampson, G. R. and Sanders, H. L., 1969. Local oil spill. *Oceanus* **15** (2): 8–10.

Hasler, A. D., Scholtz, A. T., and Horrall, R. M., 1978. Olfactory imprinting and homing in salmon. *Am. Sci.* **66**: 347–355.

Hays, B. D., 1977. Potential for parasitic disease transmission with land application of sewage plant effluents and sludges. *Water Res.* **11**: 583–595.

Hutchinson, G. E., 1957. *A Treatise on Limnology, vol. I. Geography, Physics, and Chemistry.* New York: John Wiley & Sons.

Hutchinson, G. E., 1969. Eutrophication, past and present. In National Academy of Sciences, *Eutrophication: Causes, Consequences, Correctives.* Washington: National Academy of Sciences, 17–26.

Hynes, H. B. N., 1960. *The Biology of Polluted Water.* Liverpool: Univ. of Liverpool Press.

International Joint Commission (International Lake Erie and Lake Ontario–St. Lawrence River Water Pollution Boards), 1969. *Pollution of Lake Erie, Lake Ontario, and the International Section of the St. Lawrence River,* vol. 2: Lake Erie. Washington: International Joint Commission.

Johannes, R. E., 1968. Nutrient regeneration in lakes and oceans. *Adv. Microbiol. Sea.* **1**: 203–213.

Jones, J. L., Bomberger, D. C., Jr., Lewis, F. M., and Jacknow, J., 1977. Municipal sludge disposal economics. *Env. Sci. Tech.* **11**: 968–972.

Kneese, A. V., 1963. Water quality management by regional authorities in the Ruhr area with special emphasis on the role of cost assessment. *Papers and Proceedings, Reg. Sci. Assn.* **11**: 229–250.

Kneese, A. V., 1966. The Ruhr and the Delaware. *Jour. San. Eng. Div., Proc. Amer. Soc. Civil Eng.* **92 SA5**: 83–92.

Krebs, C. T. and Burns, K. A., 1977. Long-term effects of an oil spill on populations of the salt-marsh crab, *Uca pugnax. Science* **197**: 484–487.

Latterell, J. J., Holt, R. F., and Timmons, D. R., 1971. Phosphate availability in lake sediments. *Jour. Soil and Water Conservation* **26**: 21–24.

Li, W. C., Armstrong, D. E., Williams, J. D. H., Harris, R. F., and Syers, J. K., 1972. Rate and extent of inorganic phosphate exchange in lake sediments. *Soil Sci. Soc. America Proc.* **36**: 279–295.

Lindeman, R. L., 1942. The trophic-dynamic aspect of ecology. *Ecology* **23**: 399–418.

Löf, G. O. G. and Ward, J. C., 1970. Economics of thermal pollution control. *Jour. Water Poll. Control Fed.* **42**: 2102–2116.

Lund, E., 1978. Human pathogens as potential health hazards in the reuse of water. *Ambio* **7**: 56–61.

McCabe, D. B., 1970. Water and wastewater systems to combat cholera in East Pakistan. *Jour. Water Poll. Control Fed.* **42**: 1968–1981.

Mackenthun, K. M., Keup, L. E., and Stewart, R. K., 1968. Nutrients and algae in Lake Sebasticook, Maine. *Jour. Water Poll. Control Fed.* **40**: R72–R81.

McKeown, B. A. and March, G. L., 1978. The acute effect of bunker C oil and an oil dispersant on: 1 serum glucose, serum sodium and gill morphology in both freshwater and seawater acclimated ranbow trout (*Salmo gairdneri*). *Water Res.* **12**: 157–163.

Menzel, D. W., Anderson, J., and Randke, A., 1970. Marine phytoplankton vary in their responses to chlorinated hydrocarbons. *Science* **167**: 1724–1726.

Mitrovic, V. V., Brown, V. M., Shurben, D. G., and Berryman, M. H., 1968. Some pathological effects of sub-acute and acute poisoning of rainbow trout by phenol in hard water. *Water Research* **2**: 249–254.

Mortimer, C. H., 1941, 1942. The exchange of dissolved substances between mud and water in lakes. *J. Ecol.* **29**: 280–329, **30**: 147–201.

Mortimer, C. H., 1969. Physical factors with bearing on eutrophication of lakes in general and large lakes in particular. In N.A.S., *Eutrophication: Causes, Consequences, Correctives*. Washington: National Academy of Sciences, 340–368.

Murphy, C. B., Jr, 1977. Effects of restricted use of phosphate-based detergents on Onondaga Lake. *Science* **182**: 379–381.

National Academy of Sciences, 1969. *Eutrophication: Causes, Consequences, Correctives*. Washington: National Academy of Sciences.

Patrick, W. H., Jr. and Khalid, R. A., 1974. Phosphate release and sorption by soils and sediments: effect of aerobic and anaerobic conditions. *Science* **186**: 53–55.

Pilpel, N., 1968. The natural fate of oil on the sea. *Endeavour* **27**: 11–13.

Pradt, L. A., 1971. Some recent developments in night soil treatment. *Water Research* **5**: 507–521.

Ramseier, R. O., Gantchell, G. S., and Colby, C., 1973. Oil spill at Deception Bay, Hudson Strait. Ottawa: Inland Waters Directorate, Water Resources Br., *Sci. Series* **29**.

Rukeyser, W. S., 1972. Fact and foam in the row over phosphates. *Fortune* **85** (1): 70–73, 166–170.

Ryther, J. H. and Dunstan, W. M., 1971. Nitrogen, phosphorus, and eutrophication in the coastal marine environment. *Science* **171**: 1008–1013.

Sanders, R. L. and Sprague, J. B., 1967. Effects of copper-zinc mining on a spawning migration of Atlantic salmon. *Water Research* **1**: 419–432.

Schindler, D. W., 1974. Eutrophication and recovery in experimental lakes: implications for lake management. *Science* **184**: 897–899.

Sidle, R. C., Hook, J. E., and Kardos, L. T., 1977. Accumulation of heavy metals in soils from extended wastewater irrigation. *Jour. Water Poll. Control Fed.* **49**: 311–318.

Slack, K. V., 1971. Average dissolved oxygen—measurement and water quality significance. *Jour. Water Poll. Control Fed.* **43**: 433–446.

Sopper, W. E., 1968. Waste water renovation for reuse: key to optimum use of water resources. *Water Research* **2**: 471–480.

Spangler, F. L., Fetter, C. W., Jr., and Sloey, W. E., 1977. Phosphorus accumulation–discharge cycles in marshes. *Water Res. Bull.* **13**: 1911–1201.

Spenser, E., 1956. *The Faerie Queen.* London: William Ponsonby.

Sprague, J. B., 1969; 1970; 1971. Measurement of pollutant toxicity to fish. I: Bioassay method for acute toxicity; II: Utilizing and applying bioassay results; III: Sublethal effects and "safe" concentrations. *Water Research* **3**: 793–821; **4**: 3–32; **5**: 245–266.

Sprague, J. B., and McLeese, D. W., 1968. Different toxic mechanisms in kraft pulpmill effluent for two aquatic animals. *Water Research* **2**: 761–765.

Tarr, J. A. and McMichael, F. C., 1977. Decisions about wastewater technology: 1850–1932. *Jour. Water Res. Plan. and Mgmt. Div. Proc. Am. Soc. Civil Engineers* **103** **WR1**: 47–61.

Taylor, A. W. and Kunishi, H. M., 1971. Phosphate equilibria on stream sediment and soil in a watershed draining an agricultural region. *Ag. Food Chem.* **19**: 827–831.

Walton, I., 1653. *The Compleat Angler; or the Contemplative Man's Recreation* London: Richard Marriot.

Warley, D. P. A., 1974. Toward the control of schistosomiasis in Egypt. *Span* **17 (1)**: 34–37.

Weaver, P. J., 1969. Phosphates in surface waters and detergents. *Jour. Water Poll. Control Fed.* **41**: 1647–1653.

Weibel, S. R., Anderson, R. J., and Woodward, R. L., 1964. Urban land runoff as a factor in stream pollution. *Jour. Water Poll. Control Fed.* **36**: 914–924.

Whipple, W., Jr. and Hunter, J. V., 1977. Nonpoint sources and planning for water pollution control. *Jour. Water Poll. Control Fed.* **49**: 15–23.

White, G. F., 1969. *Strategies of American Water Management.* Ann Arbor: Univ. Michigan Press.

Wielgolaski, F. E., 1975. Biological indicators on pollution. *Urban Ecology* **1**: 63–79.

Wurster, C. F., Jr., 1968. DDT reduces photosynthesis by marine phytoplankton. *Science* **159**: 1474–1475.

9/the atmosphere in human ecosystems

The atmosphere is a layer of air some 50 km. thick. It is the source of oxygen for living organisms, as well as the reservoir from which plants take carbon dioxide for photosynthesis and from which bacteria fix nitrogen. Atmospheric water vapor is an important intermediary in the hydrologic cycle. Absorption of direct and reradiated solar energy by atmospheric particles, the transfer of energy via wind, and the continual evaporation and condensation of water are largely responsible for maintaining the biosphere at a temperature at which life can exist. Atmospheric constituents are both natural and anthropogenic. Both gases and particles are involved in a broad range of chemical and physical processes. They influence the atmospheric energy balance and catalyze numerous chemical and photochemical reactions.

The lowest 10 km. of the atmosphere, the *troposphere,* has an especially significant role in the biosphere. It controls the earth's weather and receives and disperses virtually all of the airborne emissions of modern civilization. Its volume is 5 billion (5×10^9) cu. km. Even significant quantities of materials introduced into the troposphere could easily be dissipated if they were evenly distributed. But the interactions between society and the atmosphere are not evenly dispersed. Ever since the Industrial Revolution, waste emissions have been concentrated in particular areas. At first air pollution was only a local nuisance. It grew with the population and with technology until large areas are now subjected to public health hazards as a result of it. Changes in the atmosphere may have broad-scale and profound effects on the evolution of all organisms presently on earth, on local weather patterns, and even on broad regional and long-term climatic patterns.

PHYSICAL DYNAMICS

As with aquatic ecosystems, the way the atmosphere is heated causes characteristic circulation patterns that control its gross behavior. The movement of air determines the distribution of energy in the atmosphere, as well as the earth's weather and climate. It controls whether pollutants introduced into the atmosphere are mixed or stagnate in place. The atmosphere's optical properties determine the amount of light that reaches the surface of the earth and therefore the amount and spectrum of light available both for photosynthesis and for heating the lower atmosphere.

Thermal Characteristics

It is useful to compare the atmosphere with a lake. A lake is heated from above and stratifies for most of the year. Once stratified, the upper and lower portions circulate within themselves, but little or no material passes between them. The atmosphere, on the other hand, is heated from below. Solar energy is absorbed both by atmospheric particles and by the ground surface. Because the particle density is greatest near the ground, most energy absorption is at the base of the atmosphere. Some of this energy is re-emitted as infrared radiation. This may, in turn, be reabsorbed by other particles. Roughly 6% of the energy that enters the troposphere as light is intercepted and contributes to maintaining the temperature of the biosphere at a level suitable for life before it is reradiated back out into space as unavailable heat.

The atmosphere is heated from the bottom, like a kettle of water on a stove. As a result, it can circulate very freely over great heights under some conditions; at other times it is stagnant. As air rises its temperature declines, even if it gains or loses no energy in transit. The rate at which the temperature drops is roughly linear from the earth's surface to the top of the troposphere. The observed rate of this decline with increasing altitude is termed the *lapse rate*.

The lapse rate has a special significance in the hypothetical case where air is lifted without the addition or subtraction of energy. As the air rises its temperature declines at a precisely measurable rate, the *adiabatic lapse rate*. This decline is the result of the relationship of pressure, temperature, and volume of a gas. The adiabatic lapse rate is approximately 10°C per kilometer for dry air and 3.6°C per kilometer for moist air. The average is about 6.6°C per kilometer. The difference in rate between wet and dry air is caused by the fact that moist air is lighter than dry air, so that an equivalent change in altitude results in a smaller change in pressure for moist air.

The adiabatic lapse rate gives a standard against which the actual lapse rate can be compared. If the adiabatic lapse rate is greater than the actual lapse rate, this is equivalent to saying that if one were to take a quantity of real air and somehow raise it from one level to another, the temperature would drop relatively more than the actual air in the atmosphere. It would thus be relatively more dense than the gas around it, and hence would sink back to its original level. Under these conditions, the atmosphere is stable and will tend not to mix. If, on the other hand, the adiabatic lapse rate is less than the actual lapse rate, the temperature drop as one raised a quantity of air would be relatively less than would actually have been the case. The air would thus be warmer and less dense than that around it, and it would continue to rise. Under these conditions, the atmosphere is unstable and will tend to mix.

Comparing the actual and adiabatic lapse rates can tell quite a bit about the stability of the atmosphere. The air is a sufficiently fluid medium that if everything were equal it would mix until the actual lapse rate was equal to the adiabatic lapse rate. This is not the case, because of the temporal pattern by which the atmosphere is heated and because of the movements of large air masses.

Let us follow the uptake and release of energy by the atmosphere through a single day. If at the beginning of the day the actual and adiabatic lapse rates are the same, the atmosphere is fairly stable. Energy from the sun is absorbed by the soil, rocks, and the lowest portion of the atmosphere. The air near the ground is heated, causing it to expand and become less dense. It rises as a result and mixes with the air immediately above it. As the day continues, the lower atmosphere absorbs progressively more and more energy and the lapse rate continues to increase. The atmosphere is unstable, and winds tends to be moderate (Figure 9.1).

As night approaches, the amount of energy absorbed near and on the ground decreases. The lower atmosphere becomes colder as its stored energy is reradiated as infrared. Before too long the ground has cooled off, and enough energy has been redistributed that the lapse rate is equal to or less than the adiabatic lapse rate. Air does not move vertically, and the air is calm. If the air is moist the temperature may fall below the dew point, so that condensation near the ground forms an evening ground fog. It is not uncommon for the ground to cool off to such a degree that the lowest part of the atmosphere is actually cooler than the overlying portions; this is termed a *radiation inversion*. It is called an inversion because the lapse rate is positive rather than negative (Figure 9.1c). It is a radiation inversion because it is caused by the reradiation of stored energy from the ground and the absorption of the energy by relatively higher portions of the lower atmosphere.

Pressure Cells.   The radiation inversion is not the only kind of temperature inversion; nor is it the type with the most serious consequences. But before we can discuss other kinds of inversions, we must first touch on the origin and behavior of pressure

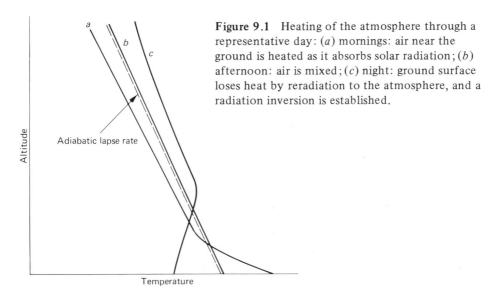

Figure 9.1   Heating of the atmosphere through a representative day: (*a*) mornings: air near the ground is heated as it absorbs solar radiation; (*b*) afternoon: air is mixed; (*c*) night: ground surface loses heat by reradiation to the atmosphere, and a radiation inversion is established.

Adiabatic lapse rate

Altitude

Temperature

cells. These are not controlled by local heating and cooling of the atmosphere. Rather they depend on its global circulation. The basic pattern of global atmospheric circulation is shown in Figure 9.2. In the equatorial regions, wind tends to blow from the east and toward the equator. In the temperate zones, the wind direction tends to be westerly and toward the equator.

Diagrams such as Figure 9.2 are oversimplified. They illustrate the aggregate picture of prevailing wind directions, but the actual pattern of wind movement in time and space is much more complex. Disruptions in atmospheric flow termed *baroclinic waves* can be initiated, causing an undulation in the boundary between two regions. The wave is often strong enough to spin off a mass of air from one zone and send it into the adjoining one. Examples include hurricanes and typhoons, which are spun off the tropical wind systems into the temperate zones, and massive cold fronts that enter the temperate zones from the polar regions. These air masses may be either low-pressure or high-pressure bodies, depending on whether the atmospheric pressure within them is greater or less than the pressure of the surrounding air.

Pressure cells have at least two significant effects. They are responsible for major changes in weather over short periods of time. The passage of a cold front, for example, can cause temperatures to drop 10° to 20°C in many parts of the temperate zone, as well as causing rain, snow, sleet, or hail. On a broad scale, spinning off pressure cells from one circulation zone into another is the main mechanism for the transfer of heat from the equator to higher latitudes. Over a year, the tropics radiate less heat than they receive in insolation, while the poles radiate much more. On a more local scale, the movement of pressure cells alters the temperature distribution of the atmosphere. When high-pressure air enters a region, it represents a greater mass of air than was previously present. Because air is a compressible fluid, the high-pressure air may ride over the lower-pressure air and compress it somewhat (Figure 9.3). If the high-pressure air is colder, the overriding is due mainly to frictional drag, and it is not extensive. The

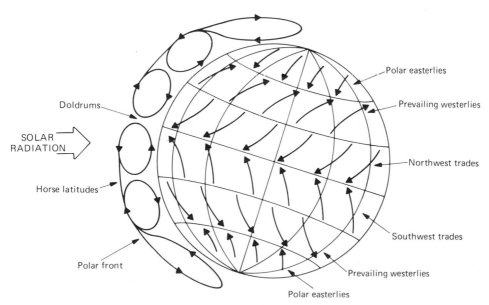

Figure 9.2 Basic patterns of global atmospheric circulation.

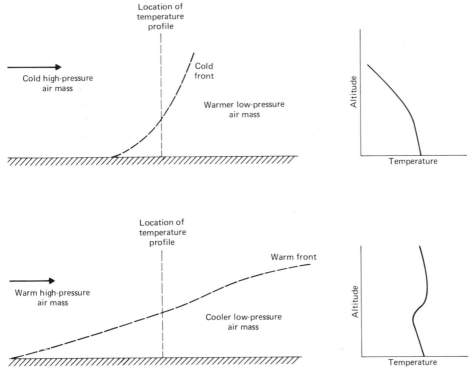

Figure 9.3 Diagram of cold and warm high-pressure cells entering an area character-ized by lower-pressure air at moderate temperature.

cold air overlying the warm air leads to a lapse rate considerably higher than the adi-abatic lapse rate, causing substantial instability and subsequent mixing. This is one rea-son for the high winds that accompany passage of a cold front.

If the high-pressure air is warmer than the air previously in the area, it advances above it. Warm high-pressure air overlying cooler air gives a lapse rate considerably less than the adiabatic rate, which tends to preclude turbulent mixing of the air masses. If the high-pressure air is warm enough, an inversion may become established. This is called a *subsidence inversion,* because the mass of warm high-pressure air enters the region and compresses (i.e., causes to subside) the cooler air already present. This type of inversion lasts longer than a radiation inversion, and it may have serious conse-quences if it occurs during a period of heavy urban air pollution.

The Atmosphere and Climatic Change. The global climate depends on the way heat is absorbed by the lower atmosphere. Both negative and positive feedback mecha-nisms exist to stabilize and to destabilize the climate as human activity changes the heat-absorption properties of the atmosphere. As its temperature increases, the amount of energy reradiated into space as infrared increases as well. This reradiation follows the Stefan-Boltzman Law and is proportional to the fourth power of the absolute tem-perature. This means that any tendency for the earth's temperature to increase or decrease would be counteracted by great increases or decreases in energy reradiated to space.

Most human emissions into the atmosphere show a positive feedback interaction with atmospheric temperature. Their effects are contradictory, however, so that their aggregate influence is not at all clear. For example, water vapor absorbs infrared radiation very strongly, converting it to atmospheric heat. The more water vapor there is in the atmosphere, the more infrared radiation is absorbed, and the warmer the atmosphere. However, as the atmosphere gets warmer, more water vapor evaporates from the surface and less condenses into clouds. So there is a very strong positive feedback interaction between atmospheric temperature and the water vapor in the atmosphere. A similar effect is shown by carbon dioxide, which also absorbs infrared radiation strongly.

Conversely, there is a strong positive feedback interaction between temperature and snow. Snow has a much higher *albedo,* or reflectivity, than most materials at the earth's surface. A decline in temperature can increase the amount of snow cover and allow it to last longer. The increased albedo would decrease the amount of energy absorbed at the surface and thereby bring further decline.

Cloudiness can either warm or cool the climate by absorbing infrared radiation or by increasing the albedo. The actual effect of clouds depends on several things including cloud height, amount of cloudiness, and the size and optical density of individual clouds. The atmosphere may respond in several different ways, and it is not at all clear what the net effect can be expected to be.

Roughly three quarters of the world is covered with oceans. Their immense size and the high heat capacity of water gives them a powerful role in regulating the earth's temperature. The oceans can store or give up immense quantities of heat, and hence confer a tremendous inertia onto incipient temperature change. This inertia is so great and so far beyond human control that it can delay warning signals of impending changes until they are inevitable. If, as many people fear, the buildup of carbon dioxide in the atmosphere is leading to an increase in heat absorption by the earth, so much of the heat would be stored in the deep ocean that global equilibrium would be delayed by decades. People would be powerless to stave off the warming of the earth to reach that equilibrium.

Optical Properties

If the energy balance of the earth is controlled by the atmosphere's thermal characteristics, the amount of the incident radiation that reaches the ground is determined by the atmosphere's optical properties. Two things may divert light radiation as it passes through the atmosphere. It may either be absorbed or get scattered by particles. In the first case, the electromagnetic radiation is transformed into kinetic energy of the absorbing molecule. In the second, it is reflected in a direction other than the original.

There is a continuous gradient of particle sizes in the atmosphere from very, very small to quite large (Figure 9.4). The smallest are on the order of 10^{-4} to 10^{-3} microns (1 micron (μ) = 10^{-6} meters). These include gas molecules such as oxygen, nitrogen, argon, and carbon dioxide as well as some small ions. At the other end of the range is dust, which comprises particles in the range of 10 to 100 μ. All of the particles below 0.1 μ are quite small relative to the wavelength of light (the wavelength of green light, for example, is 0.55 μ). They exhibit the phenomenon of Rayleigh scattering, which is characteristic of particles smaller than light waves.

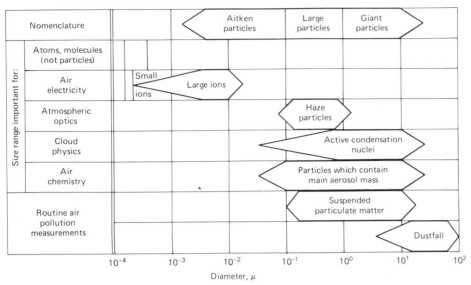

Figure 9.4 Sizes of atmospheric particulate matter of different sizes. Ranges of particle diameter are indicated in microns. [Redrawn, with permission, from Corn, Nonviable particulates in the air, Ch. 3 in Stern, ed., *Air Pollution*, 2nd ed., vol. 1. Copyright © 1968 Academic Press, Inc.]

Rayleigh scattering has little effect on the actual amount of light reaching the ground, but it causes short wavelength light to be much more intensely scattered than longer wavelength light. Thus, the portion of the visible light spectrum with the shortest wavelength (blue) is more highly scattered than the rest of the spectrum. This is why the sky is blue and also why the sky appears black from outer space, which contains no particles capable of Rayleigh scattering.

The scattering efficiency of particles over 1 μ. in diameter is inversely proportional to the wavelength of the light being scattered, so that blue light is scattered much more than the other colors of visible light. It is for this reason that the sun viewed through a dense haze may appear reddish. The shorter wavelengths have been scattered out of the path, while the red wavelengths have not. It is also why sunsets are red and are most prominently developed during dusty or hazy conditions. When the sun is very low on the horizon, even moderate scattering will remove blue light from the insolation. The spectral dependence is not very strong, however, so that the color of the light scattered by particles in this size range is often a warm gray-white.

The scattering properties of particles in the 0.1 to 1.0 μ. range are considerably more complicated than those for either the smaller or the larger particles. This size range also includes the particles of greatest interest not only with regard to light scattering but also for chemical adsorption or optical absorption. Their scattering properties include features of both extremes, and we need not go into any greater detail in this book.

The attenuation of light by airborne particles is the most significant influence of the atmosphere's optical characteristics. Remarkably small amounts of material can scatter light beyond the ability of the average eye to discriminate objects. An average of 1.2 grams of material dispersed through a cube one meter on a side attenuates light so much as to make objects virtually invisible through the cube. Or 1.2 grams of material dispersed through a column with a base area of one square meter is sufficient to render objects indistinguishable through the column. Under clear conditions, with aerosol concentrations on the order of 30 μg/m^3, visibility is on the order of 40 km. (i.e., the column would be 40 km. long). With smoggy conditions and aerosol concentrations of 1,000 μg/m^3, visibility is down to slightly over 1 km. The average figure of 1.2 gm/m^3 has been verified in numerous cities. The range extends from 0.6 to 2.4.

Nucleation Particles

Atmospheric particles serve a critical function as nucleation particles. They are the "seed" around which raindrops coalesce. Raindrops cannot form in an absolutely clean atmosphere unless the atmosphere contains several times the saturation concentration of water. This is because of the surface energy characteristics of a water droplet. Water adheres to a particle in the atmosphere very much as it adheres to a soil particle (Figure 6.2). It is easy to strip off the outer molecules, but it gets increasingly difficult as the particle itself is reached. What if there were no nucleation particle at all? Or if the nucleation particle were itself a water droplet? There is a critical nuclear size for a droplet of any pure compound. If the nucleus is larger than this, it can lose molecules and retain its identity. But when it reaches its critical size, the loss of a single additional molecule will destroy the stability of the particle and it will revert to its molecular (gaseous, in the case of water) state.

It would also be virtually impossible to start from the other end and attempt to put two water molecules together to form a particle and then add one, and then another, and so on, until the critical size was reached. Molecules of gases tend not to adhere to one another. Indeed, the repulsion among them increases with the size of the building nucleus up to the critical nuclear size. This creates a substantial energy barrier that must be crossed in order to form an airborne droplet. However, water can easily adhere to a nucleation particle that is larger than the critical size. This is especially true if the particle is hygroscopic (i.e., it attracts water), as are many of the solid particles in the air. Once a nucleation particle surface is covered by a layer of water molecules, it behaves like a water droplet of the same diameter. The energy barrier to producing the droplet is thus completely avoided.

The most obvious results of nucleation are cloud formation and rainfall. Even the distribution of rainfall appears in part a function of the distribution of nucleation particles, and the chemical properties of rainfall may also be related to their chemistry. In a sense, the formation of raindrops in the atmosphere is subject to limiting factors much as the development of biological populations is. Insufficient water vapor precludes formation of additional raindrops. But suitable nucleation particles are often limiting, and increasing their number will increase the formation of water droplets. This is the logic behind cloud-seeding, even in arid areas. The droplets formed around each nucleation particle may be too small to fall as rain by themselves, but small raindrops can coalesce into larger raindrops that can fall.

The aerosols produced by heavy concentrations of industry represent nucleation particles that would not have been there under natural conditions. The result is in-

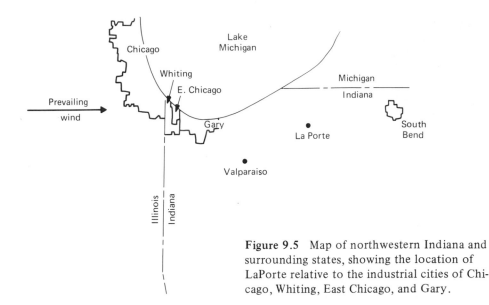

Figure 9.5 Map of northwestern Indiana and surrounding states, showing the location of LaPorte relative to the industrial cities of Chicago, Whiting, East Chicago, and Gary.

creased cloudiness downwind from the industrial center and perhaps increased precipitation. The best documented example of this is the LaPorte, Indiana, weather anomaly (Changnon, 1968). LaPorte is roughly 65 km. directly downwind from the heavy steel and petrochemical industrial districts of Chicago, Whiting, and Gary (Figure 9.5). Figure 9.6 shows a pronounced relationship between rainfall in LaPorte and the number of smoke-haze days in Chicago. The same correlation is shown neither in Valparaiso, which is southwest of LaPorte and not directly downwind from the industrial districts, nor in South Bend, which is 80 km. east of LaPorte.

It has been cogently argued by Changnon and others that nucleation particles generated by industry in the Chicago-northwest Indiana industrial area cause formation of rain droplets that would not otherwise have formed, and that they accrete to a point where they are capable of falling as rain by the time they reach LaPorte. Thunderstorms and hail are also stronger and more pronounced in the LaPorte area than they are at other meterological stations in the region. A similar effect has been seen downwind from St. Louis (Changnon, 1979).

Nucleation particles are not necessarily chemically inert. Many are derived from industrial processes and are chemically acid or can serve as adsorption substrates for acid gases and liquids. The most common examples are oxides of sulfur and nitrogen adsorbed into pieces of flyash. When raindrops form around these particles, the acid dissolves in the water, giving the raindrop a very low pH. Acid rain has often been recorded with a pH equivalent to that of vinegar, and rainfall with a pH below 2.4 has been measured in Pennsylvania and Scotland. It can be so acidic as to kill fish and plants and promote nutrient leaching from soils. Most of the acidity in the rain comes from sulfuric and nitric acids (Frohlinger and Kane, 1975), and acid rain is entirely anthropogenic in origin (Galloway et al., 1976). It is not uncommon for rainfall downwind from an industrial district to have a pH as low as 2.1, with an average of about 4 (Likens and Bormann, 1974; Likens et al., 1979). Indeed, a number of lakes in southern Sweden are in grave danger because of the toxicity of the acid rain derived from

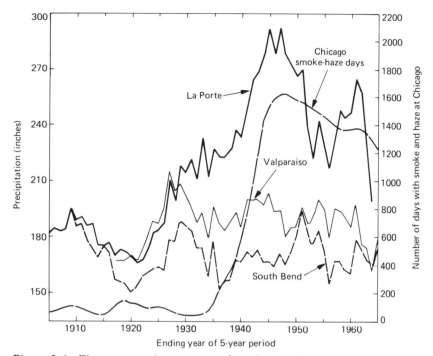

Figure 9.6   Five-year moving averages of total precipitation at several stations in north-western Indiana shown in Figure 9.5, and the number of days in Chicago with smoke or haze. Data are for a 60-year interval. [Redrawn, with permission, from S. A. Chang-non, Jr., The LaPorte weather anomaly: fact or fiction? *Bull. Am. Meteorol. Soc.,* 49: 4–11, 1968. Copyright © 1968 by American Meteorological Society.]

sources in Great Britain and Germany. Norwegian studies have confirmed the industrial sources of the acid rain (e.g., Lunde et al., 1976). In North America, acid rain has acidified several hundred lakes in the Adirondack Mountains of New York and the LaCloche Mountains of Ontario so much that they are devoid of fish. Thousands of other lakes on the continent have been threatened.

CHEMICAL CHARACTERISTICS

The normal atmosphere is composed of a wide variety of gases (Table 9.1). Most are present in very small quantities. Many of the elements have important chemical roles in the biosphere, but their average concentration in the atmosphere is fairly constant. Some of the components are capable of reacting with each other, but the reactions that are most important in human ecosystems require some input of energy. Even if a given reaction shows a net energy gain, it needs an investment of energy to allow it to take place.

The atmosphere has a potent source of energy in the form of sunlight. Photochemical reactions are powered by inputs of solar energy, and they are prominent in the

Table 9.1   Composition of the Dry Atmosphere, by Volume.

Constituent	Percentage
Nitrogen (N_2)	78.084
Oxygen (O_2)	20.9476
Argon (Ar)	0.934
Carbon Dioxide (CO_2)	0.0314*
Neon (Ne)	0.001818
Sulfur Dioxide (SO_2)	0.0001*
Helium (He)	0.000524
Methane (CH_4)	0.0002*
Krypton (Kr)	0.000114
Nitrous Oxide (N_2O)	0.00005
Hydrogen (H_2)	0.00005
Xenon (Xe)	0.0000087
Nitrogen Dioxide (NO_2)	0.000002*
Ozone (O_3)	0–0.000007*

*Highly variable.

After U.S. Air Force, 1965.

atmosphere. For example, ozone (O_3) is formed when an oxygen molecule (O_2) absorbs a photon of solar energy and breaks up into two oxygen atoms. The oxygen atom is very reactive, and it tends to react with the first thing it collides with. If that is another oxygen atom (perhaps the one from which it originally split), it will reform an oxygen molecule. It can form an ozone molecule instead, however, if it strikes an oxygen molecule. An ozone molecule can absorb a photon of light and split into an oxygen molecule and an oxygen atom. What results is a dynamic balance among oxygen atoms, molecular oxygen, and ozone, with a fairly constant and steady state level for all. This balance is entirely natural; indeed, life as we know it depends on the existence of the ozone layer in the lower stratosphere to shield the surface from ultraviolet radiation. Many anthropogenic emissions react photochemically in a similar way. Some of the most significant phenomena in air pollution result from these reactions.

The most common ways for sulfur to be introduced into the atmosphere are as hydrogen sulfide (H_2S) and sulfur dioxide (SO_2), released by combustion of sulfur-containing fuels such as coal or heavy oil. Hydrogen sulfide is released when combustion is not complete. But it is unstable in the open air and reacts very quickly to form sulfur dioxide (SO_2). This is a heavy noxious gas that is fairly toxic and combines readily with water to form sulfurous acid (H_2SO_3). Sulfur dioxide in the atmosphere does not react readily with oxygen. But it can absorb a photon of light and become "excited." This means that the molecule is characterized by a higher than normal level of energy, so that if it collides with an oxygen molecule it can break it apart and react with it to form sulfur trioxide (SO_3). This is much more toxic than sulfur dioxide, and it has a strong attraction for water molecules. These may be either liquid or vapor, and they react with the sulfur trioxide to form sulfuric acid (H_2SO_4). Sulfuric acid is a highly stable and very strong acid. It is itself hygroscopic, and a bit of sulfuric acid adsorbed onto a piece of flyash is an excellent nucleation particle. Any raindrops that form around such a particle, however, will have a very low pH.

Photochemical excitation of sulfur dioxide molecules is not the only way in which atmospheric sulfur trioxide is formed. Several catalysts can also expedite this reaction. A particle with positively charged ion exchange sites can adsorb sulfur dioxide, and it can catalyze the formation of sulfur trioxide from it. Appropriate particles include most of those produced by an industrial civilization, including flyash and steel mill emissions as well as windblown topsoil. Sulfur dioxide adsorbed onto particulate matter also has important public health connotations.

Photochemistry of Nitrogen Oxides

Nitrogen and oxygen together comprise 99% of the atmosphere. They normally occur in their molecular form (N_2 and O_2). But seven oxides of nitrogen are known, of which three are relatively common in the atmosphere: nitrous oxide (N_2O), nitric oxide (NO), and nitrogen dioxide (NO_2). The first is the most common of the three, and its concentration is essentially the same in both city and country. It is a normal constituent, and it seems not to be involved with the photochemical reactions in which the other two play such a large part.

Nitric oxide (NO) is a colorless, odorless gas that is a primary product of very high-temperature high-pressure combustion processes in which molecular oxygen and nitrogen combine. The only places in the biosphere where significant amounts of NO can form are in high-temperature combustion processes (over $1100°C$) such as the internal combustion engine or industrial furnaces. Nitric oxide can react with an oxygen molecule to form a very unstable nitrogen trioxide (NO_3) molecule. This substance commonly decomposes immediately into NO and oxygen. But if it should collide with a second NO molecule it may react to form two molecules of NO_2.

It is obviously difficult for NO_2 to form under normal atmospheric conditions, and we could ignore it entirely if atmospheric conditions in human ecosystems were normal. Indeed the high-temperature, high-pressure conditions required to form NO_2 are precisely those that are most conducive to the breakdown of NO_3. The only way one could expect the latter to be sufficiently common to react with NO would be to have a relatively high concentration of NO (a product of high temperature and pressure) together with large amounts of oxygen, and temperatures low enough so that the NO is not excessively unstable. To form NO_2 from NO and NO_3, relatively high concentrations of both reactants are essential. Few places meet these criteria. One that does is the automobile exhaust pipe. When exhaust gases are ejected into the atmosphere, they are diluted by ambient air by a factor of about 1,000 in the space of seconds. During the dilution process temperatures become much lower than in the combustion chamber, allowing a relatively high concentration of NO_3 and maintaining the concentration of NO sufficiently high that roughly 10% can be transformed to NO_2.

Photochemical Smog

Nitrogen dioxide can be regarded as the fuel that drives a series of photochemical reactions involving a host of organic compounds. Most of these compounds are hydrocarbons, but more complex molecules are formed in the atmosphere and can undergo further reactions. In addition, the photochemical interaction of NO_2 and oxygen can produce ozone. The result of these reactions is the irritating chemical soup known as photochemical (Los Angeles type) smog.

Three basic groups of hydrocarbons are found in the atmosphere (Figure 8.20). The saturated hydrocarbons include all compounds made of carbon and hydrogen in which only a single chemical bond joins adjacent carbon atoms. These are not highly reactive and play little role in atmospheric photochemistry. The unsaturated non-aromatic compounds include those that have one or more pairs of adjacent carbon atoms connected by two or three chemical bonds. These are especially important in atmospheric photochemistry. The aromatic hydrocarbons are built around the benzene ring. They contain double bonds between adjacent carbon atoms, but they behave somewhat differently from the other unsaturated hydrocarbons. The aromatics have a role in atmospheric photochemistry, but it is not as pronounced as that of the unsaturated hydrocarbons.

Nitrogen dioxide, ozone, and hydrocarbons come together to produce one of the most complex sets of chemical reactions occurring in any ecosystem save those involved in life itself. It includes both stable and unstable molecules, as well as a series of extraordinarily unstable, reactive entities called *free radicals*. Photochemical smog can be regarded as a series of reaction cycles in which reactive entities are consumed and then regenerated, occasionally producing something that either has physiological importance or is able to increase or decrease the reaction rate of one or more of the cycles.

The basic raw materials are NO_2 and hydrocarbons. The products of the airborne photochemistry include a group of reactive molecules and free radicals termed *oxidant*. This group includes ozone and is capable of attacking a broad range of materials, from rubber to plants to people's nasal tracts. Other products include irritating ketones, aldehydes, organic acids, and more complex irritants such as peroxyacetyl nitrate (PAN). Metallic catalysts found as airborne particles enable simple compounds to polymerize to form long-chain solid organic molecules. These may be taken into the lungs, where they can cause some damage, and they also reduce visibility.

The mechanism for photochemical smog generation is exceedingly complex and could not be anticipated on the basis of the normal chemistry of the primary atmospheric pollutants (hydrocarbons and NO_2). The most toxic and irritating constituents of smog are the secondary aldehydes, ketones, and PAN. The reaction is self-sustaining. Once things get started, there is a snowball effect as more NO_2 is produced within the smog. The amount of secondary pollutant is limited only by the level of hydrocarbons and NO vented into the atmosphere and by the amount of sunshine. These factors vary with traffic, industrial production, and the time of day. There is thus a diurnal cycle of smog composition (Figure 9.7). The reactions are so sensitive to so many things (including even the composition of gasoline used in automobiles; Glasson and Tuesday, 1970) that they differ strongly from place to place and from time to time. For a more

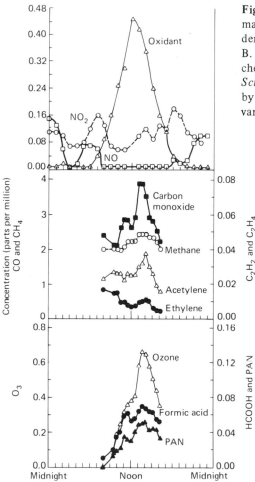

Figure 9.7 Diurnal variation of some primary and secondary pollutants in Pasadena, California, July 25, 1973. [After B. J. Finlayson and J. N. Pitts, Jr. Photochemistry of the polluted troposphere, *Science* 192: 111–119. Copyright © 1976 by the American Association for the Advancement of Science.]

detailed view of the problem the reader is referred to Leighton (1961); Cadle and Allen (1970); Altshuller and Bufalini (1971); and Finlayson and Pitts (1976).

Reducing Smog

Photochemical smog is a highly oxidizing environment characteristic of sunny places with high levels of automotive traffic or petroleum refining. Urban areas characterized by high levels of coal combustion show an entirely different type of secondary air pollution. Chemically it is much simpler than photochemical smog, and it is a reducing rather than an oxidizing environment. It is less irritating in many ways than photochemical smog, but it has been the major factor in thousands of deaths in London as well as in industrial areas of Belgium and the United States. The "killer fogs" of London go back at least to 1873, and they have caused the death of thousands of people. The air pollution disasters in the Meuse Valley of Belgium in 1930 and in Donora, Pennsylvania, in 1948 caused major loss of life and are well documented examples of this kind of smog. Most large industrial cities are very familiar with reducing or London type smog.

The mechanism is quite simple. Sulfur dioxide is produced through the combustion of sulfur containing fuels, commonly coal. Along with particulate matter, it accumulates near the ground during temperature invasions and builds up to high concentrations. Fog may also be part of the mixture trapped beneath the inversion if the air is sufficiently moist. Sulfur dioxide is toxic in its gaseous form, adsorbed onto dry particles and dissolved in fog. A sufficient concentration of solid particles practically guarantees the catalytic oxidation of SO_2 to SO_3 and therefore the formation of sulfuric acid.

These sulfur compounds irritate the respiratory tract. They may lead to coughing or discomfort in a well person; they can be fatal to the sick or elderly. The deaths that have been referred to air pollution incidents have almost without exception been of the vulnerable. Those suffering from respiratory disease, smokers, the elderly, and the very young comprise a disproportionate percentage of deaths.

It is unfortunate that photochemical (Los Angeles type) and reducing (London type) smogs are both referred to by the same word, as their chemistry is totally different. Indeed, because one is oxidizing and one is reducing, they can neutralize each other to some degree. Small amounts of SO_2 can reduce the effect of oxidant and slow the development of photochemical smog. The term *smog* was coined many years ago for the mixture of smoke and fog that characterized London and similar cities during the last few centuries. It originally referred only to reducing smog. Photochemical smog was first noticed in Los Angeles in 1942. The Los Angeles phenomenon was termed smog because it seemed superficially similar to London smog. By the time people realized how different the two phenomena are, the name had stuck.

For various reasons, London type smog is now much less common than it used to be, and photochemical smog is more so. The solid particulate matter that characterizes the former is increasingly rare, as techniques for cleaning coal prior to combustion and for removing flyash fron stack gases improve, and home heating has largely switched from coal to natural gas or oil. But every city in the world shows an increase in automobile, bus, and truck traffic, so that the concentrations of raw materials for photochemical smog are increasing.

SOCIETY AND THE ATMOSPHERE

The interactions between society and the atmosphere include the patterns by which people alter the atmosphere and the effects of those changes on society, as well as what happens to pollutants in the atmosphere.

Pollutant Generation

Practically everything done by human society generates pollutants in one way or another. Our very breathing generates carbon dioxide that would not otherwise be there, and human biological debris such as flecks of exfoliated skin can be found in urban atmospheres. But such basic biological residues are negligible. The activities that generate the bulk of atmospheric pollutants are associated with combustion, manufacturing, and excavation.

Combustion is the most important source of particulate matter, oxides of sulfur and nitrogen, hydrocarbons, carbon monoxide, and secondary pollutants such as smogs. Combustion covers a broad range of societal functions, and it includes a large number of fuels. Among the functions are transportation, space heating, electric power generation, industry, commerce, government and refuse disposal. Among the fuels are coal of all grades, petroleum and natural gas, wood, and peat. Nitrogen oxides can be generated by any type of combustion so long as the temperature is high enough. Sulfur oxide formation is limited to fuels containing sulfur. The worst offender is coal, but many petroleums contain significant amounts, and even natural gas in some regions contains small amounts of hydrogen sulfide. In the same way, particulate matter can be emitted from any fuel containing incombustible matter. Once again, coal is the worst offender. The sand, silt, and clay deposited with and incorporated into coal are released and carried along with particulate carbon out the smokestack as flyash when the coal is burned. Natural gas contains none of this kind of material, and petroleum contains very little. Unburned fuel is also released as particulate matter. Heavier petroleum fuels often produce unburned solid hydrocarbons. These are most noticeable in improperly tuned diesel and jet airplane motors.

Volatile hydrocarbons vaporize when light fuels such as gasoline and natural gas escape from storage tanks or are transferred from one tank to another. Carbon monoxide is discharged when the air-to-fuel ratio is not considerably more than that necessary for complete combustion. Most fixed combustion processes can be tuned so that sufficient air is available for complete combustion. Some CO is vented from these processes, but not in great amounts. Increasing the excess air would decrease CO production, but it would also increase the heat lost up the stack and decrease combustion efficiency. Certain mobile combustion sources such as diesel and jet engines have low fuel-to-air ratios, so that combustion is essentially complete. Table 9.2 summarizes the sources and amounts of production of various pollutants in the United States. They are quite crude, but they represent reasonable order-of-magnitude estimates of the problem.

The Atmosphere of Cities

Most forms of air pollution are urban phenomena, and cities have traits that profoundly affect the character of urban air pollution (Peterson, 1969). Clear and measurable differences between urban and rural atmospheres would exist even if pollution did not (Table 9.3). The city is warmer, drier, dustier, and cloudier. It has less insolation and wind, but greater rainfall (Landsberg, 1962). Many of these factors are interrelated. Dust generated by industries and transport facilities is one of the main causes for the reduction in insolation, and it comprises nucleation particles for clouds and thereby increases the rainfall in or downwind from the urban area.

Cities also reject a great amount of waste heat into the atmosphere. This comes from power generation, industrial activity, transportation, and space heating. Even

Table 9.2 Emissions of Air Pollutants in the U.S. by Source.

Source	Carbon Monoxide	Sulfur Oxides	Particulates	Hydrocarbons	Nitrogen Oxides	Total
Transportation	57.9/66.7	0.7/0.7	1.1/1.2	15.1/11.6	7.3/9.7	82.1/89.9
Stationary source combustion	1.7/0.8	22.1/22.0	8.1/5.4	0.6/1.5	9.1/10.0	41.6/39.7
Industrial processes	8.8/11.5	6.5/5.6	6.8/10.0	4.2/2.8	0.2/0.5	26.6/30.5
Solid waste disposal	7.1/2.2	0.1/0.0	1.0/0.5	1.5/0.5	0.5/0.1	10.2/3.3
Miscellaneous	15.3/4.6	0.5/0.1	8.7/0.7	7.7/11.1	1.5/0.1	33.8/16.6
Total	90.8/85.8	30.1/28.5	25.7/17.7	29.0/27.6	18.7/20.4	194.3/180.0

Data are in million metric tons per year, and are for the years 1968/1974.

Miscellaneous sources include forest fires, agricultural burning, coal waste fires, and gasoline production.

Totals may not add due to rounding.

Data from CEQ, 1970, 1975.

nonindustrial cities produce substantially more waste heat than the surrounding countryside simply because of the energy expended in servicing the larger concentration of people and machines. In addition, cities alter the basic physical character of the landscape. Materials such as concrete, pavement, and building stone absorb and store great quantities of thermal energy because of their high thermal admittance and because of the geometry of roads and buildings. Their energy storage capacity is much higher than that of vegetation and soil in rural areas.

Greater solar energy storage and waste heat rejection combine to make the urban area warmer than rural areas during the day. This difference increases at night. The amount of reradiation is higher, and waste heat continues to be rejected from the city throughout the night (Figure 9.8). Furthermore, most urban areas are characterized by much lower evapotranspiration than rural areas because they tend to have less surface water and because they almost always show a marked reduction in transpiration through green plants. The lower relative humidity that results also tends to increase the temperature of the city.

During the summer, the higher absorbency of the urban environment is the chief source of the higher temperature. During the winter the heat produced by human activities is more significant. In studies of Berlin and Vienna, Kratzer (1956) shows that waste heat production in urban areas is roughly a third to a sixth the energy of insolation. Figures for Sheffield, England (Garnett and Bach, 1965), and New York City (Bornstein, 1968) show similar results. In Sheffield, the average annual man-made heat is equivalent to roughly a third the total insolation. Waste heat production from combustion alone in Manhattan was 2-1/2 times the solar radiation reaching the ground during the winter. During the summer, however, waste heat production dropped to 1/6

Table 9.3 Characteristics of Urban Air Compared with Rural Air.

Temperature:	
Annual mean	.5–.8°C higher
Winter minima	1.1–1.6°C higher
Relative humidity:	
Annual mean	6% lower
Winter	2% lower
Summer	8% lower
Dust particles	10 times more
Cloudiness:	
Clouds	5–10% more
Fog, winter	100% more
Fog, summer	30% more
Radiation:	
Total insolation	15–20% less
Ultraviolet, winter	30% less
Ultraviolet, summer	5% less
Wind speed:	
Annual mean	20–30% lower
Extreme gusts	10–20% lower
Calms	5–20% more
Precipitation:	
Overall amounts	5–10% more
Days with less than .5cm	10% more

After Landsberg, 1962.

the insolation. This compares with about a sixfold decline in total daily insolation from summer to winter.

The geographic concentration of heat in urban areas is the basis of the well-known phenomenon of the *urban heat island* (Figure 9.9). But the establishment of a heat island is more complex than simply the local accumulation of heat released from combustion processes and greater absorption of solar radiation. These factors alter the local air circulation patterns to stabilize the concentration of heat and give it a permanence that it would not otherwise have. A heat island is a three-dimensional phenomenon. Circulation is contained, especially during the night, so that the wind near the ground tends to flow toward the central city from all directions. It rises in the areas of greatest heat production and settles at the periphery (Figures 9.10 and 9.11; Porter, 1963; Findley and Hirt, 1969), to entrap all the emissions of the city in the urban circulation system. The containment of circulation is especially pronounced at night when it is compounded by a radiation inversion, but it can also be maintained on windless days when aerosols at the top of the heat island form a well-defined cap known as the dust

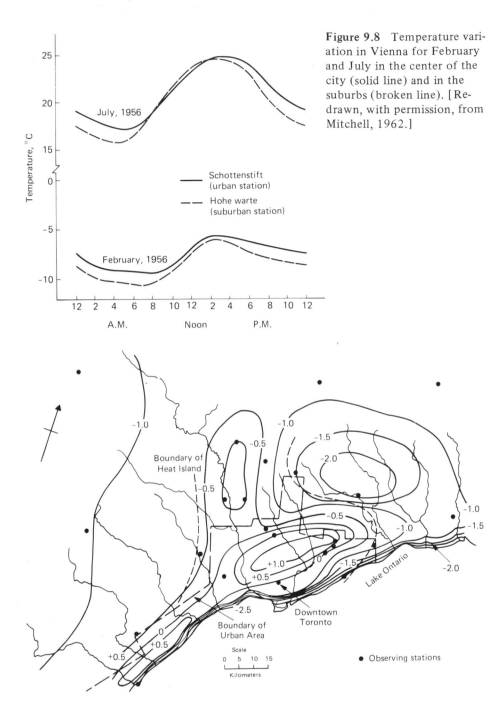

Figure 9.8 Temperature variation in Vienna for February and July in the center of the city (solid line) and in the suburbs (broken line). [Redrawn, with permission, from Mitchell, 1962.]

Figure 9.9 Heat island in Toronto, February 23, 1966. Contours show maximum temperature in degrees Celsius relative to the maximum temperature at the downtown Bloor Street gauge. The dashed line approximates the boundary of the heat island. [Redrawn, with permission, from B. F. Findlay and M. S. Hirt, An urban-induced meso-circulation, *Atmos. Environ.* 3: 537–542. Copyright © 1969 Pergamon Press, Ltd.]

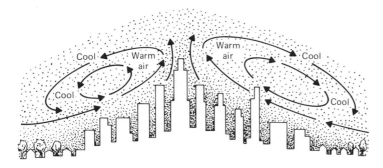

Figure 9.10 Diagram of contained air circulation in a city. [Redrawn, with permission, from American Lung Association, 1969.]

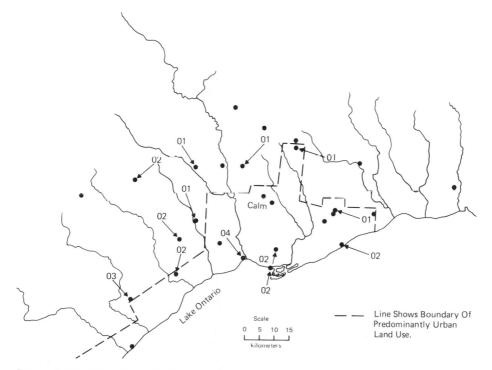

Figure 9.11 Direction of winds in Toronto with velocities in meters per second at 1:00 P.M. on February 23, 1966. Compare with Figure 9.9, which shows the surface temperatures at the same time, and Figure 9.10. [Redrawn, with permission, from B. F. Findlay and M. S. Hirt. An urban-induced meso-circulation, *Atmos. Environ.* 3: 537–542. Copyright © 1969 Pergamon Press, Ltd.]

dome or haze hood, which reflects a certain amount of solar radiation and prevents the sun from heating the surface air sufficiently to break up the heat island. This effect is most strongly developed during subsidence inversions.

Considerable work has been done on measuring vertical temperature profiles in urban and surrounding rural areas so that the three-dimensional dynamics of the heat island can be studied. Figure 9.12 shows a typical cross-section just before dawn. The normal lapse rate can be found above the dotted line. Beneath this line lies a pronounced inversion down to within 70 m. of the ground.

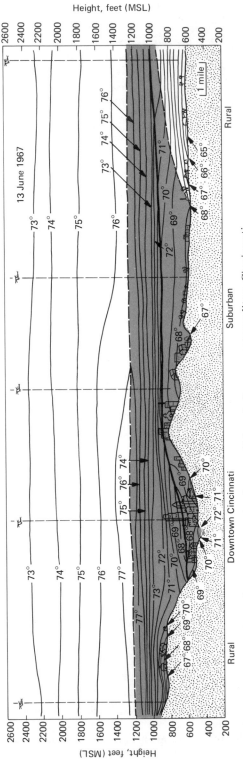

Figure 9.12 Cross section of temperature in degrees Fahrenheit over metropolitan Cincinnati about 1 hour before sunrise on June 13, 1967. The heavy solid line indicates the top of the urban boundary layer, and the dashed lines indicate a temperature discontinuity with less stable overlying stable air. Wind flow is from left to right. [Redrawn, with permission, from Clarke, 1969.]

The reinforcement of normal inversions by the urban heat island influences the distribution of air pollutants within cities. Because pollutants are produced within the city, their concentration is higher than in rural areas to begin with. But when they are trapped by an inversion layer and concentrated by local circulation cells, they build up and are not dispersed by the winds that exist at ground level in rural areas. Thus, the urban heat island magnifies pollutant concentration severalfold over what it would otherwise be.

Because the heat island is characterized by relatively stable air near the ground, it can be broken up only by relatively strong winds. The strength of the wind needed to break up a heat island is a useful measure of its intensity. One would expect *a priori* that there would be a relationship between city size and the critical wind speed needed to disperse the associated heat island. This is, in fact, the case (Figure 9.13). These data suggest that the heat island is a fundamental characteristic of all cities, and indeed of any buildup of population over roughly 2,500 people (Oke and Hannell, 1968).

Effects of Air Pollution on Property

Air pollution affects people in many ways. Some are purely economic; some are matters of public health. Of the economic impacts, some are strictly physical or chemical, while others are biological in nature.

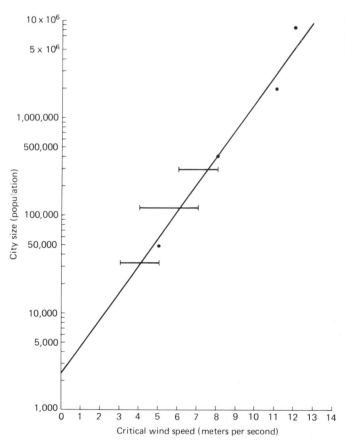

Figure 9.13 Critical wind speeds required for elimination of the heat island effect in cities of various size. [Data from Oke and Hannell, 1968.]

Perhaps the most obvious effect of air pollution is the tarnishing of buildings and implements that results from particulate deposition or chemical reaction with pollutants. From a qualitative viewpoint, no urban dweller needs to be reminded of either of these two phenomena. The dustfall on one's car, for example, is often so high that it must be washed very often. Collars get filthy after a couple of hours' wearing. Silver table utensils react with sulfide in the air to turn black. These phenomena have measurable economic cost. Steel in a polluted environment corrodes at a rate 100 times that of an unpolluted area (Hudson 1943). Different materials corrode at different rates (Table 9.4).

Building stone can be soiled by air pollution, both by deposition of particulate matter on the surface and by actual corrosion of the stone (Figure 9.14) or mortar. Indeed, atmospheric sulfur oxides can support an active and diverse community of bacteria, fungi, and yeasts within building stone, which can rapidly destroy it. (Hansen, 1980). Paint can blister or discolor. Particularly vulnerable to corrosion by acid particles common in polluted urban air are limestone, marble, and lime mortar cementing various kinds of stone. These are forms of calcium carbonate, which is quickly attacked by any acid solution. They are common building materials in many parts of the world because of their great beauty and their high resistance to corrosion in the normal atmosphere. Many modern buildings have been severely damaged by air pollution. Even

Table 9.4   Corrosivity of Atmosphere in Different Places for Steel and Zinc.

Location	Climate	Relative Corrosivity	
		Steel	*Zinc*
Norman Wells, Northwest Territory	Polar-rural	0.03	0.4
Saskatoon, Saskatchewan	Rural	0.6	0.5
Perrine, Florida	Rural	0.9	1.0
State College, Pennsylvania	Rural	1.0	1.0
Ottawa, Ontario	Semirural	1.0	1.2
Middletown, Ohio	Semi-industrial	1.2	0.9
Trail, British Columbia	Semirural	1.4	1.6
Montreal, Québec	Industrial	1.5	2.2
Point Reyes, California	Marine	1.8	1.8
Sandy Hook, New Jersey	Industrial marine	2.2	1.6
New York, New York (spring)	Industrial	3.1	3.6
Halifax, Nova Scotia	Industrial marine	3.8	18.0
New York, New York (fall)	Industrial	6.0	3.7
Daytona Beach, Florida	Marine	7.1	2.6
Kure Beach, North Carolina	Marine (25 m. from sea)	13.0	5.7

Test panels were left at each station for one year. The degree of corrosion is expressed relative to that at State College, Pennsylvania. Note that zinc is sometimes more corrodible than steel, and sometimes less so.

Figure 9.14 Damage to the caryatids of the Erechtheum of the Acropolis in Athens due to modern air pollution.

more serious is the incredible destruction of antiquities made of marble or limestone. Many significant historical buildings have had to be closed for all or most of the time because of air pollution damage.

Textiles can also be damaged by air pollution. Nylon exposed to nitrogen oxides often turns yellow; other fibers actually disintegrate in polluted air. Precisely what happens to the fabric depends mainly on its chemical composition. Open-weave fabrics tend to be more susceptible to pollution damage than tight-weave fabrics, and fibers that get charged electrostatically during normal use, such as when a person walks over certain kinds of rugs on a winter day, attract particulate matter onto them. This exacerbates both soiling by the particulate matter and chemical reactions between the fabric and anything adsorbed onto the particles.

It is difficult to ascribe monetary values to pollution damage, as it cannot be readily differentiated from the wear and tear of normal use. People are apt to accept a certain level of pollution caused damage as normal and ascribe it to ordinary wear. Dollar amounts of pollution damage based on actual observation of unquestionable pollution are almost certain to be underestimates (Liu and Yu, 1978).

One relatively unbiased study of economic losses due to air pollution (Michelson and Tourin, 1966) compares Steubenville, Ohio, and Uniontown, Pennsylvania. Both lie in the upper Ohio River Valley of the United States. Their socioeconomic and climatic data are generally comparable. Uniontown is a relatively nonindustrial city, with an average particulate concentration of 115 $\mu g/m^3$, while Steubenville is a city with a concentration of heavy industry and a particulate pollution load averaging 235 $\mu g/m^3$. Four categories of economic losses that could be ascribed to particulate pollution were identified: (1) outside maintenance of houses (frequency of painting and cleaning), (2) inside maintenance of houses and apartments (cleaning and replacing of walls, windows, drapes, curtains, venetian blinds, carpets, and furniture), (3) maintenance of clothing (laundering and dry cleaning, distinguishing between summer and winter schedules), and (4) women's hair and facial care. Three types of data were obtained for each category: frequency of the activity in question, the proportion of the population affected by pollution, and the socioeconomic characteristics of the affected popula-

Table 9.5 Differences in Cleaning Costs Incurred at Steubenville, Ohio, over and above those at Uniontown, Pennsylvania.

Activity	Cost Excesses	
	Annual	*Per capita*
Outside maintenance of houses	$ 640,000	$17
Inside maintenance of houses and apartments	1,190,000	32
Laundry and dry cleaning	900,000	25
Hair and facial care	370,000	10
Total	$3,100,000	$84

Data from Michelson and Tourin, 1966.

tion. Table 9.5 summarizes the cost differences between Steubenville and Uniontown. These total to $3,100,000 annual cost for particulate pollution alone, or $84 per capita. A third city, Martins Ferry, Ohio, has a particulate concentration roughly intermediate between those of Uniontown and Steubenville. It was shown to have a cost almost exactly intermediate between those of Uniontown and Steubenville.

In another work by the same investigators (Michelson and Tourin, 1967), three communities in the Washington, D.C., area were studied in the same way as the upper Ohio River Valley cities. Figure 9.15 shows the relationship between pollution measured in suspended particulate matter and the maintenance frequency record for the cities in both studies. There is an obvious correlation between air pollution levels and the maintenance requirements of a normal urban population.

Much damage is also done to industries and to society as a whole. The life expectancy of bridges, roads, and other public works can be substantially reduced because of air pollution. The cost of painting steel structures simply to protect them from corrosion caused by air pollution is well over $100 million per year in the United States

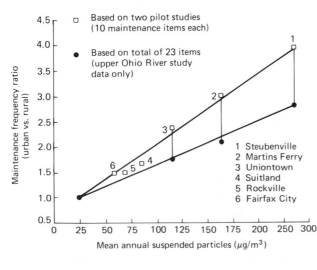

Figure 9.15 Frequency of household maintenance operations plotted against mean annual concentration of suspended particles. Points 1–3 are for 3 cities from the upper Ohio River valley; points 4–6 are for 3 Washington, D.C. area cities. [Redrawn, with permission, from NAPCA, 1969.]

alone. The annual cost of maintaining fabrics by laundering, cleaning, and dyeing is over $850 million per year. Expenditures for car washing to counteract effects of air pollution were $250 million in 1968. Not all of the impacts of air pollution can or should be reduced to dollar costs, but those that can show that the cost is very high.

Effect of Air Pollutants on Organisms

Biological damage from air pollution is varied and widespread. Plants and animals are affected, and the economic significance is high. The effects of air pollution can be seen even in semi-wilderness areas. Particulate matter is the least damaging of the air pollutants to vegetation, but even this can cause damage if dustfall is sufficiently heavy. For example, cement kilns, gypsum processing plants, and similar installations emit vast quantities of particulates that can coat plants and occasionally cause severe damage to them (Sheikh et al., 1976). Dust can prevent germination of pollen, cause reduction in photosynthesis, and reduce growth. The most severe damage to plants is not caused by the particles themselves but by pollutant gases and materials adsorbed onto particles (Kozlowski, 1980). Sulfur oxides, for example, can cause leaf necrosis, or local death of leaf tissue. Some repair can take place if there is sufficient time between fumigations. Cone setting in ponderosa pine can be virtually eliminated by SO_2, and whole forests may be eliminated altogether when sulfur emissions are extreme. This has been the case around smelters in several major mining areas whose ores were sulfide minerals.

Perhaps the most famous example of the destruction of vegetation by sulfur (and to a lesser extent arsenic) emissions is Ducktown, Tennessee, the hub of the copper basin of southeast Tennessee and northwest Georgia. Open-hearth smelting of copper ores beginning around the Civil War emitted great quantities of sulfur and arsenic oxides into the atmosphere. The effect was devastating (Figure 9.16). Some 14,000

Figure 9.16 Destruction of vegetation by smelter fumes from the copper basin of southeastern Tennessee. This photograph was taken some 120 years after the beginning of smelting in this area and at least 50 years after cessation of open hearth smelting.

hectares of timberland were severely damaged and 8,000 hectares were destroyed altogether (Hursh, 1948). Open-hearth smelting ceased many years ago, but the area's vegetation and soil were so destroyed by the original operations that much of the land is still bare, and reforestation is proceeding very slowly.

Nitrogen oxides also have pronounced effects on plant growth and yield. As with those of SO_2, these effects tend to be chronic and typically do not result in plant death. Mixtures of atmospheric pollutants may show synergistic interactions, so that more aggregate damage is done by even small amounts than would otherwise be expected. For example, the growth of pasture grasses is suppressed more by a mixture of SO_2 and NO_2 than by that of either alone (Ashendon and Mansfield, 1978).

Of the hydrocarbons, only ethylene appears to have an important effect on plants. It is an endogenous growth-regulating hormone in very low concentrations, so that plants are extremely sensitive to the relatively high concentration in which it is found in polluted air. Indeed, it has been recognized as a phytotoxicant for over 60 years.

The greatest plant damage done by any of the components of photochemical smog is from ozone and the other oxidants. Many crops are highly sensitive to ozone damage, and yields may be decreased by 50% to 60% (Thompson, quoted by Marx, 1975). Several areas show substantial vegetation damage from air pollution. The truck farming industry in southern California has been badly hurt, and over 40,000 hectares of the San Bernardino National Forest east of Los Angeles show moderate or severe damage. Truck farms in the Boston to Washington corridor have also suffered substantial damage, even though oxidant concentrations are only a third those of the Los Angeles basin. The higher humidity and soil moisture increases the susceptibility of plants to damage.

Air pollutants typically enter plants through leaf stomata. The most common result is leaf necrosis. If the pollution effects do not kill the plant they are nevertheless serious, and necrotic leafy vegetables are spotted and do not sell well at market, even if otherwise perfectly edible. In other cases air pollution leads to yield reduction, so that some areas are no longer economically competitive. These chronic effects have eliminated agriculture from a number of formerly productive areas.

Livestock is affected in a similar way. Chronic effects leading to shortened life, lessened weight gain, and greater illness are all well documented. Respiratory dysfunction in pets and livestock are known, although its extent is not well known. As with other air pollutants, death may result in extreme cases.

For one air pollutant, however, livestock death is the normal result. Airborne fluorides are released from several large-scale industrial installations, including phosphate fertilizer refining plants and aluminum refineries. They are absorbed by vegetation, which typically shows little or no response to increased fluroide content. But when cattle or other livestock eat the grasses, the fluoride is concentrated in the bones and teeth. Bones consist primarily of calcium phosphate, the mineral apatite. This mineral has a number of variants, including one, fluorapatite, which contains a considerable amount of fluorine and is much harder than other varieties. A certain amount of fluorapatite in teeth is desirable, and fluoride is commonly added to toothpastes and public water supplies to increase the fluorapatite content of teeth.

When the fluoride content is so high that it goes to bones as well, the result is serious. Fluorapatite is not only hard, it is brittle. The long bones of the legs of cattle that have fed on high-fluoride grasses are so brittle that walking may cause animals to break their legs. In addition, their jaws can become malformed and brittle. The result is death to the animal either by some accident brought on by the animal's bone structure or because the animal's owner wishes to put it out of its misery.

AIR POLLUTANTS AND PUBLIC HEALTH

Most air pollution related public health problems are respiratory. Figure 9.17 diagrams the human respiratory system. Air enters the nose and the nasal cavity, is sent through the pharynx into the larynx, down the trachea into the bronchi that lead to the two lungs. Within the lungs, each bronchus divides into several bronchioles that terminate in hundreds of small alveoli where gases pass into the bloodstream. These are thin-walled bag-like structures with a very high density of capillaries designed to facilitate the passage of gases into the bloodstream. Gaseous pollutants can enter the alveoli, where they can enter the blood. But unless the pollutant concentration is high, a large percentage is exhaled and the remainder diluted by the next breath. Thus if high pollutant concentration is brief, the resulting toxic gas entering the bloodstream is relatively small.

Particulate matter, on the other hand, can be deposited anywhere along the entire respiratory system. The body has a well-developed mechanism to minimize the deposition of particulate matter. Cilia line the entire respiratory system and beat rhythmically to force particles entering the system back out through the nose. They are fairly successful for relatively large particles (i.e., those over 1 μ in diameter) (Figure 9.18). Most of these particulates are deposited in the nasopharyngeal portion of the respiratory system and do not reach the lungs under normal conditions.

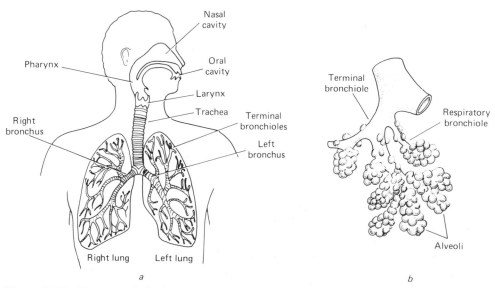

Figure 9.17 Diagram of the human respiratory system: (*a*) overall view; (*b*) detailed view of the terminal bronchioles and alveoli in the lung. [Redrawn, with permission, from NAPCA, 1969.]

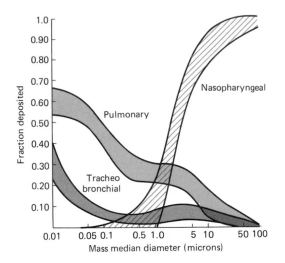

Figure 9.18 Fraction of respired particles deposited in three main parts of the respiratory system, as a function of particle diameter. [Redrawn, with permission, from Task Force on Lung Dynamics: Deposition and retention models for internal dosimetry of the human respiratory tract. *Health Phys.* 12: 173–207, 1966. Copyright © 1966 by Pergamon Press, Ltd.]

Except for gaseous pollutants, this mechanism would be sufficient to keep the lungs fairly clear of particulate air pollution. But the gases adsorbed on particles can narcotize the cilia so that they no longer beat in rhythm and thus can no longer keep particles out. The efficiency of the particle-removal mechanism deteriorates, and an increasing number of particles reach the alveoli. In the lungs as well as in the atmosphere, these particles provide a surface for adsorption of toxic materials. This is one of the main mechanisms by which sulfur and nitrogen oxides are carried into the alveoli, where they can remain long enough to enter the bloodstream.

Most of the damage done by air pollutants is to the lung itself. The most serious of the air pollution related diseases is *emphysema*. The alveoli become distended (Figure 9.19), and the overall surface area of the lungs decreases substantially. Emphysema can be severely debilitating and it can lead to death. Its economic cost (not to mention the pain and suffering it causes) runs into many millions of dollars annually.

It has several causes; the most common are smoking and occupational exposure to toxic materials. Air pollution by itself can lead to chronic emphysema, and it can be a very strong factor in emphysema in people (such as smokers) who are already at a high risk of contracting the disease. A study of autopsies from Winnipeg, Manitoba (a relatively clean city in central Canada with a population of about 265,000), and St. Louis, Missouri (a heavily industrialized city in the central U.S. with a population of 750,000), shows a clear difference that can be ascribed with some confidence to air pollution. Emphysema was 4 times as prevalent among cigarette smokers in St. Louis as in Winnipeg and even 3 times as prevalent among nonsmokers.

Other respiratory diseases caused or exacerbated by air pollution include tuberculosis, bronchitis, lung cancer, pneumonia, and a variety of others. Lave and Seskin (1970) have compared air pollution and socioeconomic factors as causes of various respiratory and other diseases. In virtually all cases air pollution was significantly correlated to disease incidence, and the relationship was closer than that of the socioeconomic factors. Data from Los Angeles County suggest a strong synergism between smoking and neighborhood air pollution as a cause of death from lung cancer (Menck et al., 1974).

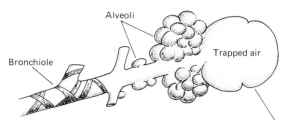

Alveoli

Trapped air

Bronchiole

Broken-down alveolar walls

Figure 9.19 Schematic diagram of the effect of pulmonary emphysema on the alveoli of the lungs. Compare with Figure 9.17. The effects of emphysema are the loss of elasticity of the alveolar walls, followed by their breakdown. [Redrawn, with permission, from American Lung Association, 1969.]

In a detailed study of Chattanooga, Tennessee, high exposure to NO_2 impaired the breathing ability of elementary school children and increased the frequency of acute respiratory illnesses. Several studies have pointed out air pollution related effects on the circulatory and other systems. Monkeys exposed to 15 to 50 ppm of NO_2 for two hours showed damage to the heart, liver, and kidneys roughly in proportion to the dosage (Henry et al., 1969). Long-term exposure of animals to NO_2 has resulted in weight loss and change in voluntary behavior. Petr and Schmidt (1967) found nitrogen oxide induced methemoglobin in the blood of Czech schoolchildren, as well as compensatory responses of the blood cell forming tissues for children exposed to nitrogen and sulfur oxides.

Perhaps the most irritating of the common air pollutants are the aromatic hydrocarbons and the derivative organic compounds produced in photochemical smog. The aromatic hydrocarbons are biochemically active, and some are quite irritating and injurious to the mucous membranes. Benzene poisoning is well known in industrial situations, with symptoms of headache, dizziness, fatigue, loss of appetite, irritability, nervousness, nosebleed, and other types of hemorrhage. Other aromatics are even more powerfully narcotic and more acutely toxic.

The aldehydes and keytones produced in photochemical smog are more reactive and toxic than the hydrocarbons from which they were produced. They attack many parts of the body. Short-chain light aldehydes tend to irritate the eyes and upper respiratory tract, while the heavier and less soluble aldehydes may reach and affect the lungs themselves. Some are allergenic. Some are anesthetics, although aldehyde metabolism in the body is rapid enough that the anesthetic effect does not often show up. Changes in the cell structure of the lung and other organs of the body have also been reported.

The two most common aldehydes in the atmosphere are formaldehyde (HCHO) and acrolein ($C_2 H_3 CHO$). Formaldehyde is very toxic in the high concentrations found in some industrial situations. At the concentrations commonly found in the atmosphere, however, toxicity is not its main effect. It can cause cessation of ciliary activity in the nasopharyngeal system. Pregnancy in rats can be prolonged 14% to 15% by 0.1 ppm, with consequent enlargement of the thymus, heart, kidneys, and adrenals of the offspring (Gofmekler, 1968). Acrolein is more irritating and toxic than formaldehyde or any of the saturated aldehydes. Irritation of eyes and nose can be caused by concentrations as low as 0.25 ppm, and the response is very rapid.

Unfortunately, there is not as much information on acrolein as there is on formaldehyde, since formaldehyde is a common industrial chemical and acrolein is not. But tests do indicate that the two aldehydes have significant synergistic influences on the

Table 9.6   Synergistic Effects of Irritant Aerosols and Several Materials.

Aerosol Synergist	Size	Formaldehyde		Acrolein	
		Concentration	ST_{50}	*Concentration*	ST_{50}
Control (no synergist)			147		87
Triethylene glycol	1.8	2,210	71*	380	73
Ethylene glycol	2.0	2,920	168	500	106
Mineral oil	2.1	1,420	72*	240	69†
Glycerin	2.0	1,280	114*	220	94
Sodium chloride	2.6	2,320	114†	390	71†
Diatomaceous earth	2.9	360	102*	60	99

Formaldehyde had a concentration of 15.375 $\mu g/1$. in all tests; acrolein had a concentration of 16.150 $\mu g/1$. in all tests.

Size refers to the size of the aerosol particles in microns. The synergist aerosols were mixed with formaldehyde and acrolein at the concentrations indicated. Mean survival time (ST_{50}) of mice in each test is noted, for comparison with the control.

*Highly significant synergism. †Moderately significant synergism.

After LaBelle et al., 1955.

irritancy or toxicity of numerous atmospheric pollutants (Table 9.6). There is also evidence that atmospheric chemicals of various sorts can act synergistically with irritants such as acrolein and formaldehyde to increase human eye irritation as well.

AIR POLLUTION CONTROL

Because such a large proportion of air pollution stems from combustion, air pollution control activities have centered on combustion sources. Other sources such as volcanoes, and farmers plowing their fields, may be substantial in some locations. However, they are either not controllable or the most appropriate means of control (e.g., soil conservation) are easier to justify for reasons other than air pollution.

Combustion source controls include precombustion measures, modifications of the combustion process, and postcombustion cleaning. Precombustion controls involve changes in refining, storing, and transporting fuels. Postcombustion controls are attempts to cleanse the exhaust stream, sometimes with some recycling or at least reclaiming some of the chemicals involved.

Precombustion Methods

The most important kinds of precombustion air pollution controls concern the automobile and coal. A certain amount of fuel tends to be lost into the atmosphere from the fuel tank of any motor vehicle. This is one major source of hydrocarbons for photochemical smog. But fuel tanks can be designed, and such design has been mandated for the United States and Canada, in such a way that significantly lower quantities of fuel escape directly into the atmosphere without being burned. Considering that 53% of the petroleum used in North America is for transportation (Hackleman, 1977), this can make a substantial difference in the flux of hydrocarbons into the atmosphere.

Coal is one of our most important fuels, and its role is likely to increase as petroleum and gas prices continue to rise. Coal is highly suited to combustion in large-scale furnaces, but it is also the dirtiest of our common fuels and the greatest single contributor to our most significant air pollution problems. As discussed in Chapter 7, coal can be cleaned so that it is a much better fuel than it is as found in the ground. Flyash consists of the clays and other mineral sediments whose specific gravities are higher than that of carbon. Likewise, sulfur is derived mainly from the mineral iron pyrites, whose specific gravity of 5.0 is considerably higher than the rest of the mineral fraction within the coal. Relatively simple techniques of washing and density separation can, at least in principle, remove most of the most important pollutants in the coal. Other approaches, such as solvent refining, gasification, or liquifaction, represent other ways of cleaning coal.

The logistic problem of cleaning coal is that an immense amount is burned every year. Even providing the water to do it is a considerable task in many areas (Josephson, 1977). It can be done, and it can result in cleaner air. But washing coal creates two other problems. First, whatever sediments (flyash) and sulfides are removed from the coal are physically transferred to the wash water. Both are water pollutants in their own right. Second, the water must be stored for treatment and reclamation for reuse. The conditions for storage of cleaning water are not always very good at mine sites, and dams constructed for the purpose have collapsed with considerable loss of life and property. Thus, cleaning coal involves shifting pollution from one sphere to another. There is an implicit tradeoff between the value of decreasing sulfur and flyash content of coal on the one hand, and greater user costs of coal, increased commitment of land and water to coal treatment, and increased probability for water pollution and dam collapse on the other. To improve conditions in the cities means to risk increased damage in the coal mining areas. This need not mean the simple export of pollution from city to country, but it may.

Other issues are involved, too. Regulations designed to reduce air pollution in cities seldom consider secondary implications, and a common strategy for air quality improvement has been to set standards for air quality or to limit coal sulfur content for specific cities or urban airsheds. Within the eastern United States, for example, this has resulted either in a conversion to oil or gas or a switch from Appalachian high-sulfur coal to the lower-sulfur coal of the Great Plains. The former exacerbates the trend to imported fuels, while the second substitutes high-ash coal for high-sulfur coal and vastly increases the fuel transport costs. It also causes a diversion within the coal industry from the depressed areas of Appalachia, where investment is needed, to a part of the country where the industry is not consistent with the lifestyles of the areas. There has been a reduction in the pollutant emissions from coal fired plants, but it has not been without cost.

Combustion Site Control of Pollution

Air pollution can be controlled to a degree by measures taken at the site of combustion. This is probably the most difficult place to control pollution, however. The experience of the automobile in North America is instructive. Because the automobile is such a small, dispersed polluter, it was virtually essential to control pollution in the engine. The first generation of controls were directed to optimizing the tune of conventional engines to minimize hydrocarbon and carbon monoxide emissions. Air-fuel mixtures were optimized and spark timing was adjusted. But gasoline consumption went up, as did nitrogen oxide production. Even so, it was clear that tuning by itself could not meet the emission requirements that were mandated for the late 1970s. So catalytic converters were put into most automobiles and light trucks sold in North America, beginning in 1975. This allowed the motor to be tuned for fuel efficiency and performance, but it required the use of unleaded fuel so that the catalysts could keep working properly. Other catalysts will probably be able to meet emission requirements for nitrogen oxides. However, the catalysts are not without problems. Their performance cannot be monitored routinely, and the motorist has no way of knowing if they are doing their job. Also, they get very hot in use and automobiles have burned when they were parked over a pile of leaves. The heat from the catalysts ignited the leaves, and the cars were consumed as well.

The only alternatives for combustion control of air pollution generation in automobiles lie in nonstandard engines. One of these, the Honda CVCC, is in widespread use and has had considerable success. Gas turbines and external combustion engines could also meet the emission standards that will be required in North America for the 1980s, but none are now in standard production.

Combustion-site control of coal emissions is not so straightforward, and few full-scale plants are capable of doing it. However, one design of boiler termed the *fluidized bed boiler* suggests that control of sulfur oxides will soon be possible (Josephson, 1978b). Coal is injected into the boiler, and the burning bed is held suspended by forced air. This expedites combustion, and it provides an environment where limestone can be fed in with the coal to react with the SO_2 and H_2S as they are formed. The reaction product is calcium sulfate ($CaSO_4$), which can be treated as a solid waste. This would be a significant development, as other coal emission problems can already be controlled adequately by postcombustion methods.

Postcombustion Control of Pollution

Exhaust gases from combustion processes are typically heavily pollutant-laden. Whatever nitrogen oxides, sulfur oxides, unburned hydrocarbons, and flyash are going to be emitted into the atmosphere are emitted at this point. Cleaning exhaust gases is the final opportunity for pollution abatement. It is not a trivial thing to clean stack gas from a stationary source. Many such installations are industrial or power plant boilers whose air throughput is huge. Control devices must be massive and dependable. Particulate matter is the easiest type of pollutant to remove. The most common particulate-removal device is the electrostatic precipitator.

A typical precipitator is a large, rectangular box through which the stack gases flow horizontally at a rate about 2 m./sec. It contains two sets of electrodes. The *discharge electrodes* are a series of vertical wires that are supplied with a very high voltage, negatively charged, pulsating direct current that forms a corona around them and ionizes the particles in the airstream. The ionized particles are repelled from the discharge electrodes and forced to the *collecting* electrodes, which are thin grounded vertical plates set parallel to the airstream. The charged particles impact on them and remain until a *rapper,* or hammer, knocks the collecting electrodes and dislodges the particles into a hopper beneath. The rappers automatically clean the collecting electrodes every 15 to 25 minutes or so.

The key to the electrostatic precipitator is that the particles in the air stream become and remain highly charged within the charged field. Some are too good as electrical conductors to hold their charge. They lose it when they hit the collecting electrode and become re-entrained in the gas stream. Such particulates commonly go through several cycles of precipitation and re-entrainment before they leave the precipitator, but by that time they have generally agglomerated into particles sufficiently large that they are easily removed by other means (Sproull, 1970, chapter 6). The efficiency of a precipitator depends on two things: its size (i.e., the length through which gases must travel) and the number of replications. The length of a precipitator is commonly increased by adding units. If a given unit is 90% efficient for a particular type of particle, then the emission from one unit contains 10% of the input. If the airstream then enters a second unit, the emission is 1% of the original input. A third unit would emit 0.1% of the original input, and so forth. The airstream is split up in large installations so that gases pass through a battery of precipitators. If one should fail, only a percentage of the treatment would be lost.

The particulates removed from the stack gases must be put somewhere. The precipitated particulate matter constitutes a solid waste, and very little of the particulate matter derived from combustion or industrial processes has a ready use. The electrostatic precipitator can be visualized, among other things, as a way of converting an air pollution problem into a solid waste problem.

A second way to remove larger particles is by the *cyclone.* This is a device that forces air to flow in a spiral fashion and generate enough centrifugal force to remove most particulate matter larger than 5 microns. Where particles are quite large, the cyclone is the cheapest control device.

Another common device for removing particles is the *baghouse.* This is a multiple bag filter consisting of several sets of thin silicone-impregnated fiberglass bags. They are about 1/2–2/3 m. in diameter and 3 to 10 m. long, open at the bottom and closed at the top, but with an opening near the top at one side of the bag. The open end has a gas-tight gate that can be opened or closed. Stack gas is blown into the bag, where the particles are trapped by the fibers much as in a vacuum cleaner. The pores become clogged fairly quickly, so that the pressure required to keep the stack gas moving becomes quite high. Every few minutes the gas flow is diverted to a different set of bags, allowing the first to collapse and drop its dust load to the bottom. Every so often the bags are shaken or cleaned by a ring that moves up and down the bag. During or after cleaning the gate at the bottom of the bag is opened to allow the collected dust to fall into a hopper, from which it can be discarded or reused. The gate is then closed, and the bag is again ready for service. There are typically several bags per unit and several units per baghouse. The exhaust gases are directed first to one unit and then to the next and then to the next, and so on until they return to the first. Each unit has a pre-cise cycle of use followed by cleaning followed again by use. The efficiency of partic-ulate removal is often well over 99%, so that a smokestack is not required.

Still another way of removing particulates—as well as some soluble gaseous contaminants—is the *wet scrubber*. Water is sprayed rapidly into the flue so that it is immediately atomized into a fine mist. The turbulent flow of the stack gases insures that particles will collide with and adhere to the water droplets, forming a slurry that can easily be removed by a cyclone. This slurry is sent to a holding pond, where the dust settles out and the clear water can be pumped back for reuse. Removal efficiency for particulate matter is 90% to 99%.

In principle, scrubbers are also useful for SO_2 removal. There are several tech-niques by which materials such as ground limestone or sodium carbonate are sprayed into the flue along with the water mist so that the SO_2 can react to form a precipitable slurry. Such techniques are required for SO_2 removal in new coal-fired power plants in the United States, but there are substantial problems in retrofitting older plants with scrubbers. The use of scrubbers for SO_2 control is controversial. They are large, expensive, and complex. Some countries, such as Canada, do not regard them as an appropriate means of pollution control for widespread installation (Shaw, 1979). Other countries, such as Japan, have had excellent results with them (Corwin, 1980). Some installations can even use the end product as a profitable commodity, as in a Japanese system that takes the calcium sulfate from the slurry and uses it to make gypsum wallboard (Josephson, 1977).

AIR POLLUTION AND LONG-RANGE CLIMATIC CHANGE

Human alterations of the atmospheric environment have significant long-range con-sequences. Compared with society's ability to wreak havoc on surface waters through water pollution and eutrophication, the long-term implications of air pollution may be very much greater.

We often think of the climate as though it were constant. It is not (Figure 9.20). Even within recorded history climatic conditions have been very different from what they are now. The last great advance of the continental ice sheets was in full swing dur-ing the Upper Paleolithic. Conditions have moderated somewhat since those times, so that by some 3,000 years ago the climate was considerably warmer than during the ice ages and indeed somewhat warmer than at the present time. It cooled off again so that the period from about 1550 to 1850 is often known as the "little ice age" (Schneider and Mesirow, 1976). Records show lower temperatures and heavier snowfall than at present.

But the fluctuations in temperature during human life on the earth are by no means the extremes shown by the geological record, nor do they even indicate the range of possibilities. The first phase of the continental glaciation was somewhat colder than the last, and there is some evidence of a major glaciation some 350 million years ago that was substantially more intense than the recent ice ages. On the other hand, tropical forests covered most of the land area of the earth as recently as 100 million years ago, and all known land areas were characterized by a milder climate than now.

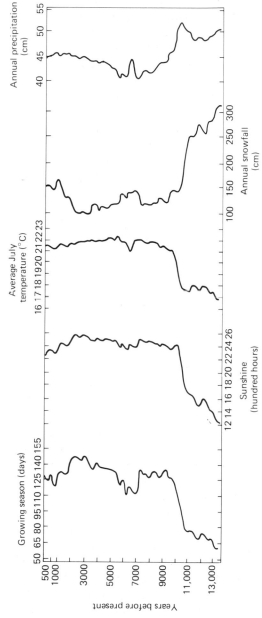

Figure 9.20 Thirteen thousand year record of length of growing season, hours of bright sunshine annually, mean July temperature, annual snowfall, and precipitation during the growing season. All data are for Kirchner Marsh, Minnesota, and are derived from pollen data by canonical transfer functions. [Redrawn, with permission, from R. A. Bryson, A perspective on climatic change, *Science* 183: 753–760. Copyright © 1974 by the American Association for the Advancement of Science.]

The earth's climate appears capable of major changes. And ecosystems are very sensitive to the earth's temperature.

Relatively small changes in average temperature can have very pronounced effects (Bryson, 1974; Wang et al., 1976). A 4°C decline would be felt differently in different places, and it would have a profound long-range effect. The temperature in tropical areas would be relatively stable at first, declining by about 2°. But temperatures in the polar regions would drop by about 8°. This would be sufficient to trigger a full-scale ice age, because of the positive feedback between the albedo of the earth and the area covered by snow. An equal rise in the average temperature would have an equally profound effect. The polar icecaps would melt and cause the sea level to rise by about 60 m. Most of the great cities of the world would be covered by water. Such changes seem extreme, but the geological record shows that the climate is an ephemeral phenomenon in geological time and that changes such as these must be considered inevitable.

Society can manipulate a number of very powerful instruments that can become part of global climate-regulating feedback devices. Some may be negative feedback loops that serve to stabilize the climate, while others may enter into a positive feedback loop in which small perturbations result in rapidly increasing change.

The temperature of the earth rose steadily from 1880 to 1940, but it has fallen equally steadily since then. The initial rise has been attributed to increased absorption of infrared reradiation by higher levels of atmospheric CO_2 resulting from high and increasing rates of combustion of fossil fuels. The fall in the last 30 years has been attributed to the overproduction of atmospheric aerosols that increase the earth's albedo and thereby reduce its insolation and consequent heat capture. Assuming that these explanations are correct, we might expect that whichever phenomenon has more staying power will be the one that determines the short-term development of world climatic trends. Air pollution control is reducing particulate pollution, but there is no parallel decline in CO_2 emissions. If synthetic fuels enter widespread use, we shall see an increase in the rate of CO_2 emissions. We can expect the greenhouse effect to begin to overwhelm the aerosol-albedo effect in that case and for the temperature to turn around again and begin to rise.

Control of the radiation balance is an extraordinarily complex matter. Most studies have concentrated strictly on aerosols and CO_2. But several other anthropogenic chemicals can also cause problems. One of the most interesting are the freons (Ramanathan, 1975), which are exceedingly stable halocarbons (CF_2Cl_2, $CFCl_3$) used in refrigeration units and aerosol cans. They absorb strongly in an infrared bond where the atmosphere is relatively transparent (8 to 13 μ). This presence of freons and related chlorocarbons (CCl_4, $CHCl_3$, CH_2Cl_2, and CH_3Cl) with similar absorption characteristics in sufficient concentrations (about 20 times these current levels) might have as pronounced an effect on atmospheric warming as increasing CO_2, and in the same direction. Such concentrations are not impossible even if their use in aerosol cans is legally proscribed, as they are exceedingly stable and virtually inert in the troposphere.

If the halocarbons rise into the stratosphere photolysis can take place, releasing very active chlorine atoms that can in turn bring about a continuous degradation of ozone to oxygen. Each chlorine atom is limited in the number of ozone molecules it can degrade only by the probability that it will abstract a hydrogen atom from a hydrocarbon and wash out of the atmosphere as HCl. Reduction of the ozone layer would be very serious, resulting in changes in stratospheric thermal characteristics and increased penetration of ultraviolet light to the ground with all of the attendant genetic, sunburn, carcinogenic, and climatic potential. This too would be likely to increase the temperature at ground level.

In the same way, nitrogen fertilizers can be metabolized by bacteria to produce numerous end products. One of these is nitrous oxide (N_2O). This is a natural component of the atmosphere, but it is rare, and its concentration is increasing. Nitrous oxide in the stratosphere can be broken down photochemically to produce oxygen atoms that can also react with and degrade ozone. It is not clear how important this effect is, but it may be serious (Platt et al., 1977). It is clear that world agriculture would be in much poorer shape without the nitrogen fertilizers that appear to be the source of the rising nitrous oxide concentration in the atmosphere.

There is more uncertainty in the interactions among people, the atmosphere, and the global climate than in virtually any other aspect of human ecosystems. We cannot be sure how any human activities will alter the atmosphere, or what will be the pattern of climatic development under human influence. It is unquestionably clear that people have the power to make extraordinary changes in the climate that may range from melting of the polar icecaps to plunging the earth into a full-fledged ice age. We know enough about the dynamics of the atmosphere to know that there is a reasonable probability of a serious problem. But we do not know enough about the atmospheric system to predict the direction or the degree to which either extreme will be approached.

The responsibilities of the policy maker are more difficult here than in virtually any other aspect of human ecosystems. Air pollution control technology is inherently difficult. The volume of air that must be treated for a given installation is typically very high, and the pollutants contained in it are dilute and difficult to handle. It is difficult to document the public health or economic consequences of air pollution—except that they unquestionably exist and that they are significant. There are no geographic boundaries to airsheds as there are in watersheds. This makes it much harder to monitor what happens to pollutants and to devise the best public policy for controlling them. The job is a difficult one. But the stakes are so high, both in the short run and in the long run, that it is critically important.

References

Air Pollution Control Office, 1971. *Air Quality Criteria for Nitrogen Oxides.* Washington: Environmental Protection Agency Pub. **AP–84.**

Altshuller, A. P. and Bufalini, J. J., 1971. Photochemical aspects of air pollution: a review. *Env. Sci. Tech.* **5**: 39–64.

American Lung Association, 1969. *Air Pollution Primer.* New York: National Tuberculosis and Respiratory Disease Assn.

Ashenden, T. W., and Mansfield, T. A., 1978. Extreme pollution sensitivity of grasses where SO_2 and NO_2 are present in the atmosphere together. *Nature* **273**: 142–143.

Blumenthal, D. L., White, W. H., and Smith, T. B., 1978. Anatomy of a Los Angeles smog episode: pollutant transport in the daytime sea breeze regime. *Atmos. Env.* **12**: 893–907.

Bornstein, R. D., 1968. Observations of the urban heat island effect in New York City. *Jour. Appl. Meteor.* **7**: 575–582.

Bryson, R. A., 1974. A perspective on climatic change. *Science* **184**: 753–760.

Cadle, R. D. and Allen, E. R., 1970. Atmospheric photochemistry. *Science* **167**: 243–249.

Changnon, S. A., Jr., 1968. The LaPorte weather anomaly—fact or fiction? *Bull. Am. Meteor. Soc.* **49**: 4–11.

Changnon, S. A., Jr., 1979. Rainfall changes in summer caused by St. Louis. *Science* **205**: 402–404.

Clarke, J. F., 1969. Nocturnal urban boundary layer over Cincinnati, Ohio. *Mon. Wea. Rev.* **97**: 582–589.

Cleveland, W. S., Kleiner, B., McRae, J. E., and Warner, J. L., 1976. Photochemical air pollution: transport from the New York City area into Connecticut and Massachusetts. *Science* **191**: 179–181.

Corn, M., 1968. Nonviable particles in the air. In Stern, A. C., ed., *Air Pollution,* 2nd ed. New York: Academic Press, Inc., 47–94.

Corwin, T. K., 1980. The economics of pollution control in Japan. *Env. Sci. Tech.* **14**: 154–157.

Council on Environmental Quality, 1970. *Environmental Quality, 1970.* Washington: U.S. Govt. Printing Office.

Council on Environmental Quality, 1975. *Environmental Quality, 1975.* Washington: U.S. Govt. Printing Office.

Findley, B. F., and Hirt, M. S., 1969. An urban-induced meso-circulation. *Atmos. Environ.* **3**: 537–542.

Finlayson, B. J. and Pitts, J. N., Jr., 1976. Photochemistry of the polluted troposphere. *Science* **192**: 111–119.

Frohlinger, J. O. and Kane, R., 1975. Precipitation: its acidic nature. *Science* **189**: 455–457. See also the extremely critical discussion and rebuttal in *Science* **194**: 643–647.

Galloway, J. N., Likens, G. E., and Edgerton, E. S., 1976. Acid precipitation in the northeastern United States: pH and acidity. *Science* **194**: 722–724.

Garnett, A. and Bach, W., 1965. An estimation of the ratio of artificial heat generation to natural radiation heat in Sheffield. *Mon. Weather Rev.* **93**: 383–385.

Glasson, W. A. and Tuesday, C. S., 1970. Hydrocarbon reactivity and the kinetics of atmospheric photooxidation of nitric oxide. *Air Poll. Contr. Assn. Jour.* **20**: 239–243.

Gofmekler, V. A., 1968. Effect of embryonic development of benzene and formaldehyde in inhalation experiments (translated from Russian). *Hyd. Sanit.* **33**: 327–332.

Hackleman, E. C., 1977. Is an electric vehicle in your future? *Env. Sci. Tech.* **11**: 858–862.

Hansen, J., 1980. Ailing Treasurers. *Science 80* **1** (6): 58–61.

Henry, M. C., Ehrlich, R., and Blair, W. H., 1969. Effect of nitrogen dioxide on resistance of squirrel monkeys to *Klebsiella pneumoniae* infection. *Arch. Environ. Health* **18**: 580–587.

Hudson, J. D., 1943. Present position of the corrosion committee's field tests on atmospheric corrosion (unpainted specimens). *Jour. Iron and Steel Inst.* **48**: 161–215.

Hursh, C. R., 1948. Local climate in the copper basin of Tennessee as modified by the removal of vegetation. U.S. Dept. of Agriculture *Circular* **744**.

Josephson, J., 1977. A new "clean image" for coal. *Env. Sci. Tech.* **11**: 1148–1149.

Josephson, J., 1978a. SOx scrubbing: clearing the air. *Env. Sci. Tech.* **12**: 16–18.

Josephson, J., 1978b. Fluidized-bed combustion's progress. *Env. Sci. Tech.* **12**: 132–134.

Kozlowski, T. T., 1980. Impacts of air pollution on forest ecosystems. *Bio Science* **30**: 88–93.

Kratzer, P., 1956. *Das Stadtklima.* Braunschweig: Friedrich Vieweg u. Sohn. English translation available through ASTIA AD 284776.

LaBelle, C. W., Long, J. E., and Christofano, E. E., 1955. Synergistic effects of aerosols. *Arch. Ind. Health* **11**: 297–304.

Landsberg, H. E., 1962. City air—better or worse. In U.S. Public Health Service, *Symposium: Air over Cities.* Cincinnati: Robt. Taft San. Eng. Ctr. *Tech. Rept.* **A62-5.**

Larrabee, C. P. and Ellis, O. B., 1959. Report of a subgroup of subcommittee VII on corrosiveness of various atmospheric test sites as measured by specimens of steel and zinc. Committee B-3, American Society for Testing Materials. *A.S.T.M. Proc.* **59**: 183–201.

Lave, L. B. and Seskin, E. P., 1970. Air pollution and human health. *Science* **169**: 723–733.

Leighton, P. A., 1961. *Photochemistry of Air Pollution.* New York: Academic Press, Inc.

Likens, G. E. and Bormann, F. H., 1974. Acid rain: a serious regional problem. *Science* **184**: 1176–1179. See also commentary and rebuttal on this article, *Science* **188**: 957–958.

Likens, G. E., Wright, R. F., Galloway, J. N., and Butler, T. J., 1979. Acid rain. *Sci. Am.* **241 (4)**: 43–51.

Liu, B. C., and Yu, E. S. H., 1978. Air pollution and material damage functions. *Jour. Env. Mgmt.* **6**: 107–115.

Lunde, G., Gether, J., Gjos, N., and Lande, M.-B. S., 1976. Organic micropollutants in precipitation in Norway. Sur Nedbørs Virkning på Skog og Fisk Prosjektet *Research Report* **9/76.**

Marx, J. L., 1975. Air pollution: effects on plants. *Science* **187**: 731–733.

Menck, H. R., Casagrande, J. T., and Henderson, B. E., 1974. Industrial air pollution: possible effect on lung cancer. *Science* **183**: 210–212.

Michelson, I. and Tourin, B., 1966. Comparative method for studying cost of air pollution. *Pub. Health Rept.* **81 (6)**: 505–511.

Michelson, I. and Tourin, B., 1967. Report of validity and extension of economic effects of air pollution data from upper Ohio River Valley to the Washington, D.C. region. *U.S. Public Health Service Contract* **PH-27-68-22.**

Mitchell, J. M., Jr. 1962. The thermal climate of cities. In U.S. Public Health Service, *Symposium: Air over Cities.* Cincinnati: Robt. Taft San. Eng. Ctr. *Tech. Rept.* **A62-5,** 131–145.

National Air Pollution Control Administration, 1969a. Air Quality Criteria for Particulate Matter. Washington: National Air Pollution Control Administration Pub. **AP-49.**

National Air Pollution Control Administration, 1969b. Air Quality Criteria for Sulfur Oxides. Washington: National Air Pollution Control Administration Pub. **AP-50.**

National Air Pollution Control Administration, 1970a. Air Quality Criteria for Carbon Monoxide. Washington: National Air Pollution Control Administration Pub. **AP-62.**

National Air Pollution Control Administration, 1970b. Air Quality Criteria for Photochemical Oxidants. Washington: National Air Pollution Control Administration Pub. **AP-63.**

National Air Pollution Control Administration, 1970c. Air Quality Criteria for Hydrocarbons. Washington: National Air Pollution Control Administration Pub. **AP-64**.

Oke, T. R. and Hannell, F. G., 1968. The form of the urban heat island in Hamilton, Canada. Paper presented at World Meteor. Org. Symposium on Urban Climates and Building Climatology. Quoted in Peterson, 1969.

Peterson, J. T., 1969. The climate of cities: a survey of recent literature. N.A.P.C.A. Pub. **AP-59**.

Petr, B. and Schmidt, P., 1967. The influence of an atmosphere contaminated with sulfur dioxide and nitrogen gases on the health of children. *Zeit. Gesamte Hyg. Grenzgeb.* **13**: 34–48.

Platt, P. F., et al., 1977. Effect of increased nitrogen fixation on stratospheric ozone. *Clim. Change* **1**: 109–136.

Ramanathan, V., 1975. Greenhouse effect due to chlorofluorocarbons: climatic implications. *Science* **190**: 50–52.

Schneider, S. H. and Mesirow, L. E., 1976. *The Genesis Strategy: Climate and Global Survival.* New York: Plenum Press.

Shaw, R. W. 1979. Acid precipitation in Atlantic Canada. *Env. Sci. Tech.* **13**: 406–411.

Sheikh, K. H., Öztürk, M. A., Secmen, Ö., and Vardar, Y., 1976. Field studies of the effects of cement dust on the growth and yield of olive trees in Turkey. *Envir. Conserv.* **3**: 117–121.

Sproull, W. T., 1970. *Air Pollution and its Control.* Jericho, N.Y.: Exposition Press, Inc.

Task Force on Lung Dynamics, 1966. Deposition and retention models for internal dosimetry of the human respiratory tract. *Health Phys.* **12**: 173–207.

U.S. Air Force, Cambridge Research Laboratories, 1965. *Handbook of Geophysics and Space Environments.* Bradford, Mass.: U.S. Air Force.

Wang, W. C., Yung, Y. L., Lacis, A. A., Mo, T., and Hanson, J. E., 1976. Greenhouse effects due to man-made perturbations of trace gases. *Science* **194**: 685–690.

10/solid wastes

Solid waste is in some ways the universal pollutant. It has been present as a part of the human condition for as long as man has been a biological species. Production of solid wastes is not only a basic biological function; it also goes with the simplest of technologies. It far predates people's ability to use fire and produce air pollution. It also predates the human pollution of watercourses to any more than the most trivial degree. During the late Middle Ages the buildup of solid wastes in the streets of Europe forced the development of modern sanitary sewers, and it has always been solid wastes (litter) that have represented "pollution" in the mind of the average citizen.

Recently, however, both air and water pollution have become far more prominent in the development of pollution technologies than solid wastes. Solid wastes have somehow not seemed as important as air pollution or water pollution. There are several reasons for this. Solid wastes have always been part of human experience, so they have never seemed exotic or new. There are relatively few ways of dealing with them and the basic types of treatment have also been around for thousands of years.

Many of the problems associated with solid wastes are very similar to those of air and water pollution. They are esthetically displeasing, they can carry diseases for man, and they represent a loss of useful resources. Their characteristics are extraordinarily varied. They may be inert, they may be highly poisonous, they may consist of valuable materials, or they may be totally worthless.

Solid wastes are endemic to both rural and urban activities, and most functions of human societies produce them. The most familiar are domestic solid wastes produced in the home. These include biological wastes not carried by the sewer system, kitchen wastes, packaging, newspapers, and other paper products. Closely related are the commercial wastes that comprise mainly packaging, paper, and so on. The composition of domestic and commercial wastes is fairly uniform throughout the world, differing mainly as a function of gross cultural practices and limited by the range of available materials. As an example, we all eat foods and we all discard the inedible parts of the food in one way or another, regardless of the culture. The major difference among cultures is that in more affluent economies food is likely to come in some kind of paper or plastic package that is itself discarded when the food is prepared. In the same way, the amount of newspaper that enters the solid waste stream depends on the amount and price of paper available to the nation as a whole. Newsprint is a much larger fraction of solid wastes in North America, where it is cheap and papers are thick, than, say, in Europe where it is expensive and newspapers are very thin.

Industrial wastes, on the other hand, tend to be unique for each instance. There are similarities among plants within each industry, but the wastes actually produced by a given plant reflect its specific constellation of raw materials, manufacturing processes, product lines, and age. Construction and demolition of buildings generate large amounts of solid wastes in the form of soil and rock from excavation, used construction materials, and building rubble. Most are fairly chemically inert, but some building materials are combustible, and asbestos is carcinogenic. These wastes are particularly concentrated in cities.

Mines are among the most prodigious producers of solid waste. Piles of mine tailings may be larger than the area of the mine itself. The tailings may be gravel of low chemical or biological activity, or they may contain materials that are very active chemically or potent biologically and that can have profound effects on adjacent ecosystems. The most important examples of the latter are acid drainage from coal mine tailings and radioactive tailings from uranium mines.

Agriculture also produces much solid waste, although it also has a considerable capacity to absorb solid wastes. The excreta of livestock may be so plentiful as to comprise a water pollution menace, especially when concentrated in the feedlot. Crop residues remaining in fields after harvest must be removed in some way or other before the next crop can be planted. This may be accomplished simply by plowing under as green manure, or planting a fall-seeded crop among the straw and leaving the straw as a mulch. Just as often, the residues represent a potent source of crop disease that must be removed if the following crop is to be successful. Sawmills produce great quantities of solid wastes, including sawdust, bark woodchips, and small pieces of wood. These are often incinerated but are even more commonly left in large piles near the sawmill.

The overall strategy of most methods of air and water pollution control is to convert the problem from one into the other or into a solid waste problem. A sewage treatment plant treats wastewater to remove as much pollutant material as possible and return it to surface waters. The remainder is retained as sludge, a solid waste. Electrostatic precipitators remove materials from flue gases in solid form that must then be disposed of or used in some way or another, while wet scrubbers remove solids as an aqueous slurry that is treated so that the solid materials are delivered as sludge. These waste conversion processes are advantageous to society if the resulting solid waste is less noxious than the air or water pollutant with which the process started. But in no way can the problem be considered to have gone away. There is no "away."

ASSOCIATED PROBLEMS

Solid wastes affect us in many ways, almost all negative. Some of these are mainly esthetic, whereas others cause tangible problems of human health or the health of human ecosystems.

Esthetic Problems

The problems that first spring to mind when we think of solid wastes are the esthetic problems associated with open dumps, their physical appearance, the smells associated with putrifying organic materials, burning of putrescible organic materials, and so on (Figure 10.1). Alternatively, we may object to the ungainly appearance of most municipal incinerators or their foul operating smells or the great quantities of unburned or semi-burned refuse they sometimes put out of their smokestacks. Construction debris may blow in the wind, be eroded by water, and cause stream siltation, in addition to its general unsightly appearance.

Mine tailings may tower many feet into the air. At the very least they pose a substantial visual blight, and they are often physically unstable as well. Some of the most serious mining-related disasters in history have happened not underground, but rather just below a mine tailings pile that gave way at the wrong time. The solid wastes from agriculture and forestry are most commonly burned off. Because this takes place in rural areas, it may escape the notice of urban populations. However, the amount of particulate material put into the air from these burning operations may be quite high. A small but significant percentage of the particulate air pollution load generated in North America comes from burning agricultural and forestry wastes.

Human Diseases

Solid wastes have an important role in disease transfer. Some diseases can survive in wastes and pass directly to people; others have one or more species of animal which act as intermediary hosts (vectors) for the pathogen between the solid wastes and people. Figure 10.2 diagrams the pathways through which diseases are carried to people via solid wastes. The most important vectors are fleas, mosquitoes, rodents, and ticks. Transfer may also be by airborne particles, drinking water, the food supply, and direct contact. The overwhelming majority of the diseases involved stem from pathogenic bacteria and viruses in either human or animal fecal materials within the solid waste stream.

Figure 10.1 Photograph of a burning garbage dump outside of Moab, Utah. [Photograph courtesy of EPA Documerica.]

Perhaps the clearest example of the relationship between solid waste management and human disease is the fly-borne diseases such as typhoid, bacterial and amoebic dysentery, diarrhea, Asiatic cholera, and African sleeping sickness (trypanosomiasis) among others (Anderson, 1964). Flies are attracted to and breed in areas of solid waste accumulation, where garbage and fecal material provide a rich and abundant source of food. Even if there are no human fecal materials, the presence of garbage guarantees fecal material from other mammals such as rats. Fecal materials are significant because pathogenic bacteria, viruses, protozoa, and so on are commonly evacuated in the feces of an infected animal. The flies pick up the pathogens both internally, where they can be spread by blood-sucking, and externally, where they can be spread by contact. Bacteria, protozoa, and viruses tend to be internally transported; worms and other small animal pathogens tend to be externally transported. The range of diseases that can be carried by flies is truly remarkable, and the details of the transfer of pathogen from waste to humans are different for almost every disease. For an engaging summary

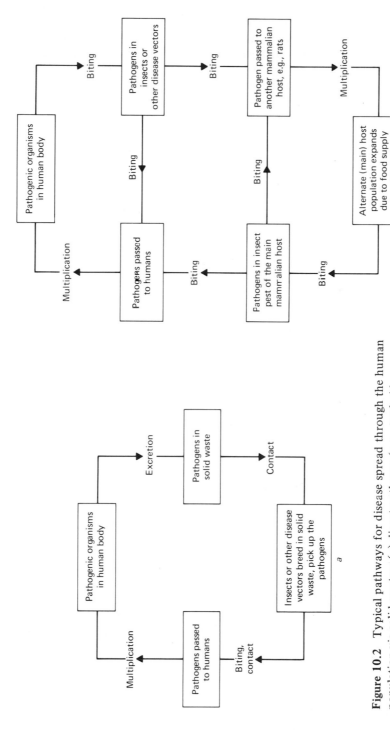

Figure 10.2 Typical pathways for disease spread through the human population via solid wastes: (*a*) direct pathway (e.g., typhoid cholera); (*b*) indirect pathway (e.g., bubonic plague, leptospirosis).

of solid waste-disease relationships, as well as for the history by which the transfer mechanisms were uncovered over the last 100 years, see Hanks (1967).

A more complex, indirect example of disease transfer from solid waste is bubonic plague, whose primary vector is the rat flea. Both wild and domestic rats are'commonly parasitized by numerous species of organisms, including several species of blood-sucking fleas. If a rat is infected with the plague, the bacillus *Pasteurella pestis* is found in great numbers in the rat's blood and is ingested with the blood by the flea. The bacterium thrives only in the bodies of warm-blooded animals, but it can survive for short periods in the body of the flea. Fleas do not normally change from one host organism to another. But the rate is highly susceptible to the plague bacillus, and once infected will generally die. The flea then attempts to find a new host as fast as it can. Most commonly, of course, this is another rat. In areas of high human habitation it is not unlikely to be a person. When the flea pierces the skin of its new human host, whatever plague bacilli are living in it can be passed into the bloodstream of the person. The reservoir for the plague bacillus, then, is the rat population. The vector is the rat flea, and the stimulus for the transfer of plague from the rat to man is the death of the plague-susceptible rat.

Pasteurella pestis requires a host. Unlike some disease entities such as typhoid or poliomyelitis, it cannot survive outside the body of a host organism in solid waste. But solid waste is a magnet for rats. Accumulations of solid wastes have three significant effects on plague. First, they encourage a relatively large number of rats to come into contact with at least one group of humans, the people who actually handle the wastes. This may include the entire population if sanitation is primitive and solid wastes accumulate in urban or built-up areas. Second, the high concentration of domestic rats creates ideal conditions for a plague epidemic to pass through the rat population. Finally, the presence of solid wastes provides a common point of contact between the domestic rat population and wild populations of rats and other rodents. In most parts of the world, the latter are both considerably larger and more diffuse than those of domestic rats. Because of these characteristics plague epidemics seldom decimate wild populations, and the disease can remain hidden, as it were, in the background within the wild rat population. When a plague-carrying wild rat comes into contact with the concentrated domestic rat population around solid waste accumulations, the disease can spread quickly to man. As a corollary, bubonic plague might never have become a serious disease for people except for large accumulations of solid wastes.

Plague is not the only disease that is carried in this manner. A class of diseases called leptospirosis is caused by a whole series of distinct species of organisms carried by rats. Once again, the effect of solid wastes is to concentrate the rat population and make contact between rats and the source of infection possible. In this case the disease agent is a spirochete passed in urine. Rats drawn by solid wastes are likely to come into contact with urine from sewer water, contaminated drinking water, and the urine of other rats. They also urinate on items that can be consumed either by humans directly or by pets. The spirochetes can then be transferred to humans through bites by infected rats or pets, as well as by any contact between people and the urine of infected animals.

Solid wastes thus have a prominent role in human disease. In some cases the wastes themselves are the repository for the disease. In others they provide an environment that is highly favorable to the disease vector. The difference between the two is very large, but either pattern can be controlled by proper sanitation of organic wastes.

Pollution of Air and Water

The treatment of noxious solid wastes can lead to substantial air and water pollution. Among the most vivid pictures of a pollution problem is the open dump being burned (Figure 10.1). Dump burning is done to reduce waste volume and to destroy harmful organic materials. But it does so at the cost of the emission into the atmosphere of great quantities of particulate matter, of which some consists of unburned garbage and represents at the very least a public health problem and source of offensive odors. Dump burning may also put significant quantities of harmful chemicals into the air, especially if the dump contains substantial amounts of tires or petroleum based wastes or industrial chemicals. These may be both harmful and foul smelling.

In the same way, dumps and sanitary landfills can contribute to local water pollution problems. Materials leached from solid waste repositories contain very high amounts of BOD and nutrients, so that landfills can be significant and all but uncontrollable contributors to oxygen depletion and eutrophication.

Incinerators. An incinerator is engineered for controlled burning of solid wastes. It is typically less offensive than an open dump, but it may still be a source for a great deal of offensive material in the atmosphere. Many municipal incinerators are quite old, and they were not designed with air pollution control devices that would now be considered appropriate. Conventional municipal incinerators have intrinsic problems that must be taken into account and that make adequate air pollution control difficult at best. Air pollution control devices are relatively sophisticated ones that operate properly only under relatively restricted conditions. An an example, stack gas temperatures and flow rates are critical variables in the performance of cleaning equipment. Most industrial boilers and furnaces are designed with operating temperatures tuned to the particular process being carried out. This constancy of temperature allows straight-

Table 10.1   Heat Content Classification of Solid Wastes.

Type	Materials	Percent Moisture	Percent Incombustible Solids	Heating Value (kwh/m.t.)
0	Trash: paper, cardboard, wood, etc.	10	5	5,550
1	Rubbish: paper, wood scraps, foliage, floor sweepings	25	10	4,200
2	Refuse: even mixture of rubbish and garbage	Up to 50	7	2,800
3	Garbage: animal and vegetable remains	Up to 70	Up to 5	1,600
4	Pathological waste: animal remains	Up to 85	5	650

Classification of the Incinerator Institute of America.

forward design of pollution control apparatus. The fuel is carefully chosen for its combustion properties, its bulk, and the waste products that it produces and that must be disposed of.

But the "fuel" for an incinerator is garbage and other solid wastes. The incinerator operator must accept whatever is given. Even if an incinerator is designed for a specific mix of waste materials, there is no way to insure that the mix of materials in the solid waste stream will remain constant over the life of the incinerator.

The changes in the mixture of solid wastes materials in the United States over the last 30 years are particularly instructive. At the end of World War II, solid wastes were predominantly garbage and newspapers. They had a high water content, and the heating value of the waste materials was relatively low (for comparison of the heat contents of various types of solid wastes, see Table 10.1). Since World War II there has been a rapid evolution in packaging materials, so that packaging plays a much more prominent role in the solid waste stream than it used to. Specifically, the water content of solid wastes has declined as the amount of foodstuff processing has increased. The amount of paper, plastics, and similar combustible items has also increased markedly. These trends have led to a very rapid and striking increase in the caloric value of solid wastes. Similar trends can be observed in Europe and presumably in other parts of the world.

Incinerators built shortly after World War II must now operate at much higher temperatures than they were designed for. As the combustion temperatures in the incinerators increased as a result of the higher energy content of the solid waste, the simple air pollution control devices that had once served became inoperative. Many just burned up. At the same time, the flow rates of air through the combustion chamber increased because of the increased operating temperatures. This made it even more likely that particles of unburned materials would be caught up in the stream of flue gas and carried out into the environment. The high repair costs and the inability of most older incinerators to meet current air pollution requirements mean that most of them have been shut down.

Forecasts of the makeup of solid waste load in the United States over the next 10 years show a continued increase in the heat content of solid wastes (Doggett et al., 1979), coupled with some major shifts in the composition of the noncombustible portions. These give the incinerator designer some guidance in what to expect, but the waste mix is not guaranteed, and the level of uncertainty does not allow a definitive choice for either temperature or conditions in the combustion chamber. Almost all societies have left decisions about the nature of packaging materials in the hands of the packagers themselves. Packagers have traditionally avoided concerning themselves with the destiny of the packaging material beyond the retail level at which it is purchased. They surely have not developed new kinds of packaging to provide for the impact on incinerators. Without some kind of overall guidelines or controls, it is difficult to design incinerators that can deal adequately with the kinds of wastes that will be produced over the next 30 to 50 years.

Solid wastes pose air pollution problems beyond the maintenance of pollution control equipment. At one point most packaging materials were based on wood or wood by-products. They included paper, paperboard, and cellulose. Plastics are now widely used for packaging and their use is expected to increase. Some are chemically quite complex. They may contain elements other than carbon, hydrogen, and oxygen, which are released when the material is incinerated. One of the most common plastics is polyvinyl chloride (PVC), a complex organic chlorohydrocarbon. Unfortunately, when this plastic is incinerated the combustion products include several toxic chlorides, including hydrochloric acid (HCl). Other plastics that are not so widely used but have similar problems include fluorochlorohydrocarbons such as teflon. Breakdown products of teflon include not only hydrochloric acid but also hydrofluoric acid, an exceedingly corrosive and dangerous chemical.

Dumps and Landfills. The simplest disposal method for solid wastes is the dump. This is little more than a place in which solid wastes are dumped without pretreatment and sometimes without management. Sometimes the materials are burned to reduce the volume and prolong the life of the dump. At best a dump is unsightly, disease-ridden, and smelly. It is really a menace, and most jurisdictions have recognized it as such and mandated its replacement by the sanitary landfill.

In principle, there is a great difference between a dump and a sanitary landfill. The former is an open area, where wastes are exposed to air, water, flies, and rats. The latter, at best, is covered every day with dirt to seal out vermin and flies and reduce the danger of disease substantially. The cover dirt is compacted so that flies cannot crawl through it. The whole landfill is a series of cells that can decompose anaerobically to a degree, but that are essentially separate from each other and from the outside (Figure 10.3). Sanitary landfills run the gamut of very good and well-managed to little better than open dumps. The biggest problem is whether, in fact, the cells are closed with dirt that has been compacted sufficiently well to seal them off adequately.

Even the best of landfills, however, are characterized by problems other than those caused by flies and vermin. Whenever solid wastes in dumps and landfills are exposed to rainfall, they absorb substantial amounts of water. This water behaves just as it would in the soil, and the concepts of field capacity, permanent wilting point, and so

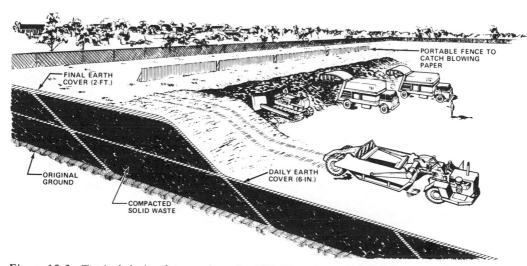

Figure 10.3 Typical design for a sanitary landfill. Wastes are concentrated in the landfill in ordered cells, covered by dirt. The size, orientation, and shape of the cells depend on the site and landfill operator. [Diagram courtesy U.S. Environmental Protection Agency.]

on, have exactly the same meanings as in a natural soil. Most importantly, when the water content of a landfill reaches the field capacity, then any additional water percolating through it must flow under the influence of gravity. Whatever materials are dissolved in the interstitial water of the landfill are carried along as the water moves.

Solid wastes are much more concentrated than air or water pollutants. Among their major constituents are the putrescible organic materials of garbage. These exert oxygen demand just as waterborne sewage does. In a shallow open dump this causes little problem, as the dump is open to highly oxygenated air. But in a sanitary landfill, the only source of the oxygen is that dissolved in the water. This is typically lost quickly by bacterial oxidation of the putrescible material. At the same time, whatever soluble materials are found in the landfill dissolve in the percolating water. This allows much higher concentrations of dissolved organic material than those of wastewater. Breakdown of organic matter produces volatile and soluble materials within the body of the landfill. Where the amount of percolating water is very low, the volatiles diffuse to the surface and the soluble materials remain in place. But where percolation is high, the water displaces volatile gases so that they reach the surface more quickly than they otherwise would, and soluble materials are carried downward by the moving water.

The process of removing soluble or colloidal organic materials by the percolation of water is termed *leaching*. Leachate may be very intensely polluted (Table 10.2), and it can be produced in large amounts. Once the water content of a landfill has reached

Table 10.2   Representative Composition of Initial Leachate from Samples of Municipal Solid Wastes.

	Low	Average	High
pH	3.7	5.6	8.5
Hardness, $CaCO_3$	200	2,310	7,600
Alkalinity, $CaCO_3$	730	5,115	9,500
Calcium	240	1,285	2,330
Magnesium	64	237	410
Iron	0.12	467	1,640
Potassium	28	864	1,700
Sodium	85	893	1,700
Chloride	47	1,208	2,350
Sulfate	20	302	730
Phosphate	0.3	40	130
Organic nitrogen	2.4	239	482
Ammonia nitrogen	0.22	165	480
Zinc	0.03	65	129
Nickel	0.15	0.48	0.81
BOD	21,700	26,000	30,300
Suspended solids	13	13,257	26,500

This table is based on two studies summarized in Brunner and Keller (1971). The "low" value is the lower low value given in either study; the "high" value is the higher high value. The "average" value is the average of the high and low values of both studies. All units are mg/1.

field capacity, any water that enters it as rain or floods must either evaporate from the surface (a relatively small amount) or leach out beneath it into the groundwater system. If the landfill is not initially at field capacity, leaching may be delayed as the landfill becomes charged with water. Thereafter there is a dynamic balance, with the water entering the landfill at the top through percolation balanced by water leaching out the bottom. Indeed, leachate may appear even before the landfill reaches field capacity, either through delivery of liquid squeezed from the organic refuse as it undergoes compaction or through channelization of some of the water due to nonuniformity of the refuse bed. In addition, the wetting front in the refuse bed is fairly broad, so that substantial increases in leachate can occur before the entire system reaches field capacity (Fungaroli and Steiner, 1971). Figure 10.4 shows the relationship between water addition to a simulated landfill and leachate production.

The chemistry of leachates changes drastically over the life of a landfill. In the beginning the leachate is dominated by carbohydrates and other easily metabolizable compounds. In an older landfill these have leached out and the organic materials in the leachate are more stable. Nevertheless, they constitute BOD, and it is much easier in principle to treat the leachate from a young landfill than it is from an older landfill (Chian, 1977).

What happens to leachate from any specific landfill depends, of course, on the geology of the landfill site. Whether leachate drains into the groundwater system or into surface water depends on the position of the water table and the land slope relative to that of the landfill (Figures 10.5, 10.6). Where leachate drains into surface waters, then the landfill is a pollutant source just as the overflow from a municipal sewer system is, except that the amounts of water are much lower and are delayed from peak rainfall conditions, and the concentration of pollutants is higher. When drainage is only into the groundwater system the result may be more or less serious, depending on geological conditions. When exchange capacity of the aquifer rocks is low, or if flow is through joint systems rather than the natural permeability of the rocks, there is little or no opportunity for removal of pollutants through adsorption. If

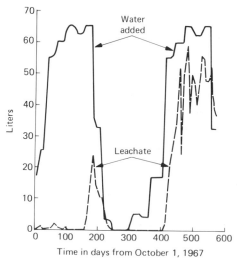

Figure 10.4 Leachate from a simulated sanitary landfill and water added as a function of time. [Redrawn, with permission, from Fungaroli and Steiner, 1971.]

Figure 10.5 Generalized movement of landfill leachate through groundwater in the hydrologic cycle. [Redrawn, with permission, from Schneider, 1970.]

the aquifer in question is tapped for use as drinking water, the wastes can be recycled rapidly to the human population. Percolation through rocks with high exchange capacity, on the other hand, can allow pollutants to become adsorbed onto rock particles and so have additional time to break down before being returned to the surface in wells or springs. If permeability of the substratum is low, as in areas overlying shale or clay rocks, percolation is restricted and pollution distribution is limited to the vicinity of the landfill.

SOLID WASTES AS RESOURCES

There is an old saying that "a waste is a resource out of place." Nowhere is this more applicable than with regard to solid wastes. Air and water pollutants are so dilute that it is generally not economically feasible to recover whatever useful materials they might contain. For example, sulfuric acid is a valuable industrial chemical. It is also the main pollutant in coal furnace flue gas, London type smog, and acid rain. Reclaimed acid from any of these sources would provide a useful commercial chemical and mitigate some major pollution problems. But the amount of material that would have to be processed to extract even small amounts of acid are overwhelming, and the costs of recovery would be astronomical, whether measured in time, money, energy, or resource terms.

Solid wastes, however, are much more concentrated. It should be easier to recover the resources in solid wastes than it would be to recover the same materials found in either air or water pollution. It is almost always easier to "mine" materials in high concentration than in low concentration, and many common constituents of solid wastes are found in considerably higher concentration than in their natural ores. But solid

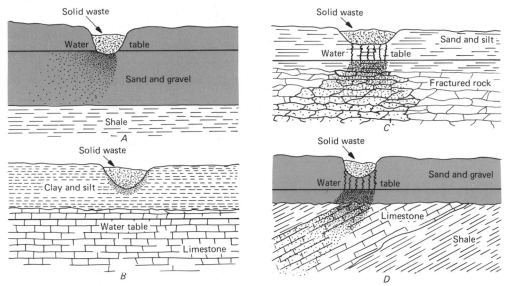

Figure 10.6 Role of subsurface structure in patterns of solid waste leachate movement: (*A*) subsurface is permeable; leachate moves freely; (*B*) subsurface is impermeable; leachate remains *in situ*; (*C*) subsurface underlain by fractured rock; leachate moves quickly, once it reaches the fractured-rock zone; (*D*) subsurface underlain by a dipping-rock aquifer; leachate moves quickly into deep groundwater areas which may be the source of potable water. [Redrawn, with permission, from Schneider, 1970.]

wastes are not consistent in their makeup, and development of solid waste management practices has not proceeded in directions that would encourage the recovery of resources that exist in solid wastes. Indeed, they have tended in the other direction.

Resource recovery is a notion that has gained considerable support throughout the developed world. Basically, it implies that waste materials can be put to some productive use rather than being disposed of as though they had no value whatever. The term has several meanings that are often confused with each other. *Reuse* means that a solid waste entity can be used over for its original purpose after cleaning, but without extensive repair or refabrication. Refillable beverage containers are the best example. *Reworking* means that solid waste entities can be used over for their original purpose after refurbishing or extensive repair. The remanufacture of auto parts or telephones and the renovation of used clothing and old buildings are all examples of reworking. *Recycling* indicates that specific materials in the solid waste stream can be refabricated to their original specifications. Aluminum or glass in beverage containers, for example, can be melted and used to make new beverage containers. *Material conversion* reclaims a material from solid waste in a form that is not usable in its original way but that retains some of the characteristics of the original material. Thus newspapers can be shredded and used to make cellulose insulation, or waste tires and crushed glass can be used as components of road-paving materials. Finally, *energy recovery* captures the heat value of the waste, either directly or indirectly.

There is an order to these notions from reuse, involving the least physical change of the waste, to energy recovery, involving the most. If everything else is equal, reuse is the most efficient method of resource recovery and energy recovery is the least. Table 10.3 summarizes the meaning of the various options on two kinds of solid waste: beverage bottles and newspapers. In both cases, the efficiency of resource recovery clearly declines from the top of the table to the bottom. Of course, other commodities may not show as clear a progression of efficiencies, and some options are not feasible for certain kinds of elements in the waste stream.

Just as there is no single type of resource recovery, there is no single way of carrying it out. Figure 10.7 shows a flow chart of the waste generation and processing system. Traditional waste management without resource recovery is indicated by the heavy line. There are at least six different loops whereby resource recovery can take place, and all have different implications.

Recycling of home scrap and recycling of prompt industrial scrap take place within industry and represent immediate recycling by the primary producer or the fabricator, respectively. Large amounts of material are involved in some cases. Since they comprise waste produced early in the manufacturing process, they tend not to be as contaminated as the same materials in final products; hence they are much easier to recycle. For example, scraps cut off the rolls of paper in a paper mill can be recycled immediately at almost no cost. The wastes from an automobile fabrication plant consists of scrap steel, copper from wires, aluminum, and other metals. These can be returned to the steel or copper mill in relatively pure state and reused as steel, copper, and so on, without any special treatment. The costs of recycling home scrap and prompt industrial scrap are low, and the value of the commodities being recycled is high.

Reuse and reworking are more complicated than industrial recycling in that they involve the return of entities from the consumer to the intermediate manufacturer, and a given intermediate manufacturer may service thousands or even millions of consumers. For the system to work, the distribution network must work both ways, and retail stores must also serve as collection and storage points for the entities to be reused or reworked. This imposes a burden on both the consumer and the retailer, as entities must be consciously saved by the consumer and returned to a retailer, who may view his function as selling rather than as being a warehouse for empty beverage bottles or burned out automobile generators. It may be necessary to sort the entities so that they can be returned to the correct intermediate manufacturer. This is especially a problem for reuse of inexpensive items such as beverage bottles, since there tend to be many different kinds of bottles, each of which must be returned to a particular bottler. Reworking is somewhat easier in that its volume tends to be smaller, and the inherent value of each entity being rebuilt is much higher than those things that are reused.

Most forms of recycling require that relatively uncontaminated materials be delivered to the reprocessor. This is most easily and cheaply done when consumers segregate their own wastes. Source-separated solid wastes can be collected by trash haulers using special trucks or trailers that preserve the segregation, or they can be taken by consumers to special pickup areas or recycling centers. Newsprint and aluminum cans are highly profitable, and steel cans and glass can often be profitably recycled under the right market conditions. Even when the market does not allow recycling of the latter materials, material conversion is often feasible.

At one time source separation was normal. But solid waste collection is a labor-intensive operation, and there has been heavy pressure to reduce labor costs. Centralization of waste collection has put a premium on reducing collection time and

Table 10.3 Representative Paths for Different Resource Recovery Options Involving Beverage Bottles and Newspapers.

Actions Done Prior to Resource Recovery in order to Make it Possible	Actions Done During Resource Recovery	Ultimate Disposition of Wastes
Reuse		
	Beverage Bottle	
Return bottle to retailer, who returns it to bottler.	Clean and refill.	Bottle refilled with beverage.
	Newspaper	
Reuse not feasible for newspapers.		
Reworking		
Reworking not feasible for beverage bottles or newspapers.		
Recycling		
	Beverage Bottle	
Take bottle to recycling center or separate from solid waste stream.	Bottle broken, remelted, refabricated.	Bottle glass broken down and remanufactured.
	Newspaper	
Take to recycling center or separate from solid waste.	Paper repulped and remanufactured.	Paper broken down and remanufactured.
Material Conversion		
	Beverage Bottle	
Take to recycling center or separate from solid waste.	Break glass, mix with asphalt.	Manufacture of road surface, "glassphalt."
	Newspaper	
Take for recycling center or separate from solid waste.	Paper shredded, mixed with fire-retardants.	Manufacture of cellulose insulation.
Energy Recovery		
	Beverage Bottle	
Energy recovery not feasible for beverage bottles.		
	Newspaper	
Solid wastes taken to energy-recovery incinerator.	Burn in energy-recovery incinerator	Energy content of newspaper recovered.
No Resource Recovery		
Solid wastes taken to landfill or standard incinerator.	Solid wastes buried in landfill or burned	No value of waste is recovered.

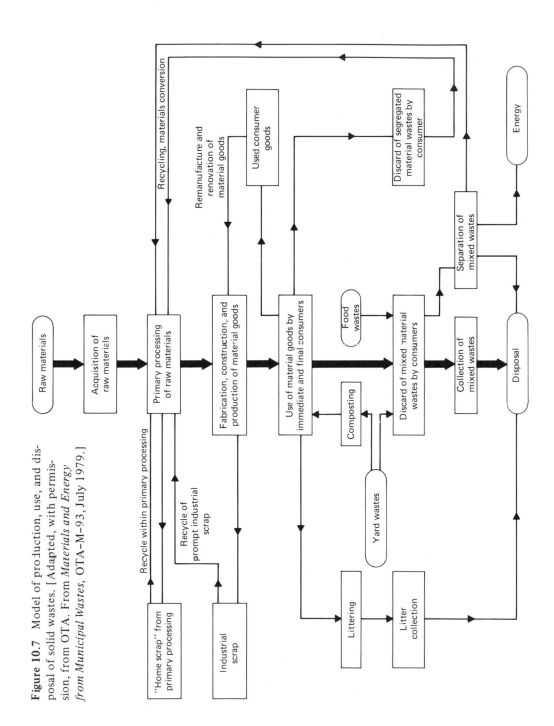

Figure 10.7 Model of production, use, and disposal of solid wastes. [Adapted, with permission, from OTA. From *Materials and Energy from Municipal Wastes*, OTA–M–93, July 1979.]

overheads. The easiest way to do this is to mix wastes, so that neither the homeowner nor the collection agency needs to consider the composition of any bag or can of solid wastes. Compacter trucks reduce the volume of wastes and allow relatively more waste to be collected in a given truck run.

By the same token, any activities by consumers that can reduce the amount of material entering the municipal solid waste load can affect the costs to the municipality. For example, beverage containers now account for about 10% of municipal solid waste. If all beverage containers were reused or recycled directly by consumers, the reduction in the cost of collection and disposal by municipalities would more than pay for the increased costs to the private sector in the increased handling costs. This is one of the strongest arguments in favor of legislation requiring deposits on beverage containers.

With the growing awareness of the economic and ecological advantages of resource recovery, serious attempts have been made to recycle materials from mixed municipal wastes. This requires an expensive separation center (Figure 10.8), where different components of the waste stream are separated mechanically through air and water density separation, as well as through magnetic and optical separators. Components such as paper, plastic, iron and steel, organic materials, aluminum, nonferrous metals, and glass can be separated in a form sufficiently pure for recycling or materials conversion after further processing. Even if the markets for recycled solid wastes were secure, the return on investment of large separation plants is low, and different types of wastes can never be sorted as efficiently or as well as in source separation.

Even with resources recovery, modern society generates solid wastes that cannot be reclaimed in a way that is both ecologically and economically sound. Some wastes will always have to be landfilled or incinerated because they have no energy or soil-building value, or because they are so toxic that they cannot be allowed into the environment at large. As with air and water pollution, the problems posed by solid waste can be reduced but they cannot be totally eliminated. Probably the best that can be hoped for is that the resources represented by solid waste are used most effectively, and that the areas that are used for ultimate disposal of solid wastes are not permanently damaged as a result. Resource recovery is a long-standing practice in Europe and the Far East. These areas of high population and relatively low natural resource endowments simply cannot afford not to recover useable resources. There are many areas of former landfills that are now valued recreational open spaces.

On the other hand, many communities landfill all of their waste or incinerate it without recovering even its energy content. Phenomena such as the "Valley of the Drums" and Love Canal, New York, are well known, where toxic wastes have leached from their containers and caused grave damage to life, property, and people's ways of life (Wilkes et al., 1980). We are still learning how best to deal with the solid wastes of a modern high-technology industrial society. We have made mistakes, and we will continue to do so. We need to recognize solid waste as a fact of life that requires a detailed understanding of chemical and biological activities over a long term as well as a feeling for the economic and policy aspects of land use, construction of central facilities, and so on. As we become increasingly aware of the problems and challenges posed by air and water pollution, we will generate increasing amounts of solid waste as a result of their treatment. There is no easy way to escape solid wastes, and they are growing throughout the world.

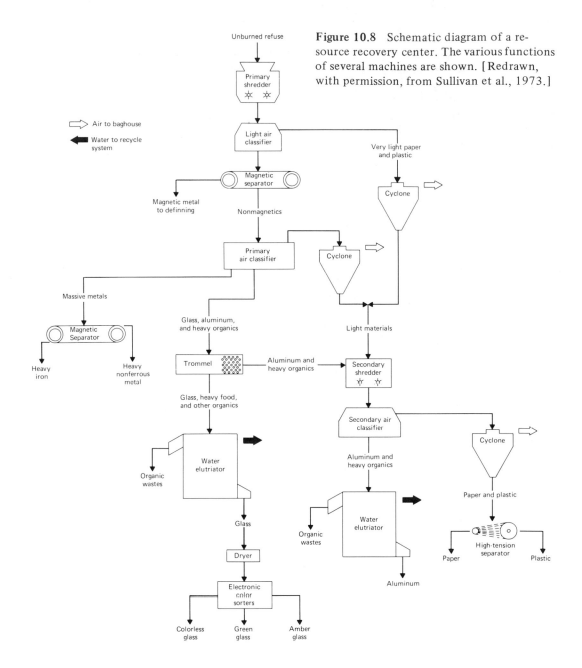

Figure 10.8 Schematic diagram of a resource recovery center. The various functions of several machines are shown. [Redrawn, with permission, from Sullivan et al., 1973.]

References

Anderson, R. J., 1964. The public health aspects of solid waste disposal. *Pub. Health Repts.* **79**: 93–96.

Brunner, D. R. and Keller, D. J., 1971. *Sanitary Landfill Design and Operation.* U.S. Environmental Protection Agency *Report* **SW–65ts.**

Chian, E. S. K., 1977. Stability of organic matter in landfill leachates. *Water Res.* **11**: 225–232.

Doggett, R. M., O'Farrell, M. K., and Watson, A. L., 1979. Forecasts of the quantity and composition of solid waste. Environmental Protection Agency Contract No. 68–03–2649.

Fungaroli, A. A. and Steiner, R. L., 1971. Laboratory study of the behavior of a sanitary landfill. *Jour. Water Poll. Control Fed.* **43**: 252–267.

Hanks, T. G., 1967. *Solid Waste/Disease Relationships: A Literature study.* U.S. Public Health Service, Solid Waste Program *Report* **SW-1c**.

Office of Technology Assessment, 1979. *Materials and Energy from Municipal Waste.* Washington: Office of Technology Assessment.

Schneider, W. J., 1970. Hydrologic implications of solid-waste disposal. U.S. Geological Survey *Circular* **601-F**.

Sullivan, P. M., Stanczyk, M. H., and Spendlove, M. J., 1973. Resource recovery from raw urban refuse. U.S. Bureau of Mines *Report of Investigations* **7760**: 1–28.

Wilkes, A., Kiefer, I., and Levine, B., 1980. Everybody's problem: hazardous waste. U.S. Environmental Protection Agency *Pub.* **SW-826**.

11/sustainability of human ecosystems

This book began with a systems view of human ecosystems. The environment and society were linked into a joint system whose integrity depended as much on the one as on the other. Most of the book has been devoted to the environment and its responses to different kinds of management. Let us now return to the theme of the integrated system.

AS GOAL-ORIENTED SYSTEMS

The structure of a human ecosystem is a function of the biological and geophysical interactions of the components of the environment, the goals and capabilities of the manager, and the practices, motivations, and capabilities of the society. The goals reflect values and aspirations, and the environment typically plays a minor role in their formation. It is often dangerous for people from one society to criticize the goals of another. For example, the Emscher River in Germany is managed as an industrial sewer for the Ruhr and given in-stream treatment before it enters the Rhine. Is this an appropriate use of a river, and does this form of management meet the needs of water users in the Ruhr area over the long term? The evidence is that it does, but such a strategy would be flatly illegal in many other developed countries.

In the same way, few people would question that agriculture was appropriate for the midwestern United States, the Canadian prairies, or the lowlands of northern France. But many might question whether one should farm the Sierra Madre of Mexico or the Andes of South America. The farming techniques available to the peasants in these areas lead quickly to rapid soil erosion, to drastic reductions in crop yields, and even to total destruction of the soil. But no alternative is available to them, given their resources. One might conclude that this situation calls for rapid rural development to provide the inhabitants of such fragile lands with technologies that would allow them to produce the food they need to keep from starving while conserving the soil resource base. One might equally well conclude that such fragile lands should not be farmed at all and that the peasants in those areas should starve (or worse), because their habitat makes successful rural development all but impossible. This is not an academic question. It is a serious policy matter concerning a large proportion of the earth's population. Both extremes have been seriously suggested (e.g., World Bank, 1975; Paddock and Paddock, 1967; 1973).

Conversely, most developed countries have placed a high priority on reserving wild areas such as national parks, wildlife refuges, scientific or protected areas, and so on. Preservation of these areas can be justified on the basis of esthetic criteria, tourism, and scientific value. It is often considered the epitome of ecologically sound thinking. But the conservation ethic carries much less weight in developing countries. Outside of east Africa, where tourism provides a major portion of national income, the preservation of natural habitat for wildlife—even for endangered species—is given lower priority than developing land for direct human uses such as food production. Many animal and plant species in the land-poor areas of south and southeast Asia are endangered precisely because their habitat is considered essential for the support of the human population.

One of the clearest examples is the Gir Forest of India, nominally a 1,250 sq. km. wildlife sanctuary some 300 km. northwest of Bombay. In addition to the wildlife, including the last remnants of the Indian lion population, the forest is inhabited by over 7,000 people and 57,000 cattle. Under these conditions, diseases can pass quickly back and forth between the domestic cattle and the native animals. Preservation of suitable wildlife habitat is virtually impossible, and the Gir Forest will soon be useless as a natural refuge (Ehrenfeld, 1972). Yet the solutions that seem most obvious, like removing the domestic cattle, are inappropriate to the situation (Berwick, 1976).

Similar conditions are found throughout the developing world. Even if a decision maker in a land-poor developing country could set aside land for a national park as in North America or Europe, it might be politically suicidal for him to do so unless it could be justified by tourist revenues. The intensity of the basic human needs in different areas simply does not allow policy makers in all societies to have the same goals. Even though wilderness, clean water, clean air, and so on are important for all people, many societies feel that they cannot afford to put a high priority on them. Even when their leaders believe they are necessary in the long run, they still feel that they cannot afford them in the short run.

STRESS, LIMITS, AND RESILIENCE

Because human ecosystems are goal-oriented, no assessment of their characteristics or dynamics can be completely free of value judgments. Perhaps the least value-laden analysis, as well as the most important for our purposes, concerns the resilience of the ecosystem. Can the system provide the resources demanded of it over the long term, be they food, timber, waste-absorptive capacity, energy, breatheable air, potable water, or amenity resources? When it cannot, what stabilizing changes can be made in the nature of the environmental domain, the techniques available to the manager, or the goals and strategies of society in general?

For example, soil erosion from farming in the Andes will bring collapse of the local farming system if it proceeds unchecked. The soil is inherently vulnerable, and its erosion potential would be high regardless of the capabilities of the farmers. In principle, the peasants could construct terraces to conserve the soil and maintain their agricultural resource base, just as the Incas did hundreds of years ago (Figure 1.3). However, the contemporary peasants have neither the capital nor the technology to build terraces on a large enough scale.

The Indian subcontinent was a land of riches in the past because it could feed itself until fairly recently, while producing coffee, tea, and spices for world trade. But its population explosion over the past century has outstripped the ability of even a well-developed agricultural system to feed the population. The dearth of other natural resources has not allowed the region to escape the burden of poverty and hunger. A major commitment to intensifying farming has been made, with greater use of fertilizer and other modern inputs. These measures have been largely successful in raising food production so far. But the raw material for most of these inputs is petroleum, and the peasants of South Asia are increasingly less able to purchase the requisites of modern agriculture as the oil price climbs.

All ecosystems have limits beyond which they cannot be pushed. Even the largest river has a maximum absorptive capacity for BOD, and a black prairie soil can be farmed too intensively. Managers with no feeling for the environment with which they deal cannot be as effective as those who recognize the danger signals and can respond to them. Long-term sustainability of human ecosystems implies not only a balance between their social and environmental domains, but also the capacity to counteract or withstand the effects of perturbations. Some environments are inherently more vulnerable than others, but they can be productive indefinitely, given proper management. The most inherently stable environment in the world can be ruined by inappropriate management. No ecosystem in the real world is ever free from stress. Environmental phenomena such as drought, floods, rain at the wrong time, late or early frosts, and disease have been plagues for millenia. Cultural phenomena such as war, economic cycles, changing ethical and religious views, and demographic change are equally omnipresent.

The factors affecting ecosystem resilience are not always obvious. They may be integral to the environment, as with the soils of mountain regions; they may relate to the management styles of the individual manager or to the organization of the society, as with the world price of petroleum and petroleum-derived products. Some of the most important are the steady, surreptitious changes in the structure of the system brought about by minor incremental adjustments made by managers and policy makers as they perceived pressures and responded to them on the basis of long-standing practice. Unfortunately, incremental decision-making of this sort seldom considers the effect of the decision on the behavior of the ecosystem. It may solve the problem temporarily but build in the need for further adjustments in the future, so that it actually decreases the ecosystem's long-range resilience. It may never be apparent that things are slipping out of control until they are almost beyond rehabilitation.

A good example is the experience of modern agriculture to chemical pest control. The early experiences with DDT and other early pesticides were so successful that the pesticide use was built into the economics of farming in developed and developing country alike. As it became increasingly clear through the 1960s and 1970s that pesticides had significant effects on nontarget organisms, regulations restricting pesticide use were issued. At the same time, the levels of pesticide application increased as genetic resistence increased in the pest populations. The most effective commercial farmers were the most strongly affected. They could afford to buy more pesticides, but at decreasing profit margins, and they either could not afford or did not know how to stop using them. The problem was compounded in that regulations intended to control pesticides impeded the development of innovative chemical alternatives to them. The registration process was much more expensive and time consuming that it had been when pesticides were first introduced. As a result, most chemical companies tended to favor the development of pesticides, whose behavior and properties they understood, rather than the development of novel alternatives that would have been able to break the cycle.

The most significant challenges to the resilience of a human ecosystem grow from within, commonly after a long buildup. Society has a great deal of experience in perceiving nascent problems and compensating for them before they become too severe. Incremental compensation for seemingly minor problems is built into the management of virtually all human ecosystems. But it is not always appropriate. We cannot assume that we will always be able to recognize significant problems in time to compensate for them. This is especially true of those that diffuse slowly through the structure of the system and that may be so devastating in conception that we consider them unthinkable. Kenneth Watt (1974) terms this the "Titanic effect." Things that we cannot or do not care to perceive can overwhelm even the most highly organized and complex of societies. One need only recall the "killer fogs" of London or the Irish potato famine of the 1840s to realize the degree to which we take human ecosystems for granted and assume that all is well simply because we have no evidence that it is not.

ETHICAL VIEWS

It seems almost self-evident that a system-wide view of human ecosystems is the only way a society can manage these very complex systems in a reasonable and creative way. But this has been an elusive goal in most developed Western countries. It is difficult to synthesize the viewpoints needed to take an adequate overview of the interactions of people and their environment. The institutions of society are not oriented to visualizing a system as complex as a human ecosystem and then acting on this view (White, 1967; Moncrief, 1970). Instead, they have tended to take a simpler view in which society and the environment are not intimately associated. Several different conceptions have served different people at different times. Let us look at some of the more important.

The Pioneer View

Perhaps the oldest view of human ecosystems is the pioneer ethic. It goes back hundreds or even thousands of years in different parts of the world. Nature places obstacles in the society's path, and it may even represent an enemy who must be conquered if people are to survive. Individuals have a responsibility to mold nature to their own ends, and success is not guaranteed. This is reflected in the Old Testament notion of "the wilderness" (untamed nature) as a place of banishment or exile. Many animist cultures whose gods are drawn from nature pray not so much as a communion between nature and man, but rather as a way of satiating the gods so that people can continue to subdue nature uninhibited by divine interference. In pre-Christian Rome, Cicero could finally boast that nature had been conquered: "we are absolute masters of . . . the earth. . . . We enjoy the mountains and the plains. The rivers are ours. We sow the seed and plant the trees. We fertilize the earth. . . . By our hands we endeavor by our various operations in this world to make it as it were another nature."

The pioneer ethic is part of our history and culture, and it is still a strong force. Especially in North America, where the early European settlers did not have the organized technical capabilities of the engineers in Cicero's Rome, the forest was a howling wilderness to be subdued (Marx, 1967). If the pioneers overstressed the environment they could always move on. At worst they were condemned to be pioneers until there was nowhere else to move to.

The vast technical capabilities of twentieth century engineers allowed people to view themselves as more powerful than nature. Practically any goal was obtainable, be it flying, sending ships to the bottom of the sea, speaking to people on the other side of the world, or traveling to the moon. Such visions from science fiction of the nineteenth century became an implicit part of our birthright in the twentieth. The technological revolution has been so fast that accelerating change has become the norm. It has known no limits so far, and it is very difficult to gauge what limits may lie ahead. Two divergent viewpoints have emerged. One, the "technological optimist," sees continuing change emerging from new technology that becomes available as it is needed. The other believes that "nature knows best," and that the environment sets boundaries that will limit the further growth of technology.

The Technological Optimist

The technological optimist believes that technology will always be available to solve the problems confronting society. As resource stocks are used up, new ones will be discovered. Resources thought to be in danger of depletion will either be replaced by substitutes or made more available as new ways of production are found. In some cases, the price of the substitute or of the material produced by the new method will be lower than that of the original. This behavior is explained by the supply and demand curves shown in Figure 7.1. Supply exhaustion is tantamount to increases in the expense of producing a material, thus shifting the supply curve to the left. The equilibrium price is thus higher per unit of production than previously. However, the higher price stimulates research into new ways of meeting the demand. When these ways are found, the market reaches an equilibrium based on the new methods. Technological advances during the interim may allow the newer methods of production to be cheaper than the older ones. One example is the replacement of hematite by taconite as the preferred iron ore in North America, as discussed in Chapter 7. Barnett and Morse (1963) cite other examples of both renewable and nonrenewable resources that have maintained an equilibrium supply in a relatively free market.

Technological optimism stems from the highly empirical discipline of resource economics. Its credibility rests on the fact that it describes our historical experience with so many commodities. Resources are highly substitutable, and economic forces do lead to further technological change. But substitutability is not infinite. All communities require a relatively small number of materials and types of energy for which substitution is either impossible or infeasible. People require certain amino acids that their bodies cannot make. Plants require available phosphorus in the soil. Fish require a certain amount of oxygen in the water they inhabit. There are no substitutes, and there never will be, regardless of the shape of the demand and supply curves.

"Nature Knows Best"

"Nature knows best" is the "third law of ecology" of Barry Commoner (1971). It holds that the natural relationships and the structure of natural communities that have emerged after 3.5 billion years of evolution are at least the best available model for human behavior and may constitute the only valid model for managing an ecosystem. People are animals whose requirements are very similar to those of other animals. They participate in the complex network of the food web, and their hegemony over other species should be no greater than that of other dominant species in other ecosystems. The widely held notion that humans are uniquely competent among animals to improve on nature is a will-o'-the wisp. History shows that most environmental planning takes far too limited a view and that major changes in ecosystems are more likely to be detrimental than beneficial. Examples include the introduction of new chemicals into the environment or forcing the extinction of species. In general, if a choice must be made between a natural way of dealing with the problem and an artificial way, the natural way should be followed. It has stood the test of time.

This conception is probably valid as far as it goes. However, the major difference between natural and human ecosystems is not the greater capability of people. It is that society can recognize or even anticipate problems and respond to them quickly. Evolution is a slow process. There are dramatic exceptions, such as the extinction of vulnerable species, but to change the structure of a natural ecosystem commonly takes many years, often measured in hundreds or thousands. Social decisions, on the other hand, can be very rapid. It is possible to reorder priorities and even the specifics of ecosystem management almost as soon as a problem is perceived. Of course, society does not always respond immediately, but it is capable of reacting quickly. As an example, the early 1970s found the lakes and rivers of industrial parts of the United States dreadfully polluted. The level and pervasiveness of pollution brought a major change in public consciousness of the environment, which led quickly to action. The Potomac

River in Washington was declared safe for swimming by 1979, and even Lake Erie, which many people had thought of as "dead," has noticeably improved.

Environmental Impact View

The environmental impact view of human ecosystems is one that has become popular since the passage of the National Environmental Policy Act in the United States in 1969. One of the key provisions of this law is that the federal government must document all significant environmental impacts of government actions, particularly when the impact is adverse or represents an irreversible or irretrievable commitment of resources. This is the famous Section 102, which provides for environmental impact statements. This provision has been copied widely, both at the state level in the United States and also in most other developed countries (Economic Commission for Europe, 1979).

The success of the environmental impact statement mechanism has been the subject of much controversy. There is evidence that it has been successful in incorporating environmental perspectives into government decision-making (CEQ, 1976). There is also evidence that it has had little effect in bringing about change in federal projects (Hill and Ortolano, 1978). It has also been cited as a disaster to the environmental movement by turning some of its best people to endless bureaucratic paper-pushing (Fairfax, 1978).

Regardless of the effectiveness and provisions of the law, it has led to the popular view that society's environmental conscience is served when people understand the effects of a project on various ecosystems. The natural characteristics of these ecosystems are the key concerns, and there is little attempt to explore the interactions between the environment and society. This is not unreasonable for projects such as airport or highway construction, where the environmental domain represents little more than the physical location of an economic activity, and minimizing the environmental impact of a project defines certain limits for engineering design to satisfy.

However, it is virtually meaningless to speak of environmental impact for agriculture, grazing land, fisheries, or timber management. The manager interacts intimately with the environment and adjusts the form of management to current conditions. The secondary changes that result from this adjustment may be more important than the original stimulus. For instance, many foreign assistance projects are oriented toward increasing the productivity of the rural poor (e.g., World Bank, 1975). The direct targets of these projects are human ecosystems: farming, grazing, and water supply systems. But development means change, often profound change, in the society as well as the environment. The dynamic evolution of the system is such that the total impact of rural development can be charted only by projecting the development of the entire ecosystem.

Another example is the recent decision by the International Whaling Commission that its members declare a moratorium on taking great whales. The environmental impact of this decision should be a rebuilding of whale populations throughout the world's oceans. However, one likely result is the proliferation of private whaling boats that are unregulated by even as weak a regulator as the International Whaling Commission and that may do more damage to whaling populations than the regulated Japanese and Soviet fleets.

An Integrated Ecosystem View

It is significant that the best and clearest examples of the close ties between society and the environment should be within poor areas of the world. The rich have the economic and technological resources to "buy their way out" of many problems. The poor do not. Rich farmers, for example, can compensate to a degree for the decline in organic content of their soil by increasing the level of chemical fertilizers. The same fertility decline for poor farmers might spell personal starvation. Technological optimism is out for them. Even if technology existed that might solve their problem, they could not afford to use it. Neither can they afford the notion of "nature knows best." They must try as hard as they can to eke as much food or other salable commodities out of the land as possible.

It is relatively easy to assert the need for a system-wide view of human ecosystems. It is much harder to carry it out. One must take sets of observations from many fields whose practitioners have different intellectual groundings and who do not always recognize the relevance of other disciplines. Ecology, economics, sociology, and policy sciences, among others, provide essential information for understanding the behavior of the overall system. All are based on empirical observations of demonstrable facts, and all have insights and models that synthesize observations into useful working hypotheses. But few of these models have been directed toward human ecosystems in a systematic way. The ecologist tends to concentrate exclusively on the environmental domain, the economist on the managerial domain, and the sociologist and policy scientist on the societal domain. When people have crossed into other domains, they have often uncritically applied their own models and views to another discipline's "turf."

This is not always the case. Biologist René Dubos (1973) has pointed out quite correctly that people can often improve on nature. He argues eloquently that they can manage an ecosystem so that many natural catastrophes can be avoided and ecological communities can exist more stably than in nature. At the same time the mosaic of differently managed landscapes can be more interesting and esthetically pleasing. In an earlier book (Dubos, 1968, p. 199) he characterizes the most useful form of conservation as "a creative interplay between man and animals, plants, and other aspects of Nature, as well as between man and his fellows." Civilized nature is to be regarded "as a kind of garden to be developed according to its own potentialities, in which human beings become what they want to be according to their own genius. Ideally, man and Nature should be joined in a nonrepressive and creative functioning order."

The economists E. J. Mishan (1970) and E. F. Schumaker (1973) have argued that the laws of nature have an important role in matters confronting society. The politician Adlai Stevenson (1965) characterized the world community as "passengers on a little space ship, dependent on its vulnerable supplies of air and soil; all committed for our safety to its security and peace, preserved from annihilation only by the care, the work, and . . . the love we give our fragile craft."

Taking a broad view of human ecosystems means understanding the requirements of living organisms, their productive capacities, and the ways they interact in biological communities. It means understanding the inanimate resources of soil, water, cycling nutrients, fuels, and economically extractible metals. It means realizing the implications of the exploitation and use of these resources, both on the environment and on society. These depend on the values of the managers and of the community to which they belong. Nothing can change the fact that the way people perceive and manage the environment is a cultural phenomenon, as is the way they adapt to change. These are as fundamental as are the laws of nature.

TAKING A SYSTEMS VIEW

A human ecosystem comprises many interconnected subsystems within each domain. Many people spend their whole lives dealing with just one of these subsystems; no one could ever develop a thorough understanding of all of them. Is it asking too much to think of human ecosystems as total systems and base a management strategy on this extremely complicated structure? Not really. The real world is a complex place, and people do not have the luxury of not making decisions simply because they do not understand everything. Decisions will be made in any case; and our goal should be to insure that they are the best ones that are humanly possible. Fortunately, it is possible to understand a great deal about the integration of the total system without needing to know everything about each of the smaller subsystems.

The domains have a specific order, and the signals passing between them are asymmetric (Figure 1.1, p. 4). The information flowing down from "higher" to "lower" represents control: agents on a "higher" level perform actions intended to bring about some directed change in the "lower" level. Conversely, information flowing up from "lower" to "higher" levels is behavioral information: the agent at the "higher" level observes the behavior of the "lower" level. The analyst can understand a great deal about the integration of the system if he can comprehend the information passing between domains.

Portraying the ecosystem as a multidimensional system provides a framework for identifying the important subsystems and the information network that links them. Experience and expert judgment are probably sufficient to gauge the behavior of individual subsystems under different conditions, at least in a qualitative or semiquantitative way. Analysts can then piece together a comprehensible picture of the gross behavior of the overall system. This does not mean that they understand it thoroughly. What is important is that they give the best possible assessment of whether the control signals passing downward in Figure 1.1 are appropriate to the behavioral signals passing upward.

As an example, let us consider a cornfield. The field, including the corn, soil, and whatever weeds and pests can be found there, is an environment that produces corn. The farmer monitors the health of the corn crop, attacks by insect pests, soil quality, soil moisture content, temperature, and so forth, and adjusts his management strategy accordingly. Other factors that influence his management activities include his perception of the market for his crop, his costs (including finance charges on machinery, mortgages on land and buildings, and outlays for all inputs from tractor fuel to fertilizer to chicken feed to electricity), and regulations limiting his management options or setting the prices he will receive for his produce. Policy makers also monitor farmers' behavior and refine farm policies to try to meet the needs of the larger society. All of the domains are dynamic entities responding to myriad signals and adapting their control to the conditions that pervade the system.

Other human ecosystems can be visualized in the same way. It is not always clear what environmental data to collect or why one should monitor factors (such as diatoms in waterways whose prime economic use is navigation) that are not of primary interest to system users or to decision makers. It is very easy to fall into the trap of refusing to collect data because the environment does not seem important enough to worry about. It is also very easy to fall into the trap of collecting data for the purpose of collecting data, without regard for what is to be done with it. One of the main uses of a systems view of a complex system is to identify the data that are most useful for a specific type of analysis.

Most analyses of human ecosystems are designed to help decision makers or managers assess the tradeoffs among different options. It is seldom possible or desirable to make decisions on the basis only of esthetic or economic values. A given decision generally concerns too many people. The economic values of fish populations, of forests, the assimilative capacities of waterways for waste, and so on, are critically important to the affected economic groups. The emotional and esthetic value of wilderness, urban parks, suburban recreation areas, and scenic landscapes is harder to quantify, but is no less significant. In deciding how to manage a particular tract of roadless wilderness, many will agree with Thoreau that "in wilderness is the preservation of the world," and opt for preserving its wilderness character. Others will agree with then California Governor Reagan's comment (about the redwoods) that "a tree is a tree. Once you've seen one you've seen them all," and support unregulated economic development. These views may be honestly held, and they are mutually exclusive. Nevertheless, some basis for a decision must be reached.

Typical decision makers do not know what factors to monitor for each subsystem within the environment. There is no real reason that they should. Their functions are as managers with broad responsibilities, not as information gatherers. Under ideal circumstances, they can design policies that allow both the environment and their constituencies to maintain a stable, constructive configuration. But unless they have both the information and the inclination to take a broad view, they will tend to address themselves to their constituents and ignore the environmental domain altogether. This is seldom beneficial to any of them in the long run, but the policy maker may have no alternative.

Our skill in managing human ecosystems should improve as we learn more about them. All of the subsystems need to be understood as completely as possible under different conditions, so that judgments can be made about the effects and ramifications of different policy options. These judgments cannot be established by decision makers or managers. Only experts in the various subsystems have sufficient in-depth insight into the individual subsystem. But the judgments must be synthesized and interpreted by people who can understand both the scientific details and the needs of the managers and decision makers. These are scientists, social scientists, planners, and policy scientists who can work with people whose interests are very different from their own.

INTERDEPENDENCE AND INTERACTIONS

Human ecosystems are open systems. They require resources, fuels, technology, markets, and so on from other places. The existence of a single city, for example, requires space and food, as well as access to forests for lumber and paper supplies. It requires water to drink, to supply industry, and to carry wastes, as well as air to breathe and to disperse emissions from automobiles, industrial plants, and electric power plants. It also requires energy and raw materials. Even a small city depends on several different kinds of human ecosystems. Some may be in or near the city; others are linked to it by the transportation network. What happens in one can affect the others, and it may not be possible to maintain all of them in their optimal state.

No metropolitan region, or any country of the world, has all of the resources needed to maintain more than the most primitive of societal structures. Virtually all areas have or can produce surpluses of some things, and all trade with each other. Even in the Old Stone Age some areas had to import stone, their basic technological resource. The interdependence of regions has increased with the complexity of society, until virtually all countries of the world are linked in a tight network. International trade is asymmetric. Some regions are raw material producers and others are manufacturers using those raw materials. In general, the first are poor and the second are rich. The only obvious exception is the petroleum producing Arab countries.

The division of the world into rich and poor, developed and developing, has several implications. Cultural differences are amplified by income disparities, and different forms of government are entrenched in different places. Population growth rates tend to be highest in poor countries (or poor areas within rich countries), and political instability is also correlated with poverty. These factors are important because of the increasing interdependence of societies. Problems in one part of the world can lead to disruption in the supply of important resources and can have repercussions throughout the world. A clear example is the impact of the Iranian revolution on world petroleum prices in 1979. Such perturbations highlight the interdependence of countries and the vulnerabilities of the system.

The interactions between people and their environment is basic to the human ecosystem. No less characteristic is the interconnectedness of ecosystems both within and among countries or regions (Figure 11.1). Different ecosystems operating under a given set of economic and political rules interact with other systems operating under different sets of rules. This network generates signals and responses that are intended to regulate or expedite the interactions of people in different places. These rules may also be significant factors constraining people's interactions with the environment even though they may have no direct connection with the environment and may not even be closely related to the characteristics of the particular society.

The environmental system is an extraordinarily complex system bound together by a worldwide network of information flow. It encompasses virtually all disciplines known to man and has for several thousand years. Barry Commoner's "first law of ecology" (Commoner, 1971), which states that "everything is connected to everything else," is true on a grand scale for human ecosystems.

The breadth and complexity of human ecosystems is confusing to many people who would prefer to treat things in a simpler way, concentrating on the phenomena of greatest interest to themselves. I would like to remind them of the story of Canute, the eleventh century King of Britain who took his throne to the seashore and commanded

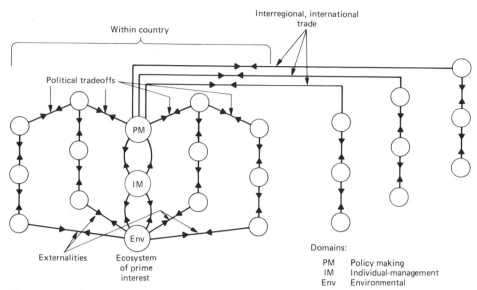

Figure 11.1 Schema for the integration of behavior of a particular human ecosystem with other ecosystems.

the tide to go back. It didn't, of course, and Canute is remembered as a model of futility. His mistake was that he did not recognize that his laws applied only to his subjects. Other kings ruled in other countries, and the environment was (and still is) governed by laws of physics and ecology that are beyond any king's power to change. Nevertheless, the legacy of Canute is still a strong force.

A democratic society can choose how to manage its landscape, but it cannot determine the environmental principles that govern the responses of the landscape to that management. Nor can it choose how others manage theirs. For example, we can choose to have wilderness or to cut virgin trees, but we cannot choose that soil will not erode once the trees are cut. We can choose to have cities that dump toxic wastes into rivers and estuaries, but we cannot choose to have salmon still swim through the polluted water to reproduce. We can choose to burn imported petroleum, but we cannot choose that our suppliers will not raise the price if they feel it is in their interest to do so. The environment and society constitute a complex system whether we like it or not, and these human ecosystems are interconnected in ways that we often cannot influence. To ask that the soil stay in place or that the salmon swim or that others ignore their own self-interest is, like Canute, to command that the tide not flow.

References

Barnett, H. J. and Morse, C., 1963. *Scarcity and Growth: The Economics of Natural Resource Availability*. Baltimore: Johns Hopkins Univ. Press.

Berwick, S., 1976. The Gir forest: An endangered ecosystem. *Am. Sci.* **64**: 28–40.

Commoner, B., 1971. *The Closing Circle: Nature, Man, and Technology*. New York: Alfred A. Knopf.

Council on Environmental Quality, 1976. Environmental impact statements: an analysis of six years' experience by seventy federal agencies. *Report of the Council on Environmental Quality*.

Dubos, R., 1968. *So Human an Animal*. New York: Charles Scribner's Sons.

Dubos, R., 1973. Humanizing the earth. *Science* **179**: 769–772.

Dubos, R., 1976. Symbiosis between the earth and humankind. *Science* **193**: 459–462.

Economic Commission for Europe, 1979. Seminar on Environmental Impact Assessment, Villach, Austria. September 24–29, 1979.

Ehrenfeld, D. W., 1972. *Conserving Life on Earth*. New York: Oxford Univ. Press.

Fairfax, S. K., 1978. A disaster in the environmental movement. *Science* **199**: 743–748.

Hill, W. W. and Ortolano, L., 1978. NEPA's effect on the consideration of alternatives: a crucial test. *Nat. Res. Jour.* **18**: 285–311.

Marx, L., 1967. *Machine in the Garden: Technology and the Pastoral Ideal in America*. New York: Oxford Univ. Press.

Mishan, E. J., 1970. *Technology and Growth: The Price We Pay*. New York: Praeger Publishers.

Moncrief, L. W., 1970. The cultural basis for our environmental crisis. *Science* **170**: 508–512.

Paddock, W., and Paddock, E., 1973. *What We Don't Know: An Independent Audit of What They Call Success in Foreign Assistance*. Ames: Iowa State Univ. Press.

Paddock, W., and Paddock, P., 1967. *Famine—1975! America's Decision: Who Will Survive*. Boston: Little, Brown and Co.

Schumacher, E. F., 1973. *Small Is Beautiful: Economics as if People Mattered*. New York: Harper & Row.

Stevenson, A. E., 1965. Speech given to the United Nations Economic and Social Council, Geneva, Switzerland, 9 July 1965.

Watt, K. E. F., 1974. *The Titanic Effect: Planning for the Unthinkable*. New York: Dutton.

White, L., Jr., 1967. The historical roots of our ecological crisis. *Science* **155**: 1203–1207.

World Bank, 1975. *The Assault on World Poverty: Problems of Rural Development*. Baltimore: Johns Hopkins Univ. Press.

index

409